D1201291

The
International Critical Commentary
on the Holy Scriptures of the Old and New Testaments.

UNDER THE PRESENT EDITORSHIP OF

THE REV. ALFRED PLUMMER, M.A., D.D.
Sometime Master of University College, Durham

PLANNED AND FOR YEARS EDITED BY

THE LATE REV. PROFESSOR SAMUEL ROLLES DRIVER, D.D., D.LITT.
THE REV. ALFRED PLUMMER, M.A., D.D.
THE LATE REV. PROFESSOR CHARLES AUGUSTUS BRIGGS, D.D., D.LITT.

THE INTERNATIONAL CRITICAL COMMENTARY

A CRITICAL AND EXEGETICAL COMMENTARY

ON THE

EPISTLE TO THE HEBREWS

BY

JAMES MOFFATT
D.D., D.Litt., Hon. M.A. (Oxon.)

Edinburgh: T. & T. CLARK, 38 George Street

PRINTED IN GREAT BRITAIN BY
MORRISON AND GIBB LIMITED
FOR
T. & T. CLARK, EDINBURGH
NEW YORK: CHARLES SCRIBNER'S SONS

FIRST EDITION . . . 1924
LATEST REPRINT . . 1968

TO THE MEMORY OF

THREE SCOTTISH EXPOSITORS OF ΠΡΟΣ ΕΒΡΑΙΟΥΣ:

A. B. BRUCE,

A. B. DAVIDSON,

AND

MARCUS DODS.

PREFACE.

It is ten years since this edition was first drafted. Various interruptions, of war and peace, have prevented me from finishing it till now, and I am bound to acknowledge the courtesy and patience of the editor and the publishers. During the ten years a number of valuable contributions to the subject have appeared. Of these as well as of their predecessors I have endeavoured to take account; if I have not referred to them often, this has been due to no lack of appreciation, but simply because, in order to be concise and readable, I have found it necessary to abstain from offering any catena of opinions in this edition. The one justification for issuing another edition of *Πρὸς Ἑβραίους* seemed to me to lie in a fresh point of view, expounded in the notes—fresh, that is, in an English edition. I am more convinced than ever that the criticism of this writing cannot hope to make any positive advance except from two negative conclusions. One is, that the identity of the author and of his readers must be left in the mist where they already lay at the beginning of the second century when the guess-work, which is honoured as "tradition," began. The other is, that the situation which called forth this remarkable piece of primitive Christian thought had nothing to do with any movement in contemporary Judaism. The writer of *Πρὸς Ἑβραίους* knew no Hebrew, and his readers were in no sense *Ἑβραῖοι*. These may sound paradoxes. I agree with those who think they are axioms. At any rate such is the point of view from which the present edition has been written; it will explain why, for example, in the Introduction there is so comparatively small space devoted to the stock questions about authorship and date.

One special reason for the delay in issuing the book has been the need of working through the materials supplied for the criticism of the text by von Soden's *Schriften des Neuen Testaments* (1913) and by some subsequent discoveries, and also the need of making a first-hand study of the Wisdom literature of Hellenistic Judaism as well as of Philo. Further, I did not feel justified in annotating *Πρὸς Ἑβραίους* without reading through the scattered ethical and philosophical tracts and treatises of the general period, like the *De Mundo* and the remains of Teles and Musonius Rufus.

"A commentary," as Dr. Johnson observed, "must arise from the fortuitous discoveries of many men in devious walks of literature." No one can leave the criticism of a work like *Πρὸς Ἑβραίους* after twelve years spent upon it, without feeling deeply indebted to such writers as Chrysostom, Calvin, Bleek, Riehm, and Riggenbach, who have directly handled it. But I owe much to some eighteenth-century writings, like L. C. Valckenaer's *Scholia* and G. D. Kypke's *Observationes Sacrae*, as well as to other scholars who have lit up special points of interpretation indirectly. Where the critical data had been already gathered in fairly complete form, I have tried to exercise an independent judgment; also I hope some fresh ground has been broken here and there in ascertaining and illustrating the text of this early Christian masterpiece.

JAMES MOFFATT.

GLASGOW, 15*th February* 1924.

CONTENTS.

INTRODUCTION.

§ 1. ORIGIN AND AIM.

(i.)

DURING the last quarter of the first century A.D. a little masterpiece of religious thought began to circulate among some of the Christian communities. The earliest trace of it appears towards the end of the century, in a pastoral letter sent by the church of Rome to the church of Corinth. The authorship of this letter is traditionally assigned to a certain Clement, who probably composed it about the last decade of the century. Evidently he knew Πρὸς Ἑβραίους (as we may, for the sake of convenience, call our writing); there are several almost verbal reminiscences (cp. Dr. A. J. Carlyle in *The New Testament in the Apostolic Fathers*, pp. 44 f., where the evidence is sifted). This is beyond dispute, and proves that our writing was known at Rome during the last quarter of the first century. A fair specimen of the indebtedness of Clement to our epistle may be seen in a passage like the following, where I have underlined the allusions:

36[2-5] ὃς ὢν ἀπαύγασμα τῆς μεγαλωσύνης αὐτοῦ, τοσούτῳ μείζων ἐστὶν ἀγγέλων, ὅσῳ διαφορώτερον ὄνομα κεκληρονόμηκεν· γέγραπται γὰρ οὕτως·

ὁ ποιῶν τοὺς ἀγγέλους αὐτοῦ πνεύματα
καὶ τοὺς λειτουργοὺς αὐτοῦ πυρὸς φλόγα.

ἐπὶ δὲ τῷ υἱῷ αὐτοῦ οὕτως εἶπεν ὁ δεσπότης·

υἱός μου εἶ σύ,
ἐγὼ σήμερον γεγέννηκά σε·

αἴτησαι παρ' ἐμοῦ, καὶ δώσω σοι ἔθνη τὴν κληρονομίαν σου καὶ τὴν κατάσχεσίν σου τὰ πέρατα τῆς γῆς.
καὶ πάλιν λέγει πρὸς αὐτόν·

κάθου ἐκ δεξιῶν μου,
ἕως ἂν θῶ τοὺς ἐχθρούς σου ὑποπόδιον τῶν ποδῶν σου.

τίνες οὖν οἱ ἐχθροί; οἱ φαῦλοι καὶ ἀντιτασσόμενοι τῷ θελήματι αὐτοῦ.

To this we may add a sentence from what precedes:

36^1 Ἰησοῦν Χριστὸν τὸν ἀρχιερέα τῶν προσφορῶν ἡμῶν, τὸν προστάτην καὶ βοηθὸν τῆς ἀσθενείας ἡμῶν.

2^{18} δύναται τοῖς πειραζομένοις βοηθῆσαι. . . . 3^1 κατανοήσατε τὸν ἀπόστολον καὶ ἀρχιερέα τῆς ὁμολογίας ἡμῶν Ἰησοῦν.

The same phrase occurs twice in later doxologies, διὰ τοῦ ἀρχιερέως καὶ προστάτου (τῶν ψυχῶν ἡμῶν, 61^3) (ἡμῶν, 64^1) Ἰησοῦ Χριστοῦ. There is no convincing proof that Ignatius or Polykarp used Πρὸς Ἑβραίους, but the so-called Epistle of Barnabas contains some traces of it (*e.g.* in $4^{9f.}$ $5^{5.6}$ and 6^{17-19}). Barnabas is a second-rate interpretation of the OT ceremonial system, partly on allegorical lines, to warn Christians against having anything to do with Judaism; its motto might be taken from 3^6 ἵνα μὴ προσρησσώμεθα ὡς προσήλυτοι (*v.l.* ἐπήλυτοι) τῷ ἐκείνων νόμῳ. In the homily called 2 Clement our writing is freely employed, *e.g.* in

11^6 ὥστε, ἀδελφοί μου, μὴ διψυχῶμεν, ἀλλὰ ἐλπίσαντες ὑπομείνωμεν, ἵνα καὶ τὸν μισθὸν κομισώμεθα. πιστὸς γάρ ἐστιν ὁ ἐπαγγειλάμενος τὰς ἀντιμισθίας ἀποδιδόναι ἑκάστῳ ἔργων αὐτοῦ.

10^{23} κατέχωμεν τὴν ὁμολογίαν τῆς ἐλπίδος ἀκλινῆ, πιστὸς γὰρ ὁ ἐπαγγειλάμενος.

1^6 ἀποθέμενοι ἐκεῖνο ὃ περικείμεθα νέφος τῇ αὐτοῦ θελήσει.

12^1 τοσοῦτον ἔχοντες περικείμενον ἡμῖν νέφος μαρτύρων, ὄγκον ἀποθέμενοι πάντα.

16^4 προσευχὴ δὲ ἐκ καλῆς συνειδήσεως.

13^{18} προσεύχεσθε περὶ ἡμῶν· πειθόμεθα γὰρ ὅτι καλὴν συνείδησιν ἔχομεν.

"It seems difficult, in view of the verbal coincidences, to resist the conclusion that the language of 2 Clement is unconsciously influenced by that of Hebrews" (Dr. A. J. Carlyle in *The New Testament in the Apostolic Fathers*, p. 126). As 2 Clement is, in all likelihood, a product either of the Roman or of the Alexandrian church, where Πρὸς Ἑβραίους was early appreciated, this becomes doubly probable.

There is no reason why Justin Martyr, who had lived at Rome, should not have known it; but the evidence for his use of it (see on 3^1 11^4 etc.) is barely beyond dispute. Hermas, however, knew it; the *Shepherd* shows repeated traces of it (cf. Zahn's edition, pp. 439 f.). It was read in the North African church, as Tertullian's allusion proves (see p. xvii), and with particular interest in the Alexandrian church, even before Clement wrote (cp. p. xviii). Clement's use of it is unmistakable, though he does not show any sympathy with its ideas about sacrifice.[1] Naturally a thinker like Marcion ignored it, though why it shared with First Peter the fate of exclusion from the Muratorian canon is inexplicable. However, the evidence of the second century upon the whole is sufficient to show that it was being widely circulated and appreciated as an edifying religious treatise, canonical or not.

(ii.)

By this time it had received the title of Πρὸς Ἑβραίους. Whatever doubts there were about the authorship, the writing never went under any title except this in the later church; which proves that, though not original, the title must be early. Ἑβραῖοι[2] was intended to mean Jewish Christians. Those who affixed this title had no idea of its original destination; otherwise they would have chosen a local term, for the writing is obviously intended for a special community. They were struck by the interest of the writing in the OT sacrifices and priests, however, and imagined in a superficial way that it must have been addressed to Jewish Christians. Ἑβραῖοι was still an archaic equivalent for Ἰουδαῖοι; and those who called our writing Πρὸς Ἑβραίους must have imagined that it had been originally meant for Jewish (*i.e.* Hebrew-speaking) Christians in Palestine, or, in a broader sense, for Christians who had been born in Judaism. The latter is more probable. Where the title originated we cannot say; the corresponding description of 1 Peter as *ad gentes* originated in the Western church, but Πρὸς Ἑβραίους is common both to the Western and the Eastern churches. The very fact that so vague and misleading a title was added, proves that by the second century all traces of the original destination of the writing had been lost. It is, like the *Ad Familiares* of Cicero's correspondence, one of the erroneous titles in ancient literature, "hardly more than a reflection of the impression produced on an early copyist" (W. Robertson Smith). The reason why the original destination had been lost sight of, was probably the fact that it was a small household church—not one of the great churches, but a more limited circle, which may have become merged in the larger local church as time went on. Had it been sent, for example, to any large church like that at Rome or Alexandria, there would have been neither the need

[1] Cp. R. B. Tollington's *Clement of Alexandria*, vol. ii. pp. 225 f.

[2] It is quite impossible to regard it as original, in an allegorical sense, as though the writer, like Philo, regarded ὁ Ἑβραῖος as the typical believer who, a second Abraham, migrated or crossed from the sensuous to the spiritual world. The writer never alludes to Abraham in this connexion; indeed he never uses Ἑβραῖος at all.

nor the opportunity for changing the title to Πρὸς Ἑβραίους. Our writing is not a manifesto to Jewish Christians in general, or to Palestinian Jewish Christians, as πρὸς Ἑβραίους would imply; indeed it is not addressed to Jewish Christians at all. Whoever were its original readers, they belonged to a definite, local group or circle. That is the first inference from the writing itself; the second is, that they were not specifically Jewish Christians. The canonical title has had an unfortunate influence upon the interpretation of the writing (an influence which is still felt in some quarters). It has been responsible for the idea, expressed in a variety of forms, that the writer is addressing Jewish Christians in Palestine or elsewhere who were tempted, *e.g.*, by the war of A.D. 66–70, to fall back into Judaism; and even those who cannot share this view sometimes regard the readers as swayed by some hereditary associations with their old faith, tempted by the fascinations of a ritual, outward system of religion, to give up the spiritual messianism of the church. All such interpretations are beside the point. The writer never mentions Jews or Christians. He views his readers without any distinction of this kind; to him they are in danger of relapsing, but there is not a suggestion that the relapse is into Judaism, or that he is trying to wean them from a preoccupation with Jewish religion. He never refers to the temple, any more than to circumcision. It is the tabernacle of the pentateuch which interests him, and all his knowledge of the Jewish ritual is gained from the LXX and later tradition. The LXX is for him and his readers the codex of their religion, the appeal to which was cogent, for Gentile Christians, in the early church. As Christians, his readers accepted the LXX as their bible. It was superfluous to argue for it; he could argue from it, as Paul had done, as a writer like Clement of Rome did afterwards. How much the LXX meant to Gentile Christians, may be seen in the case of a man like Tatian, for example, who explicitly declares that he owed to reading of the OT his conversion to Christianity (*Ad Graecos*, 29). It is true that our author, in arguing that Christ had to suffer, does not appeal to the LXX. But this is an idiosyncrasy, which does not affect the vital significance of the LXX prophecies. The Christians to whom he was writing had learned to appreciate their LXX as an authority, by their membership in the church. Their danger was not an undervaluing of the LXX as authoritative; it was a moral and mental danger, which the writer seeks to meet by showing how great their religion was intrinsically. This he could only do ultimately by assuming that they admitted the appeal to their bible, just as they admitted the divine Sonship of Jesus. There may have been Christians of Jewish birth among his readers; but he addresses his circle, irrespective of their origin, as all members of the People of God, who accept the Book of God. The writing, in short, might have been called *ad gentes* as aptly as First Peter, which also describes Gentile Christians as ὁ λαός, the People (cp. on 2^{17}). The readers were not in doubt of their religion. Its basis was unquestioned. What the trouble was, in their case, was no theoretical doubt about the codex or the contents of Christianity, but a practical failure to be loyal to their principles, which the writer seeks to meet by recalling them to the full meaning and responsibility of their faith; naturally he takes them to the common ground of the sacred LXX.

We touch here the question of the writer's aim. But, before discussing this, a word must be said about the authorship.

Had Πρὸς Ἑβραίους been addressed to Jews, the title would have been intelligible. Not only was there a [συνα]γωγὴ Ἑβρ[αίων] at Corinth (cp. Deissmann's *Light from the East*, pp. 13, 14), but a συναγωγὴ Αἰβρέων at Rome (cp. Schürer's *Geschichte des Jüd. Volkes*[3], iii. 46). Among the Jewish συναγωγαὶ mentioned in the Roman epitaphs (cp. N. Müller's *Die jüdische Katakombe am Monteverde zu Rom* . . ., Leipzig, 1912, pp. 110 f.), there is one of Ἑβρέοι, which Müller explains as in contrast to the synagogue of "vernaclorum" (Βερνάκλοι, βερνακλήσιοι), *i.e.* resident Jews as opposed to immigrants; though it seems truer, with E. Bormann (*Wiener Studien*, 1912, pp. 383 f.), to think of some Kultgemeinde which adhered to the use of Hebrew, or which, at any rate, was of Palestinian origin or connexion.

(iii.)

The knowledge of who the author was must have disappeared as soon as the knowledge of what the church was, for whom he wrote. Who wrote Πρὸς Ἑβραίους? We know as little of this as we do of the authorship of *The Whole Duty of Man*, that seventeenth-century classic of English piety. Conjectures sprang up, early in the second century, but by that time men were no wiser than we are. The mere fact that some said Barnabas, some Paul, proves that the writing had been circulating among the *adespota*. It was perhaps natural that our writing should be assigned to Barnabas, who, as a Levite, might be supposed to take a special interest in the ritual of the temple—the very reason which led to his association with the later Epistle of Barnabas. Also, he was called υἱὸς παρακλήσεως (Ac 4^{36}), which seemed to tally with He 13^{22} (τοῦ λόγου τῆς παρακλήσεως), just as the allusion to "beloved" in Ps 127^{2} (= 2 S $12^{24f.}$) was made to justify the attribution of the psalm to king Solomon. The difficulty about applying 2^{3} to a man like Barnabas was overlooked, and in North Africa, at any rate, the (Roman?) tradition of his authorship prevailed, as Tertullian's words in *de pudicitia* 20 show: "volo ex redundantia alicuius etiam comitis apostolorum testimonium superinducere, idoneum confirmandi de proximo jure disciplinam magistrorum. Extat enim et Barnabae titulus ad Hebraeos, adeo satis auctoritati viri, ut quem Paulus juxta se constituerit in abstinentiae tenore: 'aut ego solus et Barnabas non habemus hoc operandi potestatem?' (1 Co 9[6]). Et utique receptior apud ecclesias epistola Barnabae illo apocrypho Pastore moechorum. Monens itaque discipulos, omissis omnibus initiis, ad perfectionem magis tendere," etc. (quoting He 6[4f.]). What appeals to Tertullian in Πρὸς Ἑβραίους is its uncompromising denial of any second repentance. His increasing sympathy with the Montanists had led him to take a much less favourable view of the *Shepherd* of Hermas than he had once entertained; he now contrasts its lax tone with the rigour of Πρὸς Ἑβραίους, and seeks to buttress his argument on this point by insisting as much as he can on the authority of Πρὸς Ἑβραίους as a production of the apostolic Barnabas. Where this tradition originated we cannot tell. Tertullian refers to it as a fact, not as an oral tradition; he may have known some MS of the writing with the title Βαρνάβα πρὸς Ἑβραίους (ἐπιστολή), and this may have come from Montanist circles in Asia Minor, as Zahn suggests. But all this is guessing in the dark about a guess in the dark.

Since Paul was the most considerable letter-writer of the primitive church, it was natural that in some quarters this anonymous writing should be assigned to him, as was done apparently in the Alexandrian church, although even there scholarly readers felt qualms at an early period, and endeavoured to explain the idiosyncrasies of style by supposing that some disciple of Paul, like Luke, translated it from Hebrew into Greek. This Alexandrian tradition of Paul's authorship was evidently criticized in other quarters, and the controversy drew from Origen the one piece of enlightened literary criticism which the early discussions produced. Ὅτι ὁ χαρακτὴρ τῆς λέξεως τῆς πρὸς Ἑβραίους ἐπιγεγραμμένης ἐπιστολῆς οὐκ ἔχει τὸ ἐν λόγῳ ἰδιωτικὸν τοῦ ἀποστόλου, ὁμολογήσαντος ἑαυτὸν ἰδιώτην εἶναι τῷ λόγῳ (2 Co 11[6]), τουτέστι τῇ φράσει, ἀλλά ἐστιν ἡ ἐπιστολὴ συνθέσει τῆς λέξεως Ἑλληνικωτέρα, πᾶς ὁ ἐπιστάμενος κρίνειν φράσεων διαφορὰς ὁμολογήσαι ἄν. πάλιν τε αὖ ὅτι τὰ νοήματα τῆς ἐπιστολῆς θαυμάσιά ἐστι, καὶ οὐ δεύτερα τῶν ἀποστολικῶν ὁμολογουμένων γραμμάτων, καὶ τοῦτο ἂν συμφήσαι εἶναι ἀληθὲς πᾶς ὁ προσέχων τῇ ἀναγνώσει τῇ ἀποστολικῇ. . . . Ἐγὼ δὲ ἀποφαινόμενος εἴποιμ' ἂν ὅτι τὰ μὲν νοήματα τοῦ ἀποστόλου ἐστίν, ἡ δὲ φράσις καὶ ἡ σύνθεσις ἀπομνημονεύσαντός τινος τὰ ἀποστολικά, καὶ ὡσπερεὶ σχολιογραφήσαντός τινος τὰ εἰρημένα ὑπὸ τοῦ διδασκάλου. εἴ τις οὖν ἐκκλησία ἔχει ταύτην τὴν ἐπιστολὴν ὡς Παύλου, αὕτη εὐδοκιμείτω καὶ ἐπὶ τούτῳ. οὐ γὰρ εἰκῇ οἱ ἀρχαῖοι ἄνδρες ὡς Παύλου αὐτὴν παραδεδώκασι. τίς δὲ ὁ γράψας τὴν ἐπιστολήν, τὸ μὲν ἀληθὲς θεὸς οἶδεν (quoted by Eusebius, *H.E.* vi. 25. 11–14).[1] Origen is too good a scholar to notice the guess that it was a translation from Hebrew, but he adds, ἡ δὲ εἰς ἡμᾶς φθάσασα ἱστορία, ὑπό τινων μὲν λεγόντων, ὅτι Κλήμης ὁ γενόμενος ἐπίσκοπος Ῥωμαίων ἔγραψε τὴν ἐπιστολήν, ὑπό τινων δὲ ὅτι Λουκᾶς ὁ γράψας τὸ εὐαγγέλιον καὶ τὰς Πράξεις. The idea that Clement of Rome wrote it was, of course, an erroneous deduction from the echoes of it in his pages, almost as unfounded as the notion that Luke wrote it, either independently or as an amanuensis of Paul—a view probably due ultimately to the explanation of how his gospel came to be an apostolic, canonical work. Origen yields more to the "Pauline" interpretation of Πρὸς Ἑβραίους than is legitimate; but, like Erasmus at a later day,[2] he was living in an environment where the "Pauline" tradition was almost a note of orthodoxy. Even his slight scruples failed to keep the question open. In the Eastern church, any hesitation soon passed away, and the scholarly scruples of men like Clement of Alexandria and Origen made no impression on the church at large. It is significant, for example, that when even Eusebius comes to give his own opinion (*H.E.* iii. 38. 2), he alters the hypothesis about Clement of Rome, and makes him merely the translator of a Pauline Hebrew original, not the author of a Greek original. As a rule, however, Πρὸς Ἑβραίους was accepted as fully Pauline, and passed into the NT canon of the Asiatic, the Egyptian, and the Syriac churches without question. In the Syriac canon of A.D. 400 (text as in Souter's *Text and Canon of NT*, p. 226), indeed, it stands next to Romans in the list of Paul's epistles (see below, § 4). Euthalius, it is true, about the middle of the fifth century, argues for it in a way that indicates a current of opposition still flowing in certain quarters, but ecclesiastically Πρὸς Ἑβραίους in the East as a Pauline document could defy doubts. The firm conviction of the Eastern church as a whole comes out in a remark like that of Apollinarius the bishop of Laodicea, towards the close of the fourth century: ποῦ γέγραπται ὅτι χαρακτήρ ἐστι τῆς ὑποστάσεως ὁ υἱός; παρὰ τῷ ἀποστόλῳ Παύλῳ ἐν τῇ πρὸς Ἑβραίους. Οὐκ ἐκκλησιάζεται. Ἀφ' οὗ κατηγγέλη τὸ εὐαγγέλιον Χριστοῦ, Παύλου εἶναι πεπίστευται ἡ ἐπιστολή (*Dial. de sancta Trin.* 922).

It was otherwise in the Western church, where Πρὸς Ἑβραίους was for long either read simply as an edifying treatise, or, if regarded as canonical, assigned to some anonymous apostolic

[1] There is a parallel to the last words in the scoffing close of an epigram in the Greek Anthology (ix. 135): γράψε τις; οἶδε θεός· τίνος εἵνεκεν; οἶδε καὶ αὐτός.

[2] "Ut a stilo Pauli, quod ad phrasin attinet, longe lateque discrepat, ita ad spiritum ac pectus Paulinum vehementer accedit."

writer rather than to Paul. Possibly the use made of Πρὸς Ἑβραίους by the Montanists and the Novatians, who welcomed its denial of a second repentance, compromised it in certain quarters. Besides, the Roman church had never accepted the Alexandrian tradition of Paul's authorship. Hence, even when, on its merits, it was admitted to the canon, there was a strong tendency to treat it as anonymous, as may be seen, for example, in Augustine's references. Once in the canon, however, it gradually acquired a Pauline prestige, and, as Greek scholarship faded, any scruples to the contrary became less and less intelligible. It was not till the study of Greek revived again, at the dawn of the Reformation, that the question was reopened.

The data in connexion with the early fortunes of Πρὸς Ἑβραίους in church history belong to text-books on the Canon, like Zahn's *Geschichte d. NT Kanons*, i. 283 f., 577 f., ii. 160 f., 358 f.; Leipoldt's *Geschichte d. NT Kanons*, i. pp. 188 f., 219 f.; and Jacquier's *Le Nouveau Testament dans L'Église Chrétienne*, i. (1911).

Few characters mentioned in the NT have escaped the attention of those who have desired in later days to identify the author of Πρὸς Ἑβραίους. Apollos, Peter, Philip, Silvanus, and even Prisca have been suggested, besides Aristion, the alleged author of Mk 16^{9-20}. I have summarized these views elsewhere (*Introd. to Lit. of NT.*[3], pp. 438–442), and it is superfluous here to discuss hypotheses which are in the main due to an irrepressible desire to construct NT romances. Perhaps our modern pride resents being baffled by an ancient document, but it is better to admit that we are not yet wiser on this matter than Origen was, seventeen centuries ago. The author of Πρὸς Ἑβραίους cannot be identified with any figure known to us in the primitive Christian tradition. He left great prose to some little clan of early Christians, but who they were and who he was, τὸ μὲν ἀληθὲς θεὸς οἶδεν. To us he is a voice and no more. The theory which alone explains the conflicting traditions is that for a time the writing was circulated as an anonymous tract. Only on this hypothesis can the simultaneous emergence of the Barnabas and the Paul traditions in different quarters be explained, as well as the persistent tradition in the Roman church that it was anonymous. As Zahn sensibly concludes, "those into whose hands Πρὸς Ἑβραίους came either looked upon it as an anonymous writing from ancient apostolic times, or else resorted to conjecture. If Paul did not write it, they thought, then it must have been composed by some other prominent teacher of the apostolic church. Barnabas was such a man." In one sense, it was fortunate that the Pauline hypothesis prevailed so early and so extensively, for apart from this help it might have been difficult for Πρὸς Ἑβραίους to win or to retain its place in the canon. But even when it had been lodged securely inside the canon, some Western churchmen still clung for a while to the old tradition of its anonymity,[1] although they could do no more than hold this as a pious opinion. The later church was right in assigning Πρὸς Ἑβραίους a canonical position. The original reasons might be erroneous or doubtful, but even in the Western church, where they continued to be questioned, there was an increasing indisposition to challenge their canonical result.

(iv.)

Thrown back, in the absence of any reliable tradition, upon the internal evidence, we can only conclude that the writer was one of those personalities in whom the primitive church was more rich than we sometimes realize. "Si l'on a pu comparer saint Paul à Luther," says Ménégoz, "nous comparerions volontiers l'auteur de l'Épître aux Hébreux à Mélanchthon." He was a highly trained διδάσκαλος, perhaps a Jewish Christian, who had imbibed the philosophy of Alexandrian Judaism before his conversion, a man of literary culture and deep religious feeling. He writes to what is apparently a small community or circle of Christians, possibly one of the household-churches, to which he was attached. For some reason or another he was absent from them, and, although he hopes to rejoin them before long, he feels moved to send them this letter ($13^{23f.}$) to rally them. It is possible to infer from 13^{24} (see note) that they belonged to Italy; in any case, Πρὸς Ἑβραίους was written either to or from some church in Italy. Beyond the fact that the writer and his readers had been evangelized by some of the disciples of Jesus ($2^{3.\ 4}$), we know nothing more about them. The words in $2^{3.\ 4}$ do not mean that they belonged to the second generation, of course, in a chronological sense, for such words would have applied to the converts of any mission during the first thirty years or so after the crucifixion, and the only other inference to be drawn, as to the date, is from passages like $10^{32f.}$. and 13^{7}, viz. that the first readers of Πρὸς Ἑβραίους were not neophytes; they had lived through some rough experiences, and indeed their friend expects from them a maturity of experience and intelligence which he is disappointed to miss ($5^{11f.}$); also,

[1] According to Professor Souter (*Text and Canon of NT*, p. 190) the epistle is ignored by the African Canon (*c.* 360), Optatus of Mileue in Numidia (370–385), the Acts of the Donatist Controversy, Zeno of Verona, an African by birth, and Foebadius of Agen (*ob. post* 392), while "Ambrosiaster" (fourth century?) "uses the work as canonical, but always as an anonymous work."

their original leaders have died, probably as martyrs (cp. on 13^{7}). For these and other reasons, a certain sense of disillusionment had begun to creep over them. Πρὸς Ἑβραίους is a λόγος παρακλήσεως, to steady and rally people who are πειραζόμενοι, their temptation being to renounce God, or at least to hesitate and retreat, to relax the fibre of loyal faith, as if God were too difficult to follow in the new, hard situation. Once, at the outset of their Christian career, they had been exposed to mob-rioting ($10^{32f.}$), when they had suffered losses of property, for the sake of the gospel, and also the loud jeers and sneers which pagans and Jews alike heaped sometimes upon the disciples. This they had borne manfully, in the first glow of their enthusiasm. Now, the more violent forms of persecution had apparently passed; what was left was the dragging experience of contempt at the hand of outsiders, the social ostracism and shame, which were threatening to take the heart out of them. Such was their rough, disconcerting environment. Unless an illegitimate amount of imagination is applied to the internal data, they cannot be identified with what is known of any community in the primitive church, so scanty is our information. Least of all is it feasible to connect them with the supposed effects of the Jewish rebellion which culminated in A.D. 70. Πρὸς Ἑβραίους cannot be later than about A.D. 85, as the use of it in Clement of Rome's epistle proves; how much earlier it is, we cannot say, but the controversy over the Law, which marked the Pauline phase, is evidently over.

It is perhaps not yet quite superfluous to point out that the use of the present tense (*e.g.* in $7^{8.\,20}$ $8^{3f.}$ $9^{6f.}$ 13^{10}) is no clue to the date, as though this implied that the Jewish temple was still standing. The writer is simply using the historic present of actions described in scripture. It is a literary method which is common in writings long after A.D. 70, *e.g.* in Josephus, who observes (*c. Apion*, i. 7) that any priest who violates a Mosaic regulation ἀπηγόρευται μήτε τοῖς βωμοῖς παρίστασθαι μήτε μετέχειν τῆς ἄλλης ἁγιστείας (so *Ant.* iii. 6. 7–12, xiv. 2. 2, etc.). Clement of Rome similarly writes as though the Mosaic ritual were still in existence (40–41, τῷ γὰρ ἀρχιερεῖ ἴδιαι λειτουργίαι δεδομέναι εἰσίν . . . καὶ Λευΐταις ἴδιαι διακονίαι ἐπίκεινται . . . προσφέρονται θυσίαι ἐν Ἰερουσαλὴμ μόνῃ), and the author of the *Ep. ad Diognet.* 3 writes that οἱ δέ γε θυσίαις αὐτῷ δι᾽ αἵματος καὶ κνίσης καὶ ὁλοκαυτωμάτων ἐπιτελεῖν οἰόμενοι καὶ ταύταις ταῖς τιμαῖς αὐτὸν γεραίρειν, οὐδέν μοι δοκοῦσι διαφέρειν τῶν εἰς τὰ κωφὰ τὴν αὐτὴν ἐνδεικνυμένων φιλοτιμίαν. The idea that the situation of the readers was in any way connected with the crisis of A.D. 66–70 in Palestine is unfounded. Πρὸς Ἑβραίους has nothing to do with the Jewish temple, nor with Palestinian Christians. There is not a syllable in the writing which suggests that either the author or his readers had any connexion with or interest in the contemporary temple and ritual of Judaism; their existence mattered as little to his idealist method of argument as their abolition. When he observes (8^{13}) that the old διαθήκη was ἐγγὺς ἀφανισμοῦ, all he means is that the old régime, superseded now by Jesus, was decaying even in Jeremiah's age.

(v.)

The object of Πρὸς Ἑβραίους may be seen from a brief analysis of its contents. The writer opens with a stately paragraph, introducing the argument that Jesus Christ as the Son of God is superior (*κρείττων*) to angels, in the order of revelation (1^{1}–2^{18}), and this, not in spite of but because of his incarnation and sufferings. He is also superior (*κρείττων*) even to Moses ($3^{1\text{-}6a}$), as a Son is superior to a servant. Instead of pursuing the argument further, the writer then gives an impressive bible reading on the 95th psalm, to prove that the People of God have still assured to them, if they will only have faith, the divine Rest in the world to come (3^{6b}–4^{13}). Resuming his argument, the writer now begins to show how Jesus as God's Son is superior to the Aaronic high priest (4^{14}–5^{10}). This is the heart of his subject, and he stops for a moment to rouse the attention of his readers (5^{11}–6^{20}) before entering upon the high theme. By a series of skilful transitions he has passed on from the Person of the Son, which is uppermost in chs. 1–4, to the Priesthood of the Son, which dominates chs. 7–8. Jesus as High Priest mediates a superior (*κρείττων*) order of religion or *διαθήκη* than that under which Aaron and his successors did their work for the People of God, and access to God, which is the supreme need of men, is now secured fully and finally by the relation of Jesus to God, in virtue of his sacrifice (6^{20}–8^{13}). The validity of this sacrifice is then proved (9^{1}–10^{18}); it is absolutely efficacious, as no earlier sacrifice of victims could be, in securing forgiveness and fellowship for man. The remainder of the writing (10^{19}–13^{24}) is a series of impressive appeals for constancy. The first ($10^{19\text{-}31}$) is a skilful blend of encouragement and warning. He then appeals to the fine record of his readers ($10^{32f.}$), bidding them be worthy of their own past, and inciting them to faith in God by reciting a great roll-call of heroes and heroines belonging to God's People in the past, from Abel to the Maccabean martyrs ($11^{1\text{-}40}$). He further kindles their imagination and conscience by holding up Jesus as the Supreme Leader of all the faithful ($12^{1\text{-}3}$), even along the path of suffering; besides, he adds ($12^{4\text{-}11}$), suffering is God's discipline for those who belong to his household. To prefer the world ($12^{12\text{-}17}$) is to incur a fearful penalty; the one duty for us is to accept the position of fellowship with God, in a due spirit of awe and grateful confidence ($12^{18\text{-}29}$). A brief note of some ethical duties follows ($13^{1\text{-}7}$), with a sudden warning against some current tendencies to compromise their spiritual religion ($13^{8\text{-}16}$). A postscript ($13^{17\text{-}24}$), with some *personalia*, ends the epistle.

It is artificial to divide up a writing of this kind, which is not a treatise on theology, and I have therefore deliberately abstained from introducing any formal divisions and subdivisions in the commentary. The flow of thought, with its turns and windings, is best followed from point to point. So far as the general plan goes, it is determined by the idea of the finality of the Christian revelation in Jesus the Son of God. This is brought out (A) by a proof that he is superior to angels (1^{1}–2^{18}) and Moses ($3^{1\text{-}6a}$), followed by the special exhortation of 3^{6b}–4^{13}. Thus far it is what may be termed the Personality of the Son which is discussed. Next (B) comes the Son as High Priest (4^{14}–7^{28}), including the parenthetical exhortation of 5^{11}–6^{20}. The (C) Sacrifice of this High Priest in his Sanctuary then (8^{1}–10^{18}) is discussed, each of the three arguments, which are vitally connected, laying stress from one side or another upon the absolute efficacy of the revelation. This is the dominant idea of the writing, and it explains the particular line which the writer strikes out. He takes a very serious view of the position of his friends and readers. They are disheartened and discouraged for various reasons, some of which are noted in the course of the epistle. There is the strain of hardship, the unpleasant experience of being scoffed at, and the ordinary temptations of immorality, which may bring them, if they are not careful, to the verge of actual apostasy. The writer appears to feel that the only way to save them from ruining themselves is to put before them the fearful and unsuspected consequences of their failure. Hence three times over the writer draws a moving picture of the fate which awaits apostates and renegades ($6^{4f.}$ $10^{26f.}$ $12^{15f.}$). But the special line of argument which he adopts in 5–10^{18} must be connected somehow with the danger in which he felt his friends involved, and this is only to be explained if we assume that their relaxed interest in Christianity arose out of an imperfect conception of what Jesus meant for their faith. He offers no theoretical disquisition; it is to reinforce and deepen their conviction of the place of Jesus in religion, that he argues, pleads, and warns, dwelling on the privileges and responsibilities of the relationship in which Jesus had placed them. All the help they needed, all the hope they required, lay in the access to God mediated by Jesus, if they would only realize it.

This is what makes the writing of special interest. In the first place (*a*) the author is urged by a practical necessity to think out his faith, or rather to state the full content of his faith, for the benefit of his readers. Their need puts him on his mettle. "Une chose surtant," says Anatole France, "donne le l'attrait à la pensée des hommes: c'est l'inquiétude. Un esprit qui n'est point anxieux m'irrite ou m'ennuie." In a sense all the NT writers are spurred by this anxiety, but the author of Πρὸς Ἑβραίους pre-eminently. It is not anxiety about his personal faith, nor about the prospects of Christianity, but about the loyalty of those for whom he feels himself responsible; his very certainty of the absolute value of Christianity makes him anxious when he sees his friends ready to give it up, anxious on their behalf, and anxious to bring out as lucidly and persuasively as possible the full meaning of the revelation of God in Jesus. What he writes is not a theological treatise in cold blood, but a statement of the faith, alive with practical interest. The situation of his readers has stirred his own mind, and he bends all his powers of thought and emotion to rally them. There is a vital urgency behind what he writes for his circle. But (*b*), more than this, the form into which he throws his appeal answers to the situation of his readers. He feels that the word for them is the absolute worth of Jesus as the Son of God; it is to bring this out that he argues, in the middle part of his epistle, so elaborately and anxiously about the priesthood and sacrifice of Jesus. The idealistic conception of the two spheres, the real and eternal, and the phenomenal (which is the mere *σκιά* and *ὑπόδειγμα*, a *παραβολή*, an *ἀντίτυπον* of the former), is applied to the sacrifice of Jesus Christ, which inaugurates and realizes the eternal *διαθήκη* between God and man. In a series of contrasts, he brings out the superiority of this revelation to the OT *διαθήκη* with its cultus. But not because the contemporary form of the latter had any attractions for his readers. It is with the archaic *σκηνή* described in the OT that he deals, in order to elucidate the final value of Jesus and his sacrifice under the new *διαθήκη*, which was indeed the real and eternal one. To readers like his friends, with an imperfect sense of all that was contained in their faith, he says, "Come back to your bible, and see how fully it suggests the positive value of Jesus." Christians were finding Christ in the LXX, especially his sufferings in the prophetic scriptures, but our author falls back on the pentateuch and the psalter especially to illustrate the commanding position of Jesus as the Son of God in the eternal *διαθήκη*, and the duties as well as the privileges of living under such a final revelation, where the purpose and the promises of God for his People are realized as they could not be under the OT *διαθήκη*. Why the writer concentrates upon the priesthood and sacrifice of Jesus in this eternal order of things, is due in part to his general conception of religion (see pp. xliii f.). For him there could be no religion without a priest. But this idea is of direct service to his readers, as he believes. Hence the first mention of Jesus as *ἀρχιερεύς* occurs as a reason for loyalty and confidence ($2^{14f.}$). Nothing is more practical in religion than an idea, a relevant idea powerfully urged. When the writer concentrates for a while upon this cardinal idea of Jesus as ἀρχιερεύς, therefore, it is because nothing can be more vital, he thinks, for his friends than to show them the claims and resources of their faith, disclosing the rich and real nature of God's revelation to them in his Son. Access to God, confidence in God, pardon for sins of the past, and hope for the future—all this is bound up with the διαθήκη of Christ, and the writer reveals it between the lines of the LXX, to which as members of the People of God his friends naturally turned for instruction and revelation. This διαθήκη, he argues, is far superior to the earlier one, as the Son of God is superior to angels and to Moses himself; nay more, it is superior in efficacy, as the real is superior to its shadowy outline, for the sacrifice which underlies any διαθήκη is fulfilled in Christ as it could not be under the levitical cultus. The function of Christ as high priest is to mediate the direct access of the People to God, and all this has been done so fully and finally that Christians have simply to avail themselves of its provisions for their faith and need.

What the writer feels called upon to deal with, therefore, is not any sense of disappointment in his readers that they had not an impressive ritual or an outward priesthood, nor any hankering after such in contemporary Judaism; it is a failure to see that Christianity is the absolute religion, a failure which is really responsible for the unsatisfactory and even the critical situation of the readers. To meet this need, the writer argues as well as exhorts. He seeks to show from the LXX how the Christian faith alone fulfils the conditions of real religion, and as he knows no other religion than the earlier phase in Israel, he takes common ground with his readers on the LXX record of the first διαθήκη, in order to let them see even there the implications and anticipations of the higher.

But while the author never contemplates any fusion of Christianity with Jewish legalism, and while the argument betrays no trace of Jewish religion as a competing attraction for the readers, it might be argued that some speculative Judaism had affected the mind of the readers. No basis for this can be found in $13^{9f.}$. Yet if there were any proselytes among the readers, they may have felt the fascination of the Jewish system, as those did afterwards who are warned by Ignatius (*ad Philad.* 6, etc.), "Better listen to Christianity from a circumcised Christian than to Judaism from one uncircumcised." "It is monstrous to talk of Jesus Christ and ἰουδαΐζειν" (*ad Magnes.* 10). This interpretation was put forward by Häring (*Studien und Kritiken*, 1891, pp. 589 f.), and it has been most ingeniously argued by Professor Purdy (*Expositor*[8], xix. pp. 123–139), who thinks that the emphasis upon "Jesus" means that the readers were exposed to the seductions of a liberal Judaism which offered an escape from persecution and other difficulties by presenting a Christ who was spiritual, divorced from history; that this liberal, speculative Judaism came forward as "a more developed and perfected type of religion than Christianity"; and that, without being legalistic, it claimed to be a traditional, ritualistic faith, which was at once inward and ceremonial. The objection to such interpretations,[1] however, is that they explain *ignotum per ignotius*. We know little or nothing of such liberal Judaism in the first century, any more than of a tendency on the part of Jewish Christians to abandon Christianity about A.D. 70 for their ancestral faith. Indeed any influence of Jewish propaganda, ritualistic or latitudinarian, must be regarded as secondary, at the most, in the situation of the readers as that is to be inferred from Πρὸς Ἑβραίους itself. When we recognize the real method and aim of the writer, it becomes clear that he was dealing with a situation which did not require any such influence to account for it. The form taken by his argument is determined by the conception, or rather the misconception, of the faith entertained by his friends; and this in turn is due not to any political or racial factors, but to social and mental causes, such as are sufficiently indicated in Πρὸς Ἑβραίους itself. Had the danger been a relapse into Judaism of any kind, it would have implied a repudiation of Jesus Christ as messiah and divine—the very truth which the writer can assume! What he needs to do is not to defend this, but to develop it.

The writing, therefore, for all its elaborate structure, has a spontaneous aim. It is not a homily written at large, to which by some afterthought, on the part of the writer or of some editor, a few *personalia* have been appended in ch. 13. The argumentative sections bear directly and definitely upon the situation of the readers, whom the writer has in view throughout, even when he seems to be far from their situation. Which brings us to the problem of the literary structure of Πρὸς Ἑβραίους.

(vi.)

See especially W. Wrede's monograph, *Das literarische Rätsel d. Hebräerbriefs* (1906), with the essays of E. Burggaller and R. Perdelwitz in *Zeitschrift für Neutest. Wissenschaft* (1908, pp. 110f.; 1910, pp. 59f., 105f.); V. Monod's *De titulo epistulae vulgo ad Hebraeos inscriptae* (1910); C. C.

---

[1] Cp., further, Professor Dickie's article in *Expositor*[8], v. pp. 371f. The notion that the writer is controverting an external view of Christ's person, which shrank, *e.g.*, from admitting his humiliation and real humanity, had been urged by Julius Kögel in *Die Verborgenheit Jesu als des Messias* (Greifenswald, 1909) and in *Der Sohn und die Söhne, ein exegetische Studie zu Heb.* 2^{5-18} (1904).

Torrey's article in the *Journal of Biblical Literature* (1911), pp. 137–156; J. W. Slot's *De letterkundige vorm v. d. Brief aan de Hebräer* (1912), with J. Quentel's essay in *Revue Biblique* (1912, pp. 50 f.) and M. Jones' paper in *Expositor*^{8}, xii. 426 f.

The literary problem of Πρὸς Ἑβραίους is raised by the absence of any address and the presence of personal matter in ch. 13. Why (*a*) has it no introductory greeting? And why (*b*) has it a postscript? As for the former point (*a*), there may have been, in the original, an introductory title. Πρὸς Ἑβραίους opens with a great sentence ($1^{1f.}$), but Eph $1^{3f.}$ is just such another, and there is no reason why the one should not have followed a title-address any more than the other.[1] It may have been lost by accident, in the tear and wear of the manuscript, for such accidents are not unknown in ancient literature. This is, at any rate, more probable than the idea that it was suppressed because the author (Barnabas, Apollos?) was not of sufficiently apostolic rank for the canon. Had this interest been operative, it would have been perfectly easy to alter a word or two in the address itself. Besides, Πρὸς Ἑβραίους was circulating long before it was admitted to the canon, and it circulated even afterwards as non-canonical; yet not a trace of any address, Pauline or non-Pauline, has ever survived. Which, in turn, tells against the hypothesis that such ever existed—at least, against the theory that it was deleted when the writing was canonized. If the elision of the address ever took place, it must have been very early, and rather as the result of accident than deliberately. Yet there is no decisive reason why the writing should not have begun originally as it does in its present form. Nor does this imply (*b*) that the personal data in ch. 13 are irrelevant. Πρὸς Ἑβραίους has a certain originality in form as well as in content; it is neither an epistle nor a homily, pure and simple. True, down to 12^{29} (or 13^{17}) there is little or nothing that might not have been spoken by a preacher to his audience, and Valckenaer (on 4^{3}) is right, so far, in saying, "haec magnifica ad Hebraeos missa dissertatio oratio potius dicenda est quam epistola." Yet the writer is not addressing an ideal public; he is not composing a treatise for Christendom at large. It is really unreal to explain away passages like $5^{11f.}$ $10^{32f.}$ $12^{4f.}$ and 13^{1-9} as rhetorical abstractions.

Πρὸς Ἑβραίους was the work of a διδάσκαλος, who knew how to deliver a λόγος παρακλήσεως. Parts of it probably represent what he had used in preaching already (*e.g.* 3^{7}). But, while it has sometimes the tone of sermon notes written out, it is not a

[1] Ep. Barnabas begins with ἀδελφοί, οὕτως δεῖ ἡμᾶς φρονεῖν περὶ Ἰησοῦ Χριστοῦ ὡς περὶ θεοῦ, etc.; 2 Clement starts with a greeting, χαίρετε, υἱοὶ καὶ θυγατέρες, ἐν ὀνόματι κυρίου τοῦ ἀγαπήσαντος ἡμᾶς ἐν εἰρήνῃ.

sermon in the air. To strike out $13^{19. 22-24}$ or $13^{1-7. 16-19. 22f.}$ (Torrey)[1] does not reduce it from a letter or epistle to a sermon like 2 Clement. Thus, *e.g.*, a phrase like 11^{32} (see note) is as intelligible in a written work as in a spoken address. It is only by emptying passages like $5^{11f.}$ and $10^{32f.}$ of their full meaning that anyone can speak of the writer as composing a sermon at large or for an ideal public. Part of the force of $5^{11f.}$, *e.g.*, is due to the fact that the writer is dealing with a real situation, pleading that in what he is going to say he is not writing simply to display his own talent or to please himself, but for the serious, urgent need of his readers. They do not deserve what he is going to give them. But he will give it! A thoroughly pastoral touch, which is lost by being turned into a rhetorical excuse for deploying some favourite ideas of his own. According to Wrede, the author wrote in $13^{18. 19}$ on the basis of (Philem ^{22}) 2 Co $1^{11. 12}$ to make it appear as though Paul was the author, and then added 13^{23} on the basis of Ph $2^{19. 23. 24}$; but why he should mix up these reminiscences, which, according to Wrede, are contradictory, it is difficult to see. Had he wished to put a Pauline colour into the closing paragraphs, he would surely have done it in a lucid, coherent fashion, instead of leaving the supposed allusions to Paul's Roman imprisonment so enigmatic. But, though Wrede thinks that the hypothesis of a pseudonymous conclusion is the only way of explaining the phenomena of ch. 13, he agrees that to excise it entirely is out of the question. Neither the style nor the contents justify such a radical theory,[2] except on the untenable hypothesis that 1–12 is a pure treatise. The analogies of a doxology being followed by personal matter (*e.g.* 2 Ti 4^{18}, 1 P 4^{11} etc.) tell against the idea that Πρὸς Ἑβραίους must have ended with 13^{21}, and much less could it have ended with 13^{17}. To assume that the writer suddenly bethought him, at the end, of giving a Pauline appearance to what he had written, and that he therefore added $13^{22f.}$, is to credit him with too little ability. Had he wished to convey this impression, he would certainly have gone further and made changes in the earlier part. Nor is it likely that anyone added the closing verses in order to facilitate its entrance into the NT canon by bringing it into line with the other epistles. The canon was drawn up for worship, and if Πρὸς Ἑβραίους was originally a discourse, it seems very unlikely that anyone would have gone

[1] To excise 13^{1-7} as a "formless jumble of rather commonplace admonitions" is a singular misjudgment.

[2] The linguistic proof is cogently led by C. R. Williams in the *Journal of Biblical Literature* (1911), pp. 129–136, who shows that the alleged special parallels between He 13 and Paul are neither so numerous nor so significant as is commonly supposed, and that the only fair explanation of He 13 as a whole is that it was written to accompany 1–12.

out of his way, on this occasion, to add some enigmatic personal references. In short, while Πρὸς Ἑβραίους betrays here and there the interests and methods of an effective preacher, the epistolary form is not a piece of literary fiction; still less is it due (in ch. 13) to some later hand. It is hardly too much to say that the various theories about the retouching of the 13th chapter of Πρὸς Ἑβραίους are as valuable, from the standpoint of literary criticism, as Macaulay's unhesitating belief that Dr. Johnson had revised and retouched *Cecilia.*

§ 2. The Religious Ideas.

In addition to the text-books on NT theology, consult Riehm's *Lehrbegriff des Hebräerbriefs*[2] (1867), W. Milligan's *Ascension and Heavenly Priesthood of our Lord* (1891), Ménégoz's *La Théologie de l'Épître aux Hébreux* (1894), A. Seeberg's *Der Tod Christi* (1895), A. B. Bruce's *The Epistle to the Hebrews* (1899), G. Milligan's *The Theology of the Epistle to the Hebrews* (1899), G. Vos on "The Priesthood of Christ in Hebrews" (*Princeton Theological Review*, 1907, pp. 423 f., 579 f.), Du Bose's *Highpriesthood and Sacrifice* (1908), A. Nairne's *The Epistle of Priesthood* (1913), H. L. MacNeill's *Christology of the Epistle to the Hebrews* (1914), H. A. A. Kennedy's *Theology of the Epistles* (1919, pp. 182–221), and E. F. Scott's *The Epistle to the Hebrews* (1922).

Many readers who are not children will understand what Mr Edmund Gosse in *Father and Son* (pp. 89 f.) describes, in telling how his father read aloud to him the epistle. "The extraordinary beauty of the language—for instance, the matchless cadences and images of the first chapter—made a certain impression upon my imagination, and were (I think) my earliest initiation into the magic of literature. I was incapable of defining what I felt, but I certainly had a grip in the throat, which was in its essence a purely aesthetic emotion, when my father read, in his pure, large, ringing voice, such passages as 'The heavens are the work of Thy hands. They shall perish, but Thou remainest, and they shall all wax old as doth a garment, and as a vesture shalt Thou fold them up, and they shall be changed; but Thou art the same, and Thy years shall not fail.' But the dialectic parts of the epistle puzzled and confused me. Such metaphysical ideas as 'laying again the foundation of repentance from dead works' and 'crucifying the Son of God afresh' were not successfully brought down to the level of my understanding. . . . The melodious language, the divine forensic audacities, the magnificent ebb and flow of argument which make the Epistle to the Hebrews such a miracle, were far beyond my reach, and they only bewildered me." They become less bewildering when they are viewed in the right perspective. The clue to them lies in the philosophical idea which dominates the outlook of the writer, and in the symbolism which, linked to this idea, embodied his characteristic conceptions of religion. We might almost say that, next to the deflecting influence of the tradition which identified our epistle with the Pauline scheme of thought and thereby missed its original and independent contribution to early Christianity, nothing has so handicapped its appeal as the later use of it in dogmatic theology. While the author of Πρὸς Ἑβραίους often turned the literal into the figurative, his theological interpreters have been as often engaged in turning the figurative expressions of the epistle into what was literal. A due appreciation of the symbolism has been the slow gain of the historical method as applied to the classics of primitive Christianity. There is no consistent symbolism, indeed, not even in the case of the ἀρχιερεύς; in the nature of the case, there could not be. But symbolism there is, and symbolism of a unique kind.

(i.)

The author writes from a religious philosophy of his own—that is, of his own among the NT writers. The philosophical element in his view of the world and God is fundamentally Platonic. Like Philo and the author of Wisdom, he interprets the past and the present alike in terms of the old theory (cp. on 8^5 10^1) that the phenomenal is but an imperfect, shadowy transcript of what is eternal and real. He applies this principle to the past. What was all the Levitical cultus in bygone days but a faint copy of the celestial archetype, a copy that suggested by its very imperfections the future and final realization? In such arguments (chs. 7–10) he means to declare "that Christianity is eternal, just as it shall be everlasting, and that all else is only this, that the true heavenly things of which it consists thrust themselves forward on to this bank and shoal of time, and took cosmical embodiment, in order to suggest their coming everlasting manifestation."[1] The idea that the seen and material is but a poor, provisional replica of the unseen and real order of things (τὰ ἐπουράνια, τὰ ἐν τοῖς οὐρανοῖς, τὰ μὴ σαλευόμενα), pervades Πρὸς Ἑβραίους. Thus faith ($11^{1f.}$) means the conviction, the practical realization, of this world of realities, not only the belief that the universe does not arise out of mere φαινόμενα, but the conviction that life must be ordered, at all costs, by a vision of the unseen, or by obedience to a Voice unheard by any outward ear. Similarly the outward priest, sanctuary, and sacrifices of the ancient cultus were merely the shadowy copy of the real, as manifested in Jesus with his self-sacrifice, his death being, as

[1] A. B. Davidson, *Biblical and Literary Essays* (p. 317).

Sabatier says, "une fonction sacerdotale, un acte transcendant de purification rituelle, accompli hors de l'humanité" (*La Doctrine de l'Expiation*, p. 37). Such is the philosophical strain which permeates Πρὸς Ἑβραίους. The idea of heavenly counterparts is not, of course, confined to Platonism; it is Sumerian, in one of its roots (cp. on 8^5), and it had already entered apocalyptic. But our author derives it from his Alexandrian religious philosophy (transmuting the κόσμος νοητός into the more vivid and devotional figures of an οἶκος or πόλις θεοῦ, a πάτρις or even a σκηνὴ ἀληθινή), just as elsewhere he freely uses Aristotelian ideas like that of the τέλος or final end, with its τελείωσις or sequence of growth, and shows familiarity with the idea of the ἕξις (5^{14}). The τελείωσις (see on 5^9) idea is of special importance, as it denotes for men the work of Christ in putting them into their proper status towards God (see on 2^{10}). "By a single offering he has made the sanctified perfect for all time" (τετελείωκεν, 10^{14}), the offering or προσφορά being himself, and the "perfecting" being the act of putting the People into their true and final relation towards God. This the Law, with its outward organization of priests and animal sacrifices, could never do; "as the Law has a mere shadow of the bliss that is to be, instead of representing the reality of that bliss (viz. the 'perfect' relationship between God and men), it can never perfect those who draw near" (10^1).

This gives us the focus for viewing the detailed comparison between the levitical sacrifices and priests on the one hand and the κρείττων Jesus. "You see in your bible," the writer argues, "the elaborate system of ritual which was once organized for the forgiveness of sins and the access of the people to God. All this was merely provisional and ineffective, a shadow of the Reality which already existed in the mind of God, and which is now ours in the sacrifice of Jesus." Even the fanciful argument from the priesthood of Melchizedek (6^{20}–7^{17})—fanciful to us, but forcible then—swings from this conception. What the author seeks to do is not to prove that there had been from the first a natural or real priesthood, superior to the levitical, a priesthood fulfilled in Christ. His aim primarily is to discredit the levitical priesthood of bygone days; it was anticipated in the divine order by that of Melchizedek, he shows, using a chronological argument resembling that of Paul in Gal $3^{8f.}$, on the principle that what is prior is superior. But what leads him to elaborate specially the Melchizedek priesthood is that it had already played an important rôle in Jewish speculation in connexion with the messianic hope. Philo had already identified Melchizedek outright with the Logos or possibly even with the messiah. Whether the author of Πρὸς Ἑβραίους intends to contradict Philo or not, he takes a different line, falling back upon his favourite psalm, the 110th, which in the Greek version, the only one known to him, had put forward not only the belief that messiah was ἱερεὺς εἰς τὸν αἰῶνα κατὰ τὴν τάξιν Μελχισέδεκ, but the Alexandrian belief in the pre-existence of messiah (v.[3] ἐκ γαστρὸς πρὸ ἑωσφόρου ἐξεγέννησά σε). Here then, by Alexandrian methods of exegesis, in the pentateuch text combined with the psalm, he found scripture proof of an original priesthood which was not levitical, not transferable, and permanent. This priesthood of Melchizedek was, of course, not quite a perfect type of Christ's, for it did not include any sacrifice, but, as resting on personality, not on heredity,[1] it did typify, he held, that eternal priesthood of the Christ which was to supersede the levitical, for all the ancient prestige of the latter. As this prestige was wholly biblical for the writer and his readers, so it was essential that the disproof of its validity should be biblical also. Though he never uses either the idea of Melchizedek offering bread and wine to typify the elements in the eucharist, in spite of the fact that Philo once allegorized this trait (*de Leg. Alleg.* iii. 25), or the idea of Melchizedek being uncircumcised (as he would have done, had he been seriously arguing with people who were in danger of relapsing into contemporary Judaism), he does seem to glance at the combination of the sacerdotal and the royal functions. Like Philo, though more fully, he notices the religious significance of the etymology "king of righteousness" and "king of peace," the reason being that throughout his argument he endeavours repeatedly to preserve something of the primitive view of Jesus as messianic king, particularly because the idea of the divine βασιλεία plays next to no part in his scheme of thought. Sometimes the combination of the sacerdotal and royal metaphors is incongruous enough, although it is not unimpressive (*e.g.* 10[12. 13]). Primarily it is a survival of the older militant messianic category which is relevant in the first chapter (see 1[8f.]), but out of place in the argument from the priesthood; the reference is really due to the desire to reaffirm the absolute significance of Christ's work, and by way of anticipation he sounds this note even in 7[1. 2]. Later on, it opens up into an interesting instance of his relation to the primitive eschatology. To his mind, trained in the Alexandrian philosophy of religion, the present world of sense and time stands over against the world of reality, the former being merely the shadow and copy of the latter. There is an archetypal

[1] The writer is trying to express an idea which, as Prof. E. F. Scott argues (pp. 207 f.), "underlies all our modern thought—social and political as well as religious," viz. that true authority is not prescriptive but personal; "the priesthood which can bring us nearer God must be one of inherent character and personality."

order of things, eternal and divine, to which the mundane order but dimly corresponds, and only within this higher order, eternal and invisible, is access to God possible for man. On such a view as this, which ultimately (see pp. xxxi–xxxii) goes back to Platonic idealism, and which had been worked out by Philo, the real world is the transcendent order of things, which is the pattern for the phenomenal universe, so that to attain God man must pass from the lower and outward world of the senses to the inner. But how? Philo employed the Logos or Reason as the medium. Our author similarly holds that men must attain this higher world, but for him it is a σκηνή, a sanctuary, the real Presence of God, and it is entered not through ecstasy or mystic rapture, but through connexion with Jesus Christ, who has not only revealed that world but opened the way into it. The Presence of God is now attainable as it could not be under the outward cultus of the σκηνή in the OT, for the complete sacrifice has been offered "in the realm of the spirit," thus providing for the direct access of the people to their God. The full bliss of the fellowship is still in the future, indeed; it is not to be realized finally until Jesus returns for his people, for he is as yet only their πρόδρομος (6^{20}). The primitive eschatology required and received this admission from the writer, though it is hardly consonant with his deeper thought. And this is why he quotes for example the old words about Jesus waiting in heaven till his foes are crushed ($10^{12.\ 13}$). He is still near enough to the primitive period to share the forward look (see, *e.g.*, $2^{2f.}$ 9^{28} 10^{37}), and unlike Philo, he does not allow his religious idealism to evaporate his eschatology. But while this note of expectation is sounded now and then, it is held that Christians already experience the powers of the world to come. The new and final order has dawned ever since the sacrifice of Jesus was made, and the position of believers is guaranteed. "You have come to mount Sion, the city of the living God." The entrance of Jesus has made a fresh, living way for us, which is here and now open. "For all time he is able to save those who approach God through him, as he is always living to intercede on their behalf." Christians enjoy the final status of relationship to God in the world of spirit and reality, in virtue of the final sacrifice offered by Jesus the Son.

(ii.)

What was this sacrifice? How did the writer understand it? (*a*) The first thing to be said is that in his interpretation of the sacrifice of Jesus, he takes the piacular view. Calvin (*Instit.* ii. 15. 6) maintains that, as for the priesthood of Christ, "finem et usum eius esse ut sit mediator purus omni macula, qui sanctitate sua Deum nobis conciliet. Sed quia aditum occupat justa maledictio, et Deus pro judicis officio nobis infensus est, ut nobis favorem comparet sacerdos ad placandam iram ipsius Dei, piaculum intervenire necesse est. . . . Qua de re prolixe apostolus disputat in epistola ad Hebraeos a septimo capite fere ad finem usque decimi." Matthew Arnold is not often found beside Calvin, but he shares this error. "Turn it which way we will, the notion of appeasement of an offended God by vicarious sacrifice, which the Epistle to the Hebrews apparently sanctions, will never truly speak to the religious sense, or bear fruit for true religion" (*St. Paul and Protestantism*, p. 72). Arnold saves himself by the word "apparently," but the truth is that this idea is not sanctioned by Πρὸς Ἑβραίους at all. The interpretation of Calvin confuses Paul's doctrine of expiation with the piacular view of our author. The entire group of ideas about the law, the curse, and the wrath of God is alien to Πρὸς Ἑβραίους. The conception of God is indeed charged with wholesome awe (cp. on $12^{28.\,29}$); but although God is never called directly the Father of Christians, his attitude to men is one of grace, and the entire process of man's approach is initiated by him (2^{9} 13^{20}). God's wrath is reserved for the apostates ($10^{29\text{-}31}$); it does not brood over unregenerate men, to be removed by Christ. Such a notion could hardly have occurred to a man with predilections for the typical significance of the OT ritual, in which the sacrifices were not intended to avert the wrath of God so much as to reassure the people from time to time that their relations with their God had not been interrupted. The function of Christ, according to our author, is not to appease the divine wrath (see on $2^{9f.\,17}$), but to establish once and for all the direct fellowship of God with his people, and a picturesque archaic phrase like that in 12^{24} about the *αἷμα ῥαντισμοῦ* cannot be pressed into the doctrine that Jesus by his sacrifice averted or averts the just anger of God. On the other hand, while the author knows the primitive Christian idea of God's fatherhood, it is not in such terms that he expresses his own conception of God. Philo (*De Exsecrationibus*, 9) describes how the Jews in the diaspora will be encouraged to return to Israel and Israel's God, particularly by his forgiving character (*ἑνὶ μὲν εἰπεικείᾳ καὶ χρηστότητι τοῦ παρακαλουμένου συγγνώμην πρὸ τιμωρίας ἀεὶ τιθέντος*); the end of their approach to God, he adds, *οὐδὲν ἕτερον ἢ εὐαρεστεῖν τῷ θεῷ καθάπερ υἱοὺς πατρί*. But the author of Πρὸς Ἑβραίους lays no stress upon the Fatherhood of God for men; except in connexion with the discipline of suffering, he never alludes to the goodness of God as paternal, even for Christians, and indeed it is only in OT quotations that God is called even the Father of the Son (1^{5} 5^{5}). He avoids, even more strictly than Jesus, the use of love-language. The verb ἀγαπᾶν only occurs twice, both times in an OT citation; ἀγάπη is also used only twice, and never of man's attitude towards God. There is significance in such linguistic data; they corroborate the impression that the author takes a deep view (see on 12^{23}) of the homage and awe due to God. Godly reverence, εὐλάβεια (see on 5^{7}), characterized Jesus in his human life, and it is to characterize Christians towards God, *i.e.* an awe which is devoid of anything like nervous fear, an ennobling sense of the greatness of God, but still a reverential awe. This is not incompatible with humble confidence or with a serious joy, with παρρησία (cp. on 3^{16}). Indeed "all deep joy has something of the awful in it," as Carlyle says. Ἔχωμεν χάριν is the word of our author (12^{28}); the standing attitude of Christians towards their God is one of profound thankfulness for his goodness to them. Only, it is to be accompanied μετὰ εὐλαβείας καὶ δέους. We are to feel absolutely secure under God's will, whatever crises or catastrophes befall the universe, and the security is at once to thrill (see on 2^{12}) and to subdue our minds. Hence, while God's graciousness overcomes any anxiety in man, his sublimity is intended to elevate and purify human life by purging it of easy emotion and thin sentimentalism. This is not the primitive awe of religion before the terrors of the unknown supernatural; the author believes in the gracious, kindly nature of God (see on 2^{10}, also 6^{10} 13^{16} etc.), but he has an instinctive horror of anything like a shallow levity. The tone of Πρὸς Ἑβραίους resembles, indeed, that of 1 P 1^{17} (εἰ πατέρα ἐπικαλεῖσθε τὸν ἀπροσωπολήμπτως κρίνοντα κατὰ τὸ ἑκάστου ἔργον, ἐν φόβῳ τὸν τῆς παροικίας ὑμῶν χρόνον ἀναστράφητε); there may be irreverence in religion, not only in formal religion but for other reasons in spiritual religion. Yet the special aspect of our epistle is reflected in what Jesus once said to men tempted to hesitate and draw back in fear of suffering: "I will show you whom to fear—fear Him who after He has killed has power to cast you into Gehenna. Yes, I tell you, fear Him" (Lk 12^{5}). This illustrates the spirit and situation of Πρὸς Ἑβραίους, where the writer warns his friends against apostasy by reminding them of ὁ θεὸς ζῶν and of the judgment. We might almost infer that in his mind the dominant conception is God regarded as transcendental, not with regard to creation but with regard to frail, faulty human nature. What engrosses the writer is the need not so much of a medium between God and the material universe, as of a medium between his holiness and human sin (see on 12^{23}).

(*b*) As for the essence and idea of the sacrifice, while he refers to a number of OT sacrifices by way of illustration, his main analogy comes from the ritual of atonement-day in the levitical code (Lv 16), where it was prescribed that once a year the highpriest was to enter the inner shrine by himself, the shrine within which stood the sacred box or ark symbolizing the divine Presence. The elaborate sacrifices of the day are only glanced at by our author. Thus he never alludes to the famous scapegoat, which bore away the sins of the people into the desert. All he mentions is the sacrifice of certain animals, as propitiation for the highpriest's own sins and also for those of the nation. Carrying some blood of these animals, the priest was to smear the *ἱλαστήριον* or cover of the ark. This had a twofold object. (i) Blood was used to reconsecrate the sanctuary (Lv 16^{16}). This was a relic of the archaic idea that the life-bond between the god and his worshippers required to be renewed by sacred blood; "the holiness of the altar is liable to be impaired, and requires to be refreshed by an application of holy blood."[1] Our author refers to this crude practice in 9^{23}. But his dominant interest is in (ii) the action of the highpriest as he enters the inner shrine; it is not the reconsecration of the sanctuary with its altar, but the general atonement there made for the sins of the People, which engrosses him. The application of the victim's blood to the *ἱλαστήριον* by the divinely appointed highpriest was believed to propitiate Yahweh by cleansing the People from the sins which might prevent him from dwelling any longer in the land or among the People. The annual ceremony was designed to ensure his Presence among them, "to enable the close relationship between Deity and man to continue undisturbed. The logical circle—that the atoning ceremonies were ordered by God to produce their effect upon himself—was necessarily unperceived by the priestly mind" (Montefiore, *Hibbert Lectures*, p. 337). What the rite, as laid down in the bible, was intended to accomplish was simply, for the author of Πρὸς Ἑβραίους, to renew the life-bond between God and the People. This sacrifice offered by the highpriest on atonement-day was the supreme, piacular action of the levitical cultus. Once a year it availed to wipe out the guilt of all sins, whatever their nature, ritual or moral, which interrupted the relationship between God and his People.[2] For it was a sacrifice designed for the entire People as the community of God. The blood of the victims was carried into the inner shrine, on behalf of the People outside the sanctuary; this the highpriest did for them, as he passed inside the curtain which shrouded the inner shrine. Also, in contrast to the usual custom, the flesh of the victims, instead of any part being eaten as a meal, was carried out and burned up. In all this the writer finds a richly symbolic

[1] W. Robertson Smith, *The Religion of the Semites* (1907), pp. 408 f.
[2] Cp. Montefiore, *op. cit.*, pp. 334 f.

meaning ($9^{1f.}$). Jesus was both highpriest and victim, as he died and passed inside the heavenly Presence of God to establish the life-bond between God and his People. Jesus did not need to sacrifice for himself. Jesus did not need to sacrifice himself more than once for the People. Jesus secured a forgiveness which the older animal sacrifices never won. And Jesus did not leave his People outside; he opened the way for them to enter God's own presence after him, and in virtue of his self-sacrifice. So the author, from time to time, works out the details of the symbolism. He even uses the treatment of the victim's remains to prove that Christians must be unworldly ($13^{11f.}$); but this is an after-thought, for his fundamental interest lies in the sacrificial suggestiveness of the atonement-day which, external and imperfect as its ritual was, adumbrated the reality which had been manifested in the sacrifice and ascension of Jesus.

Yet this figurative category had its obvious drawbacks, two of which may be noted here. One (*a*) is, that it does not allow him to show how the sacrificial death of Jesus is connected with the inner renewal of the heart and the consequent access of man to God. He uses phrases like ἁγιάζειν (see on 2^{11}) and καθαρίζειν and τελειοῦν (this term emphasizing more than the others the idea of completeness), but we can only deduce from occasional hints like 9^{14} what he meant by the efficacy of the sacrificial death. His ritualistic category assumed that such a sacrifice availed to reinstate the People before God (cp. on 9^{22}), and this axiom sufficed for his Christian conviction that everything depended upon what Jesus is to God and to us—what he is, he is in virtue of what he did, of the sacrificial offering of himself. But the symbol or parable in the levitical cultus went no further. And it even tended to confuse the conception of what is symbolized, by its inadequacy; it necessarily separated priest and victim, and it suggested by its series of actions a time-element which is out of keeping with the eternal order. Hence the literal tendency in the interpretation of the sacrifice has led to confusion, as attempts have been made to express the continuous, timeless efficacy of the sacrifice. That the death was a sacrifice, complete and final, is assumed (*e.g.* 7^{27} 9^{14} $10^{10.\ 12.\ 14}$). Yet language is used which has suggested that in the heavenly σκηνή this sacrifice is continually presented or offered (*e.g.* 7^{25} and the vg. mistranslation of 10^{12} "hic autem unam pro peccatis offerens hostiam in sempiternum sedit"). The other drawback (*b*) is, that the idea of Jesus passing like the highpriest at once from the sacrifice into the inner sanctuary (*i.e.* through the heavens into the Presence, 4^{14}) has prevented him from making use of the Resurrection (cp. also on 13^{12}). The heavenly sphere of Jesus is so closely linked with his previous existence on earth, under the category of the sacrifice, that the author could not suggest an experience like the resurrection, which would not have tallied with this idea of continuity.

On the other hand, the concentration of interest in the symbol on the sole personality of the priest and of the single sacrifice enabled him to voice what was his predominant belief about Jesus. How profoundly he was engrossed by the idea of Christ's adequacy as mediator may be judged from his avoidance of some current religious beliefs about intercession. Over and again he comes to a point where contemporary opinions (with which he was quite familiar) suggested, *e.g.*, the intercession of angels in heaven, or of departed saints on behalf of men on earth, ideas like the merits of the fathers or the atoning efficacy of martyrdom in the past, to facilitate the approach of sinful men to God (cp. on 11^{40} $12^{17.23.24}$ etc.). These he deliberately ignores. In view of the single, sufficient sacrifice of Jesus, in the light of his eternally valid intercession, no supplementary aid was required. It is not accidental that such beliefs are left out of our author's scheme of thought. It is a fresh proof of his genuinely primitive faith in Jesus as the one mediator. The ideas of the perfect Priest and the perfect Sacrifice are a theological expression, in symbolic language, of what was vital to the classical piety of the early church; and apart from Paul no one set this out so cogently and clearly as the writer of Πρὸς Ἑβραίους.

(iii.)

Our modern symbolism does no sort of justice to the ancient idea of priesthood. Matthew Arnold says of Wordsworth:

> "He was a priest to us all,
> Of the wonder and bloom of the world,
> Which we saw with his eyes, and were glad."

That is, "priest" means interpreter, one who introduces us to a deeper vision, one who, as we might put it, opens up to us a new world of ideas. Such is not the ultimate function of Christ as ἱερεύς in our epistle. Dogmatic theology would prefer to call this the prophetic function of Christ, but the priestly office means mediation, not interpretation. The function of the high-priest is to enter and to offer: εἰσέρχεσθαι and προσφέρειν forming the complete action, and no distinction being drawn between the two, any more than between the terms "priest" and "high-priest."

The fundamental importance of this may be illustrated from the recourse made by Paul and by our author respectively to the

Jeremianic oracle of the new covenant or διαθήκη. Paul's main interest in it lies in its prediction of the Spirit, as opposed to the Law. What appeals to Paul is the inward and direct intuition of God, which forms the burden of the oracle. But to our author (8^{7-13} 10^{15-18}) it is the last sentence of the oracle which is supreme, *i.e.* the remission of sins; "I will be merciful to their iniquities, and remember their sins no more." He seizes the name and fact of a "new" covenant, as implying that the old was inadequate. But he continues: "If the blood of goats and bulls, and the ashes of a heifer, sprinkled on defiled persons, give them a holiness that bears on bodily purity, how much more will the blood of Christ, who in the spirit of the eternal offered himself as an unblemished sacrifice to God, cleanse your conscience from dead works to serve a living God? He mediates a new covenant for this reason, that those who have been called may obtain the eternal deliverance they have been promised, now that a death has occurred which redeems them from the transgressions involved in the first covenant" (9^{13-15}). That is, the conclusion of Jeremiah's oracle—that God will forgive and forget—is the real reason why our author quotes it. There can be no access without an amnesty for the past; the religious communion of the immediate future must be guaranteed by a sacrifice ratifying the pardon of God.

This difference between Paul and our author is, of course, owing to the fact that for the latter the covenant[1] or law is subordinated to the priesthood. Change the priesthood, says the writer, and *ipso facto* the law has to be changed too. The covenant is a relationship of God and men, arising out of grace, and inaugurated by some historic act; since its efficiency as an institution for forgiveness and fellowship depends on the personality and standing of the priesthood, the appearance of Jesus as the absolute Priest does away with the inferior law.

This brings us to the heart of the Christology, the sacrifice and priestly service of Christ as the mediator of this new covenant with its eternal fellowship.

Men are sons of God, and their relation of confidence and access is based upon the function of the Son κατ' ἐξόχην. The author shares with Paul the view that the Son is the Son before and during his incarnate life, and yet perhaps Son in a special sense in consequence of the resurrection—or rather, as our author would have preferred to say, in consequence of the ascension. This may be the idea underneath the compressed clauses at the opening of the epistle (1^{1-5}). "God has spoken to us by

[1] As Professor Kennedy points out, with real insight: "all the terms of the contrast which he works out are selected because of their relation to the covenant-conception" (p. 201).

a Son—a Son whom he appointed heir of the universe, as it was by him that he had created the world. He, reflecting God's bright glory and stamped with God's own character, sustains the universe by his word of power; when he had secured our purification from sins, he sat down at the right hand of the Majesty on high; and thus he is superior to the angels, as he has inherited a Name superior to theirs. For to what angel did God ever say—

'Thou art my Son,
To-day have I become thy Father'?"

(referring to the ancient notion that the king first became conscious of his latent divine sonship at his accession to the throne). The name or dignity which Christ inherits, as the result of his redemptive work, is probably that of Son; as the following quotation from the OT psalm suggests, the resurrection or exaltation may mark, as it does for Paul, the fully operative sonship of Christ, the only way to inherit or possess the universe being to endure the suffering and death which purified human sin and led to the enthronement of Christ. Our author holds that this divine being was sent into the world because he was God's Son, and that he freely undertook his mission for God's other sons on earth.

The mission was a will of God which involved sacrifice. That is the point of the quotation ($10^{5f.}$) from the 40th psalm—not to prove that obedience to God was better than sacrifice, but to bring out the truth that God's will required a higher kind of sacrifice than the levitical, namely, the personal, free self-sacrifice of Christ in the body. Even this is more than self-sacrifice in our modern sense of the term. It is "by this will," the writer argues, that "we are consecrated, because Jesus Christ once for all has offered up his body." No doubt the offering is eternal, it is not confined to the historical act on Calvary. "He has entered heaven itself, now to appear in the presence of God on our behalf" (9^{24}): "he is always living to make intercession for us" (7^{25}). Still, the author is more realistic in expression than the tradition of the *Testament of Levi* (3), which makes the angel of the Presence in the third heaven offer a spiritual and bloodless sacrifice to God in propitiation for the sins of ignorance committed by the righteous. Our author assigns entirely to Christ the intercessory functions which the piety of the later Judaism had already begun to divide among angels and departed saints, but he also makes the sacrifice of Jesus one of blood—a realism which was essential to his scheme of argument from the entrance of the OT high priest into the inner shrine.

The superior or rather the absolute efficacy of the blood of

Christ depends in turn on his absolute significance as the Son of God; it is his person and work which render his self-sacrifice valid and supreme. But this is asserted rather than explained. Indeed, it is asserted on the ground of a presupposition which was assumed as axiomatic, namely, the impossibility of communion with God apart from blood shed in sacrifice (9^{22}). For example, when the writer encourages his readers by reminding them of their position (12^{24}), that they "have come to Jesus the mediator of the new covenant and to the sprinkled blood whose message is nobler than Abel's," he does not mean to draw an antithesis between Abel's blood as a cry for vengeance and Christ's blood as a cry for intercession. The fundamental antithesis lies between exclusion and inclusion. Abel's blood demanded the excommunication of the sinner, as an outcast from God's presence; Christ's blood draws the sinner near and ratifies the covenant. The author denies to the OT cultus of sacrifice any such atoning value, but at the same time he reaffirms its basal principle, that blood in sacrifice is essential to communion with the deity. Blood offered in sacrifice does possess a religious efficacy, to expiate and purify. Without shedding of blood there is no remission. We ask, why? But the ancient world never dreamt of asking, why? What puzzles a modern was an axiom to the ancient. The argument of our epistle is pivoted on this postulate, and no attempt is made to rationalize it.

In the Law of Holiness, incorporated in Leviticus, there is indeed one incidental allusion to the rationalê of sacrifice or blood-expiation, when, in prohibiting the use of blood as a food, the taboo proceeds: "the life of the body is in the blood, and I have given it to you for the altar to make propitiation for yourselves, for the blood makes propitiation by means of the life" (*i.e.* the life inherent in it). This is reflection on the meaning of sacrifice, but it does not carry us very far, for it only explains the piacular efficacy of blood by its mysterious potency of life. Semitic scholars warn us against finding in these words (Lv 17^{11}) either the popular idea of the substitution of the victim for the sinner, or even the theory that the essential thing in sacrifice is the offering of a life to God. As far as the Hebrew text goes, this may be correct. But the former idea soon became attached to the verse, as we see from the LXX—*τὸ γὰρ αἶμα αὐτοῦ ἀντὶ τῆς ψυχῆς ἐξιλάσεται.* This view does not seem to be common in later Jewish thought, though it was corroborated by the expiatory value attached to the death of the martyrs (*e.g.* 4 Mac 17^{22}). It is in this later world, however, rather than in the primitive world of Leviticus, that the atmosphere of the idea of Πρὸς Ἑβραίους is to be sought, the idea that because Jesus was what he was, his death has such an atoning significance as to inaugurate a new and final relation between God and men, the idea that his blood purifies the conscience because it is *his* blood, the blood of the sinless Christ, who is both the priest and the sacrifice. When the author writes that Christ "in the spirit of the eternal" (9^{14}) offered himself as an unblemished sacrifice to God, he has in mind the contrast between the annual sacrifice on the day of atonement and the sacrifice of Christ which never needed to be repeated, because it had been offered in the spirit and—as we might say—in the eternal order of things. It was a sacrifice bound up with his death in history, but it belonged essentially to the higher order of absolute reality. The writer breathed the Philonic atmosphere in which the eternal Now over-shadowed the things of space and time (see on 1^{5}), but he knew this sacrifice had taken place on the cross, and his problem was one which never confronted Philo, the problem which we moderns have to face in the question: How can a single historical fact possess a timeless significance? How can Christianity claim to be final, on the basis of a specific revelation in history? Our author answered this problem in his own way for his own day.

(iv.)

For him religion is specially fellowship with God on the basis of forgiveness. He never uses the ordinary term κοινωνία, however, in this sense. It is access to God on the part of worshippers that is central to his mind; that is, he conceives religion as worship, as the approach of the human soul to the divine Presence, and Christianity is the religion which is religion since it mediates this access and thereby secures the immediate consciousness of God for man. Or, as he would prefer to say, the revelation of God in Jesus has won this right for man as it could not be won before. For, from the first, there has been a People of God seeking, and to a certain extent enjoying, this access. God has ever been revealing himself to them, so far as was possible. But now in Jesus the final revelation has come which supersedes all that went before in Israel. The writer never contemplates any other line of revelation; outside Israel of old he never looks. It is enough for him that the worship of the OT implied a revelation which was meant to elicit faith, especially through the sacrificial cultus, and that the imperfections of that revelation have now been disclosed and superseded by the revelation in Jesus the Son. Faith in this revelation is in one aspect belief ($4^{2f.}$). Indeed he describes faith simply as the conviction of the unseen world, the assurance that God has spoken and that he will make his word good, if men rely upon it; he who draws near to God must believe that he exists and that he does reward those who seek him (11^6). Faith of this noble kind, in spite of appearances to the contrary, has always characterized the People. Our author rejoices to trace it at work long before Jesus came, and he insists that it is the saving power still, a faith which in some aspects is indistinguishable from hope, since it inspires the soul to act and suffer in the conviction that God is real and sure to reward loyalty in the next world, if not in the present. Such faith characterized Jesus himself (2^{13} 12^2). It is belief in God as trustworthy, amid all the shows and changes of life, an inward conviction that, when he has spoken, the one thing for a man to do is to hold to that word and to obey it at all costs. This is the conception of faith in the early and the later sections of the writing ($3^{7f.}$ 10^{38}–12^2). The difference that Jesus has made—for the writer seems to realize that there is a difference between the primitive faith and the faith of those who are living after the revelation in Jesus—is this, that the assurance of faith has now become far more real than it was. Though even now believers have to await the full measure of their reward, though faith still is hope to some extent, yet the full realization of the fellowship with God which is the supreme object of faith has been now made through Jesus. In two ways. (i) For faith Jesus is the inspiring example; he is the great Believer who has shown in his own life on earth the possibilities of faith.[1] In order to understand what faith is, we must look to Jesus above all, to see how faith begins and continues and ends. But (ii) Jesus has not only preceded us on the line of faith; he has by his sacrifice made our access to God direct and real, as it never could be before. Hence the writer can say, "let us draw near with a full assurance of faith and a true heart, in absolute assurance of faith" since "we have a great Priest over the house of God." "We have confidence to enter the holy Presence in virtue of the blood of Jesus." He does not make Jesus the object of faith as Paul does, but he argues that only the sacrifice of Jesus opens the way into the presence of God for sinful men.

This is the argument of the central part of the writing (chs. 7–10). Religion is worship, and worship implies sacrifice; there is no access for man to God without sacrifice, and no

[1] "It was by no divine magic, no mere 'breath, turn of eye, wave of hand,' that he 'joined issue with death,' but by the power of that genuinely human faith which had inspired others in the past" (MacNeill, p. 26). Bousset's denial of this (*Theol. Literaturzeitung*, 1915, p. 431 f.: "man wird bei dem Jesus d. Hebräerbriefe so wenig wie bei dem paulinischen noch im strengen Sinne von einem subjectivem Glauben Jesu reden können") is as incomprehehsible as his desperate effort to explain He 5^{7-10} from the fixed ideas of the mystery-religions.

religion without a priest (see on 7^{11}). The relations between God and his People from the first[1] have been on the basis of sacrifice, as the bible shows, and the new revelation in Jesus simply changes the old sacrificial order with its priesthood for another. The writer starts from a profound sense of sin, as an interruption of fellowship between God and man. He thoroughly sympathizes with the instinct which underlay the ancient practice of sacrifice, that fellowship with God is not a matter of course, that God is accessible and yet difficult of access, and that human nature cannot find its way unaided into his presence. Thus he quotes the 40th psalm (see p. xli), not to prove that God's will is fellowship, and that to do the will of God is enough for man, apart from any sacrifice, but to illustrate the truth that the will of God does require a sacrifice, not simply the ethical obedience of man, but the self-sacrifice with which Jesus offered himself freely, the perfect victim and the perfect priest. All men now have to do is to avail themselves of his sacrifice in order to enjoy access to God in the fullest sense of the term. "Having a great Highpriest who has passed through the heavens, let us draw near."

The conception of religion as devotion or worship covers a wide range in Πρὸς Ἑβραίους. It helps to explain, for example (see above, p. xxxviii), why the writer represents Jesus after death not as being raised from the dead, but as passing through the heavens into the inner Presence or sanctuary of God with the sacrifice of his blood (4^{14} $9^{11f.}$). It accounts for the elaboration of a detail like that of 9^{23}, and, what is much more important, it explains the "sacrificial" delineation of the Christian life. In this *ἀληθινὴ σκηνή* (8^{2}), of God's own making, with its *θυσιαστήριον* (13^{10}), Christians worship God (*λατρεύειν*, 9^{14} 12^{28} 13^{10}); their devotion to him is expressed by the faith and loyalty which detach them from this world ($13^{13.\,14}$) and enable them to live and move under the inspiration of the upper world; indeed their ethical life of thanksgiving (see on 2^{12}) and beneficence is a sacrifice by which they honour and worship God ($13^{15.\,16}$), a sacrifice presented to God by their *ἀρχιερεύς* Jesus. The writer never suggests that the worship-regulations of the outworn cultus are to be reproduced in any rites of the church on earth; he never dreamed of this, any more than of the *ἡγούμενοι* being called "priests." The essence of priesthood, viz. the mediation of approach to God, had been absolutely fulfilled in Jesus, and in one sense all believers were enabled to follow him into the inner *σκηνή*, where they worshipped their God as the priests of old had done in their *σκηνή*, and as the People of old had never

[1] *i.e.* from the inauguration of the *διαθήκη* at Sinai, though he notes that even earlier there was sacrifice offered (11^{3}).

been able to do except through the highpriest as their representative and proxy. But, while the worship-idea is drawn out to describe Christians, in Πρὸς Ἑβραίους its primary element is that of the eternal function of Christ as ἀρχιερεύς in the heavenly σκηνή.

(v.)

Symbolism alters as the ages pass. The picture-language in which one age expresses its mental or religious conceptions often ceases to be intelligible or attractive to later generations, because the civic, ritual, or economic conditions of life which had originally suggested it have disappeared or changed their form. This well-known principle applies especially to the language of religion, and it is one reason why some of the arguments in Πρὸς Ἑβραίους are so difficult for the modern mind to follow. There are other reasons, no doubt. The exegetical methods which the author took over from the Alexandrian school are not ours. Besides, historical criticism has rendered it hard for us moderns to appreciate the naive use of the OT which prevails in some sections of Πρὸς Ἑβραίους. But, above all, the sacrificial analogies are a stumbling-block, for we have nothing to correspond to what an ancient understood by a "priest" and sacrifice. Dryden was not poetic when he translated Vergil's "sacerdos" in the third Georgic (489) by "holy butcher," but the phrase had its truth. The business of a priest was often that of a butcher; blood flowed, blood was splashed about. It was in terms of such beliefs and practices that the author of Πρὸς Ἑβραίους argued, rising above them to the spiritual conception of the self-sacrifice of Jesus, but nevertheless starting from them as axiomatic. The duty of the modern mind is to understand, in the first place, how he came by these notions; and, in the second place, what he intended to convey by the use of such symbolic terms as "blood," "highpriest," and "sacrifice."

The striking idea of Christ as the eternal ἀρχιερεύς, by whom the access of man to God is finally and fully assured, may have been a flash of inspiration, one of the notes of originality and insight which mark the writer's treatment and restatement of the faith. But originality is not depreciated by the effort to trace anticipations. What led him to this view? After all, the most brilliant flashes depend upon an atmosphere already prepared for them. They are struck out of something. In this case, it is not enough to say that the conception was merely the transference to Jesus of the Philonic predicates of the Logos, or the result of a bible-reading in the pentateuch. In the pentateuch the writer found proofs of what he brought to it, and the arguments in chs. 7–10 really buttress ideas built on other foundations.

(*a*) Once the conception of a heavenly sanctuary became current, the notion of a heavenly ἀρχιερεύς would not be far-fetched for a writer like this. Philo had, indeed, not only spoken of the Logos as a highpriest, in a metaphorical sense, *i.e.* as mediating metaphysically and psychologically the relations between the worlds of thought and sense, but in an allegorical fashion spoken of "two temples belonging to God, one being the world in which the highpriest is his own Son, the Logos, the other being the rational soul" (*de Somniis*, i. 37). Our writer is much less abstract. Like the author of the Apocalypse (see on 4^{16}), he thinks of heaven in royal and ritual imagery as well as in civic, but it is the ritual symbolism which is more prominent. During the second century B.C. the ideas of a heavenly sanctuary and a heavenly altar became current in apocalyptic piety, partly owing to the idealistic and yet realistic conception (see on 8^{5}) that in heaven the true originals were preserved, the material altar and sanctuary being, like the earthly Jerusalem, inferior representations of transcendent realities. From this it was a natural development to work out the idea of a heavenly highpriest. By "natural" I do not mean to undervalue the poetical and religious originality of the writer of Πρὸς Ἑβραίους. The author of the Apocalypse of John, for example, fails to reach this idea, and even in the enigmatic passage in the vision and confession of Levi (*Testaments of the Twelve Patriarchs*, Test. Levi 5), where the seer tells us, "I saw the holy temple, and upon a throne of glory the Most High. And he said to me, Levi, I have given thee the blessings of priesthood until I come and sojourn in the midst of Israel"—even here, though the levitical priesthood, as in our epistle, is only a temporary substitute for the presence of God, the heavenly sanctuary has no highpriest. Nevertheless it was the idea of the heavenly sanctuary which held one germ of the idea of the heavenly highpriest for the author of Πρὸς Ἑβραίους, as he desired to express the fundamental significance of Jesus for his faith.

(*b*) Another factor was the speculations of Philo about the Logos as highpriest (*de Migrat. Abrah.* 102, *de Fug.* 108 ff.), though the priestly mediation there is mainly between man and the upper world of ideas. The Logos or Reason is not only the means of creating the material cosmos after the pattern of the first and real world, but inherent in it, enabling human creatures to apprehend the invisible. This is Philo's primary use of the metaphor. It is philosophical rather than religious. Yet the increased prestige of the highpriest in the later Judaism prompted him to apply to the Logos functions which resemble intercession as well as interpretation. Vague as they are, they were familiar to the author of our epistle, and it is probable that they helped to fashion his expression of the eternal significance of Jesus as the mediator between man and God. The Logos as highpriest, says Philo (*de Somn.* ii. 28), for example, is not only ἄμωμος, ὁλόκληρος, but μεθόριός τις θεοῦ <καὶ ἀνθρώπου> φύσις, τοῦ μὲν ἐλάττων, ἀνθρώπου δὲ κρείττων. Then he quotes the LXX of Lv 16^{17}. The original says that no man is to be with the highpriest when he enters the inner shrine, but the Greek version runs, ὅταν εἰσίῃ εἰς τὰ ἅγια τῶν ἁγίων ὁ ἀρχιερεὺς, ἄνθρωπος οὐκ ἔσται, and Philo dwells on the literal, wrong sense of the last three words, as if they meant "the highpriest is not to be a man." "What will he be, if he is not a man? God? I would not say that (οὐκ ἂν εἴποιμι). . . . Nor yet is he man, but he touches both extremes (ἑκατέρων τῶν ἄκρων, ὡς ἂν βάσεως καὶ κεφαλῆς, ἐφαπτόμενος)." Later (*ibid.* 34) he remarks, "if at that time he is not a man, it is clear he is not God either, but a minister (λειτουργὸς θεοῦ) of God, belonging to creation in his mortal nature and to the uncreated world in his immortal nature." Similarly he pleads, in the *de sacerdot.* 12, that the function of the highpriest was to mediate between God and man, ἵνα διὰ μέσου τινὸς ἄνθρωποι μὲν ἱλάσκωνται θεόν, θεὸς δὲ τὰς χάριτας ἀνθρώποις ὑποδιακόνῳ τινὶ χρώμενος ὀρέγῃ καὶ χορηγῇ. Here we may feel vibrating a need of intercession, even although the idea is still somewhat theosophic.

(*c*) A third basis for the conception of Christ's priesthood lay in the combination of messianic and sacerdotal functions which is reflected in the 110th psalm (see above, p. xxxiii), which in the *Testaments of the Patriarchs* (Reuben 6^{8}) is actually applied to Hyrcanus the Maccabean priest-king, while in the *Test. Levi* (18) functions which are messianic in all but name are ascribed to a new priest, with more spiritual insight than in the psalm itself. The curious thing, however, is that this Priest discharges no sacerdotal functions. The hymn describes his divine attestation and consecration—"and in his priesthood shall sin come to an end, and he shall open the gates of paradise and shall remove the threatening sword against Adam." That is all. Probably the passing phase of expectation, that a messiah would arise from the sacerdotal Maccabees, accounts for such a fusion of messiah and priest. In any case its influence was not wide. Still, the anticipation is not unimportant for the thought of Πρὸς Ἑβραίους, which rests so much upon the mystical significance of that psalm. Paul had seen the fulfilment of Ps 110^{1} in the final triumph of Christ as messiah over his foes (1 Co $15^{24.\ 25}$ δεῖ γὰρ αὐτὸν βασιλεύειν ἄχρις οὗ θῇ πάντας τοὺς ἐχθροὺς ὑπὸ τοὺς πόδας αὐτοῦ). But meantime Christ was in living touch with his church on earth, and Paul can even speak, in a glowing outburst, of his effective intercession (Ro 8^{34} ὃς καὶ ἐντυγχάνει ὑπὲρ ἡμῶν). This is at least the idea of the highpriesthood of Christ, in almost everything except name, though Paul says as much of the Spirit (Ro 8^{27} κατὰ θεὸν ἐντυγχάνει ὑπὲρ ἁγίων). Later, in the Fourth Gospel, a similar thought reappears; Christ is represented in priestly metaphor as interceding for his People ($17^{1f.}$), and the phrases (17^{17-19}) about Jesus consecrating himself (as priest and victim) that thereby his disciples may be "consecrated" ἐν τῇ ἀληθείᾳ (*i.e.* in the sphere of Reality), indicate a use of ἁγιάζειν which expresses one of the central ideas of Πρὸς Ἑβραίους. But in the latter writing the idea is explicit and elaborate, as it is nowhere else in the NT, and explicit on the basis of a later line in the 110th psalm, which Paul ignored. Our author also knew and used the earlier couplet (10^{13}), but he draws his cardinal argument from v.[4] σὺ εἶ ἱερεὺς εἰς αἰῶνα κατὰ τὴν τάξιν Μελχισέδεκ.

(vi.)

There is a partial anticipation of all this in the Enochic conception of the Son of Man. No doubt, as Volz warns us (*Jüdische Eschatologie*, p. 90), we must not read too much into such apocalyptic phrases, since the Son of Man is an *x* quantity of personal value in the age of expected bliss and salvation. Still, the pre-existent messiah there is Son of Man as transcendent and in some sense as human; he must be human, "Man," in order to help men, and he must be transcendent in order to be a deliverer or redeemer. But the author of Πρὸς Ἑβραίους, like Paul, significantly avoids the term Son of Man, even in $2^{5f.}$; and although he has these two ideas of human sympathy and of transcendency in close connexion, he derives them from his meditation upon the real Jesus ultimately, not from any apocalyptic speculations. What he meant by the term "Son of God" is not quite plain. Philo had regarded the Logos as pre-existent and as active in the history of the people, and so he regards Christ; but while it seems clear (see on 5^{5}) that Christ is priest for him because he was already Son, the further questions, when did he become priest? and how is the Sonship compatible with the earthly life?—these are problems which remain unsolved. The interpretation of the function of Jesus through the phrase in the 2nd psalm (see on 1^{5}) hardly clears up the matter any more than in the case of Justin Martyr (*Dial.* 88). Later on, Hippolytus, or whoever wrote the homily appended (chs. xi.–xii.) to the *Epist. Diognet.*, faced the problem more boldly and beautifully by arguing that "the Word was from the very beginning, appeared new, was proved to be old, and is ever young as he is born in the hearts of the saints. He is the eternal One, who to-day was accounted Son" (ὁ σήμερον υἱὸς λογισθείς, 11^{5}). Here "to-day" refers to the Christian era;

evidently the problem left by the author of Πρὸς Ἑβραίους, with his mystical, timeless use of the 2nd psalm, was now being felt as a theological difficulty. But this is no clue to how he himself took the reference. There is a large section in his thought upon Christ as the eternal, transcendental Son which remains obscure to us, and which perhaps was indefinite to himself. He took over the idea of the divine Sonship from the primitive church, seized upon it to interpret the sufferings and sacrificial function of Jesus as well as his eternal value, and linked it to the notion of the highpriesthood; but he does not succeed in harmonizing its implications about the incarnate life with his special γνῶσις of the eternal Son within the higher sphere of divine realities.

At the same time there seems no hiatus[1] between the metaphysical and the historical in the writer's conception of Jesus, no unreconciled dualism between the speculative reconstruction and the historical tradition. In Πρὸς Ἑβραίους we have the ordinary primitive starting-point, how could a divine, reigning Christ ever have become man? The writer never hints that his readers would question this, for they were not tempted by any Jewish ideas. He uses the category of the Son quite frankly, in order to express the absolute value of the revelation in Jesus; it is his sheer sense of the reality of the incarnate life which prompts him to employ the transcendental ideas. He does not start from a modern humanist view of Jesus, but from a conviction of his eternal divine character and function as Son and as ἀρχιερεύς, and his argument is that this position was only possible upon the human experience, that Jesus became man because he was Son ($2^{10f.}$), and is ἀρχιερεύς because once he was man.

(*a*) For our author Jesus is the Son, before ever he became man, but there is no definite suggestion (see on 12^{2}) that he made a sacrifice in order to become incarnate, no suggestion that he showed his χάρις by entering our human lot (δι' ὑμᾶς ἐπτώχευσεν πλούσιος ὤν, ἑαυτὸν ἐκένωσεν ἐν ὁμοιώματι ἀνθρώπων γενόμενος). Our author feels deeply the suffering of Jesus in the days of his flesh, but it is the final sacrifice at the end of his life which is emphasized. That he suffered as the eternal Son is understood: also, that it was voluntary ($10^{5f.}$), also that it was his human experience which qualified him to offer the perfect sacrifice, by God's χάρις. But, apart from the ($2^{8f.}$) allusion to the temporary inferiority to angels, the writer does not touch the moving idea of the kenotic theories of the incarnation, viz. the "sense of sacrifice on the part of a pre-existent One."[2]

(*b*) Since he knew nothing of the sombre view of the σάρξ

[1] As H. J. Holtzmann (*Neutest. Theologie*[2], ii. 337) and Pfleiderer (p. 287) imagine.

[2] H. R. Mackintosh, *The Person of Christ*, pp. 265 f.

which pervaded the Pauline psychology, he found no difficulty in understanding how the sinless Jesus could share human flesh and blood. The sinlessness is assumed, not argued (cp. on 4^{15} 5^{7}). Yet the writer does not simply transfer it as a dogmatic predicate of messiahship to Jesus. One of the characteristics which set Πρὸς Ἑβραίους apart in the early Christian literature is the idea that Jesus did not possess sinlessness simply as a prerogative of his divine Sonship or as a requisite for the validity of his priestly function. It was not a mere endowment. The idea rather is that he had to realize and maintain it by a prolonged moral conflict *ἐν ταῖς ἡμέραις τῆς σαρκὸς αὐτοῦ*. This view goes back to direct historical tradition, with its deeply marked impression of the personality of Jesus, and no sort of justice is done to Πρὸς Ἑβραίους if its conceptions of the human Son as sinless are referred to a theoretical interest or dogmatic prepossession. Such an interpretation is bound up with the view that Πρὸς Ἑβραίους represents the more or less arbitrary fusion of an historical tradition about Jesus with a pre-Christian christology. But it is not enough to speak vaguely of materials for such a christology floating in pre-Christian Judaism and crystallizing round the person of Jesus, once Jesus was identified with the messiah. The crystallization was not fortuitous. What Πρὸς Ἑβραίους contains is a christology which implies features and characteristics in Jesus too definite to be explained away as picturesque deductions from messianic postulates or Philonic speculations. These undoubtedly enter into the statement of the christology, but the motives and interests of that christology lie everywhere. The writer's starting-point is not to be sought in some semi-metaphysical idea like that of the eternal Son as a supernatural being who dipped into humanity for a brief interval in order to rise once more and resume his celestial glory; the mere fact that the eschatology is retained, though it does not always accord with the writer's characteristic view of Christ, shows that he was working from a primitive historical tradition about Jesus (see above, pp. xliv f.). To this may be added the fact that he avoids the Hellenistic term *σωτήρ*, a term which had been associated with the notion of the appearance of a deity hitherto hidden.[1] The allusions to the historical Jesus are not numerous, but they are too detailed and direct to be explained away; he preached *σωτηρία*, the message of eschatological bliss; he belonged to the tribe of Judah; he was sorely tempted, badly

[1] He does not use the technical language of the mystery-religions (cp. on 6^{4}), and they cannot be shown to have been present continuously to his mind. If the argument from silence holds here, he probably felt for them the same aversion as the devout Philo felt (*de Sacrif.* 12), though Philo on occasion would employ their terminology for his own purposes.

treated, and finally crucified outside Jerusalem. These are the main outward traits. But they are bound up with an interpretation of the meaning of Jesus which is not a mere deduction from messianic mythology or OT prophecies, and it is unreal, in view of a passage like $5^{7f.}$, *e.g.*, to imagine that the writer was doing little more than painting in a human face among the messianic speculations about a divine Son.

(*c*) Neither is the sinlessness of Jesus connected with the circumstances of his human origin. No explanation at all is offered of how this pre-existent Son entered the world of men. It is assumed that he did not come out of humanity but that he came into it; yet, like Paul and the author of the Fourth Gospel ($1^{9f.}$), our author is not interested in questions about the human birth. Even when he describes the prototype Melchizedek as "without father and mother" (7^{3}), he is not suggesting any parallel to the Christ; the phrase is no more than a fanciful deduction from the wording or rather the silence of the legend, just as the original priest-king Gudea says to the goddess in the Sumerian tale, "I have no mother, thou art my mother; I have no father, thou art my father." It is impossible to place this allusion beside the happy misquotation in 10^{5} "a body thou hast prepared for me," and to argue, as Pfleiderer (p. 287) does, that the incarnation is conceived as purely supernatural. All we need to do is to recall the Alexandrian belief, voiced in a passage like Wisd 8^{19} ("I was the child of fine parts: to my lot there fell a good soul, or rather being good I entered a body undefiled"); the good soul is what we call the personality, the thinking self, to which God allots a body, and birth, in the ordinary human way, is not incompatible with the pre-existence of the soul or self which, prior to birth, is in the keeping of God. The author of Πρὸς Ἑβραίους could quite well think of the incarnation of Jesus along such lines, even although for him the pre-existent Christ meant much more than the pre-existent human soul.

The meaning of the incarnation is, in one aspect, to yield a perfect example of faith ($12^{2f.}$) in action; in another and, for the writer, a deeper, to prepare Jesus, by sympathy and suffering, for his sacrificial function on behalf of the People. The rationalê of his death is that it is inexplicable except upon the fact of his relationship to men as their representative and priest before God ($2^{11f.}$). From some passages like $5^{3f.}$ 7^{27}, it has been inferred that Jesus had to offer a sacrifice on his own behalf as well as on behalf of men (*i.e.* his tears and cries in Gethsemane), or that he only overcame his sinful nature when he was raised to heaven. But this is to read into the letter of the argument more than the writer ever intended it to convey. The point of his daring argument is that the sufferings of Jesus were not incompatible with his sinlessness, and at the same time that they rendered his sacrifice of himself absolutely efficacious. The writer is evidently in line with the primitive synoptic tradition, though he never proves the necessity of the sufferings from OT prophecy, as even his contemporary Peter does, preferring, with a fine intuition in the form of a religious reflection, to employ the idea of moral congruity (2^{10}).

(vii.)

The symbolism of the highpriesthood and sacrifice of Jesus in the heavenly sanctuary is therefore designed to convey the truth that the relations of men with God are based finally upon Jesus Christ. In the unseen world which is conceived in this naive idealistic way, Jesus is central; through him God is known and accessible to man, and through him man enjoys forgiveness and fellowship with God. When Paul once wrote, **τὰ ἄνω φρονεῖτε, τὰ ἄνω ζητεῖτε**, if he had stopped there he would have been saying no more than Epictetus or Marcus Aurelius might have said and did say. But when he added, **οὗ ὁ Χριστός ἐστιν (ἐν δεξιᾷ τοῦ θεοῦ καθήμενος)**, he defined the upper sphere in a new sense. So with the author of Πρὸς Ἑβραίους. In the real world of higher things, "everything is dominated by the figure of the great High Priest at the right hand of the Majesty in the Heavens, clothed in our nature, compassionate to our infirmities, able to save to the uttermost, sending timely succour to those who are in peril, pleading our cause. It is this which faith sees, this to which faith clings as the divine reality behind and beyond all that passes, all that tries, daunts, or discourages the soul: it is this in which it finds the *ens realissimum*, the very truth of things, all that is meant by God."[1]

Yet while this is the central theme (chs. 7–10), which the writer feels it is essential for his friends to grasp if they are to maintain their position, it is one proof of the primitive character of Πρὸς Ἑβραίους that it preserves traces of other and more popular ideas of Christianity. Thus (*a*) there is the primitive idea of the messiah as the heir, who at the resurrection inherits full power as the divine Son or Κληρονόμος. Strictly speaking, this does not harmonize with the conception of the Son as eternal, but it reappears now and then, thrown up from the eschatological tradition which the author retains (see above, pp. xxxiii f.). (*b*) The isolated reference to the overthrow of the devil is another allusion to ideas which were in the background of the writer's mind (see on $2^{14.15}$). (*c*) The scanty

[1] Denney, *The Death of Christ*, pp. 239, 240.

use made of the favourite conception of Jesus as the divine Κύριος (see below, p. lxiii) is also remarkable. This is not one of the writer's categories; the elements of divine authority and of a relation between the Κύριος and the divine Community are expressed otherwise, in the idea of the Highpriest and the People.

Furthermore the category of the Highpriesthood itself was not large enough for the writer's full message. (*a*) It could not be fitted in with his eschatology any more than the idea of the two worlds could be. The latter is dovetailed into his scheme by the idea of faith as practically equivalent to hope (in $10^{35f.}$); the world to come actually enters our experience here and now, but the full realization is reserved for the end, and meantime Christians must wait, holding fast to the revelation of God in the present. The former could not be adjusted to the eschatology, and the result is that when the writer passes to speak in terms of the primitive expectation of the end (10^{35}–12^{29}), he allows the idea of the Highpriesthood to fall into the background. In any case the return of Jesus is connected only with the deliverance of his own People (9^{28}). He does not come to judge; that is a function reserved for God. The end is heralded by a cataclysm which is to shake the whole universe, heaven as well as earth ($1^{11f.}$ $12^{26f.}$), another conception which, however impressive, by no means harmonizes with the idea of the two spheres. But the writer's intense consciousness of living in the last days proved too strong for his speculative theory of the eternal and the material orders. (*b*) Again, the Highpriesthood was inadequate to the ethical conceptions of the writer. It did involve ethical ideas—the cleansing of the conscience and the prompting of devotion and awe, moral consecration, and inward purity (these being the real "worship"); but when he desires to inspire his readers he instinctively turns to the vivid conception of Jesus as the ἀρχηγός, as the pioneer and supreme example of faith on earth.

The latter aspect brings out the idea of a contemplation of Jesus Christ, a vision of his reality (cp. 3^{1} $12^{1.\,2}$), which, when correlated with the idea of a participation in the higher world of reality, as embodied in the Highpriest aspect, raises the question, how far is it legitimate to speak of the writer as mystical?

(viii.)

To claim or to deny that he was a mystic is, after all, a question of words. He is devoid of the faith-mysticism which characterizes Paul. Even when he speaks once of believers being μέτοχοι Χριστοῦ (3^{14}), he means no more than their membership in the household of God over which Christ presides; there is no hint of the personal trust in Christ which distinguishes "faith" in Paul. As important is the consideration that the writer does not take the sacrifices of the levitical cultus as merely symbolizing union with God. Such is the genuinely mystical interpretation. To him, on the other hand, sacrifice is an action which bears upon man's relation to God, and it is from this point of view that he estimates and criticizes the levitical cultus. But while technically he is not a mystic, even in the sense in which that much-abused term may be applied to any NT writer, he has notes and qualities which might be called "mystical." To call him an "idealist" is the only alternative, and this is misleading, for idealism suggests a philosophical detachment which is not suitable to Πρὸς Ἑβραίους. On the other hand, his profound sense of the eternal realities, his view of religion as inspired by the unseen powers of God, his conception of fellowship with God as based on the eternal presence of Jesus in heaven—these and other elements in his mind mark him as a definitely unworldly spirit, impatient of any sensuous medium, even of a sacrificial meal, that would interpose between the human soul and God. Not that he uses any pantheistic language; he is more careful to avoid this than a writer like the author of First John. His deep moral nature conceives of God as a transcendent Majestic Being, before whom believers must feel awe and reverence, even as they rejoice and are thankful. He has a wholesome sense of God's authority, and an instinctive aversion to anything like a sentimental, presumptuous piety (see above, pp. xxxv f.). Yet as he speaks of the Rest or the City of God, as he describes the eternal Sanctuary, or the unshaken order of things, or as he delineates the present position of God's People here in their constant dependence on the unseen relation between Christ and God, he almost tempts us to call him "mystical," if "mysticism" could be restricted to the idea that the human soul may be united to Absolute Reality or God. He is certainly not mystical as Philo is;[1] there is no hint in Πρὸς Ἑβραίους, for example, of an individualistic, occasional rapture, in which the soul soars above sense and thought into the empyrean of the unconditioned. He remains in close touch with moral realities and the historical tradition. But the spirituality of his outlook, with its speculative reach and its steady openness to influences pouring from the unseen realities, hardly deserves to be denied the name of "mystical," simply because it is neither wistful nor emotional.

[1] The soundest account of Philo's "mysticism" is by Professor H. A. A. Kennedy in *Philo's Contribution to Religion*, p. 211 f.

§ 3. Style and Diction.

(i.)

Πρὸς Ἑβραίους is distinguished, among the prose works of the primitive church, by its rhythmical cadences. The writer was acquainted with the oratorical rhythms which were popularized by Isokrates, and although he uses them freely, when he uses them at all, his periods show traces of this rhetorical method. According to Aristotle's rules upon the use of paeans in prose rhythm (*Rhet.* iii. 8. 6–7), the opening ought to be –⏑⏑⏑, while ⏑⏑⏑– should be reserved for the conclusion.
⏑⏑⏑–
Our author, however, begins with *πολυμερως*, an introductory rhythm (cp. 1^{5} 3^{12}) which seems to be rather a favourite with
⏑⏑ ⏑– ⏑⏑ ⏑ – ⏑⏑⏑ –
him, *e.g.* 3^{1} *οθεν αδελφ*, 7^{10} *ετι γαρ εν τη*, 12^{25} *βλεπετε μη*, 13^{20}
⏑ ⏑ ⏑–
ο δε θεος, though he varies it with an anapaest and an iambus ⏑⏑–⏑– (*e.g.* $2^{1.\,4.\,5.\,14}$ 11^{16} *διὸ οὐκ ἐπαισχ*, 12^{12} etc.), or ––⏑–– (as in 5^{12} 6^{4} 7^{7}, see below, 13^{5} *αὐτὸς γὰρ εἴρηκ*, etc.), or ––––– (as in 2^{3} 3^{5} 11^{6} *πιστεῦσαι γὰρ δεῖ*, 11^{39} etc.), or even occasionally with three trochees –⏑–⏑–⏑ (*e.g.* 12^{8}), or –⏑––– (12^{11} 13^{13} etc.), or –⏑⏑⏑–– (*e.g.* 1^{13} 4^{12}), or even two anapaests (*e.g.* 1^{6} 5^{11} 13^{10}), or –––⏑– (13^{3}). He also likes to carry on or even to begin a new sentence or paragraph with the same or a similar rhythm as in the end of the preceding, *e.g.* –⏑⏑⏑––⏑––– in 4^{11} and 4^{12}, or ⏑⏑⏑––⏑––⏑ in 7^{21} and 7^{22}, or as in 8^{13} (––⏑–––⏓–––––⏓⏑⏑⏑––⏑–––––⏓–⏑⏑⏑––) and 9^{1} (––⏑–––⏓⏑–––⏑⏑⏑–⏓⏑⏑⏑–––⏑–), or ––⏑⏑⏑– as in 10^{10} and 10^{11}, and to repeat a rhythm twice in succession, as, *e.g.*, –⏑––⏑ in 2^{3} (*τηλικαύτης ἀ . . . ἥτις ἀρχὴν λα*), ⏑⏑––––– in 4^{10} (*ὁ γὰρ εἰσελθὼν εἰς τὴν . . . ἀπὸ τῶν ἔργων αὐτοῦ*), or –⏑–⏑–– in 12^{1} (*τοιγαροῦν καὶ ἡμεῖς τηλικοῦτ᾽ ἔχοντες*). The standard closing rhythm ⏑⏑⏑– does not clearly occur till 11^{3} (*γεγονέναι*), 11^{4} (*ἔτι λαλεῖ*), 11^{23} (*βασιλέως*), and 12^{24}; it is not so frequent as, *e.g.*, ⏑⏑–– ($7^{28.\,29}$ 9^{26} $10^{34.\,35}$ $11^{13.\,15.\,28}$ 12^{3} etc.). He also likes to close with a single or an echoing rhythm like ⏑–⏑––– in 1^{3} (*σύνης ἐν ὑψηλοῖς*), 2^{10} (*άτ ων τελειῶσαι*), 2^{18} (*πέπονθε πειρασθείς . . . μένοις βοηθῆσαι*), or ––⏑– in 7^{19} 9^{28} (*ὀφθήσεται . . . σωτηρίαν*), 11^{4} (*κεν τῷ θεῷ . . . αὐτοῦ τοῦ θεοῦ*), 11^{21} etc. A curious variety in almost parallel clauses occurs in 11^{1}

– – ⏑ – ⏑ – ⏓⏑⏑– ⏑– ⏑–
εστιν δε πιστις ελπιζομενων υποστασις
– ⏑– ⏑– ⏑ – ⏓⏑⏑–
πραγματων ελεγχος ου βλεπομενων,

where the cross cadences are plain, as in Isokrates often. But at the end of sentences, as a rule, he prefers ⏑⏑⏑–⏑ (παρα-ρυῶμεν, 2^{1} 8^{6}), or –⏑–⏓ (ἧς λαλοῦμεν, 2^{5} $7^{6.\,7}$ etc.) or –⏑––– (ων τελειῶσαι, 2^{10} 2^{18} 3^{14} $4^{3.\,11}$ 11^{21} etc.), sometimes the weighty –––– (2^{17} 8^{2} 10^{39} 11^{9} 11^{14} etc.), or ⏑–⏑– (4^{1} $5^{3.\,12}$ $10^{2.\,18.\,27}$ 11^{8}) now and then, or one or even two (5^{11}) anapaests, often ending on a short syllable.

He is true to the ancient principle of Isokrates, however, that prose should be mingled with rhythms of all sorts, especially iambic and trochaic, and there even happen to be two trimeters in 12^{14}, besides the similar rhythm in $12^{13.\,26}$. Also he secures smoothness often by avoiding the practice of making a word which begins with a vowel follow a word which ends with a vowel (δεῖ τὰ φωνήεντα μὴ συμπίπτειν). Parallelisms in sound, sense, and form are not infrequent. These σχήματα of Isokrates can be traced, *e.g.*, in $1^{2.\,3}$ where, by ἀντίθεσις, ὃν . . . πάντων answers to ὃς . . . ὑποστάσεως αὐτοῦ, as δι' οὗ . . . ἐποίησεν to φέρων . . . δυνάμεως αὐτοῦ, or as in 11^{1}, which is, however, a case of παρίσωσις or parallelism in form. As in Wisdom, the accumulation of short syllables, a characteristic of the later

⏑⏑ ⏑⏑⏑

prose, is frequent in Πρὸς Ἑβραίους (*e.g.* in $2^{1.\,2}$ ποτε παραρυ . . .

⏑⏑⏑⏑⏑⏑ ⏑–⏑ ⏑⏑⏑⏑⏑ – ⏑ ⏑⏑⏑⏑ ⏑⏑

λογος εγενετο βεβαιος, $6^{9.\,10}$ και εχομενα . . . ου γαρ αδικος ο θεος), 10^{25} $11^{12.\,19}$ $12^{8.\,9}$ 13^{4} etc.). At the same time, Πρὸς Ἑβραίους is not written in parallel rhythm, like Wisdom (cp. Thackeray's study in *Journal of Theological Studies*, vi. pp. 232 f.); it is a prose work, and, besides, we do not expect the same opportunities for using even prose-rhythms in the theological centre of the writing, though in the opening chapters and towards the close, the writer has freer play. One or two samples may be cited, *e.g.*, in the two parallel clauses of 1^{2}:

⏑ ⏑–– –⏑⏑– – –

ον εθηκεν κληρονομον παντων

⏑ – ⏑⏑––– – ––⏑

δι ου και εποιησεν τους αιωνας,

⏑⏑– – – ⏑⏑– – –

or in 1^{3} where ασεως αυτου answers to αμεως αυτου. In 2^{16} the

⏑⏑– ⏑⏑–

two clauses begin with ––– and end with επιλαμβανεται, the verb being obviously repeated to bring out the anapaestic rhythm. The "cretic" (–⏑–), which is particularly frequent, is seen clearly in a carefully wrought passage like $4^{8\text{-}10}$:

– ⏑ – – ⏑–– ⏑⏑ – –

ει γαρ αυτους Ιησους κατεπαυσεν

> – – ⌣ ⌣ – – ⌣ ⌣ – ⌣ ⌣ – – ⌣ –
> ουκ αν περι αλλης ελαλει μετα ταυτ(α) ημερας
> – ⌣ ⌣ – ⌣ – – ⌣ – – – – – – ⌣ –
> αρ(α) απολειπεται σαββατισμος τω λαω του θεου
> ⌣ ⌣ – – – – – ⌣ ⌣ – ⌣ ⌣ –
> ο γαρ εισελθων εις την καταπαυσιν αυτου
> ⌣ – – ⌣ ⌣ – ⌣
> και αυτος κατεπαυσεν
> ⌣ ⌣ – –
> απο των εργων αυτου
> – ⌣ ⌣ ⌣ – ⌣ ⌣ – ⌣ ⌣ –
> ωσπερ απο των ιδιων ο θεος.

There is a repeated attempt at balance, *e.g.* of clauses, like (11[33]):

> ⌣ ⌣ – ⌣ ⌣ –
> ηργασαντο δικαιοσυνην
> ⌣ ⌣ – ⌣ ⌣ –
> επετυχον επαγγελιων,

where both have the same number of syllables and end on the same rhythm; or, in the next verse, where δυναμιν πυρος (⌣ ⌣ – ⌣ ⌣) is echoed in εφυγον στομα (⌣ ⌣ – ⌣ ⌣), while there is a similar harmony of sound in the closing syllables of

> – ⌣ – ⌣ ⌣ –
> υροι εν πολεμω
> – ⌣ – ⌣ ⌣ –
> ιναν αλλοτριων,

and in vv.[37] and [38] the balancing is obvious in

> – ⌣ – ⌣ – –
> εν φονω μαχαιρης
> ⌣ ⌣ – ⌣ –
> περιηλθον εν
> – ⌣ – – – –
> υστερουμενοι θλιβ
> ⌣ ⌣ – ⌣ –
> εν ερημιαις

or in the chiming of [38] and [39]:

> – – – – – – ⌣ – – –
> και σπηλαιοις και τοις οπαις της γης
> – – – – – – ⌣ – – –
> και ουτοι παντες μαρτυρηθεντες δ.

As for the bearing of this rhythmical structure on the text, it does not affect the main passages in question (*e.g.* 2^{9} 6^{2}); it rather supports and indeed may explain the omission of τῷ before υἱῷ in 1^{1}, and of ὅλῳ in 2^{2}, as well as the right of μελλόντων to stand in 9^{11} and in 10^{1}; it might favour, however, ἀγγέλων γενόμενος instead of γενόμενος τῶν ἀγγέλων in 1^{4}, and the insertion of ἡ στεῖρα in 11^{11} and of ὄρει in 12^{18}, if it were pressed; while, on the other hand, as employed by Blass, it buttresses the wrong insertion of μέχρι τέλους βεβαίαν in 3^{6}, and inferior readings like συγκεκερασμένους and ἀκουσθεῖσιν in 4^{2}, ἐκδεχομένοις (D*) in 9^{28}, εἰ in 12^{7}, ἐν χολῇ in 12^{15}, and ἀνέχεσθαι in 13^{22}. But the writer is not shackled to στίχοι, though his mind evidently was familiar with the rhythms in question.

(ii.)

There are traces of vernacular Greek, but the language and style are idiomatic on the whole. Thus the perfect is sometimes employed for the sake of literary variety, to relieve a line of aorists (*e.g.* $11^{17.28}$), and indeed is often used aoristically, without any subtle intention (cp. on 7^{6} etc.); it is pedantic to press significance into the tenses, without carefully watching the contemporary Hellenistic usage. The definite article is sparingly employed. Μέν . . . δέ, on the other hand, is more common, as we might expect from the antithetical predilections of the author in his dialectic. As for the prepositions, the avoidance of σύν is remarkable (cp. on 12^{14}), all the more remarkable since our author is fond of verbs compounded with σύν. Oratorical imperatives are used with effect (*e.g.* $3^{1.12}$ 7^{4} 10^{32} etc.), also double (1^{5} $1^{13.14}$ $12^{5\text{-}7}$) and even triple ($3^{16\text{-}18}$) dramatic questions, as well as single ones ($2^{3.4}$ 7^{11} $9^{13.14}$ 10^{29} 11^{32} 12^{9}). The style is persuasive, neither diffuse nor concise. The writer shows real skill in managing his transitions, suggesting an idea before he develops it (*e.g.* in 2^{17} 5^{6}). He also employs artistically parentheses and asides, sometimes of considerable length (*e.g.* καθώς . . . κατάπαυσίν μου $3^{7\text{-}11}$ $5^{13.14}$ 8^{5} $11^{13\text{-}16}$), now and then slightly irrelevant (*e.g.* 3^{4}), but occasionally, as in Plato, of real weight (*e.g.* 2^{16} 7^{12}; οὐδὲν . . . νόμος 7^{19} 10^{4}; πιστὸς γὰρ ὁ ἐπαγγειλάμενος 10^{23}; ὧν οὐκ ἦν ἄξιος ὁ κόσμος 11^{38} 13^{14}); they frequently explain a phrase (τοῦτ' ἔστιν τὸν διάβολον 2^{14}; τοῦτ' ἔστιν τοὺς ἀδελφοὺς αὐτῶν 7^{5}; ὁ λαὸς γὰρ ἐπ' αὐτῆς νενομοθέτηται 7^{11}; ἥτις . . . ἐνεστηκότα 9^{9}; τοῦτ' ἔστιν . . . κτίσεως 9^{11}; τοῦτ' ἔστιν τῆς σαρκὸς αὐτοῦ 10^{20} 12^{20}), especially an OT citation (*e.g.* 4^{10} 6^{13} $7^{2.7}$; αἵτινες κατὰ νόμον προσφέρονται 10^{8}) on which the writer comments in passing. One outstanding feature of the style (for Πρὸς Ἑβραίους is λέξις κατεστραμμένη, not λέξις εἰρόμενη in the sense of rapid dialogue) is the number of long, carefully constructed sentences (*e.g.* $1^{1\text{-}4}$ $2^{2\text{-}4}$ $2^{14.15}$ $3^{12\text{-}15}$ $4^{12.13}$,

5^{1-3} 5^{7-10} 6^{4-6} 6^{16-20} 7^{1-3} 8^{4-6} 9^{2-5} 9^{6-10} 9^{24-26} 10^{11-13} 10^{19-25} 11^{24-26} $12^{1.2}$ 12^{18-24}). Yet his short sentences are most effective, *e.g.* 2^{18} 4^{3} 10^{18}, and once at least (3^{16-18}) there is a touch of the rapid, staccato *diatribê* style, which lent itself to the needs of popular preaching. He loves a play on words or assonance, *e.g.* καρδία πονηρὰ ἀπιστίας ἐν τῷ ἀποστῆναι (3^{12}), παρακαλεῖτε ἑαυτοὺς . . . ἄχρις οὗ τὸ σήμερον καλεῖται (3^{13}), ἔμαθεν ἀφ' ὧν ἔπαθεν (5^{8}), καλοῦ τε καὶ κακοῦ (5^{14}), ἅπαξ προσενεχθεὶς εἰς τὸ πολλῶν ἀνενεγκεῖν ἁμαρτίας (9^{28}), τοσοῦτον ἔχοντες περικείμενον ἡμῖν νέφος μαρτύρων . . . τρέχωμεν τὸν προκείμενον ἡμῖν ἀγῶνα (12^{1}), ἐκλέλησθε τῆς παρακλήσεως . . . μηδὲ ἐκλύου (12^{5}), μένουσαν πόλιν ἀλλὰ τὴν μέλλουσαν (13^{14}). Also he occasionally likes to use a term in two senses, *e.g.* ζῶν γὰρ ὁ λόγος τοῦ θεοῦ . . . πρὸς ὃν ἡμῖν ὁ λόγος ($4^{12.13}$), and διαθήκη in $9^{15f.}$ From first to last he is addicted to the gentle practice of alliteration, *e.g.* πολυμερῶς καὶ πολυτρόπως πάλαι ὁ θεὸς λαλήσας τοῖς πατράσιν ἐν τοῖς προφήταις (1^{1}), πᾶσα παράβασις καὶ παρακοή (2^{2}), ἀφῆκεν αὐτῷ ἀνυπότακτον (2^{8}), τὸν ἀπόστολον καὶ ἀρχιερέα (3^{1}), καίτοι . . . ἀπὸ καταβολῆς κόσμου (4^{3}), ἐνθυμήσεων καὶ ἐννοιῶν (4^{12}), ἀπάτωρ, ἀμήτωρ, ἀγενεαλόγητος (7^{3}), διὰ τὸ αὐτῆς ἀσθενὲς καὶ ἀνωφελές (7^{18}), εἰς τὸ παντελὲς . . . τοὺς προσερχομένους . . . πάντοτε ζῶν (7^{25}), οἱ κεκλημένοι τῆς αἰωνίου κληρονομίας (9^{15}), εἰσῆλθεν ἅγια Χριστὸς ἀντιτύπα τῶν ἀληθινῶν, ἀλλ' εἰς αὐτόν (9^{24}), ἐπεὶ ἔδει αὐτὸν πολλάκις παθεῖν ἀπὸ καταβολῆς κόσμου (9^{26}), ἅπαξ ἐπὶ συντελείᾳ τῶν αἰώνων εἰς ἀθέτησιν τῆς ἁμαρτίας (9^{26}), ἀποκεῖται τοῖς ἀνθρώποις ἅπαξ ἀποθανεῖν (9^{27}), ἐν αὐταῖς ἀνάμνησις ἁμαρτιῶν (10^{3}), ἀδύνατον γὰρ αἷμα ταύρων καὶ τράγων ἀφαιρεῖν ἁμαρτίας (10^{4}), θλίψεσιν θεατριζόμενοι (10^{33}), εἰ μὲν ἐκείνης ἐμνημόνευον ἀφ' ἧς ἐξέβησαν (11^{15}), πᾶσα μὲν παιδεία πρὸς μὲν τὸ παρόν (12^{11}), περισσοτέρως δὲ παρακαλῶ τοῦτο ποιῆσαι (13^{19}). On the other hand, he seems deliberately to avoid alliteration once by altering διεθέμην into ἐποίησα (8^{9}).

One or two other features of his style are remarkable. There is, for example, the predilection for sonorous compounds like μισθαποδοσία and εὐπερίστατος, and also the love of adjectives in α privative, which Aristotle noted as a mark of the elevated style (*Rhet.* iii. 6. 7); in Πρὸς Ἑβραίους there are no fewer than twenty-four such, while even in the historical romance miscalled 3 Mac. there are no more than twenty. Other items are the fondness for nouns ending in -ις (cp. on 2^{4}), the extensive use of periphrases (cp. on 4^{11}), and of the infinitive and the preposition (see on 3^{12}). The use of a word like τε is also noticeable. Apart from eleven occurrences of τε καί, and one doubtful case of τε . . . τε . . . καί (6^{2}), τε links (*a*) substantives without any preceding καί or δέ; (*b*) principal clauses, as in 12^{2}; and (*c*) participial clauses, as in 1^{3} 6^{4}. Emphasis is generally brought out by throwing a word forward or to the very end of the sentence.

The writer is also in the habit of interposing several words between the article or pronoun and the substantive; *e.g.*

1^{4} διαφορώτερον παρ᾽ αὐτοὺς κεκληρονόμηκεν ὄνομα.
4^{8} οὐκ ἂν περὶ ἄλλης ἐλάλει μετὰ ταῦτα ἡμέρας.
10^{11} τὰς αὐτὰς πολλάκις προσφέρων θυσίας.
10^{12} μίαν ὑπὲρ ἁμαρτιῶν προσενέγκας θυσίαν.
10^{27} πυρὸς ζῆλος ἐσθίειν μέλλοντος τοὺς ὑπεναντίους.
12^{3} τὸν τοιαύτην ὑπομεμενηκότα ὑπὸ τῶν ἁμαρτωλῶν εἰς αὐτὸν ἀντιλογίαν.

Further, his use of the genitive absolute is to be noted, *e.g.*, in—

2^{4} συνεπιμαρτυροῦντος τοῦ θεοῦ κτλ.
4^{1} καταλειπομένης . . . αὐτοῦ (seven words between μή ποτε and δοκῇ τις).
4^{3} καίτοι τῶν ἔργων . . . γενηθέντων.
7^{12} μετατιθεμένης γὰρ τῆς ἱερωσύνης.
8^{4} ὄντων τῶν προσφερόντων κατὰ νόμον τὰ δῶρα.
9^{6} τούτων δὲ οὕτω κατεσκευασμένων.
9^{8} τοῦτο δηλοῦντος τοῦ Πνεύματος τοῦ Ἁγίου . . . ἔτι τῆς πρώτης σκηνῆς ἐχούσης στάσιν.
9^{15} θανάτου γενομένου . . . παραβάσεων (ten words between ὅπως and τ. ἐ. λαβῶσιν).
9^{19} λαληθείσης γὰρ πάσης ἐντολῆς . . . Μωυσέως.
10^{26} ἑκουσίως γὰρ ἁμαρτανόντων ἡμῶν.
11^{4} μαρτυροῦντος ἐπὶ τοῖς δώροις αὐτοῦ τοῦ θεοῦ.

Finally, there is an obvious endeavour to avoid harsh hiatus, sometimes by the choice of a term (*e.g.* διότι for ὅτι, as in Polybius and Theophrastus, or ἄχρις for ἄχρι, or ὡς for ὅτι), and a distinct fondness for compound verbs; Moulton (ii. 11), reckoning by the pages of WH, finds that while Mark has 5·7 compound verbs per page, Acts 6·25, Hebrews has 8·0, and Paul only 3·8.

His vocabulary is drawn from a wide range of reading. Whether he was a Jew by birth or not, he goes far beyond the LXX. His Greek recalls that of authors like Musonius Rufus and the philosophical Greek writers, and he affects more or less technical philosophical terms like αἰσθητήριον, δημιουργός, θέλησις, μετριοπαθεῖν, τελειόω, τέλος, τιμωρία, and ὑπόδειγμα. He was acquainted with the books of the Maccabees, Wisdom, Sirach, and perhaps even Philo. This last affinity is strongly marked. The more he differs from Philo in his speculative interpretation of religion, the more I feel, after a prolonged study of Philo, that our author had probably read some of his works; it is not easy to avoid the conclusion that his acquaintance with the Hellenistic Judaism of Alexandria included an acquaintance with Philo's writings. However this may be, the terminology of the Wisdom literature was as familiar to this early Christian διδάσκαλος as to the author of James.[1]

As for the LXX, the text he used—and he uses it with some freedom in quotations—must have resembled that of A (cp. Buchel in *Studien und Kritiken*, 1906, pp. 508–591), upon the whole. It is to his acquaintance with the LXX that occasional "Semitisms" in his style may be referred, *e.g.* the ἐπ' ἐσχάτου of 1^{1}, the καρδία ἀπιστίας of 3^{12}, the ἐν τῷ λέγεσθαι of 3^{15}, the θρόνος τῆς χάριτος of 4^{16}, and the phrases in 5^{7} 9^{5} and 12^{15}. But this is a minor point. We note rather that (*a*) he sometimes uses LXX terms (*e.g.* δυναμεῖς) in a special Hellenistic sense, or in a sense of his own. (*b*) Again, it is the use of the contents of the LXX which is really significant. The nearest approach to Πρὸς Ἑβραίους, in its treatment of the OT, is the speech of Stephen, the Hellenistic Jewish Christian, in Ac 7^{1-53}, where we have a similar use of the typological method and a similar freedom in handling the OT story (cp. *EBi.* 4791, *e.g.* Ac 7^{29} = He 11^{27}), which proves how men like these writers, for all their reverence for the LXX, sat wonderfully free to the letter of the scripture and employed, without hesitation, later Jewish traditions in order to interpret it for their own purposes. But Stephen's reading of the OT is not that of Πρὸς Ἑβραίους. The latter never dwells on the crime of the Jews in putting Jesus to death (12^{3} is merely a general, passing allusion), whereas Stephen makes that crime part and parcel of the age-long obstinacy and externalism which had characterized Israel. In Πρὸς Ἑβραίους, again, the κληρονομία of Palestine is spiritualized ($3^{7f.}$), whereas Stephen merely argues that its local possession by Israel was not final. Stephen, again, argues that believers in Jesus are the true heirs of the OT spiritual revelation, not the Jews; while in Πρὸς Ἑβραίους the continuity of the People is assumed, and Christians are regarded as *ipso facto* the People of God, without any allusion to the Jews having forfeited their privileges. Here the author of Πρὸς Ἑβραίους differs even from the parable of Jesus (cp. on 1^{1}); he conveys no censure of the historical Jews who had been responsible for the crucifixion. The occasional resemblances between Stephen's speech and Πρὸς Ἑβραίους are not so significant as the difference of tone and temper between them, *e.g.* in their conceptions of Moses and of the angels (cp. on He 2^{2}). For another thing, (*c*) the conception of God derives largely

[1] On the philosophical background of ideas as well as of words, see A. R. Eagar in *Hermathena*, xi. pp. 263–287; and H. T. Andrews in *Expositor*[8], xiv. pp. 348 f.

from the element of awe and majesty in the OT (see on 1^{3} 4^{13} $10^{30.\ 31}$ 12^{29}). This has been already noted (see pp. xxxv f.). But linguistically there are characteristic elements in the various allusions to God. Apart altogether from a stately term like Μεγαλωσύνη (1^{3} 8^{1}) or Δόξα (9^{5}), we get a singular number of indirect, descriptive phrases like *δι' ὃν τὰ πάντα καὶ δι' οὗ τὰ πάντα* (2^{10}), *τῷ ποιήσαντι αὐτόν* (3^{2}), *πρὸς ὃν ἡμῖν ὁ λόγος* (4^{13}), *τὸν δυνάμενον σώζειν αὐτὸν ἐκ θανάτου* (5^{7}), *ὁ ἐπαγγειλάμενος* (10^{23} 11^{11}), *τὸν ἀόρατον* (11^{27}), *τὸν ἀπ' οὐρανῶν χρηματίζοντα* (12^{25}). After 1^{1}, indeed, there is a slight tendency to avoid the use of *ὁ θεός* and to prefer such periphrases of a solemn and even liturgical tone. It is noticeable, *e.g.*, that while *ὁ θεός* occurs about seventy-eight times in 2 Co (which is about the same length as Πρὸς Ἑβραίους), it only occurs fifty-five times in the latter writing. The title (ὁ) Κύριος is also rare; it was probably one of the reasons that suggested the quotation in $1^{10\text{f.}}$ (*κύριε*), but it is mainly applied to God (12^{14}), and almost invariably in connexion with OT quotations (7^{21} 8^{2} $8^{8\text{f.}}$ 10^{16} 10^{30} 12^{6} 13^{6}). Once only it is applied to Jesus (2^{3}), apart from the solitary use of *ὁ κύριος ἡμῶν* in 7^{14} (+Ἰησοῦς, 33. 104. 2127) and in the doxology with Ἰησοῦς (13^{20}). It is not a term to which the author attaches special significance (cp. on 7^{24}). Ἰησοῦς, as in (i) 2^{9} (*τὸν δὲ βραχύ τι παρ' ἀγγέλους ἠλαττωμένον βλέπομεν Ἰησοῦν*), (ii) 3^{1} (*κατανοήσατε τὸν ἀπόστολον καὶ ἀρχιερέα τῆς ὁμολογίας ἡμῶν Ἰησοῦν*), (iii) 4^{14} (*ἔχοντες οὖν ἀρχιερέα μέγαν διεληλυθότα τοὺς οὐρανούς, Ἰησοῦν*), (iv) 6^{20} (*ὅπου πρόδρομος ὑπὲρ ἡμῶν εἰσῆλθεν Ἰησοῦς*), (v) 7^{22} (*κατὰ τοσοῦτον καὶ κρείττονος διαθήκης γέγονεν ἔγγυος Ἰησοῦς*), (vi) 10^{19} (*ἐν τῷ αἵματι Ἰησοῦ*), (vii) 12^{2} (*τὸν τῆς πίστεως ἀρχηγὸν καὶ τελειωτὴν Ἰησοῦν*), (viii) 12^{24} (*καὶ διαθήκης νέας μεσίτῃ Ἰησοῦ*), (ix) 13^{12} (*διὸ καὶ Ἰησοῦς*), (x) 13^{20} (*τὸν ποιμένα τῶν προβάτων τὸν μέγαν ἐν αἵματι διαθήκης αἰωνίου, τὸν κύριον ἡμῶν Ἰησοῦν*), is generally the climax of an impressive phrase or phrases. The unique use of this name in such connexions soon led to liturgical or theological expansions, as, *e.g.*, 3^{1} (+Χριστόν, C^{c} K L Ψ 104. 326. 1175 syr arm Orig. Chrys.), 6^{20} (+Χριστός, D), 10^{19} (+τοῦ Χριστοῦ, 1827 vg), 13^{12} (+ὁ, 5 [as Col 3^{17}]. 330 [as Col 3^{17}]. 440 [as Ro 8^{11}]. 623. 635. 1867. 2004: +ὁ κύριος, 1836: Χριστός, 487), 13^{20} (+Χριστόν, D Ψ 5. 104. 177. 241. 323. 337. 436. 547. 623^{c}. 635. 1831. 1837. 1891 $\text{lat}^{\text{d f tol}}$ syr^{hkl} Chrys.). Χριστός (3^{6} $9^{11.\ 24}$), or ὁ Χριστός (3^{14} 5^{5} 6^{1} $9^{14.\ 28.}$ 11^{26}), has also been altered; *e.g.* 3^{14} (*κυρίου*, 256. 2127: *θεοῦ*, 635: om. *τοῦ*, 467), 5^{5} (om. *ὁ*, 462), 6^{1} (*θεοῦ*, 38. 2005: om. 429), 9^{24} (+ὁ C^{c} D Ψ 104. 256. 263. 326. 467. 1739. 2127 arm: Ἰησοῦς, 823 vg Orig.), but less seriously. Ἰησοῦς Χριστός only occurs thrice (10^{10} $13^{8.\ 21}$).

So far as vocabulary and style go, there are certain affinities between Πρὸς Ἑβραίους and (*a*) the Lucan writings, (*b*) 1 Peter, and, to a less degree, (*c*) the Pastoral Epistles; but an examination of the data indicates that the affinities are not sufficient to do more than indicate a common atmosphere of thought and expression at some points. I do not now feel it safe to go beyond this cautious verdict. The author of Πρὸς Ἑβραίους has idiosyncrasies which are much more significant than any such affinities. His literary relations with the other NT writers, if he had any, remain obscure, with two exceptions. Whether he had read Paul's epistles or not, depends in part on the question whether the quotation in 10^{30} was derived outright from Ro 12^{19} or from some *florilegium* of messianic texts; but, apart from this, there are numerous cases of what seem to be reminiscences of Paul. As for 1 Peter, our author has some connexion, which remains unsolved, with what probably was an earlier document.

To sum up. He has a sense of literary nicety, which enters into his earnest religious argument without rendering it artificial or over-elaborate. He has an art of words, which is more than an unconscious sense of rhythm. He has the style of a trained speaker; it is style, yet style at the command of a devout genius. "Of Hellenistic writers he is the freest from the monotony that is the chief fault of Hellenistic compared with literary Greek; his words do not follow each other in a mechanically necessary order, but are arranged so as to emphasize their relative importance, and to make the sentences effective as well as intelligible. One may say that he deals with the biblical language (understanding by this the Hellenistic dialect founded on the LXX, not merely his actual quotations from it) . . . as a preacher, whose first duty is to be faithful, but his second to be eloquent" (W. H. Simcox, *The Writers of the NT*, p. 43).

§ 4. Text, Commentaries, etc.

(i.)

The textual criticism of Πρὸς Ἑβραίους is bound up with the general criticism of the Pauline text (cp. *Romans* in the present series, pp. lxiii ff.), but it has one or two special features of its own, which are due in part (*a*) to the fact of its exclusion from the NT Canon in some quarters of the early church, and (*b*) also to the fact that the Pauline F (Greek text) and G are wholly, while B C H M N W p^{13} and 048 are partially, missing. It is accidental that the Philoxenian Syriac version has not survived, but the former phenomenon (*a*) accounts for the absence of Πρὸς Ἑβραίους not simply from the Gothic version, but also from the old Latin African bible-text for which Tertullian and Cyprian, the pseudo-Augustinian *Speculum* and "Ambrosiaster," furnish such valuable evidence in the case of the Pauline epistles. The (*b*) defectiveness of B, etc., on the other hand, is to some extent made up by the discovery of the two early papyrus-fragments.

The following is a list of the MSS and the main cursives, the notations of Gregory and von Soden being added in brackets, for the sake of convenience in reference :

Codicum Index.

ℵ	saec. iv. (v.)	[01 : δ 2).
A	,, v.	[02 : δ 4].
B	,, iv.	[03 : δ 1] cont. 1^{1}–9^{13}: for remainder cp. cursive 293.
C	,, v.	[04 : δ 3] cont. 2^{4}–7^{26} 9^{15}–10^{24} 12^{16}–13^{25}.
D	,, (vi.)	[06 : α 1026] cont. 1^{1}–13^{20}. Codex Claromontanus is a Graeco-Latin MS, whose Greek text is poorly[1] reproduced in the later (saec. ix.–x.) E=codex Sangermanensis. The Greek text of the latter (1^{1}–12^{8}) is therefore of no independent value (cp. Hort in WH, §§ 335–337); for its Latin text, as well as for that of F=codex Augiensis (saec. ix.), whose Greek text of Πρὸς Ἑβραίους has not been preserved, see below, p. lxix.
H	,, vi.	[015 : α 1022] cont. 1^{3-8} 2^{11-16} 3^{13-18} 4^{12-15} $10^{1-7.\ 32-38}$ 12^{10-15} 13^{24-25}: mutilated fragments, at Moscow and Paris, of codex Coislinianus.
K	,, ix.	[018 : I[1]].
L	,, ix.	[020 : α 5] cont. 1^{1}–13^{10}.
M	,, ix.	[0121 : α 1031] cont. 1^{1}–4^{3} 12^{20}–13^{25}.
N	,, ix.	[0122 : α 1030] cont. 5^{8}–6^{10}.
P	,, ix.	[025 : α 3] cont. 1^{1}–12^{8} 12^{11}–13^{25}.
p[13]	,, iv.	[α 1034] cont. 2^{14}–5^{5} 10^{8}–11^{13} 11^{28}–12^{17}: *Oxyrhynchus Papyri*, iv. (1904) 36–48. The tendency, in 2^{14}–5^{5}, to agree with B "in the omission of unessential words and phrases . . . gives the papyrus peculiar value in the later chapters, where B is deficient"; thus p[13] partially makes up for the loss of B after 9^{14}. Otherwise the text of the papyrus is closest to that of D.
p[18]	,, iv.	[α 1043] cont. 9^{12-19}: *Oxyrhynchus Papyri*, viii. (1911) 11–13.
Ψ	,, (vi. ?) viii.–ix.	[044 : δ 6] cont. 1^{1}–8^{11} 9^{19}–13^{25}.
W	,, (iv.–vi.)	[I] cont. $1^{1-3.\ 9-12}$ $2^{4-7.\ 12-14}$ $3^{4-6.\ 14-16}$ $4^{3-6.\ 12-14}$ 5^{5-7} $6^{1-3.\ 10-13.\ 20}$ $7^{1-2.\ 7-11.\ 18-20.\ 27-28}$ $8^{1.\ 7-9}$ $9^{1-4.\ 9-11.\ 16-19.\ 25-27}$ $10^{5-8.\ 16-18.\ 26-29.\ 35-38}$ $11^{6-7.\ 12-15.\ 22-24.\ 31-33.\ 38-40}$ $12^{1.\ 7-9.\ 16-18.\ 25-27}$ $13^{7-9.\ 16-18.\ 23-25}$: *NT MSS in Freer Collection, The Washington MS of the Epp. of Paul* (1918), pp. 294–306. Supports Alexandrian text, and is "quite free from Western readings."

[1] An instance may be found in 10^{33}, where a corrector of D obelized the first and last letters of ὀνειδιζόμενοι and wrote over it θεατριζόμενοι. In E we get the absurd νιδιζομενοθεατοιζομενοι (cp. Gregory's *Textkritik des NT*, i. 109).

048	saec. v.	[α 1] cont. 11^{32}–13^{4}. Codex Patiriensis is a palimpsest.
0142	,, x.	[o^{6}].
0151	,, xii.	[x^{21}].

Three specimens of how the MSS group themselves may be printed. (*a*) shows the relation between M and the papyrus p^{13}:

M agrees with p^{13} in eight places:

3^{1} Ἰησοῦν.
3^{3} δόξης οὗτος (+K L vg, alone).
3^{4} πάντα.
3^{6} ἐάν.
3^{9} ὑμῶν ἐν δοκιμασίᾳ.
3^{10} ταύτῃ.
3^{13} τις ἐξ ὑμῶν.
4^{2} συγκεκ(ε)ρασμένους.

It opposes p^{13} (+B) in

3^{2} + ὅλῳ.
3^{6} ὅς.
3^{6} + μέχρι τέλους βεβαίαν.
3^{9} + με.
4^{3} οὖν.
4^{3} + τήν before κατάπαυσιν.

M has some remarkable affinities with the text of Origen (*e.g.* 1^{3} 1^{9} 2^{1}). (*b*) exhibits the relations of א and D*, showing how A and B agree with them on the whole, and how p^{13} again falls into this group:

א and D* agree in

1^{2}	position of ἐποίησεν	A B M
1^{8}	+ καί before ἡ ῥάβδος	A B M
2^{1}	παραρυῶμεν	A B*
2^{7}	+ καὶ κατέστησας . . . σου	A
2^{15}	δουλίας	
3^{1}	om. Χριστόν	A B M p^{13}
3^{4}	πάντα	A B M p^{13}
3^{10}	ταύτῃ	A B M p^{13}
3^{19}	δι' (so 7^{9})	A B M p^{13}
4^{1}	καταλιπομένης (alone), except for p^{13}	
4^{7}	προείρηται	A (B) p^{13}
4^{15}	συνπαθῆσαι	A B*
4^{16}	ἔλεος	A B
5^{3}	δι' αὐτήν	A B
5^{3}	μερὶ ἁμαρτιῶν	A B
6^{10}	om. τοῦ κόπου	A B
6^{16}	om. μέν	A B
7^{5}	Λευί	
7^{6}	om. τόν before Ἀβραάμ	B
7^{10}	,, ὁ ,, Μελχισεδέκ	B
7^{11}	αὐτῆς	A B
7^{11}	νενομοθέτηται	A B
7^{16}	σαρκίνης	A B
7^{17}	μαρτυρεῖται	A B
8^{2}	om. καί before οὐκ ἄνθρωπος	B
8^{4}	οὖν	A B
8^{4}	om. τῶν ἱερέων	A B
8^{11}	om. αὐτῶν after μικροῦ	A B
9^{5}	χερουβίν (alone of uncials)	
9^{9}	καθ' ἥν	A B
9^{21}	ἐράντισεν	A
9^{24}	om. ὁ before Χριστός	A
10^{10}	om. οἱ ,, διά	A
10^{12}	οὗτος	A
10^{16}	διάνοιαν	A
10^{23}	λελουσμένοι	
11^{3}	τὸ βλεπόμενον	A p^{13}
11^{19}	δυνατός	
11^{29}	+ γῆς	A p^{13}
11^{30}	ἔπεσαν	A p^{13}
11^{32}	με γάρ	A
11^{34}	μαχαίρης (so 11^{37})	A
12^{5}	παιδίας	A
12^{8}	position of ἐστε	A p^{13}
12^{9}	πολύ (so 12^{25})	A
12^{21}	ἔκτρομος (alone)	
13^{3}	κακουχουμένων	A M
13^{4}	γάρ	A M
13^{8}	ἐχθές	A M
13^{21}	om. ἐργῷ	

(*c*) exhibits characteristic readings of H, with some of its main allies:

1[3]	*καθαρισμόν*		ℵ	A	B		D[b]		H*		P			vg		arm		
2[15]	*δουλίας*		ℵ				D*		H		P							
3[13]	*τις ἐξ ὑμῶν*	p[13]	ℵ	A		C			H	M	P			vg	pesh	arm	boh	
3[14]	*τοῦ Χριστοῦ γεγ.*		ℵ	A	B	C	D	W	H	M	P			vg				
3[17]	*τίσιν δέ*		ℵ		B	C	D		H		P	K	L					sah
4[12]	*ἐνεργής*		ℵ	A		C	D		H		P	K	L	vg				
4[12]	*ψυχῆς*		ℵ	A	B	C			H		P		L	(vg		arm	boh)	
4[15]	*συνπαθῆσαι*		ℵ	A	B*	C	D*		H									
10[1]	*θυσίας* (– *αὐτῶν*)			A		C	D		H			K	L	vg				
10[1]	*αἷς*						D*		H				L					
10[1]	*δυνάται*						D		H			K	L	vg			boh	
10[2]	om. *οὐκ*								H*					(vg)	pesh			
10[2]	*κεκαθαρισμένους*		ℵ				D		H		P	K						
10[6]	*ηὐδόκησας*			A		C	D*	W	H		P							
10[34]	*τοῖς δεσμίοις*	p[13]		A			D*		H					vg	pesh		boh	
10[34]	*ἑαυτούς*	p[13]	ℵ	A					H					vg			boh	
10[34]	*ὕπαρξιν*	p[13]	ℵ*	A			D*		H*					vg			boh	
10[35]	*μεγάλην μισθ.*		ℵ	A			D	W	H		P							
10[37]	*χρονιεῖ*		ℵ[c]	A			D[c]	W	H		P	K	L					
10[38]	*μου ἐκ πίστεως*		ℵ	A					H*					vg		arm		
12[11]	*πᾶσα δέ*	p[13]	ℵ[c]	A			D[c]		H			K	L	vg	pesh		boh	
12[13]	*ποιήσατε*		ℵ	A			D		H			K	L					
12[15]	*αὐτῆς*	(p[13])		A					H		P							
12[16]	*αὐτοῦ*		ℵ[c]				D*		H		P	K	L					
13[21]	om. *τῶν αἰώνων*					C[c]	D		H							arm		
13[23]	*ἡμῶν*		ℵ*	A		C	D*	W	H	M				vg	pesh	arm	boh	sah
13[25]	*ἀμήν.*		ℵ[c]	A		C	D		H	M	P	K		vg	pesh	(arm)	boh	

CURSIVES.

No.		Date		
1	saec.	x.	[δ 254]	
2	,,	xii.	[α 253]	
5	,,	xiv.	[δ 453]	
6	,,	xiii.	[δ 356]	cont. 1[1]–9[3] 10[22]–13[25]
31	,,	xi.	[α 103]	
33	,,	ix.–x.	[δ 48]	Hort's 17
35	,,	xiii.	[δ 309]	
38	,,	xiii.	[δ 355]	
47	,,	xi.	[O π[103]]	
69	,,	xv.	[δ 505]	
88	,,	xii.	[α 200]	
90	,,	xvi.	[δ 652]	
93	,,	x.	[α 51]	
103	,,	xi.	[O [28]]	
104	,,	xi.	[α 103]	
112	,,	xi.	[E π[10]]	
177	,,	xi.	[α 106]	
181	,,	xi.	[α 101]	
188	,,	xii.	[α 200]	
189	saec.	xiii.	[Θ δ [30]]	
203	,,	xii.	[α 203]	
206	,,	xiii.	[α 365]	
209	,,	xiv.	[δ 457]	
216	,,	xiv.	[α 469]	
217	,,	xi.	[α 1065]	cont. 1[1]–6[5]
218	,,	xiii.	[δ 300]	
221	,,	x.	[α 69]	
226	,,	xi.	[δ 156]	
227	,,	xii.	[α 258]	
241	,,	xi.	[δ 507]	
242	,,	xii.	[δ 206]	
253	,,	xi.	[δ 152]	
255	,,	xi.	[α 174]	
256	,,	xii.	[α 216]	
257	,,	xiv.	[α 466]	
263	,,	xiii.–xiv.	[δ 372]	
293	,,	xv.	[α 1574]	cont. 9[14]–13[25]
296	,,	xvi.	[δ 600]	
323	,,	xi.–xii.	[α 157]	

No.		Century	von Soden	Remarks
326	saec.	xii.	[α 257]	
327	,,	xiii.	[O^{36}]	
330	,,	xii.	[δ 259]	
337	,,	xii.	[α 205]	
371	,,	xiv.	[α 1431]	cont. 7^3–13^{25}
378	,,	xii.	[α 258]	
383	,,	xiii.	[α 353]	cont. 1^1–13^7
418	,,	xv. (x.)	[α 1530]	cont. 1^1–13^{17}
424	,,	xi.	[O^{12}]	Hort's 67
429	,,	xiii.–xiv.	[α 398]	
431	,,	xii.	[δ 268]	
436	,,	xi.	[α 172]	
440	,,	xii.	[δ 260]	
442	,,	xiii.	[O^{18}]	
456	,,	x. ?	[α 52]	
460	,,	xiii.–xiv.	[α 397]	
461	,,	xiii.	[α 359]	
462	,,	xv.	[α 502]	
487	,,	xi.	[α 171]	
489	,,	xiv.	[δ 459]	Hort's 102
491	,,	xi.	[δ 152]	
506	,,	xi.	[δ 101]	
522	,,	xvi.	[δ 602]	
547	,,	xi.	[δ 157]	
614	,,	xiii.	[α 364]	
623	,,	xi.	[α 173]	
633	,,	xi.	[α 161]	
639	.,	xi.	[α 169]	
642	,,	xv.	[α 552]	cont. 1^1–7^{18} 9^{13}–13^{25}
794	,,	xiv.	[δ 454]	
808	,,	xii.	[δ 203]	
823	,,	xiii.	[δ 368]	
876	,,	xiii.	[α 356]	
913	,,	xiv.	[α 470]	
915	,,	xiii.	[α 382]	
917	,,	xii.	[α 264]	
919	,,	xi.	[α 113]	
920	,,	x.	[α 55]	
927	,,	xii.	[δ 251]	
941	saec.	xiii.	[δ 369]	
999	,,	xiii.	[δ 353]	
1108	,,	xiii.	[α 370]	
1149	,,	xiii.	[δ 370]	
1175	,,	x.	[α 74]	cont. 1^1–3^5 6^8 13^{20}
1243	,,	xii.	[δ 198]	
1245	.,	xi.	[α 158]	
1288 (81)		xi.	[α 162]	
1311	,,	xi.	[α 170]	
1319	,,	xi.	[δ 180]	
1518	,,	xi.	[α 116]	
1522	,,	xiv.	[α 464]	
1525	,,	xiii.	[α 361]	cont. 1^1–7^8
1610	,,	xiv.	[α 468]	
1611	,,	xii.	[α 208]	
1739	,,	x.	[α 78]	
1758	,,	xiii.	[α 396]	cont. 1^1–13^{14}
1765	,,	xiv.	[α 486]	
1827	,,	xiii.	[α 367]	
1831	,,	xiv.	[α 472]	
1836	,,	x.	[α 65]	
1837	,,	xi.	[α 192]	
1838	,,	xi.	[α 175]	
1845	,,	x.	[α 64]	
1852	,,	xi.	[α 114]	cont. 1^1–11^{10}
1867	,,	xi.–xii.	[α 154]	
1872	.,	xii.	[α 209]	
1873	,,	xii.	[α 252]	
1891	,,	x.	[α 62]	
1898	,,	x.	[α 70]	
1906	,,	xi.	[$O\pi^{101}$]	
1908	,,	xi.	[$O\pi^{103}$]	
1912	,,	x.–xi.	[α 1066]	
2004	,,	x.	[α 56]	
2055	,,	xiv.	[α 1436]	cont. 1^1–7^2
2127	,,	xii.	[δ 202]	
2138	,,	xi.	[α 116]	
2143	,,	xi.–xii.	[α 184]	
2147	,,	xii.	[δ 299]	

Of these some like 5 and 33 and 442 and 999 and 1908, are of the first rank; von Soden pronounces 1288 "a very good representative" of his H text. Yet even the best cursives, like the uncials, may stray (see on 4^{16}). As a specimen of how one good cursive goes, I append this note of some characteristic readings in 424**:

1^3	om. *αὐτοῦ* after *δυνάμεως*		M	Orig	d e f vg
	om. *ἡμῶν*	ℵ* A B D*	M P		
2^9	*χωρὶς*		M	Orig	
3^1	om. *Χριστὸν*	ℵ A B D* C*	M P		d e f vg sah
3^6	*ὅς*	D*	M		d e f vg
3^{10}	*ταύτῃ*	ℵ A B D*	M		sah

-4^{14} πίστεως									
-5^{12} ὑμᾶς (om. τινά)									
8^{4} om. τῶν ἱερεων	ℵ	A	B	D*			P		d e f vg
9^{9} καθ' ἥν	ℵ	A	B	D*					f vg
9^{23} καθαρίζεται (ἀνάγκη)				D*				Orig	
10^{1} δύνανται	ℵ	A		D^{b}	C		P [*sc.* D*, Orig]		
10^{30} om. λέγει κύριος	ℵ*			D*			P		d e f vg
10^{34} δεσμίοις		A	H	D*				(Orig ??)	f vg
11^{5} om. αὐτοῦ	ℵ*	A		D*			P		d e f vg
12^{15} αὐτῆς		A					P		
12^{25} ἀπ' οὐρανοῦ	ℵ					M		b	
12^{26} σείσω	ℵ	A			C	M			f vg

LATIN VERSIONS.

A. Old Latin (vt), saec. ii. (?)–iv.

Hebrews is omitted in the pseudo-Augustinian *Speculum* (=*m*) and in codex Boernerianus (=*g*), but included in—

d (Latin version of D)
e (,, ,, ,, E)
f (,, ,, ,, F)
r (codex Frisingensis: saec. vi., cont. 6^{6}–7^{5} 7^{8}–8^{1} 9^{27}–11^{7})
x^2 (,, Bodleianus: ,, ix., cont. 1^{1}–11^{23})

Of these, *r* (corresponding to the text used by Augustine), with the few quotations by Priscillian, represents the African, *d* (in the main)[1] and x^2 the European, type of the Old Latin text; but *f* is predominantly vulgate, and it is doubtful whether x^2 is really Old Latin. On the other hand, some evidence for the Old Latin text is to be found occasionally in the following MSS of—

B. Vulgate (vg), saec. iv.

am (Codex Amiatinus: saec. vii.–viii.)
fuld (,, Fuldensis: ,, vi.)
cav (,, Cavensis: ,, ix.) } Spanish
tol (,, Toletanus: ,, viii.) } Spanish
harl (,, Harleianus: ,, viii.)
c (,, Colbertinus: ,, xii.)

Though *c* is an Old Latin text for the gospels, Hebrews and the rest of the NT are vulgate; but He 10–11 in *harl* (which elsewhere has affinities with *am* and *fuld*) is Old Latin, according to E. S. Buchanan (*The Epistles and Apocalypse from the codex Harleianus* [z= *Wordsworth's* Z_2], *numbered Harl.* 1772 *in the British Museum Library*, 1913). Both in *harl* and in *e*, 11^{3-33} has a special capitulation; *harl*, which adds after "the prophets" in

[1] The text of *d* corresponds to that of Lucifer of Cagliari (saec. iv.), who quotes 3^{5}–4^{10} and 4^{11-13} in his treatise *De non conueniendo cum haereticis*, xi. (*CSEL.*, vol. xiv.). According to Harnack (*Studien zur Vulgata des Hebräerbriefs*, 1920) it is *d*, not *r*, which underlies the vulgate (cp. J. Belser on "die Vulgata u. der Griech. Text im Hebräerbrief," in *Theolog. Quartalschrift*, 1906, pp. 337–369).

11^{32}—"Ananias azarias misahel daniel helias helisaeus"—apparently points to 11^{3-32} having been at one time added to the original text which ran ($11^{2.\,33}$): "in hac enim testimonium habuerunt seniores qui per fidem uicerunt regna," etc. Of these MSS, *fuld* represents an Italian text, *cav* and *tol* a Spanish (the former with some admixture of Old Latin); *am* (whose text is akin to *fuld*) is an Italian text, written in Great Britain. At an early date the Latin versions were glossed, however (cp. on 7^{1} 11^{23}).

Egyptian Versions.

sah = Sahidic (saec. iii.–iv.): *The Coptic Version of the NT in the Southern Dialect* (Oxford, 1920), vol. v. pp. 1–131.

boh = Bohairic (saec. vi.–vii.): *The Coptic Version of the NT in the Northern Dialect* (Oxford, 1905), vol. iii. pp. 472–555.

In sah Πρὸς Ἑβραίους comes very early in the Pauline canon, immediately after Romans and Corinthians, even earlier than in the first (A.D. 400) Syriac canon, whereas in boh it comes between the Pauline church letters and the Pastorals. The latter seems to have been an early (*i.e.* a fourth century) position in the Eastern or Alexandrian canon, to judge from Athanasius (*Fest. Ep.* xxxix.); it reappears in the uncials ℵ A B[1] W. Not long afterwards, at the Synod of Carthage (can. 39), in A.D. 397, it is put between the Pauline and the Catholic epistles, which seems to have been the African and even the (or, a) Roman order. This reflects at least a doubt about its right to stand under Paul's name, whereas the order in sah and the primitive Syriac canon reflects a deliberate assertion of its Pauline authorship. The Alexandrian position is intermediate.

The data of the Egyptian versions are of special interest, as several of the uncials have Egyptian affinities or an Egyptian origin, and as Πρὸς Ἑβραίους was early studied at Alexandria. Thus, to cite only one or two, boh is right, as against sah, *e.g.* in the rendering of πρός in 1^{7}, in omitting ὅλῳ (3^{5}), in rendering ὑποστάσεως as "confidence" in 3^{14}, in rendering ἐν Δαυείδ (4^{7}) "in David," in reading παθεῖν in 9^{26}, in rendering ὑπόστασις by "assurance" (so syr arm) in 11^{1}, in taking καλούμενος by itself (11^{8}), in keeping ἐλιθάσθησαν before ἐπρίσθησαν (11^{37}, though ἐπειράσθησαν, = were tempted, is inferior to sah's omission of any such term), in reading ἐπαγγελίαν (11^{39}, where sah agrees with W in reading the plural), etc. On the other hand, and in a large number of cases, sah is superior, *e.g.* at 2^{17} ("a merciful and faithful high-priest"), at 3^{6} (omitting μέχρι τέλους βεβαίαν), at 4^{2} (συγκεκερασμένος), in rendering κρατῶμεν (4^{14}) "let us hold on to," in maintaining θεός in 6^{3} (for "Lord" in boh), in omitting τοῦ κόπου in 6^{10}, in reading ἱερεῖς (with W) in 7^{28}, in reading ὑμῶν in 9^{14}, in rendering the last words of 9^{28}, in rendering ἁμ . . . ἀντιλογίαν in 12^{3} etc. Note also that sah agrees with arm in inserting τῆς before ἐπαγγελίας in 4^{1}, ὕστερον λέγει in $10^{16.\,17}$, and γάρ in 12^{4}, while boh agrees with arm in adding εἶπεν in 1^{8} and αἰώνιος at 5^{10}, and both agree with arm in omitting καί in 1^{6}. Both translate εἰσερχόμεθα (4^{3}) as a future, read ἀπιστίαν in 4^{6} (with vg and arm), omit κατὰ τὴν τ. M. in 7^{21}, take ἅγιον as an adjective in 9^{1}, read μελλόντων in 9^{11}, take ἧς in 11^{7} to mean the ark, read ἡ στεῖρα in 11^{11}, render ὄγκον by "pride" in 12^{1}, take ὑπομένετε as imperative in 12^{7}, and refer αὐτήν to τόπον μετανοίας in 12^{17}. Sah has

[1] Yet in the archetype of the capitulation system in B Πρὸς Ἑβραίους must have stood between Galatians and Ephesians, which "is the order given in the Sahidic version of the 'Festal letter' of Athanasius" (Kirsopp Lake, *The Text of the NT*, p. 53).

some curious renderings, *e.g.* "hewed out" for ἐνεκαινίσεν (10^{20}), "the place of the blood" for αἵματος in 12^{4}, and actually "hanging for them another time" (ἀνασταυροῦντας ἑαυτοῖς, 6^{6}); in general it is rather more vivid and less literal, though boh reads "through the sea of Shari" [? slaughter] in 11^{29} (sah is defective here), which is singular enough. On the other hand, sah is more idiomatic. Thus it is in sah, not in boh, that νωθροὶ γένησθε (6^{12}) is rendered by "become daunted." The differences in a passage like $12^{22f.}$ are specially instructive. Sah takes πανηγύρει with what follows, boh with ἀγγέλων ("myriads of angels keeping festival"); on the other hand, sah is right as against boh's reading of πνεύματι (v.[23]), while both render "God the judge of all." In v.[26] both render ἐπήγγελται literally by "he promised," but boh translates παραλαμβάνοντες in v.[28] as a future and χάριν as "grace," whereas sah renders correctly in both cases. In ch. 13, sah seems to read περιφέρεσθε in v.[9] ("be not tossed about"), inserts ἔργῳ (as against boh), and reads ἡμῖν in v.[21]; in v.[22] it reads ἀνέχεσθε; in v.[23], while boh renders ἀπολελυμένον by "released," sah renders "our brother Timotheos whom I sent" (which confuses the sense of the passage altogether), and, unlike boh, omits the final ἀμήν. It is significant that sah[1] often tallies with *r* as against *d*, *e.g.* in 6^{18} (ἰσχυράν), 7^{27} (ἀρχιερεῖς), though with *d* now and then against *r*, as in 11^{6} (δέ). It agrees with *d* and eth in reading πνεῦμα in 1^{7}, ὡς ἱμάτιον in 1^{12} (as well as ἑλίξεις), and καὶ τῶν τράγων in 9^{19}, but differs from *d* almost as often, and from eth in reading ταύτῃ in 3^{10}, in omitting κατὰ τ. τ. M. in 7^{21}, etc. Unexpectedly a collation of sah and of eth yields no material for a clear decision upon the relation of the texts they imply.

Syriac Versions.

For the Old Syriac, *i.e.* for the Syriac text of Hebrews prior to the vulgate revision (Peshiṭta) of the fifth century, we possess even less material than in the case of the Old Latin version. Hebrews belonged to the old Syrian canon, but the primitive text can only be recovered approximately from (i) the Armenian version,[2] which rests in part upon an Old Syriac basis—"readings of the Armenian vulgate which differ from the ordinary Greek text, especially if they are supported by the Peshiṭta, may be considered with some confidence to have been derived from the lost Old Syriac" (F. C. Burkitt, *EBi.* 5004); from (ii) the homilies of Aphraates (saec. iv), and from (iii) the Armenian translation of Ephraem Syrus (saec. iv.), *Commentarii in Epp. Pauli nunc primum ex armenio in latinum sermonem a patribus Mekitharistis translati* (Venice, 1893, pp. 200–242).

Hebrews is not extant in the Philoxenian version of A.D. 508, but the Harklean revision of that text (A.D. 616-617) is now accessible in complete form, thanks to R. L. Bensly's edition (*The Harklean Version of the Epistle to the Hebrews*, 11^{28}–13^{25}, *now edited for the first time with Introduction and Notes*, Cambridge, 1889). The Peshiṭta version is now conveniently accessible in the British and Foreign Bible Society's edition of *The New Testament in Syriac* (1920).

---

[1] It rarely goes its own way, but the omission of any adjective at all with πνεύματος in 9^{14} is most remarkable; so is the reading of ὑμᾶς for ἡμᾶς in 13^{6} (where M Orig have one of their characteristic agreements in omitting any pronoun).

[2] Mr. F. C. Conybeare kindly supplied me with a fresh collation.

The early evidence for the use of Πρὸς Ἑβραίους may be chronologically tabulated as follows:

	MSS.		Versions.	Writers.	
100–200				Clem. Rom.	
200–300			(Old Syriac)(Old Latin)	Clem. Alex.	Tertullian
				Origen (–248)	
300–400	p^{13} p^{18}			Eusebius (–340)	
				Basil (–379)	Lucifer (–371)
	B		Sahidic (?)	Cyril of Jerus. (–386)	Priscillian (–385)
				Apollinaris (–392)	Ambrose (397)
	ℵ (?)		vulgate (370–383)	Chrysostom (–407)	Jerome (–420)
				Theodore of Mopsuestia	
400–500	W (?)		peshitta (411–435)		Augustine (–430)
				Cyril of Alex. (–444)	
	A C		Armenian	Theodoret (–458)	
	048				
500–600	D	d			
		fuld	Ethiopic		Fulgentius
	H	r			
600–700			harklean (616–617)		
700–800		am	Bohairic (?)		
	Ψ	tol			
800–900	K L				
	M N	f			
	P	cav			Sedulius Scotus
900–1000		e (?)			
	0142				

ℵ A B C H M Ψ W (with p^{13}) would represent von Soden's H text (approximating to WH's Neutral), his I text (corresponding to WH's Western) being represented by K L P among the uncials. But the difference between these in the Pauline corpus are, he admits, less than in the case of the gospels. Bousset (in *Texte und Untersuchungen*, xi. 4, pp. 45 f.) has shown that $ℵ^c$ H (which tend to agree with Origen's text) have affinities with Euthalius; they carry with them a number of cursives (including 33. 69. 88. 104. 424**. 436 and 1908), and enable us to reconstruct the archetype of codex Pamphili, *i.e.* the third century recension of Origen's text. This group would therefore stand midway between B ℵ A C and the later K L (with majority of cursives). But no exact grouping of the MSS is feasible. The text has suffered early corruption at several places, *e.g.* 2^9 4^2 7^1 10^{34} 11^4 11^{37} 12^3 12^{18} and 13^{21}, though only the first of these passages is of real, religious importance. But, apart from this, the earliest MSS betray serious errors (cp. on 7^1 11^{35}), as though the text had not been well preserved. Thus B, for all its services (*e.g.* in 6^2), goes wrong repeatedly (*e.g.* 1^3 1^8 4^{12}), as does ℵ* (*e.g.* 1^5 om. αὐτῷ, 4^9 6^9 9^{17} τότε, 10^{32} ἁμαρτίας), and even p^{13} in 4^3 (ἐλεύσονται), 10^{18} (ἁμαρτίαις), 11^1 (ἀπόστασις), etc. The errors of W are mainly linguistic, but it reads ἐνθυμήσεως in 4^{12}, πίστεως in 6^{11} etc. A test passage like 2^{14}, where "blood and flesh" naturally passed into the conventional "flesh and blood," shows the inferior reading supported not only by K and L, as we might expect, but by *f* and *tol*, the peshiṭta and eth. Similarly the wrong reading μαρτυρεῖ in 7^{17} brings out not only K and L again but C D syr and a group of cursives, 256. 326. 436. 1175. 1837. 2127. In 9^{28} only arm inserts πίστει after ἀπεκδεχομένοις, but the similar homiletic gloss of διὰ πίστεως before or after εἰς σωτηρίαν turns up in A P syr^{hkl}, and in 38. 69. 218. 256. 263. 330. 436. 440. 462. 823, 1245. 1288. 1611. 1837. 1898. 2005. In 9^{14} the gloss καὶ ἀληθινῷ is supported also by A P as well as by boh and one or two cursives like 104. To take another instance, the gloss καὶ δακρύων (in 10^{28}) has only D* among the uncials, but it is an Old Latin reading, though *r* does not support it, and it was read in the original text of the harklean Syriac. Again, in 11^{12}, what B. Weiss calls the "obvious emendation" ἐγεννήθησαν is supported by ℵ L p^{13} Ψ and 1739, while in the same verse καὶ ὡς ἡ (κάθως, D) carries with it ℵ A D K L P p^{13}, and D Ψ omit ἡ παρὰ τὸ χεῖλος. When M resumes at 12^{20} it is generally in the company of ℵ A D P (as, *e.g.*, $12^{23.\,24.\,25}$ $13^{5.\,9.\,20}$), once (12^{27} om. τήν) with D* arm, once with D* (om. ἐξουσίαν, 13^{10}), once with K L P (κακοχ. 13^{3}) against ℵ A D*. Such phenomena render the problem of ascertaining any traditional text of Πρὸς Ἑβραίους unusually difficult. Even the data yielded by Clement of Alexandria[1] and the Latin and Egyptian versions do not as yet facilitate a genealogical grouping of the extant MSS or a working hypothesis as to the authorities in which a text free from Western readings may be preserved.

(ii.)

The eighteen homilies by Origen (†253) are lost, though Eusebius (cp. above, pp. xviii–xix) quotes two fragments on the style and authorship. The Ἀπολογία Ὠριγενοῦς of Pamphilus (partially extant in the Latin version of Rufinus) implies that he also wrote a commentary on the epistle, but this is lost, and the Syriac commentary of Ephraem Syrus (†373) is only extant in the Latin version of an Armenian version (cp. above, p. lxxi). We are fortunate, however, in possessing the first important exposition of Πρὸς Ἑβραίους, viz. the homilies of Chrysostom (†407), extant in the form of notes, posthumously published, which the presbyter Constantine had taken down. Chrysostom's comments are drawn upon by most of the subsequent expositors. The foremost of these Greek exegetes is Theodore of Mopsuestia (†428), who is the first to show any appreciation of historical

[1] The original text in one place at least (cp. on 11^{4}) can be restored by the help of p^{13} and Clement.

criticism (*Theodori Mopsuesteni in NT Commentaria quae reperiri potuerunt, collegit O. F. Fritzsche*, 1847, pp. 160–172). The exposition by his contemporary Theodoret of Cyrrhus (†458) is based almost entirely upon Chrysostom and Theodore of Mopsuestia (*Theod. Comm. in omnes Pauli epistolas*, ed. E. B. Pusey, 1870, ii. 132–219). Similarly, the work of Oecumenius of Tricca in Thrace (tenth century) contains large excerpts from previous writers, including Chrysostom, Theodore of Mopsuestia, and Photius (cp. Migne, *PG.* cxviii–cxix). Theophylact, archbishop of Bulgaria (end of eleventh century), also draws upon his predecessors (cp. Migne, *PG.* cxxiv), like Euthymius Zigabenus (beginning of twelfth century), a monk near Constantinople. The latter's commentary on Hebrews is in the second volume (pp. 341 f.) of his *Commentarii* (ed. N. Calogeras, Athens, 1887). In a happy hour, about the middle of the sixth century, Cassiodorus (Migne's *PL.* lxx. p. 1120) employed a scholar called Mutianus to translate Chrysostom's homilies into Latin. This version started the homilies on a fresh career in the Western church, and subsequent Latin expositions, *e.g.* by Sedulius Scotus, W. Strabo, Alcuin, and Thomas of Aquinum, build on this version and on the vulgate. An excellent account of these commentaries is now published by Riggenbach in Zahn's *Forschungen zur Gesch. des NTlichen Kanons*, vol. viii. (1907).

Since F. Bleek's great edition (1828–1840) there has been a continuous stream of commentaries; special mention may be made of those by Delitzsch (Eng. tr. 1867), Lünemann (1867, 1882), Moses Stuart⁴ (1860), Alford² (1862), Reuss (1860, 1878), Kurtz (1869), Hofmann (1873), A. B. Davidson (1882), F. Rendall (1888), C. J. Vaughan (1890), B. Weiss (in Meyer, 1897), von Soden (1899), Westcott³ (1903), Hollmann² (1907), E. J. Goodspeed (1908), A. S. Peake (*Century Bible*, n.d.), M. Dods (1910), E. C. Wickham (1910), A. Seeberg (1912), Riggenbach (1913, 1922), Windisch (1913), and Nairne (1918).

Other works referred to, in this edition,[1] are as follows:—

Bengel (Bgl.). *J. A. Bengelii Gnomon Novi Testamenti* (1742).

Blass . . F. Blass, *Grammatik des neutestamentlichen Griechisch: vierte, völlig neugearbeitete Auflage, besorgt von Albert Debrunner* (1913); also, *Brief an die Hebräer, Text mit Angabe der Rhythmen* (1903).

[1] Some references, in the textual notes, are the usual abbreviations, like Amb. = Ambrose, Ath. or Athan. = Athanasius, Cosm. = Cosmas Indicopleustes (ed. E. O. Winstedt, Cambridge, 1909), Cyr. = Cyril of Alexandria, Euth. = Euthalius, Hil. = Hilary, Lucif. = Lucifer, Sedul. = Sedulius Scotus, Thdt. = Theodoret, Theod. = Theodore of Mopsuestia, etc.

BGU. . . *Aegyptische Urkunden* (*Griechisch Urkunden*), ed. Wilcken (1895).
BM. . . *Greek Papyri in the British Museum* (1893 f.).
Diat. . . E. A. Abbott, *Diatessarica.*
EBi. . . *The Encyclopaedia Biblica* (1899–1903, ed. J. S. Black and T. K. Cheyne).
Erasmus . *Adnotationes* (1516), *In epist. Pauli apostoli ad Hebraeos paraphrasis* (1521).
ERE. . . *Encyclopaedia of Religion and Ethics* (ed. J. Hastings).
Expositor . *The Expositor.* Small superior numbers indicate the series.
GCP. . . *Grundzüge und Chrestomathie der Papyruskunde*, von L. Mitteis und U. Wilcken (1912), I. Band.
Helbing . *Grammatik der Septuaginta, Laut- und Wortlehre*, von R. Helbing (1907).
IMA. . . *Inscriptiones Graecae Insul. Maris Aegaei* (1895 f.).
Josephus . *Flavii Josephi Opera Omnia post Immanuelem Bekkerum*, recognovit S. A. Naber.
LXX . . *The Old Testament in Greek according to the Septuagint Version* (ed. H. B. Swete).
Magn. . . *Die Inschriften von Magnesia am Maeander* (ed. Kern, 1900).
Michel . . *Recueil d'Inscriptions Grecques* (ed. C. Michel, 1900).
Mitteis-Wilcken *Grundzüge u. Chrestomathie der Papyruskunde* (1912).
Moulton . J. H. Moulton's *Grammar of New Testament Greek*, vol. i. (2nd edition, 1906).
OGIS. . . Dittenberger's *Orientis Graeci Inscriptiones Selectae* (1903–1905).
OP. . . *The Oxyrhynchus Papyri* (ed. B. P. Grenfell and A. Hunt).
Pfleiderer . *Primitive Christianity*, vol. iii. (1910) pp. 272–299.
Philo . . *Philonis Alexandriai Opera Quae Supersunt* (recognoverunt L. Cohn et P. Wendland).
Radermacher. *Neutestamentliche Grammatik* (1911), in Lietzmann's *Handbuch zum Neuen Testament* (vol. i.).
Rein. P. . *Papyrus Grecs et Démotiques* (Paris, 1905), ed. Th. Reinach.
Syll. . . *Sylloge Inscriptionum Graecarum*[2] (ed. W. Dittenberger).

Tebt. P. . . *Tebtunis Papyri* (ed. Grenfell and Hunt), 1902.

Thackeray . H. St J. Thackeray, *A Grammar of the Old Testament in Greek* (1909).

Weiss . . B. Weiss, "Textkritik der paulinischen Briefe" (in *Texte und Untersuchungen zur Geschichte der altchristlichen Literatur*, vol. xiv. 3), also *Der Hebräerbrief in Zeitgeschichtlicher Beleuchtung* (1910).

WH . . Westcott and Hort's *New Testament in Greek* (1890, 1896).

Zahn . . Theodor Zahn's *Einleitung in das NT*, §§ 45–47.

COMMENTARY.

The final disclosure of God's mind and purpose has been made in his Son, who is far superior to the angels; beware then of taking it casually and carelessly (1^1–2^4)!

The epistle opens with a long sentence (vv.[1-4]), the subject being first (vv.[1. 2]) God, then (vv.[3. 4]) the Son of God; rhetorically and logically the sentence might have ended with ἐν (+ τῷ arm) υἱῷ, but the author proceeds to elaborate in a series of dependent clauses the pre-eminence of the Son within the order of creation and providence. The main thread on which these clauses about the Son's relation to God and the world are strung is ὃς . . . ἐκάθισεν ἐν δεξιᾷ τῆς μεγαλωσύνης. It is in this (including the purging of men from their sins by His sacrifice) that the final disclosure of God's mind and purpose is made; ὁ θεὸς ἐλάλησεν ἡμῖν ἐν υἱῷ . . . ὃς . . . ἐκάθισεν κτλ. But the cosmic significance of the Son is first mentioned (v.[2]); he is not created but creative, under God. Here as in 2^{10} the writer explicitly stresses the vital connexion between redemption and creation; the Son who deals with the sins of men is the Son who is over the universe. This is again the point in the insertion of φέρων τε τὰ πάντα κτλ. before καθαρισμὸν ἁμαρτιῶν ποιησάμενος. The object of insisting that the Son is also the exact counterpart of God (ὃς ὢν κτλ. [3a]), is to bring out the truth that he is not only God's organ in creation, but essentially divine as a Son. In short, since the object of the divine revelation (λαλεῖν) is fellowship between God and men, it must culminate in One who can deal with sin, as no prophet or succession of prophets could do; the line of revelation ἐν προφήταις has its climax ἐν υἱῷ, in a Son whose redeeming sacrifice was the real and effective manifestation of God's mind for communion.

As it is necessary to break up this elaborate sentence for the purpose of exposition, I print it not only in Greek but in the stately Vulgate version, in order to exhibit at the very outset the style and spirit of Πρὸς Ἑβραίους.

Πολυμερῶς καὶ πολυτρόπως πάλαι ὁ θεὸς λαλήσας τοῖς πατράσιν ἐν τοῖς προφήταις ἐπ' ἐσχάτου τῶν ἡμερῶν τούτων ἐλάλησεν ἡμῖν ἐν υἱῷ, ὃν ἔθηκε κληρονόμον πάντων, δι' οὗ καὶ ἐποίησε τοὺς αἰῶνας· ὃς ὢν ἀπαύγασμα τῆς δόξης καὶ χαρακτὴρ τῆς ὑποστάσεως αὐτοῦ, φέρων τε τὰ πάντα τῷ ῥήματι τῆς δυνάμεως αὐτοῦ, καθαρισμὸν τῶν ἁμαρτιῶν ποιησάμενος ἐκάθισεν ἐν δεξιᾷ τῆς μεγαλωσύνης ἐν ὑψηλοῖς, τοσούτῳ κρείττων γενόμενος τῶν ἀγγέλων ὅσῳ διαφορώτερον παρ' αὐτοὺς κεκληρονόμηκεν ὄνομα.

Multifariam et multis modis olim Deus loquens patribus in prophetis novissime diebus istis locutus est nobis in filio, quem constituit heredem universorum, per quem fecit et saecula, qui cum sit splendor gloriae et figura substantiae eius, portans quoque omnia verbo virtutis suae, purgationem peccatorum faciens, sedit ad dexteram majestatis in excelsis, tanto melior angelis effectus quanto differentius prae illis nomen hereditavit.

1 *Many were the forms and fashions in which God spoke of old to our fathers by the prophets,* 2 *but in these days at the end he has spoken to us by a Son—a Son whom he has appointed heir of the universe, as it was by him that he created the world.*

Greek prefaces and introductions of a rhetorical type were fond of opening with πολύς in some form or other (*e.g.* Sirach prol. πολλῶν καὶ μεγάλων κτλ.; Dion. Halic. *de oratoribus antiquis*, πολλὴν χάριν κτλ., an early instance being the third Philippic of Demosthenes, πολλῶν, ὦ ἄνδρες Ἀθηναῖοι, λόγων γιγνομένων κτλ.). Here **πολυμερῶς καὶ πολυτρόπως** is a sonorous hendiadys for "variously," as Chrysostom was the first to point out (τὸ γὰρ πολυμερῶς καὶ πολυτρόπως τουτέστι διαφόρως). A similar turn of expression occurs in 2^2 παραβάσις καὶ παρακοή. The writer does not mean to exclude variety from the Christian revelation; he expressly mentions how rich and manysided it was, in 2^4. Nor does he suggest that the revelation ἐν προφήταις was inferior because it was piecemeal and varied. There is a slight suggestion of the unity and finality of the revelation ἐν υἱῷ, as compared with the prolonged revelations made through the prophets, the Son being far more than a prophet; but there is a deeper suggestion of the unity and continuity of revelation then and now. Πολυμερῶς καὶ πολυτρόπως really "signalises the variety and fulness of the Old Testament word of God" (A. B. Davidson). On the other hand, Christ is God's last word to the world; revelation in him is complete, final and homogeneous.

Compare the comment of Eustathius on *Odyssey*, 1^1: πολυτρόπως ἀνεγνωρίσθη πᾶσιν οἷς ἦλθεν εἰς γνῶσιν, μηδενὸς ἀναγνωρισμοῦ συμπεσόντος ἑτέρῳ ἀναγνωρισμῷ τὸ σύνολον· ἄλλως γὰρ τῷ Τελεμάχῳ, ἑτέρως δὲ Εὐρυκλείᾳ, ἑτέρως τοῖς δούλοις, ἄλλον δὲ τρόπον τῷ Λαέρτῃ, καὶ ὅλως ἀνομοίως ἅπασι. Πολυμερῶς, according to Hesychius (= πολυσχέδως), differs from πολυτρόπως (διαφόρως, ποικίλως), and, strictly speaking, is the adverb of πολυμερής = manifold (Wis 7^{22}, where Wisdom is called πνεῦμα μονογενές, πολυμερές). But no such distinction is intended here.

In **πάλαι** (as opposed to ἐπ' ἐσχάτου τῶν ἡμερῶν τούτων) **θεὸς λαλήσας, λαλεῖν**, here as throughout the epistle, is practically an equivalent for λέγειν (see Anz's *Subsidia*, pp. 309–310), with a special reference to inspired and oracular utterances of God or of divinely gifted men. This sense is as old as Menander (ὁ νοῦς γάρ ἐστιν ὁ λαλήσων θέος, Kock's *Comic. Attic. Fragm.* 70). Οἱ πατέρες in contrast to ἡμεῖς means OT believers in general (cp. Jn 6^{58} 7^{22}), whereas the more usual NT sense of the term is "the patriarchs" (cp. *Diat.* 1949–1950, 2553*e*), *i.e.* Abraham, etc., though the term (3^{9} 8^{9}) covers the ancients down to Samuel or later (Mt 23^{30}). *Our fathers* or ancestors (Wis 18^{6}) means the Hebrew worthies of the far past to whom Christians as God's People, whether they had been born Jews or not (1 Co 10^{1} οἱ πατέρες ἡμῶν), look back, as the earlier Sirach did in his πατέρων ὕμνος (Sir 44^{1}–50^{23}), or the prophet in Zec 1^{5} (οἱ πατέρες ὑμῶν . . . καὶ οἱ προφῆται). For οἱ πατέρες = our fathers, cp. Prayer of Manasseh [1] (θεὸς τῶν πατέρων) and Wessely's *Studien zur Paläographie und Papyruskunde*, i. 64, where boys are reckoned in a list σὺν τοῖς πατράσι. The insertion of ἡμῶν (p^{12} 999. 1836 boh sah Clem. Alex., Chrys. Priscillian) is a correct but superfluous gloss. As for **ἐν τοῖς προφήταις**, προφῆται is used here in a broader sense than in 11^{32}; it denotes the entire succession of those who spoke for God to the People of old, both before and after Moses (Ac 3^{22} 7^{37}), who is the supreme prophet, according to Philo (*de ebriet.* 21, *de decalogo* 33). Joshua is a prophet (Sir 46^{1}), so is David (Philo, *de agric.* 12). In Ps 105^{15} the patriarchs, to whom revelations are made, are both God's προφῆται and χριστοί. Later on, the term was extended, as in Lk 13^{28} (Abraham, Isaac, and Jacob, καὶ πάντας τοὺς προφήτας, cp. He 11^{32}), and still more in Mt 5^{12} (τοὺς προφήτας τοὺς πρὸ ὑμῶν). The reason why there is no contrast between the Son and the prophets is probably because the writer felt there was no danger of rivalry; prophecy had ceased by the time that the Son came; the "prophet" belonged to a bygone order of things, so that there was no need to argue against any misconception of their function in relation to that of the Son (Bar 85^{1-3} "in former times our fathers had helpers, righteous men and holy prophets . . . but now the righteous have been gathered and the prophets have fallen asleep").

As no further use is made of the contrast between Jesus and the prophets (who are only again mentioned incidentally in 11^{32}), it was natural that ἀγγέλοις should be conjectured (S. Crellius, *Initium Ioannis Evangelii restitutum*, p. 238, independently by Spitta in *Stud. u. Kritiken*, 1913, pp. 106–109) to have been the original reading, instead of προφήταις. But "the word spoken by angels" (2^{2}) does not refer to divine communications made to the patriarchs; nor can οἱ πατέρες be identified with the patriarchs, as Spitta contends (cf. U. Holzmeister in *Zeitschrift für kathol. Theologie*, 1913, pp. 805–830), and, even if it could, προφήταις would be quite apposite (cp. Philo, *de Abrah.* 22). Why the writer selects προφήταις is not clear. But ἀνθρώποις would have been an imperfect antithesis, since the Son was human. Philo (*de Monarch.* 9: ἑρμηνεῖς γάρ εἰσιν οἱ προφῆται θεοῦ καταχρωμένου τοῖς ἐκείνων ὀργάνοις πρὸς δήλωσιν ὧν ἂν ἐθελήσῃ) views the prophets as interpreters of God in a sense that might correspond to the strict meaning of ἐν, and even (*Quaest. in Exod.* 23[22] τοῦ γὰρ λέγοντος ὁ προφήτης ἄγγελος κυρίου ἐστίν) applies ἄγγελος to the prophet. But ἐν here is a synonym for διά (Chrys. ὁρᾷς ὅτι καὶ τὸ ἐν διὰ ἐστίν), as in 1 S 28[6] (ἀπεκρίθη αὐτῷ κύριος ἐν τοῖς ἐνυπνίοις καὶ ἐν τοῖς δήλοις καὶ ἐν τοῖς προφήταις).

In Test. Dan 1[1] [acc. to the tenth cent. Paris MS 938][1] and in LXX of Nu 24[14], Jer 23[20] [B: ἐσχάτων, A Q*], 25[19] (49[39]) [B: ἐσχάτων, A Q], 37 (30) [24] [A Q: ἐσχάτων, B], Ezk 38[8] (ἐπ' ἐσχάτου ἐτῶν), Dn 10[14] [ἐσχάτῳ ? ἐσχάτων], Hos 3[5] [Q], ἐπ' ἐσχάτου τῶν ἡμερῶν appears, instead of the more common ἐπ' ἐσχάτων τῶν ἡμερῶν, as a rendering of the phrase בְּאַחֲרִית הַיָּמִים. A similar variety of reading occurs here; Origen, *e.g.*, reads ἐσχάτων without τούτων (on La 4[20]) and ἐσχάτου (fragm. on John 3[31]), while ἐσχάτων is read by 044, a few minor cursives, d and the Syriac version. The same idea is expressed in 1 P 1[20] by ἐπ' ἐσχάτου τῶν χρόνων, but the τοῦτων here is unique. The messianic mission of Jesus falls at the close of *these days*, or, as the writer says later (9[26]), ἐπὶ συντελείᾳ τῶν αἰώνων. *These days* correspond to the *present age* (ὁ νῦν αἰών); *the age* (or *world*) *to come* (ὁ μέλλων αἰών, 6[5]) is to dawn at the second coming of Christ (9[28] 10[37]). Meantime, the revelation of God ἐν υἱῷ has been made to the Christian church as God's People (ἐλάλησεν ἡμῖν); the ἡμεῖς does not mean simply the hearers of Jesus on earth, for this would exclude the writer and his readers (2[3]), and ἐλάλησεν covers more than the earthly mission of Jesus. There is no special reference in ἐλάλησεν to the teaching of Jesus; the writer is thinking of the revelation of God's redeeming purpose in Christ as manifested (vv.[3. 4]) by the (resurrection and) intercession in heaven which completed the sacrifice on the cross. This is the final revelation, now experienced by Christians.

The saying of Jesus quoted by Epiphanius (*Haer.* xxiii. 5, xli. 3, lxvi. 42), ὁ λαλῶν ἐν τοῖς προφήταις, ἰδοὺ πάρειμι, was an anti-gnostic logion based partly on this passage and partly on Is 52[6] ἐγώ εἰμι αὐτὸς ὁ λαλῶν, πάρειμι. The author of Hebrews is not conscious of any polemic against the OT revelation as inferior to and unworthy of the Christian God. He assumes that it was the same God who spoke in both Testaments: "Sed in hac diversitate unum tamen Deus nobis proponit: nequis putet Legem cum Evangelio pugnare, vel alium esse huius quam illius authorem" (Calvin).

---

[1] The Armenian reading τούτων after ἡμερῶν, instead of αὐτοῦ, is incorrect, and may even be a reminiscence of He 1[1].

In ὃν ἔθηκεν κληρονόμον πάντων there is a parallel, perhaps even an allusion, to the Synoptic parable: *finally he sent his son* (Mt 21^{37}), or, as Mark (12^{6}) and Luke (20^{13}) explicitly declare, his *beloved son*, though our author does not work out the sombre thought of the parable. There, the son is the heir (οὗτός ἐστιν ὁ κληρονόμος), though not of the universe. Here, the meaning of ὃν ἔθηκεν κληρονόμον πάντων is the same: he was "appointed" heir, he was heir by God's appointment. It is the fact of this position, not the time, that the writer has in mind, and we cannot be sure that this "appointment" corresponds to the elevation of v.^{3} (ἐκάθισεν). Probably, in our modern phrase, it describes a pre-temporal act, or rather a relationship which belongs to the eternal order. The force of the aorist ἔθηκεν is best rendered by the English perfect, "has appointed"; no definite time is necessarily intended.

"Nam ideo ille haeres, ut nos suis opibus ditet. Quin hoc elogio nunc eum ornat Apostolus ut sciamus nos sine ipso bonorum omnium esse inopes" (Calvin). The reflection of Sedulius Scotus (alii post patrem haeredes sunt, hic autem vivente Patre haeres est) is pious but irrelevant, for κληρονομεῖν in Hellenistic Greek had come to mean, like its equivalent "inherit" in Elizabethan English, no more than "possess" or "obtain"; a κληρονόμος was a "possessor," with the double *nuance* of certainty and anticipation. "Haeres" in Latin acquired the same sense; "pro haerede gerere est pro domino gerere, veteres enim 'haeredes' pro 'dominis' appellabant" (Justinian, *Instit.* ii. 19. 7).

In δι' οὗ (Griesbach conj. διότι) καὶ ἐποίησε τοὺς αἰῶνας the καί especially [1] suggests a correspondence between this and the preceding statement; what the Son was to possess was what he had been instrumental in making. Τοὺς αἰῶνας here, though never in Paul, is equivalent (*EBi.* 1147) to τὰ πάντα in v.^{3} (implied in πάντων above), *i.e.* the universe or world (11^{3}). The functions assigned by Jewish speculation to media like the Logos at creation are here claimed as the prerogative of the Son. This passing allusion to the function of Christ in relation to the universe probably originated, as in the case of Paul, in the religious conception of redemption. From the redeeming function of Christ which extended to all men, it was natural to infer His agency in relation to creation as part of his pre-existence. The notion is that "the whole course of nature and grace must find its explanation in God, not merely in an abstract divine *arbitrium*, but in that which befits the divine nature" (W. Robertson Smith), *i.e.* the thought behind $2^{9f.}$ is connected with the thought behind 1^{1-3}. This may be due to a theological reflection, but the tendency to emphasize the moral rather than the metaphysical aspect, which is noticeable in Πρὸς Ἑβραίους as

[1] An emphasis blurred by the τοὺς αἰῶνας ἐποίησεν of D^{b} K L P harkl Chrys. Theod. (Blass, von Sod.).

in the Fourth Gospel, and even in Paul, is consonant with Philo's tendency to show the function of the Logos and the other intermediate powers as religious rather than cosmical (cp. Bréhier's *Les Idées Philos. et Religieuses de Philon d'Alexandrie*, pp. 65 f., 111 f., 152, "il ne s'agit plus chez Philon d'un explication du monde mais du culte divin"; 174 f., "la thése de Philon, qui explique et produit la doctrine des intermédiaires, n'est pas l'impossibilité pour Dieu de produire le monde mais l'impossibilité pour l'âme d'atteindre Dieu directement"). Yet Philo had repeatedly claimed for his Logos, that it was the organ of creation (*e.g. de sacerdot.* 5, λόγος δ' ἐστὶν εἰκὼν θεοῦ, δι' οὗ σύμπας ὁ κόσμος ἐδημιουργεῖτο), and this is what is here, as by Paul, claimed for Christ. Only, it is a religious, not a cosmological, instinct that prompts the thought. The early Christian, who believed in the lordship of Christ over the world, felt, as a modern would put it, that the end must be implicit in the beginning, that the aim and principle of the world must be essentially Christian. This is not elaborated in "Hebrews" any more than in the Fourth Gospel (Jn 1[3]); the author elsewhere prefers the simple monotheistic expression (2[10] 11[3]). But the idea is consonant with his conception of the Son. "If pre-existence is a legitimate way of expressing the absolute significance of Jesus, then the mediation of creation through Christ is a legitimate way of putting the conviction that in the last resort, and in spite of appearances, the world in which we live is a Christian world, our ally, not our adversary" (Denney in *ERE.* viii. 516 f.).

[3] *He* (ὃς ὢν) *reflecting God's bright glory and stamped with God's own character, sustains the universe with his word of power; when he had secured our purification from sins, he sat down at the right hand of the Majesty on high;* [4] *and thus he is superior to* (κρείττων) *the angels, as he has inherited a Name superior* (διαφορώτερον, 8[6]) *to theirs.*

The unique relation of Christ to God is one of the unborrowed truths of Christianity, but it is stated here in borrowed terms. The writer is using metaphors which had been already applied in Alexandrian theology to Wisdom and the Logos. Thus Wisdom is an unalloyed emanation τῆς τοῦ παντοκράτορος δόξης, ἀπαύγασμα . . . φωτὸς αἰδίου (Wis 7[25. 26]), and ἀπαύγασμα in the same sense of "reflection" occurs in Philo, who describes the universe as οἷον ἁγίων ἀπαύγασμα, μίμημα ἀρχετύπου (*de plant.* 12), the human spirit as τύπον τινὰ καὶ χαρακτῆρα θείας δυνάμεως (*quod deter. pot. ins. sol.* 83), and similarly the Logos. χαρακτήρ is "the exact reproduction," as a statue of a person (*OGIS.* 363[60] χαρακτῆρα μορφῆς ἐμῆς); literally, the stamp or clear-cut impression made by a seal, the very facsimile of the original. The two terms ἀπαύγασμα and χαρακτήρ are therefore intended to bring out the same idea.

ὑπόστασις = the being or essence of God, which corresponds to his δόξα (= character or nature); it is a philosophical rather than a religious term, in this connexion, but enters the religious world in Wis 16^{21} (ἡ μὲν γὰρ ὑπόστασίς σου κτλ.). Its physical sense emerges in the contemporary *de Mundo*, 4, τῶν ἐν ἀέρι φαντασμάτων τὰ μέν ἐστι κατ' ἔμφασιν τὰ δὲ καθ' ὑπόστασιν. The use of it as a term for the essence or substance of a human being is not uncommon in the LXX (*e.g.* Ps 39^5 139^{15}); cp. Schlatter's *Der Glaube im NT*[3] (1905), pp. 615 f., where the linguistic data are arranged.

χαρακτήρ had already acquired a meaning corresponding to the modern "character" (*e.g.* in Menander's proverb, ἀνδρὸς χαρακτὴρ ἐκ λόγου γνωρίζεται, *Heauton Timoroumenos*, 11). The idea of χαρακτήρ as replica is further illustrated by the Bereschith rabba, 52. 3 (on Gn 21^2): "hence we learn that he (Isaac) was the splendour of his (father's) face, as like as possible to him."

An early explanation of this conception is given by Lactantius (*diuin. instit.* iv. 29), viz. that "the Father is as it were an overflowing fountain, the Son like a stream flowing from it; the Father like the sun, the Son as it were a ray extended from the sun (radius ex sole porrectus). Since he is faithful (cp. He 3^2) and dear to the most High Father, he is not separated from him, any more than the stream is from the fountain or the ray from the sun; for the water of the fountain is in the stream, and the sun's light in the ray." But our author is content to throw out his figurative expressions. How the Son could express the character of God, is a problem which he does not discuss; it is felt by the author of the Fourth Gospel, who suggests the moral and spiritual affinities that lie behind such a function of Jesus Christ, by hinting that the Son on earth taught what he had heard from the Father and lived out the life he had himself experienced and witnessed with the unseen Father. This latter thought is present to the mind of Seneca in *Epp.* $6^{5.6}$, where he observes that "Cleanthes could never have exactly reproduced Zeno, if he had simply listened to him; he shared the life of Zeno, he saw into his secret purposes" (vitae eius interfuit, secreta perspexit). The author of Hebrews, like Paul in Col 1^{15-17}, contents himself with asserting the vital community of nature between the Son and God, in virtue of which (φέρων τε) the Son holds his position in the universe.

In the next clause, **φέρων**[1] **τε τὰ πάντα** is not used in the sense in which Sappho (fragm. 95, πάντα φέρων) speaks of the evening star "bringing all things home," the sheep to their fold and children to their mother. The phrase means "upholding the universe as it moves," bearing it and bearing it on. "Thou bearest things on high and things below," Cain tells God in Bereschith rabba, 23. 2, "but thou dost not bear my sins." "Deus ille maximus potentissimusque ipse vehit omnia" (Seneca, *Epist.* 31^{10}). The idea had been already applied by Philo to the Logos (e.g. *de migrat. Abrah.* 6, ὁ λόγος . . . ὁ τῶν ὅλων κυβερνήτης πηδαλιουχεῖ τὰ σύμπαντα: *de spec. legibus*, i. 81, λόγος δ' ἐστὶν εἰκὼν θεοῦ, δι' οὗ σύμπας ὁ κόσμος ἐδημιουργεῖτο: *de plant.* 8, λόγος δὲ ὁ ἀΐδιος θεοῦ τοῦ αἰωνίου τὸ ὀχυρώτατον καὶ βεβαιότατον ἔρεισμα τῶν ὅλων ἐστί). So Chrysostom takes it: φέρων . . . τουτέστι, κυβερνῶν, τὰ διαπίπτοντα συγκρατῶν. It would certainly carry on the thought of δι' οὗ . . . αἰῶνας, however, if φέρειν here could be taken in its regular Philonic sense of "bring into existence" (e g. *quis rer. div. haer.* 7, ὁ τὰ μὴ ὄντα φέρων καὶ τὰ πάντα γεννῶν:

[1] φανερῶν is, like ἀπολεῖται in 4^9, an error of B*.

de mutat. nom. 44, πάντα φέρων σπουδαῖα ὁ θεός); this was the interpretation of Gregory of Nyssa (*MPG*. xlvi. 265), and it would give a better sense to "word of power" as the fiat of creative authority. But the ordinary interpretation is not untenable.

In **τῷ ῥήματι τῆς δυνάμεως αὐτοῦ**, the αὐτοῦ (αὑτοῦ ?) refers to the Son, not as in the preceding clause and in 11³ to God. Hence perhaps its omission by M 424** 1739 Origen.

With **καθαρισμὸν . . . ὑψηλοῖς** the writer at last touches what is for him the central truth about the Son; it is not the teaching of Jesus that interests him, but what Jesus did for sin by his sacrifice and exaltation. From this conception the main argument of the epistle flows. Καθαρισμὸν τῶν ἁμαρτιῶν is a Septuagint expression (*e.g.* Job 7²¹ ποίησω . . . καθαρισμὸν (עָבַר) τῆς ἁμαρτίας μου), though this application of κ. to sins is much more rare than that either to persons (Lv 15¹³) or places (1 Ch 23²⁶, 2 Mac 10⁵). In 2 P 1⁹ (τοῦ καθαρισμοῦ τῶν πάλαι αὐτοῦ ἁμαρτιῶν) it is filled out with the possessive pronoun, which is supplied here by some (*e.g.* ἡμῶν Dᶜ K L harkl sah arm Athan. Chrys., ὑμῶν ℵᶜ). Grammatically it = (*a*) purgation of sins, as καθαρίζω may be used of the "removal" of a disease (Mt 8³·⁴), or = (*b*) our cleansing from sins (9¹⁴ καθαριεῖ τὴν συνείδησιν ἡμῶν ἀπὸ νεκρῶν ἔργων). Before καθαρισμόν the words δι' ἑαυτοῦ (αὑτοῦ) are inserted by D H K L M 256 d harkl sah boh eth Orig. Athan. Aug. etc. **Δι' ἑαυτοῦ** = ipse, as ἑαυτῷ = sua sponte. Ἐκάθισεν ἐν δεξιᾷ is a reminiscence of a favourite psalm (110¹) of the writer, though he avoids its ἐκ δεξιῶν. It denotes entrance into a position of divine authority. "Sedere ad Patris dexteram nihil aliud est quam gubernare vice Patris" (Calvin). Ἐν ὑψηλοῖς, a phrase used by no other NT writer, is a reminiscence of the Greek psalter and equivalent to ἐν ὑψίστοις: grammatically it goes with ἐκάθισεν. (The divine attribute of μεγαλωσύνη is for the first time employed as a periphrasis for the divine *Majesty*.) This enthronement exhibits (v.⁴) the superiority of the Son to the angels. Ὄνομα is emphatic by its position at the close of the sentence; it carries the general Oriental sense of "rank" or "dignity." The precise nature of this dignity is described as that of sonship (v.⁵), but the conception widens in the following passage (vv.⁶ᶠ·), and it is needless to identify ὄνομα outright with υἱός, though υἱὲς brings out its primary meaning. In **τοσούτῳ κρείττων γενόμενος** (going closely with ἐκάθισεν) **τῶν** (accidentally omitted by B and Clem. Rom.) **ἀγγέλων** (emphatic by position) **παρ' αὐτοὺς κεκληρονόμηκεν ὄνομα**, the relative use of ὅσος in NT Greek is confined to Mk 7³⁶, but τοσούτος . . . ὅσος is a common Philonic expression. Κρείττων (for which Clement of Rome in 36² substitutes the synonymous μείζων) is an indefinite term = "superior."

Unlike Paul, the writer here and elsewhere is fond of using παρά after a comparative.

Κρείττων in this sense occurs in the contemporary (?) Aristotelian treatise *de Mundo*, 391*a* (διὰ τὸ ἀθέατοι τῶν κρειττόνων εἶναι), where τὰ κρειττόνα means the nobler Universe.

The sudden transition to a comparison between the Son and the angels implies that something is before the writer's mind. Were his readers, like the Colossians to whom Paul wrote, in danger of an undue deference to angels in their religion, a deference which threatened to impair their estimate of Christ? Or is he developing his argument in the light of some contemporary belief about angels and revelation? Probably the latter, though this does not emerge till 2². Meanwhile, seven Biblical proofs (cp. W. Robertson Smith, *Expositor*², i. pp. 5 f.) of v.⁴ are adduced; the two in v.⁵ specially explain the διαφορώτερον ὄνομα, while the five in vv.⁶⁻¹⁴ describe the meaning and force of κρείττων τῶν ἀγγέλων. The first two are:

> ⁵ *For to what angel did God ever say,*
> *"Thou art my son,*
> *to-day have I become thy father"?*
> *Or again,*
> *"I will be a father to him,*
> *and he shall be a son to me"?*

The first quotation is from the 2nd Psalm (v.⁷), read as a messianic prediction—which may have been its original meaning, and certainly was the meaning attached to it by the early Christians, if not already by some circles of Judaism:[1]

> υἱός μου εἶ σύ,
> ἐγὼ σήμερον γεγέννηκά σε.

Did the author take σήμερον here, as perhaps in 3⁷ᶠ·, though not in 13⁸, in (*a*) a mystical sense, or (*b*) with a reference to some special phase in the history of Christ? (*a*) tallies with Philo's usage: σήμερον δ' ἐστὶν ὁ ἀπέρατος καὶ ἀδιεξίτητος αἰών . . . τὸ ἀψευδὲς ὄνομα αἰῶνος (*de fuga*, 11, on Dt 4⁴), ἕως τῆς σήμερον ἡμέρας, τουτέστιν ἀεί· ὁ γὰρ αἰὼν ἅπας τῷ σήμερον παραμετρεῖται (*leg. alleg.* iii. 8 on Gn 35⁴). (*b*) might allude either to the baptism or to the resurrection of Christ in primitive Christian usage; the latter would be more congenial to our author, if it were assumed that he had any special incident in mind. But he simply quotes the text for the purpose of bringing out the title of Son as applied to Christ. When we ask what he meant by σήμερον, we are asking a question which was not present to his mind, unless, indeed, "the idea of a bright radiance streaming forth from God's glory" (v.³) pointed in the direction of (*a*), as

[1] See G. H. Box, *The Ezra-Apocalypse*, pp. lvi, lvii.

Robertson Smith thought. But the second line of the verse is merely quoted to fill out the first, which is the pivot of the proof: υἱός μου εἶ συ. *Sons of God* is not unknown as a title for angels in the Hebrew Old Testament (see *EBi.* 4691). "Sometimes Moses calls the angels sons of God," Philo observes (*Quaest. in Gen.* 6⁴—as being bodiless spirits). But the LXX is careful to translate: "sons of Elohim" by ἄγγελοι θεοῦ (*e.g.* in Gn $6^{2.4}$, Job 1^6 2^1 38^7), except in Ps 29^1 and 89^7, where *sons of God* are intended by the translator to denote human beings; and no individual angel is ever called υἱός.[1] As the author of Πρὸς Ἑβραίους and his readers knew only the Greek Bible, the proof holds good.

The second quotation is from 2 S 7^{14}:

Ἐγὼ ἔσομαι αὐτῷ εἰς πατέρα,
καὶ αὐτὸς ἔσται μοι εἰς υἱόν,

a promise cited more exactly than in 2 Co 6^{18} and Rev 21^7, but with equal indifference to its original setting. Paul and the prophet John apply it to the relationship between God and Christians; our author prefers to treat it as messianic. Indeed he only alludes twice, in OT quotations, to God as the Father of Christians (see Introd. p. xxxv).

The third quotation (v.^{6}) clinches this proof of Christ's unique authority and opens up the sense in which he is κρείττων τῶν ἀγγέλων:

and further, when introducing the Firstborn into the world, he says,
"Let all God's angels worship him."

In **ὅταν δὲ πάλιν εἰσαγάγῃ** the term πάλιν, rhetorically transferred, answers to the πάλιν of v.^{5}; it is not to be taken with εἰσαγάγῃ = "reintroduce," as if the first "introduction" of the Son had been referred to in v.$^{2f.}$. A good parallel for this usage occurs in Philo (*leg. alleg.* iii. 9: ὁ δὲ πάλιν ἀποδιδράσκων θεὸν τὸν μὲν οὐδενὸς αἴτιον φησὶν εἶναι, where πάλιν goes with φησίν). Εἰσάγειν might refer to birth,[2] as, *e.g.*, in Epictetus (iv. 1. 104, οὐχὶ ἐκεῖνός σε εἰσήγαγεν) and pseudo-Musonius, ep. 90 (Hercher's *Epist. Graeci*, 401 f.: οὐ τέκνα μόνον εἰς τὸ γένος ἄλλα καὶ τοιάδε τέκνα εἰσήγαγες), or simply to "introduction" (cp. Mitteis-Wilcken, i. 2. 141 (110 B.C.), εἰσάξω τὸν ἐμαυτοῦ υἱὸν εἰς τὴν σύνοδον). Linguistically either the incarnation or the second advent might be intended; but neither the tense of εἰσαγάγῃ (unless it be taken strictly as futuristic = ubi introduxerit) nor the proximity of

[1] It is only Theodotion who ventures in Dan $3^{25\,(92)}$ to retain the literal *son*, since from his christological point of view it could not be misunderstood in this connexion.

[2] Cp. M. Aurelius, v. 1, ποιεῖν ὧν ἕνεκεν γέγονα καὶ ὧν χάριν προῆγμαι εἰς τὸν κόσμον.

πάλιν is decisive in favour of the latter (ὅταν εἰσαγάγῃ might, by a well-known Greek idiom, be equivalent to "when he speaks of introducing, or, describes the introduction of"—Valckenaer, etc.). Πρωτότοκος is Firstborn in the sense of superior. The suggestion of Christ being higher than angels is also present in the context of the term as used by Paul (Col 1[15. 16]), but it is nowhere else used absolutely in the NT, and the writer here ignores any inference that might be drawn from it to an inferior sonship of angels. Its equivalent (cp. the *v.ll.* in Sir 36[17]) πρωτόγονος is applied by Philo to the Logos. Here it means that Christ was Son in a pre-eminent sense; the idea of priority passes into that of superiority. A πρωτότοκος υἱός had a relationship of likeness and nearness to God which was unrivalled. As the context indicates, the term brings out the pre-eminent honour and the unique relationship to God enjoyed by the Son among the heavenly host.

The notion of worship being due only to a senior reappears in the *Vita Adae et Evae* (14), where the devil declines to worship Adam: "I have no need to worship Adam . . . I will not worship an inferior being who is my junior. I am his senior in the Creation; before he was made, I was already made; it is his duty to worship me." In the *Ascensio Isaiae* (11[23f.]) the angels humbly worship Christ as he ascends through the heavens where they live; here the adoration is claimed for him as he enters ἡ οἰκουμένη.

The line **καὶ προσκυνησάτωσαν αὐτῷ πάντες ἄγγελοι θεοῦ** comes from a LXX addition to the Hebrew text of the Song of Moses in Dt 32[43], calling upon all angels to pay homage to Yahweh. But the LXX text[1] actually reads υἱοὶ θεοῦ, not ἄγγελοι θεοῦ (into which F corrects it)! Our author probably changed it into ἄγγελοι θεοῦ, recollecting the similar phrase in Ps 97[7] (προσκυνήσατε αὐτῷ πάντες οἱ ἄγγελοι αὐτοῦ),[2] unless, indeed, the change had been already made. The fact that Justin Martyr (*Dial.* 130) quotes the LXX gloss with ἄγγελοι, is an indication that this may have been the text current among the primitive Christians.

The last four (vv.[7-14]) quotations carry on the idea of the Son's superiority to the angels:

7 *While he says of angels* (πρός = with reference to),
"*Who makes his angels into winds,*
his servants into flames of fire,"
8 *he says of the Son,*
"*God is thy throne for ever and ever,*
and thy royal sceptre is the sceptre of equity:
9 *thou hast loved justice and hated lawlessness,*
therefore God, thy God, has consecrated thee
with the oil of rejoicing beyond thy comrades"—
10 *and,*
"*Thou didst found the earth at the beginning, O Lord,*

---

[1] As the song appears in A, at the close of the psalter, the reading is ἄγγελοι (υἱοί, R).

[2] Which acquired a messianic application (see *Diat.* 3134).

and the heavens are the work of thy hands:
11 *they will perish, but thou remainest,*
they will all be worn out like a garment,
12 *thou wilt roll them up like a mantle, and they will be changed,*
but thou art the same,
and thy years never fail."

In v.[7] the quotation (ὁ ποιῶν τοὺς ἀγγέλους αὐτοῦ πνεύματα| καὶ τοὺς λειτουργοὺς αὐτοῦ πυρὸς φλόγα) only differs from the LXX by the substitution of πυρὸς φλόγα [1] for πῦρ φλέγον (B: πυρὸς φλέγα A[a]). The singular in φλόγα and perhaps the recollection that πνεῦμα elsewhere in NT = "wind" only in the singular, led to the change of πνεύματα into πνεῦμα (D 1. 326. 424**. 1912. 1245. 2005 d sah eth Orig.). The author is taking the LXX translation or mistranslation of Ps 104[4] (ὁ ποιῶν κτλ., a nominative without a verb, as in 1 Co 3[19]) to mean that God can reduce angels to the elemental forces of wind and fire, so unstable is their nature, whereas the person and authority of the Son are above all change and decay. The meaning might also be that God makes angels out of wind and fire; [2] but this is less apt. Our author takes the same view as the author of 4 Esdras, who (8[21]) writes:

> "Before whom the heavenly host stands in terror,
> and at thy word change to wind and fire."

Rabbinic traditions corroborate this interpretation; *e.g.* "every day ministering angels are created from the fiery stream, and they utter a song and perish" (*Chagiga*, ed. Streane, p. 76), and the confession of the angel to Manoah in *Yalkut Shimeoni*, ii. 11. 3: "God changes us every hour . . . sometimes he makes us fire, at other times wind."

The interest of rabbinic mysticism in the nature of angels is illustrated by the second century dialogue between Hadrian, that "curiositatum omnium explorator," and R. Joshua ben Chananja (cp. W. Bacher, *Agada der Tannaiten*[2], i. 171–172). The emperor asks the rabbi what becomes of the angels whom God creates daily to sing His praise; the rabbi answers that they return to the stream of fire which flows eternally from the sweat shed by the Beasts supporting the divine throne or chariot (referring to the vision of Ezekiel and the "fiery stream" of Dn 7[10]). From this stream of fire the angels issue, and to it they return. Λειτουργούς of angels as in Ps 103[21] (λειτουργοὶ αὐτοῦ, ποιοῦντες τὸ θέλημα αὐτοῦ).

The fifth (vv.[8. 9]) quotation is from Ps 45[7. 8]—a Hebrew epithalamium for some royal personage or national hero, which our author characteristically regards as messianic.

[1] Aquila has πῦρ λάβρον, Symm. πυρίνην φλόγα.

[2] As in Apoc. Bar. 21[6] ("the holy creatures which thou didst make from the beginning out of flame and fire") and 48[8] ("Thou givest commandment to the flames and they change into spirits").

ὁ θρόνος σου ὁ θεὸς εἰς τὸν αἰῶνα τοῦ αἰῶνος,
καὶ[1] ῥάβδος τῆς εὐθύτητος ἡ ῥάβδος τῆς βασιλείας σου.[2]
ἠγάπησας δικαιοσύνην καὶ ἐμίσησας ἀνομίαν·
διὰ τοῦτο ἔχρισέ σε ὁ θεός, ὁ θεός σου,
ἔλαιον ἀγαλλιάσεως παρὰ[3] τοὺς μετόχους σου.

The quotation inserts τῆς before εὐθύτητος, follows A in preferring τὸν αἰῶνα τοῦ αἰῶνος (τοῦ αἰῶνος om. B 33) to αἰῶνα αἰῶνος (B), but prefers[4] B's ἀνομίαν (cp. 2 Co 6^{14}) to A's ἀδικίαν, and agrees with both in prefixing ἡ to the second (D K L P Cyr. Cosm. Dam.) instead of to the first (א A B M, etc.) ῥάβδος. The psalm is not quoted elsewhere in NT (apart from a possible reminiscence of $45^{5. 6}$ in Rev 6^2), and rarely cited in primitive Christian literature, although the messianic reference reappears in Irenaeus (iv. 34. 11, quoting v.[2]). Ὁ θεός (*sc.* ἐστίν rather than ἔστω) may be (*a*) nominative (subject or predicate). This interpretation ("God is thy throne," or, "thy throne is God"), which was probably responsible for the change of σοῦ after βασιλείας into αὐτοῦ (א B), has been advocated, *e.g.*, by Grotius, Ewald ("thy throne is divine"), WH ("founded on God, the immovable Rock"), and Wickham ("represents God"). Tyndale's rendering is, "God thy seat shall be." Those who find this interpretation harsh prefer to (*b*) take ὁ θεός as a vocative, which grammatically is possible (= ὦ θεέ, cp. 10^7 and Ps 3^8 138^{17} etc.); "Thy throne, O God (or, O divine One), is for ever and ever." This (so sah vg, etc.) yields an excellent sense, and may well explain the attractiveness of the text for a writer who wished to bring out the divine significance of Christ; ὁ θεός appealed to him like κύριε in the first line of the next quotation. The sense would be clear if ὁ θεός were omitted altogether, as its Hebrew equivalent ought to be in the original; but the LXX text as it stands was the text before our author, and the problem is to decide which interpretation he followed. (*b*) involves the direct application of ὁ θεός to the Son, which, in a poetical quotation, is not perhaps improbable (see Jn 1^{18} 20^{28}); in v.[9] it may involve the repetition of ὁ θεός (om. by Irenaeus, *Apost. Preaching*, 47—accidentally?) as vocative, and does involve the rendering of ὁ θεός σου as the God of the God already mentioned. The point of the citation lies in its opening and closing words: (i) the Son has a royal and lasting authority (as ὁ θεός?), in contrast

[1] The addition of this καί is not to mark a fresh quotation (as in v.[10]), but simply to introduce the parallel line (as in v.[10] καὶ ἔργα κτλ.).

[2] Cp. Ps 110^2 ῥάβδον δυνάμεως σου (om. א) ἐξαποστελεῖ κύριος.

[3] For παρά with accus. in this sense, cp. above, v.[4], and Is 53^3 ἄτιμον καὶ ἐκλιπὸν παρὰ τοὺς υἱοὺς τῶν ἀνθρώπων.

[4] ἀνομίαν, B D (Δ* ἀνομίας) M P lat harkl Ath. Eus., ἀδικίαν א A 33 38 218. 226. 919 Iren. Cosm.

to the angels, and (ii) he is anointed (ἔχρισε[1] = ὁ Χρίστος) more highly than his companions—an Oriental metaphor referring here, as in Is 61³ etc., not to coronation but to bliss. If the writer of Hebrews has anything specially in mind, it is angels (12²³) rather than human beings (3¹⁴) as μέτοχοι of the royal Prince, whose superior and supreme position is one of intense joy, based on a moral activity (as in 12², where the passive side of the moral effort is emphasized).

The sixth (vv.¹⁰⁻¹²) quotation is from Ps 102²⁶⁻²⁸ which in A runs thus:

> κατ' ἀρχὰς[2] σύ, κύριε,[3] τὴν γῆν ἐθεμελίωσας,
> καὶ ἔργα τῶν χειρῶν σού εἰσιν οἱ οὐρανοί·
> αὐτοὶ[4] ἀπολοῦνται, σὺ δὲ διαμένεις,
> καὶ πάντες ὡς ἱμάτιον παλαιωθήσονται,
> καὶ ὡσεὶ περιβόλαιον ἑλίξεις αὐτοὺς καὶ ἀλλαγήσονται·
> σοὶ δὲ ὁ αὐτὸς εἶ, καὶ τὰ ἔτη σου οὐκ ἐκλείψουσιν.

The author, for purposes of emphasis (as in 2¹³), has thrown σύ to the beginning of the sentence, and in the last line he has reverted to the more natural σύ (B). In the text of the epistle there are only two uncertain readings, for the proposed change of διαμένεις into the future διαμενεῖς (vg. permanebis) does not really affect the sense, and D*'s ὡς for ὡσεί is a merely stylistic alteration. In ¹²ᵃ two small points of textual uncertainty emerge. (*a*) ἑλίξεις (A B Dᶜ K L P M fu Syr arm sah boh eth Orig. Chrys.) has been altered into ἀλλάξεις (א* D* 327. 919 vt Tert. Ath.). The same variant occurs in LXX, where ἀλλάξεις is read by א for ἑλίξεις, which may have crept into the text from Is 34⁴, but is more likely to have been altered into ἀλλάξεις in view of ἀλλαγήσονται (ἐλιγήσονται, arm). (*b*) ὡς ἱμάτιον (א A B D* 1739 vt arm eth) after αὐτούς is omitted by Dᶜ M vg syr sah boh Chrys. Ath. Cyril Alex. Probably the words are due to homoioteleuton. If retained, a comma needs to be placed after them (so Zimmer.); they thus go with the preceding phrase, although one early rendering (D d) runs: "(and) like a garment they will be changed."

The psalm is taken as a messianic oracle (see Bacon in *Zeitschrift für die neutest. Wissenschaft*, 1902, 280–285), which the Greek version implied, or at any rate suggested; it contained welcome indications of the Son in his creative function and also of his destined triumph. The poetical suggestion of the sky as a mantle of the deity occurs in Philo, who writes (*de fuga*, 20)

[1] χρίω, in contrast to ἀλείφω, is exclusively metaphorical in NT (cp. Gray in *EBi.* 173), although neither Latin nor English is able to preserve the distinction.

[2] A classical and Philonic equivalent for ἐν ἀρχῇ (LXX again in Ps 119¹⁵²).

[3] This title, which attracted our author, is an addition of the LXX.

[4] Including ἡ γῆ, but with special reference to οἱ οὐρανοί.

that the Logos ἐνδύεται ὡς ἐσθῆτα τὸν κόσμον· γῆν γὰρ καὶ ὕδωρ καὶ ἀέρα καὶ πῦρ καὶ τὰ ἐκ τούτων ἐπαμπίσχεται. But the quotation is meant to bring out generally (i) the superiority of the Son as creative (so v.[2]) to the creation, and (ii) his permanence amid the decay of nature;[1] the world wears out,[2] even the sky (12^{26}) is cast aside, and with it the heavenly lights, but the Son remains ("thou art thou," boh); nature is at his mercy, not he at nature's. The close connexion of angels with the forces of nature (v.[7]) may have involved the thought that this transiency affects angels as well, but our author does not suggest this.

The final biblical proof (v.[13]) is taken from Ps 110^1, a psalm in which later on the writer is to find rich messianic suggestion. The quotation clinches the argument for the superiority of the Son by recalling (v.[3]) his unique divine commission and authority:

13 *To what angel did he ever say,*
"Sit at my right hand,
till I make your enemies a footstool for your feet"?
14 *Are not all angels merely spirits in the divine service, commissioned for the benefit of those who are to inherit salvation?*

The Greek couplet—

κάθου ἐκ δεξιῶν μου,
ἕως ἂν θῶ τοὺς ἐχθρούς σου ὑποπόδιον τῶν ποδῶν σου,

corresponds exactly to the LXX; D* omits ἂν as in Ac 2^{35}. The martial metaphor is (cp. Introd. pp. xxxiii f.) one of the primitive Christian expressions which survive in the writer's vocabulary (cp. 10^{12}).

The subordinate position of angels is now (v.[14]) summed up; **πάντες**—all without distinction—are simply **λειτουργικὰ πνεύματα** (without any power of ruling) **εἰς διακονίαν ἀποστελλόμενα** (commissioned, not acting on their own initiative).[3] According to the Mechilta on Ex 14^{13}, the Israelites, when crossing the Red Sea, were shown "squadrons upon squadrons of ministering angels" (תּוּרְמִיוֹת תּוּרְמִיוֹת שֶׁל מַלְאֲכֵי הַשָּׁרֵת); cp. Heb. of Sir 43^{26a}, and Dieterich's *Mithrasliturgie*, p. 6, line 14, ἡ ἀρχὴ τοῦ **λειτουργοῦντος ἀνέμου** (see above, v.[7]). Philo speaks of ἄγγελοι λειτουργοί (*de virtutibus*, 74), of τοὺς ὑποδιακόνους αὐτοῦ τῶν δυνάμεων ἀγγέλους (*de templo*, 1), and in *de plantatione*, 4: Μωσῆς δὲ ὀνόματι εὐθυβόλῳ χρώμενος ἀγγέλους προσαγορεύει, πρεσβευομένας καὶ διαγγελλούσας

[1] A pre-Christian Upanishad (*Sacred Books of East*, xv. 266) cries: "Only when men shall roll up the sky like a hide, will there be an end of misery, unless God has first been known."

[2] παλαιοῦσθαι is a common word with ἱμάτιον, and the wearing-out of clothes is a favourite metaphor for men (Is 50^9, Sir 14^{17}) as well as for nature (Is 51^6). Περιβολαῖον is any covering for the body; not simply a veil (1 Co 11^{15}), but a generic term (cp. Ps 104^6 ἄβυσσος ὡς ἱμάτιον τὸ περιβόλαιον αὐτοῦ).

[3] B reads διακονίας, as in 8^9 ἡμέραις for ἡμέρᾳ.

τά τε παρὰ τοῦ ἡγεμόνος τοῖς ὑπηκόοις ἀγαθὰ καὶ τῷ βασιλεῖ ὧν εἰσιν οἱ ὑπήκοοι χρεῖοι. "Angels of the (divine) ministry" was a common rabbinic term, and the writer concludes here that the angels serve God, not, as Philo loved to argue, in the order of nature, but in promoting the interests of God's people; this is the main object of their existence. He ignores the Jewish doctrine voiced in Test. Levi 3^{5}, that in (the sixth?) heaven the angels of the Presence (οἱ λειτουργοῦντες καὶ ἐξιλασκόμενοι πρὸς κύριον ἐπὶ πάσαις ταῖς ἀγνοίαις τῶν δικαίων) sacrifice and intercede for the saints, just as in 11^{40}–12^{1} he ignores the companion doctrine that the departed saints interceded for the living. Later Christian speculation revived the Jewish doctrine of angels interceding for men and mediating their prayers, but our author stands deliberately apart from this. Heaven has its myriads of angels (12^{23}), but the entire relation of men to God depends upon Christ. Angels are simply servants (λειτουργοί, v.^{7}) of God's saving purpose for mankind; how these "angels and ministers of grace" further it, the writer never explains. He would not have gone as far as Philo, at any rate (ἄγγελοι . . . ἱεραὶ καὶ θεῖαι φύσεις, ὑποδιάκονοι καὶ ὕπαρχοι τοῦ πρώτου θεοῦ, δι' ὧν οἷα πρεσβευτῶν ὅσα ἂν θελήσῃ τῷ γένει ἡμῶν προσθεσπίσαι διαγγέλλει, *de Abrahamo*, 23).

In **διὰ τοὺς μέλλοντας κληρονομεῖν σωτηρίαν** (κλ. σωτ. only here in NT), it is remarkable that σωτηρία is mentioned for the first time without any adjective or explanation. Evidently it had already acquired a specific Christian meaning for the readers as well as for the writer; no definition was required to differentiate the Christian significance of the term from the current usage. As σωτηρία involves the sacrificial work of Christ (who is never called σωτήρ), it cannot be applied to the pre-Christian period of revelation. Indeed in our epistle σωτηρία is invariably eschatological. The outlook in the messianic oracles already quoted is one of expectation; some future deliverance at the hands of God or his messianic representative is anticipated. **Μέλλοντας** implies a divine purpose, as in 8^{5} 11^{8}.

The phrase about **τοὺς μέλλοντας κληρονομεῖν σωτηρίαν** marks a skilful transition to the deeper theme of the next passage, viz. the relation of the Son to this σωτηρία (on 2^{1-9} cp. W. Robertson Smith in *Expositor*^{2}, i. pp. 138 f.). But the transition is worked out in a practical warning (2^{1-4}) to the readers, which not only explains the underlying interest of the preceding biblical proofs, but leads up effectively to the next aspect of truth which he has in mind:

[1] *We must therefore* (διὰ τοῦτο, in view of this pre-eminent authority of the Son) *pay closer attention to what we have heard, in case we drift away.* [2] *For if the divine word spoken by angels held good* (ἐγένετο βέβαιος, proved valid), *if transgression and disobedience met with due* (ἔνδικον=adequate, not arbitrary) *punishment in every case,* [3] *how shall we* (ἡμεῖς, emphatic) *escape*

the penalty[1] *for neglecting* (ἀμελήσαντες, if we ignore: Mt 22[5]) *a salvation which* (ἥτις, inasmuch as it) *was originally proclaimed by the Lord himself* (not by mere angels) *and guaranteed to us by those who heard him*, [4] *while God corroborated their testimony with signs and wonders and a variety of miraculous powers, distributing the holy Spirit as it pleased him* (αὐτοῦ emphatic as in Ro 3[25]).

Apart from the accidental omission of v.[1] by M 1739, Origen, and of τε (M P) in v.[4], with the variant **παραρρυῶμεν** (B[c] D[c]) for παραρυῶμεν,[2] the only textual item of any moment, and it is a minor one, is the substitution of ὑπό for διά in v.[3] by some cursives (69. 623. 1066. 1845), due either to the following ὑπό, or to the dogmatic desire of emphasizing the initiative of ὁ κύριος. But διά here as in δι' ἀγγέλων, meaning "by," is used to preserve the idea that in λαλεῖν the subject is God (1[1]). The order of words (v.[1]) δεῖ περισσοτερῶς προσέχειν ἡμᾶς has been spoiled in ℵ vg (περισσοτερῶς δεῖ) and K L P (ἡμᾶς προσέχειν).

As elsewhere in Hellenistic Greek (*e.g.* Jos. *Apion.* i. 1, ἐπεὶ δὲ συχνοὺς ὁρῶ ταῖς ὑπὸ δυσμενείας ὑπὸ τινων εἰρημέναις προσέχοντας βλασφημίαις καὶ τοῖς περὶ τὴν Ἀρχαιολογίαν ὑπ' ἐμοῦ γεγραμμένοις ἀπιστοῦντας κτλ.; Strabo, ii. 1. 7, τοῖς μὲν ἀπιστεῖν . . . ἐκείνῃ δὲ προσέχειν), **προσέχειν** (*sc.* τὸν νοῦν) is the opposite of ἀπιστεῖν: to "attend" is to believe and act upon what is heard. This is implied even in Ac 8[6] and 16[14] (προσέχειν τοῖς λαλουμένοις ὑπὸ Παύλου) where it is the attention of one who hears the gospel for the first time; here it is attention to a familiar message. **Περισσοτέρως** is almost in its elative sense of "with extreme care"; "all the more" would bring out its force here as in 13[19]. Certainly there is no idea of demanding a closer attention to the gospel than to the Law. **Ἡμᾶς** = we Christians (ἡμῖν, 1[1]), you and I, as in v.[3]. The τὰ ἀκουσθέντα (in **τοῖς ἀκουσθεῖσι**) is the revelation of the εὐαγγέλιον (a term never used by our author), *i.e.* what ὁ θεὸς ἐλάλησεν ἡμῖν ἐν υἱῷ, 1[1], and this is further defined (in vv.[3. 4]) as consisting in the initial revelation made by Jesus on earth and the transmission of this by divinely accredited envoys to the writer and his readers (εἰς ἡμᾶς ἐβεβαιώθη). In the *Ep. Aristeas*, 127, oral teaching is preferred to reading (τὸ γὰρ καλῶς ζῆν ἐν τῷ τὰ νόμιμα συντηρεῖν εἶναι· τοῦτο δὲ ἐπιτελεῖσθαι διὰ τῆς ἀκροάσεως πολλῷ μᾶλλον ἢ διὰ τῆς ἀναγνώσεως), and the evangelists of v.[4] include οἵτινες ἐλάλησαν ὑμῖν τὸν λόγον τοῦ θεοῦ (13[7]); but while the news was oral, there is no particular emphasis as that here. The author simply appeals for attentive obedience, **μή ποτε παραρυῶμεν** (2 aor. subj.), *i.e.* drift away from (literally, "be carried past" and so lose) the σωτηρία which we have heard. Παραρέω in this sense goes back to Pr 3[21] υἱέ, μὴ παραρυῇς, τήρησον δὲ ἐμὴν βουλὴν καὶ ἔννοιαν (see Clem. *Paed.* III.

[1] ἐκφευξόμεθα, without an object (κρίμα τοῦ θεοῦ, Ro 2[3]) as 12[25], Sir 16[15], 1 Th 5[3].

[2] Arm apparently read ὑστερήσωμεν, and P. Junius needlessly conjectured παρασυρῶμεν ("pervert them").

xi. 58, διὸ καὶ συστέλλειν χρὴ τὰς γυναῖκας κοσμίως καὶ περισφίγγειν αἰδοῖ σώφρονι, μὴ παραρρυῶσι τῆς ἀληθείας); indeed the writer may have had the line of Proverbs in mind, as Chrys. suggested.

The verb may have lost its figurative meaning, and may have been simply an equivalent for "going wrong," like "labi" in Latin (cp. Cicero, *De Officiis*, i. 6, "labi autem, errare . . . malum et turpe ducimus"). Anyhow προσέχειν must not be taken in a nautical sense (=moor), in order to round off the "drift away" of παραρέω, a term which carries a sombre significance here (=παραπίπτειν, 6^{6}); μήποτε παραρυῶμεν, τουτέστι μὴ ἀπολώμεθα, μὴ ἐκπέσωμεν (Chrysostom).

In vv.[2f.] we have a characteristic (*e.g.* 10^{28-31}) argument *a minori ad maius*; if, as we know from our bible (the bible being the Greek OT), every infringement of the Sinaitic legislation was strictly punished—a legislation enacted by means of angels—how much more serious will be the consequences of disregarding such a (great, τηλικαύτη) σωτηρία as that originally proclaimed by the Lord himself! The τηλικαύτη is defined as (*a*) "directly inaugurated by the Κύριος himself," and (*b*) transmitted to us unimpaired by witnesses who had a rich, supernatural endowment; it is as if the writer said, "Do not imagine that the revelation has been weakened, or that your distance from the life of Jesus puts you in any inferior position; the full power of God's Spirit has been at work in the apostolic preaching to which we owe our faith."

The reference in λόγος is to the Mosaic code, not, as Schoettgen thought, to such specific orders of angels as the admonitions to Lot and his wife.

Λόγος is used, not νόμος, in keeping with the emphasis upon the divine λαλεῖν in the context, and, instead of νόμος Μωσέως (10^{28}), ὁ δι' ἀγγέλων λαληθεὶς λόγος is chosen for argumentative reasons. Here as in Gal 3^{19} and Ac $7^{38.\ 53}$ (ἐλάβετε τὸν νόμον εἰς διαταγὰς ἀγγέλων) the function of angels in the revelation of the Law at Sinai is assumed, but without any disparaging tone such as is overheard in Paul's reference. The writer and his readers shared the belief, which first appeared in Hellenistic Judaism, that God employed angels at Sinai. Josephus (*Ant.* xv. 136, ἡμῶν δὲ τὰ κάλλιστα τῶν δογμάτων καὶ τὰ ὁσιώτατα τῶν ἐν τοῖς νόμοις δι' ἀγγέλων παρὰ τοῦ θεοῦ μαθόντων)[1] repeats this tradition, but it went back to the LXX which altered Dt 33^{2} into a definite proof of angelic co-operation (ἐκ δεξιῶν αὐτοῦ ἄγγελοι μετ' αὐτοῦ) and brought this out in Ps 68^{18}. Rabbinic tradition elaborated the idea. The writer, however, would not have claimed, like Philo (*de vita Mosis*, 2^{3}), that the Mosaic legislation was βέβαια, ἀσάλευτα, valid and supreme as long as the world endured.

[1] This is from a speech of Herod inciting the Jews to fight bravely. "In such a speech," as Robertson Smith observed, "one does not introduce doubtful points of theology." The tenet was firmly held.

Παράβασις καὶ παρακοή form one idea (see on 1[1]); as παρακοή (which is not a LXX term) denotes a disregard of orders or of appeals (cp. Clem. *Hom.* x. 13, εἰ ἐπὶ παρακοῇ λόγων κρίσις γίνεται, and the use of the verb in Mt 18[17] ἐὰν δὲ παρακούσῃ αὐτῶν κτλ., or in LXX of Is 65[12] ἐλάλησε καὶ παρηκούσατε), it represents the negative aspect, **παράβασις** the positive. **Μισθαποδοσία** is a sonorous synonym (rare in this sombre sense of κόλασις) for μισθός or for the classical μισθοδοσία. Some of the facts which the writer has in mind are mentioned in 3[17] and 10[28]. The Law proved no dead letter in the history of God's people; it enforced pains and penalties for disobedience.

In v.[3] **ἀρχὴν λαβοῦσα** is a familiar Hellenistic phrase; cp. *e.g.* Philo in *Quaest. in Exod.* 12[2] (ὅταν οἱ τῶν σπαρτῶν καρποὶ τελειωθῶσιν, οἱ τῶν δένδρων γενέσεως ἀρχὴν λαμβάνουσιν), and *de vita Mosis*, 1[14] (τὴν ἀρχὴν τοῦ γενέσθαι λάβον ἐν Αἰγύπτῳ). The writer felt, as Plutarch did about Rome, τὰ Ῥωμαίων πράγματα οὐκ ἂν ἐνταῦθα προύβη δυνάμεως, μὴ θείαν τινὰ ἀρχὴν λαβόντα καὶ μηδὲν μέγα μήδε παράδοξον ἔχουσαν. The modern mind wonders how the writer could assume that the σωτηρία, as he conceives it, was actually preached by Jesus on earth. But he was unconscious of any such difference. The Christian revelation was made through the Jesus who had lived and suffered and ascended, and the reference is not specifically to his teaching, but to his personality and career, in which God's saving purpose came to full expression. **Οἱ ἀκούσαντες** means those who heard Jesus himself, the αὐτόπται of Lk 1[1-4] (cp. the shorter conclusion to Mark's gospel: μετὰ δὲ ταῦτα καὶ αὐτὸς ὁ Ἰησοῦς . . . ἐξαπέστειλεν δι' αὐτῶν τὸ ἱερὸν καὶ ἄφθαρτον κήρυγμα τῆς αἰωνίου σωτηρίας). If the Sinaitic Law ἐγένετο βέβαιος, the Christian revelation was also confirmed or guaranteed to us—**εἰς ἡμᾶς** (1 P 1[25] τὸ ῥῆμα τὸ εὐαγγελισθὲν εἰς ὑμᾶς: Ac 2[22] Ἰησοῦν . . . ἄνδρα ἀπὸ τοῦ θεοῦ ἀποδεδειγμένον εἰς ὑμᾶς) **ἐβεβαιώθη**. It reached us, accurate and trustworthy. No wonder, when we realize the channel along which it flowed. It was authenticated by the double testimony of men[1] who had actually heard Jesus, and of God who attested and inspired them in their mission. **Συνεπιμαρτυρεῖν** means "assent" in *Ep. Aristeas*, 191, and "corroborate" in the *de Mundo*, 400*a* (συνεπιμαρτυρεῖ δὲ καὶ ὁ βίος ἅπας), as usual, but is here a sonorous religious term for συμμαρτυρεῖν (Ro 8[16]). "Coniunctio σύν . . . hunc habet sensum, nos in fide euangelii confirmari symphonia quadam Dei et hominum" (Calvin).

[1] In ὑπὸ τῶν ἀκουσάντων, ὑπό is used, as invariably throughout Πρὸς Ἑβραίους, of persons, which is a proof of good Greek. "There is no more certain test of the accuracy of individual Greek writers than their use of the passives (or equivalent forms) with ὑπό and a genitive. In the best writers this genitive almost invariably denotes *personal*, or at least *living* objects" (W. J. Hickie, on *Andocides*, *De Mysteriis*, § 14).

σημ., τερ., δυν. in the reverse order describe the miracles of Jesus in Ac 2^{22}; here they denote the miracles of the primitive evangelists as in 2 Co 12^{12}. Philo, speaking of the wonderful feats of Moses before the Pharaoh, declares that signs and wonders are a plainer proof of what God commands than any verbal injunction (ἅτε δὴ τοῦ θεοῦ τρανοτέραις χρησμῶν ἀποδείξεσι ταῖς διὰ σημείων καὶ τεράτων τὸ βούλημα δεδηλωκότος, *vit. Mos.* i. 16).

As "God" (θεοῦ) is the subject of the clause, αὐτοῦ (for which D actually reads θεοῦ) refers to him, and πνεύματος ἁγίου is the genitive of the object after μερισμοῖς (cp. 6^4). What is distributed is the Spirit, in a variety of endowments. To take αὐτοῦ with πνεύματος and make the latter the genitive of the subject, would tally with Paul's description of the Spirit διαιροῦν ἰδίᾳ ἑκάστῳ καθὼς βούλεται (1 Co 12^{11}), but would fail to explain what was distributed and would naturally require τῷ μερισμῷ. A fair parallel lies in Gal 3^5 ὁ ἐπιχορηγῶν ὑμῖν τὸ πνεῦμα καὶ ἐνεργῶν δυνάμεις ἐν ὑμῖν, where δυνάμεις also means "miraculous powers" or "mighty deeds" (a Hellenistic sense, differing from that of the LXX = "forces"). In **κατὰ τὴν αὐτοῦ θέλησιν**, as perhaps even in 7^{18} (cp. Blass, 284. 3; Abbott's *Johannine Grammar*, 2558), the possessive αὐτός is emphatic. θέλησιν is read by ℵ[ca] R for δέησιν in Ps 21^3 (cp. Ezk 28^{23} μὴ θελήσει θελήσω). It is not merely a vulgarism for θέλημα. "Θέλημα n'est pas θέλησις, volonté; θέλημα désigne le vouloir concentré sur un moment, sur un acte, l'ordre, le commandment" (Psichari, *Essai sur le grec de la Septante*, 1908, p. 171 n.). The writer is fond of such forms (*e.g.* ἀθέτησις, ἄθλησις, αἴνεσις, μετάθεσις, πρόσχυσις). Naturally the phrase has a very different meaning from the similar remark in Lucian, who makes Hesiod (*Disputatio cum Hesiode*, 4) apologize for certain omissions in his poetry, by pleading that the Muses who inspired him gave their gifts as they pleased—αἱ θεαὶ δὲ τὰς ἑαυτῶν δωρεὰς οἷς τε ἂν ἐθέλωσι.

The vital significance of the Son as the ἀρχηγός of this "salvation"[1] by means of his sufferings on earth, is now developed (vv.[5-18]). This unique element in the Son has been already hinted (1^3), but the writer now proceeds to explain it as the core of Christ's pre-eminence. The argument starts from the antithesis between the Son and angels (v.[5]); presently it passes beyond this, and angels are merely mentioned casually in a parenthesis (v.[16]). The writer is now coming to the heart of his theme, how and why the Son or Lord, of whom he has been speaking, suffered, died, and rose. Vv.[5-9] are the prelude to vv.[10-18]. The idea underlying the whole passage is this: **λαλεῖσθαι διὰ τοῦ κυρίου** meant much more than λαλεῖσθαι δι' ἀγγέλων, for the Christian revelation of σωτηρία had involved a tragic and painful experience for the Son on earth as he purged sins away. His present superiority to angels had been preceded by a period of mortal

[1] In A ℵ[ca] of Is 9^6 the messiah is called πατὴρ τοῦ μέλλοντος αἰῶνος.

experience on earth ἐν ταῖς ἡμέραις τῆς σαρκὸς αὐτοῦ. But this sojourn was only for a time; it was the vital presupposition of his triumph; it enabled him to die a death which invested him with supreme power on behalf of his fellow-men; and it taught him sympathy (cp. Zimmer, in *Studien und Kritiken*, 1882, pp. 413 f., on 2^{1-5}, and in *NTlichen Studien*, i. pp. 20–129, on 2^{6-18}).

5 *For the world to come, of which I* (ἡμεῖς of authorship) *am speaking, was not put under the control of angels* (whatever may be the case with the present world). 6 *One writer, as we know, has affirmed,*

"What is man, that thou art mindful of him?
or the son of man, that thou carest for him?
7 *For a little while thou hast put him lower than the angels,*
crowning him with glory and honour,
8 *putting all things under his feet."*

Now by[1] *"putting all things under him"*[2] *the writer meant to leave nothing out of his control. But, as it is, we do not yet see "all things controlled" by man;* 9 *what we do see is Jesus "who was put lower than the angels for a little while" to suffer death, and who has been "crowned with glory and honour," that by God's grace he might taste death for everyone.*

Οὐ γὰρ ἀγγέλοις (γάρ, as in Greek idiom, opening a new question; almost equivalent to "now": οὐ γάρ = non certe, Valckenaer) **ὑπέταξε** (*i.e.* ὁ θεός, as C vg add)—the writer is already thinking of ὑπέταξας in the quotation which he is about to make. In the light of subsequent allusions to μέλλοντα ἀγαθά (9^{11} 10^{1}) and ἡ μέλλουσα πόλις (13^{14}), we see that **τὴν οἰκουμένην τὴν μέλλουσαν** means the new order of things in which the σωτηρία of 1^{14} $2^{2.3}$ is to be realized (see 9^{28}), and from which already influences are pouring down into the life of Christians. The latter allusion is the pivot of the transition. The powers and spiritual experiences just mentioned (in v.[4]) imply this higher, future order of things (cp. $6^{4.5}$ especially δυνάμεις τε μέλλοντος αἰῶνος), from which rays stream down into the present. How the ministry of angels is connected with them, we do not learn. But the author had already urged that this service of angels was rendered to the divine authority, and that it served to benefit Christians (1^{14}). This idea starts him afresh. Who reigns in the new order? Not angels but the Son, and the Son who has come down for a time into human nature and suffered death. He begins by quoting a stanza from a psalm which seems irrelevant, because it compares men and angels. In reality this is not what occupies his mind; otherwise he might have put his argument differently and used, for example, the belief that Christians would hold sway over angels in the next world (1 Co $6^{2.3}$).

1 ἐν τῷ (*sc.* λέγειν, as 8^{13}).
2 The omission of this αὐτῷ by B d e arm does not alter the sense.

Philo (*de opificio*, 29, οὐ παρ' ὅσον ὕστατον γέγονεν ἄνθρωπος, διὰ τὴν τάξιν ἠλάττωται) argues that man is not inferior in position because he was created last in order; but this refers to man in relation to other creatures, not in relation to angels, as here.

The quotation (vv.[6-8a]) from the 8th psalm runs:

> τί ἐστιν ἄνθρωπος ὅτι μιμνήσκῃ[1] αὐτοῦ,
> ἢ υἱὸς ἀνθρώπου ὅτι ἐπισκέπτῃ αὐτόν;
> ἠλάττωσας αὐτὸν βραχύ τι παρ' ἀγγέλους,
> δόξῃ καὶ τιμῇ ἐστεφάνωσας αὐτόν.
> πάντα ὑπέταξας ὑποκάτω τῶν ποδῶν αὐτοῦ.

The LXX tr. אלהים not incorrectly by **ἀγγέλους**, since *the elohim* of the original probably included angels. This was the point of the quotation, for the author of Hebrews. The text of the quotation offers only a couple of items. (*a*) τί is changed into τίς (LXX A) by C* P 104. 917. 1288. 1319. 1891. 2127 vt boh, either in conformity to the preceding τις or owing to the feeling that the more common τίς (in questions, *e.g.* 12[7], Jn 12[34]) suited the reference to Christ better (Bleek, Zimmer). (*b*) The quotation omits καὶ κατέστησας αὐτὸν ἐπὶ τὰ ἔργα τῶν χειρῶν σου before πάντα: it is inserted by ℵ A C D* M P syr lat boh arm eth Euth. Theodt. Sedul. to complete the quotation. It is the one line in the sentence on which the writer does not comment; probably he left it out as incompatible with 1[10] (ἔργα τῶν χειρῶν σού εἰσιν οἱ οὐρανοί), although he frequently quotes more of an OT passage than is absolutely required for his particular purpose.

In **διεμαρτύρατο δέ πού τις** (v.[6]), even if the δέ is adversative, it need not be expressed in English idiom. διαμαρτυρεῖσθαι in Greek inscriptions "means primarily to address an assembly or a king" (Hicks, in *Classical Review*, i. 45). Here, the only place where it introduces an OT quotation, it = attest or affirm. Πού τις in such a formula is a literary mannerism familiar in Philo (*De Ebriet.* 14: εἶπε γάρ πού τις), and που later on (4[4]) recurs in a similar formula, as often in Philo. The τις implies no modification of the Alexandrian theory of inspiration; his words are God's words (v.[8]). The psalm intends no contrast between **ἠλάττωσας κτλ.** and **δόξῃ . . . ἐστεφάνωσας αὐτόν.** The proof that this wonderful being has been created in a position only slightly inferior to that of the divine host lies in the fact that he is crowned king of nature, invested with a divine authority over creation. The psalm is a panegyric on man, like Hamlet's ("What a piece of work is man! how noble in reason! how infinite in faculties! in form and moving how express and admirable! in action how like an angel!" etc.), but with a religious note of wonder and gratitude to God. In applying the psalm, however, our writer takes βραχύ τι

[1] μιμνήσκῃ means mindfulness shown in act, and ἐπισκέπτῃ, as always in the NT, denotes personal care.

in the sense of "temporarily" rather than "slightly," and so has to make the "inferiority" and "exaltation" two successive phases, in applying the description to the career of Jesus. He does not take this verse as part of a messianic ode; neither here nor elsewhere does he use the term "Son of Man." He points out, first of all (v.[8]) that, as things are (νῦν δὲ οὔπω: οὔ πω = οὔ πως might be read, *i.e.* "in no wise," and νῦν taken logically instead of temporally; but this is less natural and pointed), the last words are still unfulfilled; οὔπω ὁρωμεν αὐτῷ (*i.e.* man) τὰ "πάντα" (*i.e.* ἡ οἰκουμένη ἡ μέλλουσα) ὑποτεταγμένα. Human nature is not "crowned with glory and honour" at present. How can it be, when the terror of death and the devil (v.[15]) enslaves it? What is to be said, then? This, that although we do not see man triumphant, there is something that we do see: βλέπομεν Ἰησοῦν dealing triumphantly with death on man's behalf (v.[9]). The Ἰησοῦν comes in with emphasis, as in 3[1] and 12[2], at the end of a preliminary definition τὸν . . . ἠλαττωμένον.

It is less natural to take the messianic interpretation which involves the reference of αὐτῷ already to him. On this view, the writer frankly allows that the closing part of the prophecy is still unfulfilled. "We do not yet see τὰ πάντα under the sway of Jesus Christ, for *the world to come* has not yet *come*; it has only been inaugurated by the sacrifice of Christ (1[3] καθαρισμὸν τῶν ἁμαρτιῶν ποιησάμενος ἐκάθισεν ἐν δεξιᾷ τῆς μεγαλωσύνης ἐν ὑψηλοῖς). Though the Son is crowned (1[8. 9]) and enthroned (1[13] κάθου ἐκ δεξιῶν μου), his foes are still to be subdued (ἕως ἂν θῶ τοὺς ἐχθρούς σου ὑποπόδιον τῶν ποδῶν σου), and we must be content to wait for our full σωτηρία (9[28]) at his second coming; under the οὔπω ὁρῶμεν κτλ. of experience there is a deeper experience of faith." The writer rather turns back in v.[9] to the language of v.[7]; this at least has been fulfilled. *Jesus* has been put lower than the angels and he has been crowned. How and why? The writer answers the second question first. Or rather, in answering the second he suggests the answer to the first. At this point, and not till then, the messianic interpretation becomes quite natural and indeed inevitable. It is the earlier introduction of it which is unlikely. The application to the messiah of words like those quoted in v.[6] is forced, and "Hebrews" has no room for the notion of Christ as the ideal or representative Man, as is implied in the messianic interpretation of αὐτῷ in v.[8]. That interpretation yields a true idea—the thought expressed, *e.g.*, in T. E. Brown's poem, "Sad! Sad!"—

> "One thing appears to me—
>   The work is not complete;
> One world I know, and see
>   It is not at His feet—
>   Not, not! Is this the sum?"

No, our author hastens to add, it is not the sum; our outlook is not one of mere pathos; we do see Jesus enthroned, with the full prospect of ultimate triumph But the idea of the issues of Christ's triumph being still incomplete is not true here. What is relevant, and what is alone relevant, is the decisive character of his sacrifice. The argument of v.[8.9], therefore, is that, however inapplicable to man the rhapsody of the psalm is, at present, the words of the psalm are true, notwithstanding. For we see the Jesus who was "put lower than the angels for a little while" to suffer death (**διὰ τὸ πάθημα τοῦ θανάτου** must refer to the death of Jesus himself,[1] not to the general experience of death as the occasion for his incarnation), now "crowned with glory and honour." When **διὰ τὸ πάθημα τοῦ θανάτου** is connected with what follows (**δόξῃ καὶ τιμῇ ἐστεφανωμένον**), it gives the reason for the exaltation, not the object of the incarnation (= *εἰς τὸ πάσχειν*). But *διά . . . θανάτου* is elucidated in a moment by *ὅπως . . . θανάτου*. V.[9] answers the question why Jesus was lowered and exalted—it was for the sake of mankind. In v.[10] the writer proceeds to explain how he was "lowered"—it was by suffering that culminated in death. Then he recurs naturally to the "why." The mixture of quotation and comment in v.[9] leaves the meaning open to some dubiety, although the drift is plain. "But one Being referred to in the psalm (**τὸν . . . ἠλαττωμένον**) we do see—it is Jesus, and Jesus as *ἠλαττωμένον* for the purpose of suffering death, and **δόξῃ καὶ τιμῇ ἐστεφανωμένον**. Why did he die? Why was he thus humiliated and honoured? For the sake of every man; his death was *ὑπὲρ παντός*, part of the divine purpose of redemption." Thus **ὅπως . . . θανάτου** explains and expounds the idea of *διὰ τὸ πάθημα* (which consists in) *τοῦ θανάτου*, gathering up the full object and purpose of the experience which has just been predicated of Jesus. This implies a pause after *ἐστεφανωμένον*, or, as Bleek suggests, the supplying of an idea like *ὃ ἔπαθεν* before *ὅπως κτλ.*, if *γεύσηται* is to be taken, as it must be, as = "he might taste." How a *ὅπως* clause follows and elucidates *διά κτλ.* may be seen in *Ep. Arist.* 106 (*διὰ τοὺς ἐν ταῖς ἁγνείαις ὄντας, ὅπως μηδενὸς θιγγάνωσιν*).

As for v.[8a], Paul makes a similar comment (1 Co 15[27]), but excludes God from the *τὰ πάντα*. The curiously explicit language here is intended to reiterate what is possibly hinted at in v.[5], viz., that the next world has no room for the angelic control which characterizes the present. (The *τὰ πάντα* includes even angels!) This belief was familiar to readers of the Greek bible, where Dt 32[8] voices a conception of guardian-angels over the non-Jewish nations which became current in some circles of the later Judaism. Non-Jewish Christians, like the readers of our epistle, would be likely to appreciate the point of an argument which dealt with this. Note that **ἀνυπότακτον** occurs in a similar antithesis in Epictetus, ii. 10. 1, *ταύτῃ τὰ*

---

[1] But not, as the Greek fathers, etc., supposed, as if it was the fact of his death (and stay in the underworld) that lowered him (*διά* = on account of).

ἄλλα ὑποτεταγμένα, αὐτὴν δ' ἀδούλευτον καὶ ἀνυπότακτον. Our author's language reads almost like a tacit repudiation of Philo's remark on Gn 1[26] in *de opificio Mundi* (28), that God put man over all things with the exception of the heavenly beings—ὅσα γὰρ θνητὰ ἐν τοῖς τρισὶ στοιχείοις γῇ ὕδατι ἀέρι πάντα ὑπέταττεν αὐτῷ, τὰ κατ' οὐρανὸν ὑπεξελόμενος ἅτε θειοτέρας μοίρας ἐπιλαχόντα.

The closing clause of v.[9] (**ὅπως χάριτι θεοῦ ὑπὲρ παντὸς γεύσηται θανάτου**), therefore, resumes and completes the idea of διὰ τὸ πάθημα τοῦ θανάτου. Each follows a phrase from the psalm; but ὅπως . . . θανάτου does not follow ἐστεφανωμένον logically. The only possible method of thus taking ὅπως κτλ. would be by applying δόξῃ καὶ τιμῇ ἐστεφανωμένον to Christ's life prior to death, either (*a*) to his pre-incarnate existence, when "in the counsels of heaven" he was, as it were, "crowned for death" (so Rendall, who makes γεύσασθαι θανάτου cover the "inward dying" of daily self-denial and suffering which led up to Calvary), or (*b*) to his incarnate life (so, *e.g.*, Hofmann, Milligan, Bruce), as if his readiness to sacrifice himself already threw a halo round him, or (*c*) specifically to God's recognition and approval of him at the baptism and transfiguration (Dods). But the use of δόξα in v.[10] tells against such theories; it is from another angle altogether that Jesus is said in 2 P 1[17] to have received τιμὴν καὶ δόξαν from God at the transfiguration. The most natural interpretation, therefore, is to regard δόξῃ . . . ἐστεφανωμένον as almost parenthetical, rounding off the quotation from the psalm. It is unnecessary to fall back on such suggestions as (i) to assume a break in the text after ἐστεφανωμένον, some words lost which led up to ὅπως . . . θανάτου (Windisch), or (ii) to translate ὅπως by "how," as in Lk 24[20], *i.e.* "we see how Jesus tasted death" (so Blass, boldly reading ἐγεύσατο), or by "after that" or "when" (Moses Stuart), as in Soph. *Oed. Col.* 1638 (where, however, it takes the indicative as usual), etc.

In ὑπὲρ παντός, παντός was at an early stage taken as neuter, practically = the universe. This was a popular idea in Egyptian Christianity. "You know," says the risen Christ to his disciples, in a Bohairic narrative of the death of Joseph (*Texts and Studies*, iv. 2. 130), "that many times now I have told you that I must needs be crucified and taste death for the universe." The interpretation occurs first in Origen, who (*in Joan.* i. 35) writes: "He is a 'great highpriest' [referring to Heb 4[15]], having offered himself up in sacrifice once (ἅπαξ) not for human beings alone, but for the rest of rational creatures as well (ἀλλὰ καὶ ὑπὲρ τῶν λοιπῶν λογικῶν). 'For without God he tasted death for everyone' (χωρὶς γὰρ θεοῦ ὑπὲρ παντὸς ἐγεύσατο θανάτου). In some copies of the epistle to the Hebrews this passage runs: 'for by the grace of God' (χάριτι γὰρ θεοῦ). Well, if 'without God he tasted death for everyone,' he did not die simply for human beings, but for the rest of rational creatures as well; and if 'by the grace of God he tasted the death for everyone,'[1] he died for all except for God (χωρὶς θεοῦ)—for 'by the grace of God he tasted death for everyone.' It would indeed be

[1] Reading τοῦ before ὑπέρ.

preposterous (*ἄτοπον*) to say that he tasted death for human sins and not also for any other being besides man who has fallen into sin—*e.g.* for the stars. Even the stars are by no means pure before God, as we read in the book of Job: 'The stars are not pure before him,' unless this is said hyperbolically. For this reason he is a 'great highpriest,' because he restores (*ἀποκαθίστησι*) all things to his Father's kingdom, ordering it so that what is lacking in any part of creation is completed for the fulness of the Father's glory (*πρὸς τὸ χωρῆσαι δόξαν πατρικήν*)." The Greek fathers adhered steadily to this interpretation of *παντός* as equivalent to the entire universe, including especially angels. But the neuter is always expressed in "Hebrews" by the plural, with or without the article, and, as v.[16] shows, the entire interest is in human beings.

Γεύσηται after *ὑπὲρ παντός* has also been misinterpreted. *Γεύειν* in LXX, as a rendering of טָעַם, takes either genitive (1 S 14^{24}, cp. 2 Mac 6^{20}) or accusative (1 S 14^{29}, Job 34^{3}), but *γεύεσθαι θανάτου* never occurs; it is the counterpart of the rabbinic phrase טעם מיתה, and elsewhere in the NT (Mk 9^{1}=Mt 16^{28}=Lk 9^{27}, Jn 8^{52}) is used not of Jesus but of men. It means to experience (=*ἰδεῖν θάνατον*, 11^{5}). Here it is a bitter experience, not a rapid sip, as if Jesus simply "tasted" death (Chrysostom, Theophyl., Oecumenius: *οὐ γὰρ ἐνέμεινεν τῷ θανάτῳ ἀλλὰ μόνον αὐτὸν τρόπον τινὰ ἀπεγεύσατο*) quickly, or merely sipped it like a doctor sipping a drug to encourage a patient. The truer comment would be: "When I think of our Lord as tasting death it seems to me as if He alone ever truly tasted death" (M'Leod Campbell, *The Nature of the Atonement*, p. 259); *γεύσηται* does not echo *βραχύ τι*, as though all that Jesus experienced of death was slight or short.

The hardest knot of the hard passage lies in *χάριτι θεοῦ*. In the second century two forms of the text were current, ΧΩΡΙΣ ΘΕΟΥ and ΧΑΡΙΤΙ ΘΕΟΥ. This is plain from Origen's comment (see above); he himself is unwilling to rule out the latter reading, but prefers the former, which he apparently found to be the ordinary text. Theodoret assumed it to be original, as Ambrose did in the West. Jerome knew both (on Gal 3^{10}), and the eighth century Anastasius Abbas read *χωρίς* ("absque deo: sola enim divina natura non egebat"), *i.e.*, in the sense already suggested by Fulgentius and Vigilius, that Christ's divine nature did not die. On the other hand, writers like Eusebius, Athanasius, and Chrysostom never mention any other reading than *χάριτι*. Of all the supporters of *χωρίς*, the most emphatic is Theodore of Mopsuestia, who protests that it is most absurd (*γελοιότατον*) to substitute *χάριτι θεοῦ* for *χωρὶς θεοῦ*, arguing from passages like 1 Co 15^{10} and Eph $2^{8.\,9}$ that Paul's custom is not to use the former phrase *ἁπλῶς, ἀλλὰ πάντως ἀπό τινος ἀκολουθίας λόγου*. The reading suited the Nestorian view of the person of Christ, and probably the fact of its popularity among the Nestorians tended to compromise *χωρίς* in the eyes of the later church; it survives only in M 424**, though there is a trace of it (a Nestorian gloss?) in three codices of the Peshitto. But Oecumenius and Theophylact are wrong in holding that it originated among the Nestorians. This is dogmatic prejudice;

χωρίς was read in good manuscripts, if not in the best, by Origen's time, and the problem is to determine whether it or χάριτι was original. The one may be a transcriptional error for the other. In this case, the textual canon "potior lectio difficillima" would favour χωρίς. But the canon does not apply rigidly to every such case, and the final decision depends upon the internal probabilities. Long associations render it difficult for a modern to do justice to χωρὶς θεοῦ. Yet χωρίς is elsewhere used by our author in a remarkable way, *e.g.* in 9^{28} χωρὶς ἁμαρτίας ὀφθήσεται, and the question is whether χωρὶς θεοῦ here cannot be understood in an apt, although daring, sense. It may be (i) "forsaken by God," an allusion to the "dereliction" of Mk 15^{34} (B. Weiss, Zimmer), though this would rather be put as ἄτερ θεοῦ. (ii) "Apart from his divinity" (see above), *i.e.* when Christ died, his divine nature survived. But this would require a term like τῆς θεότητος. (iii) Taken with παντός, "die for everyone (everything?) except God" (Origen's view, adopted recently by moderns like Ewald and Ebrard). Of these (i) and (iii) are alone tenable. Even if (iii) be rejected, it furnishes a clue to the problem of the origin of the reading. Thus Bengel and others modify it by taking ὑπὲρ παντός = to master everything, χωρὶς θεοῦ being added to explain that "everything" does not include God. It is possible, of course, that in the Latin rendering (ut gratia Dei pro omnibus gustaret mortem) gratia is an original nominative, not an ablative, and represents χάρις (Christ = the Grace of God),[1] which came to be altered into χωρίς and χάριτι. But, if χωρὶς θεοῦ is regarded as secondary, its origin probably lies in the dogmatic scruple of some primitive scribe who wrote the words on the margin as a gloss upon παντός, or even on the margin of v.[8] opposite οὐδὲν ἀφῆκεν αὐτῷ ἀνυπότακτον, whence it slipped lower down into the text. Upon the whole, it seems fairest to assume that at some very early stage there must have been a corruption of the text, which cannot be explained upon the available data. But at any rate χάριτι fits in well with ἔπρεπει, which immediately follows, and this is one point in its favour. It was χάριτι θεοῦ that Jesus died for everyone, and this was consonant with God's character (ἔπρεπει γὰρ αὐτῷ, *i.e.* θεῷ). The nearest Latin equivalent for πρέπον, as Cicero (*de Officiis*, i. 26) said, was "decorum" (dulce et decorum est pro patria mori), and in this high sense the divine χάρις (4^{16}), shown in the wide range and object of the death of Jesus, comes out in the process and method.

[1] It was so taken by some Latin fathers like Primasius and by later theologians of the Western church like Thomas of Aquinum and Sedulius Scotus, who depended on the Vulgate version.

The writer now explains (vv.[10-18]) why Jesus had to suffer and to die. Only thus could he save his brother men who lay (whether by nature or as a punishment, we are not told) under the tyranny of death. To die for everyone meant that Jesus had to enter human life and identify himself with men; suffering is the badge and lot of the race, and a Saviour must be a sufferer, if he is to carry out God's saving purpose. The sufferings of Jesus were neither an arbitrary nor a degrading experience, but natural, in view of what he was to God and men alike. For the first time, the conception of suffering occurs, and the situation which gave rise to the author's handling of the subject arose out of what he felt to be his readers' attitude. "We are suffering hardships on account of our religion." But so did Jesus, the writer replies. "Well, but was it necessary for him any more than for us? And if so, how does that consideration help us in our plight?" To this there is a twofold answer. (*a*) Suffering made Jesus a real Saviour; it enabled him to offer his perfect sacrifice, on which fellowship with God depends. (*b*) He suffered not only for you but like you, undergoing the same temptations to faith and loyalty as you have to meet. The threefold inference is: (i) do not give way, but realize all you have in his sacrifice, and what a perfect help and sympathy you can enjoy. (ii) Remember, this is a warning as well as an encouragement; it will be a fearful thing to disparage a religious tie of such privilege. (iii) Also, let his example nerve you.

[10] *In bringing many sons to glory, it was befitting that He for whom and by whom the universe exists, should perfect the Pioneer of their salvation by suffering* (διὰ παθημάτων, echoing διὰ τὸ πάθημα τοῦ θανάτου). [11] *For sanctifier and sanctified have all one origin* (ἐξ ἑνός, *sc.* γενοῦς: neuter as Ac 17[26]). *That is why he* (ὁ ἁγιάζων) *is not ashamed to call them brothers,* [12] *saying,*

"I will proclaim thy name to my brothers,
in the midst of the church I will sing of thee";

[13] *and again,*

"I will put my trust in him";

and again,

"Here am I and the children God has given me."

[14] *Since the children then* (οὖν, resuming the thought of v.[11a]) *share blood and flesh,*[1] *he himself participated in their nature,*[2] *so that by dying he might crush him who wields the power of death* (*that is to say, the devil*), [15] *and release from thraldom those who lay under a life-long fear of death.* [16] (*For of course it is not angels that "he succours," it is "the offspring of Abraham"*). [17] *He had to resemble his brothers in every respect, in order to prove a merciful and faithful high priest in things divine, to expiate the sins of the*

---

[1] αἵματος καὶ σαρκός (Eph 6[12]) is altered into the more conventional σαρκὸς καὶ αἵματος by, *e.g.*, K L f vg syr pesh eth boh Theodoret, Aug. Jerome.

[2] αὐτῶν, *i.e.* αἵματος καὶ σαρκός, not παθημάτων, which is wrongly added by D* d syr[pal] Eus. Jerome, Theodoret.

People. [18] *It is as he suffered by his temptations that he is able to help the tempted.*

It is remarkable (cp. Introd. p. xvi) that the writer does not connect the sufferings of Jesus with OT prophecy, either generally (as, *e.g.*, Lk 24^{26} οὐχὶ ταῦτα ἔδει[1] παθεῖν τὸν Χριστόν κτλ.), or with a specific reference to Is 53. He explains them on the ground of moral congruity. Here they are viewed from God's standpoint, as in 12^2 from that of Jesus himself. God's purpose of grace made it befitting and indeed inevitable that Jesus should suffer and die in fulfilling his function as a Saviour (v.[10]); then (vv.[11f.]) it is shown how he made common cause with those whom he was to rescue.

Ἔπρεπεν γάρ κτλ. (v.[10]). Πρέπειν or πρέπον, in the sense of "seemly," is not applied to God in the LXX, but is not uncommon in later Greek, *e.g.* Lucian's *Prometheus*, 8 (οὔτε θεοῖς πρέπον οὔτε ἄλλως βασιλικόν), and the *de Mundo*, 397*b*, 398*a* (ὃ καὶ πρέπον ἐστὶ καὶ θεῷ μάλιστα ἁρμόζον—of a theory about the universe, however). The writer was familiar with it in Philo, who has several things to say about what it behoved God to do,[2] though never this thing; Philo has the phrase, not the idea. According to Aristotle (*Nic. Ethics*, iv. 2. 2, τὸ πρέπον δὴ πρὸς αὐτόν, καὶ ἐν ᾧ καὶ περὶ ὅ), what is "befitting" relates to the person himself, to the particular occasion, and to the object. Here, we might say, the idea is that it would not have done for God to save men by a method which stopped short of suffering and actual death. "Quand il est question des actes de Dieu, ce qui est *convenable* est toujours *nécessaire* au point de vue métaphysique" (Reuss). In the description of God (for **αὐτῷ** cannot be applied to Jesus in any natural sense) **δι' ὃν τὰ πάντα καὶ δι' οὗ τὰ πάντα**, the writer differs sharply from Philo. The Alexandrian Jew objects to Eve (Gn 4^1) and Joseph (Gn 40^{18}) using the phrase διὰ τοῦ θεοῦ (*Cherubim*, 35), on the ground that it makes God merely instrumental; whereas, ὁ θεὸς αἴτιον, οὐκ ὄργανον. On the contrary, we call God the creative cause (αἴτιον) of the universe, ὄργανον δὲ λόγον θεοῦ δι' οὗ κατεσκευάσθη. He then quotes Ex 14^{13} to prove, by the use of παρά, that οὐ διὰ[3] τοῦ θεοῦ ἀλλὰ παρ' αὐτοῦ ὡς αἰτίου τὸ σῴζεσθαι. But our author has no such scruples about διά, any more than Aeschylus had (*Agamemnon*, 1486, διαὶ Διὸς παναιτίου πανεργέτα). Like Paul (Ro 11^{36}) he can say δι' οὗ τὰ πάντα of God, adding, for the sake of paronomasia, δι' ὃν to cover what Paul meant by ἐξ αὐτοῦ καὶ εἰς αὐτόν. Or rather, starting with δι' ὃν τὰ πάντα he

[1] The ὤφειλεν of v.[17] is not the same as this ἔδει.

[2] Thus: πρέπει τῷ θεῷ φυτεύειν καὶ οἰκοδομεῖν ἐν ψυχῇ τὰς ἀρετάς (*Leg. alleg.* i. 15)

[3] When he does use διά (*de opificio*, 24) it is δι' αὐτοῦ μόνου, of creation.

prefers another διά with a genitive, for the sake of assonance, to the more usual equivalent ἐξ οὗ or ὑφ' οὗ. To preserve the assonance, Zimmer proposes to render: "um dessentwillen das All, und durch dessen Willen das All."

The ultimate origin of the phrase probably lies in the mystery-cults; Aristides (Εἰς τὸν Σάραπιν, 51: ed. Dindorf, i. p. 87), in an invocation of Serapis, writes to this effect, πάντα γὰρ πανταχοῦ διὰ σοῦ τε καὶ διὰ σε ἡμῖν γίγνεται. But Greek thought in Stoicism had long ago played upon the use of διά in this connexion. Possibly διά with the accusative was the primitive and regular expression, as Norden contends.[1] We call Zeus "Ζῆνα καὶ Δία" ὡς ἂν εἰ λέγοιμεν δι' ὃν ζῶμεν, says the author of *de Mundo* (401*a*), like the older Stoics (see Arnim's *Stoicorum veterum Fragmenta*, ii. pp. 305, 312), and διά with the accusative might have the same causal sense here,[2] *i.e.* "through," in which case the two phrases δι' ὅν and δι' οὗ would practically be a poetical reduplication of the same idea, or at least = "by whom and through whom." But the dominant, though not exclusive, idea of δι' ὅν here is final, "for whom"; the end of the universe, of all history and creation, lies with Him by whom it came into being and exists; He who redeems is He who has all creation at His command and under His control.

The point in adding δι' ὅν . . . τὰ πάντα to αὐτῷ is that the sufferings and death of Jesus are not accidental; they form part of the eternal world-purpose of God. Philo had explained that Moses was called up to Mount Sinai on the seventh day, because God wished to make the choice of Israel parallel to the creation of the world (*Quaest. in Exod.* 24[16] βουλόμενος ἐπιδεῖξαι ὅτι αὐτὸς καὶ τὸν κόσμον ἐδημιούργησε καὶ τὸ γένος εἵλετο. Ἡ δὲ ἀνάκλησις τοῦ προφήτου δεύτερα γένεσίς ἐστι τῆς προτέρας ἀμείνων). But our author goes deeper; redemption, he reiterates (for this had been hinted at in 1[1-4]), is not outside the order of creation. The distinction between the redeeming grace of God and the created universe was drawn afterwards by gnosticism. There is no conscious repudiation of such a view here, only a definite assertion that behind the redeeming purpose lay the full force of God the creator, that God's providence included the mysterious sufferings of Jesus His Son, and that these were in line with His will.

In **πολλοὺς υἱούς** the πολλοί is in antithesis to the one and only **ἀρχηγός**, as in Ro 8[29], Mk 14[24]. For the first time the writer calls Christians God's sons. His confidence towards the Father is in sharp contrast to Philo's touch of hesitation in *De Confus. Ling.* 28 (κἂν μηδέπω μέντοι τυγχάνῃ τις ἀξιόχρεως ὢν υἱὸς θεοῦ προσαγορεύεσθαι . . . καὶ γὰρ εἰ μήπω ἱκανοὶ θεοῦ παῖδες νομίζεσθαι γεγόναμεν). **Ἀγαγόντα** is devoid of any reference to

[1] *Agnostos Theos*, 347 f. ("Das ist die applikation der logisch-grammatischen Theorie über den Kasus, der in ältester Terminologie, ἡ κατ' αἰτίαν πτῶσις, heisst, auf die Physik: die Welt ist das Objekt der durch die höchste αἰτία ausgeübten Tätigkeit").

[2] As in Apoc. 4[11] and *Epist. Aristeas*, 16: δι' ὃν ζωοποιοῦνται τὰ πάντα καὶ γίνεται (quoting Ζῆνα καὶ Δία).

past time. The aorist participle is used adverbially, as often, to denote "an action evidently in a general way coincident in time with the action of the verb, yet not identical with it. The choice of the aorist participle rather than the present in such cases is due to the fact that the action is thought of, not as in progress, but as a simple event or fact" (Burton, *Moods and Tenses*, 149). It is accusative instead of dative, agreeing with an implied *αὐτόν* instead of *αὐτῷ*, by a common Greek assimilation (cp. *e.g.* Ac 11¹² 15²² 22¹⁷ 25²⁷). The accusative and infinitive construction prompted *ἀγαγόντα* instead of *ἀγαγόντι*. Had *ἀγαγόντα* been intended to qualify *ἀρχηγόν*, *πολλούς* would have been preceded by *τόν*. The thought is: thus do men attain the *δόξα* which had been their destiny (v.⁷), but only through a Jesus who had won it for them by suffering.

The mistaken idea that ἀγαγόντα must refer to some action previous to *τελειῶσαι*, which gave rise to the Latin rendering "qui adduxerat" (vg) or "multis filiis adductis" (vt), is responsible for the ingenious suggestion of Zimmer that *δόξα* denotes an intermediate state of bliss, where the *δίκαιοι* of the older age await the full inheritance of the messianic bliss. It is possible (see below on 11⁴⁰ 12²³) to reconstruct such an idea in the mind of the writer, but not to introduce it here.

The general idea in ἀρχηγόν is that of originator or personal source; *τουτέστι, τὸν αἴτιον τῆς σωτηρίας* (Chrysostom). It is doubtful how far the writer was determined, in choosing the term, by its varied associations, but the context, like that of 12², suggests that the "pioneer" meaning was present to his mind; Jesus was ἀρχηγὸς τῆς σωτηρίας αὐτῶν in the sense that he led the way, broke open the road for those who followed him. This meaning, common in the LXX, recurs in Ac 5³¹ (*ἀρχηγὸν καὶ σωτῆρα*), and suits *ἀγαγόντα* better than the alternative sense of the head or progenitor—as of a Greek clan or colony. In this sense *ἀρχηγός* is applied to heroes, and is even a divine title of Apollo as the head of the Seleucidae (*OGIS*. 212¹³, 219²⁶), as well as a term for the founder (=conditor) or head of a philosophical school (Athenaeus, xiii. 563 E, *τὸν ἄρχηγον ὑμῶν τῆς σοφίας Ζήνωνα*). But the other rendering is more relevant. Compare the confession (in the Acts of Maximilianus) of the soldier who was put to death in 295 A.D. (Ruinart, *Acta Martyrum*, pp. 340 f.): "huic omnes Christiani servimus, hunc sequimur vitae principem, salutis auctorem." The sufferings of Jesus as *ἀρχηγὸς σωτηρίας* had, of course, a specific value in the eyes of the writer. He did not die simply in order to show mortals how to die; he experienced death *ὑπὲρ παντός*, and by this unique suffering made it possible for "many sons" of God to enter the bliss which he had first won for them. Hence, to "perfect" (τελειῶσαι) the ἀρχηγὸς σωτηρίας is to make him adequate, completely effective. What this involved for him we are not yet told; later on (5^9 7^{28}) the writer touches the relation between the perfect ability of Christ and his ethical development through suffering (see below, v.[14]), but meantime he uses this general term. God had to "perfect" Jesus by means of suffering, that he might be equal to his task as ἀρχηγός or ἀρχιερεύς (v.[17]); the addition of αὐτῶν to σωτηρίας implies (see 7^{26}) that he himself had not to be saved from sin as they had. The underlying idea of the whole sentence is that by thus "perfecting" Jesus through suffering, God carries out his purpose of bringing "many sons" to bliss.

The verb had already acquired a tragic significance in connexion with martyrdom; in 4 Mac 7^{15} (ὃν πιστὴ θανάτου σφραγὶς ἐτελείωσεν) it is used of Eleazar's heroic death, and this reappeared in the Christian vocabulary, as, *e.g.*, in the title of the *Passio S. Perpetuae* (μαρτύριον τῆς ἁγίας Περπετούας καὶ τῶν σὺν αὐτῇ τελειωθέντων ἐν Ἀφρικῇ). But, although Philo had popularized the idea of τελευτᾶν=τελεῖσθαι, this is not present to our writer's mind; he is thinking of God's purpose to realize a complete experience of forgiveness and fellowship (σωτηρία) through the Son, and this includes and involves (as we shall see) a process of moral development for the Son.

The writer now (v.[11]) works out the idea suggested by πολλοὺς υἱούς. Since Jesus and Christians have the same spiritual origin, since they too in their own way are "sons" of God, he is proud to call them brothers and to share their lot (vv.[11-13]). The leader and his company are a unit, members of the one family of God. It is implied, though the writer does not explain the matter further, that Christ's common tie with mankind goes back to the pre-incarnate period; there was a close bond between them, even before he was born into the world; indeed the incarnation was the consequence of this solidarity or vital tie (ἐξ ἑνός, cp. Pindar, *Nem.* vi. 1, ἓν ἀνδρῶν, ἓν θεῶν γένος). Ὁ ἁγιάζων and οἱ ἁγιαζόμενοι are participles used as substantives, devoid of reference to time. Here, as at 13^{12}, Jesus is assigned the divine prerogative of ἁγιάζειν (cp. Ezk 20^{12} ἐγὼ κύριος ὁ ἁγιάζων αὐτούς, 2 Mac 1^{25}, etc.), *i.e.* of making God's People His very own, by bringing them into vital relationship with Himself. It is another sacerdotal metaphor; the thought of 1^3 (καθαρισμὸν τῶν ἁμαρτιῶν ποιησάμενος) is touched again, but the full meaning of ἁγιάζειν is not developed till $9^{13f.}$, where we see that to be "sanctified" is to be brought into the presence of God through the self-sacrifice of Christ; in other words, ἁγιάζεσθαι=προσέρχεσθαι or ἐγγίζειν τῷ θεῷ, as in Nu 16^5 where the ἅγιοι are those whom God προσηγάγετο πρὸς ἑαυτόν.

According to (Akiba?) Mechilta, 71*b* (on Ex 20^{18}), God said to the angels at Sinai, "Go down and help your brothers" (רְדוּ וְסַייְעוּ אֶת־אֲחֵיכֶם); yet it was not merely the angels, but God himself, who helped them (the proof-text being Ca 2^6!).

Δι' ἣν αἰτίαν—a phrase only used elsewhere in the NT by the author of the Pastoral epistles—**οὐκ ἐπαισχύνεται κτλ.** **Ἐπαισχύνεσθαι** implies that he was of higher rank, being somehow *υἱὸς θεοῦ* as they were not. The verb only occurs three times in LXX, twice of human shame (Ps 119[6], Is 1[29]), and once perhaps of God (= נָשָׂא) in Job 34[19]. In *Test. Jos.* 2[5] it is used passively (*οὐ γὰρ ὡς ἄνθρωπος ἐπαισχύνεται ὁ θεός*). In the gospels, besides Mk 3[34f.] and Mt 25[40], there are slight traditions of the risen Jesus calling the disciples his **ἀδελφοί** (Mt 28[10], Jn 20[17]); but the writer either did not know of them or preferred, as usual, to lead biblical proofs. He quotes three passages (vv.[12. 13]), the first from the 22nd psalm (v.[23]) taken as a messianic cry, the only change made in the LXX text being the alteration of *διηγήσομαι* into *ἀπαγγελῶ* (a synonym, see Ps 55[18]). The Son associates himself with his *ἀδελφοί* in the praise of God offered by their community (a thought which is echoed in 12[28] 13[15]).

According to Justin Martyr (*Dial.* 106), Ps 22[22. 23] foretells how the risen Jesus stood *ἐν μέσῳ τῶν ἀδελφῶν αὐτοῦ, τῶν ἀποστόλων . . . καὶ μετ' αὐτῶν διάγων ὕμνησε τὸν θεόν, ὡς καὶ ἐν τοῖς ἀπομνημονεύμασιν τῶν ἀποστόλων δηλοῦται γεγενημένον*, and in the *Acta Joannis* (11) Jesus, before going out to Gethsemane, says, *Let us sing a hymn to the Father* (*ἐν μέσῳ δὲ αὐτὸς γενόμενος*). The couplet is quoted here for the sake of the first line; the second fills it out. Our author only uses **ἐκκλησία** (12[23]) of the heavenly host, never in its ordinary sense of the "church."

The second quotation (v.[13a]) is from Is 8[17] **ἔσομαι πεποιθὼς** (a periphrastic future) **ἐπ' αὐτῷ**, but the writer prefixes *ἐγώ* to *ἔσομαι* for emphasis. The insertion of *ἐρεῖ* by the LXX at the beginning of Is 8[17] helped to suggest that the words were not spoken by the prophet himself. The fact that Jesus required to put faith in God proves that he was a human being like ourselves (see 12[2]).

In Philo trustful hope towards God is the essential mark of humanity; e.g. *quod det. pot.* 38 (on Gn 4[26]), *τοῦ δὲ κατὰ Μωυσῆν ἀνθρώπου διάθεσις ψυχῆς ἐπὶ τὸν ὄντως ὄντα θεὸν ἐλπιζούσης.*

The third quotation (v.[13b]) is from the words which immediately follow in Is 8[18], where the LXX breaks the Hebrew sentence into two, the first of which is quoted for his own purposes by the writer. The **παιδία** are God's children, the fellow *υἱοί* of Christ. It is too subtle to treat, with Zimmer, the three quotations as (*a*) a resolve to proclaim God, as a man to men; (*b*) a resolve to trust God amid the sufferings incurred in his mission, and (*c*) an anticipation of the reward of that mission. On the other hand, to omit the second *καὶ πάλιν* as a scribal gloss (Bentley) would certainly improve the sense and avoid the necessity of splitting up an Isaianic quotation into two, the first of which is not strictly apposite. But *καὶ πάλιν* is similarly[1]

[1] It is a literary device of Philo in making quotations (cp. *quis rer. div.* 1).

used in 10[30]; it is more easy to understand why such words should be omitted than inserted; and the deliberate addition of ἐγώ in the first points to an intentional use of the sentence as indirectly a confession of fellow-feeling with men on the part of the Son.

The same words of the 22nd psalm are played upon by the Od. Sol 31[4]: "and he (*i.e.* messiah or Truth) lifted up his voice to the most High, and offered to Him the sons that were with him (or, in his hands)."

In v.[14] **κεκοινώνηκεν** (here alone in the NT) takes the classical genitive, as in the LXX. An apt classical parallel occurs in the military writer Polyaenus (*Strateg.* iii. 11. 1), where Chabrias tells his troops to think of their foes merely as *ἀνθρώποις αἷμα καὶ σάρκα ἔχουσι, καὶ τῆς αὐτῆς φύσεως ἡμῖν κεκοινωνηκόσιν.* The following phrase **παραπλησίως** (= "similarly," *i.e.* almost "equally" or "also," as, *e.g.*, in Maxim. Tyr. vii. 2, *καὶ ἐστὶν καὶ ὁ ἄρχων πόλεως μέρος, καὶ οἱ ἀρχόμενοι παραπλησίως*) **μετέσχεν . . . ἵνα** *κτλ.* answers to the thought of *ἠλαττωμένον . . . διὰ τὸ πάθημα κτλ.* above. The verb is simply a synonym for *κοινωνεῖν*; in the papyri and the inscriptions *μετέχειν* is rather more common, but there is no distinction of meaning between the two.

This idea (*ἵνα κτλ.*) of crushing the devil as the wielder of death is not worked out by the writer. He alludes to it in passing as a belief current in his circle, and it must have had some context in his mind; but what this scheme of thought was, we can only guess. Evidently the devil was regarded as having a hold upon men somehow, a claim and control which meant death for them. One clue to the meaning is to be found in the religious ideas popularized by the Wisdom of Solomon, in which it is pretty clear that man was regarded as originally immortal (1[13. 14]), that death did not form part of God's scheme at the beginning, and that the devil was responsible for the introduction of death into the world (2[23. 24]); those who side with the devil encounter death (*πειράζουσιν δὲ αὐτὸν οἱ τῆς ἐκείνου μερίδος ὄντες*), which they bring upon themselves as a result of their sins. Robertson Smith (*Expositor*[2], iii. pp. 76 f.) suggests another explanation, viz., that Jesus removes the fear of death by acting as our Highpriest, since (cp. Nu 18[5]) the OT priests were responsible for averting death from the people, "the fear of death" being "specially connected with the approach of an impure worshipper before God." This certainly paves the way for v.[17], but it does not explain the allusion to the devil, for the illustration of Zech 3[5f.] is too remote.

Corroborations of this idea are to be found in more quarters than one. (*a*) There is the rabbinic notion that the angel of death has the power of inflicting death, according to Pes. Kahana, 32. 189*b*; Mechilta, 72*a* on Ex 20[20] (where Ps 82[6] is applied to Israel at Sinai, since obedience to the Torah would have exempted them from the power of the angel of death), the angel of death being identified with the devil. (*b*) There is also the apocalyptic hope that messiah at the end would crush the power of the devil, a hope expressed in the second-century conclusion (Freer-Codex) to Mark, where the risen Christ declares that "the limit (or term, ὁ ὅρος) of years for Satan's power has now expired." (*c*) Possibly the author assumed and expanded Paul's view of death as the divine punishment for sin executed by the devil, and of Christ's death as a satisfaction which, by removing this curse of the law, did away with the devil's hold on sinful mortals. Theodoret's explanation (*Dial.* iii.) is that the sinlessness of Christ's human nature freed human nature from sin, which the devil had employed to enslave men: ἐπειδὴ γὰρ τιμωρία τῶν ἁμαρτηκότων ὁ θάνατος ἦν, τὸ δὲ σῶμα τὸ Κυριακὸν οὐκ ἔχον ἁμαρτίας κηλῖδα ὃ παρὰ τὸν θεῖον νόμον ὁ θάνατος ἀδίκως ἐξήρπασεν, ἀνέστησε μὲν πρῶτον τὸ παρανόμως κατασχεθέν· ἔπειτα δὲ καὶ τοῖς ἐνδίκως καθειργμένοις ὑπέσχετο τὴν ἀπαλλαγήν.

The force of the paradox in **διὰ τοῦ θανάτου** (to which the Armenian version needlessly adds αὐτοῦ) is explained by Chrysostom: δι' οὗ ἐκράτησεν ὁ διάβολος, διὰ τούτου ἡττήθη. As the essence of σωτηρία is life, its negative aspect naturally involves emancipation from death. Ἔχειν τὸ κράτος τοῦ θανάτου means to wield the power of death, *i.e.* to have control of death. ἔχειν τὸ κράτος with the genitive in Greek denoting lordship in a certain sphere, *e.g.* Eurip. *Helena*, 68 (τίς τῶνδ' ἐρυμνῶν δωμάτων ἔχει κράτος;). **Ἀπαλλάξῃ** goes with δουλείας (as in Joseph. *Ant.* 13. 13 (363), τῆς ὑπὸ τοῖς ἐχθροῖς αὐτοὺς δουλείας . . . ἀπαλλάττειν, etc.), which is thrown to the end of the sentence for emphasis, after ὅσοι . . . ἦσαν which qualifies τούτους. Ἔνοχοι is a passive adjective, equivalent to ἐνεχόμενοι, "bound by" (as in Demosthenes, 1229), and goes with φόβῳ θανάτου, which is not a causal dative. Ὅσοι in Hellenistic Greek is no more than the ordinary relative οἵ. **Διὰ παντὸς τοῦ ζῆν**, not simply in old age, as Musonius (ed. Hense, xvii.) thinks: καὶ τό γε ἀθλιώτατον ποιοῦν τὸν βίον τοῖς γέρουσιν αὐτὸ ἐστὶν, ὁ τοῦ θανάτου φόβος. Aristeas (130, 141, 168) uses δι' ὅλου τοῦ ζῆν, but διὰ παντὸς τοῦ ζῆν is an unparalleled (in NT Greek) instance of an attribute in the same case being added to the infinitive with a preposition. There is a classical parallel in the Platonic διὰ παντὸς τοῦ εἶναι (*Parmenides*, 152 E); but τὸ ζῆν had already come to be equivalent to ὁ βίος.

The enslaving power of fear in general is described by Xenophon in the *Cyropaedia*, iii. 1. 23 f.: οἴει οὖν τι μᾶλλον καταδουλοῦσθαι ἀνθρώπους τοῦ ἰσχυροῦ φόβου; . . . οὕτω πάντων τῶν δεινῶν ὁ φόβος μάλιστα καταπλήττει τὰς ψυχάς. Here it is the fear of death, or rather of what comes after death, which is described. The Greek protest against the fear of death (cp. Epict. iii. 36. 28), as unworthy of the wise and good, is echoed by Philo (*quod omnis probus liber*, 3, ἐπαινεῖται παρά τισιν ὁ τρίμετρον ἐκεῖνο ποιήσας· "τίς ἐστι δοῦλος, τοῦ θανεῖν ἄφροντις ὤν;" ὡς μάλα συνιδὼν τὸ ἀκόλουθον. Ὑπέλαβε γάρ, ὅτι οὐδὲν οὕτω δουλοῦσθαι πέφυκε διάνοιαν, ὡς τὸ ἐπὶ θανάτῳ δέος, ἕνεκα τοῦ πρὸς τὸ ζῆν ἱμέρου). But the fear persisted, as we see from writers like Seneca ("optanda mors est sine metu mortis mori," *Troades*, 869) and Cicero; the latter deals with the fear of death in *De Finibus*, v. 11, as an almost universal emotion ("fere sic afficiuntur omnes"). Lucretius as a rationalist had denounced it magnificently in the *De Rerum Natura*, which "is from end to end a passionate argument against the fear of death and the superstition of which it was the basis. The fear which he combated was not the fear of annihilation, but one with which the writer of this Epistle could sympathize, the fear of what might come after death; 'aeternas quoniam poenas in morte timendum est' (i. 111)" (Wickham). The fear of death as death (cp. Harnack's *History of Dogma*, iii. 180) has been felt even by strong Christians like Dr. Johnson. But our author has more in view. Seneca's epistles, for example, are thickly strewn with counsels against the fear of death; he remonstrates with Lucilius on the absurdity of it, discusses the legitimacy of suicide, if things come to the worst, points out that children and lunatics have no such fear (*Ep.* xxxvi. 12), and anticipates most of the modern arguments against this terror. Nevertheless, he admits that it controls human life to a remarkable extent, even though it is the thought of death, not death itself, that we dread (*Ep.* xxx. 17); he confesses that if you take anyone, young, middle-aged, or elderly, "you will find them equally afraid of death" (xxii. 14). And his deepest consolation is that death cannot be a very serious evil, because it is the last evil of all ("quod extremum est," *Ep.* iv. 3). Now the author of Πρὸς Ἑβραίους sees more beyond death than Seneca. "After death, the judgment." The terror which he notes in men is inspired by the fact that death is not the final crisis (9^{27}). "Ultra (*i.e.* post mortem) neque curae neque gaudio locum esse," said Sallust. It was because a primitive Christian did see something "ultra mortem," that he was in fear, till his hope reassured him (9^{28}).

It is noteworthy that here (vv.[14. 15]) and elsewhere our author, not unlike the other *διδάσκαλος* who wrote the epistle of James, ignores entirely the idea of the devil as the source of temptation; he does not even imply the conception of the devil, as 1 Peter does, as the instigator of persecution.

In one of his terse parentheses the writer now (v.[16]) adds, **οὐ γὰρ δήπου ἀγγέλων ἐπιλαμβάνεται.** *Δήπου* is the classical term for "it need hardly be said" or "of course," and *ἐπιλαμβάνεσθαι* means "to succour" (Sir 4^{11} *ἡ σοφία υἱοὺς ἑαυτῇ ἀνύψωσεν, καὶ ἐπιλαμβάνεται τῶν ζητούντων αὐτήν*). If it meant "seize" or "grip," *θάνατος* (*i.e.* either death, or the angel of death, cp. v.[14]) might be taken as the nominative, the verse being still a parenthesis. This idea, favoured by some moderns, seems to lie behind the Syriac version (cp. A. Bonus, *Expository Times*, xxxiii. pp. 234–236); but *ἐπιλαμβάνεσθαι* here corresponds to βοηθῆσαι in v.[18], and is used in the same good sense as in the other quotation in 8[9]. The words ἀλλὰ σπέρματος Ἀβραὰμ ἐπιλαμβάνεται may be a reminiscence of Is 41[8. 9] where God reassures Israel: σπέρμα Ἀβραὰμ . . . οὗ ἀντελαβόμην. The archaic phrase was perhaps chosen, instead of a term like ἀνθρώπων,[1] on account of Abraham's position as the father of the faithful (see 11[8f.]). Paul had already claimed it as a title for all Christians, irrespective of their birth: οὐκ ἔνι Ἰουδαῖος οὐδὲ Ἕλλην . . . εἰ δὲ ὑμεῖς Χριστοῦ, ἄρα τοῦ Ἀβραὰμ σπέρμα ἐστέ (Gal 3[28. 29]), and our author likes these archaic, biblical periphrases. He repeats ἐπιλαμβάνεται after Ἀβραάμ to make a rhetorical antistrophe (see Introd. p. lvii).

It is a warning against the habit of taking the Greek fathers as absolute authorities for the Greek of Πρὸς Ἑβραίους, that they never suspected the real sense of ἐπιλαμβάνεται here. To them it meant "appropriates" (the nature of). When Castellio (Chatillon), the sixteenth century scholar, first pointed out the true meaning, Beza pleasantly called his opinion a piece of cursed impudence ("execranda Castellionis audacia qui ἐπιλαμβάνεται convertit 'opitulatur,' non modo falsa sed etiam inepta interpretatione"). The mere fact that the Greek fathers and the versions missed the point of the word is a consideration which bears, *e.g.*, upon the interpretation of a word like ὑπόστασις in 3[14] and 11[1].

The thought of vv.[14. 15] is now resumed in v.[17]; ὅθεν (a particle never used by Paul) ὤφειλεν (answering to ἔπρεπεν) κατὰ πάντα (emphatic by position) τοῖς ἀδελφοῖς ὁμοιωθῆναι—resembling them in reality, as one brother resembles another (so *Test. Naphtali* 1[8] ὅμοιός μου ἦν κατὰ πάντα Ἰωσήφ). In what follows, ἐλεήμων[2] is put first for emphasis (as the writer is about to speak of this first), and goes like πιστός with ἀρχιερεύς. "Quae verba sic interpretor: ut misericors esset, ideoque fidelis," Calvin argues. But this sequence of thought is not natural; loyalty to God's purpose no doubt involved compassion for men, but Christ was πίστος as he endured stedfastly the temptations incurred in his τελείωσις as ἀρχηγός. He suffered, but he never swerved in his vocation. Nor can πιστός here mean "reliable" (Seeberg, *Der Tod Christi*, 17), *i.e.* reliable because merciful; the idea of his sympathy as an encouragement to faith is otherwise put (cp. 4[14f.] 12[1f.]). The idea of τελειῶσαι in v.[10] is being explicitly stated; the sufferings of Christ on earth had a reflex influence upon himself as Saviour, fitting him for the proper discharge of his vocation. But the vocation is described from a new angle of vision; instead of ἀρχηγός or ὁ ἁγιάζων, Jesus is suddenly (see Introd. p. xxv) called ἀρχιερεύς,

[1] Cosmas Indicopleustes correctly interpreted the phrase: τουτέστι σώματος καὶ ψυχῆς λογικῆς (372 B).

[2] The seer in Enoch 40[1-10] has a vision of the four angels who intercede for Israel before God; the first is "Michael, the merciful and longsuffering."

evidently a term familiar to the readers (ἀρχιερέα τῆς ὁμολογίας ἡμῶν, 3[2]). The prestige of the highpriest in the later Judaism is plain in rabbinic (e.g. *Berachoth*, *Joma*) tradition and also in apocalyptic. The Maccabean highpriests assumed the title of ἱερεὺς τοῦ θεοῦ τοῦ ὑψίστου (Ass. Mosis, 6[1]; Jubilees, 32[1]), and the ritual of the day of atonement, when he officiated on behalf of the people, was invested with a special halo. This is the point of the allusion here, to the ἀρχιερεύς expiating the sins of the people. Philo had already used the metaphor to exalt the functions of his Logos as a mediator: ὁ δ' αὐτὸς ἱκέτης μέν ἐστι τοῦ θνητοῦ κηραίνοντος ἀεὶ πρὸς τὸ ἄφθαρτον, πρεσβευτὴς δὲ τοῦ ἡγεμόνος πρὸς τὸ ὑπήκοον (*quis rerum div. heres*, 42). But, while the term ἱκέτης does imply some idea of intercession, this is not prominent in Philo's cosmological and metaphysical scheme, as it is in our epistle, which carefully avoids the Philonic idea that men can propitiate God (βούλεται γὰρ αὐτὸν ὁ νόμος μείζονος μεμοιρᾶσθαι φύσεως ἢ κατ' ἄνθρωπον, ἐγγυτέρω προσιόντα τῆς θείας, μεθόριον, εἰ δεῖ τἀληθὲς λέγειν, ἀμφοῖν, ἵνα διὰ μέσου τινὸς ἄνθρωποι μὲν ἱλασκῶνται θεὸν, θεὸς δὲ τὰς χάριτας ἀνθρώποις ὑποδιακόνῳ τινὶ χρώμενος ὀρέγῃ καὶ χορηγῇ, *De Spec. Leg.* i. 12). Again, Philo explains (*de sacerdot.* 12) that the highpriest was forbidden to mourn, when a relative died, ἵνα . . . κρείττων οἴκτου γενόμενος, ἄλυπος εἰς ἀεὶ διατελῇ. This freedom from the ordinary affections of humanity was part of his nearer approximation to the life of God (ἐγγυτέρω προσιόντα τῆς θείας [φύσεως]). But our author looks at the function of Christ as ἀρχιερεύς differently; the first word to be used about him in this connexion is ἐλεήμων, and, before passing on to develop the idea of πιστός, the writer adds (v.[18]) another word upon the practical sympathy of Christ. In resembling his ἀδελφοὶ κατὰ παντά Christ πέπονθεν πειρασθείς. His death had achieved for them an emancipation from the dread of death (v.[14]); by entering into glory he had expiated the sins of God's People, thereby securing for them a free and intimate access to God. But the process by means of which he had thus triumphed was also of value to men; it gave him the experience which enabled him by sympathy to enter into the position of those who are tempted as he was, and to furnish them with effective help. The connexion between v.[18] (with its γάρ) and v.[17] does not rest upon the idea of Christ as ἐλεήμων καὶ πιστὸς ἀρχιερεύς, as though the effective help received from Christ were a constant proof that he expiates sins, *i.e.* maintains us in the favour and fellowship of God (Seeberg). It rests on the special idea suggested by ἐλεήμων. "His compassion is not mere pity for men racked . . . by pain in itself, however arising; it is compassion for men tempted by sufferings towards sin or unbelief" (A. B.

Davidson). What the writer has specially in mind is the agony in Gethsemane (cp. $5^{7f.}$) as the culminating experience of sorrow caused by the temptation to avoid the fear of death or the cross.

The adverbial accusative **τὰ πρὸς τὸν θεόν** here, as in 5^1, is a fairly common LXX phrase (*e.g.* Ex 4^{16} (of Moses), *σὺ δὲ αὐτῷ ἔσῃ τὰ πρὸς τὸν θεόν*). **Ἱλάσκεσθαι τὰς ἁμαρτίας** is also a LXX phrase, an expression for pardon or expiation, as in Ps 65^4 (*τὰς ἀσεβείας ἡμῶν σὺ ἱλάσῃ*), which never occurs again in the NT. When the verb (middle voice) is used of God's dealings with men, it generally takes the person of the sinner as its object in the dative (as Lk 18^{13}, the only other NT instance of *ἱλάσκεσθαι*) or else sins in the dative (*ταῖς ἁμαρτίαις* is actually read here by A 5. 33. 623. 913, Athan. Chrys. Bentley, etc.). This removal of sins as an obstacle to fellowship with God comes under the function of *ὁ ἁγιάζων*. The thought reappears in 7^{25} and in 1 Jn 2^2 (*καὶ αὐτὸς ἱλασμός ἐστιν*).

ὁ λαός (*τοῦ θεοῦ*) is the writer's favourite biblical expression for the church, from the beginning to the end; he never distinguishes Jews and Gentiles.

The introduction of the *πειρασμοί* of Jesus (v.[18]) is as abrupt as the introduction of the *ἀρχιερεύς* idea, but is thrown out by way of anticipation. **Ἐν ᾧ γάρ** = *ἐν τούτῳ ἐν ᾧ* (causal) or *ὅτι*, explaining not the sphere, but the reason of his "help," **πέπονθεν αὐτὸς πειρασθείς**—the participle defining the *πάσχειν* (a term never applied to Jesus by Paul): he suffered by his temptations, the temptations specially in view being temptations to avoid the suffering that led to the cross. This is the situation of the readers. They are in danger of slipping into apostasy, of giving up their faith on account of the hardships which it involved. **Οἱ** *πειραζόμενοι* are people tempted to flinch and falter under the pressure of suffering. Life is hard for them, and faith as hard if not harder. Courage, the writer cries, Jesus understands; he has been through it all, he knows how hard it is to bear suffering without being deflected from the will of God. Grammatically, the words might also read: "For he himself, having been tempted by what he suffered, is able to help those who are tempted." The sense is really not very different, for the particular temptations in view are those which arise out of the painful experience of having God's will cross the natural inclination to avoid pain. But the *πειρασμοί* of Jesus were not simply due to what he suffered. He was strongly tempted by experiences which were not painful at all—*e.g.* by the remonstrance of Simon Peter at Caesarea Philippi. As Ritschl puts it, "Christ was exposed to temptation simply because a temptation is always bound up with an inclination which is at the outset morally legitimate or permissible. It was the impulse, in itself lawful, of self-preservation which led to Christ's desire to be spared the suffering of death. And this gave rise to a temptation to sin, because the wish collided with his duty in his vocation. Christ, however, did not consent to this temptation. He renounced his self-preservation, because he assented to the Divine disposal of the end of his life as a consequence of his vocation" (*Rechtfertigung u. Versöhnung*, iii. 507; Eng. tr. p. 573). On the suffering that such temptation involved, see below on 5^{8}.

Βοηθεῖν and **ἱλάσκεσθαι ταῖς ἁμαρτίαις** occur side by side in the prayer of Ps 79^{9} (LXX). Are they synonymous here? Is the meaning of τὸ ἱλάσκεσθαι τὰς ἁμαρτίας τοῦ λαοῦ that Christ constantly enables us to overcome the temptations that would keep us at a distance from God or hinder us from being at peace with God? (so, *e.g.*, Kurtz and M'Leod Campbell, *The Nature of the Atonement*, pp. 172–174). The meaning is deeper. The help conveyed by the sympathy of Jesus reaches back to a sacrificial relationship, upon which everything turns. Hence the ideas of **ἐλεήμων** and **πιστός** are now developed, the latter in $3^{1\text{-}6a}$, the former in $4^{14f.}$, 3^{6b}–4^{13} being a practical application of what is urged in $3^{1\text{-}6a}$. But the writer does not work out the thought of Christ as πιστός in connexion with his function as ἀρχιερεύς, even though he mentions the latter term at the outset of his appeal, in which the stress falls on the expiatory work of Christ.

[1] *Holy brothers* (ἅγιοι = οἱ ἁγιαζόμενοι, 2^{11}), *you who participate in a heavenly calling, look at Jesus then* (ὅθεν in the light of what has just been said), *at the apostle and highpriest of our confession;* [2] *he is "faithful" to Him who appointed him. For while "Moses" also was "faithful in every department of God's house,"* [3] *Jesus* (οὗτος, as in 10^{12}) *has been adjudged greater glory* (δόξης) *than* (παρά, as 1^{4}) *Moses, inasmuch as the founder of a house enjoys greater honour* (τιμήν, a literary synonym for δόξην) *than the house itself.* [4] (*Every house is founded by some one, but God is the founder of all.*) [5] *Besides, while "Moses" was "faithful in every department of God's house" as an attendant—by way of witness to the coming revelation—*[6] *Christ is faithful as a son over God's house.*

In v.[2] **ὅλῳ** (om. p^{13} B sah boh Cyr. Amb.) may be a gloss from v.[5]. In v.[3] the emphasis on πλείονος is better maintained by οὗτος δόξης (ℵ A B C D P vt Chrys.) than by δόξης οὗτος (p^{13} K L M 6. 33. 104. 326. 1175. 1288 vg) or by the omission of οὗτος altogether (467 arm Basil). In v.[4] πάντα has been harmonized artificially with 1^{3} 2^{10} by the addition of τά (C^{c} L P Ψ 104. 326. 1175. 1128 Athan.).

For the first time the writer addresses his readers, and as **ἀδελφοὶ ἅγιοι** (only here in NT, for ἁγίοις in 1 Th 5^{27} is a later insertion), **κλήσεως ἐπουρανίου μέτοχοι** (6^{4} etc., cp. Ps 119^{63} μέτοχος ἐγώ εἰμι πάντων τῶν φοβουμένων σε, *Ep. Arist.* 207; *de Mundo*, 401*b*). In Ph 3^{14} the ἄνω κλῆσις is the prize conferred at the end upon Christian faith and faithfulness. Here there may be a side allusion to 2^{11} (ἀδελφοὺς αὐτοὺς καλεῖν). In **κατανοήσατε** (a verb used in this general sense by *Ep. Aristeas*, 3, πρὸς τὸ περιέργως τὰ θεῖα κατανοεῖν) κτλ., the writer summons his readers to consider Jesus as πιστός; but, instead of explaining why or how Jesus was loyal to God, he uses this quality to bring out two respects (the first in vv.$^{2a-4}$, the second in vv.$^{5-6a}$) in which Jesus outshone Moses, the divinely-commissioned leader and lawgiver of the People in far-off days, although there is no tone of disparagement in the comparison with Moses, as in the comparison with the angels.

In the description of Jesus as **τὸν ἀπόστολον καὶ ἀρχιερέα τῆς ὁμολογίας ἡμῶν**, ὁμολογία is almost an equivalent for "our religion," as in 4^{14} (cp. 10^{23}).[1] Through the sense of a vow (LXX) or of a legal agreement (papyri and inscriptions), it had naturally passed into the Christian vocabulary as a term for the common and solemn confession or creed of faith. Ἡμῶν is emphatic. In "*our* religion" it is Jesus who is ἀπόστολος καὶ ἀρχιερεύς, not Moses. This suits the context better than to make the antithesis one between the law and the gospel (Theophyl. οὐ γὰρ τῆς κατὰ νόμον λατρείας ἀρχιερεύς ἐστιν, ἀλλὰ τῆς ἡμετέρας πίστεως). Possibly the writer had in mind the Jewish veneration for Moses which found expression during the second century in a remark of rabbi Jose ben Chalafta upon this very phrase from Numbers (Sifre, § 110): "God calls Moses 'faithful in all His house,' and thereby he ranked higher than the ministering angels themselves." The use of **ἀπόστολος** as an epithet for Jesus shows "the fresh creative genius of the writer and the unconventional nature of his style" (Bruce). Over half a century later, Justin (in *Apol.* 1^{12}) called Jesus Christ τοῦ πατρὸς πάντων καὶ δεσπότου θεοῦ υἱὸς καὶ ἀπόστολος ὤν, and in *Apol.* 1^{63} described him as ἄγγελος καὶ ἀπόστολος· αὐτὸς γὰρ ἀπαγγέλλει ὅσα δεῖ γνωσθῆναι, καὶ ἀποστέλλεται, μηνύσων ὅσα ἀγγέλλεται (the connexion of thought here possibly explains the alteration of διηγήσομαι into ἀπαγγελῶ in He 2^{12}). Naturally Jesus was rarely called ἄγγελος; but it was all the easier for our author to call Jesus ἀπόστολος, as he avoids the term in its ecclesiastical sense (cp. 2^3). For him it carries the usual associations of authority; ἀπόστολος is Ionic for πρεσβευτής, not a mere envoy, but an ambassador or representative sent with powers, authorized to speak in the name of the person who has dispatched him. Here the allusion is to 2^3, where the parallel is with the Sinaitic legislation, just as the allusion to Jesus as **ἀρχιερεύς** recalls the ὁ ἁγιάζων of $2^{11.\,17}$. On the other hand, it is not so clear that any explicit antithesis to Moses is implied in ἀρχιερέα, for, although Philo had invested Moses with

[1] Had it not been for these other references it might have been possible to take τ. ὁ. ἡ. here as = "whom we confess." The contents of the ὁμολογία are suggested in the beliefs of $6^{1f.}$, which form the fixed principles and standards of the community, the Truth (10^{26}) to which assent was given at baptism.

highpriestly honour (*praem. et poen.* 9, τυγχάνει . . . ἀρχιερωσύνης, *de vita Mosis*, ii. 1, ἐγένετο γὰρ προνοίᾳ θεοῦ . . . ἀρχιερεύς), this is never prominent, and it is never worked out in "Hebrews."

The reason why they are to look at Jesus is (v.[2]) his faithfulness **τῷ ποιήσαντι αὐτόν**, where ποιεῖν means "to appoint" to an office (as 1 S 12[6] κύριος ὁ ποιήσας τὸν Μωυσῆν καὶ τὸν Ἀαρών, Mk 3[14] καὶ ἐποίησεν δώδεκα). This faithfulness puts him above Moses for two reasons. First (vv.[2b-4]), because he is the founder of the House or Household of God, whereas Moses is part of the House. The text the writer has in mind is Nu 12[7] (οὐχ οὕτως ὁ θεράπων μου Μωυσῆς· ἐν ὅλῳ τῷ οἴκῳ μου πιστός ἐστιν), and the argument of v.[3], where **οἶκος**, like our "house," includes the sense of household or family,[1] turns on the assumption that Moses belonged to the οἶκος in which he served so faithfully. How Jesus "founded" God's household, we are not told. But there was an οἶκος θεοῦ before Moses, as is noted later in 11[2. 25], a line of πρεσβύτεροι who lived by faith; and their existence is naturally referred to the eternal Son. The founding of the Household is part and parcel of the creation of the τὰ πάντα (1[2. 3]). **Κατασκευάζειν** includes, of course (see 9[2. 6]), the arrangement of the **οἶκος** (cp. Epict. i. 6. 7–10, where κατασκευάζω is similarly used in the argument from design). The author then adds an edifying aside, in v.[4], to explain how the οἶκος was God's (v.[2] αὐτοῦ), though Jesus had specially founded it. It would ease the connexion of thought if **θεός** meant (as in 1[8]?) "divine" as applied to Christ (so, *e.g.*, Cramer, M. Stuart), or if οὗτος could be read for θεός, as Blass actually proposes. But this is to rewrite the passage. Nor can we take **αὐτοῦ** in v.[6a] as "Christ's"; there are not two Households, and πᾶς (v.[4]) does not mean "each" (so, *e.g.*, Reuss). Αὐτοῦ in vv.[2. 5] and [6a] must mean "God's." He as creator is ultimately responsible for the House which, under him, Jesus founded and supervises.

This was a commonplace of ancient thought. Justin, *e.g.*, observes: Μενάνδρῳ τῷ κωμικῷ καὶ τοῖς ταῦτα φήσασι ταὐτὰ φράζομεν· μείζονα γὰρ τὸν δημιουργὸν τοῦ σκευαζομένου ἀπεφήνατο (*Apol.* 1[20]). It had been remarked by Philo (*De Plant.* 16): ὅσῳ γὰρ ὁ κτησάμενος τὸ κτῆμα τοῦ κτήματος ἀμείνων καὶ τὸ πεποιηκὸς τοῦ γεγονότος, τοσούτῳ βασιλικώτεροι ἀκεῖνοι, and in *Legum Allegor.* iii. 32 he argues that just as no one would ever suppose that a furnished mansion had been completed ἄνευ τέχνης καὶ δημιουργοῦ, so anyone entering and studying the universe ὥσπερ εἰς μεγίστην οἰκίαν ἢ πόλιν would naturally conclude that ἦν καὶ ἔστιν ὁ τοῦδε τοῦ παντὸς δημιουργὸς ὁ θεός.

The usual way of combining the thought of v.[4] with the context is indicated by Lactantius in proving the unity of the Father and the Son (*diuin. instit.* iv. 29): "When anyone has a son of whom he is specially fond (quem unice diligat), a son who is still in the house and under his father's authority (in manu patris)—he may grant him the name and power of lord (nomen

---

[1] Our author avoids (see on 2[12]) ἐκκλησία, unlike the author of 1 Ti 3[15] who writes ἐν οἴκῳ θεοῦ, ἥτις ἐστὶν ἐκκλησία τοῦ θεοῦ.

domini potestatemque), yet by civil law (civili iure) the house is one, and one is called lord. So this world is one house of God, and the Son and the Father, who in harmony (unanimos) dwell in the world, are one God."

The second ($^{5-6a}$) proof of the superiority of Jesus to Moses is now introduced by *καί*. It rests on the term **θεράπων** used of Moses in the context (as well as in Nu 11^{11} $12^{7.8}$ etc.; of Moses and Aaron in Wis 10^{16} 18^{21}); *θεράπων* is not the same as *δοῦλος*, but for our author it is less than *υἱός*, and he contrasts Moses as the *θεράπων ἐν τῷ οἴκῳ* with Jesus as the Son *ἐπὶ τὸν οἶκον*, *ἐπί* used as in 10^{21} (*ἱερέα μέγαν ἐπὶ τὸν οἶκον τοῦ θεοῦ*) and Mt $25^{21.23}$ (*ἐπὶ ὀλίγα ἦς πιστός*). Moses is "egregius domesticus fidei tuae" (Aug. *Conf.* xii. 23). The difficult phrase **εἰς τὸ μαρτύριον τῶν λαληθησομένων** means, like 9^9, that the position of Moses was one which pointed beyond itself to a future and higher revelation; the tabernacle was a *σκήνη τοῦ μαρτυρίου* (Nu 12^5) in a deep sense. This is much more likely than the idea that the faithfulness of Moses guaranteed the trustworthiness of anything he said, or even that Moses merely served to bear testimony of what God revealed from time to time (as if the writer was thinking of the words *στόμα κατὰ στόμα λαλήσω αὐτῷ* which follow the above-quoted text in Numbers).

The writer now passes into a long appeal for loyalty, which has three movements (3^{6b-19} 4^{1-10} 4^{11-13}). The first two are connected with a homily on Ps 95^{7-11} as a divine warning against the peril of apostasy, the story of Israel after the exodus from Egypt being chosen as a solemn instance of how easy and fatal it is to forfeit privilege by practical unbelief. It is a variant upon the theme of $2^{2.3}$, suggested by the comparison between Moses and Jesus, but there is no comparison between Jesus and Joshua; for although the former opens up the Rest for the People of to-day, the stress of the exhortation falls upon the unbelief and disobedience of the People in the past.

6 *Now we are this house of God* (οὗ, from the preceding αὐτοῦ), *if we will only keep confident and proud of our hope.* 7 *Therefore, as the holy Spirit says*:
"*Today, when* (ἐάν, as in 1 Jn 2^{28}) *you hear his voice,*
8 *harden not* (μὴ σκληρύνητε, aor. subj. of negative entreaty) *your hearts as at the Provocation,*
on the day of the Temptation in the desert,
9 *where* (οὗ = ὅπου as Dt 8^{15}) *your fathers put me to the proof,*
10 *and for forty years felt what I could do.*"
Therefore "*I grew exasperated with that generation,*
I said, '*They are always astray in their heart*';
they would not learn my ways;
11 *so* (ὡς consecutive) *I swore in my anger*
'*they shall never* (εἰ = the emphatic negative אם in oaths) *enter my Rest.*'"
12 *Brothers, take care in case there is a wicked, unbelieving heart in any of you, moving you to apostatize from the living God.* 13 *Rather admonish one another* (ἑαυτούς = ἀλλήλους) *daily, so long as this word* "*Today*" *is uttered, that none of you may be deceived by sin and* "*hardened.*" 14 *For we only*

participate in Christ provided that we keep firm to the very end the confidence with which we started, [15] *this word ever sounding in our ears:*

"*Today, when you hear his voice,*
harden not your hearts as at the Provocation."

[16] *Who heard and yet "provoked" him? Was it not all who left Egypt under the leadership of Moses?* [17] *And with whom was he exasperated for forty years? Was it not with those who sinned, whose "corpses*[1] *fell in the desert"?* [18] *And to whom "did he swear that they* (*sc.* αὐτούς) *would never enter his Rest"? To whom but those who disobeyed* (ἀπειθήσασιν, cp. Ac 19[9])? [19] *Thus* (καί consecutive) *we see it was owing to unbelief that they could not enter.*

In v.[6] (*a*) οὗ is altered into ὅς by D* M 6. 424 Lat Lucifer, Ambr. Priscillian, probably owing to the erroneous idea that the definite article (supplied by 440. 2005) would have been necessary between οὗ and οἶκος. (*b*) ἐάν is assimilated to the text of v.[14] by a change to ἐάνπερ in ℵ^c A C D^c K L W syr^{hkl} Lucifer, Chrys. etc. (von Soden). (*c*) After ἐλπίδος the words μέχρι τέλους βεβαίαν are inserted from v.[14] by a number of MSS; the shorter, correct text is preserved in p^{13} B 1739 sah eth Lucifer, Ambrose.

V.[6b] introduces the appeal, by a transition from [6a]. When Philo claims that παρρησία is the mark of intelligent religion (*quis rer. div. haeres*, 4, τοῖς μὲν οὖν ἀμαθέσι συμφέρον ἡσυχία, τοῖς δὲ ἐπιστήμης ἐφιεμένοις καὶ ἅμα φιλοδεσπότοις ἀναγκαιότατον ἡ παρρησία κτῆμα), he means by παρρησία the confidence which is not afraid to pray aloud: cp. *ib.* 5 (παρρησία δὲ φιλίας συγγενές, ἐπεὶ πρὸς τίνα ἄν τις ἢ πρὸς τὸν ἑαυτοῦ φίλον παρρησιάσαιτο;), where the prayers and remonstrances of Moses are explained as a proof that he was God's friend. But here as elsewhere in the NT παρρησία has the broader meaning of "confidence" which already appears in the LXX (*e.g.* in Job 27[10] μὴ ἔχει τινὰ παρρησίαν ἐναντίον αὐτοῦ). This confidence is the outcome of the Christian ἐλπίς (for τῆς ἐλπίδος goes with τὴν παρρησίαν as well as with τὸ καύχημα); here as in 4[16] and 10[19. 35] it denotes the believing man's attitude to a God whom he knows to be trustworthy. The idea of τὸ καύχημα τῆς ἐλπίδος is exactly that of Ro 5[2] (καυχώμεθα ἐπ' ἐλπίδι τῆς δόξης τοῦ θεοῦ), and of a saying like Ps 5[12] (καὶ εὐφρανθήτωσαν ἐπὶ σοὶ πάντες οἱ ἐλπίζοντες ἐπὶ σέ).

Διό in v.[7] goes most naturally with **μὴ σκληρύνητε** (v.[8]), the thought of which recurs in v.[13] as the central thread. The alternative, to take it with **βλέπετε** in v.[12], which turns the whole quotation into a parenthesis, seems to blunt the direct force of the admonition; it makes the parenthesis far too long, and empties the second **διό** of its meaning. **βλέπετε** is no more abrupt in v.[12] than in 12[25]; it introduces a sharp, sudden warning, without any particle like οὖν or δέ, and requires no previous term like διό. The quotation is introduced as in 10[15] by "the holy Spirit" as the Speaker, a rabbinic idea of inspiration. The quotation itself is from Ps 95[7-11] which in A runs as follows:

[1] κῶλα in this sense is from Nu 14[29. 32], a passage which the writer has in mind.

σήμερον ἐὰν τῆς φωνῆς αὐτοῦ ἀκούσητε,
 μὴ σκληρύνητε τὰς καρδίας ὑμῶν ὡς ἐν τῷ παραπικρασμῷ
 κατὰ τὴν ἡμέραν τοῦ πειρασμοῦ ἐν τῇ ἐρήμῳ·
οὗ ἐπείρασαν[1] οἱ πατέρες ὑμῶν,
 ἐδοκίμασαν με καὶ ἴδον τὰ ἔργα μου.
τεσσεράκοντα ἔτη προσώχθισα τῇ γενεᾷ ἐκείνῃ,[2]
 καὶ εἶπον·[3] ἀεὶ[4] πλανῶνται τῇ καρδίᾳ,
 αὐτοὶ δὲ οὐκ ἔγνωσαν τὰς ὁδούς μου.
ὡς ὤμοσα ἐν τῇ ὀργῇ μου,
 εἰ εἰσελεύσονται εἰς τὴν κατάπαυσίν μου.

In vv.$^{9. 10}$, though he knew (v.^{17}) the correct connexion of the LXX (cp. v.^{17a}), he alters it here for his own purpose, taking **τεσσαράκοντα ἔτη** with what precedes instead of with what follows, inserting διό (which crept into the text of R in the psalm) before **προσώχθισα** for emphasis, and altering **ἐδοκίμασαν** *με* into ἐν δοκιμασίᾳ.[5] The LXX always renders the place-names "Meriba" and "Massa" by generalizing moral terms, here by παραπικρασμός and πειρασμός, the former only here in the LXX (Aquila, 1 Sam 15^{33}; Theodotion, Prov 17^{11}). The displacement of **τεσσεράκοντα ἔτη** was all the more feasible as **εἶδον** τὰ ἔργα μου meant for him the experience of God's punishing indignation. (**Τεσσαράκοντα** is better attested than τεσσεράκοντα (Moulton, ii. 66) for the first century.) There is no hint that the writer was conscious of the rabbinic tradition, deduced from this psalm, that the period of messiah would last for forty years, still less that he had any idea of comparing this term with the period between the crucifixion and 70 A.D. What he really does is to manipulate the LXX text in order to bring out his idea that the entire forty years in the desert were a "day of temptation,"[6] during which the People exasperated God. Hence (in v.^{9}) he transfers the "forty years" to **εἶδον τὰ ἔργα** *μου*, in order to emphasize the truth that the stay of the People in the desert was one long provocation of God; for εἶδον τὰ ἔργα μου is not an aggravation of their offence

[1] ℵ^{ca} adds με (so T), which has crept (needlessly, for πειράζειν may be used absolutely as in 1 Co 10^{9}) into the text of Hebrews through ℵ^{c} D^{c} M vg pesh harkl boh arm Apollin.

[2] In some texts of Hebrews (p^{13} ℵ A B D* M 33. 424** vg Clem. Apollin.) this becomes (under the influence of the literal view of forty years?) ταύτῃ (ἐκείνῃ in C D^{c} K L P syr sah boh arm eth Eus. Cyril, Chrys.).

[3] The Ionic form εἶπα (B) has slipped into some texts of Hebrews (A D 33. 206. 489. 1288. 1518. 1836).

[4] The LXX is stronger than the Hebrew; it appears to translate not the עם of the MT, but עלם (cp. Flashar in *Zeits. für alt. Wiss.*, 1912, 84–85).

[5] ἐδοκίμασαν (με) is read in the text of Hebrews, by assimilation, in ℵ^{c} D^{c} K L vg syr arm eth Apollin. Lucifer, Ambr. Chrys. etc. *i.e.* Ε̄ΔΟΚΙ-ΜΑCΙΑ was altered into ΕΔΟΚΙΜΑCᾹ.

[6] The κατά in κατὰ τὴν ἡμέραν (v.^{8}) is temporal as in 1^{10} 7^{27}, not "after the manner of" ("secundum," vg).

("though they felt what I could do for them"), but a reminder that all along God let them feel how he could punish them for their disobedience. Finally, their long-continued obstinacy led him to exclude them from the land of Rest. This "finally" does not mean that the divine oath of exclusion was pronounced at the end of the forty years in the desert, but that as the result of God's experience he gradually killed off (v.[17]) all those who had left Egypt. This retribution was forced upon him by the conviction αὐτοὶ δὲ οὐκ ἔγνωσαν τὰς ὁδούς μου (*i.e.* would not learn my laws for life, cared not to take my road).

The rabbinic interpretation of Ps 95 as messianic appears in the legend (T.B. *Sanhedrim*, 98*a*) of R. Joshua ben Levi and Elijah. When the rabbi was sent by Elijah to messiah at the gates of Rome, he asked, "*Lord, when comest thou?*" *He answered,* "*To-day.*" *Joshua returned to Elijah, who inquired of him:* "*What said He to thee?*" *Joshua:* "*Peace be with thee, son of Levi.*" *Elijah:* "*Thereby He has assured to thee and thy father a prospect of attaining the world to come.*" *Joshua:* "*But He has deceived me, by telling me He would come to-day.*" *Elijah:* "*Not so, what He meant was, To-day, if you will hear His voice.*" The severe view of the fate of the wilderness-generation also appears in *Sanh.* 110*b*, where it is proved that the generation of the wilderness have no part in the world to come, from Nu 14[35] and also from Ps 95 (*as I swore in my anger that they should not enter into my Rest*). This was rabbi Akiba's stern reading of the text. But rabbinic opinion, as reflected in the Mishna (cp. W. Bacher, *Agada der Tannaiten*[2], i. 135 f.), varied on the question of the fate assigned to the generation of Israelites during the forty years of wandering in the desert. While some authorities took Ps 95[11] strictly, as if the "rest" meant the rest after death, and these Israelites were by the divine oath excluded from the world to come, others endeavoured to minimize the text; God's oath only referred to the incredulous spies, they argued, or it was uttered in the haste of anger and recalled. In defence of the latter milder view Ps 50[5] was quoted, and Isa 35[10]. Our author takes the sterner view, reproduced later by Dante (*Purgatorio*, xviii. 133–135), for example, who makes the Israelites an example of sloth; "the folk for whom the sea opened were dead ere Jordan saw the heirs of promise." He never speaks of men "tempting God," apart from this quotation, and indeed, except in 11[17], God's πειρασμός or probation of men is confined to the human life of Jesus.

For **διό** in v.[10] Clem. Alex. (*Protrept.* 9) reads δι' ὅ. **Προσωχθίζειν** is a LXX term for the indignant loathing excited by some defiance of God's will, here by a discontented, critical attitude towards him. In v.[11] **κατάπαυσις** is used of Canaan as the promised land of settled peace, as only in Dt 12[9] (οὐ γὰρ ἥκατε . . . εἰς τὴν κατάπαυσιν) and 1 K 8[56] (εὐλογητὸς Κύριος σήμερον, ὃς ἔδωκεν κατάπαυσιν τῷ λαῷ αὐτοῦ). The mystical sense is developed in 4[3f.].

The application (vv.[12f.]) opens with **βλέπετε** (for the classical ὁρᾶτε) **μὴ . . . ἔσται** (as in Col 2[8] (βλέπετε μὴ . . . ἔσται), the reason for the future being probably "because the verb εἰμί has no aorist, which is the tense required," Field, *Notes on Translation of N.T.*, p. 38) **ἔν τινι ὑμῶν**—the same concern for individuals as in 4^{11} 10^{25} 12^{15}—καρδία ἀπιστίας (genitive of quality—a Semitism here). Ἀπιστία must mean more than "incredulity"; the assonance with ἀποστῆναι was all the more apt as ἀπιστία denoted the unbelief which issues in action, ἐν τῷ ἀποστῆναι—the idea as in Ezk 20^{8} καὶ ἀπέστησαν ἀπ' ἐμοῦ, καὶ οὐκ ἠθέλησαν εἰσακοῦσαι μου, though the preposition ἀπό was not needed, as may be seen, *e.g.*, in Wis 3^{10} (οἱ . . . τοῦ κυρίου ἀποστάντες). Our author is fond of this construction, the infinitive with a preposition. "The living God" suggests what they lose by their apostasy, and what they bring upon themselves by way of retribution (10^{31}), especially the latter (cp. 4^{12}). There is no real distinction between θεοῦ ζῶντος and τοῦ θεοῦ ζῶντος, for the article could be dropped, as in the case of θεὸς πατήρ and κύριος Ἰησοῦς, once the expression became stamped and current.

In v.[13] παρακαλεῖτε . . . καθ' ἑκάστην ἡμέραν (cp. *Test. Levi* 9^{8} ἦν καθ' ἑκάστην ἡμέραν συνετίζων με) emphasizes the keen, constant care of the community for its members, which is one feature of the epistle. In ἄχρις οὗ (elsewhere in NT with aorist or future), which is not a common phrase among Attic historians and orators, ἄχρις is a Hellenistic form of ἄχρι (p^{13} M) used sometimes when a vowel followed. Σήμερον is "God's instant men call years" (Browning), and the paronomasia in καλεῖται[1] . . . παρακαλεῖτε led the writer to prefer καλεῖται to a term like κηρύσσεται. The period (see 4^{7}) is that during which God's call and opportunity still hold out, and the same idea is expressed in ἐν τῷ λέγεσθαι Σήμερον κτλ. (v.[15]). ἐξ ὑμῶν is sufficiently emphatic as it stands, without being shifted forward before τις (B D K L d e etc. harkl Theodt. Dam.) in order to contrast ὑμεῖς with οἱ πατέρες ὑμῶν (v.[9]). As for ἡ ἁμαρτία, it is the sin of apostasy (12^{4}), which like all sin deceives men (Ro 7^{11}), in this case by persuading them that they will be better off if they allow themselves to abandon the exacting demands of God. The responsibility of their position is expressed in ἵνα μὴ σκληρυνθῇ, a passive with a middle meaning; men can harden themselves or let lower considerations harden them against the call of God. As Clement of Alexandria (*Protrept.* ix.) explains: ὁρᾶτε τὴν ἀπειλήν· ὁρᾶτε τὴν προτροπήν· ὁρᾶτε τὴν τιμήν. τί δὴ οὖν ἔτι τὴν χάριν εἰς ὀργὴν μεταλλάσσομεν . . .; μεγάλη γὰρ τῆς ἐπαγγελίας αὐτοῦ ἡ χάρις, "ἐὰν σήμερον τῆς φωνῆς αὐτοῦ ἀκουσῶμεν"· τὸ δὲ σήμερον τῆς φωνῆς αὐτοῦ αὔξεται τὴν ἡμέραν, ἔστ' ἂν ἡ σήμερον ὀνομάζηται.

In v.[14] μέτοχοι τοῦ Χριστοῦ (which is not an equivalent for the Pauline ἐν Χριστῷ, but rather means to have a personal interest in him) answers to μέτοχοι κλήσεως ἐπουρανίου in v.[1] and to μετόχους πνεύματος ἁγίου in 6^{4}; γεγόναμεν betrays the predilection of the writer for γέγονα rather than its equivalent εἶναι. Ἐάνπερ

[1] The common confusion between αι and ει led to the variant καλεῖτε (A C).

an intensive particle (for ἐάν, v.[6]) τὴν ἀρχὴν τῆς ὑποστάσεως (genitive of apposition)—*i.e.* "our initial confidence" (the idea of 10[32])—**κατάσχωμεν** (echoing v.[6b]). The misinterpretation of **ὑποστάσεως** as (Christ's) "substance"[1] led to the addition of αὐτοῦ (A 588. 623. 1827. 1912 vg). But ὑπόστασις here as in 11[1] denotes a firm, confident conviction or resolute hope (in LXX, *e.g.*, Ru 1[12] ἔστιν μοι ὑπόστασις τοῦ γενηθῆναι με ἀνδρί, rendering תקוה, which is translated by ἐλπίς in Pr 11[7]), with the associations of steadfast patience under trying discouragements. This psychological meaning was already current (cp. 2 Co 9[4] μὴ . . . καταισχυνθῶμεν ἡμεῖς ἐν τῇ ὑποστάσει ταύτῃ), alongside of the physical or metaphysical. What a man bases himself on, as he confronts the future, is his ὑπόστασις, which here in sound and even (by contrast) in thought answers to ἀποστῆναι.

It is possible to regard v.[14] as a parenthesis, and connect **ἐν τῷ λέγεσθαι** (v.[15]) closely with **παρακαλεῖτε** or **ἵνα μὴ . . . ἁμαρτίας** (v.[13]), but this is less natural; ἐν τῷ λέγεσθαι ("while it is said," as in Ps 42[4] ἐν τῷ λέγεσθαι) connects easily and aptly with κατάσχωμεν, and vv.[14. 15] thus carry on positively the thought of v.[13], viz. that the writer and his readers are still within the sound of God's call to his οἶκος to be πιστός.

The pointed questions which now follow (vv.[16-18]) are a favourite device of the diatribe style. **Παραπικραίνειν** (Hesych. παροργίζειν)[2] in v.[16] seems to have been coined by the LXX to express "rebellious" with a further sense of provoking or angering God; *e.g.* Dt 31[27] παραπικραίνοντες ἦτε τὰ πρὸς τὸν θεόν (translating מרה), and Dt 32[16] ἐν βδελύγμασιν αὐτῶν παρεπίκρανάν με (translating כעס). The sense of "disobey" recurs occasionally in the LXX psalter (*e.g.* 104[28], 106[11]); indeed the term involves a disobedience which stirs up the divine anger against rebels, the flagrant disobedience (cp. παραβαίνειν for מרה in Dt 1[43], Nu 27[14]) which rouses exasperation in God. **'Αλλ'**, one rhetorical question being answered by another (as Lk 17[8]), logically presupposes τινές, but τίνες must be read in the previous question. By writing **πάντες** the writer does not stop to allow for the faithful minority, as Paul does (1 Co 10[7f.] τινες αὐτῶν). In the grave conclusion (v.[19]) **δι' ἀπιστίαν** (from v.[12]) is thrown to the end for the sake of emphasis.

But, the author continues (4[1f.]), the promised rest is still available; it is open to faith, though only to faith ([1-3]). No matter how certainly all has been done upon God's part ([3-5]), and no matter how sure some human beings are to share his

[1] Another early error was to regard it as "our substance," so that ἡ ἀρχὴ τῆς ὑποστάσεως meant faith as "the beginning of our true nature" (a view already current in Chrysostom).

[2] In Dt 32[16] it is parallel to παροξύνειν; cp. Flashar's discussion in *Zeitschrift für alt. Wiss.*, 1912, 185 f. It does not always require an object (God).

Rest (v.[6]), it does not follow that *we* shall, unless we take warning by this failure of our fathers in the past and have faith in God. Such is the urgent general idea of this paragraph. But the argument is compressed; the writer complicates it by defining the divine Rest as the sabbath-rest of eternity, and also by introducing an allusion to Joshua. That is, he (*a*) explains God's κατάπαυσις in Ps 95 by the σαββατισμός of Gn 2[2], and then (*b*) draws an inference from the fact that the psalm-promise is long subsequent to the announcement of the σαββατισμός. He assumes that there is only one Rest mentioned, the κατάπαυσις into which God entered when he finished the work of creation, to which οἱ πατέρες ὑμῶν were called under Moses, and to which Christians are now called. They must never lose faith in it, whatever be appearances to the contrary.

[1] *Well then, as the promise of entrance into his Rest is still left to us, let us be afraid of anyone being judged to have missed it.* [2] *For* (καὶ γάρ = etenim) *we have had the good news as well as they* (ἐκεῖνοι = 3[8-19]); *only, the message they heard was of no use to them, because it did not meet with faith in the hearers.* [3] *For we do "enter the Rest" by our faith: according to his word,*

"As I swore in my anger,
they shall never enter my Rest"—

although "his works" were all over by the foundation of the world. [4] *For he says somewhere about the seventh* (*sc.* ἡμέρας) *day: "And God rested from all his works on the seventh day."* [5] *And again in this* (ἐν τούτῳ, *sc.* τόπῳ) *passage, "they shall never enter my Rest."* [6] *Since then it is reserved* (ἀπολείπεται, a variant for καταλειπ. v.[1]) *for some "to enter it," and since those who formerly got the good news failed to "enter" owing to their disobedience,*[1] [7] *he again fixes a day; "today"—as he says in "David" after so long an interval, and as has been already quoted:*

"Today, when you hear his voice,
harden not your hearts."

[8] *Thus if Joshua had given them Rest, God would not speak later about another day. There is a sabbath-Rest, then, reserved* (ἀπολείπεται, as in [6]) *still for the People of God* (*for once "a man enters his* (αὐτοῦ, *i.e.* God's) *rest," he "rests from work" just as God did*).

Ἐπαγγελία (v.[1]) is not common in the LXX, though it mistranslates סִפְרָה in Ps 56[8], and is occasionally the term for a human promise. In the Prayer of Manasseh ([6]) it is the divine promise (τὸ ἔλεος τῆς ἐπαγγελίας σου), and recurs in the plural, of the divine promises, in *Test. Jos.* 20[1] (ὁ θεὸς ποιήσει τὴν ἐκδίκησιν ὑμῶν καὶ ἐπάξει ὑμᾶς εἰς τὰς ἐπαγγελίας τῶν πατέρων ὑμῶν) and Ps. Sol 12[8] (ὅσιοι κυρίου κληρονομήσαιεν ἐπαγγελίας κυρίου—the first occurrence of this phrase κλ. ἐπ., cp. below on 6[12]). **Καταλειπομένης ἐπαγγελίας** (+τῆς D* 255, from 6[15. 17] 11[9]) is a genitive absolute. **Ἐπαγγελίας εἰσελθεῖν** (like ὁρμὴ . . . ὑβρίσαι in Ac 14[5]) κτλ.: the basis of the appeal is (*a*) that the divine promise of Rest has been neither fulfilled nor withdrawn (still τὸ "σήμερον" καλεῖται); and (*b*) that the punishment which befalls

[1] Ἀπείθειαν, altered into ἀπιστίαν by ℵ* vg sah boh arm Cyr.

others is a warning to ourselves (cp. Philo, *ad Gaium*, 1: *αἱ γὰρ ἑτέρων τιμωρίαι βελτιοῦσι τοὺς πολλούς, φόβῳ τοῦ μὴ παραπλήσια παθεῖν*). By a well-known literary device **μή ποτε**, like *μή* in 12[15], takes a present (*δοκῇ*), instead of the more usual aorist, subjunctive. **Δοκῇ** means "judged" or "adjudged," as in Josephus, *Ant.* viii. 32, *κἂν ἀλλότριον δοκῇ*. This is common in the LXX, *e.g.* in Pr 17[28] *ἐνεὸν δέ τις ἑαυτὸν ποιήσας δόξει φρόνιμος εἶναι* (where *δόξει* is paralleled by *λογισθήσεται*), 27[14] (*καταρωμένου οὐδὲν διαφέρειν δόξει*); indeed it is an ordinary Attic use which goes back to Plato (*e.g. Phaedo*, 113 D, of the souls in the under-world, *οἳ μὲν ἂν δόξωσι μέσως βεβιωκέναι*) and Demosthenes (629. 17, *οἱ δεδογμένοι ἀνδροφόνοι* = the convicted murderers). The searching scrutiny which passes this verdict upon lack of faith is the work of the divine Logos (in v.[12]).

In v.[2] **εὐηγγελισμένοι** is remarkable. Our author, who never uses *εὐαγγέλιον* (preferring *ἐπαγγελία* here as an equivalent), employs the passive of *εὐαγγελίζειν*[1] (as in v.[6]) in the broad sense of "having good news brought to one." The passive occurs in LXX of 2 S 18[31] (*εὐαγγελισθήτω ὁ κύριός μου ὁ βασιλεύς*) and in Mt 11[5] (*πτωχοὶ εὐαγγελίζονται*). The *καί* after **καθάπερ** emphasizes as usual the idea of correspondence. The reason for the failure of the past generation was that they merely heard what God said, and did not believe him; **ὁ λόγος τῆς ἀκοῆς** (*ἀκοῆς*, passive = "sermo auditus," vg), which is another (see 3[12]) instance of the Semitic genitive of quality, is defined as **μή** (causal particle as in 11[27] *μὴ φοβηθείς*) **συγκεκ(ε)ρα(σ)μένος τῇ πίστει τοῖς ἀκούσασιν**, since it did not get blended with faith in (the case of) those who heard it. Or *τῇ πίστει* may be an instrumental dative: "since it did not enter vitally into the hearers by means of the faith which it normally awakens in men." The fault lies, as in the parable of the Sower, not with the message but with the hearers. The phrase *λόγος . . . συγκεκρασμένος* may be illustrated from Menander (Stob. *Serm.* 42, p. 302), *τὴν τοῦ λόγου μὲν δύναμιν οὐκ ἐπίφθονον ἤθει δὲ χρηστῷ συγκεκραμένην ἔχειν*, and Plutarch, *non posse suauiter vivi secundum Epicurum*, 1101, *βέλτιον γὰρ ἐνυπάρχειν τι καὶ συγκεκρᾶσθαι τῇ περὶ θεῶν δόξῃ κοινὸν αἰδοῦς καὶ φόβου πάθος κτλ*. The use of *λόγος* with such verbs is illustrated by Plutarch, *Vit. Cleom.* 2 (*ὁ δὲ Στωϊκὸς λόγος . . . βάθει δὲ καὶ πρᾴῳ κεραννύμενος ἤθει μάλιστα εἰς τὸ οἰκεῖον ἀγαθὸν ἐπιδίδωσιν*). *Κρᾶσις* occurs in Philo's definition of *φιλία* (*Quaest. in Gen.* 2[18]) as consisting [*οὐκ*] *ἐν τῷ χρειώδει μᾶλλον ἢ κράσει καὶ συμφωνίᾳ βεβαίῳ τῶν ἠθῶν*, and *συγκεκρᾶσθαι* in his description of the union of spirit and blood in the human body (*Quaest. in Gen.* 9[4] *πνεῦμα . . . ἐμφέρεσθαι καὶ συγκεκρᾶσθαι αἵματι*).

[1] An almost contemporary instance (*εὐαγγελίζοντι τὰ τῆς νείκης αὐτοῦ καὶ προκοπῆς*) of the active verb is cited by Mitteis-Wilcken, i. 2. 29.

The original reading συγκεκ(ε)ρα(σ)μένος (ℵ 114 vt pesh Lucif.) was soon assimilated (after ἐκείνους) into the accusative -ους (p[13] A B C D K L M P vg boh syr[hkl] etc. Chrys. Theod.-Mops. Aug.), and this led to the alteration of τοῖς ἀκούσασιν into τῶν ἀκουσάντων (D* 104. 1611. 2005 d syr[hkl mg] Lucif.), or τοῖς ἀκουσθεῖσιν (1912 vg Theod.-Mops.), or τοῖς ἀκούουσιν (1891). The absence of any allusion elsewhere to the faithful minority (Caleb, Joshua) tells decisively against συγκεκρασμένους ("since they did not mix with the believing hearers"); for the writer (see above) never takes them into account, and, to make any sense, this reading implies them. How could the majority be blamed for not associating with believing hearers when *ex hypothesi* there were none such ?

The writer now (vv.[3-10]) lays emphasis upon the reality of the Rest. "We have had this good news too as well as they," for (γάρ) we believers do enter into God's Rest; it is prepared and open, it has been ready ever since the world began—ἄρα ἀπολείπεται σαββατισμὸς τῷ λαῷ τοῦ θεοῦ. Εἰσερχόμεθα is the emphatic word in v.[3]: "we do (we are sure to) enter," the futuristic present ("ingrediemur," vg). When God excluded that unbelieving generation from his Rest, he was already himself in his Rest. The κατάπαυσις was already in existence; the reason why these men did not gain entrance was their own unbelief, not any failure on God's part to have the Rest ready. Long ago it had been brought into being (this is the force of καίτοι in v.[3]), for what prevents it from being realized is not that any ἔργα of God require still to be done. Κατάπαυσις is the sequel to ἔργα. The creative ἔργα leading up to this κατάπαυσις have been completed centuries ago; God enjoys his κατάπαυσις, and if his People do not, the fault lies with themselves, with man's disbelief.

Here, as in Ro 3[28], there is a choice of reading between οὖν (ℵ A C M 1908 boh) and γάρ (p[13] B D K L P Ψ 6. 33 lat syr[hkl] eth Chrys. Lucif. etc.); the colourless δέ (syr[pesh] arm) may be neglected. The context is decisive in favour of γάρ. Probably the misinterpretation which produced οὖν led to the change of εἰσερχόμεθα into εἰσερχώμεθα[1] (A C 33. 69*: future in vg sah boh Lucif.). The insertion of τήν (the first) may be due to the same interpretation, but not necessarily; p[13] B D* om., but B omits the article sometimes without cause (*e.g.* 7[15]). The omission of εἰ (p[13] D* 2. 330. 440. 623. 642. 1288. 1319. 1912) was due to the following εἰ in εἰσελεύσονται.

Καίτοι (with gen. absol., as *OP.* 898[26]) is equivalent here to καίτοιγε for which it is a *v.l.* in Ac 17[27] (A E, with ptc.). "Καίτοι, ut antiquiores καίπερ, passim cum participio iungunt scriptores aetatis hellenisticae" (Herwerden, *Appendix Lexici Graeci*, 249). Καταβολή is not a LXX term, but appears in *Ep. Aristeas*, 129 and 2 Mac 2[29] (τῆς ὅλης καταβολῆς = the entire edifice); in the NT always, except He 11[11], in the phrase ἀπό or πρὸ καταβολῆς κόσμου.

The writer then (v.[4]) quotes Gn 2[2], inserting ὁ θεὸς ἐν (exactly as Philo had done, *de poster. Caini*, 18), as a proof that the κατά-

[1] A similar error of A C in 6[2].

παυσις had originated immediately after the six days of creation. In **εἴρηκε που** the **που** is another literary mannerism (as in Philo); instead of quoting definitely he makes a vague allusion (cp. 2^6). The psalm-threat is then (v.[5]) combined with it, and (v.[6]) the deduction drawn, that the threat (v.[7]) implies a promise (though not as if v.[1] meant, "lest anyone imagine he has come too late for it"—an interpretation as old as Schöttgen, and still advocated, *e.g.*, by Dods).

The title of the 92nd psalm, "for the sabbath-day," was discussed about the middle of the 2nd century by R. Jehuda and R. Nehemia; the former interpreted it to mean the great Day of the world to come, which was to be one perfect sabbath, but R. Nehemia's rabbinical tradition preferred to make it the seventh day of creation on which God rested (see W. Bacher's *Agada der Tannaiten*[2], i. pp. 328–329). The author of the Epistle of Barnabas (15) sees the fulfilment of Gn 2^2 in the millennium: "he rested on the seventh day" means that "when his Son arrives he will destroy the time of the lawless one, and condemn the impious, and alter sun and moon and stars; then he will really rest on the seventh day," and Christians cannot enjoy their rest till then. Our author's line is different—different even from the Jewish interpretation in the *Vita Adae et Evae* (li. 1), which makes the seventh day symbolize "the resurrection and the rest of the age to come; on the seventh day the Lord rested from all his works."

In v.[7] **μετὰ τοσοῦτον χρόνον**, like **μετὰ ταῦτα** (v.[8]), denotes the interval of centuries between the desert and the psalm of David, for **ἐν Δαυεὶδ** means "in the psalter" (like ἐν Ἠλίᾳ, Ro 11^2); the 95th psalm is headed *αἶνος ᾠδῆς τῷ Δαυείδ* in the Greek bible, but the writer throughout ($3^{7f.}$) treats it as a direct, divine word. **Προείρηται** (the author alluding to his previous quotation) is the original text (p[13] A C D* P 6. 33. 1611. 1908. 2004. 2005 lat syr Chrys. Cyr. Lucif.); *προείρηκεν* (B 256. 263. 436. 442. 999. 1739. 1837 arm sah boh Orig.) suggests that God or David spoke these words before the oath (v.[7] comes before v.[11]!), while *εἴρηται* (D[c] K L eth etc. Theophyl.) is simply a formula of quotation. From the combination of Ps $95^{7.8}$ with Ps 95^{11} and Gn 2^2 (vv.[3-7]) the practical inference is now drawn (v.[8f.]). Like Sirach ($46^{1.2}$ *κραταιὸς ἐν πολέμοις Ἰησοῦς Ναυή . . . ὃς ἐγένετο κατὰ τὸ ὄνομα αὐτοῦ μέγας ἐπὶ σωτηρίᾳ ἐκλεκτῶν αὐτοῦ*), Philo (*de mutatione nominum*, 21, *Ἰησοῦς δὲ* [*ἑρμηνεύεται*] *σωτηρία κυρίου, ἕξεως ὄνομα τῆς ἀρίστης*) had commented on the religious significance of the name Joshua; but our author ignores this, and even uses the name Ἰησοῦς freely, since Ἰησοῦς is never applied by him to Christ before the incarnation (Aquila naturally avoids Ἰησοῦς and prefers Ἰωσουα). The author of Ep. Barnabas plays on the fact that "Joshua" and "Jesus" are the same names: *ἐλπίσατε ἐπὶ τὸν ἐν σαρκὶ μέλλοντα φανεροῦσθαι ὑμῖν Ἰησοῦν* (6^9), *i.e.* not on the "Jesus" who led Israel into the land of rest, but on the true, divine "Joshua." Such, he declares, is the inner meaning of Is 28[16] (ὃς ἐλπίσει ἐπ' αὐτὸν ζήσεται εἰς τὸν αἰῶνα). But the author of Πρὸς Ἑβραίους takes his own line, starting from the transitive use of **καταπαύειν** (Jos 1[13] κύριος ὁ θεὸς ὑμῶν κατέπαυσεν ὑμᾶς καὶ ἔδωκεν ὑμῖν τὴν γῆν ταύτην, etc.); not that he reads subtle meanings into the transitive and intransitive usages of καταπαύειν, like Philo. Nor does he philosophize upon the relevance of κατάπαυσις to God. Philo, in *De Cherubim* (26), explains why Moses calls the sabbath (ἑρμηνεύεται δ' ἀνάπαυσις) the "sabbath of God" in Ex 20[10] etc.; the only thing which really rests is God—"rest (ἀνάπαυλαν) meaning not inactivity in good (ἀπραξίαν καλῶν)—for the cause of all things which is active by nature never ceases doing what is best, but—an energy devoid of laboriousness, devoid of suffering, and moving with absolute ease." The movement and changes of creation point to labour, but "what is free from weakness, even though it moves all things, will never cease to rest: ὥστε οἰκειοτόρατον μόνῳ θεῷ τὸ ἀναπαύεσθαι." So in *De Sacrif. Abelis et Caini*, 8, τὸν τοσοῦτον κόσμον ἄνευ πόνων πάλαι μὲν εἰργάζετο, νυνὶ δὲ καὶ εἰσαεὶ συνέχων οὐδέποτε λήγει [cp. He 1[3] φέρων τε τὰ πάντα], θεῷ γὰρ τὸ ἀκάματον ἁρμοδιώτατον. All such speculations are remote from our author. He simply assumes (*a*) that God's promise of κατάπαυσις is spiritual; it was not fulfilled, it was never meant to be fulfilled, in the peaceful settlement of the Hebrew clans in Canaan; (*b*) as a corollary of this, he assumes that it is eschatological.

In v.[9] **ἄρα**, as in 12[8], Lk 11[48], Ac 11[18], Ro 10[17], is thrown to the beginning by an unclassical turn ("müsste dem gebildeten Hellenen hochgradig anstössig erscheinen," Radermacher, 20). **Σαββατισμός**, apparently[1] a word coined by the writer, is a Semitic-Greek compound. The use of σαββατισμός for **κατάπαυσις** is then (v.[10]) justified in language to which the closest parallel is Apoc 14[13]. "Rest" throughout all this passage—and the writer never refers to it again—is the blissful existence of God's faithful in the next world. As a contemporary apocalyptist put it, in 4 Es 8[52]: "for you paradise is opened, the tree of life planted, the future age prepared, abundance made ready, a City built, a Rest appointed" (κατέσταθη?). In **ἀπὸ τῶν ἰδίων**, as in **διὰ τοῦ ἰδίου αἵματος** (13[12]), ἴδιος is slightly emphatic owing to the context; it is not quite equivalent to the possessive pronoun.

When Maximus of Tyre speaks of life as a long, arduous path to the goal of bliss and perfection, he describes in semi-mystical language how tired souls, longing for the land to which this straight and narrow and little-frequented way leads, at length reach it and "rest from their labour" (*Dissert.* xxiii.).

---

[1] The only classical instance is uncertain; Bernadakis suspects it in the text of Plutarch, *de superstit.* 166 A.

The lesson thus drawn from the reading of the OT passages is pressed home (vv.[11-13]) with a skilful blend of encouragement and warning.

[11] *Let us be eager then to "enter that Rest," in case anyone falls into the same sort of disobedience.* [12] *For the Logos of God is a living thing, active and more cutting than any sword with double edge, penetrating to the very division of soul and spirit, joints and marrow—scrutinizing the very thoughts and conceptions of the heart.* [13] *And no created thing is hidden from him; all things lie open and exposed before the eyes of him with whom we have to reckon* (ὁ λόγος).

In v.[11] the position of **τις**, as, *e.g.*, in Lk 18[18], is due to "the tendency which is to be noted early in Greek as well as in cognate languages, to bring unemphasized (enclitic) pronouns as near to the beginning of the sentence as possible" (Blass, § 473. 1). For **πίπτειν ἐν**, cp. Epict. iii. 22. 48, *πότε ὑμῶν εἶδέν μέ τις . . . ἐν ἐκκλίσει περιπίπτοντα.* This Hellenistic equivalent for *πίπτειν εἰς* goes back to earlier usage, *e.g.* Eurip. *Herc.* 1091, 1092, *ἐν κλύδωνι καὶ φρενῶν ταράγματι πέπτωκα δεινῷ.* In Hellenistic Greek *ὑπόδειγμα* came to have the sense of *παράδειγμα*, and is used here loosely for "kind" or "sort"; take care of falling into disobedience like that of which these *πατέρες ὑμῶν* yield such a tragic example. The writer, with his fondness for periphrases of this kind, writes **ἐν τῷ αὐτῷ ὑποδείγματι τῆς ἀπειθείας**, where *ἐν τῇ αὐτῇ ἀπειθείᾳ* would have served. In passing away from the text about Rest, he drops this last warning reference to the classical example of *ἀπείθεια* in the far past of the People.

The connexion of thought in vv.[11f.] is suggested by what has been already hinted in v.[1], where the writer pled for anxiety, *μή ποτε δοκῇ τις ἐξ ὑμῶν ὑστερηκέναι.* He repeats *ἵνα μὴ . . . τις . . . πέσῃ*, and enlarges upon what lies behind the term *δοκῇ*. Then, after the passage on the relentless scrutiny of the divine Logos, he effects a transition to the direct thought of God (v.[13]), with which the paragraph closes. **Σπουδάσωμεν**—we have to put heart and soul into our religion, for we are in touch with a God whom nothing escapes; **ζῶν γάρ κτλ.** (v.[12]). The term *ζῶν* echoes *θεὸς ζῶν* in 3[12] (men do not disobey God with impunity), just as *καρδίας* echoes *καρδία πονηρὰ ἀπιστίας.* God is swift to mark any departure from his will in human thought—the thought that issues in action.

The personifying of the divine **λόγος**, in a passage which described God in action, had already been attempted. In Wis 18[15], for example, the plagues of Egypt are described as the effect of God's *λόγος* coming into play: *ὁ παντοδύναμός σου λόγος ἀπ' οὐρανῶν . . . ξίφος ὀξὺ τὴν ἀνυπόκριτον ἐπιταγήν σου φέρων.* In Wis 1[6], again, the *φιλάνθρωπον πνεῦμα σοφία*, which cannot tolerate blasphemy, reacts against it: *ὅτι τῶν νεφρῶν αὐτοῦ* (the blasphemer) *μάρτυς ὁ θεός, καὶ τῆς καρδίας αὐτοῦ ἐπίσκοπος ἀληθής,* so that no muttering of rebellion is unmarked. Here the writer poetically personifies the revelation of God for a moment. Ὁ λόγος τοῦ θεοῦ is God speaking, and speaking in words which are charged with doom and promise ($3^{7f.}$). The revelation, however, is broader than the scripture; it includes the revelation of God's purpose in Jesus ($1^{1f.}$). The free application of ὁ λόγος (τοῦ θεοῦ) in primitive Christianity is seen in 1 P $1^{23f.}$, Ja $1^{18f.}$, quite apart from the specific application of the term to the person of Christ (Jn 1^{1-18}). Here it denotes the Christian gospel declared authoritatively by men like the writer, an inspired message which carries on the OT revelation of God's promises and threats, and which is vitally effective. No dead letter, this λόγος! The rhetorical outburst in vv.$^{12f.}$ is a preacher's equivalent for the common idea that the sense of God's all-seeing scrutiny should deter men from evil-doing, as, *e.g.*, in Plautus (*Captivi*, ii. 2. 63, "est profecto deu', qui quae nos gerimus auditque et uidet"). This had been deepened by ethical writers like Seneca (*Ep.* lxxxiii. 1, "nihil deo clusum est, interest animis nostris et cogitationibus mediis intervenit"), Epictetus (ii. 14. 11, οὐκ ἔστι λαθεῖν αὐτὸν οὐ μόνον ποιοῦντα ἀλλ' οὐδὲ διανοούμενον ἢ ἐνθυμούμενον), and the author of the *Epistle of Aristeas* (132–133: Moses teaches ὅτι μόνος ὁ θεός ἐστι . . . καὶ οὐθὲν αὐτὸν λανθάνει τῶν ἐπὶ γῆς γινομένων ὑπ' ἀνθρώπων κρυφίως . . . κἂν ἐννοηθῇ τις κακίαν ἐπιτελεῖν, οὐκ ἂν λάθοι, μὴ ὅτι καὶ πράξας, and 210: the characteristic note of piety is τὸ διαλαμβάνειν ὅτι πάντα διαπαντὸς ὁ θεὸς ἐνεργεῖ καὶ γινώσκει, καὶ οὐθὲν ἂν λάθοι ἄδικον ποιήσας ἢ κακὸν ἐργασάμενος ἄνθρωπος), as well as by apocalyptists like the author of Baruch (83^3: He will assuredly examine the secret thoughts and that which is laid up in the secret chambers of all the members of man). But our author has one particular affinity. Take Philo's interpretation of διεῖλεν αὐτὰ μέσα in Gn 15^{10}. Scripture means, he explains (*quis rer. div. haeres*, 26) that it was God who divided them, τῷ τομιεῖ τῶ συμπάντων ἑαυτοῦ λόγῳ, ὃς εἰς τὴν ὀξυτάτην ἀκονηθεὶς ἀκμὴν διαιρῶν οὐδέποτε λήγει. τὰ γὰρ αἰσθητὰ πάντα ἐπειδὰν μέχρι τῶν ἀτόμων καὶ λεγομένων ἀμερῶν διεξέλθῃ, πάλιν ἀπὸ τούτων τὰ λόγῳ θεωρητὰ εἰς ἀμυθήτους καὶ ἀπεριγράφους μοίρας ἄρχεται διαιρεῖν οὗτος ὁ τομεύς. He returns (in 48) to this analytic function of the Logos in God and man, and in *De mutatione nominum* (18) speaks of ἠκονημένον καὶ ὀξὺν λόγον, μαστεύειν καὶ ἀναζητεῖν ἕκαστα ἱκανόν. Still, the Logos is τομεύς as the principle of differentiation in the universe, rather than as an ethical force; and when Philo connects the latter with ὁ λόγος, as he does in *quod deter. pot.* 29, *Cherub.* 9, etc., ὁ λόγος is the human faculty of reason. Obviously, our author is using Philonic language rather than Philonic ideas.

Ἐνεργής (for which B, by another blunder, has ἐναργής=

evidens) is not a LXX term, but denotes in Greek vital activity (cp. Schol. on Soph. *Oed. Tyr.* 45, ζώσας ἀντὶ ἐνεργεστέρας). Neither is τομώτερος a LXX term; the comparison of ὁ λόγος to a sword arose through the resemblance between the tongue and a "dagger," though μάχαιρα had by this time come to mean a sword of any size, whether long (ῥομφαία) or short.[1] The comparative is followed (cp. Lk 16^8) by ὑπέρ, as elsewhere by παρά, and the "cutting" power of ὁ λόγος extends or penetrates to the innermost recesses of human nature—**ἄχρι μερισμοῦ ψυχῆς καὶ πνεύματος,**[2] **ἁρμῶν τε καὶ μυελῶν** (the conj. μελῶν = limbs is neat but superfluous, for μυελῶν was in the text known to Clem. Alex. *quis dives*, 41). D K here (as in 11^{32}) insert τε before the first καί, but there is no idea of distinguishing the psychical and the physical spheres; ἁρμων . . . μυελῶν is merely a metaphorical equivalent for ψυχῆς καὶ πνεύματος. Μερισμός (only in LXX in Jb 11^{23}, 2 Es 6^{18}) means here "division," not "distribution" (2^4); the subtlest relations of human personality, the very border-line between the ψυχή and the πνεῦμα, all this is open to ὁ λόγος. The metaphorical use of μυελῶν in this sense is as old as Euripides, who speaks of μὴ πρὸς ἄκρον μυελὸν ψυχῆς (*Hippolytus*, 255).

According to Philo (*De Cherubim*, 8. 9), the flaming sword of Gn 3^{24} is a symbol either of the sun, as the swiftest of existences (circling the whole world in a single day), or of reason, ὀξυκινητότατον γὰρ καὶ θέρμον λόγος καὶ μάλιστα ὁ τοῦ αἰτίου. Learn from the fiery sword, o my soul, he adds, to note the presence and power of this divine Reason, ὃς οὐδέποτε λήγει κινούμενος σπουδῇ πάσῃ πρὸς αἵρεσιν μὲν τῶν καλῶν, φυγὴν δὲ τῶν ἐναντίων. But there is a still better parallel to the thought in Lucian's account of the impression made by the address (ὁ λόγος) of a philosopher: οὐ γὰρ ἐξ ἐπιπολῆς οὐδ' ὡς ἔτυχεν ἡμῶν ὁ λόγος καθίκετο, βαθεῖα δὲ καὶ καίριος ἡ πληγὴ ἐγένετο, καὶ μάλα εὐστόχως ἐνεχθεὶς ὁ λόγος αὐτήν, εἰ οἷόν τε εἰπεῖν, διέκοψε τὴν ψυχήν (*Nigr.* 35). Only, Lucian proceeds to compare the soul of a cultured person to a target at which the words of the wise are aimed. Similarly, in pseudo-Phocylides, 124: ὅπλον τοι λόγος ἀνδρὶ τομώτερόν ἐστι σιδήρου, and Od. Sol. 12^5: for the swiftness of the Word is inexpressible, and like its expression is its swiftness and force, and its course knows no limit.

The **μερισμοῦ . . . μυελῶν** passage is "a mere rhetorical accumulation of terms to describe the whole mental nature of man" (A. B. Davidson); the climax is καρδία, for what underlies human failure is καρδία πονηρὰ ἀπίστιας (3^{12}), and the writer's warning all along has been against hardening the heart, *i.e.* obdurate disobedience. Hence the point of **καὶ κριτικὸς κτλ.** Κριτικός is another of his terms which are classical, not religious; it is used by Aristotle (*Eth. Nik.* vi. 10) of ἡ σύνεσις, the intelligence of man being κριτική in the sense that it discerns. If

[1] The description was familiar to readers of the LXX, *e.g.* Pr 5^4 ἠκονημένον μᾶλλον μαχαίρας διστόμου.

[2] The subtlety of thought led afterwards to the change of πνεύματος into σώματος (2. 38. 257. 547. 1245).

there is any distinction between **ἐνθυμήσεων** (ἐνθυμήσεως C* D* W vt Lucifer) and **ἐννοιῶν**, it is between impulses and reflections, but contemporary usage hardly distinguished them; indeed ἔννοια could mean "purpose" as well as "conception." The two words are another alliterative phrase for "thought and conception," ἔννοια, unlike ἐνθύμησις, being a LXX term.

In v.[13] **καὶ οὐκ ἔστιν κτίσις ἀφανής κτλ.**, κτίσις means anything created (as in Ro 8[39]), and **αὐτοῦ** is "God's." The negative side is followed by the positive, **πάντα δὲ γυμνὰ καὶ τετραχηλισμένα.** The nearest verbal parallel is in En 9[5] πάντα ἐνώπιόν σου φανερὰ καὶ ἀκάλυπτα, where the context points as here to secret sins. The general idea was familiar; *e.g.* (above, p. 55) "nihil deo clusum est, interest animis nostris et cogitationibus mediis intervenit." Μόνῳ γὰρ ἔξεστι θεῷ, ψυχὴν ἰδεῖν (Philo, *de Abrahamo*, 21). But what the writer had in mind was a passage like that in *de Cherub.* 5, where Philo explains Dt 29[29] (τὰ κρυπτὰ κυρίῳ τῷ θεῷ, τὰ δὲ φανερὰ γενέσει γνώριμα) by arguing, γενητὸς δὲ οὐδεὶς ἱκανὸς γνώμης ἀφανοῦς κατιδεῖν ἐνθύμημα, μόνος δὲ ὁ θεός. Hence, he adds, the injunction (Nu 5[18]) τὴν ψυχὴν "ἐναντίον τοῦ θεοῦ στῆσαι" with head uncovered; which means, the soul τὸ κεφάλαιον δόγμα γυμνωθεῖσαν καὶ τὴν γνώμην ᾗ κέχρηται ἀπαμφιασθεῖσαν, ἵν' ὄψεσι ταῖς ἀκριβεστάταις ἐπικριθεῖσα τοῦ ἀδεκάστου θεοῦ κτλ., the closing description of God being τῷ μόνῳ γυμνὴν ψυχὴν ἰδεῖν δυναμένῳ. For γυμνά see also M. Aurel. 12[2] ὁ θεὸς πάντα τὰ ἡγεμονικὰ γυμνὰ τῶν ὑλικῶν ἀγγείων . . . ὁρᾷ. **Τετραχηλισμένα** must mean something similar, "exposed" or "bared" ("aperta," vg; πεφανερωμένα, Hesych.).

Though τραχηλίζω does not occur in the LXX, the writer was familiar with it in Philo, where it suggests a wrestler "downing" his opponent by seizing his throat. How this metaphorical use of throttling or tormenting could yield the metaphorical passive sense of "exposed," is not easy to see. The Philonic sense of "depressed" or "bent down" would yield here the meaning "abashed," *i.e.* hanging down the head in shame ("conscientia male factorum in ruborem aguntur caputque mittunt," Wettstein). But this is hardly on a level with γυμνά. The most probable clue is to be found in the practice of exposing an offender's face by pushing his head back, as if the word were an equivalent for the Latin "resupinata" in the sense of "manifesta." The bending back of the neck produced this exposure. Thus when Vitellius was dragged along the Via Sacra to be murdered, it was "reducto coma capite, ceu noxii solent, atque etiam mento mucrone gladii subrecto, ut visendam praeberet faciem" (Suet. *Vit. Vitell.* 17).

In the last five words, **πρὸς ὃν ἡμῖν ὁ λόγος**, which are impressive by their bare simplicity, there is a slight play on the term λόγος here and in v.[12], although in view of the flexible use of the term, *e.g.* in 5[11] and 13[17], it might be even doubtful if the writer intended more than a verbal assonance. The general sense of the phrase is best conveyed by "with whom we have to reckon." (*a*) This rendering, "to whom we have to account (or, to render our account)," was adopted without question by the Greek fathers from

Chrysostom (αὐτῷ μέλλομεν δοῦναι εὐθύνας τῶν πεπραγμένων) onwards, and the papyri support the origin of the phrase as a commercial metaphor; *e.g.* *OP.* 1188[5] (A.D. 13) ὡς πρὸς σὲ τοῦ περὶ τῶν ἀγνοη[θέντων] ζη[τήματος] ἐσο[μένου] (*sc.* λόγου), and Hibeh Papyri, 53[4] (246 B.C.) πειρῶ οὖν ἀσφολῶς ὡς πρὸς σὲ τοῦ λόγου ἐσομένου. (*b*) The alternative rendering, "with whom we have to do," has equal support in Gk. usage; *e.g.* in the LXX phrase λόγος μοι πρός σε (1 K 2^{14}, 2 K 9^{5}) and in Jg 17^{7} (μακράν εἰσιν Σιδωνίων, καὶ λόγον οὐκ ἔχουσιν πρὸς ἄνθρωπον). The former idea is predominant, however, as the context suggests (cp. Ignat. *ad Magn.* 3, τὸ δὲ τοιοῦτον οὐ πρὸς σάρκα ὁ λόγος, ἀλλὰ πρὸς θεὸν τὸν τὰ κρύφια εἰδότα), and includes the latter. It is plainly the view of the early anti-Marcionite treatise, which has been preserved among the works of Ephraem Syrus (cp. Preuschen, *Zeitschrift für die neutest. Wissenschaft*, 1911, pp. 243–269), where the passage is quoted from a text like this: ὡς καὶ ὁ Παῦλος λέγει, ζῶν ὁ λόγος τοῦ θεοῦ καὶ τομώτερος ὑπὲρ πᾶσαν μάχαιραν δίστομον, διϊκνούμενον μέχρι μερισμοῦ πνεύματος καὶ σαρκός, μέχρι ἁρμῶν τε καὶ μυελῶν, καὶ κριτικός ἐστιν ἐνθυμήσεων καὶ ἐννοιῶν καρδίας· καὶ οὐκ ἔστιν κτίσις ἀφανὴς ἐνώπιον αὐτοῦ, ἀλλὰ πάντα ἐμφανῆ ἐνώπιον αὐτοῦ, ὅτι γυμνοὶ καὶ τετραχηλισμένοι ἐσμὲν ἐν τοῖς ὀφθαλμοῖς αὐτοῦ ἕκαστος ἡμῶν λόγον αὐτῷ ἀποδιδόναι. The rendering, "who is our subject, of whom we are speaking" (πρός = with reference to, and ἡμῖν ὁ λόγος as in 5^{11}), is impossibly flat.

At this point the writer effects a transition to the main theme, which is to occupy him till 10^{18}, *i.e.* Christ as ἀρχιερεύς. He begins, however, by a practical appeal (vv.[14-16]) which catches up the ideas of $2^{17.18}$ 3^{1}.

[14] *As we have a great highpriest, then, who has passed through the heavens, Jesus the Son of God, let us hold fast to our confession;* [15] *for ours is no high priest who is incapable* (μὴ δυν. as in 9^{9}) *of sympathizing with our weaknesses, but one who has been tempted in every respect like ourselves* (*sc.* πρὸς ἡμᾶς), *yet without sinning.* [16] *So let us approach the throne of grace with confidence* (μετὰ παρρησίας, 3^{6}), *that we may receive mercy and find grace to help us in the hour of need.*

Μέγας is a favourite adjective for ἀρχιερεύς in Philo,[1] but when the writer adds, ἔχοντες οὖν ἀρχιερέα μέγαν διεληλυθότα τοὺς οὐρανούς, he is developing a thought of his own. The greatness of Jesus as ἀρχιερεύς consists in his access to God not through any material veil, but through the upper heavens; he has penetrated to the very throne of God, in virtue of his perfect self-sacrifice. This idea is not elaborated till later (cp. $6^{19f.}$ $9^{24f.}$), in the sacerdotal sense. But it has been already mentioned in $2^{9.10}$, where Jesus the Son of God saves men by his entrance into the full divine glory. Κρατῶμεν here as in 6^{18} with the genitive

[1] ὁ μὲν δὴ μέγας ἀρχιερεύς (*de Somn.* i. 38), even of the Logos.

(ὁμολογιάς, see 3^1); in Paul it takes the accusative. The writer now (v.[15]) reiterates the truth of $2^{11f.}$; the exalted Jesus is well able to sympathize with weak men on earth, since he has shared their experience of temptation. It is put negatively, then positively. **Συμπαθῆσαι** is used of Jesus[1] as in *Acta Pauli et Theclae*, 17 (ὃς μόνος συνεπάθησεν πλανωμένῳ κόσμῳ); see below, on 10^{34}. Origen (*in Matt.* xiii. 2) quotes a saying of Jesus: διὰ τοὺς ἀσθενοῦντας ἠσθένουν καὶ διὰ τοὺς πεινῶντας ἐπείνων καὶ διὰ τοὺς διψῶντας ἐδίψων, the first part of which may go back to Mt 8^{17} (αὐτὸς τὰς ἀσθενείας ἔλαβεν); cp. also Mt $25^{35f.}$. Philo uses the term even of the Mosaic law (*de spec. leg.* ii. 13, τῷ δὲ ἀπόρως ἔχοντι συνεπάθησε), but here it is more than "to be considerate." The aid afforded by Jesus as **ἀρχιερεύς** is far more than official; it is inspired by fellow-feeling **ταῖς ἀσθενείαις ἡμῶν**. "Verius sentiunt qui simul cum externis aerumnis comprehendunt animi affectus, quales sunt metus, tristitia, horror mortis, et similes" (Calvin). These ἀσθένειαι are the sources of temptation. Ἡ σὰρξ ἀσθενής, as Jesus had said to his disciples, warning them against temptation. Jesus was tempted κατὰ πάντα ($2^{17.18}$) **καθ' ὁμοιότητα** (a psychological Stoic term; the phrase occurs in *OP.* ix. 1202^{24} and *BGU.* 1028^{15}, in second-century inscriptions) **χωρὶς ἁμαρτίας**, without yielding to sin. Which is a real ground for encouragement, for the best help is that afforded by those who have stood where we slip and faced the onset of temptation without yielding to it. The special reference is to temptations leading to apostasy or disobedience to the will of God. It is true that χωρὶς ἁμαρτίας does exclude some temptations. Strictly speaking, κατὰ πάντα is modified by this restriction, since a number of our worst temptations arise out of sin previously committed. But this is not in the writer's mind at all. He is too eager, to enter into any psychological analysis.

Philo deduces from Lv 4^3 (μόνον οὐκ ἄντικρυς ἀναδιδάσκων, ὅτι ὁ πρὸς ἀλήθειαν ἀρχιερεὺς καὶ μὴ ψευδώνυμος ἀμέτοχος ἁμαρτημάτων ἐστίν) that the ideal highpriest is practically sinless (*de Victimis*, 10); but this is a thought with which he wistfully toys, and the idea of the Logos as unstained by contact with the material universe is very different from this conception of Jesus as actually tempted and scatheless. Nor would the transference of the idea of messiah as sinless account for our writer's view. To him and his readers Jesus is sinless, not in virtue of a divine prerogative, but as the result of a real human experience which proved successful in the field of temptation.

Hence (v.[16]) **προσερχώμεθα οὖν μετὰ παρρησίας**. Philo (*quis rer. div. haeres*, 2) makes παρρησία the reward of a good conscience, which enables a loyal servant of God to approach him frankly.

[1] Of God in 4 Mac 5^{25} κατὰ φύσιν ἡμῖν συμπαθεῖ νομοθετῶν ὁ τοῦ κτίστης, but in the weaker sense of consideration. It is curious that 4 Mac., like Hebrews, uses the word twice, once of God and once of men (cp. 4 Mac 13^{23} οὕτως δὴ τοίνυν καθεστηκυίας τῆς φιλαδελφίας συμπαθούσης).

But here (cp. *ERE.* ii. 786) παρρησία is not freedom of utterance so much as resolute confidence (cp. on 3^6). Our writer certainly includes prayer in this conception of approaching God, but it is prayer as the outcome of faith and hope. Seneca bids Lucilius pray boldly to God, if his prayers are for soundness of soul and body, not for any selfish and material end: "audacter deum roga; nihil illum de alieno rogaturus es" (*Ep.* x. 4). But even this is not the meaning of παρρησία here. The Roman argues that a man can only pray aloud and confidently if his desires are such as he is not ashamed to have others hear, whereas the majority of people "whisper basest of prayers to God." Our author does not mean "palam" by παρρησία.

Our approach (προσερχώμεθα: the verb in the sense of applying to a court or authority, *e.g.* in *OP.* 1119^8 προσήλθομεν τῇ κρατίστῃ βουλῇ, *BGU.* 1022) is **τῷ θρονῷ τῆς χάριτος**, for grace is now enthroned (see $2^{9f.}$). For the phrase see Is 16^5 διορθωθήσεται μετ' ἐλέους θρόνος. Our author (cp. Introd. p. xlvii), like those who shared the faith of apocalyptic as well as of rabbinic piety, regarded heaven as God's royal presence and also as the σκηνή where he was worshipped, an idea which dated from Is $6^{1f.}$ and Ps 29 (cp. Mechilta on Ex 15^{17}), though he only alludes incidentally (12^{22}) to the worship of God by the host of angels in the upper sanctuary. He is far from the pathetic cry of Azariah (Dn 3^{38}): ὠκ ἔστιν ἐν τῷ καιρῷ τούτῳ . . . οὐδὲ τόπος τοῦ καρπῶσαι ἐνώπιόν σου καὶ εὑρεῖν ἔλεος. He rather shares Philo's feeling (*de Exsecrat.* 9) that οἱ ἀνασῳζόμενοι can rely upon the compassionate character of God (ἑνὶ μὲν ἐπιεικείᾳ καὶ χρηστότητι τοῦ παρακαλουμένου συγγνώμην πρὸ τιμωρίας ἀεὶ τιθέντος), though he regards this mercy as conditioned by the sacrifice of Jesus. The twofold object of the approach is (*a*) **λαμβάνειν ἔλεος**, which is used for the passive of ἐλεῶ (which is rare), and (*b*) **χάριν εὑρίσκειν κτλ.**, an echo of the LXX phrase (*e.g.* Gn 6^8) εὑρίσκειν χάριν ἐναντίον κυρίου (τοῦ θεοῦ). In the writer's text (A) of the LXX, Prov 8^{17} ran οἱ δὲ ἐμὲ ζητοῦντες εὑρήσουσι χάριν.[1] **Εἰς εὔκαιρον βοήθειαν** recalls τοῖς πειραζομένοις βοηθῆσαι in 2^{18}; it signifies "for assistance in the hour of need." Εὔκαιρος means literally "seasonable," as in Ps 104^{27} (δοῦναι τὴν τροφὴν αὐτοῖς εὔκαιρον), "fitting" or "opportune" (*Ep. Aristeas*, 203, 236). The "sympathy" of Jesus is shown by practical aid to the tempted, which is suitable to their situation, suitable above all because it is timely (εὔκαιρον being almost equivalent to ἐν καιρῷ

[1] Aristotle argues that χάρις or benevolence must be spontaneous and disinterested; also, that its value is enhanced by necessitous circumstances (ἔστω δὴ χάρις, καθ' ἣν ὁ ἔχων λέγεται χάριν ὑπουργεῖν δεομένῳ μὴ ἀντί τινος, μηδ' ἵνα τι αὐτῷ τῷ ὑπουργοῦντι ἀλλ' ἵν' ἐκείνῳ τι· μεγάλη δ' ἂν ᾖ σφόδρα δεομένῳ, ἢ μεγάλων καὶ χαλεπῶν, ἢ ἐν καιροῖς τοιουτοῖς, ἢ μόνος ἢ πρῶτος ἢ μάλιστα, *Rhet.* ii. 7. 2).

χρείας, Sir 8[9]). Philo (*de sacrificantibus*, 10) shows how God, for all his greatness, cherishes compassion (ἔλεον καὶ οἶκτον λαμβάνει τῶν ἐν ἐνδείαις ἀπορωτάτων) for needy folk, especially for poor proselytes, who, in their devotion to him, are rewarded by his help (καρπὸν εὑράμενοι τῆς ἐπὶ τὸν θεὸν καταφυγῆς τὴν ἀπʼ αὐτοῦ βοήθειαν). But the best illustration of the phrase is in Aristides, Εἰς τὸν Σάραπιν 50: σὲ γὰρ δὴ πᾶς τις ἐν παντὶ καιρῷ βοηθὸν καλεῖ, Σάραπι.

How widely even good cursives may be found supporting a wrong reading is shown by the evidence for προσερχόμεθα: 6. 38. 88. 104. 177. 206*. 241. 255. 263. 337. 378. 383. 440. 462. 467. 487. 489. 623. 635. 639. 642. 915. 919. 920. 927. 1149. 1245. 1288. 1518. 1836. 1852. 1872. 1891. 2004. For ἔλεος (the Hellenistic neuter, cp. Cronert's *Memoria Graeca Herculanensis*, 176[1]), the Attic ἔλεον (ἔλεος, masc.) is substituted by L and a few minuscules (Chrys. Theodoret). B om. εὕρωμεν.

He now (5[1-10]) for the first time begins to explain the qualifications of the true ἀρχιερεύς.

(*a*) First, he must be humane as well as human:

[1] *Every highpriest who is selected from men and appointed to act on behalf of men in things divine, offering gifts and sacrifices for sin,* [2] *can deal gently with those who err through ignorance, since he himself is beset with weakness—* [3] *which obliges him to present offerings for his own sins as well as for those of the People.*

(*b*) Second, he must not be self-appointed.

[4] *Also, it is an office which no one elects to take for himself; he is called to it by God, just as Aaron was.*

The writer now proceeds to apply these two conditions to Jesus, but he takes them in reverse order, beginning with (*b*).

[5] *Similarly Christ was not raised to the glory of the priesthood by himself, but by Him who declared to him,*

> "*Thou art my son,*
> *to-day have I become thy father.*"

[6] *Just as elsewhere* (ἐν ἑτέρῳ, *sc.* τόπῳ) *he says,*

> "*Thou art a priest for ever, with the rank of Melchizedek.*"

He then goes back to (*a*):

[7] *In the days of his flesh, with bitter cries and tears, he offered prayers and supplications to Him who was able to save him from death; and he was heard, because of his godly fear.* [8] *Thus, Son though he was, he learned by* (ἀφʼ ὧν = ἀπὸ τούτων ἅ) *all he suffered how to obey,* [9] *and by being thus perfected he became the source of eternal salvation for all who obey him,* [10] *being designated by God highpriest "with the rank of Melchizedek."*

Πᾶς γὰρ ἀρχιερεύς (dealing only with Hebrew highpriests, and only with what is said of them in the LXX) **ἐξ ἀνθρώπων λαμβανόμενος** (Nu 8[6] λάβε τοὺς Λευείτας ἐκ μέσου υἱῶν Ἰσραήλ) **καθίσταται**—passive, in the light of 7[28] (ὁ νόμος γὰρ ἀνθρώπους καθίστησιν ἀρχιερεῖς ἔχοντας ἀσθένειαν) and of the Philonic usage (e.g. *de vit. Mosis*, ii. 11, τῷ μέλλοντι ἀρχιερεῖ καθίστασθαι). The middle may indeed be used transitively, as, *e.g.*, in Eurip. *Supplic.* 522 (πόλεμον δὲ τοῦτον οὐκ ἐγὼ καθίσταμαι), and is so taken here by some (*e.g.* Calvin, Kypke). But τὰ πρὸς τὸν θεόν is an adverbial accusative as in 2[17], not the object of καθίσταται in an active sense. In **δωρά τε καὶ θυσίας**, here as in 8[3] and 9[9], the writer goes back to the LXX (A) rendering of 1 K 8^{64} (*καὶ τὸ δῶρον καὶ τὰς θυσίας*). The phrase recurs in *Ep. Aristeas*, 234 (*οὐ δώροις οὐδὲ θυσίαις*), and is a generic term for sacrifices or offerings, without any distinction. The early omission of **τε** (B D^b K Lat boh pesh) was due to the idea that *θυσίας* should be closely connected with **ἁμαρτιῶν** ("ut offerat dona, et sacrificia pro peccatis," vg). Instead of writing *εἰς τὸ προσφέρειν*, our author departs from his favourite construction of *εἰς* with the infinitive and writes **ἵνα προσφέρῃ**, in order to introduce **μετριοπαθεῖν δυνάμενος.** This, although a participial clause, contains the leading idea of the sentence. The *ἀρχιερεύς* is able to deal gently with the erring People whom he represents, since he shares their **ἀσθένεια**, their common infirmity or liability to temptation.

Μετριοπαθεῖν in v.^{2} is a term coined by ethical philosophy. It is used by Philo to describe the mean between extravagant grief and stoic apathy, in the case of Abraham's sorrow for the death of his wife (*τὸ δὲ μέσον πρὸ τῶν ἄκρων ἑλόμενον μετριοπαθεῖν*, *De Abrah.* 44); so Plutarch (*Consol. ad Apoll.* 22) speaks of *τῆς κατὰ φύσιν ἐν τοιούτοις μετριοπαθείας.* But here it denotes gentleness and forbearance, the moderation of anger in a person who is provoked and indignant—as in Plut. *de Cohib. ira*, 10, *ἀναστῆσαι δὲ καὶ σῶσαι, καὶ φείσασθαι καὶ καρτερῆσαι, πραότητός ἐστι καὶ συγγνώμης καὶ μετριοπαθείας.* Josephus (*Ant.* xii. 3. 2) praises this quality in Vespasian and Titus (*μετριοπαθησάντων*), who acted magnanimously and generously towards the unruly Jews; Dionysius Halicarnassus accuses Marcius (*Ant.* 8. 529) of lacking *τὸ εὐδιάλλακτον καὶ μετριοπαθές, ὁπότε δι' ὀργῆς τῷ γένοιτο.* And so on. The term is allied to *πραότης*. The sins of others are apt to irritate us, either because they are repeated or because they are flagrant; they excite emotions of disgust, impatience, and exasperation, and tempt us to be hard and harsh (Gal 6^1). The thought of excess here is excessive severity rather than excessive leniency. The objects of this **μετριοπαθεῖν** are **τοῖς ἀγνοοῦσιν καὶ πλανωμένοις**, *i.e.*, people who sin through yielding to the weaknesses of human nature. For such offenders alone the *piacula* of atonement-day (which the writer has in mind) availed. Those who sinned **ἑκουσίως** (10^{26}), not *ἀκουσίως*, were without the pale; for such presumptuous sins, which our writer regards specially under the category of deliberate apostasy (3^{12} 10^{26}), there is no pardon possible. The phrase here is practically a hendiadys, for *τοῖς ἐξ ἀγνοίας πλανωμένοις*: the People err through their *ἄγνοια*. Thus *ἀγνοεῖν* becomes an equivalent for *ἁμαρτάνειν* (Sir 23^2 etc.), just as the noun *ἀγνόημα* comes to imply sin (cp. 9^7 and Jth 5^{20} *εἰ μέν ἐστιν ἀγνόημα ἐν τῷ λαῷ τούτῳ καὶ ἁμαρτάνουσι εἰς τὸν θεὸν αὐτῶν*, with Tebt. Pap. 124^4 (118 B.C.) and 5^3—a proclamation by king Euergetes and queen Cleopatra declaring "an amnesty to all their subjects for all errors, crimes," etc., except wilful murder and sacrilege). In the *Martyr. Pauli*, 4, the apostle addresses his pagan audience as ἄνδρες οἱ ὄντες ἐν τῇ ἀγνωσίᾳ καὶ τῇ πλάνῃ ταύτῃ.

(*a*) Strictly speaking, only such sins could be pardoned (Lv 4^{2} $5^{21.22}$, Nu 15^{22-31}, Dt 17^{12}) as were unintentional. Wilful sins were not covered by the ordinary ritual of sacrifice (10^{26}, cp. Nu 12^{11}).

(*b*) The term **περίκειμαι** only occurs in the LXX in Ep. Jer. 23. 57 and in 4 Mac 12^{3} (τὰ δεσμὰ περικείμενον), and in both places in its literal sense (Symm. Is 61^{10}), as in Ac 28^{20}. But Seneca says of the body, "hoc quoque natura ut quemdam vestem animo circumdedit" (*Epist.* 92), and the metaphorical sense is as old as Theocritus ($23^{13.14}$ φεῦγε δ' ἀπὸ χρὼς ὕβριν τᾶς ὀργᾶς περικείμενος).

The **ἀρχιερεύς**, therefore (v.[3]), requires to offer sacrifice for his own sins as well as for those of the People, **καθὼς περὶ τοῦ λαοῦ οὕτω καὶ περὶ ἑαυτοῦ.** This twofold sacrifice is recognized by Philo (*de vit. Mosis*, ii. 1), who notes that the holder of the ἱερωσύνη must ἐπὶ τελείοις ἱεροῖς beseech God for blessing αὐτῷ τε καὶ τῆς ἀρχομένοις. The regulations for atonement-day (Lv 16^{6-17}) provided that the ἀρχιερεύς sacrificed for himself and his household as well as for the People (καὶ προσάξει Ἀαρὼν τὸν μόσχον τὸν περὶ τῆς ἁμαρτίας αὐτοῦ καὶ ἐξιλάσεται περὶ αὐτοῦ καὶ τοῦ οἴκου αὐτοῦ . . . καὶ περὶ πάσης συναγωγῆς υἱῶν Ἰσραήλ). But our author now turns from the idea of the solidarity between priest and People to the idea of the priest's commission from God. **Τὴν τιμήν** (in v.[4]) means position or office, as often, *e.g.* ἐπίτροπος λαμβάνει ταύτην τὴν τιμήν (*i.e.* of supervising the household slaves), Arist. *Pol.* i. 7, τιμὰς γὰρ λέγομεν εἶναι τὰς ἀρχάς, *ib.* iii. 10, περὶ τῶν ἀρχιερέων πῶς τ' ἤρξαντο καὶ τίσιν ἔξεστι τῆς τιμῆς ταύτης μεταλαμβάνειν, Joseph. *Ant.* xx. 10. 1. **Ἀλλὰ** (*sc.* λαμβάνει) **καλούμενος**, but takes it when (or, as) he is called. The terseness of the phrase led to the alteration (C^{c} L) of ἀλλά into ἀλλ' ὁ (as in v.[5]). **Καθώσπερ καὶ Ἀαρών.** In Josephus (*Ant.* iii. 8. 1), Moses tells the Israelites, νῦν δ' αὐτὸς ὁ θεὸς Ἀαρῶνα τῆς τιμῆς ταύτης ἄξιον ἔκρινε καὶ τοῦτον ᾕρηται ἱερέα.

περὶ (before **ἁμαρτιῶν** in v.[3]) has been changed to ὑπέρ in C^{c} D^{c} K L etc. (conforming to 5^{1}). There is no difference in meaning (cp. περί, Mt 26^{28} = ὑπέρ, Mk. and Lk.), for περί (see $10^{6.8.18.26}$ 13^{11}) has taken over the sense of ὑπέρ.

For καθώσπερ (ℵ* A B D* 33) in v.[4], $ℵ^{c}$ D^{c} K L P Ψ 6. 1288. 1739 read the more obvious καθάπερ (C? syr^{hkl} Chrys. Cyr. Alex. Procopius: καθώς).

In v.[5] **οὐχ ἑαυτὸν ἐδόξασεν**, while the term δόξα was specially applicable to the highpriestly office (cf. 2 Mac 14^{7} ὅθεν ἀφελόμενος τὴν προγονικὴν δόξαν, λέγω δὴ τὴν ἀρχιερωσύνην), the phrase is quite general, as in the parallel Jn 8^{54}. The following **γενηθῆναι** is an epexegetic infinitive, which recurs in the Lucan writings (Lk $1^{54.72}$, Ac 15^{10}) and in the earlier Psalter of Solomon ($2^{28.40}$ etc.). After ἀλλ' we must supply some words like **αὐτὸν ἐδόξασεν**.

The argument runs thus: We have a great **ἀρχιερεύς**, Jesus the Son of God (4^{14}), and it is as he is Son that he carries out the vocation of *ἀρχιερεύς*. There is something vital, for the writer's mind, in the connexion of *ἀρχιερεύς* and **Υἱός**. Hence he quotes (v.[5]) his favourite text from Ps 2^7 before the more apposite one (in v.[6]) from Ps 110^4, implying that the position of divine Son carried with it, in some sense, the rôle of *ἀρχιερεύς*. This had been already suggested in $1^{2.3}$ where the activities of the Son include the purification of men from their sins. Here the second quotation only mentions *ἱερεύς*, it is true; but the writer drew no sharp distinction between **ἱερεύς** and *ἀρχιερεύς*. In **κατὰ τὴς τάξιν Μελχισεδέκ**, *τάξις* for the writer, as 7^{15} proves (*κατὰ τὴν ὁμοιότητα* Μελχισεδέκ), has a general meaning;[1] Jesus has the rank of a Melchizedek, he is a priest of the Melchizedek sort or order, though in the strict sense of the term there was no *τάξις* or succession of Melchizedek priests.

Τάξις in the papyri is often a list or register; in *OP.* 1266^{24} (A.D. 98) *ἐν τάξει* means "in the class" (of people). It had acquired a sacerdotal nuance, *e.g.* Michel $735^{125f.}$ (the regulations of Antiochus I.), *ὅστις τε ἂν ὑστέρωι χρόνωι τάξιν λάβῃ ταύτην*, and occasionally denoted a post or office (*e.g.* Tebt. P 297^8, A.D. 123).

Ὃς *κτλ.* Some editors (*e.g.* A. B. Davidson, Lünemann, Peake, Hollmann) take vv.[7-10] as a further proof of (*b*). But the writer is here casting back to (*a*), not hinting that the trying experiences of Jesus on earth proved that his vocation was not self-sought, but using these to illustrate the thoroughness with which he had identified himself with men. He does this, although the parallel naturally broke down at one point. Indeed his conception of Christ was too large for the categories he had been employing, and this accounts for the tone and language of the passage. (*a*) Jesus being *χωρὶς ἁμαρτίας* did not require to offer any sacrifices on his own behalf; and (*b*) the case of Melchizedek offered no suggestion of suffering as a vital element in the vocation of an *ἀρχιερεύς*. As for the former point, while the writer uses *προσενέγκας* in speaking of the prayers of Jesus, this is at most a subconscious echo of *προσφέρειν* in vv.[1-3]; there is no equivalent in Jesus to the sacrifice offered by the OT *ἀρχιερεύς*, *περὶ ἑαυτοῦ . . . περὶ ἁμαρτιῶν*. The writer starts with his parallel, for *ἐν ταῖς ἡμέραις τῆς σαρκὸς αὐτοῦ* corresponds to *περικεῖται ἀσθένειαν* (v.[2]); but instead of developing the idea of sympathy in an official (*μετριοπαθεῖν δυνάμενος κτλ.*), he passes to the deeper idea that Jesus qualified himself by a moral discipline

[1] As in 2 Mac 9^{18} *ἐπιστολὴν ἔχουσαν ἱκετηρίας τάξιν*, *Ep. Arist.* 69, *κρηπῖδος ἔχουσα τάξιν*.

to be ἀρχιερεύς in a pre-eminent sense. He mentions the prayers and tears of Jesus here, as the faith of Jesus in $2^{12f.}$, for the express purpose of showing how truly he shared the lot of man on earth, using **δεήσεις τε καὶ ἱκετηρίας**, a phrase which the writer may have found in his text (A) of Jb $40^{22\,(27)}$ δεήσεις καὶ ἱκετηρίας, but which was classical (*e.g.* Isokrates, *de Pace*, 46, πολλας ἱκετηρίας καὶ δεήσεις ποιούμενοι). Ἱκετηρία had become an equivalent for **ἱκεσία**, which is actually the reading here in 1 (δεήσεις τε καὶ ἱκεισίας). The phrase recurs in a Ptolemaic papyrus (Brunet de Presle et E. Egger's *Papyrus Grecs du Musée du Louvre*, 27^{22}), χαίρειν σε ἀξιῶ μετὰ δεήσεως καὶ ἱκετείας, though in a weakened sense. The addition of **μετὰ κραυγῆς** (here a cry of anguish) **ἰσχυρᾶς καὶ δακρύων** may be a touch of pathos, due to his own imagination,[1] or suggested by the phraseology of the 22nd psalm, which was a messianic prediction for him (cp. above, 2^{12}) as for the early church; the words of v.[3] in that psalm would hardly suit (κεκράξομαι ἡμέρας πρὸς σὲ καὶ οὐκ εἰσακούσῃ), but phrases like that of v.[6] (πρὸς σὲ ἐκέκραξαν καὶ ἐσώθησαν) and v.[25] (ἐν τῷ κεκραγέναι με πρὸς αὐτὸν ἐπήκουσέν μου) might have been in his mind. Tears were added before long to the Lucan account of the passion, at 22^{44} (Epiph. *Ancor.* 31, ἀλλὰ "καὶ ἔκλαυσεν" κεῖται ἐν τῷ κατὰ Λουκᾶν εὐαγγελίῳ ἐν τοῖς ἀδιορθώτοις ἀντιγράφοις). It is one of the passages which prove how deeply the writer was impressed by the historical Jesus; the intense faith and courage and pitifulness of Jesus must have deeply moved his mind. He seeks to bring out the full significance of this for the saving work of Jesus as Son. His methods of proof may be remote and artificial, to our taste, but the religious interest which prompted them is fundamental. No theoretical reflection on the qualification of priests or upon the dogma of messiah's sinlessness could have produced such passages as this.

Later Rabbinic piety laid stress on tears, *e.g.* in Sohar Exod. fol. 5. 19, "Rabbi Jehuda said, all things of this world depend on penitence and prayers, which men offer to God (Blessed be He!), especially if one sheds tears along with his prayers"; and in Synopsis Sohar, p. 33, n. 2, "There are three kinds of prayers, entreaty, crying, and tears. Entreaty is offered in a quiet voice, crying with a raised voice, but tears are higher than all."

In **ἀπὸ τῆς εὐλαβείας**, the sense of εὐλαβεία in 12^{28} and of εὐλαβεῖσθαι in 11^{7} shows that ἀπό here means "on account of" (as is common in Hellenistic Greek), and that ἀπὸ τῆς εὐλαβείας must be taken, as the Greek fathers took it, "on account of his reverent fear of God," *pro sua reverentia* (vg), "because he had

[1] Like that of Hos 12^{4}, where tears are added to the primitive story (Gn 32^{26}) of Jacob's prayer (ἐνίσχυσεν μετὰ ἀγγέλου καὶ ἠδυνάσθη· ἔκλαυσαν καὶ ἐδεήθησάν μου). In 2 Mac 11^{6} the Maccabean army μετὰ ὀδυρμῶν καὶ δακρύων ἱκέτευον τὸν κύριον.

God in reverence" (Tyndale; "in honoure," Coverdale). The writer is thinking of the moving tradition about Jesus in Gethsemane, which is now preserved in the synoptic gospels, where Jesus entreats God to be spared death: Ἀββᾶ ὁ πατήρ, πάντα δυνατά σοι· παρένεγκε τὸ ποτήριον ἀπ' ἐμοῦ τοῦτο (Mk 14^{36}). This repeated supplication corresponds to the "bitter tears and cries." Then Jesus adds, ἀλλ' οὐ τί ἐγὼ θέλω, ἀλλὰ τί σύ. This is his εὐλάβεια, the godly fear which leaves everything to the will of God. Such is the discipline which issues in ὑπακοή. Compare Ps. Sol 6^8 καὶ κύριος εἰσήκουσε προσευχὴν παντὸς ἐν φόβῳ θεοῦ.

(*a*) The alternative sense of "fear" appears as early as the Old Latin version (d=exauditus a metu). This meaning of εὐλαβεία (Beza: "liberatus ex metu") occurs in Joseph. *Ant.* xi. 6. 9, εὐλαβείας αὐτὴν (Esther) ἀπολύων. Indeed εὐλαβεία (cp. Anz, 359) and its verb εὐλαβεῖσθαι are common in this sense; cp. *e.g.* 2 Mac 8^{16} μὴ καταπλαγῆναι τοῖς δεσμίοις μηδὲ εὐλαβεῖσθαι τὴν . . . πολυπληθείαν: Sir 41^3 μὴ εὐλαβοῦ κρῖμα θανάτου: Wis 17^8 οὗτοι καταγέλαστον εὐλάβειαν ἐνόσουν. But here the deeper, religious sense is more relevant to the context. "In any case the answer consisted . . . in courage given to face death. . . . The point to be emphasized is, not so much that the prayer of Jesus was heard, as that it *needed* to be heard" (A. B. Bruce, p. 186).

(*b*) Some (*e.g.* Linden in *Studien und Kritiken*, 1860, 753 f., and Blass, § 211) take ἀπὸ τῆς εὐλαβείας with what follows; this was the interpretation of the Peshitto ("and, although he was a son, he learned obedience from fear and the sufferings which he bore"). But the separation of ἀπὸ τῆς εὐλαβείας from ἀφ' ὧν and the necessity of introducing a καί before the latter phrase point to the artificiality of this construction.

In v.[8] καίπερ ὢν υἱός (καίπερ being used with a participle as in 7^5 12^{17}) means, "Son though he was," not "son though he was." The writer knows that painful discipline is to be expected by all who are sons of God the Father; he points out, in $12^{5f.}$, that every son, because he is a son, has to suffer. Here the remarkable thing is that Jesus had to suffer, not because but although he was υἱός, which shows that Jesus is Son in a unique sense; as applied to Jesus υἱός means something special. As divine υἱός in the sense of $1^{1f.}$, it might have been expected that he would be exempt from such a discipline. Ὃς . . . ἔμαθεν . . . ὑπακοήν is the main thread of the sentence, but καίπερ ὢν υἱός attaches itself to ἔμαθεν κτλ. rather than to the preceding participles προσενέγκας and εἰσακουσθείς (Chrys. Theophyl.). With a daring stroke the author adds, ἔμαθεν ἀφ' ὧν ἔπαθε τὴν ὑπακοήν. The paronomasia goes back to a common Greek phrase which is as old as Aeschylus (*Agam.* 177 f.), who describes Zeus as τὸν πάθει μάθος θέντα κυρίως ἔχειν, and tells how (W. Headlam)—

"The heart in time of sleep renews
Aching remembrance of her bruise,
And chastening wisdom enters wills that most refuse"—

which, the poet adds, is a sort of χάρις βίαιος from the gods. This moral doctrine, that πάθος brings μάθος, is echoed by Pindar (*Isthm.* i. 40, ὁ πονήσαις δὲ νόῳ καὶ προμάθειαν φέρει) and other writers, notably by Philo (*de vit. Mos.* iii. 38, τούτους οὐ λόγος ἀλλ' ἔργα παιδεύει· παθόντες εἴσονται τὸ ἐμὸν ἀψευδὲς, ἐπεὶ μαθόντες οὐκ ἔγνωσαν: *de spec. leg.* iii. 6, ἵν' ἐκ τοῦ παθεῖν μάθῃ κτλ.: *de somn.* ii. 15, ὁ παθὼν ἀκριβῶς ἔμαθεν, ὅτι τοῦ θεοῦ (Gn 50[19]) ἐστιν). But in the Greek authors and in Philo it is almost invariably applied to "the thoughtless or stupid, and to open and deliberate offenders" (Abbott, *Diat.* 3208*a*), to people who can only be taught by suffering. Our writer ventures, therefore, to apply to the sinless Jesus an idea which mainly referred to young or wilful or undisciplined natures. The term ὑπακοή only occurs once in the LXX, at 2 S 22[36] (καὶ ὑπακοή σου ἐπλήθυνέν με, A), where it translates עֲנָוָה. The general idea corresponds to that of 10[5-9] below, where Jesus enters the world submissively to do the will of God, a vocation which involved suffering and self-sacrifice. But the closest parallel is the argument of Paul in Ph 2[6-8], that Jesus, born in human form, ἐταπείνωσεν ἑαυτὸν γενόμενος ὑπήκοος (*sc.* τῷ θεῷ) μέχρι θανάτου, and the conception of the ὑπακοή of Jesus (Ro 5[18. 19]) in contrast to the παρακοή of Adam. What our writer means to bring out here, as in 2[10f.], is the practical initiation of Jesus into his vocation for God and men. "Wherever there is a vocation, growth and process are inevitable. . . . Personal relations are of necessity relations into which one grows; the relation can be fully and practically constituted only in the practical exercise of the calling in which it is involved. So it was with Christ. He had, so to speak, to work Himself into His place in the plan of salvation, to go down among the brethren whom He was to lead to glory and fully to identify Himself with them, not of course by sharing their individual vocation, but in the practice of obedience in the far harder vocation given to Him. That obedience had to be learned, not because His will was not at every moment perfect . . . but simply because it was a concrete, many-sided obedience" (W. Robertson Smith, *Expositor*[2], ii. pp. 425, 426). Τελειωθείς in v.[9] recalls and expands the remark of 2[10], that God "perfected" Jesus by suffering as τὸν ἀρχηγὸν τῆς σωτηρίας αὐτῶν, and the argument of 2[17. 18]. The writer avoids the technical Stoic terms προκόπτειν and προκοπή. He prefers τελειοῦν and τελείωσις, not on account of their associations with the sacerdotal consecration of the OT ritual, but in order to suggest the moral ripening which enabled Jesus to offer a perfect self-sacrifice, and also perhaps with a side-allusion here to the death-association of these terms.

Philo (*de Abrah.* 11) observes that nature, instruction, and practice are the three things essential πρὸς τελειότητα τοῦ βιοῦ, οὔτε γὰρ διδασκαλίαν ἄνευ φύσεως ἢ ἀσκήσεως τελειωθῆναι δυνατὸν οὔτε φύσις ἐπὶ πέρας ἐστὶν ἐλθεῖν ἱκανὴ δίχα τοῦ μαθεῖν.

Αἴτιος σωτηρίας was a common Greek phrase. Thus Philo speaks of the brazen serpent as αἴτιος σωτηρίας γενόμενος παντελοῦς τοῖς θεασαμένοις (*de Agric.* 22), Aeschines (*in Ctesiph.* 57) has τῆς μὲν σωτηρίαν τῇ πόλει τοὺς θεοὺς αἰτίους γεγενήμενους, and in the *de Mundo*, 398*b*, the writer declares that it is fitting for God αἴτιον τε γίνεσθαι τοῖς ἐπὶ τῆς γῆς σωτηρίας. **Σωτηρία αἰωνίος** is a LXX phrase (Is 45[17]), but not in the sense intended here (cp. 2[3]). The collocation of Jesus learning how to obey God and of thus proving a saviour **τοῖς ὑπακούουσιν αὐτῷ** is remarkable. At first sight there is a clue to the sense in Philo, who declares that "the man who is morally earnest," receiving God's kingdom, "does not prove a source of evil to anyone (αἴτιος γίνεται), but proves a source of the acquisition and use of good things for all who obey him" (πᾶσι τοῖς ὑπηκόοις, *de Abrah.* 45). This refers to Abraham, but to the incident of Gn 23[6], not to that of Melchizedek; Philo is spiritualizing the idea of the good man as king, and the ὑπηκόοι are the members of his household under his authority. The parallel is merely verbal. Here by **πᾶσιν τοῖς ὑπακούουσιν αὐτῷ** the writer means οἱ πιστεύσαντες (4[3]), but with a special reference to their loyalty to Christ. Disobedience to Christ or to God (3[18] 4[6. 11]) is the practical expression of disbelief. It is a refusal to take Christ for what he is, as God's appointed ἀρχιερεύς. The writer then adds (v.[10]) **προσαγορευθεὶς ὑπὸ τοῦ θεοῦ ἀρχιερεὺς κατὰ τὴν τάξιν Μελχισεδέκ**, in order to explain how, thus commissioned, he brought the σωτηρία αἰωνίος. The paragraph is thus rounded off, like that of vv.[5. 6], with a reference to the Melchizedek priesthood, which the writer regards as of profound importance, and to which he now proposes to advance. Though προσαγορεύω is not used in this sense ("hail," "designate") in the LXX, the usage is common in Hellenistic writings like 2 Maccabees (1[36] 4[7] 10[9]) and Josephus (e.g. *c. Apion.* i. 311). But the Melchizedek type of priesthood is not discussed till 6[20] 7[1f.]. The interlude between 5[10] and 6[20] is devoted to a stirring exhortation; for this interpretation of the Son as priest is a piece of γνῶσις which can only be imparted to those who have mastered the elementary truths of the Christian religion, and the writer feels and fears that his readers are still so immature that they may be unable or unwilling to grasp the higher and fuller teaching about Christ. The admonition has three movements of thought, 5[11-14], 6[1-8], and 6[9-19].

[11] *On this point I* (ἡμῖν, plural of authorship, as 2[5]) *have a great deal to say, which it is hard to make intelligible to you. For* (καὶ γάρ=etenim) *you have*

grown dull of hearing. [12] *Though by this time you should be teaching other people, you still need someone to teach you once more the rudimentary principles of the divine revelation. You are in need of milk, not of solid food.* [13] (*For anyone who is fed on milk is unskilled in moral truth; he is*[1] *a mere babe.* [14] *Whereas solid food is for the mature, for those who have their faculties trained by exercise to distinguish good and evil.*) 6[1] *Let us pass on then to what is mature, leaving elementary Christian doctrine behind, instead of laying the foundation over again with repentance from dead works, with faith in God,* [2] *with instruction about ablutions and the laying on of hands, about the resurrection of the dead and eternal punishment.* [3] *With God's permission we will take this step.*

Περὶ οὗ (*i.e.* on ἀρχιερεὺς κατὰ τὴν τάξιν M.) **πολύς** κτλ. (v.[11]). The entire paragraph (vv.[11-14]) is full of ideas and terms current in the ethical and especially the Stoic philosophy of the day. Thus, to begin with, πολύς (*sc.* ἐστι) **ὁ λόγος** is a common literary phrase for "there is much to say"; *e.g.* Dion. Hal. *ad Amm.* i. 3, πολὺς γὰρ ὁ περὶ αὐτῶν λόγος, and Lysias *in Pancleonem*, 11, ὅσα μὲν οὖν αὐτόθι ἐρρήθη, πολὺς ἂν εἴη μοι λόγος δεηγεῖσθαι. Πολύς and δυσερμήνευτος are separated, as elsewhere adjectives are (*e.g.* 2[17]). For the general sense of **δυσερμήνευτος λέγειν**, see Philo, *de migrat. Abrah.* 18, ἧς τὰ μὲν ἄλλα μακροτέρων ἢ κατὰ τὸν παρόντα καιρὸν δεῖται λόγων καὶ ὑπερθετέον, and Dion. Halic. *de Comp.* viii. περὶ ὧν καὶ πολὺς ὁ λόγος καὶ βαθεῖα ἡ θεωρία. Δυσερμήνευτος occurs in an obscure and interpolated passage of Philo's *de Somniis* (i. 32, ἀλέκτῳ τινι καὶ δυσερμηνεύτῳ θέᾳ), and Artemidorus (*Oneirocr.* iii. 67, οἱ ὄνειροι . . . ποικίλοι καὶ πολλοῖς δυσερμήνευτοι) uses it of dreams. **Ἐπεί** κτλ. (explaining δυσερμήνευτοι) for the fault lies with you, not with the subject. **Νωθρός** only occurs once in the LXX, and not in this sense (Pr 22[29] ἀνδράσι νωθροῖς, tr. חָשֻׁךְ); even in Sir 4[29] 11[12] it means no more than slack or backward (as below in 6[12]). It is a common Greek ethical term for sluggishness, used with the accusative or the (locative) dative. With ἀκοή it denotes dulness. The literal sense occurs in Heliodorus (v. 10: ἐγὼ μὲν οὖν ᾐσθόμην . . . τάχα μέν που καὶ δι' ἡλικίαν νωθρότερος ὢν τὴν ἀκοήν· νόσος γὰρ ἄλλων τε καὶ ὤτων τὸ γῆρας), and the metaphorical sense of ἀκοαί is illustrated by Philo's remark in *quis rer. div. haer.* 3: ἐν ἀψύχοις ἀνδριᾶσιν, οἷς ὦτα μὲν ἐστιν, ἀκοαὶ δ' οὐκ ἔνεισιν.

Why (**καὶ γάρ**, v.[12]), the writer continues, instead of being teachers you still need a teacher. For χρεία with the article and infinitive (**τοῦ διδάσκειν**[2] κτλ.), cp. the similar use of χρέων in *OP.* 1488[25]. In what follows, **τινά**, the masculine singular, gives a better sense than **τίνα**, the neuter plural. "Ye again have need of (one) to teach you what are the elements" (sah boh); but it

[1] D* inserts ἀκμήν (Mt 15[16]) between γάρ and ἐστιν: "he is *still* a mere babe." Blass adopts this, for reasons of rhythm.

[2] 1912 and Origen read (with 462) διδάσκεσθαι, and omit ὑμᾶς.

is the elementary truths themselves, not what they are, that need to be taught. **Τὰ στοιχεῖα** here means the ABC or elementary principles (see Burton's *Galatians*, pp. 510 f.), such as he mentions in $6^{1.2}$. He defines them further as **τῆς ἀρχῆς τῶν λογίων θεοῦ**, where *τὰ λογία θεοῦ* means not the OT but the divine revelation in general, so that *τὰ σ. τ. ἀρχῆς* corresponds to the Latin phrase "prima elementa." The words **ὀφείλοντες εἶναι διδάσκαλοι** simply charge the readers with backwardness. "The expression, 'to be teachers,' affirms no more than that the readers ought to be ripe in Christian knowledge. Once a man is ripe or mature, the qualification for teaching is present" (Wrede, p. 32). The use of the phrase in Greek proves that it is a general expression for stirring people up to acquaint themselves with what should be familiar. See Epict. *Enchir.* 51, *ποῖον οὖν ἔτι διδάσκαλον προσδοκᾷς; . . . οὐκ ἔτι εἶ μειράκιον, ἀλλὰ ἀνὴρ ἤδη τέλειος.* It was quite a favourite ethical maxim in antiquity. Thus Cyrus tells the Persian chiefs that he would be ashamed to give them advice on the eve of battle: *οἶδα γὰρ ὑμᾶς ταῦτα ἐπισταμένους καὶ μεμελετηκότας καὶ ἀσκοῦντας διὰ τέλους οἷάπερ ἐγώ, ὥστε κἂν ἄλλους εἰκότως ἂν διδάσκοιτε* (*Cyrop.* iii. 3. 35). Similarly we have the remark of Aristophanes in Plato, *Sympos.* 189*d*, *ἐγὼ οὖν πειράσομαι ὑμῖν εἰσηγήσασθαι τὴν δύναμιν αὐτοῦ, ὑμεῖς δὲ τῶν ἄλλων διδάσκαλοι ἔσεσθε*, and the reply given by Apollonius of Tyana to a person who asked why he never put questions to anybody: *ὅτι μειράκιον ὢν ἐζήτησα, νῦν δὲ οὐ χρὴ ζητεῖν ἀλλὰ διδάσκειν ἃ εὕρηκα* (Philostratus, *Vita Apoll.* i. 17). Seneca tells Lucilius the same truth: "quousque disces? iam et praecipe (*Ep.* 33^9). Thus the phrase here offers no support whatever to any theories about the readers of Πρὸς Ἑβραίους being a group of teachers, or a small, specially cultured community. The author, himself a διδάσκαλος, as he is in possession of this mature *γνῶσις*, is trying to shame his friends out of their imperfect grasp of their religion. That is all. **Γεγόνατε χρείαν ἔχοντες** is a rhetorical variant for *χρείαν ἔχετε*, due to the writer's fondness for *γεγόνα*. If there is any special meaning in the larger phrase, it is that detected by Chrysostom, who argues that the writer chose it deliberately: *τουτέστιν, ὑμεῖς ἠθελήσατε, ὑμεῖς ἑαυτοὺς εἰς τοῦτο κατεστήσατε, εἰς ταύτην τὴν χρείαν.* They are responsible for this second childhood of theirs. The comparison [1] of milk and solid food is one of the most common in Greek

[1] Origen (*Philocalia*, xviii. 23) uses this passage neatly to answer Celsus, who had declared that Christians were afraid to appeal to an educated and intelligent audience. He quotes $5^{12f.}$ as well as 1 Co $3^{2f.}$, arguing that in the light of them it must be admitted *ἡμεῖς, ὅση δύναμις, πάντα πράττομεν ὑπὲρ τοῦ φρονίμων ἀνδρῶν γενέσθαι τὸν σύλλογον ἡμῶν· καὶ τὰ ἐν ἡμῖν μάλιστα καλὰ καὶ θεῖα τότε τολμῶμεν ἐν τοῖς πρὸς τὸ κοινὸν διαλόγοις φέρειν εἰς μέσον, ὅτ' εὐποροῦμεν συνετῶν ἀκροατῶν.*

ethical philosophy, as in Epictetus, *e.g.* ii. 16. 39, οὐ θέλεις ἤδη ὡς τὰ παιδία ἀπογαλακτισθῆναι καὶ ἅπτεσθαι τροφῆς στερεωτέρας, and iii. 24. 9, οὐκ ἀπογαλακτίσομεν ἤδη ποθ' ἑαυτούς, and particularly in Philo. A characteristic passage from the latter writer is the sentence in *de agric.* 2 : ἐπεὶ δὲ νηπίοις μὲν ἐστι γάλα τροφή, τελείοις δὲ τὰ ἐκ πυρῶν πέμματα, καὶ ψυχῆς γαλακτώδεις μὲν ἂν εἶεν τροφαὶ κατὰ τὴν παιδικὴν ἡλικίαν τὰ τῆς ἐγκυκλίου μουσικῆς προπαιδεύματα, τέλειαι δὲ καὶ ἀνδράσιν ἐμπρεπεῖς αἱ διὰ φρονήσεως καὶ σωφροσύνης καὶ ἁπάσης ἀρετῆς ὑφηγήσεις. Our writer adopts the metaphor, as Paul had done (1 Co 3[1. 2]), and adds a general aside (vv.[13. 14]) in order to enforce his remonstrance. He does not use the term γνῶσις, and the plight of his friends is not due to the same causes as operated in the Corinthian church, but he evidently regards his interpretation of the priesthood of Christ as mature instruction, **στερεὰ τροφή**. **Ὁ μετέχων γάλακτος** is one whose only food (μετέχειν as in 1 Co 10[17] etc.) is milk; **ἄπειρος** is "inexperienced," and therefore "unskilled," in **λόγου δικαιοσύνης**—an ethical phrase for what moderns would call "moral truth," almost as in Xen. *Cyrop.* i. 6. 31, ἀνὴρ διδάσκαλος τῶν παίδων, ὃς ἐδίδασκεν ἄρα τοὺς παῖδας τὴν δικαιοσύνην κτλ., or in M. Aurelius xi. 10, xii. 1. Thus, while **δικαιοσύνη** here is not a religious term, the phrase means more than (*a*) "incapable of talking correctly" (Delitzsch, B. Weiss, von Soden), which is, no doubt, the mark of a νήπιος, but irrelevant in this connexion; or (*b*) "incapable of understanding normal speech," such as grown-up people use (Riggenbach). **Τελείων δέ** κτλ. (v.[14]). The clearest statement of what contemporary ethical teachers meant by **τέλειος** as mature, is (cp. p. 70) in Epict. *Enchirid.* 51, "how long (εἰς ποῖον ἔτι χρόνον) will you defer thinking of yourself as worthy of the very best . . . ? You have received the precepts you ought to accept, and have accepted them. Why then do you still wait for a teacher (διδάσκαλον προσδοκᾷς), that you may put off amending yourself till he comes? You are a lad no longer, you are a full-grown man now (οὐκ ἔτι εἶ μειράκιον, ἀλλὰ ἀνὴρ ἤδη τέλειος). . . . Make up your mind, ere it is too late, to live ὡς τέλειον καὶ προκόπτοντα." Then he adds, in words that recall He 12[1f.]: "and when you meet anything stiff or sweet, glorious or inglorious, remember that νῦν ὁ ἀγὼν καὶ ἤδη πάρεστι τὰ Ὀλύμπια." As Pythagoras divided his pupils into νήπιοι and **τέλειοι**, so our author distinguishes between the immature and the mature (cp. 1 Co 2[6] ἐν τοῖς τελείοις, 3[1] νηπίοις). In **διὰ τὴν ἕξιν** (vg. "pro consuetudine") he uses ἕξις much as does the writer of the prologue to Sirach (ἱκανὴν ἕξιν περιποιησάμενος), for facility or practice.[1] It is not an equivalent for mental faculties here,

[1] "Firma quaedam facilitas quae apud Graecos ἕξις nominatur" (Quint. *Instit. Orat.* 10. 1).

but for the exercise of our powers. These powers or faculties are called **τὰ αἰσθητήρια.** *Αἰσθητήριον* was a Stoic term for an organ of the senses, and, like its English equivalent "sense," easily acquired an ethical significance, as in Jer 4[19] *τὰ αἰσθητήρια τῆς καρδίας μου.* The phrase **γεγυμνασμένα αἰσθητήρια** may be illustrated from Galen (*de dign. puls.* iii. 2, ὃς μὲν γὰρ ἂν εὐαισθητότατον φύσιν τε καὶ τὸ αἰσθητήριον ἔχῃ γεγυμνασμένον ἱκανῶς . . . οὗτος ἂν ἄριστος εἴη γνώμων τῶν ἐντὸς ὑποκειμένων, and *de complexu*, ii. : λελογισμένου μὲν ἐστιν ἀνδρὸς τοὺς λογισμοὺς οὓς εἴρηκα καὶ γεγυμνασμένα τὴν αἴσθησιν ἐν πολλῇ τῇ κατὰ μέρος ἐμπειρίᾳ κτλ.), *γεγυμνασμένα* being a perfect participle used predicatively, like *πεφυτευμένην* in Lk 13[6], and *γεγυμνασμένον* above. Compare what Marcus Aurelius (iii. 1) says about old age; it may come upon us, bringing not physical failure, but a premature decay of the mental and moral faculties, *e.g.*, of self-control, of the sense of duty, *καὶ ὅσα τοιαῦτα λογισμοῦ συγγεγυμνασμένου πάνυ χρῄζει.* Elsewhere (ii. 13) he declares that ignorance of moral distinctions (*ἄγνοια ἀγαθῶν καὶ κακῶν*) is a blindness as serious as any inability to distinguish black and white. The power of moral discrimination (**πρὸς διάκρισιν καλοῦ τε καὶ κακοῦ**) is the mark of maturity, in contrast to childhood (cp. *e.g.* Dt 1[39] *πᾶν παιδίον νέον ὅστις οὐκ οἶδεν σήμερον ἀγαθὸν ἢ κακόν*). Compare the definition of *τὸ ἠθικόν* in Sextus Empiricus (*Hyp. Pyrrh.* iii. 168): *ὅπερ δοκεῖ περὶ τὴν διάκρισιν τῶν τε καλῶν καὶ κακῶν καὶ ἀδιαφόρων καταγίγνεσθαι.*

In spite of Resch's arguments (*Texte u. Untersuchungen*, xxx. 3. 112 f.), there is no reason to hear any echo of the well-known saying attributed to Jesus: *γίνεσθε δὲ δόκιμοι τραπεζῖται, τὰ μὲν ἀποδοκιμάζοντες, τὸ δὲ καλὸν κατέχοντες.*

Διὸ—well then (as in 12[12. 28])—**ἐπὶ τὸν τελειότητα φερώμεθα** (6[1]). It is a moral duty to grow up, and the duty involves an effort. The *τελειότης* in question is the mature mental grasp of the truth about Christ as *ἀρχιερεύς*, a truth which the writer is disappointed that his friends still find it difficult to understand. However, *διὰ τὸν χρόνον* they ought to understand it. He has every reason to expect an effort from them, and therefore he follows up his remonstrance with a word of encouragement. Instead of the sharp, severe tone of vv.[11f.], he now speaks more hopefully. The connexion is not easy. We expect "however" instead of "well then." But the connexion is not made more easy by regarding 6[1f.] as a resolve of the writer: "since you are so immature, I am going on myself to develop the higher teaching." It would be senseless for a teacher to take this line, and it is not facilitated by reading *φερόμεθα*. The plural is not the literary plural as in 5[11]. The writer wishes to carry his readers along with him. "If you want anyone to instruct you over again in rudimentary Christianity, I am not the man; I propose to carry you forward into a higher course of lessons. Come, let us advance, you and I together." The underlying thought, which explains the transition, is revealed in the next paragraph (vv.$^{4f.}$), where the writer practically tells his readers that they must either advance or lose their present position of faith,[1] in which latter case there is no second chance for them. In spite of his unqualified censure in 5^{12}, he shows, in $6^{9f.}$, that they are really capable of doing what he summons them to try in $6^{1f.}$, *i.e.* to think out the full significance of Jesus in relation to faith and forgiveness. Only thus, he argues, can quicken the faint pulse of your religious life. "Religion is something different from mere strenuous thinking on the great religious questions. Yet it still remains true that faith and knowledge are inseparable, and that both grow stronger as they react on one another. More often than we know, the failure of religion, as a moral power, is due to no other cause than intellectual sloth" (E. F. Scott, p. 44). After the parenthesis of $5^{13.14}$, the writer resumes the thought with which he started in 5^{11a} "you must make an effort to enter into this larger appreciation of what Christ means." **Ἀφεντες . . . φερώμεθα** is a phrase illustrated by Eurip. *Androm.* 392–393, *τὴν ἀρχὴν ἀφεὶς | πρὸς τὴν τελευτὴν ὑστέραν οὖσαν φέρῃ*: by *ἀφέντες* the writer means "leaving behind," and by *φερώμεθα* "let us advance." Ἀφίημι might even mean "to omit" ("not mentioning"); it is so used with *λόγον* (=to pass over without mentioning), *e.g.* in Plutarch's *an seni respublica gerenda sit*, 18, *ἀλλ' ἀφέντες, εἰ βούλει, τὸν ἀποσπῶντα τῆς πολιτείας λόγον ἐκεῖνο σκοπῶμεν ἤδη κτλ.*, and even independently (cp. Epict. iv. 1. 15, *τὸν μὲν Καίσαρα πρὸς τὸ παρὸν ἀφῶμεν*, and Theophrastus, *prooem. ἀφεὶς τὸ προοιμιάζεσθαι καὶ πολλὰ περὶ τοῦ πράγματος λέγειν*). In what follows, **τὸν τῆς ἀρχῆς τοῦ Χριστοῦ λόγον** is a variant for *τὰ στοιχεῖα τῆς ἀρχῆς τῶν λογίων τοῦ θεοῦ* (5^{12}). Τοῦ Χριστοῦ is an objective genitive; the writer is not thinking of injunctions issued by Christ (so Harnack, *Constitution and Law of the Church*, p. 344). Blass follows L in reading *λοιπόν* after *λόγον*—needlessly.

The use of the **θεμέλιον** metaphor after **τῆς ἀρχῆς** was natural; it occurs in Epictetus (ii. 15. 8, *οὐ θέλεις τὴν ἀρχὴν στῆσαι καὶ τὸν θεμέλιον*) and in Philo (*de spec. leg.* ii. 13, *ἀρχὴν ταύτην βαλλόμενος ὥσπερ θεμέλιόν τινα*). Indeed the *θεμέλιον* metaphor is particularly common in Philo, as, *e.g.*, in the *de vita contempl.* 476 (*ἐγκράτειαν δὲ ὥσπερ τινὰ θεμέλιον προκαταβαλλόμενοι ψυχῆς*). This basis (**θεμέλιον**) of Christian instruction is now described; the contents are arranged in three pairs, but, as the middle pair are not distinctively Christian ideas (v.^{2}), the writer puts in

[1] Compare the motto which Cromwell is said to have written on his pocket-bible, "qui cessat esse melior cessat esse bonus."

διδαχήν or **διδαχῆς**. The *θεμέλιον* of instruction consists of *μετανοίας . . . καὶ πίστεως* (genitives of quality), while *διδαχήν*, which is in apposition to it ("I mean, instruction about"), controls the other four genitives. **Μετάνοια** and **πίστις, βαπτισμοί** and **ἐπιθέσις χειρῶν, ἀνάστασις** and **κρίμα αἰώνιον**, are the fundamental truths. Μετάνοια[1] *ἀπό* is like *μετανοεῖν ἀπό* (Ac 8^{22}), and *πίστις ἐπὶ θεόν* like *πιστεύειν ἐπί* (*e.g.* Wis 12^{2} *ἵνα ἀπαλλαγέντες τῆς κακίας πιστεύσωμεν ἐπὶ σέ, κύριε*). These two requirements were foremost in the programme of the Christian mission. The other side of repentance is described in 9^{14} *πόσῳ μᾶλλον τὸ αἷμα τοῦ Χριστοῦ . . . καθαριεῖ τὴν συνείδησιν ἡμῶν ἀπὸ νεκρῶν ἔργων εἰς τὸ λατρεύειν θεῷ ζῶντι*, where the last word indicates that *νεκρὰ ἔργα* mean the conduct of those who are outside the real life and service of God. Practically, therefore, *νεκρὰ ἔργα* are sins, as the Greek fathers assumed; the man who wrote 11^{25} (*θεοῦ . . . ἁμαρτίας*) would hardly have hesitated to call them such. He has coined this phrase to suggest that such *ἔργα* have no principle of life in them,[2] or that they lead to death. The origin of the phrase has not been explained, though Chrysostom and Oecumenius were right in suggesting that the metaphor of 9^{14} was derived from the contamination incurred by touching a corpse (see Nu $19^{1f.}$ 31^{19}). Its exact meaning is less clear. The one thing that is clear about it is that these *ἔργα νεκρά* were not habitual sins of Christians; they were moral offences from which a man had to break away, in order to become a Christian at all. They denote not the lifeless, formal ceremonies of Judaism, but occupations, interests, and pleasures, which lay within the sphere of moral death, where, as a contemporary Christian writer put it (Eph 2^{1}), pagans lay *νεκροὶ τοῖς παραπτώμασιν καὶ ταῖς ἁμαρτίαις*. The phrase might cover Jewish Christians, if there were any such in the community to which this homily is addressed, but it is a general phrase. Whatever is evil is *νεκρόν*, for our author, and *ἔργα νεκρά* render any Christian *πίστις* or *λατρεύειν* impossible (cp. *Expositor*, Jan. 1918, pp. 1–18), because they belong to the profane, contaminating sphere of the world.

In v.[2] **διδαχήν** is read, instead of **διδαχῆς**, by B syr^{harkl} and the Old Latin, a very small group—yet the reading is probably

[1] According to Philo (*de Abrah.* 2, 3), next to hope, which is the *ἄρχη μετουσίας ἀγαθῶν*, comes *ἡ ἐπὶ ἁμαρτανομένοις μετάνοια καὶ βελτίωσις*. Only, he adds (*ibid.* 4), repentance is second to *τελειότης, ὥσπερ καὶ ἀνόσου σώματος ἡ πρὸς ὑγιείαν ἐξ ἀσθενείας μεταβολὴ . . . ἡ δ' ἀπό τινος χρόνου βελτίωσις ἴδιον ἀγαθὸν εὐφυοῦς ψυχῆς ἐστι μὴ τοῖς παιδικοῖς ἐπιμενούσης ἀλλ' ἁδροτέροις καὶ ἀνδρὸς ὄντως φρονήμασιν ἐπιζητούσης εὔδιον κατάστασιν [ψυχῆς] καὶ τῇ φαντασίᾳ τῶν καλῶν ἐπιτρεχούσης.*

[2] Cp. the use of *νεκρός* in Epict. iii. 23. 28, *καὶ μὴν ἂν μὴ ταῦτα ἐμποιῇ ὁ τοῦ φιλοσόφου λόγος, νεκρός ἐστι καὶ αὐτὸς καὶ ὁ λέγων.* This passage indicates how *νεκρός* could pass from the vivid application to persons (Mt 8^{22}, Lk 15^{32}, cp. Col 2^{13}), into a secondary application to their sphere and conduct.

original; the surrounding genitives led to its alteration into διδαχῆς. However, it makes no difference to the sense, which reading is chosen. Even διδαχῆς depends on θεμέλιον as a qualifying genitive. But the change of διδαχήν into διδαχῆς is much more likely than the reverse process. Διδαχήν follows βαπτισμῶν like κόσμος in 1 P 3[3] (ἐνδύσεως ἱματίων κόσμος). **Βαπτισμοί** by itself does not mean specifically Christian baptism either in this epistle (9[10]) or elsewhere (Mk 7[4]), but ablutions or immersions such as the mystery religions and the Jewish cultus required for initiates, proselytes, and worshippers in general. The singular might mean Christian baptism (as in Col 2[12]), but why does the writer employ the plural here? Not because in some primitive Christian circles the catechumen was thrice sprinkled or immersed in the name of the Trinity (Didache 7[1-3]), but because ancient religions, such as those familiar to the readers, had all manner of purification rites connected with water (see on 10[22]). The distinctively Christian uses of water had to be grasped by new adherents. That is, at baptism, *e.g.*, the catechumen would be specially instructed about the difference between this Christian rite, with its symbolic purification from sins of which one repented, and (*a*) the similar rites in connexion with Jewish proselytes on their reception into the synagogue or with adherents who were initiated into various cults, and (*b*) the ablutions which were required from Christians in subsequent worship. The latter practice may be alluded to in 10[22] (λελουσμένοι τὸ σῶμα ὕδατι καθαρῷ). Justin (*Apol.* i. 62) regards these lustrations of the cults as devilish caricatures of real baptism: καὶ τὸ λουτρὸν δὴ τοῦτο ἀκούσαντες οἱ δαίμονες . . . ἐνήργησαν καὶ ῥαντίζειν ἑαυτοὺς τοὺς εἰς τὰ ἱερὰ αὐτῶν ἐπιβαίνοντας καὶ προσιέναι αὐτοῖς μέλλοντας, λοιβὰς καὶ κνίσας ἀποτελοῦντας τέλεον δὲ καὶ λούεσθαι ἐπιόντας πρὶν ἐλθεῖν ἐπὶ τὰ ἱερά, ἔνθα ἵδρυνται, ἐνεργοῦσι. The **ἐπιθέσις χειρῶν** which often followed baptism in primitive days (*e.g.* Ac 8[17f.] 19[6]), though it is ignored by the Didache and Justin, was supposed to confer the holy Spirit (see v.[4]). Tertullian witnesses to the custom (*de baptismo*, 18, *de carnis resurrectione*, 8), and Cyprian corroborates it (*Ep.* lxxiv. 5, "manus baptizato imponitur ad accipiendum spiritum sanctum"). The rite was employed in blessing, in exorcising, and at "ordination," afterwards at the reception of penitents and heretics; here it is mentioned in connexion with baptism particularly (*ERE.* vi. 494*b*).

The subject is discussed in monographs like A. J. Mason's *The Relation of Confirmation to Baptism* (1891), and J. Behm's *Die Handauflegung im Urchristenthum* (1911).

The final pair of doctrines is **ἀναστάσεως νεκρῶν καὶ κρίματος** (2[14. 15] 9[27]) **αἰωνίου** (as in Ac 24[15. 25]). **Τε** is added after ἀναστάσεως mechanically (to conform with the preceding τε) by ℵ A C K L Lat arm syr[hkl pesh], just as it is added after βαπτισμῶν by harkl. In the rather elliptical style and loose construction of the whole sentence, "notwithstanding its graceful rhythmical structure," it is possible to see, with Bruce (p. 203), "an oratorical device to express a feeling of impatience" with people who need to have such *principia* mentioned. At any rate the writer hastens forward. V.[3] is not a parenthesis ("I will do this," *i.e.* go over such elementary truths with you, "if God permits," when I reach you, 13[23]); the **τοῦτο** refers to the advance proposed in v.[1], and after **ποιήσομεν** the author adds reverently, "if God permits," **ἐάνπερ ἐπιτρέπῃ ὁ θεός**, almost as a contemporary rhetorician might say in a pious aside: ἐὰν δὲ σῴζῃ τὸ δαιμόνιον ἡμᾶς (Dion. Halicarn. *De Admir. Vi dicendi in Dem.* 58), or θεῶν ἡμᾶς φυλαττόντων ἀσινεῖς τέ καὶ ἀνόσους (*De Composit. Verborum*, 1). The papyri show that similar phrases were current in the correspondence of the day (cp. Deissmann's *Bible Studies*, p. 80), and Josephus (*Ant.* XX. 11. 2) uses κἂν τὸ θεῖον ἐπιτρεπῇ.

ποιήσομεν (ℵ B K L N 1. 2. 5. 6. 33. 69. 88. 216. 218. 221. 226. 242. 255. 337. 429. 489. 919. 920. 1149. 1518. 1739. 1758. 1827. 1867. 2127. 2143. Lat sah boh Chrys.) has been changed into ποιήσωμεν by A C D P arm, etc., though the latter may have been originally, like φερόμεθα in v.[1], an orthographical variant, ο and ω being frequently confused.

[4] *For in the case of people who have been once enlightened, who tasted the heavenly Gift, who participated in the holy Spirit,* [5] *who tasted the goodness of God's word and the powers of the world to come,* [6] *and then fell away—it is impossible to make them repent afresh, since they crucify the Son of God in their own persons and hold him up to obloquy.* [7] *For "land" which absorbs the rain that often falls on it, and bears "plants" that are useful to those for whom it is tilled, receives a blessing from God;* [8] *whereas, if it* (*sc.* ἡ γῆ) *"produces thorns and thistles," it is reprobate and on the verge of being cursed—its fate is to be burned.*

Vv.[4-6] put the reason for **τοῦτο ποιήσομεν** (v.[3]), and vv.[7. 8] give the reason for **ἀδύνατον . . . ἀνακαινίζειν εἰς μετάνοιαν** (vv.[4-6]). **Ἀδύνατον γάρ** κτλ. (v.[4]); there are four impossible things in the epistle: this and the three noted in vv.[18] 10[4] and 11[6]. **Τοὺς . . . αἰῶνος** ([4. 5a]) is a long description of people who have been initiated into Christianity; then comes the tragic **καὶ παραπεσόντας**. What makes the latter so fatal is explained in (v.[6]) **ἀνασταυροῦντας . . . παραδειγματίζοντας**. Logically **πάλιν ἀνακαινίζειν εἰς μετάνοιαν** ought to come immediately after **ἀδύνατον γάρ**, but the writer delayed the phrase in order to break up the sequence of participles. The passage is charged with an austerity which shows how seriously the writer took life. Seneca quotes (*Ep.* xxiii. 9-11) to Lucilius the saying of Epicurus, that "it is irksome always to be starting life over again," and that "they live badly who are always beginning to live." The reason is: "quia semper illis imperfecta vita est." But our writer takes a much more sombre view of the position of his friends. He urges them to develop their ideas of Christianity. "You need some one to teach you the rudimentary lessons of the faith all over again," he had said. "Yes," he now adds, "and in some cases that is impossible. Relaying a foundation of repentance, etc.! That cannot be done for deliberate apostates." The implication is that his readers are in danger of this sin, as indeed he has hinted already (in 3^7–4^{14}), and that one of the things that is weakening them is their religious inability to realize the supreme significance of Jesus. To remain as they are is fatal; it means the possibility of a relapse altogether. "Come on," the writer bids them, "for if you do not you will fall back, and to fall back is to be ruined." The connexion between this passage and the foregoing, therefore, is that to rest content with their present elementary hold upon Christian truth is to have an inadequate grasp of it; the force of temptation is so strong that this rudimentary acquaintance with it will not prevent them from falling away altogether, and the one thing to ensure their religious position is to see the full meaning of what Jesus is and does. This meaning he is anxious to impart, not as an extra but as an essential. The situation is so serious, he implies, that only those who fully realize what Jesus means for forgiveness and fellowship will be able to hold out. And once you relapse, he argues, once you let go your faith, it is fatal; people who deliberately abandon their Christian confession of faith are beyond recovery. Such a view of apostasy as a heinous offence, which destroyed all hope of recovery, is characteristic of Πρὸς Ἑβραίους. It was not confined to this writer. That certain persons could not repent of their sins was, *e.g.*, an idea admitted in rabbinic Judaism. "Over and over again we have the saying: 'For him who sins and causes others to sin no repentance is allowed or possible' (Aboth v. 26; Sanhedrin, 107*b*). 'He who is wholly given up to sin is unable to repent, and there is no forgiveness to him for ever' (Midrash Tehillim on Ps 1 *ad fin.*)."[1] There is a partial parallel to this passage in the idea thrown out by Philo in *de agricultura*, 28, as he comments upon Gn 9^{20}: "Noah began to till the earth." Evidently, says Philo, this means that he was merely working at the ἄρχαι of the subject. Ἀρχὴ δ', ὁ τῶν παλαιῶν λόγος, ἥμισυ τοῦ πάντος, ὡς ἂν ἡμίσει πρὸς τὸ τέλος ἀφεστηκυῖα, οὗ μὴ προσγενομένου καὶ τὸ ἄρξασθαι πολλάκις μεγάλα πολλοὺς ἔβλαψεν. His point is that it is dangerous to stop short in any moral endeavour. But our author is more rigorous in his outlook. His warning is modified, however. (*a*) It is put in the form of a general statement.

[1] C. G. Montefiore, in *Jewish Quarterly Review* (1904), p. 225.

(*b*) It contains a note of encouragement in v.[7]; and (*c*) it is at once followed up by an eager hope that the readers will disappoint their friend and teacher's fear (v.[9]). In the later church this feature of Πρὸς Ἑβραίους entered into the ecclesiastical question of penance (cp. *ERE.* ix. 716, and *Journal of Theological Studies*, iv. 321 f.), and seriously affected the vogue of the epistle (cp. Introd. p. xx).

The fourfold description of believers ([4. 5a]) begins with **ἅπαξ φωτισθέντας**, where φωτισθέντας corresponds to λαβεῖν τὴν ἐπίγνωσιν τῆς ἀληθείας (10[26]), in the general sense of LXX (*e.g.* Ps 118[130] ἡ δήλωσις τῶν λόγων σου φωτιεῖ, καὶ συνετεῖ νηπίους), *i.e.* "enlightened" in the sense of having their eyes opened (Eph 1[18]) to the Christian God. Subsequently, earlier even than Justin Martyr, the verb, with its noun φωτισμός, came to be used of baptism specifically (cp. *ERE.* viii. 54, 55). Ἅπαξ is prefixed, in contrast to **πάλιν** (v.[6]); once for all men enter Christianity, it is an experience which, like their own death (9[27]) and the death of Jesus (9[28]), can never be repeated. In **καλὸν γευσαμένους θεοῦ ῥῆμα** ("experienced how good the gospel is") the construction resembles that of Herod. vii. 46, where the active voice is used with the accusative (ὁ δὲ θεὸς γλυκὺν γεύσας τὸν αἰῶνα, φθονερὸς ἐν αὐτῷ εὑρίσκεται ἐών), and the adj. is put first: "the deity, who let us taste the sweetness of life (or, that life is sweet), is found to be spiteful in so doing." The similar use of the middle here as in Pr 29[36] and Jn 2[9] probably points to the same meaning (cp., however, *Diat.* 2016–2018), *i.e.*, practically as if it were ὅτι κτλ. (cp. Ps 34[8] γεύσασθε καὶ ἴδετε ὅτι χρηστὸς ὁ κύριος, 1 P 2[3]), in contrast to the more common construction with the genitive (v.[4] 2[9]). The writer uses genitive and accusative indifferently, for the sake of literary variety; and καλόν here is the same as καλοῦ in 5[14]. **Γευσαμένους κτλ.** recalls the partiality of Philo for this metaphor (e.g. *de Abrah.* 19; *de Somniis*, i. 26), but indeed it is common (cp. *e.g.* Jos. *Ant.* iv. 6. 9, ἅπαξ τὸ νέον γευσαμένον ξενικῶν ἐθισμῶν ἀπλήστως αὐτῶν ἐνεφορεῖτο) throughout contemporary Hellenistic Greek as a metaphor for experiencing. Probably **γευσαμένους . . . ἐπουρανίου, μετόχους . . . ἁγίου,** and **καλὸν γευσαμένους αἰῶνος** are three rhetorical expressions for the initial experience described in **ἅπαξ φωτισθέντας.** "The heavenly Gift" (τῆς δωρεᾶς τῆς ἐπουρανίου) may be the Christian salvation in general, which is then viewed as the impartation of the holy Spirit, and finally as the revelation of the higher world which even already is partly realized in the experience of faith. Note that **φωτισθέντας** is followed by **γευσαμένους κτλ.**, as the light-metaphor is followed by the food-metaphor in Philo's (*de fuga et invent.* 25) remarks upon the manna (Ex 16[15. 16]): ἡ θεία σύνταξις αὕτη τὴν ὁρατικὴν ψυχὴν φωτίζει τε καὶ ὁμοῦ καὶ γλυκαίνει . . . τοὺς διψῶντας καὶ πεινῶντας καλοκἀγαθίας ἐφηδύνουσα. Also, that **δυνάμεις τε μέλλοντος αἰῶνος**[1] includes the thrilling experiences mentioned in 2⁴. The dramatic turn comes in (v.[6]) **καὶ παραπεσόντας**. Παραπίπτειν is here used in its most sinister sense; it corresponds to ἀποστῆναι (3[12]), and indeed both verbs are used in the LXX to translate the same term פעל. The usage in Wis 6[9] (μὴ παραπέσητε) 12[2] (τοὺς παραπίπτσοντας) paves the way for this sense of a deliberate renunciation of the Christian God, which is equivalent to ἑκουσίως ἁμαρτάνειν in 10[26]. The sin against the holy Spirit, which Jesus regarded as unpardonable, the mysterious ἁμαρτία πρὸς θάνατον of 1 Jn 5[16], and this sin of apostasy, are on the same level. The writer never hints at what his friends might relapse into. Anything that ignored Christ was to him hopeless.

'Αδύνατον (*sc.* ἐστι) is now (v.[6]) taken up in **ἀνακαινίζειν** (for which Paul prefers the form ἀνακαινοῦν), a LXX term (*e.g.* Ps 51[12]) which is actually used for the Christian start in life by Barnabas (6[11] ἀνακαινίσας ἡμᾶς ἐν τῇ ἀφέσει τῶν ἁμαρτιῶν), and naturally of the divine action. **Πάλιν** is prefixed for emphasis, as in Isokr. *Areopag.* 3, τῆς ἔχθρας τῆς πρὸς τὸν βασιλέα πάλιν ἀνακεκαινισμένης.

There have been various, vain efforts to explain the apparent harshness of the statement. Erasmus took ἀδύνατον (like d=difficile) as "difficult"; Grotius said it was impossible "per legem Mosis"; others take ἀνακαινίζειν to mean "keep on renewing," while some, like Schoettgen, Bengel, and Wickham, fall back on the old view that while men could not, God might effect it. But even the last-named idea is out of the question. If the writer thought of any subject to ἀνακαινίζειν, it was probably a Christian διδάσκαλος like himself; but the efforts of such a Christian are assumed to be the channel of the divine power, and no renewal could take place without God. There is not the faintest suggestion that a second repentance might be produced by God when human effort failed. The tenor of passages like 10[28f.] and 12[17] tells finally against this modification of the language. A similarly ominous tone is heard in Philo's comment on Nu 30[10] in *quod deter. pot. insid.* 40: φήσομεν διάνοιαν . . . ἐκβεβλῆσθαι καὶ χήραν θεοῦ, ἥτις ἢ γονὰς θείας οὐ παρεδέξατο ἢ παραδεξαμένη ἑκουσίως αὖθις ἐξήμβλωσε . . . ἡ δ' ἅπαξ διαζευχθεῖσα καὶ διοικισθεῖσα ὡς ἄσπονδος μέχρι τοῦ παντὸς αἰῶνος ἐκτετόξευται, εἰς τὸν ἀρχαῖον οἶκον ἐπανελθεῖν ἀδυνατοῦσα.

The reason why a second repentance is impossible is given in **ἀνασταυροῦντας . . . παραδειγματίζοντας**, where **ἀνασταυροῦντας** is used instead of σταυροῦντας, for the sake of assonance (after ἀνακαινίζειν), but with the same meaning. 'Ανασταυροῦν simply means "to crucify," as, *e.g.*, in Plato's *Gorgias*, 28 (τοὺς αὐτοῦ ἐπιδὼν

[1] Tertullian's translation, "occidente iam aevo" (*de Pudicitia*, 20) shows that his Greek text had omitted a line by accident:

ΝΟΥΣΘ̅Υ̅ΡΗΜΑΔΥΝ
ΑΜΕΙΣΤΕΜΕΛΛ
ΟΝΤΟΣΑΙΩΝΟCΚΑΙ,

i.e. δυν[άμεις τε μέλλ]οντος αἰῶνος.

παῖδας τε καὶ γυναῖκα τὸ ἔσχατον ἀνασταυρωθῇ ἢ καταπιττωθῇ); Thucyd. i. 110 (Ἰνάρως . . . προδοσίᾳ ληφθεὶς ἀνεσταυρώθη); Josephus (*Ant.* xi. 6. 10, ἀνασταυρῶσαι τὸν Μαρδοχαῖον), etc. The ἀνα = sursum, not rursum, though the Greek fathers (*e.g.* Chrys. τὶ δέ ἐστιν ἀνασταυροῦντας; ἄνωθεν πάλιν σταυροῦντας), and several of the versions (*e.g.* vg "rursum crucifigentes"), took it in the sense of re-crucify. **Ἑαυτοῖς**: it is *their* crucifixion of Jesus. "The thought is that of wilfulness rather than of detriment" (Vaughan).

In the story of Jesus and Peter at Rome, which Origen mentions as part of the Acts of Paul (*in Joh.* xx. 12), the phrase, "to be crucified over again" occurs in a different sense (*Texte u. Unters.* xxx. 3, pp. 271–272). Καὶ ὁ κύριος αὐτῷ εἶπεν· εἰσέρχομαι εἰς τὴν Ῥώμην σταυρωθῆναι. Καὶ ὁ Πέτρος εἶπεν αὐτῷ· Κύριε, πάλιν σταυροῦσαι; εἶπεν αὐτῷ· ναί, Πέτρε, πάλιν σταυροῦμαι. Origen, quoting this as Ἄνωθεν μέλλω σταυροῦσθαι, holds that such is the meaning of ἀνασταυροῦν in He 6^{6}.

The meaning of the vivid phrase is that they put Jesus out of their life, they break off all connexion with him; he is dead to them. This is the decisive force of σταυροῦσθαι in Gal 6^{14}. The writer adds an equally vivid touch in **καὶ παραδειγματίζοντας** (= τὸν υἱὸν θεοῦ καταπατήσας κτλ., 10^{29})—as if he is not worth their loyalty! Their repudiation of him proclaims to the world that they consider him useless, and that the best thing they can do for themselves is to put him out of their life. **Παραδειγματίζειν** is used in its Hellenistic sense, which is represented by τιθέναι εἰς παράδειγμα in the LXX (Nah 3^{6}). Possibly the term was already associated with impaling (cp. Nu 25^{4} παραδειγμάτισον αὐτοὺς Κυρίῳ),[1] but our author does not use it in the LXX sense of "make an example of" (by punishing); the idea is of exposing to contemptuous ignominy, in public (as in Mt 1^{19}).

The Bithynians who had renounced Christianity proved to Pliny their desertion by maligning Christ—one of the things which, as he observed, no real Christian would do ("quorum nihil posse cogi dicuntur qui sunt re vera Christiani"). "Omnes . . . Christi male dixerunt." When the proconsul urges Polykarp to abandon Christianity, he tells the bishop, λοιδόρησον τὸν Χριστόν (*Mart. Polyk.* ix. 3). The language of **Πρὸς Ἑβραίους** is echoed in the saying of Jesus quoted in *Apost. Const.* vi. 18: οὗτοί εἰσι περὶ ὧν καὶ ὁ κύριος πικρῶς καὶ ἀποτόμως ἀπεφήνατο λέγων ὅτι εἰσὶ ψευδόχριστοι καὶ ψευδοδιδάσκαλοι, οἱ βλασφημήσαντες τὸ πνεῦμα τῆς χάριτος καὶ ἀποπτύσαντες τὴν παρ' αὐτοῦ δωρεὰν μετὰ τὴν χάριν, οἷς οὐκ ἀφεθήσεται οὔτε ἐν τῷ αἰῶνι τούτῳ οὔτε ἐν τῷ μέλλοντι. In Sir 31^{30} (βαπτιζόμενος ἀπὸ νεκροῦ καὶ πάλιν ἁπτόμενος αὐτοῦ, τί ὠφέλησεν τῷ λουτρῷ αὐτοῦ;) the allusion is to the taboo-law of Nu $19^{11.\,12}$; the parallel is verbal rather than real. But there is a true parallel in Mongolian Buddhism, which ranks five sins as certain "to be followed by a hell of intense sufferings, and that without cessation . . . patricide, matricide, killing a Doctor of Divinity (*i.e.* a lama), bleeding Buddha, sowing hatred among priests. . . . Drawing blood from the body of Buddha is a figurative expression, after the manner of He 6^{6}" (J. Gilmour, *Among the Mongols*, pp. 233, 234).

[1] In alluding to the gibbeting law of Dt $21^{22f.}$, Josephus (*Bell. Jud.* iv. 5. 2) speaks of ἀνασταυροῦν.

In the little illustration (vv.[7.8]), which corresponds to what Jesus might have put in the form of a parable, there are reminiscences of the language about God's curse upon the ground (Gn 3[17.18]): ἐπικατάρατος ἡ γῆ . . . ἀκάνθας καὶ τριβόλους ἀνατελεῖ, and also of the words in Gn 1[12] καὶ ἐξήνεγκεν ἡ γῆ βοτάνην χόρτου, though the writer uses ἐκφέρειν for ἀνατέλλειν, and prefers τίκτειν to ἐκφέρειν (in v.[7]). The image of a plot or field is mentioned by Quintilian (*Instit. Orat.* v. 11. 24) as a common instance of the παραβολή: "ut, si animum dicas excolendum, similitudine utaris terrae quae neglecta spinas ac dumos, culta fructus creat." The best Greek instance is in Euripides (*Hecuba*, 592 f.: οὔκουν δεινόν, εἰ γῆ μὲν κακὴ | τυχοῦσα καιροῦ θεόθεν εὖ στάχυν φέρει, | χρηστὴ δ' ἁμαρτοῦσ' ὧν χρεὼν αὐτὴν τυχεῖν | κακὸν δίδωσι καρπόν κτλ.). **Πιοῦσα** of land, as, *e.g.*, in Dt 11[11] γῆ . . . ἐκ τοῦ ὑετοῦ τοῦ οὐρανοῦ πίεται ὕδωρ: Is 55[10f.] etc. As **εὔθετος** generally takes εἰς with the accusative, it is possible that **τίκτουσα** was meant to go with ἐκείνοις. **Γεωργεῖται**, of land being worked or cultivated, is a common term in the papyri (*e.g. Syll.* 429[9] τά τε χωρία εἰ γεωργεῖται) as well as in the LXX.

(*a*) Origen's homiletical comment (*Philocalia*, xxi. 9) is, τὰ γινόμενα ὑπὸ τοῦ θεοῦ τεράστια οἱονεὶ ὑετός ἐστιν· αἱ δὲ προαιρέσεις αἱ διάφοροι οἱονεὶ ἡ γεγεωργημένη γῆ ἐστι καὶ ἡ ἠμελημένη, μιᾷ τῇ φύσει ὡς γῆ τυγχάνουσα—an idea similar to that of Jerome (*tractatus de psalmo xcvi.*, Anecdota Maredsolana, iii. 3. 90: "apostolorum epistolae nostrae pluviae sunt spiritales. Quid enim dicit Paulus in epistola ad Hebraeos? Terra enim saepe venientem super se bibens imbrem, et reliqua"). (*b*) The Mishna directs that at the repetition of the second of the Eighteen Blessings the worshipper should think of the heavy rain and pray for it at the ninth Blessing (Berachoth, 5[1]), evidently because the second declares, "Blessed art thou, O Lord, who restorest the dead" (rain quickening the earth), and the ninth runs, "Bless to us, O Lord our God, this year and grant us a rich harvest and bring a blessing on our land." Also, "on the occasion of the rains and good news, one says, Blessed be He who is good and does good" (Berachoth, 9[2]). Cp. Marcus Aurelius, v. 7, εὐχὴ Ἀθηναίων· ὗσον, ὗσον, ὦ φίλε Ζεῦ, κατὰ τῆς ἀρούρας τῆς Ἀθηναίων καὶ τῶν πεδίων.

Μεταλαμβάνει (= participate in) is not a LXX term, but occurs in this sense in Wis 18[9] etc.; **εὐλογίας** occurs again in 12[17] (of Esau the apostate missing his εὐλογία), and there is a subtle suggestion here, that those alone who make use of their divine privileges are rewarded. What the writer has in mind is brought out in v.[10]; that he was thinking of the Esau-story here is shown by the reminiscence of ἀγροῦ ὃν ηὐλόγησεν Κύριος (Gn 27[27]).

The reverse side of the picture is now shown (v.[8]).

Commenting on Gn 3[18] Philo fancifully plays on the derivation of the word **τρίβολος** (like "trefoil"): ἕκαστον δὲ τῶν παθῶν τριβόλια εἴρηκεν, ἐπειδὴ τριττά ἐστιν, αὐτό τε καὶ τὸ ποιητικὸν καὶ τὸ ἐκ τούτων ἀποτέλεσμα (*leg. alleg.* 3[89]). He also compares the eradication of evil desires in the soul to a gardener or farmer burning down weeds (*de Agric.* 4, πάντ' ἐκκόψω, ἐκτεμῶ . . . καὶ ἐπικαύσω καὶ τὰς ῥίζας αὐτῶν ἐφιεῖσ' ἄχρι τῶν ὑστάτων τῆς γῆς φλογὸς ῥιπήν); but in our epistle, as in Jn 15[6], the burning is a final doom, not a process of severe discipline.

Ἀδόκιμος is used as in 1 Co 9[27]; the moral sense breaks through, as in the next clause, where the meaning of **εἰς καῦσιν** may be illustrated by Dt 29[22] and by Philo's more elaborate description of the thunderstorm which destroyed Sodom (*de Abrah.* 27); God, he says, showered a blast οὐχ ὕδατος ἀλλά πυρός upon the city and its fields, by way of punishment, and everything was consumed, ἐπεὶ δὲ τὰ ἐν φανερῷ καὶ ὑπὲρ γῆς ἅπαντα κατανάλωσεν ἡ φλόξ, ἤδη καὶ τὴν γῆν αὐτὴν ἔκαιε . . . ὑπὲρ τοῦ μηδ' αὖθίς ποτε καρπὸν ἐνεγκεῖν ἢ χλοηφορῆσαι τὸ παράπαν δονηθῆναι. The metaphor otherwise is inexact, for the reference cannot be to the burning of a field in order to eradicate weeds; our author is thinking of final punishment (=κρίματος αἰωνίου, 6[2]), which he associates as usual with fire (10[26. 27] 12[29]). The moral application thus impinges on the figurative sketch. The words **κατάρας ἐγγύς** actually occur in Aristides (*Orat. in Rom.* 370: τὸ μὲν προχωρεῖν αὐτοῖς ἃ ἐβούλοντο, ἀμήχανον καὶ κατάρας ἐγγύς).[1] There is no thought of mildness in the term ἐγγύς, it being used, as in 8[13], of imminent doom, which is only a matter of time. Meanwhile there is the ἐκδοχή (10[27]).

Later on, this conception of unpardonable sins led to the whole system of penance, which really starts from the discussion by Hermas in the second century. But for our author the unpardonable sin is apostasy, and his view is that of a missionary. Modern analogies are not awanting. Thus, in Dr. G. Warneck's book, *The Living Forces of the Gospel* (p. 248), we read that "the Battak Christians would have even serious transgressions forgiven; but if a Christian should again sacrifice to ancestors or have anything to do with magic, no earnest Christian will speak in his favour; he is regarded as one who has fallen back into heathenism, and therefore as lost."

[9] *Though I say this, beloved, I feel sure you will take the better*[2] *course that means salvation.* [10] *God is not unfair; he will not forget what you have done, or the love you have shown for his sake in ministering, as you still do, to the saints.* [11] *It is my heart's desire that each of you would prove equally keen upon realizing your full* (πληροφορίαν, 10[22]) *hope to the very end,* [12] *so that instead of being slack you may imitate those who inherit the promises by their steadfast faith.*

The ground for his confident hope about his "dear friends" (Tyndale, v.[9]) lies in the fact that they are really fruitful (v.[7]) in what is the saving quality of a Christian community, viz. brotherly love (v.[10]). The God who blesses a faithful life (v.[7]) will be sure to reward them for that; stern though he may be, in punishing the disloyal, he never overlooks good service. Only (vv.[11. 12]),

[1] Cp. Eurip. *Hippolytus*, 1070: αἰαῖ, πρὸς ἧπαρ· δακρύων ἐγγὺς τόδε.

[2] For some reason the softer linguistic form κρείσσονα is used here, as at 10[34], in preference to κρείττονα.

the writer adds, put as much heart and soul into your realization of what Christianity means as you are putting into your brotherly love; by thus taking the better course, you are sure of God's blessing. As ἀγαπητοί indicates (the only time he uses it), the writer's affection leads him to hope for the best; he is deeply concerned about the condition of his friends, but he does not believe their case is desperate (v.[4]). He has good hopes of them, and he wishes to encourage them by assuring them that he still believes in them. We may compare the remarks of Seneca to Lucilius, *Ep.* xxix. 3, about a mutual friend, Marcellinus, about whom both of them were anxious. Seneca says he has not yet lost hope of Marcellinus. For wisdom or philosophy "is an art; let it aim at some definite object, choosing those who will make progress (profecturos) and withdrawing from those of whom it despairs—yet not abandoning them quickly, rather trying drastic remedies when everything seems hopeless." Elsewhere, he encourages Lucilius himself by assuring him of his friend's confidence and hope (*Ep.* xxxii. 2: "habeo quidem fiduciam non posse te detorqueri mansurumque in proposito"), and, in connexion with another case, observes that he will not be deterred from attempting to reform certain people (*Ep.* xxv. 2): "I would rather lack success than lack faith."

In καὶ (epexegetic) ἐχόμενα (*sc.* *πράγματα*) σωτηρίας, *ἐχόμενα*, thus employed, is a common Greek phrase (cp. *e.g.* Marc. Aurel. i. 6, *ὅσα τοιαῦτα τῆς Ἑλληνικῆς ἀγωγῆς ἐχόμενα*: Musonius (ed. Hense), xi., *ζητεῖν παιδείας ἐχόμενα* (*v.l.* *ἐχόμενον*): Philo, *de Agric.* 22, *τὰ δὲ καρτερίας καὶ σωφροσύνης . . . ἐχόμενα*) for what has a bearing upon, or is connected with; here, for what pertains to and therefore promotes *σωτηρία* (the opposite of κατάρα and καῦσις). The reason for this confidence, with which he seeks to hearten his readers, lies in their good record of practical service (*τοῦ ἔργου ὑμῶν κτλ.*) which God is far too just to ignore. After all, they had some fruits as well as roots of Christianity (v.[10]). Ἐπιλαθέσθαι is an infinitive of conceived result (Burton's *Moods and Tenses*, 371*c*; Blass, § 391. 4), instead of ἵνα c. subj., as, *e.g.*, in 1 Jn 1[9], or *ὥστε* c. infinitive; cp. Xen. *Cyrop.* iv. 1. 20, *δίκαιος εἶ ἀντιχαρίζεσθαι.*[1] The text of τοῦ ἔργου ὑμῶν καὶ τῆς ἀγάπης was soon harmonized with that of 1 Th 1[3] by the insertion of *τοῦ κόπου* after *καὶ* (so D[c] K L 69*. 256. 263. 1611*. 2005. 2127 boh Theodoret, etc.). The relative ἧν after ἀγάπης has been attracted into the genitive ἧς (as in 9[20]). One practical form of this διακονεῖν is mentioned in 10[33. 34]. Here εἰς τὸ ὄνομα αὐτοῦ goes closely with διακονήσαντες *κτλ.*, as well as with ἐνεδείξασθε, in the sense of "for his sake." In *Pirke Aboth*,

[1] See Dolon's remark in the *Rhesus* of Euripides (161, 162): *οὐκοῦν πονεῖν μὲν χρή, πονοῦντα δ' ἄξιον μισθὸν φέρεσθαι.*

2[16], R. Jose's saying is quoted, "Let all thy works be done for the sake of heaven" (literally לְשֵׁם, *i.e.* εἰς ὄνομα, as here and in Ign. *Rom.* 9[3] ἡ ἀγάπη τῶν ἐκκλησιῶν τῶν δεξαμένων με εἰς ὄνομα Ἰησοῦ Χριστοῦ). **Τοῖς ἁγίοις**, the only place (except 13[24]) where the writer uses this common term for "fellow-Christians"; God will never be so unjust as to overlook kindness shown to "his own."

The personal affection of the writer comes out not only in the **ἀγαπητοί** of v.[9], but again (v.[11]) in the deep **ἐπιθυμοῦμεν**, a term charged with intense yearning (as Chrysostom says, πατρικῆς φιλοστοργίας), and in the individualizing **ἕκαστον** (cp. 3[12. 13]). He is urgent that they should display **τὴν αὐτὴν σπουδήν** with regard to their Christian **ἐλπίς** as they display in the sphere of their Christian **ἀγάπη**. This does not mean that he wishes them to be more concerned about saving their own souls or about heaven than about their duties of brotherly love; his point is that the higher knowledge which he presses upon their minds is the one security for a Christian life at all. Just as Paul cannot assume that the warm mutual affection of the Thessalonian Christians implied a strict social morality (see below on 13[4]), or that the same quality in the Philippian Christians implied moral discrimination (Ph 1[9]), so our author pleads with his friends to complete their brotherly love by a mature grasp of what their faith implied. He reiterates later on the need of φιλαδελφία (13[1]), and he is careful to show how it is inspired by the very devotion to Christ for which he pleads (10[19-24]). **Πληροφορία** (not a LXX term) here is less subjective than in 10[22], where it denotes the complete assurance which comes from a realization of all that is involved in some object. Here it is the latter sense of fulness, scope and depth in their—ἐλπίς.[1] This is part and parcel of the τελειότης to which he is summoning them to advance (6[1]). The result of this grasp of what is involved in their faith will be (v.[12]) a vigorous constancy, without which even a kindly, unselfish spirit is inadequate. For **ἐνδείκνυσθαι σπουδήν** compare Herodian's remark that the soldiers of Severus in A.D. 193 πᾶσαν ἐνεδείκνυντο προθυμίαν καὶ σπουδήν (ii. 10. 19), Magn. 53[61] (iii. B.C.), ἀπόδειξιν ποιούμενος τῆς περὶ τὰ μέγιστα σπουδῆς, and *Syll.* 342[41] (i. B.C.) τὴν μεγίστην ἐνδείκνυται σπουδὴν εἰς τὴν ὑπὲρ τῆς πατρίδος σωτηρίαν. The Greeks used the verb as we use "display," in speaking of some inward quality. This ardour has to be kept up **ἄχρι τέλους** (cp. pseudo-Musonius, *Epp.* 1, in Hercher's *Epistolog. Graeci*, 401 f.: τηροῦντας δὲ ἣν ἔχουσι νῦν πρόθεσιν ἄχρι τέλους φιλοσοφῆσαι); it is the sustained interest in essential Christian truth which issues practically in **μακροθυμία** (v.[12]), or in the confident attitude of hope (3[6. 14]).

[1] For ἐλπίδος, πίστεως is read in W 1867.

Aristotle, in *Rhet.* ii. 19. 5, argues that *οὗ ἡ ἀρχὴ δύναται γενέσθαι, καὶ τὸ τέλος· οὐδὲν γὰρ γίγνεται οὐδ' ἄρχεται γίγνεσθαι τῶν ἀδυνάτων*, a paradox which really means that "if you want to know whether the end of any course of action, plan, scheme, or indeed of anything—is possible, you must look to the beginning: beginning implies end: if it can be begun, it can also be brought to an end" (Cope).

In v.[12] the appeal is rounded off with **ἵνα μὴ νωθροὶ γένησθε**, that you may not prove remiss (repeating *νωθροί* from 5^{11}, but in a slightly different sense: they are to be alert not simply to understand, but to act upon the solid truths of their faith), **μιμηταὶ δέ** *κτλ.* Hitherto he has only mentioned people who were a warning; now he encourages them by pointing out that they had predecessors in the line of loyalty. This incentive is left over for the time being; the writer returns to it in his panegyric upon faith in chapter 11. Meanwhile he is content to emphasize the steadfast faith (*πίστεως καὶ μακροθυμίας*, a hendiadys) that characterizes this loyalty. **Μακροθυμία** means here (as in Ja $5^{7f.}$) the tenacity with which faith holds out. Compare Menander's couplet (Kock's *Com. Attic. Fragm.* 549), *ἄνθρωπος ὢν μηδέποτε τὴν ἀλυπίαν | αἰτοῦ παρὰ θεῶν, ἀλλὰ τὴν μακροθυμίαν*, and *Test. Jos.* 2^7 *μέγα φάρμακόν ἐστιν ἡ μακροθυμία | καὶ πολλὰ ἀγαθὰ δίδωσιν ἡ ὑπομονή*. But this aspect of *πίστις* is not brought forward till $10^{35f.}$, after the discussion of the priesthood and sacrifice of Christ. In **κληρονομούντων τὰς ἐπαγγελίας** the writer implies that hope is invariably sustained by a promise or promises. He has already mentioned *ἡ ἐπαγγελία* (4^1). *Κληρονομεῖν τὰς ἐπαγγελίας* can hardly mean "get a promise of something"; as the appended **διὰ πίστεως καὶ μακροθυμίας** suggests, it denotes "coming into possession of what is promised." This is proved by the equivalent **ἐπέτυχε τῆς ἐπαγγελίας** in v.[15].

Taking Abraham as the first or as a typical instance of steadfast faith in God's promises, the writer now (vv.[13-19]) lays stress not upon the human quality, but upon the divine basis for this undaunted reliance. Constancy means an effort. But it is evoked by a divine revelation; what stirs and sustains it is a word of God. From the first the supreme Promise of God has been guaranteed by him to men so securely that there need be no uncertainty or hesitation in committing oneself to this Hope. The paragraph carries on the thought of vv.[11. 12]; at the end, by a dexterous turn, the writer regains the line of argument which he had dropped when he turned aside to incite and reprove his readers ($5^{11f.}$).

[13] *For in making a promise to Abraham God "swore by himself" (since he could swear by none greater),* [14] *"I will indeed bless you and multiply you."* [15] *Thus it was* (*i.e.* thanks to the divine Oath) *that Abraham by his steadfastness obtained* (so 11^{33}) *what he had been promised.* [16] *For as*[1] *men swear by*

[1] To make the connexion clear, some inferior texts (C D^c K L 6. 33. 104 1610, etc.) add *μέν*.

a greater than themselves, and as an oath means to them a guarantee that ends any dispute, [17] *God, in his desire to afford the heirs of the Promise a special proof of the solid character of his purpose, interposed with an oath;* [18] *so that by these two solid facts* (the Promise and the Oath), *where it is impossible for God to be false, we refugees might have strong encouragement* (παράκλησιν, see on 12[5]) *to seize the hope set before us,* [19] *anchoring the soul to it safe and sure, as it "enters the inner" Presence "behind the veil."*

As usual, he likes to give a biblical proof or illustration (vv.[13. 14]), God's famous promise to Abraham, but the main point in it is that God ratified the promise with an oath.

Our author takes the OT references to God's oath quite naively. Others had felt a difficulty, as is shown by Philo's treatise *de Abrahamo* (46): "God, enamoured of this man [*i.e.* Abraham], for his faith (πίστιν) in him, gives him in return a pledge (πίστιν), guaranteeing by an oath (τὴν δι' ὅρκου βεβαίωσιν) the gifts he had promised . . . for he says, 'I swear by myself' (Gn 22[16])—and with him a word is an oath—for the sake of confirming his mind more steadfastly and immovably than ever before." But the references to God's oaths were a perplexity to Philo; his mystical mind was embarrassed by their realism. In *de sacrif. Abelis et Caini* (28, 29) he returns to the subject. Hosts of people, he admits, regard the literal sense of these OT words as inconsistent with God's character, since an oath implies (μαρτυρία θεοῦ περὶ πράγματος ἀμφισβητουμένου) God giving evidence in a disputed matter; whereas θεῷ οὐδὲν ἄδηλον οὐδὲ ἀμφισβητούμενον, God's mere word ought to be enough: ὁ δὲ θεὸς καὶ λέγων πιστός ἐστιν, ὥστε καὶ τοὺς λόγους αὐτοῦ βεβαιότητος ἕνεκα μηδὲν ὅρκων διαφέρειν. He inclines to regard the OT references to God's oaths as a condescension of the sacred writer to dull minds rather than as a condescension upon God's part. In *Leg. Allegor.* iii. 72 he quotes this very passage (Gn 22[16. 17]), adding: εὖ καὶ τὸ ὅρκῳ βεβαιῶσαι τὴν ὑπόσχεσιν καὶ ὅρκῳ θεοπρεπεῖ· ὁρᾷς γὰρ ὅτι οὐ καθ' ἑτέρου ὀμνύει θεός, οὐδὲν γὰρ αὐτοῦ κρεῖττον, ἀλλὰ καθ' ἑαυτοῦ, ὅς ἐστι πάντων ἄριστος. But he feels bound to explain it. Some of his contemporaries had begun to take exception to such representations of God, on the ground that God's word required no formal confirmation—it confirmed itself by being fulfilled—and that it was absurd (ἄτοπον) to speak of God swearing by himself, in order to bear testimony to himself.[1] Philo (*ibid.* 73) attempts to meet this objection by urging that only God can bear testimony to himself, since no one else knows the divine nature truly; consequently it is appropriate for him to add confirmation to his word, although the latter by itself is amply deserving of belief. In Berachoth, 32. 1 (on Ex 32[13]), it is asked, "What means בך? R. Eleazar answered: 'Thus saith Moses to God (Blessed be He!), 'Lord of all the world, hadst thou sworn by heaven and earth, I would say, even as heaven and earth shall perish, so too thine oath shall perish. But now thou hast sworn by thy Great Name, which lives and lasts for ever and ever; so shall thine oath also last for ever and ever.'"

Εἶχε (v.[13]) with infin. = ἐδύνατο as usual. **Ὤμοσεν. . . . εἰ μήν . . . εὐλογήσω.** Both the LXX (Thackeray, pp. 83, 84) and the papyri (Deissmann, *Bible Studies*, 205 f.) show that εἶ μήν after ὀμνύειν in oaths is common as an asseveration; in some cases, as here, the classical form ἦ μήν, from which εἰ μήν arose by itacism, is textually possible. The quotation (v.[14]) is from the promise made to Abraham after the sacrifice of Isaac (Gn 22[16. 17]): κατ' ἐμαυτοῦ ὤμοσα . . . εἰ μὴν εὐλογῶν εὐλογήσω σε, καὶ πλη-

[1] This is the point raised in Jn 8[13f.]

θύνων πληθυνῶ τὸ σπέρμα σου. The practical religious value of God's promise being thus (v.[15]) confirmed is now brought out for the present generation (vv.[16f.]—another long sentence). **Κατὰ τοῦ μείζονος,** *i.e.* by God. Which, Philo argues, is irreverent: *ἀσεβεῖς ἂν νομισθεῖεν οἱ φάσκοντες ὀμνύναι κατὰ θεοῦ* (*Leg. Allegor.* iii. 73), since only swearing by the Name of God is permissible (cp. Dt 6[13]). But our author has no such scruples (see above). And he is quite unconscious of any objection to oaths, such as some early Christian teachers felt (*e.g.* Ja 5[12]); he speaks of the practice of taking oaths without any scruples. "Hic locus . . . docet aliquem inter Christianos jurisjurandi usum esse legitimum . . . porro non dicit olim fuisse in usu, sed adhuc vigere pronuntiat" (Calvin). **Ἀντιλογίας,** dispute or quarrel (the derived sense in 7[7] *χωρὶς πάσης ἀντιλογίας,* there is no disputing). **Εἰς βεβαίωσιν** only occurs once in the LXX (Lv 25[23]), but is a current phrase in the papyri (cp. Deissmann's *Bible Studies,* 163 f.) for "by way of guarantee"; it is opposed to *εἰς ἀθέτησιν,* and used here as in Wis 6[19] *προσοχὴ δὲ νόμων βεβαίωσις ἀφθαρσίας.* In Philo (see on v.[13]) it is the oath which is guaranteed; here the oath guarantees. The general idea of v.[17] is that of *OGIS.* (ii. B.C.), *ὅπως ἂν εἰς τὸν ἅπαντα χρόνον ἀκίνητα καὶ ἀμετάθετα μένηι τά τε πρὸς τὸν θεὸν τίμια καὶ τὰ πρὸς τὸν Ἀθήναιον φιλάνθρωπα.* **Ἐν ᾧ** (=*διό,* Theophylact), such being the case. **Περισσότερον,** which goes with **ἐπιδεῖξαι,** is illustrated by what Philo says in *de Abrahamo,* 46 (see above): "abundantius quam sine juramento factum videretur" (Bengel). It is an equivalent for *περισσοτερῶς,* which, indeed, B reads here. **Ἐπιδεῖξαι** (cp. Elephantine-Papyri [1907] 1[7] (iv. B.C.) *ἐπιδειξάτω δὲ Ἡρακλείδης ὅτι ἂν ἐγκαλῆι Δημητρίαι ἐναντίον ἀνδρῶν τριῶν*): the verb, which is only once used of God in the LXX (Is 37[26] *νῦν δὲ ἐπέδειξα ἐξερημῶσαι ἔθνη κτλ.*), means here "to afford proof of." The writer uses the general plural, **τοῖς κληρονόμοις τῆς ἐπαγγελίας,**[1] instead of the singular "Abraham," since the Promise in its mystical sense applied to the entire People, who had faith like that of Abraham. The reference is not specifically to Isaac and Jacob, although these are called his **συγκληρονόμοι** in 11[9]. In **τὸ ἀμετάθετον τῆς βουλῆς** our author evidently chooses *βουλῆς* for the sake of the assonance with **βουλόμενος. Ἀμετάθετος** is a synonym for *ἀκίνητος* (cp. above on v.[17] and Schol. on Soph. *Antig.* 1027), and, as the papyri show, had a frequent connexion with wills in the sense of "irrevocable." Here, in connexion with *βουλῆς,* it implies final determination (cp. 3 Mac 5[11. 12]); the purpose had a fixed

[1] Eusebius once (*Dem.* iv. 15. 40) omits *τῆς ἐπαγγελίας,* and once (*ibid.* v. 3. 21) reads *τῆς βασιλείας,* either accidentally or with a recollection of Ja 2[5].

character or solidity about it. The verb ἐμεσίτευσεν ("intervened") does not occur in the LXX, and is here used intransitively, instead of, as usual (cp. *e.g.* Dion. Halic. *Ant.* ix. 59. 5; *OGIS.* 437[76] etc.), with some accusative like συνθήκας. In Jos. *Ant.* vii. 8. 5 it is used intransitively, but in the sense of "interceding" (πεισθεὶς δ' ὁ Ἰώαβος καὶ τὴν ἀνάγκην αὐτοῦ κατοικτείρας ἐμεσίτευσε πρὸς τὸν βασιλέα). The oath is almost certainly that just mentioned. Less probable is the interpretation (Delitzsch, Hofmann, M. Stuart, von Soden, Peake, Seeberg, Wickham) which regards the oath referred to in vv.[16f.] as the oath in the writer's favourite psalm, 110[4]:

> ὤμοσεν Κύριος καὶ οὐ μεταμεληθήσεται
> Σὺ εἶ ἱερεὺς εἰς τὸν αἰῶνα κατὰ τὴν τάξιν Μελχισέδεκ.

This oath does refer to the priesthood of Jesus, which the writer is about to re-introduce (in v.[20]); but it is not a thought which is brought forward till 7[20. 21. 28]; and the second line of the couplet has been already quoted (5[6]) without any allusion to the first.

In v.[18] **καταφεύγειν** and **ἐλπίς** are connected, but not as in Wis 14[6] (Noah = ἡ ἐλπὶς τοῦ κόσμου ἐπὶ σχεδίας, καταφυγοῦσα). Here, as **ἐλπίς** means what is hoped for, *i.e.* the object of expectation, "the only thought is that we are moored to an immoveable object" (A. B. Davidson). The details of the anchor-metaphor are not to be pressed (v.[19]); the writer simply argues that we are meant to fix ourselves to what has been fixed for us by God and in God. To change the metaphor, our hope roots itself in the eternal order. What we hope for is unseen, being out of sight, but it is secure and real, and we can grasp it by faith.

(*a*) Philo (*Quaest. in Exod.* 22[20]) ascribes the survival and success of the Israelites in Egypt διὰ τὴν ἐπὶ τὸν σωτῆρα θεὸν καταφυγήν, ὃς ἐξ ἀπόρων καὶ ἀμηχάνων ἐπιπέμψας τὴν εὐεργέτιν δύναμιν ἐρρύσατο τοὺς ἱκέτας. (*b*) **τόν** is inserted in v.[18] before **θεόν** (by ℵ* A C P 33. 1245. 1739. 1827. 2005 Ath. Chrys.), probably to harmonize with ὁ θεός in v.[17] (where 1912 omits ὁ). But θεόν ("one who is God") is quite apposite.

Παράκλησιν goes with **κρατῆσαι** (aor. = "seize," rather than "hold fast to," like κρατεῖν in 4[14]), and **οἱ καταφυγόντες** stands by itself, though there is no need to conjecture οἱ κατὰ φυγὴν ὄντες = in our flight (so J. J. Reiske, etc.). Is not eternal life, Philo asks, ἡ πρὸς τὸ ὂν καταφυγή (*de fuga*, 15)? In **τῆς προκειμένης ἐλπίδος**, προκειμένης must have the same sense as in 12[2]; the colloquial sense of "aforesaid," which is common in the papyri (*e.g. OP.* 1275[25] εἰς τὴν προκιμένην κώμην), would be flat. **Ἀσφαλῆ τε καὶ βεβαίαν** reflects one of the ordinary phrases in Greek ethics which the writer is so fond of employing. Cp.

Plutarch, *de comm. not.* 1061c, καίτοι πᾶσα κατάληψις ἐν τῷ σοφῷ καὶ μνήμη τὸ ἀσφαλὲς ἔχουσα καὶ βέβαιον κτλ.: Sextus Empir. *adv. log.* ii. 374, ἐς τὸ ὑποτιθέμενον ᾗ ὑποτίθεται βέβαιον ἐστι καὶ ἀσφαλές: and Philo, *quis rer. div.* 62, κατάληφις ἀσφαλὴς καὶ βεβαία. The **ἄγκυρα** of hope is safe and sure, as it is fixed in eternity. All hope for the Christian rests in what Jesus has done in the eternal order by his sacrifice.

Chrysostom's comment on the "anchor" metaphor is all that is needed: ὥσπερ γὰρ ἡ ἄγκυρα ἐξαρτηθεῖσα τοῦ πλοίου, οὐκ ἀφίησεν αὐτὸ περιφέρεσθαι, κἂν μυρίοι παρασαλεύωσιν ἄνεμοι, ἀλλ' ἐξαρτηθεῖσα ἑδραῖον ποιεῖ· οὕτω καὶ ἡ ἐλπίς. The anchor of hope was a fairly common metaphor in the later Greek ethic (*e.g.* Heliod. vii. 25, πᾶσα ἐλπίδος ἄγκυρα παντοίως ἀνέσπασται, and Epict. *Fragm.* (30) 89, οὔτε ναῦν ἐξ ἑνὸς ἀγκυρίου οὔτε βίον ἐκ μιᾶς ἐλπίδος ὁρμιστέον), but our author may have taken the religious application from Philo, who writes (*de Somniis*, i. 39),[1] οὐ χρὴ κατεπτηχέναι τὸν ἐλπίδι θείας συμμαχίας ἐφορμοῦντα (lies moored to). He does not use it as a metaphor for stability, however, like most of the Greeks from Euripides (*e.g. Helena*, 277, ἄγκυρα δ' ἥ μου τὰς τύχας ὤχει μόνη) and Aristophanes (*e.g. Knights*, 1244, λεπτή τις ἐλπίς ἐστ' ἐφ' ἧς ὀχούμεθα) onwards, as, *e.g.*, in the most famous use of the anchor-metaphor,[2] that by Pythagoras (Stob. *Eclog.* 3: πλοῦτος ἀσθενὴς ἄγκυρα, δόξα ἔτι ἀσθενεστέρα . . . τίνες οὖν ἄγκυραι δυναταί; φρόνησις, μεγαλοψυχία, ἀνδρία· ταύτας οὐθεὶς χειμὼν σαλεύει).

Suddenly he breaks the metaphor,[3] in order to regain the idea of the priesthood of Jesus in the invisible world. Hope enters the unseen world; the Christian hope, as he conceives it, is bound up with the sacrifice and intercession of Jesus in the Presence of God, and so he uses language from the ritual of Lv 16$^{2f.}$ about Aaron "passing inside the veil," or curtain that screened the innermost shrine. To this conception he returns in 9$^{3f.}$ after he has described the vital functions of Jesus as ἱερεύς (6$^{20f.}$). For at last he has reached what he regards as the cardinal theme of his homily. The first paragraph (7$^{1-3}$), which is one long sentence in Greek, applies and expands **εἰς τὸν αἰῶνα**, the first note of Melchizedek's priesthood being that it is perpetual, thus typifying the priesthood of Jesus. The next is (7$^{4-10}$), that it is prior and superior to the levitical priesthood; this is

[1] The comparison between hope and a voyage in *de Abrahamo*, 9, is different: ὁ δὲ ἐλπίζων, ὡς αὐτὸ δηλοῖ τοὔνομα, ἐλλιπής, ἐφιέμενος μὲν ἀεὶ τοῦ καλοῦ, μήπω δ' ἐφικέσθαι τούτου δεδυνημένος, ἀλλ' ἐοικὼς τοῖς πλέουσιν, οἳ σπεύδοντες εἰς λιμένας καταίρειν θαλαττεύουσιν ἐνορμίσασθαι μὴ δυνάμενοι. This is nearer to the thought of Ro 8$^{24.25}$.

[2] For the anchor as a symbol on tombs, pagan and Christian, see Le Blant's *Inscr. Chrét. de Gaule*, ii. 158, 312. Contrast with He 6$^{18.19}$ the bitter melancholy of the epitaph in the Greek Anthology (ix. 49): ἐλπὶς καὶ σύ, Τύχη, μέγα χαίρετε· τὸν λιμέν' εὗρον· | οὐδὲν ἐμοί χ' ὑμῖν· παίζετε τοὺς μετ' ἐμέ.

[3] A similar mixture of metaphor in *Ep. Aristeas*, 230 (σὲ μὲν οὐ δυνατόν ἐστι πταῖσαι, πᾶσι γὰρ χάριτας ἔσπαρκας αἳ βλαστάνουσιν εὔνοιαν, ἣ τὰ μέγιστα τῶν ὅπλων κατισχύουσα περιλαμβάνει τὴν μεγίστην ἀσφάλειαν), and Philo, *de praemiis*, 2 (ταύτης δ' ὁ πρῶτος σπόρος ἐστὶν ἐλπίς, ἡ πηγὴ τῶν βίων).

implied in the former claim, but the writer works it out fancifully from the allusion to tithes.

[20] *There* (ὅπου for the classical ὅποι) *Jesus entered for us in advance, when he became highpriest "for ever with the rank of Melchizedek."* [1] *For "Melchizedek, the king of Salem, a priest of the Most High God," who "met Abraham on his return from the slaughter of the kings and blessed him"*.— [2] *who had "a tenth part* (δεκάτην, *sc.* μοῖραν) *of everything" assigned him by Abraham—this Melchizedek is* (*sc.* ὤν) *primarily a "king of righteousness" (that is the meaning of his name); then, besides that, "king of Salem" (which means, king of peace).* [3] *He has neither father nor mother nor genealogy, neither a beginning to his days nor an end to his life, but, resembling the Son of God, continues to be "priest" permanently.*

This paragraph and that which follows (vv.[4-10]) are another little sermon, this time on the story of Gn 14[18-20]. In 6[20]–7[3] the writer starts from the idea that Jesus is ἀρχιερεὺς εἰς τὸν αἰῶνα κατὰ τὴν τάξιν Μελχισεδέκ, and shows how the Melchizedek priesthood was εἰς τὸν αἰῶνα, *i.e.* explaining Ps 110[4] from Gn 14[18-20]. **Εἰσῆλθεν** in 6[20] is explained later, in 9[12f.]. **Πρόδρομος** recalls ἀρχηγός (2[10]), with its suggestion of pioneering. The term is only used in the LXX of the days ἔαρος, πρόδρομοι σταφυλῆς (Nu 13[22]), or of early fruit (ὡς πρόδρομος σύκου, Is 28[4]); the present sense occurs, however, in Wis 12[8], where wasps or hornets are called the **πρόδρομοι** of God's avenging host. The thought here is of Christ entering heaven as we are destined to do, after him, once like him (5[9]) we are "perfected." Vv.[1-3] in ch. 7 are another of the writer's long sentences: **οὗτος ὁ Μελχισεδέκ . . . μένει ἱερεὺς εἰς τὸ διηνεκές** is the central thought, but the subject is overloaded with quotations and comments, including a long **μέν . . . δέ** clause. The length of the sentence and the difficulty of applying μένει ἱερεὺς εἰς τὸ διηνεκές to Melchizedek have led some editors to make Jesus the subject of the sentence: οὗτος (Jesus) γὰρ (ὁ Μελχισεδέκ . . . τῷ υἱῷ θεοῦ) μένει ἱερεὺς εἰς τὸν αἰῶνα. But the οὗτος, as v.[4] shows, is Melchizedek, and the theory is wrecked upon v.[8], for it is quite impossible to take ἐκεῖ κτλ. as "in the upper sanctuary (*sc.* ἐστιν) there is One of whom the record is that He lives." There is a slight but characteristic freedom at the very outset in the use of the story, *e.g.* in **ὁ συναντήσας** κτλ. The story implies this, but does not say it. It was the king of Sodom who ἐξῆλθεν εἰς συνάντησιν αὐτῷ μετὰ τὸ ὑποστρέψαι αὐτὸν ἀπὸ τῆς κοπῆς, but as Melchizedek is immediately said to have brought the conquering hero bread and wine, our writer assumed that he also met Abraham.

An interesting example of the original reading being preserved in an inferior group of MSS is afforded by **ὁ συναντήσας** (C* L P). The variant ὃς συναντήσας (ℵ A B C² D K W 33. 436. 794. 1831. 1837. 1912), which makes a pointless anacolouthon, was due to the accidental reduplication of C

(OCCYN for OCYN), though attempts have been made to justify this reading by assuming an anacolouthon in the sentence, or a parenthesis in ὅς . . . Ἀβραάμ, or carelessness on the part of the writer who began with a relative and forgot to carry on the proper construction. Some curious homiletic expansions have crept into the text of vv.[1. 2]. After βασιλέων two late minuscules (456. 460) read ὅτι ἐδίωξεν τοὺς ἀλλοφύλους καὶ ἐξείλατο Λὼτ μετὰ πάσης αἰχμαλωσίας, and after αὐτόν, D* vt 330. 440. 823 put καὶ (Ἀβραὰμ) εὐλογησθεὶς ὑπ' αὐτοῦ. The latter is another (cp. 11[23]) of the glosses which were thrown up by the Latin versions.

In v.[2] ἐμέρισεν is substituted for the ἔδωκεν of the LXX (which reappears in v.[4]), in order to make it clear that Abraham's gift was a sort of tithe. Tithes were not paid by the Hebrews from spoils of war; this was a pagan custom. But such is the interpretation of the story in Philo, *e.g.* in his fragment on Gn 14[18] (*Fragments of Philo*, ed. J. Rendel Harris, p. 72): τὰ γὰρ τοῦ πολέμου ἀριστεῖα δίδωσι τῷ ἱερεῖ καὶ τὰς τῆς νίκης ἀπαρχάς. ἱεροπρεπεστάτη δὲ καὶ ἁγιωτάτη πασῶν ἀπαρχῶν ἡ δεκάτη διὰ τὸ παντέλειον εἶναι τὸν ἀριθμόν, ἀφ' οὗ καὶ τοῖς ἱερεῦσι καὶ νεωκόροις αἱ δεκάται προστάξει νόμου καρπῶν καὶ θρεμμάτων ἀποδίδονται, ἄρξαντος τῆς ἀπαρχῆς Ἀβραάμ, ὃς καὶ τοῦ γένους ἀρχηγέτης ἐστίν. Or again in *de congressu*, 17, where he describes the same incident as Abraham offering God τὰς δεκάτας χαριστήρια τῆς νίκης.

The fantastic interpretation of the Melchizedek episode is all the writer's own. What use, if any, was made of Melchizedek in pre-Christian Judaism, is no longer to be ascertained. Apparently the book of Jubilees contained a reference to this episode in Abraham's career, but it has been excised for some reason (see R. H. Charles' note on Jub 13[25]). Josephus makes little of the story (*Ant.* i. 10. 2). He simply recounts how, when Abraham returned from the rout of the Assyrians, ἀπήντησε δ' αὐτῷ ὁ τῶν Σοδομιτῶν βασιλεὺς εἰς τόπον τινὰ ὃν καλοῦσι Πεδίον βασιλικόν· ἔνθα ὁ τῆς Σολυμᾶ πόλεως ὑποδέχεται βασιλεὺς αὐτὸν Μελχισεδέκης. σημαίνει δὲ τοῦτο βασιλεὺς δίκαιος· καὶ ἦν δὲ τοιοῦτος ὁμολογουμένως, ὡς διὰ ταύτην αὐτὸν τὴν αἰτίαν καὶ ἱερέα γινέσθαι τοῦ θεοῦ. τὴν μέντοι Σολυμᾶ ὕστερον ἐκάλεσαν Ἱεροσόλυμα. ἐχορήγησε δὲ οὗτος ὁ Μελχισεδέκης τῷ Ἀβράμου στρατῷ ξένια καὶ πολλὴν ἀφθονίαν τῶν ἐπιτηδείων παρέσχε, καὶ παρὰ τὴν εὐωχίαν αὐτόν τ' ἐπαινεῖν ἤρξατο καὶ τὸν θεὸν εὐλογεῖν ὑποχειρίους αὐτῷ ποιήσαντα τοὺς ἐχθρούς. Ἀβράμου δὲ διδόντος καὶ τὴν δεκάτην τῆς λείας αὐτῷ, προσδέχεται τὴν δόσιν κτλ. In the later Judaism, however, more interest was taken in Melchizedek (cp. M. Friedländer in *Revue des Études Juives*, v. pp. 1 f.). Thus some applied the 110th psalm to Abraham (Mechilta on Ex 15[7], r. Gen. 55. 6), who was ranked as the priest after the order of Melchizedek, while Melchizedek was supposed to have been degraded because he (Gn 14[19]) mentioned the name of Abraham before that of God! This, as Bacher conjectures, represented a protest against the Christian view of Melchizedek (*Agada der Tannaiten*[2], i. p. 259). It denotes the influence of Πρὸς Ἑβραίους. Philo, as we might expect, had already made more of the episode than Josephus, and it is Philo's method of interpretation which gives the clue to our writer's use of the story. Thus in *Leg. Alleg.* iii. 25, 26. he points out (*a*) that Μελχισεδὲκ βασιλέα τε τῆς εἰρήνης—Σαλὴμ τοῦτο γὰρ ἑρμηνεύεται—καὶ ἱερέα ἑαυτοῦ πεποίηκεν[1] ὁ θεός (in Gn 14[18]), and allegorizes the reference into a panegyric upon the peaceful, persuasive influence of the really royal mind. He then (*b*) does the same with the sacerdotal reference. Ἀλλ'

[1] The same sort of perfect as recurs in Πρὸς Ἑβραίους (*e.g.* 7[6] and 11[28]).

ὁ μὲν Μελχισεδὲκ ἀντὶ ὕδατος οἶνον προσφερέτω καὶ ποτιζέτω καὶ ἀκρατιζέτω ψυχάς, ἵνα κατάσχετοι γένωνται θείᾳ μέθῃ νηφαλεωτέρᾳ νήψεως αὐτῆς. ἱερεὺς γάρ ἐστι λόγος κλῆρον ἔχων τὸν ὄντα καὶ ὑψηλῶς περὶ αὐτοῦ καὶ ὑπερόγκως καὶ μεγαλοπρεπῶς λογιζόμενος· τοῦ γὰρ ὑψίστου ἐστὶν ἱερεύς, quoting Gn 14[18] and hastening to add, οὐχ ὅτι ἐστί τις ἄλλος οὐχ ὕψιστος. Philo points out thus the symbolism of wine (not water) as the divine intoxication which raises the soul to lofty thought of God; but our author does not even mention the food and drink, though later on there was a tendency to regard them as symbolizing the elements in the eucharist. His interest in Melchizedek lies in the parallel to Christ. This leads him along a line of his own, though, like Philo, he sees immense significance not only in what scripture says, but in what it does not say, about this mysterious figure in the early dawn of history.

In vv.[1. 2] the only points in the original tale which are specially noted are (*a*) that his name means **βασιλεὺς δικαιοσύνης**; (*b*) that **Σαλήμ**, his capital, means **εἰρήνη**; and (*c*) inferentially that this primitive ideal priest was also a king. Yet none of these is developed. Thus, the writer has no interest in identifying Σαλήμ. All that matters is its meaning. He quotes ἱερεὺς τοῦ θεοῦ τοῦ ὑψίστου, but it is ἱερεύς alone that interests him. The fact about the tithes (**ᾧ καὶ δεκάτην ἀπὸ πάντων ἐμέρισεν Ἀβραάμ**) is certainly significant, but it is held over until v.[4]. What strikes him as far more vital is the silence of the record about the birth and death of Melchizedek (v.[3]). **Δικαιοσύνη** as a royal characteristic (see Introd. pp. xxxii f.) had been already noted in connexion with Christ (1[8f.]); but he does not connect it with **εἰρήνη**, as Philo does, though the traditional association of δικαιοσύνη καὶ εἰρήνη with the messianic reign may have been in his mind. In the alliteration (v.[3]) of **ἀπάτωρ, ἀμήτωρ, ἀγενεαλόγητος**, the third term is apparently coined by himself; it does not mean "of no pedigree," nor "without successors," but simply (cp. v.[6]) "devoid of any genealogy." Having no beginning (since none is mentioned), M. has no end. **Ἀπάτωρ** and **ἀμήτωρ** are boldly lifted from their pagan associations. In the brief episode of Gn 14[18-20], this mysterious Melchizedek appears only as a priest of God; his birth is never mentioned, neither is his death; unlike the Aaronic priests, with whom a pure family descent was vital, this priest has no progenitors. Reading the record in the light of Ps 110[4], and on the Alexandrian principle that the very silence of scripture is charged with meaning, the writer divines in Melchizedek a priest who is permanent. This method of interpretation had been popularized by Philo. In *quod det. pot.* 48, *e.g.*, he calls attention to the fact that Moses does not explain in Gn 4[15] what was the mark put by God upon Cain. Why? Because the mark was to prevent him from being killed. Now Moses never mentions the death of Cain διὰ πάσης τῆς νομοθεσίας, suggesting that ὥσπερ ἡ μεμυθευμένη Σκύλλα, κακὸν ἀθάνατον ἐστιν ἀφροσύνη. Again (*de Ebriet.* 14) εἶπε γάρ πού τις "καὶ γὰρ ἀληθῶς ἀδελφή μού ἐστιν ἐκ πατρός, ἀλλ' οὐκ ἐκ μητρός" (Gn 20[12])—

Abraham's evasive description of Sarah—is most significant; she had no mother, *i.e.* she had no connexion with the material world of the senses.

'Απάτωρ and ἀμήτωρ were applied to (*a*) waifs, whose parents were unknown; or (*b*) to illegitimate children; or (*c*) to people of low origin; or (*d*) to deities who were supposed to have been born, like Athenê and Hephaestus, from only one sex. Lactantius (*diuin. instit.* i. 7) quotes the Delphic oracle, which described Apollo as ἀμήτωρ, and insists that such terms refer only to God (*ibid.* iv. 13). "As God the Father, the origin and source of things, is without parentage, he is most accurately called ἀπάτωρ and ἀμήτωρ by Trismegistus, since he was not begotten by anyone. Hence it was fitting that the Son also should be twice born, that he too should become ἀπάτωρ and ἀμήτωρ." His argument apparently[1] is that the pre-existent Son was ἀμήτωρ and that He became ἀπάτωρ by the Virgin-birth (so Theodore of Mopsuestia). Lactantius proves the priesthood of Christ from Ps 110[4] among other passages, but he ignores the deduction from the Melchizedek of Gn 14; indeed he gives a rival derivation of Jerusalem as if from ἱερὸν Σολομών. Theodoret, who (*Dial.* ii.) explains that the incarnate Son was ἀμήτωρ, with respect to his divine nature, and ἀγενεαλόγητος in fulfilment of Is 53[8], faces the difficulty of Melchizedek with characteristic frankness. Melchizedek, he explains, is described as ἀπάτωρ, ἀμήτωρ, simply because scripture does not record his parentage or lineage. Εἰ ἀληθῶς ἀπάτωρ ἦν καὶ ἀμήτωρ, οὐκ ἂν ἦν εἰκών, ἀλλ' ἀλήθεια. 'Επειδὴ δὲ οὐ φύσει ταῦτ' ἔχει, ἀλλὰ κατὰ τὴν τῆς θείας Γραφῆς οἰκονομίαν, δείκνυσι τῆς ἀληθείας τὸν τύπον. In his commentary he explains that μένει ἱερεὺς εἰς τὸ διηνεκές means τὴν ἱερωσύνην οὐ παρέπεμψεν εἰς παῖδας, καθάπερ 'Ααρὼν καὶ 'Ελεάζαρ καὶ Φινεές.

'Αφωμοιωμένος in v.[3] means "resembling," as, *e.g.*, in *Ep. Jerem.*[70] νεκρῷ ἐρριμένῳ ἐν σκότει ἀφωμοίωνται οἱ θεοὶ αὐτῶν, though it might even be taken as a strict passive, "made to resemble" (*i.e.* in scripture), the Son of God being understood to be eternal. **Εἰς τὸ διηνεκές** is a classical equivalent for εἰς τὸν αἰῶνα, a phrase which is always to be understood in the light of its context. Here it could not be simply "ad vitam"; the foregoing phrases and the fact that even the levitical priests were appointed for life, rule out such an interpretation.

The writer now (vv.[4-10]) moralizes upon the statement that Abraham paid tithes to Melchizedek and received his blessing, which proves the supreme dignity of the Melchizedek priesthood, and, inferentially, its superiority to the levitical.

[4] *Now mark the dignity of this man. The patriarch "Abraham paid" him "a tenth" of the spoils.* [5] *Those sons of Levi, who receive the priestly office, are indeed ordered by law to tithe the people (that is, their brothers), although the latter are descended from Abraham;* [6] *but he who had no levitical* (ἐξ αὐτῶν = ἐκ τῶν υἱῶν Λευεί) *genealogy actually tithed Abraham and "blessed" the possessor of the promises!* [7] *(And there is no question that it is the inferior who is blessed by the superior.)* [8] *Again, it is mortal men in the one case who receive tithes, while in the other it is one of whom the witness is that "he lives."* [9] *In fact, we might almost say that even Levi the receiver of tithes paid tithes through Abraham;* [10] *for he was still in the loins of his father when Melchizedek met him.*

---

[1] In iv. 25 he says that "as God was the Father of his spirit without a mother, so a virgin was the mother of his body without a father."

Θεωρεῖτε (v.[4]) is an oratorical imperative as in 4 Mac 14[13] (*θεωρεῖτε δὲ πῶς πολύπλοκός ἐστιν ἡ τῆς φιλοτεκνίας στοργή*); **πηλίκος** is a rare word, often used for *ἡλίκος* after vowels, though not in Zec 2[6] (*τοῦ ἰδεῖν πηλίκον τὸ πλάτος αὐτῆς ἐστιν*), where alone it occurs in the LXX. The *οὗτος* (om. D* 67**. 1739 Blass) repeats the *οὗτος* of v.[1]. We have now a triple proof of the inferiority of the levitical priesthood to Melchizedek. (*a*) Melchizedek, though not in levitical orders, took tithes from and gave a blessing to Abraham himself (vv.[4-7]); (*b*) he is never recorded to have lost his priesthood by death (v.[8]); and (*c*) indeed, in his ancestor Abraham, Levi yet unborn did homage to Melchizedek ([9. 10]). **Τὰ ἀκροθίνια** (v.[4]), which this alone of NT writers has occasion to use, explains the *πάντα* of v.[2]; it is one of the classical terms for which he went outside the LXX. **Ὁ πατριάρχης** is thrown to the end of the sentence for emphasis. In v.[5] **ἱερατείαν** is chosen instead of *ἱερωσύνην* for the sake of assonance with **Λευεί**. The LXX does not distinguish them sharply. The general statement about tithing, **κατὰ τὸν νόμον** (the *ἐντολή* of Nu 18[20. 21]), is intended to throw the spontaneous action of Abraham into relief; **ἀποδεκατοῦν** of "tithing" persons occurs in 1 S 8[15f.], but usually means "to pay tithes," like the more common **δεκατοῦν** (v.[6]), the classical form being *δεκατεύειν*. In v.[6] the perfect **εὐλογήκε** is like the Philonic perfect (see above). In describing the incident (*de Abrahamo*, 40), Philo lays stress upon the fact that *ὁ μέγας ἱερεὺς τοῦ μεγίστου θεοῦ* offered *ἐπινίκια* and feasted the conquerors; he omits both the blessing and the offering of tithes, though he soon allegorizes the latter (41).

Moulton calls attention to "the beautiful parallel in Plato's *Apol.* 28*c*, for the characteristic perfect in Hebrews, describing what *stands written* in Scripture," holding that "*ὅσοι ἐν Τροίᾳ τετελευτήκασι* (as is written in the Athenians' Bible) is exactly like He 7[6] 11[17. 28]." But these perfects are simply aoristic (see above, p. 91, note).

V.[7] is a parenthetical comment on what blessing and being blessed imply; the neuter (**ἔλαττον**) is used, as usual in Greek (cp. Blass, § 138. 1), in a general statement, especially in a collective sense, about persons. Then the writer rapidly summarizes, from vv.[1-4], the contrast between the levitical priests who die off and Melchizedek whose record (*μαρτυρούμενος* in scripture, cp. 11[5]) is "he lives" (*μήτε ζωῆς τέλος . . . μένει εἰς τὸ διηνεκές*). Finally (vv.[9. 10]), he ventures (*ὡς ἔπος εἰπεῖν*, a literary phrase, much affected by Philo) on what he seems to feel may be regarded as a forced and fanciful remark, that Levi was committed **δι' Ἀβραάμ** (genitive) to a position of respectful deference towards the prince-priest of Salem. In v.[5] **καίπερ ἐληλυθότας ἐκ τῆς ὀσφύος Ἀβραάμ** (the Semitic expression for descendants, chosen here in view of what he was going to say in v.[10] ἐν τῇ ὀσφύϊ τοῦ πατρός) is another imaginative touch added in order to signalize the pre-eminent honour of the levitical priests over their fellow-countrymen. Such is their high authority. And yet Melchizedek's is higher still!

(*a*) In v.[6] "forte legendum, ὁ δὲ μὴ γενεαλογούμενος αὐτὸν δεδεκάτωκε τὸν Ἀβραάμ, ipsum Abrahamam" (Bentley). But ἐξ αὐτῶν explains itself, and the stress which αὐτόν would convey is already brought out by the emphatic position of Ἀβραάμ, and by the comment καὶ τὸν ἔχοντα κτλ. (*b*) In v.[4] **καὶ** is inserted after ᾧ, in conformity with v.[2], by ℵ A C D^c K L P syr^{hkl} arm, etc. For **ἀποδεκατοῦν** in v.[5] the termination (cp. Thackeray, 244) ἀποδεκατοῖν is read by B D (as κατασκηνοῖν in Mt 13^{32}). In v.[6] the more common (11^{20}) aorist, **εὐλόγησε**, is read by A C P 6. 104. 242. 263. 326. 383. 1288. 1739. 2004. 2143, Chrys. for εὐλόγηκε.

He now (vv.[11f.]) turns to prove his point further, by glancing at the text from the 110th psalm. "It is no use to plead that Melchizedek was succeeded by the imposing Aaronic priesthood; this priesthood belonged to an order of religion which had to be superseded by the Melchizedek-order of priesthood." He argues here, as already, from the fact that the psalter is later than the pentateuch; the point of 7^{11} is exactly that of 4$^{7f.}$.

[11] *Further, if the levitical priesthood had been the means of reaching perfection (for it was on the basis of that priesthood that the Law was enacted for the People), why was it still necessary for another sort of priest to emerge "with the rank of Melchizedek," instead of simply with the rank of Aaron* ([12]*for when the priesthood is changed, a change of law necessarily follows*)*?* [13] *He who is thus* (*i.e.* "with the rank of M.") *described belongs to another tribe, no member of which ever devoted himself to the altar;* [14]*for it is evident that our Lord sprang from Judah, and Moses never mentioned priesthood in connexion with that tribe.* [15] *This becomes all the more plain when* (εἰ = ἐπεί) *another priest emerges "resembling Melchizedek,"* [16] *one who has become a priest by the power of an indissoluble* (ἀκαταλύτου, *i.e.* by death) *Life and not by the Law of an external command;* [17] *for the witness to him is,*
"Thou art priest for ever, with the rank of Melchizedek."
[18] *A previous command is set aside on account of its weakness and uselessness* [19] (*for the Law made nothing perfect*), *and there is introduced a better Hope, by means of which we can draw near to God.*

Εἰ μέν οὖν (without any δέ to follow, as in 8^4) **τελείωσις** ("perfection" in the sense of a perfectly adequate relation to God; see v.[19]) **διὰ τῆς Λευειτικῆς ἱερωσύνης** κτλ. Λευειτικῆς is a rare word, found in Philo (*de fuga*, ἡ Λευιτικὴ μόνη), but never in the LXX except in the title of Leviticus; ἱερωσύνη does occur in the LXX, and is not distinguishable from ἱερατεία (v.[5]). In the parenthetical remark **ὁ λαὸς γὰρ ἐπ᾽ αὐτῆς νενομοθέτηται, αὐτῆς** was changed into αὐτήν (6. 242. 330. 378. 383. 440. 462. 467. 489. 491. 999. 1610. 1836 Theophyl.), or αὐτῇ (K L 326. 1288, etc. Chrys.) after 8^6 (where again we have this curious passive), and **νενομοθετήται** altered into the pluperfect ἐνενομοθέτητο (K L, etc.). The less obvious genitive (cp. Ex. 34^{27} ἐπὶ γὰρ τῶν λόγων τούτων τέθειμαι σοὶ διαθήκην καὶ τῷ Ἰσραήλ) **ἐπ᾽ αὐτῆς**

is not "in the time of," for the levitical priesthood was not in existence prior to the Law; it might mean "in connexion with," since ἐπί and περί have a similar force with this genitive, but the incorrect dative correctly explains the genitive. The Mosaic νόμος could not be worked for the λαός without a priesthood, to deal with the offences incurred. The idea of the writer always is that a νόμος or διαθήκη depends for its validity and effectiveness upon the ἱερεύς or ἱερεῖς by whom it is administered. Their personal character and position are the essential thing. Every consideration is subordinated to that of the priesthood. As a change in that involves a change in the νόμος (v.[12]), the meaning of the parenthesis in v.[11] must be that the priesthood was the basis for the νόμος, though, no doubt, the writer has put his points in vv.[11. 12] somewhat intricately; this parenthetical remark would have been better placed after the other in v.[12], as indeed van d. Sande Bakhuyzen proposes. Three times over (cp. v.[19]) he puts in depreciatory remarks about the Law, the reason being that the Law and the priesthood went together. It is as if he meant here: "the levitical priesthood (which, of course, implies the Law, for the Law rested on the priesthood)." The inference that the νόμος is antiquated for Christians reaches the same end as Paul does by his dialectic, but by a very different route. **Ἀνίστασθαι** (= appear on the scene, as v.[15]) and **λέγεσθαι** refer to Ps 110[4], which is regarded as marking a new departure, with far-reaching effects, involving (v.[12]) an alteration of the **νόμος** as well as of the **ἱερωσύνη**. In **καὶ οὐ . . . λέγεσθαι** the οὐ negatives the infinitive as μή usually does; **Ἀαρών**, like Κανᾶ (Jn 21[2]), has become indeclinable, though Josephus still employs the ordinary genitive **Ἀαρῶνος**. In v.[12] **μετάθεσις**, which is not a LXX term, though it occurs in 2 Mac 11[24], is practically equivalent here (cp. 12[27]) to **ἀθέτησις** in v.[18]. A close parallel occurs in *de Mundo*, 6, νόμος μὲν γὰρ ἡμῖν ἰσοκλινὴς ὁ θεός, οὐδεμίαν ἐπιδεχόμενος διόρθωσιν ἢ μετάθεσιν, and a similar phrase is employed by Josephus to describe the arbitrary transference of the highpriesthood (*Ant.* xii. 9. 7, ὑπὸ Λυσίου πεισθεὶς, μεταθεῖναι τὴν τιμὴν ἀπὸ ταύτης τῆς οἰκίας εἰς ἕτερον).

We now (vv.[13f.]) get an account of what was meant by **οὐ κατὰ τὴν τάξιν Ἀαρών** or **ἕτερος** ("another," in the sense of "a different") **ἱερεύς** in v.[11]; Jesus, this ἱερεὺς κατὰ τὴν τάξιν Μελχισεδέκ, came from the non-sacerdotal tribe of Judah, not from that of Levi. **Ἐφ᾽ ὅν** is another instance of the extension of this metaphorical use of ἐπί from the Attic dative to the accusative. The perfect **μετέσχηκεν** may be used in an aoristic sense, like ἔσχηκα, or simply for the sake of assonance with προσέσχηκεν, and it means no more than μετέσχεν in 2[14]; indeed μετέσχεν is read here by P 489. 623*. 1912 arm, as προσέσχεν is (by A C

33. 1288) for προσέσχηκεν. The conjecture of Erasmus, προσέστηκεν, is ingenious, but προσέχειν in the sense of "attend" is quite classical. The rule referred to in εἰς ἣν φυλήν (ἐξ ἧς φυλῆς, arm?), *i.e.* ἐκ φυλῆς εἰς ἥν (as Lk 10[10]) κτλ. is noted in Josephus, *Ant.* xx. 10. 1, πάτριόν ἐστι μηδένα τοῦ θεοῦ τὴν ἀρχιερωσύνην λαμβάνειν ἢ τὸν ἐξ αἵματος τοῦ Ἀαρῶνος. No tribe except Levi supplied priests. (**Πρόδηλον** in v.[14] is not a LXX term, but occurs in this sense in 2 Mac 3[17] (δι' ὧν πρόδηλον ἐγίνετο) and 14[39], as well as in Judith 8[29].) In *Test. Levi* 8[14] it is predicted (cp. Introd. p. xlviii) that βασιλεὺς ἐκ τοῦ Ἰούδα ἀναστήσεται καὶ ποιήσει ἱερατείαν νέαν: but this is a purely verbal parallel, the βασιλεύς is Hyrcanus and the reference is to the Maccabean priest-kings who succeed the Aaronic priesthood. **Ἀνατέλλειν** is a synonym for ἀνίστασθαι (v.[15]), as in Nu 24[17], though it is just possible that ἀνατέταλκεν is a subtle allusion to the messianic title of Ἀνατολή in Zec 6[12]; in commenting on that verse Philo observes (*de confus. ling.* 14): τοῦτον μὲν γὰρ πρεσβύτατον υἱὸν ὁ τῶν ὅλων ἀνέτειλε πατήρ. (For ἱερέων the abstract equivalent ἱερωσύνης, from v.[12], is substituted by D[c] K L.) The title **ὁ κύριος ἡμῶν** is one of the links between the vocabulary of this epistle and that of the pastorals (1 Ti 1[14], 2 Ti 1[8]). As the result of all this, what is it that becomes (v.[15]) **περισσότερον** (for περισσότερως) **κατάδηλον**?[1] The provisional character of the levitical priesthood, or the μετάθεσις νόμου? Probably the latter, though the writer would not have distinguished the one from the other. In v.[15] **κατὰ τὴν ὁμοιότητα** linguistically has the same sense as ἀφωμοιώμενος (v.[3]). In v.[16] **σαρκίνης** (for which σαρκικῆς is substituted by C[c] D K Ψ 104. 326. 1175, etc.) hints at the contrast which is to be worked out later (in 9[1-14]) between the external and the inward or spiritual, the sacerdotal **ἐντολή** being dismissed as merely σαρκίνη, since it laid down physical descent as a requisite for office. Hereditary succession is opposed to the inherent personality of the Son (= 9[14]). The distinction between σαρκικός (= fleshly, with the nature and qualities of σάρξ) and σάρκινος (fleshy, composed of σάρξ) is blurred in Hellenistic Greek of the period, where adjectives in -ινος tend to take over the sense of those in -ικος, and *vice versa.* In v.[17] **μαρτυρεῖται** (cp. μαρτυρούμενος, v.[8]) is altered to the active (10[15]) μαρτυρεῖ by C D K L 256. 326. 436. 1175. 1837. 2127 syr[hkl] vg arm Chrys.

The **μετάθεσις** of v.[12] is now explained negatively (**ἀθέτησις**) and positively (ἐπεισαγωγή) in vv.[18. 19]. **Ἀθέτησις** (one of his juristic metaphors, cp. 9[26]) γίνεται (*i.e.* by the promulgation of Ps 110[4]) **προαγούσης** (cp. *IMA.* iii. 247, τὰ προάγοντα ψαψίσματα: προάγειν is

[1] Κατάδηλον is the classical intensive form of δῆλον, used here for the sake of assonance with the following κατά.

not used by the LXX in this sense of "fore-going") ἐντολῆς (v.[16]) διὰ τὸ αὐτῆς (unemphatic) ἀσθενὲς καὶ ἀνωφελές (alliteration). Ἀνωφελές is a word common in such connexions, e.g. *Ep. Arist.* 253, ὅπερ ἀνωφελὲς καὶ ἀλγεινόν ἐστιν: Polyb. xii. 25[9] ἄζηλον καὶ ἀνωφελές. The uselessness of the Law lay in its failure to secure an adequate forgiveness of sins, without which a real access or fellowship (ἐγγίζειν τῷ θεῷ) was impossible; οὐδὲν ἐτελείωσεν, it led to no absolute order of communion between men and God, no τελείωσις. The positive contrast (v.[19]) is introduced by the striking compound ἐπεισαγωγή (with γίνεται), a term used by Josephus for the replacing of Vashti by Esther (*Ant.* xi. 6. 2, σβέννυσθαι γὰρ τὸ πρὸς τὴν προτήραν φιλόστοργον ἑτέρας ἐπεισαγωγῇ, καὶ τὸ πρὸς ἐκείνην εὔνουν ἀποσπώμενον κατὰ μικρὸν γίγνεσθαι τῆς συνούσης); there is no force here in the ἐπει, as if it meant "fresh" or "further." The new ἐλπίς is κρείττων by its effectiveness (6[18]); it accomplishes what the νόμος and its ἱερωσύνη had failed to realize for men, viz. a direct and lasting access to God. In what follows the writer ceases to use the term ἐλπίς, and concentrates upon the ἐγγίζειν τῷ θεῷ, since the essence of the ἐλπίς lies in the priesthood and sacrifice of Jesus the Son. With this allusion to the κρείττων ἐλπίς, he really resumes the thought of 6[18. 19]; but he has another word to say upon the superiority of the Melchizedek priest, and in this connexion he recalls another oath of God, viz. at the inauguration or consecration mentioned in Ps 110[4], a solemn divine oath, which was absent from the ritual of the levitical priesthood, and which ratifies the new priesthood of Jesus as permanent (vv.[20-22]), enabling him to do for men what the levitical priests one after another failed to accomplish (vv.[23-25]).

[20] *A better Hope, because it was not promised apart from an oath. Previous priests* (οἱ μέν = levitical priests) *became priests apart from any oath,* [21] *but he has an oath from Him who said to him,*

> *"The Lord has sworn, and he will not change his mind,*
> *thou art a priest for ever."*

[22] *And this makes Jesus surety for a superior covenant.* [23] *Also, while they* (οἱ μέν) *became priests in large numbers, since death prevents them from continuing to serve,* [24] *he holds his priesthood without any successor, since he continues for ever.* [25] *Hence for all time he is able to save those who approach God through him, as he is always living to intercede on their behalf.*

The long sentence (vv.[20-22]) closes with Ἰησοῦς in an emphatic position. After καὶ καθ' ὅσον οὐ χωρὶς ὁρκωμοσίας, which connect (*sc.* τοῦτο γίνεται) with ἐπεισαγωγὴ κρείττονος ἐλπίδος, there is a long explanatory parenthesis οἱ μὲν γὰρ . . . εἰς τὸν αἰῶνα, exactly in the literary style of Philo (e.g. *quis rer. div.* 17, ἐφ' ὅσον γὰρ οἶμαι κτλ.—νοῦς μὲν γὰρ . . . αἴσθησις—ἐπὶ τοσοῦτον κτλ.). In v.[20] ὁρκωμοσία (oath-taking) is a neuter plural (cp. *Syll.* 593[29], *OGIS.* 229[82]) which, like ἀντωμοσία, has become a feminine singular of the first declension, and εἰσὶν γεγονότες is simply an analytic form of the perfect tense, adopted as more sonorous than *γεγόνασι*. As we have already seen (on 6[13]), Philo (*de sacrific.* 28–29) discusses such references to God swearing. Thousands of people, he observes, regard an oath as inconsistent with the character of God, who requires no witness to his character. "Men who are disbelieved have recourse to an oath in order to win credence, but God's mere word must be believed (*ὁ δὲ θεὸς καὶ λέγων πιστός ἐστιν*); hence, his words are in no sense different from oaths, as far as assurance goes." He concludes that the idea of God swearing an oath is simply an anthropomorphism which is necessary on account of human weakness. Our author takes the OT language in Ps 110[4] more naively, detecting a profound significance in the line **ὤμοσεν κύριος καὶ οὐ μεταμεληθήσεται** (in the Hellenistic sense of "regret" = change his mind). The allusion is, of course, to the levitical priests. But Roman readers could understand from their former religion how oaths were needful in such a matter. Claudius, says Suetonius (*Vit. Claud.* 22), "in co-optandis per collegia sacerdotibus neminem nisi juratus (*i.e.* that they were suitable) nominavit."

The superfluous addition of **κατὰ τὴν τάξιν Μελχιζεδέκ** was soon made, after **εἰς τὸν αἰῶνα,** by ℵ[c] A D K L P vt Syr[pesh hkl] boh eth Eus (Dem. iv. 15. 40), etc.

Παραμένειν means to remain in office or serve (a common euphemism in the papyri). The priestly office could last in a family (cp. Jos. *Ant.* xi. 8. 2, *τῆς ἱερατικῆς τιμῆς μεγίστης οὔσης καὶ ἐν τῷ γένει παραμενούσης*), but mortal men (*ἀποθνήσκοντες*, v.[8]) could not *παραμένειν* as priests, whereas (v.[24]) Jesus remains a perpetual **ἱερεύς, διὰ τὸ μένειν** (= **πάντοτε ζῶν**, v.[25]) **αὐτόν** (superfluous as in Lk 2[4] *διὰ τὸ αὐτὸν εἶναι*). **Ἀπαράβατον**, a legal adjective for "inviolable," is here used in the uncommon sense of non-transferable (boh Chrys. **οὐκ ἔχει** *διάδοχον*, Oecumenius, etc. *ἀδιάδοχον*), as an equivalent for *μὴ παραβαίνουσαν εἰς ἄλλον*, and contrasts Jesus with the long succession of the levitical priests (*πλείονές*). The passive sense of "not to be infringed" (cp. Justin Martyr, *Apol.* i. 43, *εἱμαρμένην φαμὲν ἀπαράβατον ταύτην εἶναι*, where the adjective = ineluctabile) or "unbroken" does not suit the context, for Jesus had no rivals and the word can hardly refer to the invasion of death. Like **γεγυμνασμένα** in 5[14], also after **ἔχειν**, it has a predicative force, marked by the absence of the article. Philo (*quis rer. div. heres*, 6) finds a similar significance in the etymology of *κύριος* as a divine title: *κύριος μὲν γὰρ παρὰ τὸ κῦρος, ὃ δὴ βέβαιόν ἐστιν, εἴρηται, κατ' ἐναντιότητα ἀβεβαίου καὶ ἀκύρου.* But our author does not discover any basis for the perpetuity of *ὁ κύριος ἡμῶν* in the etymology of *κύριος*, and is content (in vv.[22-24]) to stress the line of the psalm, in order to prove that Jesus guaranteed a superior **διαθήκη** (*i.e.* order of religious fellowship). Ἔγγυος is one of the juristic terms (vg, sponsor) which he uses in a general sense; here it is "surety" or "pledge." Διαθήκη is discussed by him later on; it is a term put in here as often to excite interest and anticipation. How readily ἔγγυος could be associated with a term like σώζειν (v.[25]) may be understood from Sir 29[15f.]:

> χάριτας ἐγγύου μὴ ἐπιλάθῃ,
> ἔδωκεν γὰρ τὴν ψυχὴν αὐτοῦ ὑπὲρ σου.
> ἀγαθὰ ἐγγύου ἀνατρέψει ἁμαρτωλός,
> καὶ ἀχάριστος ἐν διανοίᾳ ἐγκαταλείψει ῥυσάμενον.

Our author might have written μεσίτης here as well as in 8[6]; he prefers ἔγγυος probably for the sake of assonance with γέγονεν or even ἐγγίζομεν. As μεσιτεύειν means to vouch for the truth of a promise or statement (cp. 6[17]), so ἔγγυος means one who vouches for the fulfilment of a promise, and therefore is a synonym for μεσίτης here. The conclusion (v.[25]) is put in simple and effective language. Εἰς τὸ παντελές is to be taken in the temporal sense of the phrase, as in *BM.* iii. 161[11] (A.D. 212) ἀπὸ τοῦ νῦν εἰς τὸ παντελές, being simply a literary variant for πάντοτε. The alternative rendering "utterly" suits Lk 13[11] better than this passage. This full and final ἱερωσύνη of Jesus is the κρείττων ἐλπίς (v.[19]), the τελείωσις which the levitical priesthood failed to supply, a perfect access to God's Presence. His intercession (ἐντυγχάνειν, *sc.* θεῷ as in Ro 8[34] ὃς καὶ ἐντύγχανει ὑπὲρ ἡμῶν) has red blood in it, unlike Philo's conception, *e.g.* in *Vit. Mos.* iii. 14, ἀναγκαῖον γὰρ ἦν τὸν ἱερωμένον (the highpriest) τῷ τοῦ κόσμου πατρὶ παρακλήτῳ χρῆσθαι τελειοτάτῳ τὴν ἀρετὴν υἱῷ (*i.e.* the Logos) πρός τε ἀμνηστίαν ἁμαρημάτων καὶ χορηγίαν ἀφθονωτάτων ἀγαθῶν, and in *quis rer. div.* 42, where the Logos is ἱκέτης τοῦ θνητοῦ κηραίνοντος ἀεὶ πρὸς τὸ ἄφθαρτον παρὰ δὲ τῷ φύντι πρὸς εὐελπιστίαν τοῦ μήποτε τὸν ἵλεω θεὸν περιιδεῖν τὸ ἴδιον ἔργον. The function of intercession in heaven for the People, which originally (see p. 37) was the prerogative of Michael the angelic guardian of Israel, or generally of angels (see on 1[14]), is thus transferred to Jesus, to One who is no mere angel but who has sacrificed himself for the People. The author deliberately excludes any other mediator or semi-mediator in the heavenly sphere (see p. xxxix).

A triumphant little summary (vv.[26-28]) now rounds off the argument of 6[19f.]–7[25]:

[26] *Such was the highpriest for us, saintly, innocent, unstained, far from all contact with the sinful, lifted high above the heavens,* [27] *one who has no need, like yonder highpriests, day by day to offer sacrifices first for their own sins and then for* (the preposition is omitted as in Ac 26[18]) *those of the People—he did that once for all in offering up himself.* [28] *For the Law appoints human beings in their weakness to the priesthood; but the word of the Oath* (which came after the Law) *appoints a Son who is made perfect for ever.*

The text of this paragraph has only a few variants, none of any importance. After ἡμῖν in v.[26] καί is added by A B D 1739 syr[pesh hkl] Eusebius ("was exactly the one for us"). In v.[27] it makes no difference to the sense whether προσενέγκας (א A W 33. 256. 436. 442. 1837. 2004. 2127 arm Cyr.) or ἀνενέγκας (B C D K L P etc. Chrys.) is read; the latter may have been suggested by ἀναφέρειν, or προσενέγκας may have appealed to later scribes as the more usual and technical term in the epistle. The technical distinction between ἀναφέρειν (action of people) and προσφέρειν (action of the priest) had long been blurred; both verbs mean what we mean by "offer up" or "sacrifice." In v.[28] the original ἱερεῖς (D* r vg) was soon changed (to conform with ἀρχιερεῖς in v.[27]) into ἀρχιερεῖς. The reason why ἱερεῦς and ἱερεῖς have been used in 7[1f.] is that Melchizedek was called ἱερεύς, not ἀρχιερεύς. Once the category is levitical, the interchange of ἀρχιερεύς and ἱερεύς becomes natural.

The words τοιοῦτος γὰρ ἡμῖν ἔπρεπεν (another daring use of ἔπρεπεν, cp. 2[10]) ἀρχιερεύς (v.[26]) might be bracketed as one of the author's parentheses, in which case ὅσιος κτλ. would carry on πάντοτε ζῶν . . . αὐτῶν. But ὅς in Greek often follows τοιοῦτος, and the usual construction is quite satisfactory. Γάρ is intensive, as often. It is generally misleading to parse a rhapsody, but there is a certain sequence of thought in ὅσιος κτλ., where the positive adjective ὅσιος is followed by two negative terms in alliteration (ἄκακος, ἀμίαντος), and κεχωρισμένος ἀπὸ τῶν ἁμαρτωλῶν is further defined by ὑψηλότερος τῶν οὐρανῶν γενόμενος (the same idea as in 4[14] διεληλυθότα τοὺς οὐρανούς). He is ὅσιος, pious or saintly (cp. *ERE*. vi. 743), in virtue of qualities like his reverence, obedience, faith, loyalty, and humility, already noted. Ἄκακος is innocent (as in Job 8[20], Jer 11[19]), one of the LXX equivalents for תָּם or תָּמִים, not simply = devoid of evil feeling towards men; like ἀμίαντος, it denotes a character χωρὶς ἁμαρτίας. Ἀμίαντος is used of the untainted Isis in *OP*. 1380 (ἐν Πόντῳ ἀμίαντος). The language may be intended to suggest a contrast between the deep ethical purity of Jesus and the ritual purity of the levitical highpriest, who had to take extreme precautions against outward defilement (cp. Lv 21[10-15] for the regulations, and the details in Josephus, *Ant*. iii. 12. 2, μὴ μόνον δὲ περὶ τὰς ἱερουργίας καθαροὺς εἶναι, σπουδάζειν δὲ καὶ περὶ τὴν αὐτῶν δίαιταν, ὡς αὐτὴν ἄμεμπτον εἶναι· καὶ διὰ ταύτην τὴν αἰτίαν, οἱ τὴν ἱερατικὴν στολὴν φοροῦντες ἄμωμοι τε εἰσι καὶ περὶ πάντα καθαροὶ καὶ νηφάλιοι), and had to avoid human contact for seven days before the ceremony of atonement-day. The next two phrases go together. Κεχωρισμένος ἀπὸ τῶν ἁμαρτωλῶν is intelligible in the light of 9[28]; Jesus has ἅπαξ sacrificed himself for the sins of men, and in that sense his connexion with ἁμαρτωλοί is done. He is no levitical highpriest who is in daily contact with them, and therefore obliged to sacrifice repeatedly. Hence the writer at once adds (v.[27]) a word to explain and expand this pregnant thought; the sphere in which Jesus now lives (ὑψηλότερος κτλ.) is not one in which, as on earth, he had to suffer the contagion or the hostility of **ἁμαρτωλοί** (12²) and to die for human sins.

> "He has outsoared the shadow of our night;
> Envy and calumny and hate and pain . . .
> Can touch him not and torture not again;
> From the contagion of the world's slow stain
> He is secure."

This is vital[1] to the sympathy and intercession of Jesus; it is in virtue of this position before God that he aids his people, as **τετελειωμένος**, and therefore able to do all for them. His priesthood is, in modern phrase, absolute. As eternal **ἀρχιερεύς** in the supreme sense, and as no longer in daily contact with sinners, Jesus is far above the routine ministry of the levitical **ἀρχιερεῖς**. The writer blends loosely in his description (v.²⁷) the annual sacrifice of the highpriest on atonement-day (to which he has already referred in 5³) and the daily sacrifices offered by priests. Strictly speaking the *ἀρχιερεῖς* did not require to offer sacrifices *καθ' ἡμέραν*, and the accurate phrase would have been *κατ' ἐνιαυτόν*. According to Lv 6¹⁹⁻²³ the highpriest had indeed to offer a cereal offering morning and evening; but the text is uncertain, for it is to be offered both on the day of his consecration and also *διὰ πάντος*. Besides, this section was not in the LXX text of A, so that the writer of Hebrews did not know of it. Neither had he any knowledge of the later Jewish ritual, according to which the highpriest did offer this offering twice a day. Possibly, however, his expression here was suggested by Philo's statement about this offering, viz. that the highpriest did offer a daily sacrifice (*quis rer. div.* 36: *τὰς ἐνδελεχεῖς θυσίας . . . ἥν τε ὑπὲρ ἑαυτῶν οἱ ἱερεῖς προσφέρουσι τῆς σεμιδάλεως καὶ τὴν ὑπὲρ τοῦ ἔθνους τῶν δυεῖν ἀμνῶν, de spec. leg.* iii. 23, *ὁ ἀρχιερεύς . . . εὐχὰς δὲ καὶ θυσίας τελῶν καθ' ἑκάστην ἡμέραν*). It is true that this offering **ὑπέρ ἑαυτῶν** was not a sin-offering, only an offering of cereals; still it was reckoned a *θυσία*, and in Sir 45¹⁴ it is counted as such. **Τοῦτο γὰρ ἐποίησεν** refers then to his sacrifice for sins (9²⁸), not, of course, including any sins of his own (see on 5³); it means **ὑπὲρ τῶν ἁμαρτιῶν τοῦ λαοῦ**, and the writer could afford to be technically inexact in his parallelism without fear of being misunderstood. "Jesus offered his sacrifice," "Jesus did all that a highpriest has to do,"—this was what he intended. The Greek fathers rightly referred **τοῦτο** to **ἔπειτα τῶν τοῦ λαοῦ**, as if the writer meant "*this*, not that **πρότερον**." It is doubtful if he had such a sharp distinction in his mind, but when he wrote **τοῦτο**

[1] Thus Philo quotes (*de Fug.* 12) with enthusiasm what Plato says in the *Theatetus*: *οὔτ' ἀπολέσθαι τὰ κακὰ δυνατόν—ὑπεναντίον γάρ τι τῷ ἀγαθῷ ἀεὶ εἶναι ἀνάγκη—οὔτε ἐν θείοις αὐτὰ ἱδρῦσθαι.*

he was thinking of τῶν τοῦ λαοῦ, and of that alone. An effort is sometimes made to evade this interpretation by confining καθ' ἡμέραν to ὃς οὐκ ἔχει and understanding "yearly" after οἱ ἀρχιερεῖς, as if the idea were that Christ's daily intercession required no daily sacrifice like the annual sacrifice on atonement-day. But, as the text stands, ἀνάγκην is knit to *καθ' ἡμέραν*, and these words must all be taken along with ὥσπερ οἱ ἀρχιερεῖς (*ἔχουσι*).

Compare the common assurance of the votaries of Serapis, *e.g.* *BGU.* ii. 385 (ii/iii A.D.), *τὸ προσκύνημά σου ποιῶ κατ' ἑκάστην ἡμέραν παρὰ τῷ κυρίῳ Σαράπιδι καὶ τοῖς συννέοις θεοῖς.*

A deep impression is made by the words ἑαυτὸν ἀνενέγκας, "pro nobis tibi uictor et uictima, et ideo uictor, quia uictima, pro nobis tibi sacerdos et sacrificium, et ideo sacerdos, quia sacrificium" (Aug. *Conf.* x. 43). What is meant by this the writer holds over till he reaches the question of the sacrifice of Jesus as ἀρχιερεύς ($9^{1f.}$). As usual, he prepares the way for a further idea by dropping an enigmatic allusion to it. Meantime (v.[28]) a general statement sums up the argument. Καθίστησιν is used as in 1 Mac 10^{20} (*καθεστάκαμέν σε σήμερον ἀρχιερέα τοῦ ἔθνους σου*), and *ἀσθένειαν* recalls 5^{2} (*περίκειται ἀσθένειαν*), in the special sense that such weakness involved a sacrifice for one's personal sins (*ὑπὲρ τῶν ἰδίων ἁμαρτιῶν*). Whereas Jesus the Son of God (as opposed to *ἀνθρώπους ἀσθενεῖς*) was appointed by a divine order which superseded the Law (*μετὰ τὸν νόμον* = vv.[11-19]), and appointed as one who was τετελειωμένος (in the sense of 2^{10}) εἰς τὸν αἰῶνα. It is implied that he was appointed ἀρχιερεύς, between which and *ἱερεύς* there is no difference.

The writer now picks up the thought (7^{22}) of the superior διαθήκη which Jesus as ἀρχιερεύς in the eternal σκηνή or sanctuary mediates for the People. This forms the transition between the discussion of the priesthood (5–8) and the sacrifice of Jesus (9^{1}–10^{17}). The absolute sacrifice offered by Jesus as the absolute priest (vv.[1-6]) ratifies the new *διαθήκη* which has superseded the old (vv.[7-13]) with its imperfect sacrifices.

[1] *The point of all this is, we do have such a highpriest, one who is "seated at the right hand" of the throne of Majesty* (see 1^{3}) *in the heavens,* [2] *and who officiates in the sanctuary or "true tabernacle set up by the Lord" and not by man.* [3] *Now, as every highpriest is appointed to offer gifts and sacrifices, he too must have something to offer.* [4] *Were he on earth, he would not be a priest at all, for there are priests already to offer the gifts prescribed by Law* ([5] *men who serve a mere outline and shadow of the heavenly—as Moses was instructed when he was about to execute the building of the tabernacle: "see," God said, "that* (sc. ὅπως) *you make everything on the pattern shown you upon the mountain").* [6] *As it is, however, the divine service he has obtained is superior, owing to the fact that he mediates a superior covenant, enacted with superior promises.*

The terseness of the clause ἣν ἔπηξεν ὁ κύριος, οὐκ ἄνθρωπος (v.[1]) is spoiled by the insertion of **καί** before **οὐκ** (A K L P vg boh syr arm eth Cosm.). In v.[4] **οὖν** becomes *γάρ* in D^c K L syr^{hkl} arm Chrys. Theod., and a similar group of authorities add *ἱερέων* after *ὄντων*. **Τόν** is prefixed needlessly to *νόμον* by ℵ^c D K L P Chrys. Dam. to conform to the usage in 7^5 9^{22}; but the sense is really unaffected, for the only legal regulation conceivable is that of the Law. In v.[6] *νῦν* and **νυνί** (9^{26}) are both attested; the former is more common in the papyri. The Hellenistic (from Aristotle onwards) form *τέτευχεν* (ℵ^c B D^c 5. 226. 467. 623. 920. 927. 1311. 1827. 1836. 1873. 2004. 2143, etc.: or *τέτυχεν*, ℵ^c A D* K L) has been corrected in P Ψ 6. 33. 1908 Orig. to the Attic *τετύχηκεν*. Before **κρείττονός**, **καί** is omitted by D* 69. 436. 462 arm Thdt.

Κεφάλαιον ("the pith," Coverdale), which is nominative absolute, is used as in Cic. *ad Attic.* v. 18: "et multa, immo omnia, quorum *κεφάλαιον*," etc., Dem. xiii. 36: *ἔστι δ', ὦ ἄνδρες Ἀθηναῖοι, κεφάλαιον ἁπάντων τῶν εἰρημένων* (at the close of a speech); Musonius (ed. Hense, 67 f.) *βίου καὶ γενέσεως παίδων κοινωνίαν κεφάλαιον εἶναι γάμου*, etc. The word in this sense is common throughout literature and the more colloquial papyri, here with **ἐπὶ τοῖς λεγομένοις** (concerning what has been said). In passing from the intricate argument about the Melchizedek priesthood, which is now dropped, the writer disentangles the salient and central truth of the discussion, in order to continue his exposition of Jesus as highpriest. "Such, I have said, was the **ἀρχιερεύς** for us, and such is the *ἀρχιερεύς* we have—One who is enthroned, **ἐν τοῖς οὐρανοῖς**, next to God himself." While Philo spiritualizes the highpriesthood, not unlike Paul (Ro $12^{1f.}$), by arguing that devotion to God is the real highpriesthood (*τὸ γὰρ θεραπευτικὸν γένος ἀνάθημά ἐστι θεοῦ, ἱερώμενον τὴν μεγάλην ἀρχιερωσύνην αὐτῷ μόνῳ, de Fug.* 7), our author sees its essential functions transcended by Jesus in the spiritual order.

The phrase in v.[2] **τῶν ἁγίων λειτουργός**, offers two points of interest. First, the linguistic form *λειτουργός*. The *ει* form stands between the older *η* or *ηι*, which waned apparently from the third cent. B.C., and the later *ι* form; "*λειτουργός* sim. socios habet omnium temporum papyros praeter perpaucas recentiores quae sacris fere cum libris conspirantes *λιτουργὸς λιτουργία* scribunt" (Crönert, *Memoria Graeca Hercul.* 39). Then, the meaning of *τῶν ἁγίων*. Philo has the phrase, in *Leg. Alleg.* iii. 46, *τοιοῦτος δὲ ὁ θεραπευτὴς καὶ λειτουργὸς τῶν ἁγίων*, where *τῶν ἁγίων* means "sacred things," as in *de Fug.* 17, where the Levites are described as priests *οἷς ἡ τῶν ἁγίων ἀνακεῖται λειτουργία.* This might be the meaning here. But the writer uses *τὰ ἅγια* elsewhere ($9^{8f.}$ 10^{19} 13^{11}) of "the sanctuary," a rendering favoured by the context. By *τὰ ἅγια* he means, as often in the LXX, the sanctuary in general, without any reference to the distinction (cp. $9^{2f.}$) between the outer and the inner shrine. The LXX avoids the pagan term *ἱερόν* in this connexion, though *τὸ ἅγιον* itself was already in use among ethnic writers (*e.g.* the edict of

Ptolemy III., καὶ καθιδρῦσαι ἐν τῶν ἁγίωι = "in sacrario templi," Dittenberger, *OGIS*. 56[59]). It is here defined (καί epexegetic) as the true or real σκηνή, ἣν[1] ἔπηξεν ὁ κύριος (a reminiscence of Nu 24[6] σκηναὶ ἃς ἔπηξεν Κύριος, and of Ex 33[7] καὶ λαβὼν Μωυσῆς τὴν σκηνὴν αὐτοῦ ἔπηξεν). The reality and authenticity of the writer's faith come out in a term like ἀληθινός. What he means by it he will explain in a moment (v.[5]). Meanwhile he turns to the λειτουργία of Jesus in this ideal sanctuary. This ἀρχιερεύς of ours, in his vocation (v.[3], cp. 5[1]), must have (ἀναγκαῖον, *sc*. ἐστίν) some sacrifice to present before God, though what this offering is, the writer does not definitely say, even later in 9[24]. The analogy of a highpriest carrying the blood of an animal inside the sacred shrine had its obvious limitations, for Jesus was both ἀρχιερεύς and offering, by his self-sacrifice. Προσενέγκῃ is the Hellenistic aorist subjunctive, where classical Greek would have employed a future indicative (Radermacher, 138). The writer proceeds to argue that this λειτουργία is far superior to the levitical cultus (vv.[4f.]). Even in the heavenly sanctuary there must be sacrifice of some kind—for sacrifice is essential to communion, in his view. It is not a sacrifice according to the levitical ritual; indeed Jesus on this level would not be in levitical orders at all. But so far from that being any drawback or disqualification to our ἀρχιερεύς, it is a proof of his superiority, for the bible itself indicates that the levitical cultus is only an inferior copy of the heavenly order to which Jesus belongs.

Instead of contrasting at this point (v.[4]) τὰ δῶρα (sacrifices, as in 11[4]) of the levitical priests with the spiritual sacrifice of Jesus, he hints that the mere fact of these sacrifices being made ἐπὶ γῆς is a proof of their inferiority. This is put into a parenthesis (v.[5]); but, though a grammatical aside, it contains one of the writer's fundamental ideas about religion (Eusebius, in *Praep. Evang*. xii. 19, after quoting He 8[5], refers to the similar Platonic view in the sixth book of the *Republic*). Such priests (οἵτινες, the simple relative as in 9[2] 10[8. 11] 12[5]) λατρεύουσι (with dative as in 13[10]) ὑποδείγματι καὶ σκιᾷ τῶν ἐπουρανίων (cp. 9[23]). Ὑπόδειγμα here as in 9[23] is a mere outline or copy (the only analogous instance in the LXX being Ezk 42[15] τὸ ὑπόδειγμα τοῦ οἴκου); the phrase is practically a hendiadys for "a shadowy outline," a second-hand, inferior reproduction. The proof of this is given in a reference to Ex 25[40]: Καθὼς κεχρημάτισται Μωυσῆς—χρηματίζω,[2] as often in the LXX and the papyri, of divine

[1] ἣν is not assimilated, though ἧς might have been written; the practice varied (cp. *e.g.* Dt 5[31] ἐν τῇ γῇ ἣν ἐγὼ δίδωμι, and 12[1] ἐν τῇ γῇ ᾗ Κύριος δίδωσιν).

[2] Passively in the NT in Ac 10[22], but the exact parallel is in Josephus, *Ant*. iii. 8. 8, Μωϋσῆς . . . εἰς τὴν σκηνὴν εἰσιὼν ἐχρηματίζετο περὶ ὧν ἐδεῖτο παρὰ τοῦ θεοῦ.

revelations as well as of royal instructions—μέλλων ἐπιτελεῖν τὴν σκηνήν. The subject of the φησι is God, understood from κεχρημάτισται, and the γάρ[1] introduces the quotation, in which the writer, following Philo (*Leg. Alleg.* iii. 33), as probably codex Ambrosianus (F) of the LXX followed him, adds πάντα. He also substitutes δειχθέντα for δεδειγμένον, which Philo keeps (κατὰ τὸ παράδειγμα τὸ δεδειγμένον σοι ἐν τῷ ὄρει πάντα ποιήσεις), and retains the LXX τύπον (like Stephen in Ac 7^{44}). The idea was current in Alexandrian Judaism, under the influence of Platonism, that this σκηνή on earth had been but a reproduction of the pre-existent heavenly sanctuary. Thus the author of Wisdom makes Solomon remind God that he had been told to build the temple (νάον . . . καὶ θυσιαστήριον) as μίμημα σκηνῆς ἁγίας ἣν προητοίμασας ἀπ' ἀρχῆς (9^8), where σκηνὴ ἁγία is plainly the heavenly sanctuary as the eternal archetype. This idealism determines the thought of our writer (see Introd. pp. xxxi f.). Above the shows and shadows of material things he sees the real order of being, and it is most real to him on account of Jesus being there, for the entire relationship between God and man depends upon this function and vocation of Jesus in the eternal sanctuary.

Such ideas were not unknown in other circles. Seneca (*Ep.* lviii. 18–19) had just explained to Lucilius that the Platonic ideas were "what all visible things were created from, and what formed the pattern for all things," quoting the Parmenides, 132 D, to prove that the Platonic idea was the ever-lasting pattern of all things in nature. The metaphor is more than once used by Cicero, e.g. *Tusc.* iii. 2. 3, and in *de Officiis*, iii. 17, where he writes: "We have no real and life-like (solidam et expressam effigiem) likeness of real law and genuine justice; all we enjoy is shadow and sketch (umbra et imaginibus). Would that we were true even to these! For they are taken from the excellent patterns provided by nature and truth." But our author's thought is deeper. In the contemporary Syriac Apocalypse of Baruch the idea of Ex 25^{40} is developed into the thought that the heavenly Jerusalem was also revealed to Moses along with the patterns of the σκηνή and its utensils ($4^{4f.}$); God also showed Moses "the pattern of Zion and its measures, in the pattern of which the sanctuary of the present time was to be made" (Charles' tr.). The origin of this notion is very ancient; it goes back to Sumerian sources, for Gudea the prince-priest of Lagash (*c.* 3000 B.C.) receives in a vision the plan of the temple which he is commanded to build (cp. A. Jeremias, *Babylonisches im NT*, pp. 62 f.). It is to this fundamental conception that the author of Πρὸς Ἑβραίους recurs, only to elaborate it in an altogether new form, which went far beyond Philo. Philo's argument (*Leg. Alleg.* iii. 33), on this very verse of Exodus, is that Bezaleel only constructed an imitation (μιμήματα) of τὰ ἀρχέτυπα given to Moses; the latter was called up to the mountain to receive the direct idea of God, whereas the former worked simply ἀπὸ σκιᾶς τῶν γενομένων. In *de Plant.* 6 he observes that the very name of Bezaleel (בְּצַל אֵל) means "one who works in shadows" (ἐν σκιαῖς ποιῶν); in *De Somniis*, i. 35, he defines it as "in the shadow of God," and again contrasts Bezaleel with Moses: ὁ μὲν οἷα σκιὰς ὑπεγράφετο, ὁ δ' οὐ σκιάς,

[1] Put before φησι, because the point is not that the oracle was given, but what the oracle contained.

αὐτὰς δὲ τὰς ἀρχετύπους ἐδημιούργει φύσεις. In *Vit. Mos.* iii. 3 he argues that in building the σκηνή Moses designed to produce καθάπερ ἀπ' ἀρχετύπου γραφῆς καὶ νοητῶν παραδειγμάτων αἰσθητὰ μιμήματα . . . ὁ μὲν οὖν τύπος τοῦ παραδείγματος ἐνεσφραγίζετο τῇ διανοίᾳ τοῦ προφήτου . . . τὸ δ' ἀποτέλεσμα πρὸς τὸν τύπον ἐδημιουργεῖτο.

He then continues (v.^{6} **νῦν δέ**, logical as in 2^{8} 9^{26}, answering to **εἰ μέν** in v.^{4}) the thought of Christ's superior **λειτουργία** by describing him again (cp. 7^{22}) in connexion with the superior **διαθήκη**, and using now not ἔγγυος but **μεσίτης**. Μεσίτης (see on Gal 3^{19}) commonly means an arbitrator (*e.g.* Job 9^{33}, *Rein. P.* 44^{3} [A.D. 104] ὁ κατασταθεὶς κριτὴς μεσίτης) or intermediary in some civil transaction (*OP.* 1298^{19}); but this writer's use of it, always in connexion with **διαθήκη** (9^{15} 12^{24})[1] and always as a description of Jesus (as in 1 Ti 2^{5}), implies that it is practically (see on 7^{22}) a synonym for **ἔγγυος**. Indeed, linguistically, it is a Hellenistic equivalent for the Attic μετέγγυος, and in Diod. Siculus, iv. 54 (τοῦτον γὰρ μεσίτην γεγονότα τῶν ὁμολογιῶν ἐν Κόλχοις ἐπηγγέλθαι βοηθήσειν αὐτῇ παρασπονδουμένῃ), its meaning corresponds to that of ἔγγυος. The sense is plain, even before the writer develops his ideas about the new διαθήκη, for, whenever the idea of reconciliation emerges, terms like μεσίτης and μεσιτεύειν are natural. Μεσίτης καὶ διαλλακτής is Philo's phrase[2] for Moses (*Vit. Mos.* iii. 19). And as a διαθήκη was a gracious order of religious fellowship, inaugurated upon some historical occasion by sacrifice, it was natural to speak of Jesus as the One who mediated this new διαθήκη of Christianity. He gave it (Theophyl. μεσίτης καὶ δότης); he it was who realized it for men and who maintains it for men. All that the writer has to say meantime about the διαθήκη is that it has been enacted (v.^{6}) **ἐπὶ κρείττοσιν ἐπαγγελίαις**. This passive use of **νομοθετεῖν** is not unexampled; cf. *e.g.* *OGIS.* 493^{55} (ii A.D.) καὶ ταῦτα μὲν ὑμεῖν ὀρθῶς καὶ καλῶς . . . νενομοθετήσθω. It is implied, of course, that God is ὁ νομοθετῶν (as in LXX Ps 83^{7}). What the "better promises" are, he now proceeds to explain, by a contrast between their διαθήκη and its predecessor. The superiority of the new διαθήκη is shown by the fact that God thereby superseded the διαθήκη with which the levitical cultus was bound up; the writer quotes an oracle from Jeremiah, again laying stress on the fact that it came after the older διαθήκη (vv.$^{7-13}$), and enumerating its promises as contained in a new διαθήκη.

[1] In these two latter passages, at least, there may be an allusion to the contemporary description of Moses as "mediator of the covenant" ("arbiter testamenti," *Ass. Mosis*, i. 14). The writer does not contrast Jesus with Michael, who was the great angelic mediator in some circles of Jewish piety (cp. Jub 1^{29}, Test. Dan 6).

[2] Josephus (*Ant.* xvi. 2. 2) says that Herod τῶν παρ' Ἀγρίππα τισὶν ἐπιζητουμένων **μεσίτης** ἦν, and that his influence moved πρὸς τὰς εὐεργεσίας οὐ βραδύνοντα τὸν Ἀγρίππαν. Ἰλιεῦσι μὲν γὰρ αὐτὸν **διήλλαξεν** ὀργιζόμενον.

[7] *For if that first covenant had been faultless, there would have been no occasion for a second.* [8] *Whereas God does find fault with the people of that covenant, when he says:*

"The day is coming, saith the Lord,
when I will conclude a new covenant with the house of Israel and with the house of Judah.
[9] *It will not be on the lines of the covenant I made with their fathers,*
on the day when I took them by the hand to lead them out of Egypt's Land;
for they would not hold to my covenant,
so I left them alone, saith the Lord.
[10] *This is the covenant I will make with the house of Israel when that* ("the day" of v.[8]) *day comes, saith the Lord;*
I will set my laws within their mind,
inscribing them upon their hearts;
I will be a God (εἰς θεόν, *i.e.* all that men can expect a God to be) *to them,*
and they shall be a People to me;
[11] *one citizen will no longer teach his fellow,*
one man will no longer teach his brother (τὸν ἀδελφὸν αὐτοῦ, *i.e.* one another, Ex 10[23]),
saying, "Know the Lord."
for all shall know me, low and high together.
[12] *I will be merciful to their iniquities,*
and remember their sins no more.
[13] *By saying "a new covenant," he antiquates the first. And whatever is antiquated and aged is on the verge of vanishing.*

The contents of the prediction of a **καινὴ διαθήκη** by God, and the very fact that such was necessary, prove the defectiveness of the first διαθήκη. The writer is struck by the mention of a new διαθήκη even in the OT itself, and he now explains the significance of this. As for **ἡ πρώτη** (*sc.* διαθήκη) **ἐκείνη, εἰ . . . ἄμεμπτος** (if no fault could have been found with it), **οὐκ ἂν δευτέρας ἐζητεῖτο τόπος. Δευτέρας** is replaced by ἑτέρας in B* (so B. Weiss, Blass); but, while ἕτερος could follow πρῶτος (Mt 21[30]), δεύτερος is the term chosen in 10[9], and B* is far too slender evidence by itself. **Ζητεῖν τόπον** is one of those idiomatic phrases, like εὑρεῖν τόπον and λαβεῖν τόπον, of which the writer was fond. The force of the **γάρ** after **μεμφόμενος** is: "and there was occasion for a second διαθήκη, the first was not **ἄμεμπτος**, since," etc. It need make little or no difference to the sense whether we read **αὐτοῖς** (ℵ[c] B D[c] L 6. 38. 88. 104. 256. 436. 467. 999. 1311. 1319. 1739. 1837. 1845. 1912. 2004. 2127 Origen) or αὐτούς (ℵ* A D* K P W 33 vg arm), for μεμφόμενος can take a dative as well as an accusative (cf. Arist. *Rhet.* i. 6. 24, Κορινθίοις δ' οὐ μέμφεται τὸ Ἴλιον: Aesch. *Prom.* 63, οὐδεὶς ἐνδίκως μέμψαιτο μοι) in the sense of "censuring" or "finding fault with," and μεμφόμενος naturally goes with αὐτοῖς or αὐτούς. The objection to taking **αὐτοῖς** with **λέγει** [1]

[1] μεμφόμενος is then "by way of censure," and some think the writer purposely avoided adding αὐτήν. Which, in view of what he says in v.[13], is doubtful; besides, he has just said that the former διαθήκη was not ἄμεμπτος.

is that the quotation is not addressed directly to the people, but spoken at large. Thus the parallel from 2 Mac 2^7 (*μεμψάμενος αὐτοῖς εἶπεν*) is not decisive, and the vg is probably correct in rendering "vituperans enim eos dicit." The context explains here as in 4^8 and 11^{28} who are meant by *αὐτούς*. The real interest of the writer in this Jeremianic oracle is shown when he returns to it in 10^{16-18}; what arrests him is the promise of a free, full pardon at the close. But he quotes it at length, partly because it did imply the supersession of the older *διαθήκη* and partly because it contained high promises (vv.$^{10-12}$), higher than had yet been given to the People. No doubt it also contains a warning (v.^{9}), like the text from the 95th psalm ($3^{7f.}$), but this is not why he recites it (see p. xl).

The text of Jer 38^{31-34} (31^{31-34}) as he read it in his bible (*i.e.* in A) ran thus:

ἰδοὺ ἡμέραι ἔρχονται, λέγει Κύριος,
καὶ διαθήσομαι τῷ οἴκω Ἰσραὴλ καὶ τῷ οἴκῳ Ἰούδα διαθήκην καινήν,
οὐ κατὰ τὴν διαθήκην ἣν διεθέμην τοῖς πατράσιν αὐτῶν
ἐν ἡμέρᾳ ἐπιλαβομένου μου τῆς χειρὸς αὐτῶν ἐξαγαγεῖν αὐτοὺς ἐκ γῆς Αἰγύπτου,
ὅτι αὐτοὶ οὐκ ἐνέμειναν ἐν τῇ διαθήκῃ μου,
κἀγὼ ἠμέλησα αὐτῶν, φησὶν Κύριος.
ὅτι αὕτη ἡ διαθήκη ἣν διαθήσομαι τῷ οἴκῳ Ἰσραήλ
μετὰ τὰς ἡμέρας ἐκείνας, φησὶν Κύριος,
διδοὺς νόμους μου εἰς τὴν διάνοιαν αὐτῶν
καὶ ἐπιγράψω αὐτοὺς ἐπὶ τὰς καρδίας αὐτῶν,
καὶ ὄψομαι αὐτοὺς
καὶ ἔσομαι αὐτοῖς εἰς θεόν.
καὶ αὐτοὶ ἔσονταί μοι εἰς λαόν.
καὶ οὐ μὴ[1] διδάξωσιν ἕκαστος τὸν ἀδελφὸν αὐτοῦ
καὶ ἕκαστος τὸν πλησίον αὐτοῦ λέγων· γνῶθι τὸν Κύριον,
ὅτι πάντες ἰδήσουσιν με
ἀπὸ μικροῦ ἕως μεγάλου αὐτῶν,
ὅτι ἵλεως ἔσομαι ταῖς ἀδικίαις αὐτῶν
καὶ τῶν ἁμαρτιῶν αὐτῶν οὐ μὴ μνησθῶ ἔτι.

Our author follows as usual the text of A upon the whole (*e.g.* λέγει for *φησίν* in v.^{31}, *κἀγώ* in v.^{32}, the omission of *μου* after *διαθήκη* and of *δώσω* after *διδούς* in v.^{33}, *οὐ μὴ διδάξωσιν* for *οὐ διδάξουσιν* in v.^{34} and the omission of *αὐτῶν* after *μικροῦ*), but substitutes *συντελέσω ἐπὶ τὸν οἶκον* (bis) for *διαθήσομαι τῷ οἴκῳ* in v.^{31}, reads λέγει for *φησίν* in v.^{32} and v.^{33}, alters *διεθέμην* into *ἐποίησα* (Q*), and follows B in reading *καὶ ἐπὶ κ. αὐτῶν* before the verb (v.^{33}), and *πολίτην . . . ἀδελφόν* in v.^{34}, as well as in omitting *καὶ ὄψ. αὐτούς* (A א) in the former verse; in v.^{34} he reads *εἰδήσουσιν* (א Q) instead of

[1] *οὐ μή* only occurs in Hebrews in quotations (here, 10^{17} 13^5); out of about ninety-six occurrences in the NT, only eight are with the future.

ἰδήσουσιν, the forms of οἶδα and εἶδον being repeatedly confused (cp. Thackeray, 278). These minor changes may be partly due to the fact that he is quoting from memory. In some cases his own text has been conformed to other versions of the LXX; *e.g.* A D Ψ boh restore μου in v.[10], ℵ* K vg Clem. Chrys. read καρδίαν (with ℵ in LXX), though the singular[1] is plainly a conformation to διάνοιαν ("Für den Plural sprechen ausser A D L noch B, wo nur das C in ϵ verschrieben und daraus ϵπι καρδια ϵαυτων geworden ist, und P, wo der Dat. in den Acc. verwandelt," B. Weiss in *Texte u. Untersuchungen*, xiv. 3. 16, 55); B Ψ arm revive the LXX (B) variant γράψω; the LXX (Q) variant πλησίον is substituted for πολίτην by P vg syr^hkl eth 38. 206. 218. 226. 257. 547. 642. 1288. 1311. 1912, etc. Cyril, and the LXX (B Q ℵ) αὐτῶν restored after μικροῦ by D^c L syr boh eth, etc. On the other hand, a trait like the reading ἐποίησα in the LXX text of Q* may be due to the influence of Hebrews itself. The addition of καὶ τῶν ἀνομιῶν αὐτῶν after or before καὶ τῶν ἁμαρτιῶν αὐτῶν in v.[12] is a homiletic gloss from 10[17], though strongly entrenched in ℵ^c A C D K L P Ψ 6. 104. 326, etc. vg pesh arm Clem.

Συντελέσω διαθήκην, a literary LXX variant for ποιήσω διαθήκην, recalls the phrase συντελέσαι διαθήκην (Jer 41[8] (34[8])), and, as 12[24] (**νέας διαθήκης**) shows, the writer draws no distinction between καινός and νέος (v.[8]). In v.[9] the genitive absolute (**ἐπιλαβομένου μου**) after **ἡμέρᾳ**, instead of ἐν ᾗ ἐπελαβόμην (as Justin correctly puts it, *Dial.* xi.), is a Hellenistic innovation, due here to translation, but paralleled in Bar 2[28] ἐν ἡμέρᾳ ἐντειλαμένου σου αὐτῷ); in **ὅτι** (causal only here and in v.[10]) . . . ἐνέμειναν, the latter is our "abide by," in the sense of obey or practise, exactly as in Isokrates, κατὰ τῶν Σοφιστῶν, 20: οἷς εἴ τις ἐπὶ τῶν πράξεων ἐμμείνειεν. Bengel has a crisp comment on **αὐτοὶ . . . κἀγώ** here and on **ἔσομαι . . . καὶ αὐτοί** ("correlata . . . sed ratione inversa; populus fecerat initium tollendi foederis prius, in novo omnia et incipit et perficit Deus"); and, as it happens, there is a dramatic contrast between **ἠμέλησα** here and the only other use of the verb in this epistle (2[3]). In v.[10] **διδούς**, by the omission of δώσω, is left hanging in the air; but (cp. Moulton, 222) such participles could be taken as finite verbs in popular Greek of the period (cp. *e.g.* χειροτονηθείς in 2 Co 8[19]). The **καινὴ διαθήκη** is to be on entirely fresh lines, not a mere revival of the past; it is to realize a knowledge of God which is inward and intuitive (vv.[10. 11]). There is significance in the promise, **καὶ ἔσομαι αὐτοῖς . . . εἰς λαόν**. A διαθήκη was always between God and his people, and this had been the object even of the former διαθήκη (Ex. 6[7]); now it is to be realized at last. Philo's sentence ("even if we are sluggish, however, He is not sluggish about taking to Himself those who are fit for His service; for He says, 'I will take you to be a people for myself, and I will be your God,'" *De Sacrif. Abelis et Caini*, 26) is an apt comment; but our author, who sees the new διαθήκη fulfilled in Christianity, has

[1] That ἐπί takes the accusative here is shown by 10[16]; καρδίας cannot be the genitive singular alongside of an accusative.

his own views about how such a promise and purpose was attainable, for while the oracle ignores the sacrificial ritual altogether, he cannot conceive any pardon apart from sacrifice, nor any διαθήκη apart from a basal sacrifice. These ideas he is to develop in his next paragraphs, for it is the closing promise of pardon[1] which is to him the supreme boon. Meanwhile, before passing on to explain how this had been mediated by Jesus, he (v.[13]) drives home the truth of the contrast between old and new (see Introd., p. xxxix). **Ἐν τῷ λέγειν** (same construction as in 2[8])—when the word **καινὴν** (*sc.* διαθήκην) was pronounced, it sealed the doom of the old διαθήκη. **Παλαιόω** (**πεπαλαίωκε**) in this transitive sense ("he hath abrogat," Tyndale) is known to the LXX (Job 9[5], La 3[4], both times of God in action); **γηράσκειν** is practically equivalent to μαραίνεσθαι, and implies decay (see Wilamowitz on Eur. *Herakles*, 1223). The two words **ἐγγὺς** (as in 6[8]) **ἀφανισμοῦ**, at the end of the paragraph, sound like the notes of a knell, though they have no contemporary reference; the writer simply means that the end of the old διαθήκη was at hand (p. xxii). The new would soon follow, as it had done ἐν υἱῷ (1[1]). The verb ἀφανίζειν (-εσθαι) is applied to legislation (*e.g.*, Lysias, 868, τὴν ὑμέτεραν νομοθεσίαν ἀφανίζοντας) in the sense of abolition, lapsing or falling into desuetude, Dion. Hal. *Ant.* iii. 178, ἃς (*i.e.* Numa's laws) ἀφανισθῆναι συνέβη τῷ χρόνῳ, the opposite of ἀφανίζειν being γράφειν (*ibid.* ix. 608, κατὰ τοὺς νόμους, οὓς οὐ νεωστὶ δεήσει γράφειν πάλαι γὰρ ἐγράφησαν, καὶ οὐδεὶς αὐτοὺς ἠφάνιζε χρόνος), and the sense of disappearance in ἀφανισμός appears already in the LXX (*e.g.* Jer 28[37] καὶ ἔσται Βαβυλὼν εἰς ἀφανισμόν).

But the new διαθήκη is also superior to the old by its sacrifice (9[1f.]), sacrifice being essential to any forgiveness such as has been promised. The older διαθήκη had its sanctuary and ritual (vv.[1-5]), but even these (vv.[6f.]) indicated a defect.

[1] *The first covenant had indeed its regulations for worship and a material sanctuary.* [2] *A tent was set up* (κατασκευάζω as in 3[3]), *the outer tent, containing the lampstand, the table, and the loaves of the Presence; this is called the Holy place.* [3] *But behind* (μετά only here in NT of place) *the second veil was the tent called the Holy of Holies,* [4] *containing the golden altar of incense, and also the ark of the covenant covered all over with gold, which held the golden pot of manna, the rod of Aaron that once blossomed, and the tablets of the covenant;* [5] *above this were the cherubim of the Glory overshadowing the mercy-seat—matters which* (*i.e.* all in [2-5]) *it is impossible for me to discuss at present in detail.*

---

[1] With τῶν ἁμαρτιῶν αὐτῶν οὐ μὴ μνησθῶ ἔτι compare the parable of R. Jochanan and R. Eliezer on God's readiness to forget the sinful nature of his servants: "There is a parable concerning a king of flesh and blood, who said to his servants, Build me a great palace on the dunghill. They went and built it for him. It was not thenceforward the king's pleasure to remember the dunghill which had been there" (Chagiga, 16 a. i. 27).

The **καινὴ διαθήκη** of 8^{7-13} had been realized by the arrival of Christ (9^{11}); hence the older *διαθήκη* was superseded, and the writer speaks of it in the past tense, **εἶχε**. As for **ἡ πρώτη** (*sc.* *διαθήκη*) of which he has been just speaking (8^{13}), the antithesis of the entire passage is between **ἡ πρώτη διαθήκη** (vv.$^{1-10}$) and **ἡ καινὴ διαθήκη** (vv.$^{11-22}$), as is explicitly stated in v.^{15}. The **καί** (om. B 38. 206*. 216*. 489. 547. 1739. 1827 boh pesh Origen) before **ἡ πρώτη** emphasizes the fact that the old had this in common with the new, viz. worship and a sanctuary. This is, of course, out of keeping with the Jeremianic oracle of the new *διαθήκη*, which does not contemplate any such provision, but the writer takes a special view of *διαθήκη* which involves a celestial counterpart to the ritual provisions of the old order.

The former *διαθήκη*, then, embraced **δικαιώματα**, *i.e.* regulations, as in Lk 1^{6} and 1 Mac $2^{21.\ 22}$ (*ἵλεως ἡμῖν καταλείπειν νόμον καὶ δικαιώματα τὸν νόμον τοῦ βασιλέως οὐκ ἀκουσόμεθα, παρελθεῖν τὴν λατρίαν ἡμῶν*), rather than rights or privileges (as, *e.g.*, *OP.* 1119^{15} *τῶν ἐξαιρέτων τῆς ἡμετέρας πατρίδος δικαιωμάτων*), arrangements for the cultus. **Λατρείας** grammatically might be accusative plural (as in v.^{6}), but is probably the genitive, after *δικαιώματα*, which it defines. *Λατρεία* or (as spelt in W) *λατρία* (cp. Thackeray, 87) is the cultus (Ro 9^{4}), or any specific part of it (Ex $12^{25.\ 27}$). The close connexion between worship and a sanctuary (already in $8^{2.\ 3}$) leads to the addition of **τό τε** (as in 1^{3} 6^{5}) **ἅγιον κοσμικόν.** By **τὸ ἅγιον** the author means the entire sanctuary (so, *e.g.*, Ex 36^{3}, Nu 3^{38}), not the innermost sacred shrine or *ἅγια ἁγίων*. This is clear. What is not so clear is the meaning of **κοσμικόν**, and the meaning of its position after the noun without an article. Primarily *κοσμικός* here as in Ti 2^{12} (*τὰς κοσμικὰς ἐπιθυμίας*) is an equivalent for *ἐπὶ γῆς* (8^{3}), *i.e.* mundane or material, as opposed to **ἐπουράνιον** or **οὐ ταύτης τῆς κτίσεως** (v.^{11}). A fair parallel to this occurs in *Test. Jos.* 17^{8}, *διὰ τὴν κοσμικήν μου δόξαν*. But did our author use it with a further suggestion? It would have been quite irrelevant to his purpose to suggest the "public" aspect of the sanctuary, although Jews like Philo and Josephus might speak of the temple as *κοσμικός* in this sense, *i.e.* in contrast to synagogues and *προσευχαί*, which were of local importance (Philo, *ad Caium*, 1019), or simply as a place of public worship (*e.g.* Jos. *Bell.* iv. 5. 2, *τῆς κοσμικῆς θρησκείας κατάρχοντας, προσκυνουμένους τε τοῖς ἐκ τῆς οἰκουμένης παραβάλλουσιν εἰς τὴν πόλιν*). Neither would our author have called the sanctuary *κοσμικός* as symbolic of the *κόσμος*, though Philo (*Vit. Mosis*, iii. 3–10) and Josephus (*Ant.* iii. 6. 4, iii. 7. 7, *ἕκαστα γὰρ τούτων εἰς ἀπομίμησιν καὶ διατύπωσιν τῶν ὅλων*) also play with this fancy. He views the sanctuary as a dim representation of the divine sanctuary, not of the universe. Yet he might have employed κοσμικόν in a similar sense, if we interpret the obscure phrase μυστήριον κοσμικὸν ἐκκλησίας in Did. 11[11] (see the notes of Dr. C. Taylor and Dr. Rendel Harris in their editions) as a spiritual or heavenly idea, "depicted in the world of sense by emblematic actions or material objects," "a symbol or action wrought upon the stage of this world to illustrate what was doing or to be done on a higher plane." Thus, in the context of the Didache, marriage would be a μυστήριον κοσμικόν (cp. Eph 5[32]) of the spiritual relation between Christ and his church. This early Christian usage may have determined the choice of κοσμικόν here, the sanctuary being κοσμικόν because it is the material representation or parabolic outward expression of the true, heavenly sanctuary. But at best it is a secondary suggestion; unless κοσμικόν could be taken as "ornamented," the controlling idea is that the sanctuary and its ritual were external and material (δικαιώματα σαρκὸς, χειροποιήτου, χειροποίητα). The very position of κοσμικόν denotes, as often in Greek, a stress such as might be conveyed in English by "a sanctuary, material indeed."

The ἅγιον is now described (v.[2f.]), after Ex 25–26. It consisted of two parts, each called a σκηνή. The large outer tent, the first (ἡ πρώτη) to be entered, was called Ἅγια (neut. plur., not fem. sing.). The phrase, ἥτις λέγεται Ἅγια[1] would have been in a better position immediately after ἡ πρώτη, where, indeed, Chrysostom (followed by Blass) reads it, instead of after the list of the furniture. The lampstand stood in front (to the south) of the sacred table on which twelve loaves or cakes of wheaten flour were piled (ἡ πρόθεσις τῶν ἄρτων = οἱ ἄρτοι τῆς προθέσεως), the Hebrew counterpart of the well-known lectisternia: ἡ τράπεζα . . . ἄρτων is a hendiadys for "the table with its loaves of the Presence." Such was the furniture of the outer σκηνή. Then (vv.[3-5]) follows a larger catalogue (cp. *Joma* 2[4]) of what lay inside the inner shrine (ἅγια ἁγίων) behind the curtain (Ex 27[16]) which screened this from the outer tent, and which is called δεύτερον καταπέτασμα, δεύτερον, because the first was a curtain hung at the entrance to the larger tent, and καταπέτασμα, either because that is the term used in Ex 26[31f.] (the particular passage the writer has in mind here), the term elsewhere being usually κάλυμμα or ἐπίσπαστρον (Ex 26[36] etc.), or because Philo had expressly distinguished the outer curtain as κάλυμμα, the inner as καταπέτασμα (*de vita Mosis*, iii. 9). This inner shrine contained (v.[4]) χρυσοῦν θυμιατήριον, *i.e.* a wooden box, overlaid with gold, on which incense (θυμίαμα) was offered twice daily by the priests. The LXX calls this θυσιαστήριον τοῦ θυμιάματος (Ex 30[1-10]), but our writer follows the usage of Philo, which is also,

[1] Τὰ Ἅγια (B arm) is an attempt to reproduce exactly the LXX phrase.

on the whole, that of Josephus, in calling it *θυμιατήριον* (so Symm. Theodotion, Ex 30^1 31^8); *θυμιατήριον*, in the non-biblical papyri, denotes articles like censers in a sanctuary, but is never used in the LXX of levitical censers, though Josephus occasionally describes them thus, like the author of 4 Mac 7^{11}. The ordinary view was that this **θυμιατήριον** stood beside the **λυχνία** and the sacred **τράπεζα** in the outer sanctuary. Both Philo (e.g. *quis rer. div.* 46, *τριῶν ὄντων ἐν τοῖς ἁγίοις σκευεῶν, λυχνίας, τραπέζης, θυμιατηρίου*: *de vita Mos.* iii. 9 f., in the outer tent, *τὰ λοιπὰ τρία σκευή . . . μέσον μὲν τὸ θυμιατήριον . . . τὴν δὲ λυχνίαν . . . ἡ δὲ τράπεζα*) and Josephus (*Ant.* iii. 6. 4 f.; cp. viii. 4. 1 for the reproduction in Solomon's temple) are quite explicit on this. Indeed no other position was possible for an altar which required daily service from the priests; inside the *ἅγια τῶν ἁγίων* it would have been useless. But another tradition, which appears in the contemporary (Syriac) apocalypse of Baruch (6^7), placed the altar of incense[1] inside the **ἅγια ἁγίων**, a view reflected as early as the Samaritan text of the pentateuch, which put Ex 30^{1-10} (the description of the altar of incense) after 26^{35}, where logically it ought to stand, inserting a לפני יהוה in Ex 40^{27} (where the altar of incense is placed "before the veil"). The earliest hint of this tradition seems to be given in the Hebrew text of 1 K 6^{22}, where Solomon is said to have overlaid with gold "the altar that is by the oracle" (*i.e.* the *ἅγια ἁγίων*). But our author could not have been influenced by this, for it is absent from the LXX text. His inaccuracy was rendered possible by the vague language of the pentateuch about the position of the altar of incense, *ἀπέναντι τοῦ καταπετάσματος τοῦ ὄντος ἐπὶ τῆς κιβωτοῦ τῶν μαρτυριῶν* (Ex 30^6), where *ἀπέναντι* may mean "opposite" or "close in front of" the curtain—but on which side of it? In Ex 37 the *τράπεζα*, the *λυχνία*, and the altar of incense are described successively after the items in the *ἅγια ἁγίων*; but then the LXX did not contain the section on the altar of incense, so that this passage offered no clue to our writer. In Ex 40^5 it is merely put *ἐναντίον τῆς κιβωτοῦ*. This vagueness is due to the fact that in the original source the sketch of the *σκηνή* had no altar of incense at all; the latter is a later accretion, hence the curious position of Ex 30^{1-10} in a sort of appendix, and the ambiguity about its site.

After all it is only an antiquarian detail for our author. It has been suggested that he regarded the *ἅγια τῶν ἁγίων*, irrespective of the veil, as symbolizing the heavenly sanctuary, and that he therefore thought it must include the altar of incense as symbolizing the prayers of the saints. But there is no trace of such a symbolism elsewhere in the epistle; it is confined to the author of the Apocalypse ($8^{3f.}$). The suggestion that he meant **ἔχουσα**

[1] Whether the language means this or a censer is disputed.

to express only a close or ideal connexion between the inner shrine and the altar of incense, is popular (*e.g.* Delitzsch, Zahn, Peake, Seeberg) but quite unacceptable; ἔχουσα as applied to the other items could not mean this,[1] and what applies to them applies to the θυμιατήριον. Besides, the point of the whole passage is to distinguish between the contents of the two compartments. Still less tenable is the idea that θυμιατήριον really means "censer" or "incense pan." This way out of the difficulty was started very early (in the peshiṭta, the vulgate), but a censer is far too minor a utensil to be included in this inventory; even the censer afterwards used on atonement-day did not belong to the ἅγια τῶν ἁγίων, neither was it golden. What the σκηνή had was merely a brazier (πυρεῖον, Lv 16^{12}). Since it is not possible that so important an object as the altar of incense could have been left out, we may assume without much hesitation that the writer did mean to describe it by θυμιατήριον,[2] and that the irregularity of placing it on the wrong side of the curtain is simply another of his inaccuracies in describing what he only knew from the text of the LXX. In B the slip is boldly corrected by the transference of (καὶ) χρυσοῦν θυμιατήριον to v.^{2}, immediately after ἄρτων (so Blass).

The second item is τὴν κιβωτὸν τῆς διαθήκης covered with gold all over (πάντοθεν: Philo's phrase is ἔνδοθεν καὶ ἔξωθεν, *de Ebriet.* 21), a chest or box about 4 feet long and 2½ feet broad and high (Ex 25$^{10f.}$), which held three sacred treasures, (*a*) the golden pot (στάμνος, Attic feminine) of manna (Ex 16$^{32-34}$); (*b*) Aaron's rod ἡ βλαστήσασα (in the story of Nu 17$^{1-11}$, which attested the sacerdotal monopoly of the clan of Levi); and (*c*) αἱ πλάκες τῆς διαθήκης (Ex 25$^{16f.}$ 31^{18}), *i.e.* the two stone tablets on which the decalogue was written (πλάκας διαθήκης, Dt 9^9; ἐνέβαλον τὰς πλάκας εἰς τὴν κιβωτόν, 10^5), the decalogue summarizing the terms of the διαθήκη for the People. In adding χρυσῆ to στάμνος the writer follows the later tradition of the LXX and of Philo (*de congressu*, 18); the pot is not golden in the Hebrew original. He also infers, as later Jewish tradition did, that the ark contained this pot, although, like Aaron's rod, it simply lay in front of the ark (Ex 16$^{33.34}$, Nu 17^{10}). He would gather from 1 K 8^9 that the ark contained the tablets of the covenant. He then (v.^{5}) mentions the χερουβείν (Aramaic form) or χερουβεὶμ (Hebrew form) δόξης, two small winged figures (Ex 25$^{18-20}$), whose pinions extended over a rectangular gold slab, called τὸ ἱλαστήριον, laid on the top of the ark, which it fitted exactly. They are called cherubim Δόξης, which is like Μεγαλωσύνης (1^3 8^1) a divine title, applied to Jesus in Ja 2^1, but here used as in Ro 9^4. The cherubim on the ἱλαστήριον represented the divine Presence as accessible in mercy; the mystery of this is suggested by the couplet in Sir 49$^{8\,(10)}$:

> Ἰεζεκιήλ, ὃς εἶδεν ὅρασιν Δόξης
> ἣν ὑπέδειξεν αὐτῷ ἐπὶ ἅρματος χερουβείμ.

[1] The change from ἐν ᾗ to ἔχουσα is purely stylistic, and ἔχουσα in both instances means "containing."

[2] χρυσοῦν θυμιατήριον lacks the article, like στάμνος χρυσῆ.

Philo's account of **τὸ ἱλαστήριον** is given in *de vita Mosis*, iii. 8, ἡ δὲ κιβωτὸς . . . κεχρυσωμένη πολυτελῶς ἔνδοθέν τε καὶ ἔξωθεν, ἧς ἐπίθεμα ὡσανεὶ πῶμα τὸ λεγόμενον ἐν ἱεραῖς βίβλοις ἱλαστήριον . . . ὅπερ ἔοικεν εἶναι σύμβολον φυσικώτερον μὲν τῆς ἵλεω τοῦ θεοῦ δυνάμεως. Lower down, in the same paragraph, he speaks of τὸ ἐπίθεμα τὸ προσαγορευόμενον ἱλαστήριον, and **τὸ ἱλαστήριον** is similarly used in *De Cherub.* 8 (on the basis of Ex 25[19]). The **ἐπίθεμα** or covering of the ark was splashed with blood on atonement-day; perhaps, even apart from that, its Hebrew original meant "means of propitiation," and was not incorrectly named **ἱλαστήριον** (cp. Deissmann in *EBi.* 3027–3035), but our author simply uses it in its LXX sense of "mercy-seat." He does not enter into any details about its significance; in his scheme of sacrificial thought such a conception had no place. Philo also allegorizes the overshadowing wings of the cherubim as a symbol of God's creative and royal powers protecting the cosmos, and explains Ex 25[22] as follows (*Quaest. in Exod.* 25[22]): τὰ μὲν οὖν περὶ τὴν κιβωτὸν κατὰ μέρος εἴρηται· δεῖ δὲ συλλήβδην ἄνωθεν ἀναλαβόντα τοῦ γνωρίσαι χάριν τίνων ταῦτά ἐστι σύμβολα διεξελθεῖν· ἦν δὲ ταῦτα συμβολικά· κιβωτὸς καὶ τὰ ἐν αὐτῇ θησαυριζόμενα νόμιμα καὶ ἐπὶ ταύτης τὸ ἱλαστήριον καὶ τὰ ἐπὶ τοῦ ἱλαστηρίου Χαλδαίων γλώττῃ λεγόμενα χερουβίμ, ὑπὲρ δὲ τούτων κατὰ τὸ μέσον φωνὴ καὶ λόγος καὶ ὑπεράνω ὁ λέγων κτλ. But our author does not enter into any such details. He has no time for further discussion of the furniture, he observes; whether he would have allegorized these items of antiquarian ritual, if or when he had leisure, we cannot tell. The only one he does employ mystically is the **καταπέτασμα** (10[20]), and his use of it is not particularly happy. He now breaks off, almost as Philo does (*quis rer. div.* 45, πολὺν δ' ὄντα τὸν περὶ ἑκάστου λόγον ὑπερθέτεον εἰσαῦθις) on the same subject. **Κατὰ μέρος** is the ordinary literary phrase in this connexion (*e.g.* 2 Mac 2[30]; Polybius, i. 67. 11, περὶ ὧν οὐχ οἷόν τε διὰ τῆς γραφῆς τὸν κατὰ μέρος ἀποδοῦναι λόγον, and Poimandres [ed. Reitzenstein, p. 84] περὶ ὧν ὁ κατὰ μέρος λόγος ἐστὶ πολύς). **Οὐκ ἔστιν** as in 1 Co 11[20].

Worship in a sanctuary like this shows that access to God was defective (vv.[6-8]), as was inevitable when the sacrifices were external (vv.[8-10]). Having first shown this, the writer gets back to the main line of his argument (8[2]), viz. the sacrifice of Jesus as pre-eminent and final (v.[11f.]).

[6] *Such were the arrangements for worship. The priests constantly enter the first tent* (v.[2]) *in the discharge of their ritual duties,* [7] *but the second tent is entered only once a year by the highpriest alone—and it must not be without blood, which he presents on behalf of* (cp. 5[3]) *himself and the errors of the People.* [8] *By this the holy Spirit means that the way into the Holiest Presence was not yet disclosed so long as the first tent* [9] (*which foreshadowed the present age*) *was still standing, with its offerings of gifts and sacrifices which cannot* (μή as in 4[2]) *possibly make the conscience of the worshipper*

perfect, [10] *since they relate* (*sc.* οὖσαι) *merely to food and drink and a variety of ablutions—outward regulations for the body, that only hold till the period of the New Order.*

In v.[6] **διὰ παντός** = continually, as in *BM.* i. 42[6] (ii B.C.) οἱ ἐν οἴκῳ πάντες σου διαπαντὸς μνείαν ποιούμενοι. **Εἰσίασιν** (which might even be the present with a futuristic sense, the writer placing himself and his readers back at the inauguration of the sanctuary: "Now, this being all ready, the priests will enter," etc.) **ἐπιτελοῦντες** (a regular sacerdotal or ritual term in Philo) **λατρείας** (morning and evening, to trim the lamps and offer incense on the golden altar, Ex 27[21] 30[7f.] etc.; weekly, to change the bread of the Presence, Lv 24[8f.], Jos. *Ant.* iii. 6. 6). The ritual of the inner shrine (v.[3]) is now described (v.[7], cp. *Joma* 5[3]); the place is entered by the highpriest **ἅπαξ τοῦ ἐνιαυτοῦ**, on the annual day of atonement (Lv 16[29. 34], Ex 30[10]): only once, and he must be alone (μόνος, Lv 16[17]), this one individual out of all the priests. Even he dare not enter **χωρὶς αἵματος** (Lv 16[14f.]), *i.e.* without carrying in blood from the sacrifice offered for his own and the nation's **ἀγνοημάτων**. In Gn 43[12] ἀγνόημα is "an oversight," but in Jg 5[20] Tob 3[3], 1 Mac 13[39], Sir 23[2] ἀγνοήματα and "sins" are bracketed together (see above on 5[2]), and the word occurs alone in Polyb. xxxviii. 1. 5 as an equivalent for "offences" or "errors" in the moral sense. There is no hint that people were not responsible for them, or that they were not serious; on the contrary, they had to be atoned for. **Ὑπέρ κτλ.**; for a similarly loose construction cp. 1 Jn 2[2] (οὐ περὶ ἡμετέρων [ἁμαρτιῶν] δὲ μόνον, ἀλλὰ καὶ περὶ ὅλου τοῦ κόσμου).

Rabbi Ismael b. Elischa, the distinguished exegete of i–ii A.D., classified sins as follows (*Tos. Joma* 5[6]): Transgressions of positive enactments were atoned for by repentance, involving a purpose of new obedience, according to Jer 22[23] ("Return, ye backsliding children, and I will heal your backslidings"). The day of atonement, however, was necessary for the full pardon of offences against divine prohibitions: according to Lv 16[30] ("On that day shall the priest make atonement for you, to cleanse you, that ye may be clean from all your sins"). An offender whose wrongdoing deserved severe or capital punishment could only be restored by means of sufferings: according to Ps 89[32] ("Then will I visit their transgression with the rod, and their iniquity with stripes"). But desecration of the divine Name could not be atoned for by any of these three methods; death alone wiped out this sin (Jer 24[4]).

The author now (v.[8]) proceeds to find a spiritual significance in this ceremonial. **Δηλοῦντος** is used of a divine meaning as in 12[27], here conveyed by outward facts. In 1 P 1[11] the verb is again used of the Spirit, and this is the idea here; Josephus (*Ant.* iii. 7. 7, δηλοῖ δὲ καὶ τὸν ἥλιον καὶ τὴν σελήνην τῶν σαρδονύχων ἑκάτερος) uses the same verb for the mystic significance of the jewels worn by the highpriest, but our author's interpretation of the significance of the **σκηνή** is naturally very different from that of Josephus, who regards the unapproachable character of the ἄδυτον or inner shrine as symbolizing heaven itself (*Ant.* iii. 6. 4 and 7. 7, ὃ τοῖς ἱερεῦσιν ἦν ἄβατον, ὡς οὐρανὸς ἄνειτο τῷ θεῷ . . . διὰ τὸ καὶ τὸν οὐρανὸν ἀνεπίβατον εἶναι ἀνθρώποις). For ὁδόν with gen. in sense of "way to," cp. Gn 3^{24} (τὴν ὁδὸν τοῦ ξύλου τῆς ζωῆς), Jg 5^{14} (εἰς ὁδὸν τοῦ Σινά). **Τῶν ἁγίων** here (like τὰ ἅγια in vv.$^{12. 25}$, cp. 13^{11}) as in 10^{19} means the very Presence of God, an archaic liturgical phrase suggested by the context. The word **φανεροῦσθαι** was not found by the writer in his text of the LXX; it only occurs in the LXX in Jer 40 $(33)^6$, and the Latin phrase "iter patefieri" (*e.g.* Caesar, *de Bello Gall.* iii. 1) is merely a verbal parallel. In **τῆς πρώτης σκηνῆς ἐχούσης στάσιν** (v.^{9}), the writer has chosen στάσιν for the sake of assonance with ἐνεστηκότα, but ἔχειν στάσιν is a good Greek phrase for "to be in existence." The parenthesis **ἥτις**[1] **παραβολὴ** (here = τύπος, as Chrysostom saw) **εἰς τὸν καιρὸν τὸν ἐνεστηκότα** means that the first σκηνή was merely provisional, as it did no more than adumbrate the heavenly reality, and provisional εἰς (as in Ac 4^3 εἰς τὴν αὔριον) τὸν καιρὸν τὸν ἐνεστηκότα, *i.e.* the period in which the writer and his readers lived, the period inaugurated by the advent of Jesus with his new **διαθήκη**. This had meant the supersession of the older διαθήκη with its sanctuary and **δικαιώματα**, which only lasted **μέχρι καιροῦ διορθώσεως**. But, so long as they lasted, they were intended by God to foreshadow the permanent order of religion; they were, as the writer says later (v.^{23}), **ὑποδείγματα τῶν ἐν τοῖς οὐρανοῖς**, mere copies but still copies. This is why he calls the fore-tent a **παραβολή**. For now, as he adds triumphantly, in a daring, imaginative expression, our **ἀρχιερεύς** has passed through his heavenly fore-tent (v.^{11}), and his heavenly sanctuary corresponds to a heavenly (*i.e.* a full and final) sacrifice. In the levitical ritual the highpriest on atonement-day took the blood of the victim through the fore-tent into the inner shrine. Little that accomplished! It was but a dim emblem of what our highpriest was to do and has done, in the New Order of things.

When readers failed to see that **ἥτις . . . ἐνεστηκότα** was a parenthesis, it was natural that καθ' ἥν should be changed into **καθ' ὅν** (D^c K L P, so Blass).

The failure of animal sacrifices ($^{9b-10}$) lies **κατὰ συνείδησιν**. As the inner consciousness here is a consciousness of sin, "conscience" fairly represents the Greek term συνείδησις. Now, the levitical sacrifices were ineffective as regards the conscience of worshippers; they were merely **ἐπὶ βρώμασιν καὶ πόμασιν καὶ διαφόροις βαπτισμοῖς**, a striking phrase (cp. 13^9) of scorn for the mass of

[1] *Sc.* ἦν. The construction was explained by the addition of καθέστηκεν after ἐνεστηκότα (so 69. 104. 330. 436. 440. 462. 491. 823. 1319. 1836. 1837. 1898. 2005. 2127, etc.).

minute regulations about what might or might not be eaten or drunk, and about baths, etc. Food and ablutions are intelligible; a book like Leviticus is full of regulations about them. But πόμασιν? Well, the writer adds this as naturally as the author of *Ep. Aristeas* does, in describing the levitical code. "I suppose most people feel some curiosity about the enactments of our law περί τε τῶν βρωτῶν καὶ ποτῶν" (128); it was to safeguard us from pagan defilement that παντόθεν ἡμᾶς περιέφραξεν ἁγνείαις καὶ διὰ βρωτῶν καὶ ποτῶν (142), ἐπὶ τῶν βρωτῶν καὶ ποτῶν ἀπαρξαμένους εὐθέως τότε συγχρῆσθαι κελεύει (158). It is curious that this defence of the levitical code contains an allusion which is a verbal parallel to our writer's disparaging remark here; the author asserts that intelligent Egyptian priests call the Jews "men of God," a title only applicable to one who σέβεται τὸν κατὰ ἀλήθειαν θεόν, since all others are ἄνθρωποι βρωτῶν καὶ ποτῶν καὶ σκέπης, ἡ γὰρ πᾶσα διάθεσις αὐτῶν ἐπὶ ταῦτα καταφεύγει. τοῖς δὲ παρ' ἡμῶν ἐν οὐδενὶ ταῦτα λελόγισται (140. 141). Libations of wine accompanied certain levitical sacrifices (*e.g.* Nu 5^{15} $6^{15.17}$ $28^{7f.}$), but no ritual regulations were laid down for them, and they were never offered independently (cp. *EBi.* 4193, 4209). It is because the whole question of sacrifice is now to be restated that he throws in these disparaging comments upon the **δῶρά τε καὶ θυσίαι** and their accompaniments in the older **σκηνή**. Such sacrifices were part and parcel of a system connected with (v.[10]) external ritual, and in concluding the discussion he catches up the term with which he had opened it: all such rites are **δικαιώματα σαρκός**, connected with the sensuous side of life and therefore provisional, **μέχρι καιροῦ διορθώσεως ἐπικείμενα.** Here ἐπικείμενα is "prescribed," as in the description of workmen on strike, in *Tebt. P.* 26^{17} (114 B.C.) ἐγκαταλείποντας τὴν ἐπικειμένην ἀσχολίαν. Διόρθωσις means a "reconstruction" of religion, such as the new διαθήκη (8^{13}) involved; the use of the term in Polybius, iii. 118. 12 (πρὸς τὰς τῶν πολιτευμάτων διορθώσεις), indicates how our author could seize on it for his own purposes.

The comma might be omitted after **βαπτισμοῖς**, and **δικαιώματα** taken closely with **μόνον**: "gifts and sacrifices, which (μόνον κτλ. in apposition) are merely (the subject of) outward regulations for the body," ἐπί being taken as cumulative (Lk 3^{20})—"besides," etc. This gets over the difficulty that the levitical offerings had a wider scope than food, drink, and ablutions; but ἐπί is not natural in this sense here, and ἐπὶ . . . βαπτισμοῖς is not a parenthetical clause. The insertion of καί before δικαιώματα (by ℵ^{c} B D^{c} etc. vg hkl Chrys.), = "even" or "in particular" (which is the only natural sense), is pointless. Δικαιώμασιν (D^{c} K L vg hkl) was an easy conformation to the previous datives, which would logically involve ἐπικειμένοις (as the vg implies: "et justitiis carnis usque ad tempus correctionis impositis"), otherwise ἐπικείμενα would be extremely awkward, after δυνάμεναι, in apposition to δῶρα τε καὶ θυσίαι.

Now for the better sanctuary and especially the better sacrifice of Christ as our ἀρχιερεύς (vv.[11-28])!

[11] *But when Christ arrived as the highpriest of the bliss that was to be, he passed through the greater and more perfect tent which no hands had made* (*no part, that is to say, of the present order*), [12] *not* (οὐδέ = nor yet) *taking any blood of goats and calves but his own blood, and entered once for all into the Holy place. He secured an eternal redemption.* [13] *For if the blood of goats and bulls and the ashes of a heifer, sprinkled on defiled persons, give them a holiness that bears on bodily purity,* [14] *how much more shall* (καθαριεῖ, logical future) *the blood of Christ, who in the spirit of the eternal offered himself as an unblemished sacrifice to God, cleanse your conscience from dead works to serve a living God."*

This paragraph consists of two long sentences (vv.[11. 12], [13. 14]). The second is an explanation of αἰωνίαν λύτρωσιν εὑράμενος at the close of the first. In the first, the sphere, the action, and the object of the sacrifice are noted, as a parallel to vv.[6. 7]; but in vv.[13. 14] the sphere is no longer mentioned, the stress falling upon the other two elements. The writer does not return to the question of the sphere till vv.[21f.]

Χριστὸς δὲ παραγενόμενος (v.[11]). But Christ came on the scene,[1] and all was changed. He arrived as ἀρχιερεύς, and the author carries on the thought by an imaginative description of him passing through the upper heavens (no hand-made, mundane fore-court this!) into the innermost Presence. It is a more detailed account of what he had meant by ἔχοντες ἀρχιερέα μέγαν διεληλυθότα τοὺς οὐρανούς (4[14]). Χειροποιήτου, like χειροποίητα (v.[24]), means "manufactured," not "fictitious" (as applied to idols or idol-temples by the LXX and Philo). Τουτ' ἔστιν οὐ ταύτης τῆς κτίσεως reads like the gloss of a scribe, but the writer is fond of this phrase τουτ' ἔστιν, and, though it adds nothing to οὐ χειροποιήτου, it may stand. Κτίσις, in this sense of creation or created order, was familiar to him (*e.g.* Wis 5[17] 19[6]). Μελλόντων, before ἀγαθῶν, was soon altered into γενομένων (by B D* 1611. 1739. 2005 vt syr Orig. Chrys.), either owing to a scribe being misled by παραγενόμενος or owing to a pious feeling that μελλόντων here (though not in 10[1]) was too eschatological. The ἄγαθα were μέλλοντα in a sense even for Christians, but already they had begun to be realized; *e.g.* in the λύτρωσις. This full range was still to be disclosed (2[5] 13[14]), but they were realities of which Christians had here and now some vital experience (see on 6[5]).

Some editors (*e.g.* Rendall, Nairne) take τῶν γενομένων ἀγαθῶν with what follows, as if the writer meant to say that "Christ appeared as highpriest of the good things which came by the greater and more perfect tabernacle (not made with hands—that is, not of this creation)." This involves, (*a*) the interpretation of οὐδέ as = "not by the blood of goats and calves either," the term carrying on παραγενόμενος; and (*b*) διά in a double sense. There is no objection to (*b*), but (*a*) is weak; the bliss and benefit are mediated not through the sphere but through what Jesus does in the sphere of the eternal σκηνή. Others (*e.g.* Westcott, von Soden, Dods, Seeberg) take διὰ τῆς

[1] Παραγενόμενος (as Lk 12[51], Mt 3[1] suggest) is more active than the πεφανέρωται of v.[26].

σκηνῆς with Χριστός, "Christ by means of the . . . sanctuary." This sense of διά is better than that of (*a*) above, and it keeps διά the same for vv.[11] and [12]. But the context (παραγενόμενος . . . εἰσῆλθεν) points to the local use of διά in διὰ τῆς . . . σκηνῆς, rather than to the instrumental; and it is no objection that the writer immediately uses διά in another sense (δι' αἵματος), for this is one of his literary methods (cp. διά with gen. and accus. in 2[1. 2] 2[9. 10] 7[18. 19. 23. 24. 25]).

Continuing the description of Christ's sacrifice, he adds (v.[12]) **οὐδὲ δι' αἵματος τράγων** (for the People) **καὶ μόσχων** (for himself), which according to the programme in Lv 16 the priest smeared on the east side of the ἱλαστήριον. The later Jewish procedure is described in the Mishna tractate *Joma*, but our author simply draws upon the LXX text, though (like Aquila and Symmachus) he uses μόσχων instead of χίμαρων. Διά is graphically used in **διὰ τοῦ ἰδίου αἵματος**, as in **δι' αἵματος τράγων καὶ μόσχων**, but the idea is the self-sacrifice, the surrender of his own life, in virtue of which[1] he redeemed his People, the αἷμα or sacrifice being redemptive as it was his. The single sacrifice had eternal value, owing to his personality. The term **ἐφάπαξ**, a stronger form of ἅπαξ, which is unknown to the LXX, is reserved by our author for the sacrifice of Jesus, which he now describes as issuing in a λύτρωσις—an archaic religious term which he never uses elsewhere; it is practically the same as **ἀπολύτρωσις** (v.[15]), but he puts into it a much deeper meaning than the LXX or than Luke (1[68] 2[38]), the only other NT writer who employs the term. Though he avoids the verb, his meaning is really that of 1 P 1[18] (ἐλυτρώθητε τιμίῳ αἵματι ὡς ἀμνοῦ ἀμώμου καὶ ἀσπίλου Χριστοῦ) or of Ti 2[14] (ὃς ἔδωκεν ἑαυτὸν ὑπὲρ ἡμῶν, ἵνα λυτρωσήται ἡμᾶς ἀπὸ πάσης ἀνομίας καὶ καθαρίσῃ ἑαυτῷ λαὸν περιούσιον).

In this compressed phrase, **αἰωνίαν λύτρωσιν εὑράμενος**, (*a*) αἰωνίαν offers the only instance of αἰώνιος being modified in this epistle. (*b*) Εὑράμενος, in the sense of Dion. Hal. *Ant.* v. 293 (οὔτε διαλλαγὰς εὕρατο τοῖς ἀνδράσι καὶ κάθοδον), and Jos. *Ant.* i. 19. 1 (πάππου δόξαν ἀρετῆς μεγάλης εὑράμενου), is a participle (for its form,[2] cp. Moulton, i. p. 51), which, though middle, is not meant to suggest any personal effort like "by himself," much less "for himself"; the middle in Hellenistic Greek had come to mean what the active meant. What he secured, he secured for us (cp. Aelian, *Var. Hist.* iii. 17, καὶ αὐτοῖς σωτηρίαν εὕραντο). The aorist has not a past sense; it either means "to secure" (like εὑράμενοι in 4 Mac 3[13] and ἐπισκεψάμενοι in 2 Mac 11[36]), after a verb of motion (cp. Ac 25[13]), or "securing" (by what grammarians call "coincident action").

The last three words of v.[12] are now (vv.[13. 14]) explained by an *a fortiori* argument. Why was Christ's redemption eternal? What gave it this absolute character and final force? In v.[13]

[1] The διά here as in διὰ πνεύματος αἰωνίου suggest the state in which a certain thing is done, and inferentially the use becomes instrumental, as we say, "he came *in* power."

[2] The Attic form εὑρόμενος is preferred by D* 226. 436. 920.

τράγων καὶ ταύρων reverses the order in 10[4], and *ταύρων* is now substituted for *μόσχων*. The former led to *ταύρων καὶ τράγων* being read (by the K L P group, Athanasius, Cyril, etc.), but "the blood of goats and bulls" was a biblical generalization (Ps 50[13], Is 1[11]), chosen here as a literary variation, perhaps for the sake of the alliteration, though some editors see in *ταύρων* a subtle, deliberate antithesis to the feminine **δάμαλις**. According to the directions of Nu 19[9f.] a red cow was slaughtered and then burned; the ashes (**ἡ σπόδος τῆς δαμάλεως**) were mixed with fresh water and sprinkled upon any worshipper who had touched a dead body and thus incurred ceremonial impurity, contact with the dead being regarded as a disqualification for intercourse with men or God (see above on 6[1]). This mixture was called *ὕδωρ ῥαντισμοῦ*. The rite supplies the metaphors of the argument in vv.[14. 15]; it was one of the ablutions (v.[10]) which restored the contaminated person (**τοὺς κεκοινωμένους**) to the worshipping community of the Lord. The cow is described as **ἄμωμον**, the purified person as **καθαρός**; but our author goes ouside the LXX for *κεκοινωμένους*, and even *ῥαντίζειν* is rare in the LXX. "The red colour of the cow and the scarlet cloth burnt on the pyre with the aromatic woods, suggest the colour of blood; the aromatic woods are also probably connected with primitive ideas of the cathartic value of odours such as they produce" (R. A. S. Macalister in *ERE*. xi. 36*a*). The lustration had no connexion whatever with atonement-day, and it was only in later rabbinic tradition that it was associated with the functions of the high-priest. According to *Pesikta* 40*a*, a pagan inquirer once pointed out to Rabbi Jochanan ben Zakkai the superstitious character of such rites. His disciples considered his reply unsatisfactory, and afterwards pressed him to explain to them the meaning of the ashes and the sprinkling, but all he could say was that it had been appointed by the Holy One, and that men must not inquire into His reasons (cp. Bacher's *Agada d. Pal. Amoräer*, i. 556; *Agada der Tannaiten*[2], i. 37, 38). Our author does not go into details, like the author of *Ep. Barnabas* (8), who allegorizes the ritual freely in the light of the Jewish tradition; he merely points out that, according to the bible, the rite, like the similar rite of blood on atonement-day, restored the worshipper to outward communion with God. **Ἁγιάζει** means this and no more.

The removal of the religious tabu upon persons contaminated by contact with the dead was familiar to non-Jews. The writer goes back to the OT for his illustration, but it would be quite intelligible to his Gentile Christian readers (cp. Marett's *The Evolution of Religion*, pp. 115 f.; *ERE*. iv. 434, x. 456, 483, 485, 501), in a world where physical contact with the dead was a *μίασμα*. Philo's exposition (*de spec. legibus*. i. *περὶ θυόντων*, 1 f.) of the rite is that the primary concern is for the purity of the soul; the attention needed for securing that the victim is *ἄμωμον*, or, as he says, *παντελῶς μούμων ἀμέτοχον*, is a figurative expression for moral sensitiveness on the part of the worshipper; it is a regulation really intended for rational beings. *Οὐ τῶν θυομένων φροντίς ἐστιν . . . ἀλλὰ τῶν θυόντων, ἵνα περὶ μηδὲν πάθος κηραίνωσι.* The bodily cleansing is only secondary, and even this he ingeniously allegorizes into a demand for self-knowledge, since the water and ashes should remind us how worthless our natures are, and knowledge of this kind is a wholesome purge for conceit! Thus, according to Philo, the rite did purge soul as well as body: *ἀναγκαῖον τοὺς μέλλοντας φοιτᾶν εἰς τὸ ἱερὸν ἐπὶ μετουσίᾳ θυσίας τὸ τε σῶμα φαιδρύνεσθαι καὶ τὴν ψυχὴν πρὸ τοῦ σώματος.* Our author does not share this favourable view (cp. Seeberg's *Der Tod Christi*, pp. 53 f.; O. Schmitz's *Die Opferanschauung des späteren Judentums*, pp. 281 f.). He would not have denied that the levitical cultus aimed at spiritual good; what he did deny was that it attained its end. Till a perfect sacrifice was offered, such an end was unattainable. The levitical cultus "provided a ritual cleansing for the community, a cleansing which, for devout minds that could penetrate beneath the letter to the spirit, must have often meant a sense of restoration to God's community. But at best the machinery was cumbrous: at best the pathway into God's presence was dimly lighted" (H. A. A. Kennedy, *The Theology of the Epistles*, p. 213).

Our author does not explain how the blood of goats and bulls could free the worshiper from ceremonial impurity; the cathartic efficacy of blood is assumed. From the comparative study of religion we know now that this belief was due to the notion that "the animal that has been consecrated by contact with the altar becomes charged with a divine potency, and its sacred blood, poured over the impure man, absorbs and disperses his impurity" (Marett, *The Evolution of Religion*, p. 121). But in Πρὸς Ἑβραίους, (*a*) though the blood of goats and bulls is applied to the people as well as to the altar, and is regarded as atoning (see below), the writer offers no rationale of sacrifice. Χωρὶς αἱματεκχυσίας οὐ γίνεται ἄφεσις. He does not argue, he takes for granted, that access to God involves sacrifice, *i.e.* blood shed. (*b*) He uses the rite of Nu 19 to suggest the cathartic process, the point of this lustration being the use of "water made holy by being mingled with the ashes of the heifer that had been burnt." "The final point is reached," no doubt (Marett, *op. cit.* 123), "when it is realized that the blood of bulls and goats cannot wash away sin, that nothing external can defile the heart or soul, but only evil thoughts and evil will." Yet our writer insists that even this inward defilement requires a sacrifice, the sacrifice of Christ's blood. This is now (v.[14]) urged in the phrase ἑαυτὸν προσήνεγκεν, where we at last see what was intended by προσφέρειν τι in 8[3]. We are not to think of the risen or ascended Christ presenting himself to God, but of his giving himself up to die as a sacrifice. The blood of Christ means his life given up for the sake of men. He did die, but it was a voluntary death—not the slaughter of an unconscious, reluctant victim; and he who died lives. More than that, he lives with the power of that death or sacrifice. This profound thought is further developed by (*a*) the term **ἄμωμον**, which is in apposition to *ἑαυτόν*; and (*b*) by **διὰ πνεύματος αἰωνίου**, which goes with **προσήνεγκεν**. (*a*) Paul calls Christians, or calls them to be, *ἄμωμοι*; but our writer, like the author of 1 P (1^{19}), calls Christ *ἄμωμος* as a victim. It is a poetic synonym for *ἀμώμητος*, taken over as the technical term (LXX) for the unblemished (מוּם) animals which alone could be employed in sacrifice; here it denotes the stainless personality, the sinless nature which rendered the self-sacrifice of Jesus eternally valid. Then (*b*) the pregnant phrase *διὰ πνεύματος αἰωνίου*, which qualifies *ἑαυτὸν προσήνεγκεν*, means that this sacrifice was offered in the realm or order of the inward spirit, not of the outward and material; it was no *δικαίωμα σαρκός*, but carried out *διὰ πνεύματος*, *i.e.* in, or in virtue of, his spiritual nature. What the author had called *ζωὴ ἀκατάλυτος* (7^{16}) he now calls **πνεῦμα αἰώνιον.** The sacrificial blood had a mystical efficacy; it resulted in an eternal **λύτρωσις** because it operated in an eternal order of spirit, the sacrifice of Jesus purifying the inner personality (*τὴν συνείδησιν*) because it was the action of a personality, and of a sinless personality which belonged by nature to the order of spirit or eternity. Christ was both priest and victim; as Son of God he was eternal and spiritual, unlike mortal highpriests (7^{16}), and, on the other side, unlike a mortal victim. The implication (which underlies all the epistle) is that even in his earthly life Jesus possessed eternal life. Hence what took place in time upon the cross, the writer means, took place really in the eternal, absolute order. Christ sacrificed himself **ἐφάπαξ**, and the single sacrifice needed no repetition, since it possessed absolute, eternal value as the action of One who belonged to the eternal order. He died—he had to die—but only once (9^{15}–10^{18}), for his sacrifice, by its eternal significance, accomplished at a stroke what no amount of animal sacrifices could have secured, viz. the forgiveness of sins. It is as trivial to exhaust the meaning of **πνεῦμα αἰώνιον** in a contrast with the animal sacrifices of the levitical cultus as it is irrelevant to drag in the dogma of the trinity. **Αἰωνίου** closely describes **πνεύματος** (hence it has no article). What is in the writer's mind is the truth that what Jesus did by dying can never be exhausted or transcended. His sacrifice, like his **διαθήκη**, like the *λύτρωσις* or *σωτηρία* which he secures, is **αἰώνιος** or lasting, because it is at the heart of things. It was because Jesus was what he was by nature that his sacrifice had such final value; its atoning significance lay in his vital connexion with the realm of absolute realities; it embodied all that his divine personality meant for men in relation to God. In short, his self-sacrifice "was something beyond which nothing could be, or could be conceived to be, as a response to God's mind and requirement in relation to sin . . . an intelligent and loving response to the holy and gracious will of God, and to the terrible situation of man" (Denney, *The Death of Christ*, p. 228).

A later parallel from rabbinic religion occurs in the Midrash Tehillim on Ps 31: "formerly you were redeemed with flesh and blood, which to-day is and to-morrow is buried; wherefore your redemption was temporal (גאולת שעה). But now I will redeem you by myself, who live and remain for ever; wherefore your redemption will be eternal redemption (גאולת עולם, cp. Is 45^{17})."

One or two minor textual items may be noted in v.[14].

πνεύματος] J. J. Reiske's conjecture *ἁγνεύματος* (purity) is singularly prosaic. **Αἰωνίου** (א* A B D^c K L syr$^{vg\ hkl}$ arm Ath) is altered into the conventional *ἁγίου* by א^c D* P 35. 88. 206. 326. 547, etc. lat boh Chrys. Cyril. Liturgical usage altered **ὑμῶν** into *ἡμῶν* (A D* P 5. 38. 218. 241. 256. 263. 378. 506. 1319. 1831. 1836*. 1912. 2004. 2127 vt syr^{vg} boh Cyr.), and, to *ζῶντι, καὶ ἀληθινῷ* (a gloss from 1 Th 1^9) is added in A P 104 boh Chrys. etc.

In the closing words of v.[14] **καθαριεῖ** is a form which is rare (Mt 3^{12}, Ja 4^8?) in the NT, so rare that *καθαρίσει* is read here by 206. 221. 1831 Did. Ath. It is a Hellenistic verb, used in the inscriptions (with *ἀπό*) exactly in the ceremonial sense underlying the metaphor of this passage (Deissmann, *Bible Studies*, 216 f.). The cleansing of the conscience (cp. v.[9]) is **ἀπὸ νεκρῶν ἔργων**, from far more serious flaws and stains than ceremonial pollution by contact with a corpse (see above, and in 6^1). As Dods puts it, "a pause might be made before *ἔργων*, from dead—(not bodies but) works." The object is **εἰς τὸ λατρεύειν θεῷ ζῶντι**. The writer uses the sacerdotal term (8^5) here as in 10^2 and 12^{28}, probably like Paul in a general sense; if he thought of Christians as priests, *i.e.* as possessing the right of access to God, he never says so. Religion for him is access to God, and ritual metaphors are freely used to express the thought. When others would say "fellowship," he says "worship." It is fundamental for him that forgiveness is essential to such fellowship, and forgiveness is what is meant by "purifying the conscience." As absolute forgiveness was the boon of the new *διαθήκη* (8^{12}), our author now proceeds (vv.[15f.]) to show how Christ's sacrifice was necessary and efficacious under that **διαθήκη**. A sacrifice, involving death, is essential to any *διαθήκη*: this principle, which applies to the new **διαθήκη** (v.[15]), is illustrated first generally (vv.[16. 17]) and then specifically, with reference to the former **διαθήκη** (vv.[18-22]).

15 *He mediates a new covenant for this reason, that those who have been called may obtain the eternal inheritances they have been promised, now that a death has occurred which redeems them from the transgressions involved in the first covenant.* 16 *Thus in the case of a will, the death of the testator must be announced.* 17 *A will only holds in cases of death, it is never valid so long as the testator is alive.* 18 *Hence even the first* (ἡ πρώτη, *sc.* διαθήκη as in 9^1) *covenant of God's will was not inaugurated apart from blood;* 19 *for after Moses had announced every command in the Law to all the people, he took the*

blood of calves and goats, together with water, scarlet wool and hyssop, sprinkling the book and all the people, and saying, [20] *"This is the blood of that covenant which is God's command for you."* [21] *He even* (καὶ . . . δέ, only here in Heb.) *sprinkled with blood the tent and all the utensils of worship in the same way.* [22] *In fact, one might almost say that by Law everything is cleansed with blood. No blood shed no remission of sins!*

The writer thus weaves together the idea of the new διαθήκη (9^{15} echoes 8^{6}) and the idea of sacrifice which he has just been developing. In v.[15] διὰ τοῦτο carries a forward reference ("now this is why Christ mediates a new διαθήκη, ὅπως κτλ."), as, *e.g.*, in Xen. *Cyrop.* ii. 1. 21, οἱ σύμμαχοι οὐδὲ δι' ἓν ἄλλο τρέφονται ἢ ὅπως μαχοῦνται ὑπὲρ τῶν τρεφόντων. As the climax of the promises in the new διαθήκη is pardon (8^{12}), so here its purpose is described as ἀπολύτρωσις, which obviously is equivalent to full forgiveness (Eph 1^{7} τὴν ἀπολύτρωσιν διὰ τοῦ αἵματος αὐτοῦ, τὴν ἄφεσιν τῶν παραπτωμάτων). Ἀπολύτρωσιν τῶν . . . παραβάσεων is like καθαρισμὸν τῶν ἁμαρτιῶν in 1^{3}. But pardon is only the means to fellowship, and the full scope of what has been promised is still to be realized. Yet it is now certain; the "bliss to be" is an eternal κληρονομία, assured by Christ. Note that the ἐπί in ἐπὶ τῇ πρώτῃ διαθήκῃ is not exactly temporal = "under," *i.e.* during the period of (cp. ἐπὶ συντελείᾳ τῶν αἰωνῶν in v.[26]), but causal. The transgressions, which had arisen "in connexion with" the first διαθήκη, like unbelief and disobedience, are conceived as having taken their place among men; they are the standing temptations of life towards God. The writer does not say, with Paul, that sin became guilt in view of the law, but this is near to his meaning; with the first διαθήκη sins started, the sins that haunt the People. They are removed, for the penitent, by the atoning death of Jesus, so that the People are now unencumbered. There is a similar thought in Ac $13^{38. 39}$, where Paul tells some Jews that through Jesus Christ ὑμῖν ἄφεσις ἁμαρτιῶν καταγγέλλεται, καὶ ἀπὸ πάντων ὧν οὐκ ἠδυνήθητε ἐν νόμῳ Μωϋσέως δικαιωθῆναι, ἐν τούτῳ πᾶς ὁ πιστεύων δικαιοῦται. For the sake of emphasis, τὴν ἐπαγγελίαν is thrown forward, away from κληρονομίας, like θάνατον in the next verse.

Ἀπολύτρωσις, which in 11^{35} is used in its non-technical sense of "release" from death (at the cost of some unworthy compliance), is used here in its LXX religious sense of a redemption which costs much, which can only be had at the cost of sacrifice. The primitive idea of "ransom" had already begun to fade out of it (cp. Dn 4^{32}; Philo, *quod omnis probus*, 17), leaving "liberation" at some cost as the predominant idea (so in Clem. Alex. *Strom* vii. 56). Here it is a synonym for λύτρωσις (v.[12]), or as Theophylact put it, for deliverance. But its reference is not eschatological; the retrospective reference is uppermost.

For the first and only time he employs οἱ κεκλημένοι to describe those whom he had already hailed as κλήσεως ἐπουρανίου μέτοχοι (3^1). To be "called" was indispensable to receiving God's boon (11^8), so that κεκλημένοι here is an appropriate term for those who are no longer hampered by any obstacles of an inadequate pardon. The κεκλημένοι are the faithful People; "the objects of redemption are united in one category, for the One and Only Sacrifice is not of the sphere of time" (Wickham). It is not an aoristic perfect (=κλήθεντες), as if the κεκλημένοι were simply those under the old διαθήκη, though these are included, for the sacrificial death of Jesus has a retrospective value; it clears off the accumulated offences of the past. The writer does not work out this, any more than Paul does in Ro $3^{25f.}$; but it may be implied in 11^{40} 12^{23} (see below), where the "perfecting" of the older believers is connected with the atonement. However, the special point here of **θανάτου . . . παραβάσεων** is that the death which inaugurates the new διαθήκη deals effectively with the hindrances left by the former διαθήκη. Not that this is its exclusive function. That the death inaugurates an order of grace in which forgiveness is still required and bestowed, is taken for granted (*e.g.* 4^{16}); but the **κληρονομία**, which from the beginning has been held out to the People of God, has only become attainable since the sacrifice of Jesus, and therefore (*a*) his death avails even for those who in the past hoped for it, yet could not obtain it, and also (*b*) deals with the παράβασεις set up by the older διαθήκη among men.

But how was a death necessary to a διαθήκη? The answer is given in v.$^{16f.}$ through a characteristic play on the term. In **ὅπου γὰρ** (*sc.* ἐστι) **διαθήκη** κτλ. he uses διαθήκη as equivalent to "will" or testamentary disposition, playing effectively upon the double sense of the term, as Paul had already done in Gal $3^{15f.}$. The point of his illustration (vv.$^{16. 17}$) depends upon this; **βεβαία** and **ἰσχύει** are purposely used in a juristic sense, applicable to wills as well as to laws, and **ὁ διαθέμενος** is the technical term for "testator." The illustration has its defects, but only when it is pressed beyond what the writer means to imply. A will does not come into force during the lifetime of the testator, and yet Jesus was living! True, but he had died, and died inaugurating a **διαθήκη** in words which the writer has in mind (v.^{20}); indeed, according to one tradition he had spoken of himself figuratively as assigning rights to his disciples (κἀγὼ διατίθεμαι ὑμῖν, Lk 22^{29}). The slight incongruity in this illustration is not more than that involved in making Jesus both priest and victim. It is a curious equivoque, this double use of διαθήκη, the common idea of both meanings being that benefits are "disponed," and that the διαθήκη only takes effect after a death. The continuity of argument is less obvious in English, where no single word conveys the different nuances which διαθήκη bore for Greek readers.

Hence in v.[18] some periphrasis like "the first covenant of God's will" is desirable.

That διαθήκη in vv.[16. 17] is equivalent to "testamentary disposition," is essential to the argument. No natural interpretation of vv.[15-20] is possible, when διαθήκη is understood rigidly either as "covenant" or as "will." The classical juristic sense is richly illustrated in the papyri and contemporary Hellenistic Greek, while the "covenant" meaning prevails throughout the LXX; but Philo had already used it in both senses, and here the juristic sense of κληρονομία (v.[15]) paved the way for the juristic sense which v.[17] demands. The linguistic materials are collected, with a variety of interpretations, by Norton in *A Lexicographical and Historical Study of Διαθήκη* (Chicago, 1908), Behm (*Der Begriff Διαθήκη im Neuen Testament*, Naumburg, 1912), Lohmeyer (*Διαθήκη: ein Beitrag zür Erklärung des Neutestamentlichen Begriffs*, Leipzig, 1913), and G. Vos in *Princeton Theological Review* (1915, pp. 587 f.; 1916, pp. 1–61).

In v.[16] φέρεσθαι is "announced," almost in the sense of "proved" (as often in Greek); in v.[17] μή ποτε (cp. on οὔπω in 2[8]) is not equivalent to μήπω (nondum, vg) but simply means "never" (non unquam), as, *e.g.*, in Eurip. *Hipp.* 823, ὥστε μήποτε ἐκπνεῦσαι πάλιν, μή here following the causal particle ἐπεί, like ὅτι in Jn 3[18]; it had begun to displace οὐ in later Greek. Moulton quotes *BGU.* 530 (i A.D.), μέμφεταί σε ἐπ(ε)ὶ μὴ ἀντέγραψας αὐτῇ, and Radermacher (171) suggests that the change was sometimes due to a desire of avoiding the hiatus. Ἰσχύει has the same force as in Gal 5[6], cp. *Tebt. P.* 286[7] (ii A.D.) νομὴ ἄδικος [οὐ]δὲν εἰσχύει. Some needless difficulties have been felt with regard to the construction of the whole sentence. Thus (*a*) ἐπεὶ . . . διαθέμενος might be a question, it is urged: "For is it ever valid so long as the testator is alive?" In Jn 7[26] μήποτε is so used interrogatively, but there it opens the sentence. This construction goes back to the Greek fathers Oecumenius and Theophylact; possibly it was due to the feeling that μήποτε could not be used in a statement like this. (*b*) Isidore of Pelusium (*Ep.* iv. 113) declares that πότε is a corruption of τότε (Π from Τ, a stroke being added by accident), and that he found τότε "ἐν παλαιοῖς ἀντιγράφοις." Two old MSS (ℵ* D*) do happen to preserve this reading, which is in reality a corruption of πότε.

Why, it may be asked, finally, does not the writer refer outright to the new διαθήκη as inaugurated at the last supper? The reason is plain. Here as throughout the epistle he ignores the passover or eucharist. As a non-sacerdotal feast, the passover would not have suited his argument. Every Israelite was his own priest then, as Philo remarks (*De Decalogo*, 30, πάσχα . . . ἐν ᾗ θύουσι πανδημεὶ αὐτῶν ἕκαστος τοὺς ἱερεῖς αὐτῶν οὐκ ἀναμένοντες, ἱερωσύνην τοῦ νόμου χαρισαμένου τῷ ἔθνει παντὶ κατὰ μίαν ἡμέραν κτλ.). Hence the absence of a passover ritual from the entire argument of the epistle, and also perhaps his failure to employ it here, where it would have been extremely apt.

Reverting now to the other and biblical sense of **διαθήκη**, the writer (vv.[18f.]) recalls how the *διαθήκη* at Sinai was inaugurated with blood. **Ὅθεν**—since *διαθήκη* and *θάνατος* are correlative—**οὐδὲ ἡ πρώτη** (*sc.* *διαθήκη*) **χωρὶς αἵματος ἐνκεκαίνισται** (the verb here and in 10[20] being used in its ordinary LXX sense, *e.g.*, 1 K 11[14] *ἐγκαινίσωμεν ἐκεῖ τὴν βασιλείαν*, 1 Mac 4[36] *ἀναβῶμεν καθαρίσαι τὰ ἅγια καὶ ἐνκαινίσαι*). This fresh illustration of death or blood being required in order to inaugurate a *διαθήκη*, is taken from the story in Ex 24[3f.], but he treats it with characteristic freedom. Five points may be noted. (i) He inserts[1] **τὸ αἷμα . . . τῶν τράγων**, a slip which was conscientiously corrected by a number of MSS which omitted **καὶ τῶν τράγων** (ℵ[c] K L Ψ 5. 181. 203. 242. 487. 489. 506. 623. 794. 917. 1311. 1319. 1739. 1827. 1836. 1845. 1898. 2143) as well as by syr Origen and Chrysostom. Moses merely had **μοσχάρια** slaughtered; our author adds goats, perhaps because the full phrase had become common for OT sacrifices (see on v.[13]). (ii) He inserts **μετὰ ὕδατος καὶ ἐρίου κοκκίνου καὶ ὑσσώπου**, as these were associated in his mind with the general ritual of sprinkling; water, hyssop, and scarlet thread (**κόκκινον**), for example, he remembered from the description of another part of the ritual in Nu 19. The water was used to dilute the blood; and stems of a small wall plant called "hyssop" were tied with scarlet wool (**κεκλωσμένον κόκκινον**) to form a sprinkler in the rite of cleansing a leper (Lv 14[6f.]), or for sprinkling blood (Ex 12[22]). But of this wisp or bunch there is not a word in Ex 24[3f.]. (iii) Nor is it said in the OT that Moses sprinkled[2] **αὐτὸ τὸ βιβλίον**. He simply splashed half of the blood *πρὸς τὸ θυσιαστήριον, καὶ λαβὼν τὸ βιβλίον* (*i.e.* the scroll containing the primitive code) **τῆς διαθήκης**, read it aloud to the people, who promised obedience; whereupon *λαβὼν δὲ Μωυσῆς τὸ αἷμα κατεσκέδασεν τοῦ λαοῦ καὶ εἶπεν κτλ.* An ingenious but impracticable attempt to correct this error is to take **αὐτό τε τὸ βιβλίον** with **λαβών**, but the **τε** goes with the next **καὶ πάντα τὸν λαόν**. The *βιβλίον* may have been included, since as a human product, for all its divine contents, it was considered to require cleansing; in which case the mention of it would lead up to v.[21], and **αὐτό τε τὸ βιβλίον** might be rendered "the book itself." This intensive use of *αὐτός* occurs just below in **αὐτὰ τὰ ἐπουράνια**. But *αὐτός* may be, according to the usage of Hellenistic Greek,

[1] In *πάσης ἐντολῆς κατὰ τὸν* (om. ℵ* K P) *νόμον* ("lecto omni mandato legis," vg) the *κατά* means "throughout" rather than "by."

[2] For *κατεσκέδασεν* he substitutes *ἐρράντισεν*, from *ῥαντίζω*, which is comparatively rare in the LXX (Lv 6[27], 2 K 9[33], Ps 51[7], Aquila and Symm. in Is 63[3], Aquila and Theodotion in Is 52[15]).

unemphatic, as, *e.g.*, in 11[11] καὶ αὐτὴ Σάρρα, Jn 2[24] αὐτὸς δὲ ὁ Ἰησοῦς. (iv) In quoting the LXX ἰδοὺ τὸ αἷμα τῆς διαθήκης ἧς διέθετο Κύριος πρὸς ὑμᾶς (= ὑμῖν), he changes ἰδού into τοῦτο (possibly a reminiscence of the synoptic tradition in Mk 14[22]), διέθετο into ἐνετείλατο (after ἐντολῆς in v.[19]; but the phrase occurs elsewhere, though with the dative, *e.g.* Jos 23[16]), and κύριος πρὸς ὑμᾶς into πρὸς ἡμᾶς ὁ θεός. This is a minor alteration. It is more significant that, (v) following a later Jewish tradition, which reappears in Josephus (*Ant.* iii. 8. 6 [Moses cleansed Aaron and his sons] τήν τε σκηνὴν καὶ τὰ περὶ αὐτὴν σκεύη ἐλαίῳ τε προθυμιωμένῳ καθὼς εἶπον, καὶ τῷ αἵματι τῶν ταύρων καὶ κριῶν σφαγέντων κτλ.), he makes Moses use blood to sprinkle the σκηνή and all τὰ σκεύη τῆς λειτουργίας (a phrase from 1 Ch 9[28]). The account of Ex 40[9. 10] mentions oil only; Josephus adds blood, because the tradition he followed fused the oil-dedication of the σκηνή in Ex 40[9. 10] with the (oil) sprinkling at the consecration of the priests (Lv 8[10f.]), which was followed by a blood-sprinkling of the altar alone. Philo had previously combined the oil-dedication of the σκηνή with the consecration of the priests (*vit. Mos.* iii. 17); but he, too, is careful to confine any blood-sprinkling to the altar. Our author, with his predilection for blood as a cathartic, omits the oil altogether, and extends the blood to everything.

This second illustration (vv.[18f.]) is not quite parallel to the first; the death in the one case is of a human being in the course of nature, in the other case of animals slaughtered. But αἷμα and θάνατος were correlative terms for the writer. The vital necessity of αἷμα in this connexion is reiterated in the summary of v.[22]. Σχεδόν, he begins—for there were exceptions to the rule that atonement for sins needed an animal sacrifice (*e.g.* Lv 5[11-13], where a poverty-stricken offender could get remission by presenting a handful of flour, and Nu 31[22f.], where certain articles, spoils of war, are purified by fire or water). But the general rule was that πάντα, *i.e.* everything connected with the ritual and every worshipper, priest, or layman, had to be ceremonially purified by means of blood (καθαρίζεται as the result of ἐρράντισεν). The Greek readers of the epistle would be familiar with the similar rite of αἱμάσσειν τοὺς βωμούς (Theokr. *Epigr.* i. 5, etc.). Finally, he sums up the position under the first διαθήκη by coining a term αἱματεκχυσία (from ἔκχυσις αἵματος, 1 K 18[28] etc.) for the shedding of an animal victim's blood in sacrifice; χωρὶς αἱματεκχυσίας οὐ γίνεται ἄφεσις, *i.e.* even the limited pardon, in the shape of "cleansing," which was possible under the old order. Ἄφεσις here as in Mk 3[29] has no genitive following, but the sense is indubitable, in view of 10[18] ὅπου δὲ ἄφεσις τούτων (*i.e.* of sins). The latter passage voices a feeling which seems to contradict the possibility of any forgiveness prior to the sacrifice of Christ (cp. 9^{15} $10^{4f.}$), but the writer knew from his bible that there had been an ἄφεσις under the old régime as the result of animal sacrifice; καὶ ἐξιλάσεται περὶ (or περὶ τῆς ἁμαρτίας) αὐτοῦ ὁ ἱερεὺς . . . καὶ ἀφεθήσεται αὐτῷ was the formula (cp. Lv $5^{10. 16. 18}$ etc.). The underlying principle of the argument is practically (cp. Introd., p. xlii) that laid down in the Jewish tract *Joma* v. 1 ("there is no expiation except by blood"), which quotes Lv 17^{11}, a text known to the writer of Hebrews in this form: ἡ γὰρ ψυχὴ πάσης σαρκὸς αἷμα αὐτοῦ ἐστίν, καὶ ἐγὼ δέδωκα αὐτὸ ὑμῖν ἐπὶ τοῦ θυσιαστηρίου ἐξιλάσκεσθαι περὶ τῶν ψυχῶν ὑμῶν· τὸ γὰρ αἷμα αὐτοῦ ἀντὶ τῆς ψυχῆς ἐξιλάσεται. Blood as food is prohibited, since blood contains the vital principle; as there is a mysterious potency in it, which is to be reserved for rites of purification and expiation, by virtue of the life in it, this fluid is efficacious as an atonement. The Greek version would readily suggest to a reader like our author that the piacular efficacy of αἷμα was valid universally, and that the αἷμα or sacrificial death of Christ was required in order that human sin might be removed. Why such a sacrifice, why sacrifice at all, was essential, he did not ask. It was commanded by God in the bible; that was sufficient for him. The vital point for him was that, under this category of sacrifice, the αἷμα of Christ superseded all previous arrangements for securing pardon.

After the swift aside of v.[22], the writer now pictures the appearance of Christ in the perfect sanctuary of heaven with the perfect sacrifice (vv.[25f.]) which, being perfect or absolute, needs no repetition.

[23] *Now, while the copies of the heavenly things had* (ἀνάγκη, sc. ἦν or ἐστίν) *to be cleansed with sacrifices like these, the heavenly things themselves required nobler sacrifices.* [24] *For Christ has not entered a holy place which human hands have made* (*a mere type of the reality!*); *he has entered heaven itself, now to appear in the presence of God on our behalf.* [25] *Nor was it* (sc. εἰσῆλθεν) *to offer himself repeatedly, like the highpriest entering the holy place every year with blood that was not his own:* [26] *for in that case he would have had to suffer repeatedly ever since the world was founded. Nay, once for all, at the end of the world, he has appeared with his self-sacrifice to abolish sin.* [27] *And just as it is appointed for men to die once and after that to be judged,* [28] *so Christ, after being once sacrificed to bear the sins of many, will appear again, not to deal with sin, but for the saving of those who look out for him.*

The higher σκηνή requires a nobler kind of sacrifice than its material copy on earth (v.[23]).[1] This would be intelligible enough;

[1] For ἀνάγκη . . . καθαρίζεσθαι an early variant was ἀνάγκη . . . καθαρίζεται (D* 424** Origen), which Blass adopts. But our author prefers the nominative (v.[16]) to the dative, and καθαρίζεται is no more than a conformation to the καθαρίζεται of v.[22]. The τε, which some cursives (33. 1245. 2005) substitute for δέ between αὐτά and τὰ ἐπουράνια, is due to alliteration.

but when the writer pushes the analogy so far as to suggest that the sacrifice of Christ had, among other effects, to purify heaven itself, the idea becomes almost fantastic. The nearest parallel to this notion occurs in Col 1[20]; but the idea here is really unique, as though the constant work of forgiving sinners in the upper *σκηνή* rendered even that in some sense defiled. The slight touch of disparagement in **τούτοις** (=*τοῖς ἀλόγοις*, Theodoret) may be conveyed by "like these" or "such," and **θυσίαις** is the plural of category (like **νεκροῖς** in v.[17]). After this passing lapse into the prosaic, the writer quickly recovers himself in a passage of high insight (vv.[24f.]) upon the nobler sacrifice of Jesus. Indeed, even as he compares it with the levitical sacrifices, its incomparable power becomes more and more evident. In v.[24] (=vv.[11. 12]) by **ἀντίτυπα τῶν ἀληθινῶν** he means a counterpart (*ἀντίτυπον* in reverse sense in 1 P 3[21]) of reality (cp. 8[2]), *ἀντίτυπα* being a synonym here for *ὑποδείγματα*, literally = "answering to the *τύπος*" which was shown to Moses (cp. 2 Clem. 14[3] *οὐδεὶς οὖν τὸ ἀντίτυπον φθείρας τὸ αὐθεντικὸν μεταλήψεται*). Christ has entered the heavenly sphere **νῦν** (emphatic, "now at last" = 1[2]) **ἐμφανισθῆναι** *κτλ.* In **ἐμφανισθῆναι τῷ προσώπῳ τοῦ θεοῦ** (cp. Ps 42[3] *ὀφθήσομαι τῷ προσώπῳ τοῦ θεοῦ*) we have *ἐμφανίζειν* used in its Johannine sense (14[21. 22]), though passively as in Wis 1[2] (*ἐμφανίζεται τοῖς μὴ πιστεύουσιν αὐτῷ*). But the appearance is before God on behalf of men, and the meaning is brought out in 7[26] 10[12f.]. Christ's sacrifice, it is held, provides men with a close and continuous access to God such as no cultus could effect; it is of absolute value, and therefore need not be repeated (vv.[25. 26]), as the levitical sacrifices had to be. **Οὐδ' ἵνα πολλάκις προσφέρῃ ἑαυτόν**] What is meant precisely by *προσφέρειν ἑαυτόν* here (as in v.[14]) is shown by **παθεῖν** in v.[26]. "There is no difference between entering in and offering. The act of entering in and offering is one highpriestly act" (A. B. Davidson), and *προσφέρειν ἑαυτόν* is inseparably connected with the suffering of death upon the cross. The contrast between his self-sacrifice and the highpriest entering with **αἵματι ἀλλοτρίῳ** (as opposed to **ἰδίῳ**, v.[12]) is thrown in, as a reminiscence of vv.[7f.], but the writer does not dwell on this; it is the **ἅπαξ** (cp. v.[12] and 1 P 3[18] *Χριστὸς ἅπαξ περὶ ἁμαρτιῶν ἀπέθανεν*) which engrosses his mind in v.[26], **ἐπεὶ** ("alioquin," vg) **ἔδει** (the *ἄν* being omitted as, *e.g.*, in 1 Co 5[10] *ἐπεὶ ὠφείλετε . . . ἐξελθεῖν*) **κτλ.** According to his outlook, there would be no time to repeat Christ's incarnation and sacrifice before the end of the world, for that was imminent; hence he uses the past, not the future, for his *reductio ad absurdum* argument. If Christ's sacrifice had not been of absolute, final value, *i.e.* if it had merely availed for a brief time, as a temporary provision, it would have had to be done over and over again in previous ages, since from the first sinful man has needed sacrifice; whereas the only time he was seen on earth was once, late in the evening of the world. It is implied that Christ as the Son of God was eternal and pre-existent; also that when his sacrifice did take place, it covered sins of the past (see v.^{15}), the single sacrifice of Christ in our day availing for all sin, past as well as present and future. Had it not been so, God could not have left it till so late in the world's history; it would have had to be done over and over again to meet the needs of men from the outset of history. **Νυνὶ δέ** (logical, as in 8^{6}, not temporal) **ἐπὶ συντελείᾳ** (for which Blass arbitrarily reads *τέλει*) **τῶν αἰώνων** (= *ἐπ' ἐσχάτου τῶν ἡμερῶν τούτων*, 1^{2}) **κτλ.** **Συντέλεια** is employed in its ordinary Hellenistic sense of "conclusion" (e.g. *Test. Benj.* xi. 3, *ἕως συντελείας τοῦ αἰῶνος*: *Test. Levi* x. 2, *ἐπὶ τῇ συντελείᾳ τῶν αἰώνων*); in Matthew's gospel, where alone in the NT it occurs, the genitive is *τοῦ αἰῶνος*. **Πεφανέρωται**, as in the primitive hymn or confession of faith (1 Ti 3^{16} *ἐφανερώθη ἐν σαρκί*); but the closest parallel is in 1 P 1^{20} *Χριστοῦ προεγνωσμένου μὲν πρὸ καταβολῆς κόσμου, φανερωθέντος δὲ ἐπ' ἐσχάτου τῶν χρόνων*. The object of the incarnation is, as in 2^{9}, the atonement.

The thought of the first "appearance" of Christ naturally suggests that of the second, and the thought of Jesus dying **ἅπαξ** also suggests that men have to die *ἅπαξ* as well. Hence the parenthesis of vv.$^{27.\ 28}$, for 10^{1} carries on the argument from 9^{26}. It is a parenthesis, yet a parenthesis of central importance for the primitive religious eschatology which formed part of the writer's inheritance, however inconsistent with his deeper views of faith and fellowship. "As surely as men have once to die and then to face the judgment, so Christ, once sacrificed for the sins of men, will reappear to complete the salvation of his own." **Ἀπόκειται** (cp. Longinus, *de sublim.* 9^{7} *ἀλλ' ἡμῖν μὲν δυσδαιμονοῦσιν ἀπόκειται λιμὴν κακῶν ὁ θάνατος*, and 4 Mac 8^{11} *οὐδὲν ὑμῖν ἀπειθήσασιν πλὴν τοῦ μετὰ στρεβλῶν ἀποθανεῖν ἀποκεῖται*) **τοῖς ἀνθρώποις ἅπαξ ἀποθανεῖν.** The *ἅπαξ* here is not by way of relief, although the Greeks consoled themselves by reflecting that they had not to die twice; as they could only live once, they drew from this the conclusion that life must be "all the sweeter, as an experience that never can be repeated" (A. C. Pearson on Sophocles' *Fragments*, n. 67). But our author (see on 2^{14}) sees that death is not the last thing to be faced by men; **μετὰ δὲ τοῦτο κρίσις.** This was what added seriousness to the prospect of death for early Christians. The Greek mind was exempt from such a dread; for them death ended the anxieties of life, and if there was one thing of which the Greek was sure, it was that "dead men rise up never."

Aeschylus, for example, makes Apollo declare (*Eumenides*, 647, 648):

> ἀνδρὸς δ᾽ ἐπειδὰν αἷμ᾽ ἀνασπάσῃ κόνις
> ἅπαξ θανόντος, οὔτις ἔστ᾽ ἀνάστασις.

Even in the sense of a return to life, there is no ἀνάστασις (Eurip. *Heracles*, 297; *Alcestis*, 1076; *Supplices*, 775). **Κρίσις** in En $1^{7f.}$ (καὶ κρίσις ἔσται κατὰ πάντων), as the context shows, is the eschatological catastrophe which spares the elect on earth, just as in En 5^{6}, which parallels He 9^{28}, sinners are threatened thus: πᾶσιν ὑμῖν τοῖς ἁμαρτωλοῖς οὐχ ὑπάρξει σωτηρία ἀλλὰ ἐπὶ πάντας ὑμᾶς κατάλυσις, κατάρα. In 10^{27} below **κρίσις** means the doom of the rebellious, but that is due to the context; here it is judgment in general, to which all **ἄνθρωποι** alike are liable (12^{23} κριτῇ θεῷ πάντων). Only, some have the happy experience of Christ's return (v.^{28}), in the saving power of his sacrifice. There is (as in 1 P 2^{24}) an echo of Is 53^{12} (καὶ αὐτὸς ἁμαρτίας πολλῶν ἀνήνεγκεν) in **εἰς τὸ πολλῶν** (cp. above on 2^{10}) **ἀνενεγκεῖν ἁμαρτίας**. **Προσενεχθείς** may be chosen to parallel men's passive experience of death. At any rate his suffering of death was vicarious suffering; he took upon himself the consequences and responsibilities of our sins. Such is the Christ who **ἐκ δευτέρου ὀφθήσεται**. In 1 P 5^{4} **φανεροῦσθαι** is used of the second appearance as well as of the first, but our author prefers a variety (see on v.^{26}) of expression. The striking phrase **χωρὶς ἁμαρτίας** rests on the idea that the one atonement had been final (εἰς ἀθέτησιν τῆς ἁμαρτίας), and that Christ was now **κεχωρισμένος ἀπὸ τῶν ἁμαρτωλῶν** (7^{26}). He is not coming back to die, and without death sin could not be dealt with. The homiletic (from 2 Ti 3^{15}) addition of **διὰ** (τῆς, 1611. 2005) **πίστεως**, either after **ἀπεκδεχομένοις** (by 38. 68. 218. 256. 263. 330. 436. 440. 462. 823. 1837 arm. etc.) or after **σωτηρίαν** (by A P 1245. 1898 syr^{hkl}), is connected with the mistaken idea that εἰς σωτηρίαν goes with ἀπεκδεχομένοις (cp. Phil 3^{20}) instead of with **ὀφθήσεται**. There is a very different kind of **ἐκδοχή** (10^{27}) for some **ἄνθρωποι**, even for some who once belonged to the People!

He now resumes the idea of $9^{25.\,26}$, expanding it by showing how the personal sacrifice of Jesus was final. This is done by quoting a passage from the 40th psalm which predicted the supersession of animal sacrifices (vv.$^{5-10}$). The latter are inadequate, as is seen from the fact of their annual repetition; and they are annual because they are animal sacrifices.

[1] *For as the Law has a mere shadow of the bliss that is to be, instead of representing the reality of that bliss, it never can perfect those who draw near with the same annual sacrifices that are perpetually offered.* [2] *Otherwise, they would have surely ceased to be offered; for the worshippers, once cleansed, would no longer be conscious of sins!* [3] *As it is, they are an annual reminder*

of sins 4 *(for the blood of bulls and goats cannot possibly remove sins!).*
5 *Hence, on entering the world he says,*

> *"Thou hast no desire for sacrifice or offering;*
> *it is a body thou hast prepared for me—*
> 6 *in holocausts and sin-offerings* (περὶ ἁμαρτίας as 13^{11}) *thou takest no delight.*
> 7 *So* (τότε) *I said, 'Here I come—in the roll of the book this is written of me—*
> *I come to do thy will, O God.'"*

8 *He begins by saying, "Thou hast no desire for, thou takest no delight in,*
sacrifices and offerings and holocausts and sin-offerings" (and those are what
are offered in terms of the Law); 9 *he then* (τότε) *adds, "Here I come to do*
thy will." He does away with the first in order to establish the second.
10 *And it is by this "will" that we are consecrated, because Jesus Christ once*
for all has "offered" up his "body."

This is the author's final verdict on the levitical cultus, "rapid in utterance, lofty in tone, rising from the didactic style of the theological doctor to the oracular speech of the Hebrew prophet, as in that peremptory sentence: 'It is not possible that the blood of bulls and of goats should take away sins.' The notable thing in it is, not any new line of argument, though that element is not wanting, but the series of spiritual intuitions it contains, stated or hinted, in brief, pithy phrases" (A. B. Bruce, pp. 373, 374). In **σκιὰν . . . οὐκ εἰκόνα τῶν πραγμάτων** (v.^{1}) the writer uses a Platonic phrase (Cratylus, 306 E, *εἰκόνας τῶν πραγμάτων*); **εἰκών** (=*ἀλήθεια*, Chrysostom) is contrasted with *σκιά* as the real expression or representation of substance is opposed to the faint shadow. The addition of *τῶν πραγμάτων* (=*τῶν μέλλοντων ἀγαθῶν*) emphasizes this sense; what represents solid realities is itself real, as compared to a mere *σκιά*. The **μέλλοντα ἀγαθά** (9^{11}) are the boons and blessings still to be realized in their fulness for Christians, being thought of from the standpoint of the new *διαθήκη*, not of the Law. The Law is for the writer no more than the regulations which provided for the cultus; the centre of gravity in the Law lies in the priesthood (7^{11}) and its sacrifices, not in what were the real provisions of the Law historically. The writer rarely speaks of the Law by itself. When he does so, as here, it is in this special ritual aspect, and what really bulks in his view is the contrast between the old and the new *διαθήκη*, *i.e.* the inadequate and the adequate forms of relationship to God. Once the former was superseded, the Law collapsed, and under the new *διαθήκη* there is no new Law. Even while the Law lasted, it was shadowy and ineffective, *i.e.* as a means of securing due access to God. And this is the point here made against the Law, not as Paul conceived it, but as the system of atoning animal sacrifices.

The text of v.^{1} has been tampered with at an early stage, though the variants affect the grammar rather than the general sense. Unless **δύναται**

(D H K L Ψ 2. 5. 35. 88. 181. 206. 226. 241. 242. 255. 326. 383. 429. 431. 547. 623. 794. 915. 917. 927. 1311. 1518. 1739. 1827. 1836. 1845. 1867. 1873. 1898. 2143 lat boh Orig. Chrys. Thdt. Oec.) is read for *δύνανται*, ὁ *νόμος* is a hanging nominative, and an awkward anacolouthon results. Hort suggests that the original form of the text was: *καθ' ἣν κατ' ἐνιαυτὸν τὰς αὐτὰς θυσίας προσφέρουσιν, αἳ εἰς τὸ διηνεκὲς οὐδέποτε δύνανται τοὺς προσερχομένους τελειῶσαι*. As in 9^{9}, *καθ' ἣν* (dropped out by a scribe accidentally, owing to the resemblance between ΚΑΘΗΝ and ΚΑΘΕΝ) would connect with a previous noun (here *σκιάν*), ΑΙ similarly fell out before ΕΙ (ΕΙϹ), and ΑϹ was changed into ΑΙϹ in the three consecutive words after *ἐνιαυτόν*. This still leaves ὁ *νόμος* without a verb, however, and is no improvement upon the sense gained either (*a*) by treating **ὁ νόμος** as a nominative absolute, and *δύνανται* as an irregular plural depending on *αἵ* understood[1] from *θυσίαις*; or (*b*) by simply reading *δύναται* (so Delitzsch, Weiss, Westcott, Peake, Riggenbach, Blass), which clears up everything. A desire to smooth out the grammar or to bring out some private interpretation may be underneath changes like the addition of **αὐτῶν** after **θυσίαις** (א P), or the substitution of *αὐτῶν* for *αὐταῖς* (69. 1319), or the omission of *αὐταῖς* altogether (2. 177. 206. 642. 920. 1518. 1872), as well as the omission of *ἃς* (A 33. 1611. 2005) or *αἷς* altogether, like the Syriac and Armenian versions, and the change of **τελειῶσαι** (*τελεῶσαι*, Blass) into *καθαρίσαι* (D vt).

Προσφέρουσιν is an idiomatic use of the plural (Mt 2^{20} *τεθνήκασιν*, Lk 12^{20} *αἰτοῦσιν*), "where there is such a suppression of the subject in bringing emphasis upon the action, that we get the effect of a passive, or of French *on*, German *man*" (Moulton, i. 58). The allusion is to the yearly sacrifice on atonement-day, for *προσφέρουσιν* goes with **κατ' ἐνιαυτόν**, the latter phrase being thrown forward for the sake of emphasis, and also in order to avoid bringing **εἰς τὸ διηνεκές** too near it. *Εἰς τὸ διηνεκές* also goes with *προσφέρουσιν*, not (as in v.^{14}) with **τελειοῦν**. **Οὐδέποτε** here as in v.^{11} before **δύνα(ν)ται** (never elsewhere in the epistle) is doubly emphatic from its position. The constant repetition of these sacrifices proves that their effect is only temporary; they cannot possibly bring about a lasting, adequate relationship to God. So our author denies the belief of Judaism that atonement-day availed for the pardon of the People, a belief explicitly put forward, *e.g.*, in Jub $5^{17.18}$ ("If they turn to Him in righteousness, He will forgive all their transgressions, and pardon all their sins. It is written and ordained that He will show mercy to all who turn from their guilt once a year"). He reiterates this in v.^{2}, where **ἐπεί** (as in 9^{26} = alioquin) is followed by **οὐκ**, which implies a question. "Would they not, otherwise, have ceased to be offered?" When this was not seen, either **οὐκ** was omitted (H* vg? syr 206. 1245. 1518 Primasius, etc.), leaving **ἄν** out of its proper place, or it was suggested—as would never have occurred to the author—that the OT sacrifices ceased to be valid

[1] It is inserted by A** 31. 366. 472. 1319 syr^{hkl} arm. If the relative pronoun were assimilated, *i.e.* if *αἷς* (D* H L 5. 88. 257. 547, etc.) were read for *ἅς*, the accidental omission of *αἱ* would be more intelligible.

when the Christian sacrifice took place. In **οὐκ ἂν ἐπαύσαντο προσφερόμεναι** (for construction see Gn 11^{8} *ἐπαύσαντο οἰκοδομοῦντες*) the *ἂν* is retained (see on 9^{26}). **Κεκαθαρισμένους** has been altered into *κεκαθάρμενους* (L), but *καθαρίζω*, not the Attic *καθαίρω*, is the general NT form. If our author spelt like his LXX codex, however, *κεκαθερισμένους* would be original (cp. Thackeray, 74). **Συνείδησις** is again used (9^{9}) in connexion with "the worshipper(s)," but the writer adds **ἁμαρτιῶν** (*i.e.* sins still needing to be pardoned). For the genitive, compare Philo's fine remark in *quod det. pot.* 40, *ἱκετεύωμεν οὖν τὸν θεὸν οἱ συνειδήσει τῶν οἰκείων ἀδικημάτων ἐλεγχόμενοι, κολάσαι μᾶλλον ἡμᾶς ἢ παρεῖναι.* In v.^{3} **ἀνάμνησις** means that public notice had to be taken of such sins ("commemoratio," vg).

There is possibly an echo here of a passage like Nu 5^{15} (*θυσία μνημοσύνου ἀναμιμνήσκουσα ἁμαρτίαν*), quoted by Philo in *de Plant.* 25 to illustrate his statement that the sacrifices of the wicked simply serve to recall their misdeeds (*ὑπομιμνήσκουσαι τὰς ἑκάστων ἀγνοίας τε καὶ διαμαρτίας*). In *vita Mosis*, iii. 10, he repeats this; if the sacrificer was ignorant and wicked, the sacrifices were no sacrifices (. . . *οὐ λύσιν ἁμαρτημάτων, ἀλλ' ὑπόμνησιν ἐργάζονται*). What Philo declares is the result of sacrifices offered by the wicked, the author of Hebrews declares was the result of all sacrifices; they only served to bring sin to mind. So in *de Victimis*, 7, *εὔηθες γὰρ τὰς θυσίας ὑπόμνησιν ἁμαρτημάτων ἀλλὰ μὴ λήθην αὐτῶν κατασκευάζειν*—what Philo declares absurd, our author pronounces inevitable.

The ringing assertion of v.^{4} voices a sentiment which would appeal strongly to readers who had been familiar with the classical and contemporary protests (cp. *ERE.* iii. 770^{a}), against ritual and external sacrifice as a means of moral purification (see above on 9^{13}). **Ἀφαιρεῖν**, a LXX verb in this connexion (*e.g.* Num 14^{18} *ἀφαιρῶν ἀνομίας καὶ ἀδικίας καὶ ἁμαρτίας*), becomes *ἀφελεῖν* in L (so Blass), the aoristic and commoner form; the verb is never used elsewhere in the NT, though Paul once quotes Is 27^{9} *ὅταν ἀφέλωμαι ἁμαρτίας* (Ro 11^{27}). All this inherent defectiveness of animal sacrifices necessitated a new sacrifice altogether (v.^{5} *διό*), the self-sacrifice of Jesus. So the writer quotes Ps 40$^{7-9}$, which in A runs as follows:

θυσίαν καὶ προσφορὰν οὐκ ἠθέλησας,
σῶμα δὲ κατηρτίσω μοι·
ὁλοκαυτώματα καὶ περὶ ἁμαρτίας οὐκ ἐζήτησας.
τότε εἶπον· ἰδοὺ ἥκω,
(ἐν κεφαλίδι βιβλίου γέγραπται περὶ ἐμοῦ)
τοῦ ποιῆσαι τὸ θέλημά σου, ὁ θεός μου, ἠβουλήθην.

Our author reads *εὐδόκησας* for *ἐζήτησας*,[1] shifts *ὁ θεός* (omitting *μου*) to

---

[1] Which is replaced in the text of Hebrews by Ψ (*ἐκζητήσεις*) 623*. 1836. The augment spelling *ηὐδόκησας* reappears here as occasionally at v.^{8} in a small group (A C D* W, etc.), and the singular *θυσίαν κ. προσφοράν* is kept at v.^{8} by ℵ^{c} D^{c} K L W, etc.

a position after ποιῆσαι, in order to emphasize τὸ θέλημά σου, and by omitting ἐβουλήθην (replaced by W in v.[7]), connects τοῦ ποιῆσαι closely with ἥκω. A recollection of Ps 51[18] εἰ ἠθέλησας θυσίαν . . . ὁλοκαυτώματα οὐκ εὐδοκήσεις may have suggested εὐδόκησας, which takes the accusative as often in LXX. Κεφαλίς is the roll or scroll, literally the knob or tip of the stick round which the papyrus sheet was rolled (cp. Ezek 2[9] κεφαλὶς βιβλίου).

This is taken as an avowal of Christ on entering the world, and the LXX mistranslation in σῶμα is the pivot of the argument. The more correct translation would be ὠτία δέ, for the psalmist declared that God had given him ears for the purpose of attending to the divine monition to do the will of God, instead of relying upon sacrifices. Whether ὠτία was corrupted into σῶμα, or whether the latter was an independent translation, is of no moment; the evidence of the LXX text is indecisive. Our author found σῶμα in his LXX text and seized upon it; Jesus came with his body to do God's will, *i.e.* to die for the sins of men. The parenthetical phrase **ἐν κεφαλίδι βιβλίου γέγραπται περὶ ἐμοῦ**, which originally referred to the Deuteronomic code prescribing obedience to God's will, now becomes a general reference to the OT as a prediction of Christ's higher sacrifice; that is, if the writer really meant anything by it (he does not transcribe it, when he comes to the interpretation, vv.[8f.]). Though the LXX mistranslated the psalm, however, it did not alter its general sense. The Greek text meant practically what the original had meant, and it made this interpretation or application possible, namely, that there was a sacrifice which answered to the will of God as no animal sacrifice could. Only, our author takes the will of God as requiring some sacrifice. The point of his argument is not a contrast between animal sacrifices and moral obedience to the will of God; it is a contrast between the death of an animal which cannot enter into the meaning of what is being done, and the death of Jesus which means the free acceptance by him of all that God requires for the expiation of human sin. To do the will of God is, for our author, a sacrificial action, which involved for Jesus an atoning death, and this is the thought underlying his exposition and application of the psalm (vv.[8-10]). In v.[8] **ἀνώτερον** is "above" or "higher up" in the quotation (v.[6]). The interpretation of the oracle which follows is plain; there are no textual variants worth notice,[1] and the language is clear. Thus **εἴρηκεν** in v.[9] is the perfect of a completed action, = the saying stands on record, and **ἀναιρεῖ** has its common juristic sense of "abrogate," the opposite of ἵστημι. The general idea is: Jesus entered the world fully conscious that the various sacrifices of the Law were unavailing as means of atonement, and ready to sacrifice himself in order

[1] The vocative ὁ θεός is sometimes repeated after ποιῆσαι by ℵ[c] L 104. 1288. 1739 vg syr[hkl and pesh] etc., or after σου (*e.g.* 1. 1311 harl, arm).

to carry out the redeeming will of God. God's will was to bring his People into close fellowship with himself (2[10]); this necessitated a sacrifice such as that which the σῶμα of Christ could alone provide. The triumphant conclusion is that this divine will, which had no interest in ordinary sacrifices, has been fulfilled in the **προσφορά** of Christ; what the Law could not do (v.[1]) has been achieved by the single self-sacrifice of Christ; it is by what he suffered in his body, not by any animal sacrifices, that we are **ἡγιασμένοι** (v.[10]). Jesus chose to obey God's will; but, while the Psalmist simply ranked moral obedience higher than any animal sacrifice, our writer ranks the moral obedience of Jesus as redeemer above all such sacrifices. "Christ did not come into the world to be a good man: it was not for this that a body was prepared for him. He came to be a great High Priest, and the body was prepared for him, that by the offering of it he might put sinful men for ever into the perfect religious relation to God" (Denney, *The Death of Christ*, p. 234).

In conclusion ([11-18]) the writer interprets ([11-14]) a phrase which he has not yet noticed expressly, namely, that Christ *sat down at the right hand of God* (1[3. 13]); this proves afresh that his sacrifice was final. Then, having quoted from the pentateuch and the psalter, he reverts to the prophets ([15-18]), citing again the oracle about the new διαθήκη with its prediction, now fulfilled, of a final pardon.

[11] *Again, while every priest stands daily at his service, offering the same sacrifices repeatedly, sacrifices which never can take sins away*—[12] *He offered a single sacrifice for sins and then "seated himself" for all time "at the right hand of God,"* [13] *to wait "until his enemies are made a footstool for his feet."* [14] *For by a single offering he has made the sanctified perfect for all time.* [15] *Besides, we have the testimony of the holy Spirit; for after saying,*
[16] *"This is the covenant I will make with them when that day comes,*
saith the Lord,
I will set my laws upon their hearts,
inscribing them upon their minds,"

he adds,

[17] *"And their sins and breaches of the law I will remember no more."*
[18] *Now where these are remitted* (ἄφεσις, as 9[22]), *an offering for sin exists* (sc. ἔστι) *no longer.*

One or two textual difficulties emerge in this passage. In v.[11] **ἱερεύς** was altered (after 5[1] 8[3]) into ἀρχιερεύς (A C P 5. 69. 88. 206. 241. 256. 263. 436. 462. 467. 489. 623. 642. 794. 917. 920. 927. 999. 1836. 1837. 1898 syr[hkl*] sah arm eth Cyr. Cosm.). In v.[12] **αὐτός** (K L 104. 326 boh Theod. Oec. Theophyl.) is no improvement upon οὗτος. A curious variant (boh Ephr.) in the following words is ἑαυτὸν μίαν ὑπὲρ ἁμαρτιῶν προσενέγκας θυσίαν. In v.[14] boh ("for one offering will complete them, who will be sanctified, for ever") appears to have read μιᾷ γὰρ προσφορᾷ (so Bgl.) τελειώσει κτλ. In v.[16] **τῶν διανοιῶν** is read by K L Ψ d r syr sah boh arm.

The decisive consideration in favour of **ἱερεύς** (v.[11]) is not that the ἀρχιερεύς did not sacrifice daily (for the writer believed this, see on 7[27]), but the adjective πᾶς. Περιελεῖν is a literary synonym for ἀφαιρεῖν (v.[4]); there is no special emphasis in the verb here any more than, *e.g.*, in 2 Co 3[16], for the (Zeph 3[15] περιεῖλε κύριος τὰ ἀδικήματά σου) metaphorical idea of stripping no longer attached to the term, and the περί had ceased to mean "entirely" or "altogether." The contrast between this repeated and ineffective ritual of the priests and the solitary, valid sacrifice of Jesus is now drawn in v.[12], where εἰς τὸ διηνεκές goes more effectively with ἐκάθισεν than with προσενέγκας θυσίαν, since the idea in the latter collocation is at once expressed in v.[14] At the opening of the writer's favourite psalm (110[1]) lay a promise of God to his Son, which further proved that this sacrifice of Christ was final:

> εἶπεν ὁ κύριος τῷ κυρίῳ μου Κάθου ἐκ δεξιῶν μου
> ἕως ἂν θῶ τοὺς ἐχθρούς σου ὑποπόδιον τῶν ποδῶν σου.

Κάθου—a unique privilege; so Christ's priestly sacrifice must be done and over, all that remains for him being to await the submission and homage of his foes. As for the obedient (5[9]), they are perfected "finally," *i.e.* brought into the closest relation to God, by what he has done for them; no need for him to stand at any priestly service on their behalf, like the levitical drudges! The contrast is between ἐκάθισεν and ἕστηκεν (the attitude of a priest who has to be always ready for some sacrifice). Who the foes of Christ are, the writer never says.[1] This militant metaphor was not quite congruous with the sacerdotal metaphor, although he found the two side by side in the 110th psalm. If he interpreted the prediction as Paul did in 1 Co 15[25f.], we might think of the devil (2[14]) and such supernatural powers of evil; but this is not an idea which is worked out in Πρὸς Ἑβραίους. The conception belonged to the primitive messianic faith of the church, and the writer takes it up for a special purpose of his own, but he cannot interpret it, as Paul does, of an active reign of Christ during the brief interval before the end. Christ must reign actively, Paul argues. Christ must sit, says our writer.

The usual variation between the LXX ἐκ δεξιῶν and ἐν δεξιᾷ is reproduced in Πρὸς Ἑβραίους: the author prefers the latter, when he is not definitely quoting from the LXX as in 1[13]. As this is a reminiscence rather than a citation, ἐν δεξιᾷ is the true reading, though ἐκ δεξιῶν is introduced by A 104 Athanasius. The theological significance of the idea is discussed in Dr. A. J. Tait's monograph on *The Heavenly Session of our Lord* (1912), in which he points out the misleading influence of the Vulgate's mistranslation of 10[12] ("hic autem unam pro peccatis offerens hostiam in sempiternum sedit") upon the notion that Christ pleads his passion in heaven.

---

[1] In Clem. Rom. 36[5. 6] they are οἱ φαῦλοι καὶ ἀντιτασσόμενοι τῷ θελήματι αὐτοῦ.

After reiterating the single sacrifice in v.[14] (where **τοὺς ἁγιαζομένους** is "the sanctified," precisely as in 2^{11}), he adds (v.[15]) an additional proof from scripture. **Μαρτυρεῖ δὲ ἡμῖν καὶ τὸ πνεῦμα τὸ ἅγιον**, a biblical proof as usual clinching the argument. **Ἡμῖν** is "you and me," "us Christians," not the literary plural, as if he meant "what I say is attested or confirmed by the inspired book." **Μαρτυρεῖν** is a common Philonic term in this connexion, e.g. *Leg. Alleg.* iii. 2, *μαρτυρεῖ δὲ καὶ ἐν ἑτέροις λέγων κτλ.* (introducing Dt 4^{39} and Ex 17^{6}); similarly in Xen. *Mem.* i. 2. 20, *μαρτυρεῖ δὲ καὶ τῶν ποιητῶν ὁ λέγων.* The quotation, which is obviously from memory, is part of the oracle already quoted upon the new *διαθήκη* (8^{8-12}); the salient sentence is the closing promise of pardon in v.[17], but he leads up to it by citing some of the introductory lines. The opening, **μετὰ γὰρ τὸ εἰρηκέναι**, implies that some verb follows or was meant to follow, but the only one in the extant text is **λέγει κύριος** (v.[16]). Hence, before v.[17] we must understand something like *μαρτυρεῖ* or **λέγει** or *προσέθηκεν καί φησιν* (Oecumenius) or *τότε εἴρηκεν*, although the evidence for any such phrase, *e.g.* for *ὕστερον λέγει* (31. 37. 55. 67. 71. 73. 80. 161) is highly precarious. In v.[17] **μνησθήσομαι** has been corrected into *μνησθῶ* by ℵ^{c} D^{c} K L P, etc., since **μνησθῶ** was the LXX reading and also better grammar, the future after **οὐ μή** being rare (cp. *Diat.* 2255, and above on 8^{11}). The oracle, even in the LXX version, contemplates no sacrifice whatever as a condition of pardon; but our author (see above, p. 131) assumes that such an absolute forgiveness was conditioned by some sacrifice.

The writer now (10^{19}–12^{29}) proceeds to apply his arguments practically to the situation of his readers, urging their privileges and their responsibilities under the new order of religion which he has just outlined. In 10^{19-31}, which is the first paragraph, encouragement (vv.[19-25]) passes into warning ([26-31]).

[19] *Brothers* (ἀδελφοί, not since $3^{1.\ 12}$), *since we have confidence to enter the holy Presence in virtue of the blood of Jesus,* [20] *by the fresh, living way which he has inaugurated for us through the veil* (*that is, through his flesh*), [21] *and since we have "a great Priest over the house of God,"* [22] *let us draw near with a true heart, in absolute assurance of faith, our hearts sprinkled clean from a bad conscience, and our bodies washed in pure water;* [23] *let us hold the hope we avow without wavering* (*for we can rely on him who gave us the Promise*); [24] *and let us consider how to stir one another up to love and good deeds*—[25] *not ceasing to meet together, as is the habit of some, but admonishing one another* (sc. ἑαυτούς, as 3^{13}), *all the more so, as you see the Day coming near.*

The writer (**ἔχοντες οὖν**) presses the weighty arguments of 6^{20}–10^{18}, but he returns with them to reinforce the appeal of 3^{1}–4^{16}; after 10^{19-21} the conception of Jesus as the *ἱερεύς* falls more into the background. The passage is one long sentence,

ἔχοντες . . . προσερχώμεθα . . . κατέχωμεν . . . καὶ κατανοῶμεν . . . Ἔχοντες οὖν (as in 4^{14}) since the way is now open (9^{8}) through the sacrifice of Jesus, whose atoning blood is for us the means of entering God's presence; **παρρησίαν**, "a fre sure intraunce" (Coverdale), echoing 4^{16}. But the writer fills out the appeal of $4^{14\text{-}16}$ with the idea of the sanctuary and the sacrifice which he had broken off, in $5^{1f.}$, to develop. Though the appeal still is **προσερχώμεθα** ($^{23} = 4^{16}$), the special motives are twofold: (*a*) **παρρησία** for access in virtue of the sacrifice of Jesus (vv.$^{19.\ 20}$), and (*b*) the possession of Jesus as the supreme **ἱερεύς** (v.^{21}). (*a*) The religious sense of **παρρησία** emerges in the early gloss inserted after Sir 18^{29}:

> *κρείσσων παρρησία ἐν δεσπότῃ μόνῳ*
> *ἢ νεκρὰ καρδία νεκρῶν ἀντέχεσθαι.*

Here *παρρησία* means confident trust, the unhesitating adherence of a human soul to God as its only Master, but our author specially defines it as **παρρησία εἰς** (cp. 2 P 1^{11} *ἡ εἴσοδος εἰς τὴν αἰώνιον βασιλείαν*) **εἴσοδον** (with gen. as *ὁδόν* in 9^{8}, but not a synonym for *ὁδόν*), *i.e.* for access to (**τῶν ἁγίων**) the holy Presence, **ἐν τῷ αἵματι Ἰησοῦ** (qualifying *εἴσοδον*).[1] This resumes the thought of $9^{24\text{-}26}$ $10^{10\text{-}12}$ (*ἐν αἵματι* as in 9^{25}). Compare for the phrase and general idea the words on the self-sacrifice of Decius Mus in Florus, i. 15. 3: "quasi monitu deorum, capite uelato, primam ante aciem dis manibus se devoverit, ut in confertissima se hostium tela iaculatus nouum ad uictoriam iter sanguinis sui semita aperiret." This *εἴσοδος τῶν ἁγίων ἐν τῷ αἵματι Ἰησοῦ* is further described in v.^{20}; we enter by (*ἥν*, with *ὁδὸν . . . ζῶσαν* in apposition) a way which Jesus has inaugurated by his sacrifice ($9^{18.\ 24.\ 25}$). This way is called recent or fresh and also living. In **πρόσφατος**, as in the case of other compounds (*e.g. κελαινεφής*), the literal sense of the second element had been long forgotten (cp. Holden's note on Plutarch's *Themistocles*, 24); *πρόσφατος* simply means "fresh," without any sacrificial allusion ("freshly-killed"). Galen (*de Hipp. et Plat. plac.* iv. 7) quotes the well-known saying that *λύπη ἐστὶ δόξα πρόσφατος κακοῦ παρουσίας*, and the word (*i.e. τὸ ἀρτίως γενόμενον, νέον, νεαρόν*, Hesychius), as is plain from other passages like Arist. *Magna Moralia*, 1203*b* (*ὁ ἐκ τῆς προσφάτου φαντασίας ἀκρατής κτλ.*), and Eccles 1^{9} (*οὐκ ἔστιν πᾶν πρόσφατον ὑπὸ τὸν ἥλιον*), had no longer any of the specific sacrificial sense suggested etymologically by its second part. It is the thought of *ἐχθές* in 13^{8}, though the writer means

[1] Hence the idea is not put in quite the same way as in Eph 3^{12} (*ἐν ᾧ ἔχομεν τὴν παρρησίαν καὶ τὴν προσαγωγήν*). In Sir 25^{25} *μηδὲ* (*δῷς*) *γυναικὶ πονηρᾷ ἐξουσίαν*, ℵ A read *παρρησίαν* for B's *ἐξουσίαν*, which proves how deeply the idea of liberty was rooted in *παρρησία*.

particularly (as in 1^{1-2} 9^{8-11}) to suggest that a long period had elapsed before the perfect fellowship was inaugurated finally; it is πρόσφατος, not ἀρχαῖος. Ζῶσαν means, in the light of 7^{25} (cp. Jn 14^{6}), that access to God is mediated by the living Christ in virtue of his sacrificial intercession; the contrast is not so much with what is transient, as though ζῶσαν were equivalent to μένουσαν (Chrysostom, Cosm. 415*a*), as with the dead victims of the OT cultus or "the lifeless pavement trodden by the highpriest" (Delitzsch). He entered God's presence thus διὰ τοῦ καταπετάσματος (6^{19} 9^{3}), τοῦτ᾽ ἔστιν τοῦ σαρκὸς αὐτοῦ—a ritual expression for the idea of 6^{19}. Διά is local, and, whether a verb like εἰσελθών is supplied or not, διὰ τ. κ. goes with ἐνεκαίνισεν, the idea being that Jesus had to die, in order to bring us into a living fellowship with God; the shedding of his blood meant that he had a body (10^{5-10}) to offer in sacrifice (cp. 9^{14}). The writer, however, elaborates his argument with a fresh detail of symbolism, suggested by the ritual of the tabernacle which he has already described in $9^{2f.}$. There, the very existence of a veil hanging between the outer and the inner sanctuary was interpreted as a proof that access to God's presence was as yet imperfectly realized. The highpriest carried once a year inside the veil the blood of victims slain outside it; that was all. Jesus, on the other hand, sheds his own blood as a perfect sacrifice, and thus wins entrance for us into the presence of God. Only, instead of saying that his sacrificial death meant the rending of the veil (like the author of Mk 15^{38}), *i.e.* the supersession of the OT barriers between God and man, he allegorizes the veil here as the flesh of Christ; this had to be rent before the blood could be shed, which enabled him to enter and open God's presence for the people. It is a daring, poetical touch, and the parallelism is not to be prosaically pressed into any suggestion that the human nature in Jesus hid God from men ἐν ταῖς ἡμέραις τῆς σαρκὸς αὐτοῦ, or that he ceased to be truly human when he sacrificed himself.

The idea already suggested in ζῶσαν is now (*b*) developed (in v.[21]) by (ἔχοντες) καὶ ἱερέα μέγαν ἐπὶ τὸν οἶκον τοῦ θεοῦ, another echo of the earlier passage (cp. 3^{1-6} 4^{14}), ἱερεὺς μέγας being a sonorous LXX equivalent for ἀρχιερεύς. Then comes the triple appeal, προσερχώμεθα . . . κατέχωμεν . . . καὶ κατανοῶμεν . . . The metaphor of προσερχώμεθα κτλ. (v.[22]), breaks down upon the fact that the Israelites never entered the innermost shrine, except as represented by their highpriest who entered once a year ἐν αἵματι ἀλλοτρίῳ ($9^{7.\,25}$), which he took with him in order to atone for the sins that interrupted the communion of God and the people. In Πρὸς Ἑβραίους the point is that, in virtue of the blood of Christ, Christians enjoy continuous fellowship with

God; the sacrifice of Christ enables them to approach God's presence, since their sins have been once and for all removed The entrance of the OT highpriest therefore corresponds both to the sacrifice of Christ and to that access of Christians which the blood of Christ secures. On the one hand, Christ is our highpriest (v.[21]); through his self-sacrifice in death the presence of God has been thrown open to us (vv.[19. 20]). This is the primary thought. But in order to express our use of this privilege, the writer has also to fall back upon language which suggests the entrance of the OT highpriest (cp. v.[19] ἐν τῷ αἵματι Ἰησοῦ with 9[25]). He does not mean that Christians are priests, with the right of entry in virtue of a sacrifice which they present, but, as to approach God was a priestly prerogative under the older order, he describes the Christian access to God in sacerdotal metaphors. Προσερχώμεθα is one of these. It is amplified first by a μετά clause, and then by two participial clauses. The approach to God must be whole-hearted, μετὰ ἀληθινῆς καρδίας,[1] without any hesitation or doubt, ἐν πληροφορίᾳ (6[11]) πίστεως.[2] This thought of πίστις as man's genuine answer to the realities of divine revelation, is presently to be developed at length (10[38f.]). Meantime the writer throws in the double participial clause, ῥεραντισμένοι . . . καθαρῷ. The metaphors are sacerdotal; as priests were sprinkled with blood and bathed in water, to qualify them for their sacred service, so Christians may approach God with all confidence, on the basis of Christ's sacrifice, since they have been ῥεραντισμένοι (*i.e.* sprinkled and so purified from—a frequent use of the verb) ἀπὸ συνειδήσεως πονηρᾶς (=συνειδήσεως ἁμαρτιῶν, 10[2]) in their hearts (τὰς καρδίας—no external cleansing). Then the writer adds, καὶ λελουσμένοι τὸ σῶμα ὕδατι καθαρῷ, suggesting that baptism corresponded to the bathing of priests (*e.g.* in Lev 16[4]). Once and for all, at baptism (cp. 1 P 3[21]), Christians have been thus purified from guilty stains by the efficacy of Christ's sacrifice.[3] What room then can there be in their minds for anything but faith, a confident faith that draws near to God, sure that there is no longer anything between Him and them?

The distinctive feature which marked off the Christian βαπτισμός from all similar ablutions (6[2] 9[10]) was that it meant something more than a cleansing of the body; it was part and parcel of an inward cleansing of the καρδία, effected by τὸ αἷμα

[1] The phrase ἐν ἀληθινῇ καρδίᾳ occurs in *Test. Dan* 5[3] (*v.l.* καθαρᾷ) and in Is 38[3] (ἐν. κ. ἀ.).

[2] There is a verbal parallel in the account of Isis-worship given by Apuleius (*Metamorph.* xi. 28: "ergo igitur cunctis adfatim praeparatis . . . principalis dei nocturnis orgiis inlustratus, *plena iam fiducia* germanae religionis obsequium diuinum frequentabam").

[3] More specifically, by the αἷμα ῥαντισμοῦ of 12[24].

τῆς διαθήκης (v.[29]).[1] Hence this as the vital element is put first, though the body had also its place and part in the cleansing experience. The *καρδία* and the *σῶμα* are a full, plastic expression for the entire personality, as an ancient conceived it. Ancient religious literature[2] is full of orders for the penitent to approach the gods only after moral contrition and bodily cleansing, with a clean heart and a clean body, in clean clothes even. But, apart from other things, such ablutions had to be repeated, while the Christian **βαπτισμός** was a single ceremony, lying at the source and start of the religious experience. And what our author is thinking of particularly is not this or that pagan rite, but the OT ritual for priests as described in Ex 29[20f.], Lv 8[23f.] 14[5f.] etc. (cp. *Joma* 3).

Three specimens of the anxious care for bodily purity in ancient religious ritual may be given. First (i) the ritual directions for worship in *Syll.* 567 (ii A.D.): *πρῶτον μὲν καὶ τὸ μέγιστον, χεῖρας καὶ γνώμην καθαροὺς καὶ ὑγιεῖς ὑπάρχοντας καὶ μηδὲν αὑτοῖς δεινὸν συνειδότας.* Second (ii) the stress laid on it by a writer like Philo, who (*quod deus sit immutabilis*, 2), after pleading that we should honour God by purifying ourselves from evil deeds and washing off the stains of life, adds: *καὶ γὰρ εὔηθες εἰς μὲν τὰ ἱερὰ μὴ ἐξεῖναι βαδίζειν, ὃς ἂν μὴ πρότερον λουσάμενος φαιδρύνηται τὸ σῶμα, εὔχεσθαι δὲ καὶ θύειν ἐπιχειρεῖν ἔτι κηλιδωμένῃ καὶ πεφυρμένῃ διανοίᾳ.* His argument is that if the body requires ablutions (*περιρραντηρίοις καὶ καθαρσίοις ἀγνευτικοῖς*) before touching an external shrine, how can anyone who is morally impure draw near (*προσελθεῖν τῷ θεῷ*) the most pure God, unless he means to repent? Ὁ *μὲν γὰρ πρὸς τῷ μηδὲν ἐπεξεργάσασθαι κακὸν καὶ τὰ παλαιὰ ἐκνίψασθαι δικαιώσας γεγηθὼς προσίτω* [cp. He 10[19. 22]], *ὁ δ' ἄνευ τούτων δυσκάθαρτος ὢν ἀφιστάσθω· λήσεται γὰρ οὐδέποτε τὸν τὰ ἐν μυχοῖς τῆς διανοίας ὁρῶντα* [cp. He 4[13]] *καὶ τοῖς ἀδύτοις αὐτῆς ἐμπεριπατοῦντα.* Or again in *de Plant.* 39: *σώματα καὶ ψυχὰς καθηράμενοι, τὰ μὲν λουτροῖς, τὰ δὲ νόμων καὶ παιδείας ὀρθῆς ῥεύμασι.* In *de Cherub.* 28 he denounces the ostentatious religion of the worldly, who in addition to their other faults, *τὰ μὲν σώματα λουτροῖς καὶ καθαρσίοις ἀπορρύπτονται, τὰ δὲ ψυχῆς ἐκνίψασθαι πάθη, οἷς καταρρυπαίνεται ὁ βίος, οὔτε βούλονται οὔτε ἐπιτηδεύουσι,* are very particular about their outward religious practices[3] but careless about a clean soul. Finally, (iii) there is the saying of Epictetus (iv. 10. 3): *ἐπεὶ γὰρ ἐκεῖνοι* (*i.e.* the gods) *φύσει καθαροὶ καὶ ἀκήρατοι, ἐφ' ὅσον ἠγγίκασιν αὐτοῖς οἱ ἄνθρωποι κατὰ τὸν λόγον, ἐπὶ τοσοῦτον καὶ τοῦ καθαροῦ καὶ τοῦ καθαρίου εἰσὶν ἀνθεκτικοί.*

For the exceptional *ῥεραντισμένοι* (א* A C D*), א^c D^c etc. have substituted *ἐρραντισμένοι* (so Theodoret). The λελουσμένοι of א B D P is the more common *κοινή* form of the Attic λελουμένοι (A C D^c etc.).

The next appeal (v.[23]), **κατέχωμεν τὴν ὁμολογίαν τῆς ἐλπίδος** (to which א* vg pesh eth add the gloss of *ἡμῶν*), echoes 4[14]

[1] Τὸ αἷμα τῆς διαθήκης ἐν ᾧ ἡγιάσθη, as 1 Co 6[11] ἀλλὰ ἀπελούσασθε, ἀλλὰ ἡγιάσθητε.

[2] Cp. Eugen Fehrle's *Die Kultische Keuschheit im Altertum* (1910), pp. 26 f., 131 f.; Sir J. G. Frazer's *Adonis, Attis, Osiris* (1907), pp. 407 f.

[3] According to a recently discovered (first century) inscription on a Palestinian synagogue (cp. *Revue Biblique*, 1921, pp. 247 f.), the synagogue was furnished with *τὸν ξενῶνα* (for hospitality, cp. below, 13[2]) *καὶ τὰ χρηστήρια τῶν ὑδάτων* (baths for ritual ablutions).

(κρατῶμεν τῆς ὁμολογίας) and 3^6 (ἐὰν τὴν παρρησίαν καὶ τὸ καύχημα τῆς ἐλπίδος . . . κατάσχωμεν). This hope for the future was first confessed at baptism, and rests upon God's promise[1] (as already explained in $6^{17.18}$). It is to be held ἀκλινής, a term applied by Philo to the word of a good man (ὁ γὰρ τοῦ σπουδαίου, φησί, λόγος ὅρκος ἔστω, βέβαιος, ἀκλινής, ἀψευδέστατος, ἐρηρεισμένος ἀληθείᾳ, *de Spec. Leg.* ii. 1); in Irenaeus it recurs in a similar connexion (i. 88, ed. Harvey: ὁ τὸν κανόνα τῆς ἀληθείας ἀκλινῆ ἐν ἑαυτῷ κατέχων, ὃν διὰ τοῦ βαπτίσματος εἴληφε). The old Wycliffite version translates finely: "hold we the confessioun of oure hope bowynge to no side." The close connexion between ῥεραντισμένοι κτλ. and λελουσμένοι κτλ. makes it inadvisable to begin the second appeal with καὶ λελουσμένοι τὸ σῶμα ὕδατι καθαρῷ (Erasmus, Beza, Bengel, Lachmann, Lünemann, von Soden, B. Weiss, etc.). A more plausible suggestion, first offered by Theodoret and adopted recently by Hofmann and Seeberg, is to begin the second appeal after πίστεως, making κατεχῶμεν carry ῥεραντισμένοι . . . καθαρῷ. This yields a good sense, for it brings together the allusions to the baptismal confession. But the ordinary view is more probable; the asyndeton in κατεχῶμεν is impressive, and if it is objected that the κατεχῶμεν clause is left with less content than the other two, the answer is that its eschatological outlook is reiterated in the third clause, and that by itself its brevity has a telling force. Besides, ἔχοντες κτλ. ($^{19-21}$) introduce κατεχῶμεν as well as προσερχώμεθα.

The third appeal ($^{24.25}$) turns on love (cp. 6^{10}), as the first on faith, and the second on hope. The members of the circle or community are to stir up one another to the practice of Christian love. Since this is only possible when common worship and fellowship are maintained, the writer warns them against following the bad example of abandoning such gatherings; καὶ κατανοῶμεν ἀλλήλους, for, if we are to κατανοεῖν Christ (3^1), we are also bound to keep an eye on one another εἰς παροξυσμὸν ἀγαπῆς καὶ καλῶν ἔργων (*i.e.* an active, attractive moral life, inspired by Christian love). This good sense of παροξυσμός as stimulus seems to be an original touch; in Greek elsewhere it bears the bad sense of provocation or exasperation (cp. Ac 15^{39}), although the verb παροξύνειν had already acquired a good sense (*e.g.* in Josephus, *Ant.* xvi. 125, παροξῦναι τὴν εὔνοιαν: in Pr 6^3 ἴσθι μὴ ἐκλυόμενος, παρόξυνε δὲ καὶ τὸν φίλον σου ὃν ἐνεγυήσω: and in Xen. *Cyrop.* vi. 2. 5, καὶ τούτους ἐπαινῶν τε παρώξυνε). Pliny's words at the close of his letter to Caninius Rufus (iii. 7) illustrate what is meant by παροξυσμός in this sense: "Scio te stimulis non egere; me tamen tui caritas evocat ut currentem

[1] An instance of this is quoted in 11^{11}.

quoque instigem, sicut tu soles me. Ἀγαθὴ δ' ἔρις, cum invicem se mutuis exhortationibus amici ad amorem immortalitatis exacuunt." How the παροξυσμός is to be carried out, the writer does not say. By setting a good example? By definite exhortations (παρακαλοῦντες, v.[25], like 13[1])? Μὴ ἐγκαταλείποντες—do not do to one another what God never does to you (13[5]), do not leave your fellow-members in the lurch (the force of ἐγκαταλείπειν, especially in the κοινή)—τὴν ἐπισυναγωγὴν ἑαυτῶν (reflexive pronoun in the genitive = ἡμῶν). Ἐπισυναγωγή in the κοινή (cp. Deissmann's *Light from the East*, 102 f.) means a collection (of money), but had already in Jewish Greek (*e.g.* 2 Mac 2[7] ἕως ἂν συνάγῃ ὁ θεὸς ἐπισυναγωγὴν τοῦ λαοῦ) begun to acquire the present sense of a popular "gathering." Καθὼς ἔθος (*sc.* ἐστιν) τισίν. But who are these? What does this abandonment of common fellowship mean? (*a*) Perhaps that some were growing ashamed of their faith; it was so insignificant and unpopular, even dangerous to anyone who identified himself with it openly. They may have begun to grow tired of the sacrifices and hardships involved in membership of the local church. This is certainly the thought of 10[32f.], and it is better than to suppose (*b*) the leaders were a small group of teachers or more intelligent Christians, who felt able, in a false superiority, to do without common worship; they did not require to mix with the ordinary members! The author in any case is warning people against the dangers of individualism, a warning on the lines of the best Greek and Jewish ethics, *e.g.* Isokrates, *ad Demon.* 13, τιμὰ τὸ δαιμόνιον ἀεὶ μέν, μάλιστα δὲ μετὰ τῆς πόλεως, and the rabbinic counsel in Taanith, 11. 1 ("whenever the Israelites suffer distress, and one of them withdraws from the rest, two angels come to him and, laying their hands upon his head, say, this man who separates himself from the assembly shall not see the consolation which is to visit the congregation"), or in Hillel's saying (*Pirke Aboth* 2[5]): "Separate not thyself from the congregation, and trust not in thyself until the day of thy death." The loyal Jews are described in Ps.-Sol 17[18] as οἱ ἀγαπῶντες συναγωγὰς ὁσίων, and a similar thought occurs also (if "his" and not "my" is the correct reading) in Od. Sol 3[2]: "His members are with Him, and on them do I hang." Any early Christian who attempted to live like a pious particle without the support of the community ran serious risks in an age when there was no public opinion to support him. His isolation, whatever its motive—fear, fastidiousness, self-conceit, or anything else—exposed him to the danger of losing his faith altogether. These are possible explanations of the writer's grave tone in the passage before us. Some critics, like Zahn (§ 46), even think that (*c*) such unsatisfactory Christians left their own little congregation for another, in a spirit of lawless pique, or to gratify their own tastes selfishly; but ἑαυτῶν is not emphatic, and in any congregation of Christians the duties of love would be pressed. Separatist tendencies were not absent from the early church; thus some members considered themselves too good to require common worship, as several warnings prove, *e.g.* in Barn 4[10] μὴ καθ' ἑαυτοὺς ἐνδύνοντες μονάζετε ὡς ἤδη δεδικαιωμένοι, ἀλλ' ἐπὶ τὸ αὐτὸ συνερχόμενοι συνζητεῖτε περὶ τοῦ κοινῇ συμφέροντος) and Ign. *Eph.* 5[3] (ὁ οὖν μὴ ἐρχόμενος ἐπὶ τὸ αὐτὸ οὗτος ἤδη ὑπερηφανεῖ καὶ ἑαυτὸν διέκρινεν). But in our epistle (*d*) the warning is directed specially against people who combined Christianity with a number of mystery-cults, patronizing them in turn, or who withdrew from Christian fellowship, feeling that they had exhausted the Christian faith and that it required to be supplemented by some other cult. "At first and indeed always there were naturally some people who imagined that one could secure the sacred contents and blessings of Christianity as one did those of Isis or the Magna Mater, and then withdraw" (Harnack, *Expansion of Christianity*, bk. iii. c. 4; cp. Reitzenstein's *Hellen. Mysterienreligionen*, 94). This was serious, for, as the writer realized, it implied that they did not regard Christianity as the final and full revelation; their action proved that the Christian faith ranked no higher with them than one of the numerous Oriental cults which one by one might interest the mind, but which were not necessarily in any case the last word on life. The argument of the epistle has been directed against this misconception of Christianity, and the writer here notes a practical illustration of it in the conduct of adherents who were holding aloof, or who were in danger of holding aloof, from the common worship. Hence the austere warning which follows. Such a practice, or indeed any failure to "draw near" by the way of Jesus, is an insult to God, which spells hopeless ruin for the offender. And evidently this retribution is near. Christians are to be specially on their guard against conduct that means apostasy, for βλέπετε (how, he does not say) ἐγγίζουσαν (as in Ro 13[12]) τὴν ἡμέραν (here, as in 1 Co 3[13], without ἐκείνη or τοῦ κυρίου). This eschatological setting distinguishes the next warning (vv.[26-31]) from the earlier in 6[4-6].

[26] *For if we sin deliberately after receiving the knowledge of the Truth, there is no longer any sacrifice for sins left,* [27] *nothing but an awful outlook of doom, that "burning Wrath" which will "consume the foes"* (see v.[13]) *of God.* [28] *Anyone who has rejected the law of Moses "dies" without mercy, "on the evidence of two or of three witnesses."* [29] *How much heavier, do you suppose, will be the punishment assigned* (*i.e.* by God) *to him who has spurned the Son of God, who has profaned "the covenant-blood"* (9[20]) *with which he was sanctified* (10[10]), *who has insulted the Spirit of grace?* [30] *We know who said, "Vengeance is mine, I will exact a requital": and again* (πάλιν, as in

2[13]), "*The Lord will pass sentence on his people.*" [31] *It is an awful thing to fall into the hands of the living God.*

Apostasy like withdrawal from the church on the ground already mentioned, is treated as one of the deliberate (ἑκουσίως) sins which (cp. on 5[2]), under the OT order of religion, were beyond any atonement. Wilful offences, like rebellion and blasphemy against God, were reckoned unpardonable. "In the case of one who, by his sin, intentionally disowns the covenant itself, there can be no question of sacrifice. He has himself cut away the ground on which it would have been possible for him to obtain reconciliation" (Schultz, *OT Theology*, ii. 88). There is an equivalent to this, under the new διαθήκη, our author declares. To abandon Christianity is to avow that it is inadequate, and this denial of God's perfect revelation in Jesus Christ is fatal to the apostate. In ἑκουσίως ἁμαρτόντων ἡμῶν ([26]), ἑκουσίως is put first for the sake of emphasis, and ἁμαρτόντων means the sin of ἀποστῆναι ἀπὸ θεοῦ ζῶντος (3[12]) or of παραπίπτειν (6[6]), the present tense implying that such people persist in this attitude. Ἑκουσίως is the keynote to the warning. Its force may be felt in a passage like Thuc. iv. 98, where the Athenians remind the Boeotians that God pardons what is done under the stress of war and peril, καὶ γὰρ τῶν ἀκουσίων ἁμαρτημάτων καταφυγὴν εἶναι τοὺς βωμούς, and that it is wanton and presumptuous crimes alone which are heinous. Philo (*vit. Mos.* i. 49) describes Balaam praying for forgiveness from God on the ground that he had sinned ὑπ' ἀγνοίας ἀλλ' οὐ καθ' ἑκούσιον γνώμην. The adverb occurs in 2 Mac 14[3] (Ἄλκιμος . . . ἑκουσίως δὲ μεμολυσμένος). The general idea of the entire warning is that the moral order punishes all who wantonly and wilfully flout it; as Menander once put it (Kock's *Com. Attic. Fragm.* 700):

> νόμος φυλαχθεὶς οὐδέν ἐστιν ἢ νόμος·
> ὁ μὴ φυλαχθεὶς καὶ νόμος καὶ δήμιος.

Our author expresses this law of retribution in personal terms drawn from the OT, which prove how deeply moral and reverent his religious faith was, and how he dreaded anything like presuming upon God's kindness and mercy. The easy-going man thinks God easy going; he is not very serious about his religious duties, and he cannot imagine how God can take them very seriously either. "We know" better, says the author of Πρὸς Ἑβραίους!

Christianity is described (in v.[26]) as τὸ λαβεῖν τὴν ἐπίγνωσιν τῆς ἀληθείας, a semi-technical phrase of the day, which recurs in the Pastoral Epistles (though with ἐλθεῖν εἰς instead of λαβεῖν). It is not one of our author's favourite expressions,[1] but the phrase

[1] Here it is an equivalent for the phrases used in 6[4. 5]; there is no distinction between ἐπίγνωσις and γνῶσις (θεοῦ) any more than in the LXX, and

is partly used by Epictetus in its most general sense (*λαβών τις παρὰ τῆς φύσεως μέτρα καὶ κανόνας εἰς ἐπίγνωσιν τῆς ἀληθείας κτλ.*, ii. 20. 21), when upbraiding the wretched academic philosophers (*οἱ ἀταλαίπωροι Ἀκαδημαϊκοί*) for discrediting the senses as organs of knowledge, instead of using and improving them. All that renegades can expect (v.[27]) is **φοβερά τις** (= quidam, deepening the idea with its touch of vagueness) **ἐκδοχή** (a sense coined by the writer for this term, after his use of *ἐκδέχεσθαι* in 10[13]) **κρίσεως**, for they have thrown over the only sacrifice that saves men from *κρίσις* (9[27]). This is expanded in a loose[1] reminiscence of Is 26[11] (*ζῆλος λήμψεται λαὸν ἀπαίδευτον, καὶ νῦν πῦρ τοὺς ὑπεναντίους ἔδεται*), though the phrase **πυρὸς ζῆλος** recalls Zeph 1[19] (3[8]) *ἐν πυρὶ ζήλου αὐτοῦ καταναλωθήσεται πᾶσα ἡ γῆ*. The contemporary Jewish Apocalypse of Baruch (48[39. 40]) contains a similar threat to wilful sinners:

"Therefore shall a fire consume their thoughts,
and in flame shall the meditations of their reins be tried;
for the Judge shall come and will not tarry—
because each of earth's inhabitant knew when he was transgressing."

The penalty for the wilful rejection (**ἀθετήσας**) of the Mosaic law[2] was severe (Dt 17[2-17]), but not more severe than the penalty to be inflicted on renegades from Christianity (vv.[28-31]). The former penalty was merciless, **χωρὶς οἰκτιρμῶν** (to which, at an early period, *καὶ δακρύων* was added by D, most old Latin texts, and syr[hkl]). It is described in a reminiscence of Dt 17[6] *ἐπὶ δυσὶν μάρτυσιν ἢ ἐπὶ τρισὶν μάρτυσιν ἀποθανεῖται ὁ ἀποθνήσκων* (*i.e.* the apostate who has yielded to idolatry). The witnesses executed the punishment for the sin of which they had given evidence (Dt 17[7], Ac 7[57f.], Jn 8[7], Sanhedrim 6[4]), but this is not before the writer's mind; *ἐπί* with the dative simply means "on the ground of (the evidence given by)." In **πόσῳ δοκεῖτε κτλ.** (v.[29]), *δοκεῖτε* is intercalated as in Aristoph. *Acharn.* 12 (*πῶς τοῦτ' ἔσεισέ μου δοκεῖς τὴν καρδίαν;*), and Herm. *Sim.* ix. 28. 8 (*εἰ τὰ ἔθνη τοὺς δούλους αὐτῶν κολάζουσιν, ἐάν τις ἀρνήσηται τὸν κύριον ἑαυτοῦ, τί δοκεῖτε ποιήσει ὁ κύριος ὑμῖν;*). *Πόσῳ* (cp. 9[14]) introduces an

ἀλήθεια had been already stamped by Philo (e.g. *de Justitia*, 6, where the proselyte is said *μεταναστὰς εἰς ἀλήθειαν*) as a term for the true religion, which moulds the life of those who become members of the People. Compare the study of the phrase by M. Dibelius in *NT Studien für G. Heinrici* (1914), pp. 176-189.

[1] Probably it was the awkwardness of *ζῆλος*, coming after *πυρός*, which led to its omission in W. Sah reads simply "the flame of the fire."

[2] According to the later rabbinic theory of inspiration, even to assert that Moses uttered one word of the Torah on his own authority was to despise the Torah (Sifre 112, on Nu 15[31]).

argument from the less to the greater, which was the first of Hillel's seven rules for exegesis, and which is similarly used by Philo in *de Fuga*, 16, where, after quoting Ex 21[15], he adds that Moses here practically denies that there is any pardon for those who blaspheme God (*εἰ γὰρ οἱ τοὺς θνητοὺς κακηγορήσαντες γονεῖς ἀπάγονται τὴν ἐπὶ θανάτῳ, τίνος ἀξίους χρὴ νομίζειν τιμωρίας τοὺς τῶν ὅλων πατέρα καὶ ποιητὴν βλασφημεῖν ὑπομένοντας;*). There is also a passage in *de Spec. Legibus* (ii. 254, 255) where Philo asks, "If a man *μὴ προσηκόντως ὀμνύς* is guilty, *πόσης ἄξιος τιμωρίας ὁ τὸν ὄντως ὄντα θεὸν ἀρνούμενος;*"

τιμωρία originally meant vengeance. *Διαφέρει δὲ τιμωρία καὶ κόλασις· ἡ μὲν γὰρ κόλασις τοῦ πάσχοντος ἕνεκα ἐστιν, ἡ δὲ τιμωρία τοῦ ποιοῦντος, ἵνα ἀποπληρωθῇ* (Arist. *Rhetoric*, i. 10. 11; see Cope's *Introduction*, p. 232). But it became broadened into the general sense of punishment, and this obtained in Hellenistic Greek.

The threefold description of what is involved in the sin of apostasy begins: **ὁ τὸν υἱὸν τοῦ θεοῦ καταπατήσας**, another expression for the thought of 6[6], which recalls Zec 12[3] (*λίθον καταπατούμενον πᾶσιν τοῖς ἔθνεσιν· πᾶς ὁ καταπατῶν αὐτὴν ἐμπαίζων ἐμπαίξεται*). *Καταπατεῖν ὅρκια* was the phrase for breaking oaths (*Iliad*, 4[157]); with a personal object, the verb denotes contempt of the most flagrant kind. Another aspect of the sin is that a man has thereby **κοινὸν**[1] **ἡγησάμενος** the sacrifice of Jesus; his action means that it is no more to him than an ordinary death ("communem," *d*), instead of a divine sacrifice which makes him a partaker of the divine fellowship (see p. 145). Where Christ is rejected, he is first despised; outward abandonment of him springs from some inward depreciation or disparagement. The third aspect, **καὶ τὸ πνεῦμα τῆς χάριτος** (not **τὸν** *νόμον* Μωυσέως) **ἐνυβρίσας**, suggests that the writer had in mind the language of Zec 12[10] (*ἐκχεῶ . . . πνεῦμα χάριτος καὶ οἰκτιρμοῦ*), but **πνεῦμα χάριτος** (contrasted here, as in Jn 1[17], with the *νόμος* Μωυσέως) is a periphrasis for *πνεῦμα ἅγιον* (6[4]), *χάρις* being chosen (4[16] 12[15]) to bring out the personal, gracious nature of the power so wantonly insulted.[2] **Ἐνυβρίζειν** is not a LXX term, and it generally takes the dative. (**Ἐν ᾧ ἡγιάσθη** after **ἡγησάμενος** is omitted by A and some MSS of Chrysostom.)

The sombre close (vv.[30. 31]) of the warning is a reminder that the living God punishes renegades. **Φοβερόν** (v.[31]) re-echoes the *φοβερά* of v.[27], and the awful nature of the doom is brought out by two quotations adapted from the OT. **Ἐμοὶ ἐκδίκησις,**

[1] Once in the LXX (Pr 15[23]) in this sense.

[2] In *Test. Jud.* 18[2] the *πνεῦμα χάριτος* poured out upon men is the Spirit as a gracious gift of God. But in He 10[29], as in Eph 4[30], it is the divine Spirit wounded or outraged, the active retribution, however, being ascribed not to the Spirit itself but to God.

ἐγὼ ἀνταποδώσω, is the same form of Dt 32^{35} as is quoted in Ro 12^{19}; it reproduces the Hebrew original more closely than the LXX (*ἐν ἡμέρᾳ ἐκδικήσεως ἀνταποδώσω*), perhaps from some current Greek version, unless the author of Hebrews borrowed it from Paul.[1] Some of the same authorities as in 8^{12} indeed add, from Ro 12^{19}, **λέγει κύριος** (ℵ^c A D^c K L arm Theodoret, Damasus, etc.). **Κρινεῖ Κύριος τὸν λαὸν αὐτοῦ** is from Dt 32^{36}. The thought of the original, in both passages, is God avenging his people on their foes and championing them, not punishing them; but here this fate is assigned to all who put themselves outside the range of God's mercy in the sacrifice of Jesus Christ; they fall under God's retribution. **Τὸ ἐμπεσεῖν εἰς χεῖρας θεοῦ** is a phrase used in a very different sense in 2 S 24^{14}, Sir 2^{18}; here it means, to fall into the grasp of the God who punishes the disloyal[2] or rebels against his authority. Thus the tyrant Antiochus is threatened, in 2 Mac 7^{31}, *οὐ μὴ διαφύγῃς τὰς χεῖρας τοῦ θεοῦ*. As in 3^{12}, **ζῶντος** is added to **θεοῦ** to suggest that he is quick and alive to inflict retribution. The writer is impressively reticent on the nature of God's **τιμωρία**, even more reticent than Plato, in one of the gravest warnings in Greek literature, the famous passage in the *Leges* (904, 905) about the divine *δίκη*: *Ταύτης τῆς δίκης οὔτε σὺ μὴ πότε οὔτε εἰ ἄλλος ἀτυχὴς γενόμενος ἐπεύξηται περιγενέσθαι θεῶν· ἣν πασῶν δικῶν διαφερόντως ἔταξάν τε οἱ τάξαντες χρεών τε ἐξευλαβεῖσθαι τὸ παράπαν. οὐ γὰρ ἀμεληθήσῃ ποτὲ ὑπ' αὐτῆς· οὐχ οὕτω σμικρὸς ὢν δύσῃ κατὰ τὸ τῆς γῆς βάθος, οὐδ' ὑψηλὸς γενόμενος εἰς τὸν οὐρανὸν ἀναπτήσῃ, τείσεις δὲ αὐτῶν τὴν προσήκουσαν τιμωρίαν εἴτ' ἐνθάδε μένων εἴτε καὶ ἐν Αἵδου διαπορευθείς.* Plato altered the Homeric term *δίκη θεῶν* to suit his purpose; what meant "way" or "habit," he turned into a weighty word for "justice." The alteration is justified from his "preaching" point of view, and the solemn note of the Greek sage's warning is that of He $10^{26f.}$; you cannot play fast and loose with God.

Yet, as at 6^9, so here, the writer swiftly turns from warning to encouragement, appealing to his readers to do better than he feared, and appealing to all that was best in them. "Why throw away the gains of your fine record in the past? You have not long to wait for your reward. Hold on for a little longer." This is the theme of vv.$^{32-39}$:

[1] Paul cites the saying to prove that private Christians need not and must not take revenge into their own hands, since God is sure to avenge his people on their adversaries. Which is close to the idea of the original. Our author uses the text to clinch a warning that God will punish (*κρινεῖ*="punibit," not "judicabit") his people for defying and deserting him.

[2] So the martyr Eleazar protests in 2 Mac 6^{26}, as he refuses to save his life by unworthy compromise: *εἰ γὰρ καὶ ἐπὶ τοῦ παρόντος ἐξελοῦμαι τὴν ἐξ ἀνθρώπων τιμωρίαν, ἀλλὰ τὰς τοῦ παντοκράτορος χεῖρας οὔτε ζῶν οὔτε ἀποθανὼν ἐκφεύξομαι.*

32 *Recall the former days when, after you were enlightened* (φωτισθέντες,
as 6^{4}), *you endured a hard struggle of suffering,* 33 *partly by being held up*
yourselves to obloquy and anguish, partly by making common cause with those
who fared in this way; 34 *for you did sympathize with the prisoners, and you*
took the confiscation of your own belongings cheerfully, conscious that elsewhere
you had higher, you had lasting possessions. 35 *Now do not drop that con-*
fidence of yours; it (ἥτις, as in 2^{3}) *carries with it a rich hope of reward.*
36 *Steady patience is what you need, so that after doing the will of God you*
may (like Abraham, 6^{15}) *get what you have been promised.* 37 *For "in a*
little, a very little" now,

> *"The Coming One* (9^{29}) *will arrive without delay.*
> 38 *Meantime my just man shall live on by his faith;*
> *if he shrinks back, my soul takes no delight in him."*

39 *We are not the men to shrink back and be lost, but to have faith and so to*
win our souls.

The excellent record of these Christians in the past consisted in their common brotherliness (6^{10}), which is now viewed in the light of the hardships they had had to endure, soon after they became Christians. The storm burst on them early; they weathered it nobly; why give up the voyage, when it is nearly done? It is implied that any trouble at present is nothing to what they once passed through. **Ἀναμιμνήσκεσθε δὲ τὰς πρότερον ἡμέρας** (v.[32]): memory plays a large part in the religious experience, and is often as here a stimulus. In these earlier days they had (vv.[32. 33]) two equally creditable experiences (**τοῦτο μέν . . . τοῦτο δέ**, a good classical idiom); they bore obloquy and hardship manfully themselves, and they also made common cause with their fellow-sufferers. By saying **ἄθλησιν παθημάτων**, the writer means, that the *παθήματα* made the **ἄθλησις** which tested their powers (2^{10}). Ἄθλησις—the metaphor is athletic, as in 12^{1}—came to denote a martyr's death in the early church; but no such red significance attaches to it here. Apparently the persecution was not pushed to the last extreme (12^{4}); all survived it. Hence there can be no allusion to the "ludibria" of Nero's outburst against the Roman Christians, in (v.[33]) **θεατριζόμενοι**, which is used in a purely figurative sense (so *θέατρον* in 1 Co 4^{9}), like **ἐκθεατρίζειν** in Polybius (*e.g.* iii. 91. 10, *διόπερ ἔμελλον . . . ἐκθεατριεῖν δὲ τοὺς πολεμίους φυγομαχοῦντας*). The meaning is that they had been held up to public derision, scoffed and sneered at, accused of crime and vice, unjustly suspected and denounced. All this had been, the writer knew, a real ordeal, particularly because the stinging contempt and insults had had to be borne in the open. *Ὅταν μὲν γάρ τις ὀνειδίζηται καθ' ἑαυτὸν, λυπηρὸν μὲν, πολλῷ δὲ πλέον, ὅταν ἐπὶ πάντων* (Chrysostom). They had been exposed to **ὀνειδισμοῖς τε καὶ θλίψεσι**, taunts and scorn that tempted one to feel shame (an experience which our author evidently felt keenly), as well as to wider hardships, both insults and injuries. All this they had stood manfully. Better still, their personal troubles had not rendered them indisposed to care for their fellow-sufferers, **τῶν οὕτως** (*i.e.* in the *παθήματα*) **ἀναστρεφομένων** (13^{18}). They exhibited the virtue of practical sympathy, urged in 13^{3}, at any risk or cost to themselves (**κοινωνοὶ . . . γενηθέντες** with the genitive, as in LXX of Pr 28^{14}, Is 1^{23}).

The ideas of v.[33] are now (v.[34]) taken up in the reverse order (as in 5^{1-7}). **Καὶ γὰρ τοῖς δεσμίοις συνεπαθήσατε**, imprisonment being for some a form of their *παθήματα*. Christians in prison had to be visited and fed by their fellow-members. For **συμπαθεῖν** (cp. 4^{15}) as between man and man, see *Test. Sym.* 3^{6} *καὶ λοιπὸν συμπαθεῖ τῷ φθονουμένῳ*: *Test. Benj.* 4^{4} *τῷ ἀσθενοῦντι συμπάσχει*: Ign. *Rom.* 6^{4} *συμπαθείτω μοι*: and the saying which is quoted in Meineke's *Frag. Comic. Graec.* iv. 52, *ἐκ τοῦ παθεῖν γίγνωσκε καὶ τὸ συμπαθεῖν· καὶ σοὶ γὰρ ἄλλος συμπαθήσεται παθών.* They had also borne their own losses with more than equanimity,[1] with actual gladness (**μετὰ χαρᾶς**, the same thought as in Ro 5^{3}, though differently worked out), **γινώσκοντες** (with accus. and infinitive) **ἔχειν ἑαυτούς** (= *ὑμᾶς*, which is actually read here by Cosmas Indicopleustes, 348*a*; **ἑαυτούς** is not emphatic any more than **ἑαυτῶν** in v.[25]) **κρείσσονα** (a favourite term of the author) **ὕπαρξιν** (Ac 2^{35}) **καὶ μένουσαν** (13^{14}, the thought of Mt 6^{20}). **Τὴν ἁρπαγὴν τῶν ὑπαρχόντων ὑμῶν** (cp. Polybius, iv. 17. 4, *ἁρπαγὰς ὑπαρχόντων*) implies that their own property had been either confiscated by the authorities or plundered in some mob-riot. Note the paronomasia of *ὑπαρχόντων* and *ὕπαρξιν*, and the place of this loss in the list of human evils as described in the *Laches*, 195 E (*εἴτε τῷ θάνατος εἴτε νόσος εἴτε ἀποβολὴ χρημάτων ἔσται*).

There is no question of retaliation; the primitive Christians whom the author has in view had no means of returning injuries for injuries, or even of claiming redress. Thus the problem raised and solved by contemporary moralists does not present itself to the writer; he does not argue, as, *e.g.*, Maximus of Tyre did in the next century (*Dissert.* ii.), that the good man should treat the loss of property as a trifle, and despise the futile attempts of his enemies to injure him thus, the soul or real self being beyond the reach of such evil-doers. The tone is rather that of Tob 4^{21} (*μὴ φοβοῦ, παιδίον, ὅτι ἐπτωχεύσαμεν· ὑπάρχει σοὶ πολλά, ἐὰν φοβηθῇς τὸν θεόν κτλ.*), except that our author notes the glow (*μετὰ χαρᾶς*) of an enthusiastic unworldliness, which was more than any Stoic resignation or even any quiet acquiescence in providence; he suggests in *ἑαυτούς* that, while others might seize and hold their property, they themselves had a possession of which no one could rob them. Seneca (*Ep.* ix. 18–19) quotes the famous reply of the philosophic Stilpo to Demetrius Poliorketes, who asked him, after the siege and sack of Megara, if he had lost anything in the widespread ruin, Stilpo answered that he had suffered no loss; "omnia bona mecum sunt." That is, Seneca explains, he did not consider anything as "good" which could be taken from him. This helps to illustrate what the author of Πρὸς Ἑβραίους means. As Epictetus put it, there are more losses than the loss of property (ii. 10. 14,

[1] This is not conveyed in *προσεδέξασθε*, which here, as in 11^{35}, simply means "accepted," not "welcomed."

ἀλλὰ δεῖ σε κέρμα ἀπολέσαι, ἵνα ζημιωθῇς, ἄλλου <δ'> οὐδενὸς ἀπώλεια ζημιοῖ τὸν ἄνθρωπον ;). A similar view pervades the fine homiletic misinterpretation of Dt 6^5 in *Berachoth* 9^5 "Man is bound to bless [God] for evil as for good, for it is said, *Thou shalt love Jahweh thy God with all thy heart and with all thy soul and with all thy strength. With all thy heart* means, with both yetzers, the good and the bad alike: *with all thy soul* means, even if he deprive thee of thy soul: *with all thy strength* means, with all thy possessions." A similar view is cited in Sifre 32. Apollonius, in the last quarter of the second century, declares: "We do not resent having our goods taken from us, because we know that, whether we live or die, we are the Lord's" (Conybeare, *Monuments of Early Christianity*, p. 44).

No persecution known to us in the primitive church answers to the data of this passage. But some sidelights are thrown upon it by Philo's vivid account of the earlier anti-Semite riots in Alexandria. He notes that even those who sympathized with the persecuted were punished: τῶν δ' ὡς ἀλθῶς πεπονθότων φίλοι καὶ συγγενεῖς, ὅτι μόνον ταῖς τῶν προσηκόντων συμφόραις συνήλγησαν, ἀπήγοντο, ἐμαστιγοῦντο, ἐτροχίζοντο, καὶ μετὰ πάσας τὰς αἰκίας, ὅσας ἐδύνατο χωρῆσαι τὰ σώματα αὐτοῖς, ἡ τελευταία καὶ ἔφεδρος τιμωρία σταυρὸς ἦν (*in Flaccum*, 7: *n. b.* neither here nor in $11^{35f.}$ does the author of Πρὸς Ἑβραίους mention the cross as a punishment for sufferers). Philo (*ibid.* 9) continues: πενία χαλεπὸν μέν, καὶ μάλισθ' ὅταν κατασκευάζηται πρὸς ἐχθρῶν, ἔλαττον δὲ τῆς εἰς τὰ σώματα ὕβρεως, κἂν ᾖ βραχυτάτη. He repeats this (10), telling how Flaccus maltreated Jews who had been already stripped of their property, ἵνα οἱ μὲν ὑπομενῶσι διττὰς συμφορὰς, πενίαν ὁμοῦ καὶ τὴν ἐν τοῖς σώμασιν ὕβριν, καὶ οἱ μὲν δρῶντες, ὥσπερ ἐν τοῖς θεατρίκοις μίμοις καθυπερκρίνοντο τοὺς πάσχοντας.

Three items of textual corruption occur in v.[34]. (*a*) **δεσμίοις** (p^{13} A D* H 33. 104. 241. 424**. 635. 1245. 1288. 1739. 1908. 1912. 2005 r vg syr^{hkl} boh arm Chrys.) was eventually corrupted into δεσμοῖς (μου) in ℵ D^c Ψ 256. 1288* etc. vt eth Clem. Orig.), a misspelling (*i.e.* δεσμοῖς) which, with μου added to make sense, contributed to the impression that Paul had written the epistle (Ph $1^{7. 15f.}$, Col 4^{18}). Compare the text implied in the (Pelagian?) prologue to Paul's epp. in vg: "nam et vinctis compassi estis, et rapinam bonorum vestrorum cum gaudio suscepistis."

(*b*) **ἑαυτούς** (p^{13} ℵ A H lat boh Clem. Orig. etc.) suffered in the course of transmission; it was either omitted (by C) or altered into ἑαυτοῖς (D K L Ψ, etc., Chrys.) or ἐν ἑαυτοῖς (1. 467. 489. 642. 920. 937. 1867. 1873), the dative being an attempt to bring out the idea that they had in their own religious personalities a possession beyond the reach of harm and loss, an idea pushed by some editors even into ἑαυτούς, but too subtle for the context.

(*c*) **ὕπαρξιν** was eventually defined by the addition of **ἐν (τοῖς) οὐρανοῖς** (from Ph 3^{20}?) in $ℵ^c$ D^c H** Ψ 6. 203. 326. 506. 1288. 1739 syr arm Chrys. etc.

The reminder of vv.[32-34] is now ([35-39]) pressed home. **Μὴ ἀποβάλητε οὖν τὴν παρρησίαν ὑμῶν**, as evinced in **μετὰ χαρᾶς . . . γινώσκοντες κτλ.** The phrase occurs in Dio Chrys. *Orat.* 34^{39} (δέδοικα μὴ τελέως ἀποβάλητε τὴν παρρησίαν) and elsewhere in the sense of losing courage, but παρρησία retains its special force (3^6) here, and ἀποβάλλειν is the opposite of κατέχειν ("nolite itaque amittere," vg). The παρρησία is to be maintained, ἥτις ἔχει μεγάλην μισθαποδοσίαν (as 11^{26}), it is so sure of bringing its reward in the bliss promised by God to cheerful loyalty. Compare the saying of the contemporary rabbi Tarphon: "faithful is the Master of thy work, who will pay thee the reward of thy work, and know thou that the recompense of the reward of the righteous is for the time to come" (*Pirke Aboth* 2^{19}).

Epictetus makes a similar appeal, in iv. 3. 3 f., not to throw away all that one has gained in character by failing to maintain one's philosophical principles when one has suffered some loss of property. When you lose any outward possession, recollect what you gain instead of it (τί ἀντ' αὐτοῦ περιποιῇ); otherwise, you imperil the results of all your past conscientiousness (ὅσα νῦν προσέχεις σεαυτῷ, μέλλεις ἐκχεῖν ἅπαντα ταῦτα καὶ ἀνατρέπειν). And it takes so little to do this; a mere swerve from reasonable principle (μικρᾶς ἀποστροφῆς τοῦ λόγου), a slight drowsiness, and all is lost (ἀπῆλθεν πάντα τὰ μέχρι νῦν συνειλεγμένα). No outward possession is worth having, Epictetus continues, if it means that one ceases to be free, to be God's friend, to serve God willingly. I must not set my heart on anything else; God does not allow that, for if He had chosen, He would have made such outward goods good for me (ἀγαθὰ πεποιήκει αὐτὰ ἂν ἐμοί). Maximus of Tyre again argued that while, for example, men might be willing to endure pain and discomfort for the sake and hope of regaining health, "if you take away the hope of good to come, you also take away the power of enduring present ills" (εἰ ἀφέλοις τινὰ ἐλπίδα τῶν μέλλοντων ἀγαθῶν, ἀφαιρήσεις καὶ τινὰ αἵρεσιν τῶν παρόντων κακῶν, *Diss.* xxxiii).

To retain the Christian παρρησία means still ὑπομένειν, no longer perhaps in the earlier sense (ὑπεμείνατε, v.[32]), and yet sometimes what has to be borne is harder, for sensitive people, than any actual loss. Such obedience to the will of God assumes many phases, from endurance of suffering to sheer waiting, and the latter is now urged (v.[36]). Ὑπομονῆς γὰρ ἔχετε χρείαν (5^{12}) ἵνα τὸ θέλημα τοῦ θεοῦ ποιήσαντες (suggested by 10^{7-9}) κομίσησθε τὴν επαγγελίαν (6^{12} 10^{23}). "Though the purpose of ὑπομονή is contained in the clause ἵνα . . . ἐπαγγελίαν, yet the function of this clause in the sentence is not telic. Its office is not to express the purpose of the principal clause, but to set forth a result (conceived, not actual) of which the possesion of ὑπομονή is the necessary condition" (Burton, *NT Moods and Tenses*, p. 93). Ὑπομονή and ὑπομένειν echo through this passage and 12^{1-7}, the idea of tenacity being expressed in 10^{38}–11^{40} by πίστις. Ὑπομονή here as in the LXX (cp. *Diat.* 3548*a–c*) implies the conviction of "hope that the evil endured will be either remedied or proved to be no evil." Κομίσησθε does not mean to get back or recover, nor to gather in, but simply as in the κοινή to receive, to get what has been promised (τὴν ἐπαγγελίαν) rather than to get it as our due (which is the idea of μισθαποδοσίαν), though what is promised is in one sense our due, since the promise can only be fulfilled for those who carry out its conditions (6^{10}). And it will soon be fulfilled. "Have patience; it is not long now." Again he clinches his appeal with an OT word, this time from the prophets (vv.$^{37. 38}$). Ἔτι γὰρ (om. p^{13}) μικρὸν (*sc.* ἔστιν) ὅσον ὅσον. In *de mutat. nomin.* 44, Philo comments upon the aptness and significance of the word *ναί* in the promise of Gn 17^{19} (*τὶ γὰρ εὐπρεπέστερον ἢ τἀγαθὰ ἐπινεύειν θεῷ καὶ ταχέως ὁμολογεῖν;*). Our author has a similar idea in mind, though he is eschatological, as Philo is not. Ὅσον ὅσον is a variant in D (on Lk 5^{3}) for *ὀλίγον*. The phrase occurs in Aristoph. *Wasps*, 213 (*τί οὐκ ἀπεκοιμηθήσαν ὅσον ὅσον στίλην*), and elsewhere, but here it is a reminiscence of the LXX of Is 26^{20} (*μικρὸν ὅσον ὅσον*). Hence, although μικρὸν ὅσον is also used, as by Philo, the omission of the second *ὅσον* in the text of Hebrews by some cursives (*e.g.* 6. 181. 326. 1836) and Eusebius is unjustified. The words serve to introduce the real citation, apparently suggested by the term ὑπομονῆς (v.^{36}), from Hab $2^{3. 4}$ *ἐὰν ὑστερήσῃ, ὑπόμεινον αὐτόν, ὅτι ἐρχόμενος ἥξει καὶ οὐ μὴ χρονίσῃ· ἐὰν ὑποστείληται, οὐκ εὐδοκεῖ ἡ ψυχή μου ἐν αὐτῷ· ὁ δὲ δίκαιος ἐκ πίστεώς μου ζήσεται*, especially as the LXX makes the object of patient hope not the fulfilment of the vision, *i.e.* the speedy downfall of the foreign power, but either messiah or God. (*a*) The author of Hebrews further adds ὁ to ἐρχόμενος, applying the words to Christ; (*b*) changes οὐ μὴ χρονίσῃ into οὐ χρονεῖ:[1] (*c*) reverses the order of the last two clauses, and (*d*) shifts μου in front of ἐκ πίστεως, as in the A text of the LXX. In the MSS of Hebrews, *μου* is entirely omitted by p^{13} D H K L P W cop eth Chrys. etc., to conform the text to the Pauline quotation (Ro 1^{17}, Gal 3^{11}), while the original LXX text, with *μου* after *πίστεως*, is preserved in D* d syr$^{\text{pesh hkl}}$ etc. This text, or at any rate its Hebrew original, meant that the just man (*i.e.* the Israelite) lived by God being faithful to his covenant with the nation. In Πρὸς Ἑβραίους the idea is that the just man of God is to live by his own πίστις or loyalty, as he holds on and holds out till the end, timidity meaning ἀπώλεια (v.^{39}), while the *ζωή* promised by God as the reward of human loyalty is the outcome of *πίστις* (ἐκ πίστεως). But our author is interested in *πίστις* rather than in *ζωή*. The latter is not one of his categories, in the sense of eternal life; this idea he prefers to express otherwise. What he quotes the verse for is its combination of God's speedy recompense and of the stress on human *πίστις*, which he proceeds to develop at length. The note struck in ὁ δὲ δικαιός μου also echoes on and on through the following passage (11^{4} Ἄβελ . . . ἐμαρτυρήθη εἶναι δίκαιος, 11^{7} Νῶε . . .

[1] This second future, or *χρονίσει*, p^{13} ℵ* D*, is read by some editors (*e.g.* Tregelles, W-H, B. Weiss).

τῆς κατὰ πίστιν δικαιοσύνης, 11[33] ἠργάσαντο δικαιοσύνην, 12[11] καρπὸν ἀποδίδωσιν δικαιοσύνης, 12[23] πνεύμασι δικαίων τετελειωμένων). The aim of (*c*) was to make it clear, as it is not clear in the LXX, that the subject of ὑποστείληται was ὁ δίκαιος, and also to make the warning against apostasy the climax. Καὶ ἐὰν ὑποστείληται—not simply in fear (as, *e.g.*, Dem. *adv. Pant.* 630, *μηδὲν ὑποστελλόμενον μηδ' αἰσχυνόμενον*), but in the fear which makes men (cp. Gal 2[12]) withdraw from their duty or abandon their convictions—οὐκ εὐδοκεῖ ἡ ψυχή μου ἐν αὐτῷ. It is a fresh proof of the freedom which the writer uses, that he refers these last seven words to God as the speaker; in Habakkuk the words are uttered by the prophet himself. Then, with a ringing, rallying note, he expresses himself confident about the issue. Ἡμεῖς δὲ οὐκ ἐσμὲν ὑποστολῆς (predicate genitive, as in 12[11], unless *ἄνδρες* or *ἐκ* is supplied) εἰς ἀπώλειαν, ἀλλὰ πίστεως εἰς περιποίησιν ψυχῆς (=ζήσεται, v.[38]). Περιποίησις occurs three times in the LXX (2 Ch 14[13], Hag 2[9], Mal 3[17]) and several times in the NT, but never with ψυχῆς, though the exact phrase was known to classical Greek as an equivalent for saving one's own life. *Ὑποστόλη*, its antithesis, which in Jos. *B.J.* ii. 277 means dissimulation, has this new sense stamped on it, after ὑποστείληται.

The exhortation is renewed in 12[1f.], but only after a long paean on πίστις, with historical illustrations, to prove that *πίστις* has always meant hope and patience for loyal members of the People (11[1-40]). The historical résumé (11[3-40]), by which the writer seeks to kindle the imagination and conscience of his readers, is prefaced by a brief introduction (11[1-3]):

[1] *Now faith means we are confident of what we hope for, convinced of what we do not see.* [2] *It was for this that the men of old won their record.* [3] *It is by faith we understand that the world was fashioned by the word of God, and thus the visible was made out of the invisible.*

Calvin rightly protested against any division here, as an interruption to the thought: "quisquis hic fecit initium capitis undecimi, perperam contextum abrupit." The following argument of 11[1-40] flows directly out of 10[35-39]: *ὑμομονή* is justified and sustained by *πίστις*, and we have now a *λόγος παρακλήσεως* on *μιμηταὶ τῶν διὰ πίστεως καὶ μακροθυμίας κληρονομούντων τὰς ἐπαγγελίας* (6[12]). Hitherto the only historical characters who have been mentioned have been Abraham, Melchizedek, Moses, Aaron, and Joshua; and Abraham alone has been mentioned for his *πίστις*; now a long list of heroes and heroines of *πίστει* is put forward, from Abel to the Maccabean martyrs. But first (vv.[1-3]) a general word on faith. Ἔστιν δὲ πίστις *κτλ.* (v.[1]). It is needless to put a comma after *πίστις*, *i.e.*, "there is such a thing as faith, faith really exists." *Εἰμί* at the beginning of a sentence does not necessarily carry this meaning; cp. *e.g.* Wis 7[1] εἰμὶ μὲν κἀγὼ θνητός, Lk 8[11] ἔστιν δὲ αὕτη ἡ παραβολή (Jn 21[25] and 1 Jn 5[17] etc.). Ἔστιν here is simply the copula, πίστις being the subject, and ἐλπιζομένων ὑπόστασις the predicate. This turn of phrase is common in Philo, who puts ἔστι first in descriptions or definitions (e.g. *Leg. Allegor.* iii. 75, ἔστι δὲ στεναγμὸς σφοδρὰ καὶ ἐπιτεταμένη λύπη: *quod deus immut.* 19, ἔστι δὲ εὐχὴ μὲν αἴτησις ἀγαθῶν παρὰ θεοῦ κτλ.). Needless difficulties have been raised about what follows. Ὑπόστασις is to be understood in the sense of 3[14] "une assurance certaine" (Ménégoz); "faith is a sure confidence of thynges which are hoped for, and a certaynetie of thynges which are not seyne" (Tyndale), the opposite of ὑποστόλη. In the parallel clause, πράγματων ἔλεγχος οὐ βλεπομένων (which in Attic Greek would have been ὧν ἄν τις μὴ ὁρᾷ), grammatically πράγματων might go with ἐλπιζομένων instead of with βλεπομένων, for the sake of emphasis (so Chrysostom, Oecumenius, von Soden, etc.); the sense would be unaffected, but the balance of the rhythm would be upset. Ἔλεγχος is used in a fresh sense, as the subjective "conviction" (the English word has acquired the same double sense as the Greek); as Euthymius said, it is an equivalent for πραγμάτων ἀοράτων πληροφορία (so syr arm eth). The writer could find no Greek term for the idea, and therefore struck out a fresh application for ἔλεγχος. As for ἐλπιζομένων . . . οὐ βλεπομένων (ὃ γὰρ βλέπει τις, τί ἐλπίζει; εἰ δὲ ὃ οὐ βλέπομεν ἐλπίζομεν δι' ὑπομονῆς ἀπεκδεχόμεθα, Ro 8[24. 25]), the unseen realities of which faith is confident are almost entirely in the future as promised by God, though, as the sequel shows, τὰ οὐ βλεπόμενα (*e.g.* vv.[3. 7. 8. 27]) are not precisely the same as τὰ ἐλπιζόμενα. It cannot be too emphatically pointed out that the writer did not mean to say: (*a*) that faith gave substance or reality to unseen hopes, though this is the interpretation of the Greek fathers (Chrysostom, for example, argues: ἐπειδὴ τὰ ἐν ἐλπίδι ἀνυπόστατα εἶναι δοκεῖ, ἡ πίστις ὑπόστασιν αὐτοῖς χαρίζεται· μᾶλλον δὲ οὐ χαρίζεται ἀλλ' αὐτό ἐστιν οὐσία αὐτῶν). When the writer declares that it is by faith we understand that the world was created, he does not mean that faith imparts reality to the creation; nor, when he says, *e.g.*, the patriarchs lived in the expectation of a celestial Fatherland, that they thereby made this more real to themselves. No doubt this was true in a sense; but the author's point is that just because these objects of hope were real, because, *e.g.*, God had prepared for them a City, therefore they were justified in having faith. It is faith as the reflex of eternal realities or rewards promised by God which is fundamental in this chapter, the faith by which a good man lives. (*b*) Similarly, faith is not the ἔλεγχος of things unseen in the sense of "proof," which could only mean that it tests, or rather attests, their reality. The existence of human faith no doubt proves that there is some unseen object which calls it out, but the writer wishes to show, not the reality of these unseen ends of God—he assumes these—but the fact and force of believing in them with absolute confidence. Such erroneous interpretations arise out of the notion that the writer is giving an abstract definition of **πίστις**, whereas he is describing it, in view of what follows, as an active conviction which moves and moulds human conduct. The happiest description of it is, "seeing Him who is invisible" (v.[27]); and this idea is applied widely; sometimes it is belief in God as against the world and its forces, particularly the forces of human injustice or of death, sometimes belief in the spirit as against the senses, sometimes again (and this is prominent in 11[5f.]) belief in the future as against the present.

In the papyri (*e.g.* in *OP.* ii. pp. 153, 176, where in the plural it = "the whole body of documents bearing on the ownership of a person's property . . . deposited in the archives, and forming the evidence of ownership") **ὑπόστασις** means occasionally the entire collection of title-deeds by which a man establishes his right to some property (cp. Moulton in *Manchester Theological Essays*, i. 174; *Expositor*, Dec. 1903, pp. 438 f.); but while this might suggest the metaphor, the metaphor means "confident assurance." The original sense of substance or reality, as in the *de Mundo*, 4 (*συλλήβδην δὲ τῶν ἐν ἀέρι φαντασμάτων τὰ μέν ἐστι κατ' ἔμφασιν τὰ δὲ καθ' ὑπόστασιν*), survives in Dante's interpretation (*Paradiso*, xxiv. 61 f.). He quotes the words as a definition of faith:

> "Fede è sustanzia di cose sperate,
> ed argumento delle non parventi,"

adding that he understands this to be its "quidity" or essence. But the notion that faith imparts a real existence to its object is read into the text. Faith as *ὑπόστασις* is "realization" of the unseen, but "realization" only in our popular, psychological sense of the term. The legal or logical sense of **ἔλεγχος**, as proof (in classical Greek and elsewhere, *e.g.* Jos. *BJ.* iv. 5. 4, *ἦν δ' οὔτ' ἔλεγχος τις τῶν κατηγορουμένων, οὔτε τεκμήριον*) is out of place here. The existence of human faith is in one sense a proof that an invisible order exists, which can alone explain men acting as they do *ἐν πίστει*. But the writer assumes that, and declares that *πίστις* lives and moves in the steady light of the unseen realities. The sense of "test," as in Epictetus, iii. 10. 11 (*ἐνθάδ' ὁ ἔλεγχος τοῦ πράγματος, ἡ δοκιμασία τοῦ φιλοσοφοῦντος*), is as impossible here as that of "rebuke"; the force of *πίστις* in 11[3-40] rests on its subjective sense as an inner conviction, which forms a motive for human life, and this determines the meaning of *ὑπόστασις* and *ἔλεγχος* as applied to it in the introductory description.

This connexion of faith with the future is emphasized by Philo in *de Migratione Abrahami*, 9, commenting on Gn 12[1] *ἣν σοι δείξω*. It is *δείξω*, not *δείκνυμι*, he points out—*εἰς μαρτυρίαν πίστεως ἣν ἐπίστευσεν ἡ ψυχὴ θεῷ, οὐκ ἐκ τῶν ἀποτελεσμάτων ἐπιδεικνυμένη τὸ εὐχάριστον, ἀλλ' ἐκ προσδοκίας τῶν μελλόντων . . . νομίσασα ἤδη παρεῖναι τὰ μὴ παρόντα διὰ τὴν τοῦ ὑποσχο-*

μένου βεβαιότητα πίστιν [cp. He 10[23]], ἀγαθὸν τέλειον, ἆθλον εὕρηται. Faith thus relies upon God's promise and eagerly expects what is to come; indeed it lives for and in the future. So our writer uses **πίστις**, almost as Paul used **ἐλπίς** (psychologically the two being often indistinguishable). Nor is this *πίστις* a novelty in our religion (v.[2]), he adds, **ἐν ταύτῃ γὰρ ἐμαρτυρήθησαν** (7[8]) **οἱ πρεσβύτεροι.** Ἐν = διά (ταύτης) as in 4[6] 6[16] 9[22] 10[10]; δι' ἧς ἐμαρτυρήθη (v.[4]), μαρτυρηθέντες διὰ τῆς πίστεως (v.[39]). **Οἱ πρεσβύτεροι** (= οἱ πατέρες, 1[1]) never bears this exact sense elsewhere in the NT, the nearest[1] parallel being Mt 15[2] = Mk 7[3. 5] (τὴν παράδοσιν τῶν πρεσβυτέρων). Philo (*de Abrahamo* 46), indeed, noting that Abraham the man of faith is the first man called πρεσβύτερος in scripture (Gn 24[1]), reflects that this is significant; ὁ γὰρ ἀληθείᾳ πρεσβύτερος οὐκ ἐν μήκει χρόνων ἀλλ' ἐν ἐπαινετῷ καὶ τελείῳ βίῳ θεωρεῖται. Aged worldly people can only be called longlived children, τὸν δὲ φρονήσεως καὶ σοφίας καὶ τῆς πρὸς θεὸν πίστεως ἐρασθέντα λέγοι τις ἂν ἐνδίκως εἶναι πρεσβύτερον. But our author weaves no such fancies round the word, though he probably understood the term in an honorific sense (cp. Philo, *de Sobrietate*, 4, πρεσβύτερον . . . τὸν γέρως καὶ τιμῆς ἄξιον ὀνομάζει). For **ἐμαρτυρήθησαν** in this sense of getting a good report, cp. B. Latyschev's *Inscript. Antiquae Orae Septent.* i. 21[26f.] ἐμαρτυρήθη τοὺς ὑπὲρ φιλίας κινδύνους . . . παραβολευσάμενος: *Syll.* 366[28] (i A.D.) ἀρχιτέκτονας μαρτυρηθέντας ὑπὸ τῆς σεμνοτάτης [βουλῆς], and the instances quoted in Deissmann's *Bible Studies* (265).

Before describing the scriptural record of the **πρεσβύτεροι**, however, the writer pauses to point out the supreme proof of **πίστις** as **πραγμάτων ἔλεγχος οὐ βλεπομένων.** The very world within which they showed their faith and within which we are to show our faith, was the outcome of what is invisible (v.[3]), and this conviction itself is an act of faith. **Πίστει νοοῦμεν** (cp. Ro 1[20]: "νοεῖν is in Hellenistic Greek the current word for the apprehension of the divine in nature," A. T. Goodrick on Wis 13[4]) **κατηρτίσθαι** (of creation, Ps 73[16] σὺ κατηρτίσω ἥλιον καὶ σελήνην) **τοὺς αἰῶνας** (1[2]) **ῥήματι θεοῦ** (the divine fiat here), **εἰς** (with consecutive infinitive) **τὸ μὴ ἐκ φαινομένων τὸ βλεπόμενον γεγονέναι** (perfect of permanence). The μή goes with φαινομένων, but is thrown before the preposition as, *e.g.*, in Ac 1[5] οὐ μετὰ πολλὰς ταύτας ἡμέρας (according to a familiar classical construction, Blass, § 433. 3).[2] Faith always answers to revelation,

[1] W. Brandt (*Jüdische Reinheitslehre und ihre Beschreibung in den Evangelien*, 1910, pp. 2, 3) thinks that this expression might apply to the more recent teachers as well as to the ancient authorities.

[2] In 2 Mac 7[28] οὐκ ἐξ ὄντων ἐποιήσεν αὐτὰ ὁ θεός (A), the οὐκ goes with the verb.

and creation is the first revelation of God to man. Creation by the fiat of God was the orthodox doctrine of Judaism, and anyone who read the OT would accept it as the one theory about the origin of the world (cp. *e.g.* the description of God in the Mechilta, 33*b*, on Ex 14^{31} etc. as "He who spoke and the world was," שֶׁאָמַן וְהָיָה הָעוֹלָם, and Apoc. Bar. 14^{17}: "when of old there was no world with its inhabitants, Thou didst devise and speak with a word, and forthwith the works of creation stood before Thee"). But the explicitness of this sentence about creation out of what is invisible, suggests that the writer had other views in mind, which he desired to repudiate. Possibly Greek theories like those hinted at in Wis 10^{17} about the world[1] being created ἐξ ἀμόρφου ὕλης, or the statement in the *de aeternitate mundi*, 2, where Philo declares ἐκ τοῦ μὴ ὄντος οὐδὲν γίνεται, quoting Empedocles to this effect, though elsewhere Philo does agree that the world was made out of nothing, as, *e.g.*, in the *de Somniis*, i. 13 (ὁ θεὸς τὰ πάντα γεννήσας οὐ μόνον εἰς τοὐμφανὲς ἤγαγεν ἀλλὰ καὶ ἃ πρότερον οὐκ ἦν ἐποίησεν, οὐ δημιουργὸς μόνον ἀλλὰ καὶ κτίστης αὐτὸς ὤν, cp. also Apoc. Bar. 21^4: "O Thou . . . that hast called from the beginning of the world that which did not yet exist," and Slav. En. 24^2: "I will tell thee now what things I created from the non-existent, and what visible things from the invisible"). What the μὴ φαινόμενα were, our author does not suggest. R. Akiba is said to have applied the words of Ps 101^7 to anyone who rashly speculated on the original material of the world. Our author does not speculate; it is very doubtful if he intends (Windisch, M'Neill) to agree with Philo's idea (in the *de opificio Mundi*, 16, *de confus. ling.* 34) of the φαινόμενος οὗτος κόσμος being modelled on the ἀσώματος καὶ νοητός or archetypal ideas, for the language of 8^5 is insufficient to bear the weight of this inference.

To take εἰς τὸ . . . γεγονέναι as final, is a forced construction. The phrase does not describe the motive of κατηρτίσθαι, and if the writer had meant, "so that we might know the seen came from the unseen,"[2] he would have written this, instead of allowing the vital words *might know* to be supplied.

The roll-call of the πρεσβύτεροι (vv.[4f.]) opens with Abel and Enoch, two men who showed their πίστις before the deluge (vv.[4-6]). One was murdered, the other, as the story went, never died; and the writer uses both tales to illustrate his point about πίστις.

[1] LXX of Gn 1^2 ἡ δὲ γῆ ἦν ἀόρατος καὶ ἀκατασκεύαστος.

[2] At an early period τὸ βλεπόμενον was altered into τὰ βλεπόμενα (D K L Ψ 6. 104. 218. 326. 1288. r vg syr arm), to conform with the previous plurals βλεπομένων and φαινομένων.

[4] *It was by faith* (πίστει, the rhetorical anaphora repeated throughout the section) *that Abel offered God a richer sacrifice than Cain did, and thus* (δι' ἧς, sc. πίστεως) *won from God the record of being "just," on the score of what he gave; he died, but by his faith he is speaking to us still.* [5] *It was by faith that Enoch was taken to heaven, so that he never died* (*"he was not overtaken by death, for God had taken him away"*). *For before he was taken to heaven, his record was that "he had satisfied God";* [6] *and apart from faith it is impossible* (ἀδύνατον, sc. ἐστι) *"to satisfy him," for the man who draws near to God must believe that he exists, and that he does reward those who seek him.*

The faith of Abel and of Enoch is not **πίστις ἐλπιζομένων**, which is not introduced till v.[7]. In 4 Mac 16[20f.] the illustrations of steadfast faith are (*a*) Abraham sacrificing Isaac, (*b*) Daniel in the den of lions, and (*c*) the three men in the fiery furnace; but in 18[11f.] the list of noble sufferers includes (*a*) Abel, (*b*) Isaac, (*c*) Joseph in prison, (*d*) Phinehas, (*e*) the three men in the fiery furnace, and (*f*) Daniel. Sirach's eulogy of famous men in Israel (44–50) has a wider sweep: Enoch, Noah, Abraham, Isaac, Jacob, Moses, Aaron, Phinehas, Joshua, Caleb, the judges, Samuel, David, Solomon, Elijah, Elisha, Hezekiah, Isaiah, Josiah, Jeremiah, Ezekiel, Job, the twelve prophets, Zerubbabel, Joshua the son of Josedek, Nehemiah, and the highpriest Simon (*i.e.* down to the second century B.C.).

The first illustration (v.[4]) is much less natural than most of those that follow. In the story of Gn 4[4-8], ἔπιδεν ὁ θεὸς ἐπὶ Ἄβελ καὶ ἐπὶ τοῖς δώροις αὐτοῦ. But why God disregarded Cain's sacrifice and preferred Abel's, our author does not explain. Josephus (*Ant.* i. 54) thought that an offering of milk and animals was more acceptable to God as being natural (τοῖς αὐτομάτοις καὶ κατὰ φύσιν γεγονόσι) than Cain's cereal offering, which was wrung out of the ground by a covetous man; our author simply argues that the πλείων θυσία of Abel at the very dawn of history was prompted by faith. He does not enter into the nature of this **πλείονα** (in sense of Mt 6[25] or Mk 12[43] ἡ χήρα αὕτη ἡ πτωχὴ πλεῖον πάντων βέβληκεν) **θυσίαν παρὰ** (as in 1[4]) **Κάϊν**, offered at the first act of worship recorded in scripture. What seems to be implied is that faith must inspire any worship that is to be acceptable to God from anyone who is to be God's **δίκαιος** (10[38]). Josephus held that Abel δικαιοσύνης ἐπιμελεῖτο, the blood of Ἄβελ τοῦ δικαίου is noted in Mt 23[35], and the Genesis-words ἔπιδεν ὁ θεός are here expanded by our author into **ἐμαρτυρήθη εἶναι δίκαιος.** Note the practical equivalence of δῶρα and θυσία, as already in 5[1] etc. There is nothing in **Πρὸς Ἑβραίους** like Philo's effort (*Quaest. in Gen.* 4[4]) to distinguish between δῶρα and θυσίας as follows: ὁ μὲν θύων ἐπιδιαιρεῖ, τὸ μὲν αἷμα τῷ βωμῷ προχέων, τὰ δὲ κρέα οἴκαδε κομίζων· ὁ δὲ δωρούμενος ὅλον ἔοικε παραχωρεῖν τῷ λαμβάνοντι· ὁ μὲν οὖν φίλαυτος διανομεὺς οἷος ὁ Κάϊν, ὁ δὲ φιλόθεος δώρηται οἷον ὁ Ἄβελ.

Πλείονα: of the conjectural emendations, ΠΙΟΝΑ and ΗΔΙΟΝΑ (Cobet, Vollgraff), the latter is favoured by Justin's reference in *Dial.* 29 (*εὐδόκησε γὰρ καὶ εἰς τὰ ἔθνη, καὶ τὰς θυσίας ἥδιον παρ' ἡμῖν ἢ παρ' ὑμῶν λαμβάνει· τίς οὖν ἔτι μοι περιτομῆς λόγος, ὑπὸ τοῦ θεοῦ μαρτυρηθέντι;*), and is admitted into the text by Baljon and Blass (so Maynard in *Exp.*[7] vii. 164 f., who infers from *μαρτυρηθέντι* that Justin knew Πρὸς Ἑβραίους, the original text of the latter being *αὐτῷ τοῦ θεοῦ*). In Demosth. *Prooem.* 23, *ἥδιον* has been corrupted into *πλεῖον*.

In what follows, (*a*) the original text (**μαρτυροῦντος . . . αὐτῷ τοῦ θεοῦ**) is preserved in p[13] Clem. (om. *τῷ θεῷ*). (*b*) *αὐτῷ* then became *αὐτοῦ* under the influence of the LXX, and *τῷ θεῷ* was inserted after *προσήνεγκε* to complete the sense (ℵ[c] D[c] K L P r vg syr boh arm Orig. Chrys. etc.). Finally, (*c*) *τοῦ θεοῦ* became assimilated to the preceding *τῷ θεῷ*, and *μαρτυροῦντος . . . αὐτοῦ τῷ θεῷ* (ℵ* A D* 33. 104. 326. 1311. 1836. eth) became current, as though Abel witnessed to God, instead of God witnessing to Abel. Thus after *προσήνεγκε* the Greek originally ran: **δι' ἧς ἐμαρτυρήθη εἶναι δίκαιος, μαρτυροῦντος ἐπὶ τοῖς δώροις αὐτῷ τοῦ θεοῦ.** Then another application of the LXX was added. The phrase in Gn 4[10] (*φωνὴ αἵματος τοῦ ἀδελφοῦ σου βοᾷ πρός με*) had already suggested to Philo that Abel was in a sense still living (*quod det. potiori insid. soleat*, 14: *ὁ Ἄβελ, τὸ παραδοξότατον, ἀνῄρηταί τε καὶ ζῇ· ἀνῄρηται μὲν ἐκ τῆς τοῦ ἄφρονος διανοίας, ζῇ δὲ τὴν ἐν θεῷ ζωὴν εὐδαίμονα· μαρτυρήσει δὲ τὸ χρησθὲν λόγιον, ἐν ᾧ "φωνῇ" χρώμενος καὶ "βοῶν"* (Gen 4[10]) *ἃ πέπονθεν ὑπὸ κακοῦ συνδέτου τηλαυγῶς εὑρίσκεται· πῶς γὰρ ὁ μηκέτ' ὢν διαλέγεσθαι δυνατός;*). Our author takes a similar line here: **καὶ δι' αὐτῆς** (*i.e.* **πίστεως**) **ἀποθανὼν ἔτι λαλεῖ.** Even after death, Abel's cry is represented as reaching God, so Philo puts it (*ibid.* 20), *ζῇ μὲν γάρ, ὡς καὶ πρότερον ἔφην, ὁ τεθνάναι δοκῶν, εἴ γε καὶ ἱκέτης ὢν θεοῦ καὶ φωνῇ χρώμενος εὑρίσκεται.* Only, it is not the fact that the cry was one for retribution (12[24]) which is stressed here, not the fact that his blood cried to God after he died; but, as *λαλεῖν* is never used of speaking to God, what the writer means to suggest (as in 3[15]) is that Abel's faith still speaks to us (*λαλεῖ*, not the historic present, but = in the record). Not even in 12[24] does he adopt the idea of a divine nemesis for the sufferings of the pious in past generations. He does not represent the blood of martyrs like Abel as crying from the ground for personal vengeance; he has nothing of the spirit which prompted the weird vision of the wronged souls under the altar crying out for retribution (Rev 6[10]). **Ἔτι λαλεῖ** means, in a general sense, that he is an eloquent, living witness to all ages (so recently Seeberg). Primasius ("qui enim alios suo exemplo admonet ut justi sint, quomodo non loquitur?") and Chrysostom (*τοῦτο καὶ τοῦ ζῆν σημεῖον ἐστι, καὶ τοῦ παρὰ πάντων ᾄδεσθαι, θαυμάζεσθαι καὶ μακαρίζεσθαι· ὁ γὰρ παραινῶν τοῖς ἄλλοις δικαίοις εἶναι λαλεῖ*) put this well. The witness is that *πίστις* may have to face the last extreme of death (12^4), and that it is not abandoned by God; **ἀποθανών** is never the last word upon a **δίκαιος**. Compare Tertullian's argument from Abel, in *De Scorpiace*, 8: "a primordio enim justitia vim patitur. Statim ut coli Deus coepit, invidiam religio sortita est: qui Deo placuerat, occiditur, et quidem a fratre; quo proclivius impietas alienum sanguinem sectaretur, a suo auspicata est. Denique non modo justorum, verum etiam et prophetarum."

The difficulty of *λαλεῖ* led to the tame correction *λαλεῖται* in D K L d eth, etc. *Λαλεῖται* as passive (=*λέγεται*) is nearly as impossible as middle; to say that Abel, even after death, is still spoken of, is a tepid idea. The writer of Hebrews meant more than an immortal memory, more even than Epictetus when he declared that by dying *ὅτε ἔδει καὶ ὡς ἔδει* one may do even more good to men than he did in life, like Socrates (iv. 1. 169, *καὶ νῦν Σωκράτους ἀποθανόντος οὐθὲν ἧττον ἢ καὶ πλεῖον ὠφέλιμός ἐστιν ἀνθρώποις ἡ μνήμη ὧν ἔτι ζῶν ἔπραξεν ἢ εἶπεν*).

The **πίστις Ἐνώχ** (vv.[5. 6]) is conveyed in an interpretation of the LXX of Gn 5^{24} *καὶ εὐηρέστησεν Ἐνὼχ τῷ θεῷ· καὶ οὐχ ηὑρίσκετο, διότι μετέθηκεν αὐτὸν ὁ θεός.* The writer takes the two clauses in reverse order. Enoch **μετετέθη τοῦ** (with infinitive of result) **μὴ ἰδεῖν θάνατον** (Lk 2^{26}) **καὶ** ("indeed," introducing the quotation) **οὐχ ηὑρίσκετο** (on this Attic augmented form, which became rare in the *κοινή*, see Thackeray, 200) **διότι μετέθηκεν αὐτὸν ὁ θεός, πρὸ γὰρ** (resuming *πίστει μετετέθη*) **τῆς μεταθέσεως μεμαρτύρηται** (in the scripture record; hence the perfect, which here is practically aoristic) **εὐηρεστηκέναι τῷ θεοῦ** (*εὐαρεστεῖν* in its ordinary Hellenistic sense of a servant giving satisfaction to his master). For **εὑρίσκεσθαι** = die (be overtaken or surprised by death),[1] cp. Epict. iii. 5. 5 f., *οὐκ οἶδας ὅτι καὶ νόσος καὶ θάνατος καταλαβεῖν ἡμᾶς ὀφείλουσίν τί ποτε ποιοῦντας; . . . ἐμοὶ μὲν γὰρ καταληφθῆναι γένοιτο μηδενὸς ἄλλου ἐπιμελουμένῳ ἢ τῆς προαιρέσεως τῆς ἐμῆς . . . ταῦτα ἐπιτηδεύων θέλω εὑρεθῆναι*: iv. 10. 12, *ἀγαθὸς ὢν ἀποθανῇ, γενναίαν πρᾶξιν ἐπιτελῶν. ἐπεὶ γὰρ δεῖ πάντως ἀποθανεῖν, ἀνάγκη τί ποτε ποιοῦντα εὑρεθῆναι . . . τί οὖν θέλεις ποιῶν εὑρεθῆναι ὑπὸ τοῦ θανάτου;* Here *εὑρεθῆναι* (with or without *τοῦ θανάτου*) is a synonym for *καταληφθῆναι* or *ἀποθανεῖν*, as in Ph 3^9 (*εὑρεθῶ ἐν αὐτῷ*).

Both Clem. Rom. (9^2) and Origen, like Tertullian, appear to have read *οὐχ εὑρέθη αὐτοῦ θάνατος* in Gn 5^{24}; and Blass therefore reads here *οὐχ ηὑρίσκετ(ο) αὐτοῦ θάνατος*, especially as it suits his scheme of rhythm. This is linguistically possible, as *εὑρίσκεσθαι* = be (cp. Fr. *se trouver*), *e.g.* in Lk 17^{18}, Ph 2^8. **Μετέθηκεν** was turned into the pluperfect *μετετέθηκεν* by א* D^c L 5. 203. 256. 257. 326. 337. 378. 383. 491. 506. 623. 1611, etc.

Traditions varied upon Enoch (*EBi.* 1295*a*), and even Alexandrian Judaism did not always canonize him in this way. (*a*)

[1] In Sifre Deut. 304, the angel of death sought Moses, but found him not (וְלֹא מְצָאוֹ).

The author of Wis $4^{10f.}$, without mentioning his name, quotes Gn 5^{24} as if it meant that God removed Enoch from life early (*καὶ ζῶν μεταξὺ ἁμαρτωλῶν μετετέθη*) in order to prevent him from sharing the sin of his age (*ἡρπάγη, μὴ κακία ἀλλάξῃ σύνεσιν αὐτοῦ, ἢ δόλος ἀπατήσῃ ψυχὴν αὐτοῦ*); he departed young, but his removal was a boon mercifully granted by God to his youthful piety. (*b*) Philo views him in *de Abrahamo*, 3 (cp. *de praem.* 3–4), as a type of μετάνοια. Quoting Gn 5^{24} he points out that μετάθεσις means a change for the better, and that *οὐχ ηὑρίσκετο* is therefore appropriate, τῷ τὸν ἀρχαῖον καὶ ἐπίληπτον ἀπαληλίφθαι βίον καὶ ἠφανίσθαι καὶ μηκέθ' εὑρίσκεσθαι, καθάπερ εἰ μηδὲ τὴν ἀρχὴν ἐγένετο. The Greek version of Sir 44^{16} echoes the same tradition (*Ἐνωχ εὐηρέστησεν Κυρίῳ καὶ μετετέθη, ὑπόδειγμα μετανοίας ταῖς γενεαῖς*), viz. that μετέθηκεν implies the effacement of Enoch's blameable past, or at any rate that he was enrolled in better company. Our author does not share this view. His general deduction in v.^{6} expands the description of **πίστις** in v.^{1}. To say that a man has satisfied God is to pronounce the highest possible eulogy upon him, says Philo[1] (*de Abrahamo*, 6, "*τῷ θεῷ εὐηρέστησεν*·" οὗ τί γένοιτ' ἂν ἐν τῇ ψύσει κρεῖττον; τίς καλοκἀγαθίας ἐναργέστερος ἔλεγχος;), though he is referring to Noah, not to Enoch. Our author explains that to satisfy God necessarily implies *πίστις* (v.^{6}) in the sense of 10^{35}. **Πιστεῦσαι γὰρ δεῖ τὸν προσερχόμενον τῷ θεῷ** (4^{16} etc.) **ὅτι ἔστιν** (so *Epict.* iii. 26. 15, *ὅτι καὶ ἔστι καὶ καλῶς διοικεῖ τὰ ὅλα*) **καὶ τοῖς ἐκζητοῦσιν αὐτὸν μισθαποδότης** (cf. v.^{26} 10^{35}) **γίνεται.** As for the first element of belief, in the existence of God (*ὅτι ἔστιν*), the early commentators, from Chrysostom (*ὅτι ἔστιν· οὐ τὸ τί ἐστιν*: cp. Tert. *adv. Marc.* i. 17, "primo enim quaeritur an sit, et ita qualis sit") and Jerome (on Is $6^{1\text{-}7}$, in *Anecdota Maredsolana*, iii. 3. 110: "cumque idem apostolus Paulus scribit in alio loco, Credere oportet accedentem ad Deum quia est, non posuit quis et qualis sit debere cognosci, sed tantum quod sit. Scimus enim esse Deum, scimusque quid non sit; quid autem et qualis sit, scire non possumus") onwards, emphasize the fact that it is God's existence, not his nature, which is the primary element of faith. Philo does declare that the two main problems of enquiry are into God's existence and into his essence (*de Monarch.* i. 4–6), but our author takes the more practical, religious line, and he does not suggest how faith in

[1] Philo fancifully allegorizes the phrase in the *de mutat. nomin.* 4: *φθείρεται οὖν εἰκότως τὸ γεῶδες καὶ καταλύεται, ὅταν ὅλος δι' ὅλων ὁ νοῦς εὐαρεστεῖν προέληται θεῷ· σπάνιον δὲ καὶ τὸ γένος καὶ μόλις εὑρισκόμενον, πλὴν οὐκ ἀδύνατον γενέσθαι· δηλοῖ δὲ τὸ χρησθὲν ἐπὶ τοῦ Ἐνὼχ λόγιον τόδε· εὐηρέστησε δὲ Ἐνὼχ τῷ θεῷ καὶ οὐχ εὑρισκετο· ποῦ γὰρ <ἂν> σκεψάμενός τις εὕροι τἀγαθὸν τοῦτο; . . . οὐχ εὑρίσκετο ὁ εὐαρηστήσα sτρόπος τῷ θεῷ, ὡς ἂν δήπου ὑπαρκτὸς μὲν ὤν, ἀποκρυπτόμενος δὲ καὶ τὴν εἰς ταὐτὸ σύνοδον ἡμῶι ἀποδιδράσκων, ἐπειδὴ καὶ μετατεθῆναι λέγεται.*

God's existence is to be won or kept. When objectors asked him why he believed in the existence of the gods, Marcus Aurelius used to reply: *πρῶτον μὲν καὶ ὄψει ὁρατοί εἰσιν· ἔπειτα μέντοι οὐδὲ τὴν ψυχὴν τὴν ἐμαυτοῦ ἑώρακα καὶ ὅμως τιμῶ· οὕτως οὖν καὶ τοὺς θεούς, ἐξ ὧν τῆς δυνάμεως αὐτῶν ἑκάστοτε πειρῶμαι, ἐκ τούτων ὅτι τε εἰσὶ καταλαμβάνω καὶ αἰδοῦμαι* (xii. 28). We have no such argument against atheism here; only the reminder that faith does imply a belief in the existence of God—a reminder which would appeal specially to those of the readers who had been born outside Judaism. Belief in the existence of God is for our author, however, one of the elementary principles of the Christian religion (6[1]); the stress here falls on the second element, **καὶ . . . μισθαποδότης γίνεται.** When the Stoics spoke about belief in the divine existence, they generally associated it with belief in providence; both Seneca (*Ep.* xcv. 50, "primus est deorum cultus deos credere . . . scire illos esse qui praesident mundo, quia universa vi sua temperant, qui humani generis tutelam gerunt interdum curiosi singulorum") and Epictetus (*e.g.* ii. 14. 11, *λέγουσιν οἱ φιλόσοφοι ὅτι μαθεῖν δεῖ πρῶτον τοῦτο, ὅτι ἔστι θεὸς καὶ προνοεῖ τῶν ὅλων*: *Enchir.* xxxi. 1, *τῆς περὶ τοὺς θεοὺς εὐσεβείας ἴσθω ὅτι τὸ κυριώτατον ἐκεῖνό ἐστιν ὀρθὰς ὑπολήψεις περὶ αὐτῶν ἔχειν ὡς ὄντων καὶ διοικούντων τὰ ὅλα καλῶς καὶ δικαίως*) are contemporary witnesses to this connexion of ideas, which, indeed, is as old as Plato (*Leges*, 905*d*, *ὅτι μὲν γὰρ θεοί τ' εἰσὶν καὶ ἀνθρώπων ἐπιμελοῦνται*).

Τοῖς ἐκζητοῦσιν αὐτόν (for which p[13] P read the simple *ζητοῦσιν*) denotes, not philosophic enquiry, but the practical religious quest, as in the OT (*e.g.* Ac 15[17], Ro 3[11]). This is not Philo's view, *e.g.*, in the *Leg. Alleg.* 3[15] *εἰ δὲ ζητοῦσα εὑρήσεις θεὸν ἄδηλον, πολλοῖς γὰρ οὐκ ἐφανέρωσεν ἑαυτὸν, ἀλλ' ἀτελῆ τὴν σπουδὴν ἄχρι παντὸς ἔσχον· ἐξαρκεῖ μέντοι πρὸς μετουσίαν ἀγαθῶν καὶ ψιλὸν τὸ ζητεῖν μόνον, ἀεὶ γὰρ αἱ ἐπὶ τὰ καλὰ ὁρμαὶ κἂν τοῦ τέλους ἀτυχῶσι τοὺς χρωμένους προευφραίνουσιν.* But our author has a simpler belief; he is sure that the quest of faith is always successful. By God's reward he means that the faith of man reaching out to God is never left to itself, but met by a real satisfaction; God proves its rewarder. Such faith is a conviction which illustrates 11[1], for the being of God is an unseen reality and his full reward is at present to be hoped for.

A still more apt illustration of **πίστις** as the *ἔλεγχος πράγματων οὐ βλεπομένων* which becomes a motive in human life, now occurs in (v.[7]) the faith which Noah showed at the deluge when he believed, against all appearances to the contrary, that he must obey God's order and build an ark, although it is true that in this case the unseen was revealed and realized within the lifetime of the **δίκαιος.** Like Philo, our author passes from Enoch tc

Noah, although for a different reason. Philo ranks Noah as the lover of God and virtue, next to Enoch the typical penitent (*de Abrah.* 3, 5, εἰκότως τῷ μετανενοηκότι τάττει κατὰ τὸ ἑξῆς τὸν θεοφιλῆ καὶ φιλάρετον); here both are grouped as examples of **πίστις**. Sirach ($44^{17f.}$) also passes at once from Enoch to Noah the **δίκαιος**.

[7] *It was by faith* (πίστει) *that Noah, after being told by God* (χρηματισθείς, 8^5, sc. παρὰ τοῦ θεοῦ) *of what was still unseen* (τῶν μηδέπω βλεπομένων, *i.e.* the deluge), *reverently* (εὐλαβηθείς, cp. 5^7) *constructed* (κατεσκεύασεν, as 1 P 3^{20}) *an ark to save his household; thus he condemned the world and became heir of the righteousness that follows faith.*

The writer recalls, though he does not quote from, the story of Gn $6^{13f.}$. **Πίστει** goes closely with **εὐλάβηθεὶς κατεσκεύασεν**, and **περὶ τ. μ. βλεπομένων** goes with **χρηματισθείς** (as Jos. *Ant.* iv. 102, ἐχρηματίζετο περὶ ὧν ἐδεῖτο), not with εὐλαβηθείς, which is not a synonym for φοβηθείς—the writer is at pains always to exclude fear or dread from faith (cp. vv.[23. 27]). **Εἰς** σωτηρίαν is to be taken as = "to save alive" (Ac 27^{20} πᾶσα ἐλπὶς τοῦ σώζεσθαι ἡμᾶς, 27^{34} τοῦτο γὰρ πρὸς τῆς ὑμετέρας σωτηρίας ὑπάρχει). **Δι'** ἧς (*i.e.* by the faith he thus exhibited; as both of the following clauses depend on this, it cannot refer to the ark, which would suit only the first) **κατέκρινε τὸν** κόσμον, where κατέκρινεν corresponds to what is probably the meaning of Wis 4^{16} κατακρινεῖ δὲ δίκαιος καμὼν τοὺς ζῶντας ἀσεβεῖς, though καμών (= θανών) is not the point of Hebrews, which regards Noah's action as shaming the world, throwing its dark scepticism into relief against his own shining faith in God (Josephus, in *Ant.* i. 75, puts it less pointedly: ὁ δὲ θεὸς τοῦτον μὲν τῆς δικαιοσύνης ἠγάπησε, κατεδίκαζε δ' **ἐκείνους**); **κόσμος** here (as in v.[38]) means sinful humanity, almost in the sense so common in the Johannine vocabulary, the κόσμος ἀσεβῶν of 2 P 2^5. Philo (*de congressu erudit.* 17) notes that Noah was the first man in the OT to be specially called (Gn 6^9) **δίκαιος**; but our author, who has already called Abel and Noah δίκαιος, does not use this fact; he contents himself with saying that **τῆς κατὰ πίστιν δικαιοσύνης ἐγένετο κληρόνομος**, *i.e.* he became entitled to, came into possession of, the δικαιοσύνη which is the outcome or property (κατά κτλ., as in Hellenistic Greek, cp. Eph 1^{15}, a periphrasis for the possessive genitive) of such faith as he showed. **Δικαιοσύνη** here is the state of one who is God's δίκαιος (ὁ δίκαιος μου, 10^{38}). A vivid description of Noah's faith is given in Mark Rutherford's novel, *The Deliverance*, pp. 162, 163.

The faith of Abraham, as might be expected, receives more attention than that of any other (cp. Ac $7^{2f.}$). It is described in three phases ([8. 9-10. 17-19]); the faith of his wife Sara is attached to his ([11-12]), and a general statement about his immediate descendants is interpolated ([13-16]) before the writer passes from the second to the third phase. As in Sirach and Philo, Abraham follows Noah. "Ten generations were there from Noah to Abraham, to show how great was His longsuffering; for all the generations were provoking Him, till Abraham our father came and received the reward of them all" (*Pirke Aboth* 5[3]).

[8] *It was by faith that Abraham obeyed his call to go forth to a place which he would receive as an inheritance; he went forth, although he did not know where he was to go.* [9] *It was by faith that he "sojourned" in the promised land, as in a foreign country, residing in tents, as did Isaac and Jacob, who were co-heirs with him of the same promise;* [10] *he was waiting for the City with its fixed foundations, whose builder and maker is God.*

The first phase (v.[8]) is the call to leave Mesopotamia and travel West, which is described in Gn 12[1f.]. The writer does not dwell, like Philo (*de Abrahamo*, 14), on the wrench of tearing oneself from one's home. But, as Philo says that Abraham started ἅμα τῷ κελευσθῆναι, our author begins with **καλούμενος**. When the call came, he obeyed it—**ὑπήκουσεν ἐξελθεῖν** (epexegetic infinitive), a reminiscence of Gn 12[1. 4] καὶ εἶπεν κύριος τῷ Ἀβρὰμ, Ἔξελθε . . . καὶ ἐπορεύθη Ἀβρὰμ καθάπερ ἐλάλησεν αὐτῷ κύριος. He went out from Mesopotamia, **μὴ ἐπιστάμενος ποῦ ἔρχεται**, his faith being tested by this uncertainty. So Philo (*de Migr. Abrah.* 9) notes the point of the future δείξω in Gn 12[1]; it is εἰς μαρτυρίαν πίστεως ἣν ἐπίστευσεν ἡ ψυχὴ θεῷ.

The insertion of ὁ before καλούμενος (A D 33. 256. 467. 1739. 2127 sah boh arm Thdt.) turns the phrase into an allusion to Abraham's change of name in Gn 17[5], which is irrelevant to his earlier call to leave the far East.

The second phase (vv.[9. 10]) is the trial of patience. He did not lose heart or hope, even when he did reach the country appointed to him, although he had to wander up and down it as a mere foreigner, **εἰς** (= ἐν, Mk 13[16], Ac 8[40]) . . . **ἀλλοτρίαν**. He found the land he had been promised still in the hands of aliens, and yet he lived there, lived as an alien in his own country! **Παρῴκησεν** is the opposite of **κατῴκησεν** (as in Gn 37[1]), and with a fine touch of paradox the writer therefore goes on to describe Abraham as **ἐν σκηναῖς κατοικήσας**, contented patiently to lead a wandering, unsettled life. Such was all the "residence" he ever had! What sustained him was his **πίστις** (v.[10]), his eager outlook for the City, **ἧς τεχνίτης καὶ δημιουργὸς ὁ θεός**. Compare the scholion on Lucian's *Jov. Trag.* 38: ὃν δὴ θεὸν καὶ δημιουργὸν ὁ εὐσεβὴς ἀνευρηκὼς λογισμὸς ἔφορον καὶ τεχνίτην τοῦ παντὸς προευτρέπισεν. Τεχνίτης is not a LXX term, and only began to be used of God in Alexandrian Judaism (*e.g.* in Wis 13[1]). This is the one place in the NT where it is applied to God; afterwards (*e.g.* Did. 12[3]; Diognetus, 7[2]) it became more common. **Δημιουργός** is equally unique as a NT term for God, but it occurs in 2 Mac 4[1], and was used in classical literature frequently for a subordinate deity (cp. Schermann, *Texte u. Untersuchungen*, xxxiv. 2*b*. 23). In Apoc. Esdrae (ed. Tisch. 32) the phrase occurs, ὁ πάσης τῆς κτίσεως δημιουργός. Our author simply writes **τεχνίτης καὶ δημιουργός** as a rhetorical expression for maker or creator (8[2]), without differentiating the one term from the other, as "designer" and "constructor" (cp. Philo, *quis rer. div.* 27, ὁ τεχνίτης . . . ἡνίκα τὸν κόσμον ἐδημιούργει: *de mut. nom.* 4, ἔθηκε τὰ πάντα ὁ γεννήσας καὶ τεχνιτεύσας πατήρ, ὥστε τὸ "ἐγώ εἰμι θεὸς σὸς" ἴσον ἐστὶ τῷ "ἐγώ εἰμι ποιητὴς καὶ δημιουργός").

In [9b] the writer adds a new touch (as if to suggest that Abraham propagated his πίστις) in **μετὰ Ἰσαὰκ καὶ Ἰακώβ** [1]—who shared the same outlook—**τῶν συγκληρονόμων** (a κοινή, though not a LXX, term for co-heir) **τῆς ἐπαγγελίας τῆς αὐτῆς**. Their individual faith is noted later (vv.[20. 21]). In sketching his fine mystical interpretation of Abraham's hope, the author ignores the fact that Jacob, according to Gn 33[17] (ἐποίησεν αὐτῷ ἐκεῖ οἰκίας), did erect a permanent settlement for himself at Sukkoth. His immediate interest is not in Isaac and Jacob but in Abraham, and in the contrast of the tent-life with the stable, settled existence in a city—the idea which recurs in 12[22] 13[14]. It is a Philonic thought in germ, for Philo (*Leg. Alleg.* 3[27]) declares that the land promised by God to Abraham is a πόλις ἀγαθὴ καὶ πολλὴ καὶ σφόδρα εὐδαίμων, typifying the higher contemplation of divine truth in which alone the soul is at home, or that the soul lives for a while in the body as in a foreign land (*de Somniis*, 1[31]), till God in pity conducts it safe to **μητρόπολις** or immortality. The historical Abraham never dreamed of a **πόλις**, but our author imaginatively allegorizes the promised land once more (cp. 4[3f.]), this time as (12[22]) a celestial πόλις or Jerusalem, like Paul and the apocalyptists. According to later tradition in Judaism, the celestial Jerusalem was shown in a vision to Abraham at the scene of Gn 15[9-21] (Apoc. Bar. 4[4]), or to Jacob at Bethel (Beresh. rabba on Gn 28[17]). **Ἐξεδέχετο γὰρ**—and this showed the steady patience(10[36]) and inward expectation (11[1]) of his faith—**τὴν τοὺς θεμελίους** (τούς, because it was such foundations that the tents lacked) **ἔχουσαν πόλιν**. No doubt there was something promised by God which Abraham expected and did get, in this life; the writer admits that (6[13-15]). But, in a deeper sense, Abraham had yearnings for a higher, spiritual bliss, for heaven as his true home. The fulfilment of the promise about his family was not everything; indeed, his real faith was in an unseen future order of being (11[1]). However, the realization of the one promise about Isaac (6[13-15]) suggests a passing word upon the faith of Sara (vv.[11. 12]).

[1] According to Jubilees 19[16f.] Abraham lived to see Jacob's manhood.

11 *It was by faith that even* (καὶ) *Sara got strength to conceive, bearing a son when she was past the age for it—because she considered she could rely on Him who gave the promise.* 12 *Thus a single man, though* (καὶ ταῦτα) *he was physically impotent, had issue in number "like the stars in heaven, countless as the sand on the seashore."*

This is the first instance of a woman's faith recorded, and she is a married woman. Paul (Ro 4[19f.]) ignores any faith on her part. Philo again praises Sarah, but not for her faith; it is her loyalty and affection for her husband which he singles out for commendation, particularly her magnanimity in the incident of Gn 16[2] (*de Abrahamo*, 42–44). Our author declares that even in spite of her physical condition (καὶ αὐτὴ Σάρρα), she believed God when he promised her a child. The allusion is to the tale of Gn 17[15]–21[7], which the readers are assumed to know, with its stress on the renewal of sexual functions in a woman of her age. This is the point of καὶ αὐτή, not "mere woman that she was" (Chrysostom, Oec., Bengel), nor "in spite of her incredulity" (Bleek), nor "Sara likewise," *i.e.* as well as Abraham (Delitzsch, Hofmann, von Soden, Vaughan), owing to her close connexion with Abraham (Westcott, Seeberg), though the notion of "likewise" is not excluded from the author's meaning, since the husband also was an old man. A gloss (στεῖρα, ἡ στεῖρα, ἡ στεῖρα οὖσα) was soon inserted by D* P, nearly all the versions, and Origen. This is superfluous, however, and probably arose from dittography (ΣΑΡΡΑΣΤΕΙΡΑ). The general idea is plain, though there is a difficulty in δύναμιν ἔλαβεν (*i.e.* from God) εἰς καταβολὴν σπέρματος = εἰς τὸ καταβάλλεσθαι σπέρμα, *i.e.* for Abraham the male to do the work of generation upon her. This is how the text was understood in the versions, *e.g.* the Latin ("in conceptionem seminis"). Probably it was what the writer meant, though the expression is rather awkward, for καταβολὴ σπέρματος means the act of the male; εἰς ὑποδοχὴν σπέρματος would have been the correct words. This has been overcome (*a*) by omitting καὶ αὐτὴ Σάρρα as a gloss, or (*b*) by reading αὐτῇ Σάρρᾳ. (*a*) certainly clears up the verse, leaving Abraham as the subject of both verses (so Field in *Notes on Transl. of NT*, p. 232, and Windisch); (*b*) is read by Michaelis, Storr, Rendall, Hort, and Riggenbach, the latter interpreting it not as "dativus commodi," but = "along with." If the ordinary text is retained, the idea suggested in καὶ αὐτὴ Σάρρα is made explicit in παρὰ καιρὸν ἡλικίας. What rendered such faith hard for her was her physical condition. Philo (*de Abrah.* 22) applies this to both parents (ἤδη γὰρ ὑπερήλικες γεγονότες διὰ μακρὸν γῆρας ἀπέγνωσαν παιδὸς σποράν), and a woman in the period of life described in Gn 18[11. 12] is called by Josephus γύναιον τὴν ἡλικίαν ἤδη προβεβληκός (*Ant.* vii. 8. 4).

Εἰς τὸ τεκνῶσαι (D* P 69. 436. 462. 1245. 1288. 2005 syr[hkl]) after ἔλαβεν is a harmless gloss. The addition of ἔτεκεν (ℵ[c] K L P lat arm) after ἡλικίας was made when the force of καί (=even) before παρὰ καιρόν was missed.

Πιστὸν ἡγήσατο τὸν ἐπαγγειλάμενον (10[23]) is an assertion which shows that the author ignores her sceptical laughter in Gn 18[12]; he does not hesitate (cp. v.[27]) to deal freely with the ancient story in order to make his point, and indeed ignores the equally sceptical attitude of Abraham himself (Gn 17[17]). To be πιστός in this connexion is to be true to one's word, as Cicero observes in the *de Officiis* (i. 7: "fundamentum autem justitiae fides, id est dictorum conventorumque constantia et veritas"). The promise was fulfilled in this life, so that Sara's faith resembles that of Noah (v.[7]). The fulfilment is described in v.[12], where, after διὸ καὶ ἀφ' ἑνὸς (*i.e.* Abraham),[1] ἐγεννήθησαν (p[13] ℵ L Ψ 1739, etc.) is read by some authorities for ἐγενήθησαν (A D K P etc.), though the latter suits the ἀπό in ἀφ' ἑνός rather better. In either case something like τέκνα must be understood. Ἀφ' ἑνός is resumed in καὶ ταῦτα (a *v.l.* in 1 Co 6[8] for the less common καὶ τοῦτο) νενεκρωμένου (in the sense of Ro 4[19]). Gen. r. on Gn 25[1] applies Job 14[7-9] to Abraham, but the plain sense is given in Augustine's comment (*Civit. Dei*, xvi. 28): "sicut aiunt, qui scripserunt interpretationes nominum Hebraeorum, quae his sacris literis continentur, Sara interpretatur princeps mea, Sarra autem uirtus. Unde scriptum est in epistula ad Hebraeos: Fide et ipsa Sarra uirtutem accepit ad emissionem seminis. Ambo enim seniores erant, sicut scriptura testatur; sed illa etiam sterilis et cruore menstruo iam destituta, propter quod iam parere non posset, etiam si sterilis non fuisset. Porro si femina sit prouectioris aetatis, ut ei solita mulierum adhuc fluant, de iuuene parere potest, de seniore non potest; quamuis adhuc possit ille senior, sed de adulescentula gignere, sicut Abraham post mortem Sarrae de Cettura potuit [Gn 25[1]], quia uiuidam eius inuenit aetatem. Hoc ergo est, quod mirum commendat apostolus, et ad hoc dicit Abrahae iam fuisse corpus emortuum, quoniam non ex omni femina, cui adhuc esset aliquod pariendi tempus extremum, generare ipse in illa aetate adhuc posset." This elucidates He 11[11. 12a]. In what follows, the author is quoting from the divine promise in Gn 22[17], a passage much used in later Jewish literature,[2] though this is the only full allusion to it in the NT (cf. Ro 9[27]).

Before passing to the third phase of Abraham's faith, the writer adds (vv.[13-16]) a general reflection on the faith of the patriarchs, an application of vv.[9. 10]. There were promises which

[1] Is 51[2] ἐμβλέψατε εἰς Ἀβραὰμ τὸν πατέρα ὑμῶν . . . ὅτι εἷς ἦν.

[2] The comparison of a vast number to stars and sands is common in Greek and Latin literature; cp. *e.g.* Pindar's *Olymp.* 2[98], and Catullus, 61[202f.].

could not be fulfilled in the present life, and this aspect of faith is now presented.

[13] (*These all died in faith without obtaining the promises; they only saw them far away and hailed them, owning they were "strangers and exiles" upon earth.* [14] *Now people who speak in this way plainly show they are in search of a fatherland.* [15] *If they thought of the land they have left behind, they would have time to go back,* [16] *but they really aspire to the better land in heaven. That is why God is not ashamed to be called their God; he has prepared a City for them.*)

Οὗτοι πάντες (those first mentioned in [9-12], particularly the three patriarchs) died as well as lived **κατὰ πίστιν**, which is substituted here for *πίστει* either as a literary variety of expression, or in order to suggest *πίστις* as the sphere and standard of their characters. The writer argues that the patriarchs already possessed a *πίστις* in eternal life beyond the grave; their very language proves that. **Μὴ κομισάμενοι** explains the *πίστις* in which they died; this is the force of *μή*. All they had was a far-off vision of what had been promised them, but a vision which produced in them a glad belief—**ἰδόντες καὶ ἀσπασάμενοι**, the latter ptc. meaning that they hailed the prospect with delight, sure that it was no mirage. The verb here is less metaphorical than, *e.g.*, in Musonius (ed. Hense), vi. : *τὴν δὲ ζωὴν ὡς τῶν ἀγαθῶν μέγιστον ἀσπαζόμεθα*, or Philo (*ἀγάπησον οὖν ἀρετὰς καὶ ἄσπασαι ψυχῇ τῇ σεαυτοῦ*, *quis rer. div. heres*, 8). Two interesting classical parallels may be cited, from Euripides (*Ion*, 585–587:

> οὐ ταὐτὸν εἶδος φαίνεται τῶν πραγμάτων
> πρόσωθεν ὄντων ἐγγύθεν θ' ὁρωμένων.
> ἐγὼ δὲ τὴν μὲν συμφορὰν ἀσπάζομαι)

and Vergil (*Aen.* 3^{524} "Italiam laeto socii clamore salutant"). Chrysostom prettily but needlessly urges that the whole metaphor is nautical (*τῶν πλεόντων καὶ πόῤῥωθεν ὁρώντων τὰς πόλεις τὰς ποθουμένας, ἃς πρὶν ἢ εἰσελθεῖν εἰς αὐτὰς τῇ προσρήσει λαβόντες αὐτὰς οἰκειοῦνται*).

Κομισάμενοι (p^{13} ℵ* P W 33, etc.) is more likely to be original than a conformation to 10^{36} 11^{39}; the sense is unaffected if we read the more common *λαβόντες* ($ℵ^c$ D K L Ψ 6. 104. 1739, Orig.). The reading of A arm (*προσδεξάμενοι*) makes no sense.

Καὶ ὁμολογήσαντες, for to reside abroad carried with it a certain stigma, according to ancient opinion (cp. e.g. *Ep. Aristeae*, 249, *καλὸν ἐν ἰδίᾳ καὶ ζῆν καὶ τελευτᾶν. ἡ δὲ ξενία τοῖς μὲν πένησι καταφρόνησιν ἐργάζεται, τοῖς δὲ πλουσίοις ὄνειδος, ὡς διὰ κακίαν ἐκπεπτωκόσιν*: Sir 29^{22-28} etc.). The admission, **ὅτι ξένοι καὶ παρεπίδημοί εἰσιν ἐπὶ γῆς**, is a generalization from the Oriental deprecation of Jacob in Gn 47^{9} (*εἶπεν Ἰακὼβ τῷ Φαραώ, αἱ ἡμέραι τῶν ἐτῶν τῆς ζωῆς μου ἃς παροικῶ κτλ.*), and the similar confession of Abraham in Gn 23^{4} to the sons of Heth, *πάροικος* καὶ παρεπίδημος ἐγώ εἰμι μεθ' ὑμῶν. The ἐπὶ γῆς is a homiletic touch, as in Ps 119[19] (πάροικός εἰμι ἐν τῇ γῇ). In both cases this ὁμολογία τῆς ἐλπίδος (10[23]) is made before outsiders, and the words ἐπὶ τῆς γῆς start the inference (vv.[14-16a]) that the true home of these confessors was in heaven. Such a mystical significance of **ξένοι καὶ παρεπίδημοι**, which had already been voiced in the psalter, is richly and romantically developed by Philo, but it never became prominent in primitive Christianity. Paul's nearest approach to it is worded differently (Phil 3[20], where τὸ πολίτευμα corresponds to πατρίς here). In Eph 2[12-19], indeed, Christians are no longer ξένοι καὶ πάροικοι, for these terms are applied literally to pagans out of connexion with the chosen People of God. The only parallel to the thought of Hebrews is in 1 P, where Christians are παρεπιδήμοι (1[1]) and παροίκοι καὶ παρεπιδήμοι (2[11]). The term ξένοι is used here as a synonym for πάροικοι, which (cp. Eph 2[12. 19]) would be specially intelligible to Gentile Christians. Παρεπίδημος only occurs in the LXX in Gn 23[4], Ps 39[13]; in the Egyptian papyri παρεπιδημοῦντες (consistentes) denotes foreigners who settled and acquired a domicile in townships or cities like Alexandria (*GCP.* i. 40, 55; cp. A. Peyron's *Papyri graeci R. Taur. Musei Aegyptii*, 8[13] τῶν παρεπιδημοῦντων καὶ [κα]τοικούντων ἐ[ν] [τ]αύται[ς] ξένων), and for ξένοι = peregrini, *Ep. Arist.* 109 f. The use of such metaphorical terms became fairly common in the moral vocabulary of the age, quite apart from the OT, *e.g.* Marcus Aurelius, ii. 17 (ὁ δὲ βιὸς πόλεμος καὶ ξένου ἐπιδημία). A similar symbolism recurs in the argument of Epictetus (ii. 23, 36 f.) against the prevalent idea that logic, style, and eloquence are the end of philosophy: οἷον εἴ τις ἀπιὼν εἰς τὴν πατρίδα τὴν ἑαυτοῦ καὶ διοδεύων πανδοκεῖον καλὸν ἀρέσαντος αὐτῷ τοῦ πανδοκείου καταμένοι ἐν τῷ πανδοκείῳ. ἄνθρωπε, ἐπελάθου σου τῆς προθέσεως· οὐκ εἰς τοῦτο ὥδευες, ἀλλὰ διὰ τούτου . . . τὸ δὲ προκείμενον ἐκεῖνο· εἰς τὴν πατρίδα ἐπανελθεῖν. In a more specifically religious sense, it is expressed in the saying of Anaxagoras quoted by Diogenes Laertius (ii. 3. 7, πρὸς τὸν εἰπόντα, "οὐδέν σοι μέλει τῆς πατρίδος," "εὐφήμει" ἔφη, "ἔμοι γὰρ καὶ σφόδρα μέλει τῆς πατρίδος," δείξας τὸν οὐρανόν). According to Philo, the confession that they were strangers and pilgrims meant that the soul in this world longed to return to its pre-existent state in the eternal order, and could never feel at home among things material. So, e.g., *de confus. ling.* 17, διὰ τοῦτο οἱ κατὰ Μωυσῆν σοφοὶ πάντες εἰσάγονται "παροικοῦντες·" αἱ γὰρ τούτων ψυχαὶ στέλλονται μὲν ἀποικίαν οὐδέποτε τὴν ἐξ οὐρανοῦ, εἰώθασι δὲ ἕνεκα τοῦ φιλοθεάμονος καὶ φιλομαθοῦς εἰς τὴν περίγειον φύσιν ἀποδημεῖν . . . ἐπανέρχονται ἐκεῖσε πάλιν, ὅθεν ὡρμήθησαν τὸ πρῶτον, πατρίδα μὲν τὸν οὐράνιον χῶρον ἐν ᾧ πολιτεύονται, ξένην δὲ τὸν περίγειον ἐν ᾧ παρῴκησαν νομίζουσαι κτλ. In *Cherub.* 33, 34, commenting on πάροικοι in Lv 25[23], he argues that this is the real position of all wise souls towards God, since each of us is a stranger and sojourner in the foreign city of the world where God has for a time placed us till we return to Him.

The metaphor had been applied, in a derogatory sense, by Sallust to the lazy and sensual men who never know what real life means, but who pass through it heedlessly: "many human beings, given over to sensuality and sloth ('ventri atque somno'), uneducated, and uncultured, have gone through life like travellers" ("vitam sicuti peregrinantes transiere," *Catil.* 2).

Such a confession proves (v.[14]) that the men in question are not satisfied with the present outward order of things; **ἐμφανίζουσιν** (Esth 2[22] καὶ αὐτὴ ἐνεφάνισεν τῷ βασιλεῖ τὰ τῆς ἐπιβουλῆς: Ac 23[15], *OGIS.* (iii A.D.) 42[9], *Syll.* 226[85] τήν τε παρουσίαν ἐμφανισάντων τοῦ βασίλεως), they thus avow or affirm, **ὅτι πατρίδα ἐπιζητοῦσιν** (Valckenaer's conjecture, ἔτι ζητοῦσι, is ingenious but needless, cp. 13[14]). For **πάτρις** in a mystical sense, compare Philo, *de Agric.* 14, commenting on Gn 47[4]): τῷ γὰρ ὄντι πᾶσα ψυχὴ σοφοῦ πατρίδα μὲν οὐρανόν, ξένην δὲ γῆν ἔλαχε, καὶ νομίζει τὸν μὲν σοφίας οἶκον ἴδιον, τὸν δὲ σώματος ὀθνεῖον, ᾧ καὶ παρεπιδημεῖν οἴεται. Here it is "heaven, the heart's true home." The creditable feature in this kind of life was that these men had deliberately chosen it.[1] Had they liked, they might have taken another and a less exacting line (v.[15]). **Εἰ μὲν** (as in 8[4]) **ἐμνημόνευον** (referring to the continuous past) κτλ. The μνημονεύουσιν of ℵ* D* was due to the influence of the preceding presents, just as ἐμνημόνευσαν (33. 104. 216 Cosm.) to the influence of ἐξέβησαν, which in turn was smoothed out into the usual NT term ἐξῆλθον (ℵ^c D K L Ψ 436. 919. 1288. 1739). Μνημόνευειν here has the sense of "giving a thought to," as in Jos. *Ant.* vi. 37, οὔτε τροφῆς ἐμνημόνευσεν οὔθ' ὕπνου, and below in v.[22]. Time (as Ac 24[25]), as elsewhere in Hebrews, rather than opportunity (1 Mac 15[34] ἡμεῖς δὲ καιρὸν ἔχοντες ἀντεχόμεθα τῆς κληρονομίας ἡμῶν καὶ τῶν πατέρων ἡμῶν), is the idea of **εἶχον ἂν καιρὸν, καιρός** taking an infinitive **ἀνακάμψαι** (so Codex A in Jg 11[39] καὶ ἀνεκάμψεν πρὸς τὸν πατέρα αὐτῆς, for the ἀπέστρεψεν of B), as in Eurip. *Rhesus*, 10 (καιρὸς γὰρ ἀκοῦσαι).

Philo remarks of Abraham: τίς δ' οὐκ ἂν μετατραπόμενος παλινδρόμησεν οἴκαδε, βραχέα μὲν φροντίσας τῶν μελλουσῶν ἐλπίδων, τὴν δὲ παροῦσαν ἀπορίαν σπεύδων ἐκφυγεῖν (*de Abrahamo*, 18).

> "Sometimes he wished his aims had been
> To gather gain like other men;
> Then thanked his God he'd traced his track
> Too far for wish to drag him back."
> (THOMAS HARDY, *The Two Men.*)

On the contrary (v.[16]), so far from that, they held on, the writer

[1] Cp. *Test. Job* xxxiii. (οὕτω κἀγὼ ἡγησάμην τὰ ἐμά, ἀντ' οὐδένος πρὸς ἐκείνην τὴν πόλιν περὶ ἧς λελάληκέν μοι ὁ ἄγγελος).

adds; **νῦν δέ** (logical, as in 8^6, not temporal) **κρείττονος ὀρέγονται, τοῦτ' ἔστιν ἐπουρανίου** (so God is described in 2 Mac 3^{39} as *ὁ τὴν κατοικίαν ἐπουράνιον ἔχων*). **Διὸ οὐκ ἐπαισχύνεται** (compare 2^{11}) **αὐτοὺς ὁ θεὸς "θεὸς" ἐπικαλεῖσθαι** (epexegetic infinitive) "**αὐτῶν**," referring to Ex 3^6, *Ἐγώ εἰμι . . . θεὸς Ἀβραὰμ καὶ θεὸς Ἰσαὰκ καὶ θεὸς Ἰακώβ*, which the writer[1] interprets (cp. Mk $12^{26.27}$) as an assurance of immortality. Their hope of a *πατρίς* or heavenly home was no illusion; it was because God had such a *πόλις* (v.[10]) all ready for them that he could call himself their God. He might have been ashamed to call himself such, had he not made this provision for their needs and prepared this reward for their faith (*ἡτοίμασεν*, cp. Mt 23^{34}).

The third phase of the faith of Abraham (vv.[17-19]) is now chronicled, followed by three instances of faith at the end of life, in Isaac, Jacob, and Joseph (vv.[20-22]).

17 *It was by faith* (πίστει), "*when Abraham was put to the test, that he sacrificed Isaac*"; *he was ready to sacrifice* "*his only son*," *although he had received the promises*, 18 *and had been told* (πρὸς ὅν, as 5^5) *that* (ὅτι recitative) "*it is through Isaac* (not Ishmael) *that your offspring shall be reckoned*"— 19 *for he considered God was able even to raise men from the dead. Hence* (ὅθεν, causal) *he did get him back, by what was a parable of the resurrection.* 20 *It was by faith that Isaac blessed Jacob and Esau in connection with the future.* 21 *It was by faith that, when Jacob was dying* (ἀποθνήσκων), *he blessed each of the sons of Joseph*, "*bending in prayer over the head of his staff.*" 22 *It was by faith that Joseph at his end* (τελευτῶν only here) *thought about the exodus of the sons of Israel, and gave orders about his own bones.*

The supreme test of Abraham's **πίστις** is found in the story of Gn 22^{1-18}, which Jewish tradition always reckoned as the last and sorest of his ten trials (*Pirke Aboth* 5^4). It is cited in 4 Mac 16^{18-20} as a classical example of **ὑπομονή** (*ὀφείλετε πάντα πόνον ὑπομένειν διὰ τὸν θεόν, δι' ὃν καὶ ὁ πατὴρ ἡμῶν Ἀβραὰμ ἔσπευδεν τὸν ἐθνοπάτορα υἱὸν σφαγιάσαι Ἰσαάκ κτλ.*). In v.[17] the perfect tense **προσενήνοχεν** may mean "the ideally accomplished sacrifice, as permanently recorded in scripture" (Moulton, so *Diat.* 2751); but it is more likely to be aoristic (cp. Simcox, *Lang. of NT.*, pp. 104, 126). **Πειραζόμενος** echoes Gn 22^1 (*ὁ θεὸς ἐπείραζεν τὸν Ἀβραάμ*). **Καὶ** (epexegetic) **τὸν μονογενῆ** (a Lucan use of the term in the NT)[2] **προσέφερεν** (conative imperfect of interrupted action, like *ἐκάλουν* in Lk 1^{59}) **ὁ τὰς ἐπαγγελίας ἀναδεξάμενος**, *i.e.* the promises of a son, of a numerous line of descendants (v.[12]), and of a blessing thus coming to all nations.

[1] Origen (*Joh.* ii. 17): *μεγάλη γὰρ δωρεὰ τοῖς πατριάρχαις τὸ τὸν θεὸν ἀντὶ ὀνόματος προσάψαι τὴν ἐκείνων ὀνομασίαν τῇ* >*θεὸς*< *ἰδίᾳ αὐτοῦ προσηγορίᾳ.*

[2] The LXX of Gn 22^2 reads *τὸν ἀγαπητόν*, but perhaps the writer of *Πρὸς Ἑβραίους* read a text like that underlying Aquila (*τὸν μονογενῆ*), Josephus (*τὸν μονογενῆ*, *Ant.* i. 3. 1), and Symmachus (*τὸν μόνον*). *Μονογενής* and *ἀγαπητός*, as applied to a son, tended to shade into one another. Philo reads *ἀγαπητὸς καὶ μόνος* (*quod deus immut.* 4, etc.).

This is made explicit in v.[18], with its quotation from Gn 21[12]. For ἀναδέχομαι in the sense of "secure," see the line from Sophocles' "Ichneutae," in *Oxyrh. Papyri*, vii. 25 (ὃν Φοῖβος ὑμῖν εἶπε κ[ά]νεδέξατο).

In v.[19] **λογισάμενος** (as Ro 8[18] etc.) explains why he had the courage to sacrifice Isaac, although the action seemed certain to wreck the fulfilment of what God had promised him. He held **ὅτι καὶ ἐκ νεκρῶν ἐγείρειν** (weakened into ἐγεῖραι by A P, etc.) **δυνατός** (Dan 3[17] ὅς ἐστι δυνατὸς ἐξελέσθαι ἡμᾶς κτλ., and Ro 4[21]) *sc.* ἔστιν **ὁ θεός**. Abraham, says Philo (*de Abrahamo*, 22), πάντα ᾔδει θεῷ δυνατὰ σχεδὸν ἐξ ἔτι σπαργάνων τουτὶ τὸ δόγμα προμαθοῦσα. Later (32) he speaks of this sacrifice as the most outstanding action in Abraham's life—ὀλίγου γὰρ δέω φάναι πάσας ὅσαι θεοφιλεῖς ὑπερβάλλει. It was "a complicated and brilliant act of faith" (A. B. Davidson), for God seemed to contradict God, and the command ran counter to the highest human affection (Wis 10[6] σοφία . . . ἐπὶ τέκνου σπλάγχνοις ἰσχυρὸν ἐφύλαξεν). As Chrysostom put it, this was the special trial, τὰ γὰρ τοῦ θεοῦ ἐδόκει τοῖς τοῦ θεοῦ μάχεσθαι, καὶ πίστις ἐμάχετο πίστει, καὶ πρόσταγμα ἐπαγγελίᾳ. Hence (**ὅθεν**, in return for this superb faith) **ἐκομίσατο**, he did recover him (κομίζεσθαι, as in Gn 38[20] etc., of getting back what belongs to you),[1] in a way that prefigured the resurrection (κρείττονος ἀναστάσεως, v.[35]). Such is the meaning of **ἐν παραβολῇ** (cp. 9[9]). Isaac's restoration was to Abraham a sort[2] of resurrection (v.[35a] "quaedam resurrectionis fuit species, quod subito liberatus fuit ex media morte," Calvin). Ἐν παραβολῇ has been taken sometimes in two other ways. (*a*) = παραβολῶς, *i.e.* beyond all expectation, almost παραδόξως, παρ' ἐλπίδα(s), or in a desperate peril, as Polybius says of Hannibal (i. 23. 7, ἀνελπίστως καὶ παραβόλως αὐτὸς ἐν τῇ σκάφῃ διέφυγε). This is at any rate less far-fetched than—(*b*) "whence he had originally got him, figuratively-speaking," as if the allusion was to νενεκρωμένου (in v.[12])! Against (*a*) is the fact that παραβολή never occurs in this sense.

Augustine's comment is (*Civit. Dei*, xvi. 32): "non haesitauit, quod sibi reddi poterat immolatus, qui dari potuit non speratus. Sic intellectum est et in epistula ad Hebraeos, et sic expositum [He 11[17-19]] . . . cuius similitudinem, nisi illius unde dicit apostolus: Qui proprio filio non pepercit, sed pro nobis omnibus tradidit eum?" He makes Isaac carrying the wood a type of Christ carrying his cross, and the ram caught in the thicket typical of Christ crowned with thorns. According to the later Jewish tradition (*Pirqe R. Eliezer*, 31), Isaac's soul, which had left his body as his father's sword

---

[1] Josephus (*Ant.* i. 13. 4) describes the father and son as παρ' ἐλπίδας ἑαυτοὺς κεκομισμένοι. Philo (*de Josepho*, 35, τὸ κομίσασθαι τὸν ἀδελφόν) has the same usage.

[2] Aelian (*Var. Hist.* iii. 33) speaks of Satyrus the flautist, τρόπον τινὰ τὴν τέχνην ἐκφαυλίζων παραβολῇ τῇ πρὸς φιλοσοφίαν.

was falling, returned at the words, "Lay not thy hand on the lad"; thus Abraham and Isaac "learned that God would raise the dead."

The next three instances are of **πίστις** as *ὑπόστασις ἐλπιζομένων*, the hope being one to be realized in the destiny of the race (vv.[20-22]).

The solitary instance of **πίστις** in Isaac (v.[20]) is that mentioned in Gn 27[28. 29. 39. 40], a faith which (11[1]) anticipated a future for his two sons. **Εὐλόγησεν**, of one man blessing another, as in 7[1f.] In **καὶ περὶ μελλόντων** (*sc. πραγμάτων*), where *μέλλειν* refers to a future in this world, the *καί* simply[1] emphasizes *περὶ μελλόντων* **εὐλόγησεν**, and the whole phrase goes with *εὐλόγησεν*, not with *πίστει*. The very fact that he blessed his two sons proved that he believed the divine promises to them would be realized in the future. The next two instances of faith are taken from death-beds; it is faith, not in personal immortality, but in the continuance of the chosen race. In v.[21] the writer quotes from Gn 47[31] *καὶ προσεκύνησεν Ἰσραὴλ ἐπὶ τὸ ἄκρον τῆς ῥάβδου αὐτοῦ*, where the LXX by mistake has read הַמַּטֶּה (staff) instead of הַמִּטָּה (bed), and the incident is loosely transferred to the later situation (Gn 48[9f.]), when Jacob blessed the two sons of Joseph. Supporting himself on[2] his staff, he bowed reverently before God, as he blessed the lads. (In the Ep. Barnabas 13[4-6], the writer interprets Jacob's preference for the younger son as a proof that Christians, not Jews, were the real heirs of God's blessing!) In v.[22] the argument draws upon Gn 50[24. 25] (Ex 13[19], Jos 24[32]), where Joseph makes the Israelites swear to remove his remains from Egypt to the promised land, so confident was he that God's promise to the people would one day be fulfilled. **Τελευτῶν** (Gn 50[26] *καὶ ἐτελεύτησεν Ἰωσήφ*) **περὶ τῆς ἐξόδου** (only here in this sense in NT) **τῶν υἱῶν Ἰσραὴλ ἐμνημόνευσε** (called to mind, as v.[15]) **καὶ περὶ τῶν ὀστέων** (uncontracted form as in LXX and Mt 23[27], Lk 24[39]; cp. Crönert, *Mem. Graeca Hercul.* 166[4]) **αὐτοῦ ἐνετείλατο.** Joseph's faith also was shown in his conviction of the future promised by God to Israel, but it found a practical expression in the instructions about conveying his mummy out of Egypt (Sir 49[18] *καὶ τὰ ὀστᾶ αὐτοῦ ἐπεσκέπησαν*).

The ninth example of **πίστις** is Moses, of whom almost as much is made as of Abraham. Five instances of faith are mentioned in connexion with his career (vv.[23-29]).

[23] *It was by faith that Moses was "hidden for three months"* (*τρίμηνον, sc. χρόνον*) *after birth by his parents, because "they saw" the child was*

---

[1] To suggest that it means "even" is flat for a blessing, *ex hypothesi*, referred to the future. Its omission (by א K L P, the eastern versions, etc.) is more easily explained than its insertion.

[2] 1 K 1[47] *προσεκύνησεν ὁ βασιλεὺς ἐπὶ τὴν κοίτην*, *ἐπί* has the same local sense.

"beautiful" (Ac 7[20]), *and had no fear of the royal decree.* [24] *It was by faith that Moses refused, "when he had grown up," to be called the son of Pharaoh's daughter;* [25] *ill-treatment with God's people he preferred to the passing pleasures of sin,* [26] *considering obloquy with the messiah to be richer wealth than all Egypt's treasures—for he had an eye to the Reward.* [27] *It was by faith that he left Egypt, not from any fear of the king's wrath; like one who saw the King Invisible, he never flinched.* [28] *It was by faith that he celebrated "the passover" and performed the sprinkling by blood, so that "the destroying angel"* (cf. 1 Co 10[10]) *might not touch Israel's firstborn.* [29] *It was by faith that they crossed the Red Sea* (Ac 7[36]) *like dry land—and when the Egyptians attempted it, they were drowned.*

Moses (v.[23]) owed the preservation of his life as an infant to the courageous **πίστις** of his parents (**πατέρων** = γονεῖς, *parentes*, like *patres* in Ovid's *Metam.* 4[61], and Plato's *Leges*, vi. 772 E, ἀγαθῶν πατέρων φύντι). The writer quotes from Ex 2[2. 3], adding that, as the result of their faith, they had no fear of the royal edict (διάταγμα as in Jos. *Ant.* xvi. 16. 5; Wis 11[7] etc.). This is the main point of their πίστις. On ἀστεῖον see Philo's *vit. Mos.* i. 3: γεννηθεὶς οὖν ὁ παῖς εὐθὺς ὄψιν ἐνέφαινεν ἀστειοτέραν ἢ κατ' ἰδιώτην, ὡς καὶ τῶν τοῦ τυράννου κηρυγμάτων, ἐφ' ὅσον οἷόν τε ἦν, τοὺς γονεῖς ἀλογῆσαι). The Hebrew text makes the mother act alone, but the LXX gives the credit to both parents; and this tradition is followed by Philo and Josephus (*Ant.* ii. 9. 4), as by our author.

The parents of Moses are the first anonymous people in the roll-call of faith's representatives. Calvin rather severely ranks their faith on a lower level, because the parents of Moses were moved by the external appearance of their child, and because they ought to have brought him up themselves ("notandum est fidem quae hîc laudatur ualde fuisse imbecillam. Nam quum posthabito mortis suae metu Mosen deberent educare, eum exponunt. Patet igitur illorum fidem breui non tantum uacillasse sed fuisse collapsam"). Still, he reflects that this is after all an encouragement, since it proves that even weak faith is not despised by God. Chrysostom's comment is kinder; the writer, he thinks, means to afford additional encouragement to his readers by adducing not only heroes, but commonplace people as examples of faith (ἀσήμων, ἀνωνύμων).

Another (7[2]) gloss has been inserted here, after v.[23], by D* 1827 and nearly all the MSS of the Latin versions, viz. πίστει μέγας γενόμενος Μωυσῆς ἀνεῖλεν τὸν Αἰγύπτιον κατανοῶν τὴν ταπείνωσιν τῶν ἀδελφῶν αὐτοῦ, a homiletical application of Ex 2[11. 12] (used in Ac 7[23f.]).

The second item of faith (v.[24]) is the first individual proof by Moses himself. Josephus (*Ant.* ii. 9. 7) makes Moses refuse the Pharaoh's crown when a baby. The Pharaoh's daughter placed the child in her father's arms; he took it, pressed it to his bosom, and to please his daughter graciously put the crown upon its head. But the child threw it to the ground and stamped on it. Which seemed ominous to the king! The writer of Hebrews avoids such fancies, and simply summarizes Ex 2[11f.], where Moses **μέγας γενόμενος** (from Ex 2[11]; *i.e.*, as Calvin points out, when his refusal could not be set down to childish ignorance of the world, nor to youthful impetuousness) **ἠρνήσατο** (with infinitive as in Wis 12^{27} 16^{16} 17^{10}) **λέγεσθαι υἱὸς θυγατρὸς Φαραώ.** His religious motive in declining the title and position of son to an Egyptian princess (Jub 47^{9}) is now given (v.^{25}); **μᾶλλον ἑλόμενος** (for the construction and idea, cp. *OGIS.* 669^{15} *μᾶλλον τὴν τῶν προτέρων ἐπάρχων αἰώνιον συνήθειαν φυλάσσων ἢ<ι> τὴν πρόσκαιρόν τινος ἀδικίαν μειμησάμενος*) **συγκακουχεῖσθαι** (a new compound, unknown to the LXX) **τῷ λαῷ τοῦ θεοῦ ἢ πρόσκαιρον** (a non-LXX term [1] which first occurs in 4 Mac $15^{2.8.23}$, and passed into the early Christian vocabulary as an antithesis to *αἰώνιος*) **ἔχειν ἁμαρτίας ἀπόλαυσιν.** The *ἁμαρτία* is the sin which he would have committed in proving disloyal to the People of God; that might have been pleasant for the time being, but **πίστις** looks to higher and lasting issues (10^{34} 11^{1}). It would have been "sin" for him to choose a high political career at court, the "sin" of apostasy; he did what others in their own way had done afterwards (10^{35}, cp. 13^{3}).

For **ἀπόλαυσις** see Antipater of Tarsus (Stob. *Florileg.* lxvii. 25): *τὸν δ' ἤθεον <βίον>, ἐξουσίαν διδόντα πρὸς ἀκολασίαν καὶ ποικίλων ἡδονῶν ἀπόλαυσιν ἀγεννῶν καὶ μικροχαρῶν, ἰσόθεον νομίζουσι,* and 4 Mac 5^{8}, where the tyrant taunts the conscientious Jews, *καὶ γὰρ ἀνόητον τοῦτο τὸ μὴ ἀπολαύειν τῶν χωρὶς ὀνείδους ἡδέων.* Philo (*vit. Mos.* i. 6: *γενόμενός τε διαφερόντως ἀσκητὴς ὀλιγοδεείας καὶ τὸν ἁβροδίαιτον βίον ὡς οὐδεὶς ἕτερος χλευάσας—ψυχῇ γὰρ ἐπόθει μόνῃ ζῆν, οὐ σώματι*) praises the asceticism of Moses in the palace of the Pharaoh, but gives an interpretation of his reward which is lower than that of our author; he declares (i. 27) that as Moses renounced the high position of authority which he might have enjoyed in Egypt (*ἐπειδὴ γὰρ τὴν Αἰγύπτου κατέλιπεν ἡγεμονίαν, θυγατριδοῦς τοῦ τότε βασιλεύοντος ὤν*), because he disapproved of the local injustice, God rewarded him with authority over a greater nation.

In v.^{26} the reason for this renunciation of the world is explained. **Μείζονα πλοῦτον ἡγησάμενος** (cp. v.^{11} and *λογισάμενος* in v.^{19}) **τῶν Αἰγύπτου θησαυρῶν τὸν ὀνειδισμὸν τοῦ Χριστοῦ** (as involved in *συγκακουχεῖσθαι τῷ λαῷ τοῦ θεοῦ*). This is one of the writer's dinting phrases. There is a special obloquy in being connected with Christ. It is one of the things which Christians have to face to-day (13^{13}), and, the writer argues, it has always been so; Moses himself, the leader of God's people at the first, showed his *πίστις* by deliberately meeting it. The obloquy was part of the human experience of Jesus himself (12^{2} 13^{12}), but the point here in **τὸν ὀνειδισμὸν τοῦ Χριστοῦ** is that, by identifying himself with God's people in Egypt, Moses encountered the same *ὀνειδισμός* as their very messiah afterwards was to endure. He thus faced what the writer, from his own standpoint, does not hesitate to call *τὸν ὀνειδισμὸν τοῦ Χριστοῦ.* Whether he had in mind anything further, *e.g.* the idea that *ὁ Χριστός* here

[1] It recurs in an edict of Caracalla (215 A.D.), quoted by Mitteis-Wilcken, i. 2. 39.

means the pre-incarnate Logos, as though a mystical sense like that of 1 Co 10[4] underlay the words, is uncertain and rather unlikely, though the idea that Christ was suffering in the person of the Israelites, or that they represented him, might be regarded as justified by the language, *e.g.*, of Ps 89[51] (τοῦ ὀνειδισμοῦ τῶν δούλων σου . . . οὗ ὠνείδισαν τὸ ἀντάλλαγμα τοῦ Χριστοῦ σου). The experiences of ingratitude and insulting treatment which Moses suffered at the hands of Israel illustrate Chrysostom's definition of τὸν ὀνειδισμὸν τοῦ Χριστοῦ: τὸ μέχρι τέλους καὶ ἐσχάτης ἀναπνοῆς πάσχειν κακῶς . . . τοῦτο ἐστιν ὀνειδισμὸς τοῦ Χριστοῦ, ὅταν τις παρ' ὧν εὐεργετεῖ ὀνειδίζηται (citing Mt 27[40]). The basis of this estimate of life is now given: **ἀπέβλεπεν γὰρ εἰς τὴν μισθαποδοσίαν**, as the writer desired his readers to do (10[35] 11[6]). Ἀποβλέπειν εἰς is a common phrase for keeping one's eye upon, having regard to, *e.g.* Theophrastus, ii. 10, καὶ εἰς ἐκεῖνον ἀποβλέπων: Josephus, *Bell. Jud.* ii. 15. 1, ὁ μὲν . . . εἰς μόνον τὸ λυσιτελὲς τὸ ἐκ τῶν ἁρπαγῶν ἀποβλέπων, παρήκουσεν. Mr. Starkie, in his note on Arist. *Acharn.* 32, suggests that ἀποβλέπειν, which is common in the comic poets and is also a philosophical term (*e.g.* Plato's *Phaedo*, 115 C; *Phaedrus*, 234 D), "was used like 'to prescind' in English," *i.e.* to fix one's gaze on a single object by withdrawing it from everything else.

The third act of faith in his life (v.[27]) is his withdrawal from Egypt to Midian (Ex 2[14f.] = Ac 7[29]). In **μὴ φοβηθεὶς τὸν θυμὸν τοῦ βασιλέως** the author ignores the statement of the OT that Moses did fly from Egypt, in terror of being punished by the king for having murdered the Egyptian (ὄργην ἀμείλικτον βασιλέως ἀποδιδράσκων, Philo, *de vit. Mos.* i. 9). Josephus in his own way also (*Ant.* ii. 10. 1) eliminates the motive of fear. Our author declares that if Moses did retreat from Egypt, it was from no fear of Pharaoh, but in the faith that God had a future and a mission for him still; he had as little fear of Pharaoh as his parents had had, **τὸν γὰρ ἀόρατον** (*sc.* βασιλέα) **ὡς ὁρῶν ἐκαρτέρησεν** (cp. Sir 2[2] εὔθυνον τὴν καρδίαν σου καὶ καρτέρησον). "The courage to abandon work on which one's heart is set, and accept inaction cheerfully as the will of God, is of the rarest and highest kind, and can be created and sustained only by the clearest spiritual vision" (Peake). The language and thought are illustrated by Epict. ii. 16. 45–46: ἐκ τῆς διανοίας ἔκβαλε . . . λύπην, φόβον, ἐπιθυμίαν, φθόνον, ἐπιχαιρεκακίαν, φιλαργυρίαν, μαλακίαν, ἀκρασίαν. Ταῦτα δ' οὐκ ἔστιν ἄλλως ἐκβαλεῖν, εἰ μὴ πρὸς μόνον τὸν θεὸν ἀποβλέποντα, ἐκείνῳ μόνῳ προσπεπονθότα, τοῖς ἐκείνου προστάγμασι καθωσιωμένον. The phrase ὡς ὁρῶν means the inward vision where, as Marcus Aurelius observes (x. 26), ὁρῶμεν, οὐχὶ τοῖς ὀφθαλμοῖς, ἀλλ' οὐχ ἧττον ἐναργῶς. In the *de Mundo*, 399*a*, God is described as ἀόρατος ὢν ἄλλῳ πλὴν λογισμῷ. Philo had already singled out this trait in Moses, e.g. *de mutat. nomin.* 2: Μωυσῆς ὁ τῆς ἀειδοῦς φύσεως θεατὴς καὶ θεόπτης—εἰς γὰρ τὸν γνόφον φασὶν αὐτὸν οἱ θεῖοι χρησμοὶ εἰσελθεῖν (Ex 20^{21}), τὴν ἀόρατον καὶ ἀσώματον οὐσίαν αἰνιττόμενοι. In *vit. Mos.* i. 15 he declares that the Pharaoh had no notion of any invisible God (μηδένα τὸ παράπαν νοητὸν θεὸν ἔξω τῶν ὁρατῶν νομίζων), and later on, commenting on Ex 20^{21} (i. 28), he adds that Moses entered the darkness, τουτέστιν εἰς τὴν ἀειδῆ καὶ ἀόρατον καὶ ἀσώματον τῶν ὄντων παραδειγματικὴν οὐσίαν, τὰ ἀθέατα φύσει θνητῇ κατανοῶν.

On μὴ φοβηθεὶς τὸν θυμὸν τοῦ βασιλέως, it may be noted that the Stoics took the prudential line of arguing that one ought not needlessly to provoke a tyrant: "sapiens nunquam potentium iras provocabit, immo declinabit, non aliter quam in navigando procellam" (Seneca, *Ep.* xiv. 7). Various attempts have been made to explain away the contradiction between this statement and that of Ex 2^{14}. (*a*) Some think they are not irreconcilable; "so far as his life was concerned, he feared, but in a higher region he had no fear" (A. B. Davidson), *i.e.* he was certain God would ultimately intervene to thwart Pharaoh, and so took precautions to save his own life in the interest of the cause. This is rather artificial, however, though maintained by some good critics like Lünemann. (*b*) Or, the θυμός may be not anger at the murder of the Egyptian, but the resentment of Moses' action in refusing a court position and withdrawing from Egypt (Vaughan, Dods, Delitzsch, etc.). (*c*) A more favourite method is to deny that the writer is alluding to Ex $2^{14.\,15}$ at all, and to refer the passage to the real Exodus later (so Calvin, Bleek, Westcott, Seeberg, and many other edd.); but this is to anticipate v.[28], and the Israelites were ordered out of Egypt by Pharaoh, not exposed to any anger of his.

The fourth act of faith (v.[28]) is his obedience to the divine orders of Ex 12^{12-48} (cp. Wis 18^{5-9}), which proved that he believed, in spite of appearances, that God had protection and a future for the People. Πεποίηκεν is another aoristic perfect; πρόσχυσις is not a LXX term, and θίγγανω (θίγῃ) only occurs in LXX in Ex 19^{13} (= Heb 12^{20}). As θίγγανω may take a genitive (12^{20}) as well as an accusative, ὀλοθρεύων might go with πρωτότοκα (*i.e.* of the Egyptians) and θίγῃ with αὐτῶν (the Israelites). Note the alliteration in πίστει πεπ. πάσχα . . . πρόσχυσιν The ἵνα μή clause explains τὴν πρόσχυσιν τοῦ αἵματος.

By one Old Latin, or at any rate a non-Vulgate, text of this passage, in Codex Harleianus (ed. E. S. Buchanan, *Sacred Latin Texts*, i., 1912), a gloss is inserted at this point: "fide praedaverunt Aegyptios exeuntes" (Ex $12^{35.\,36}$), which was evidently known to Sedulius Scotus (Migne, ciii. 268 C), who quotes it as "fide praedaverunt Aegyptios, quia crediderunt se iterum in Aegyptum non reversuros."

The fifth act of faith (v.[29]) is the crossing of the Red Sea (Ex $14^{16f.}$). Strictly speaking, this is an act of faith on the part of the Israelites; the διέβησαν depends on, for its subject, the αὐτῶν of v.[28]. But those who crossed were οἱ ἐξελθόντες ἐξ Αἰγύπτου διὰ Μωϋσέως (3^{16}), and the action is the direct sequel to that of v.[28], though Moses is now included in the People. διὰ ξηρᾶς γῆς is from Ex 14^{29}; διαβαίνειν goes with the genitive as well as with the accusative. The Israelites took a risk, in obedience to God's order, and so proved their πίστις. But there are some things which are possible only to faith. Ἧς (*i.e.* ἐρυθρὰ θάλασση) πεῖραν λαβόντες οἱ Αἰγύπτιοι κατεπόθησαν (from Ex 15^4 κατεπόθησαν ἐν ἐρυθρᾷ θαλάσσῃ, B), *i.e.* the Egyptians tried it and were swallowed up in the sea. Here πεῖραν λαμβάνειν is a classical phrase for (*a*) making an attempt, almost in the sense of testing or risking. They "ventured on" (cp. Dt 28^{56} ἡ τρυφερά, ἧς οὐχὶ πεῖραν ἔλαβεν ὁ ποὺς αὐτῆς βαίνειν ἐπὶ τῆς γῆς), or tried it (cp. Jos. *Ant.* 8. 6. 5, σοφίας βουλομένη λαβεῖν πεῖραν, etc.). The other meaning is that (*b*) of getting experience (so in v.[36]), which is often the sad result of (*a*); so, *e.g.*, Demosth. *in Aristocratem*, 131, λαβὼν ἔργῳ τῆς ἐκείνου φιλίας πεῖραν. The writer ignores the legendary embroidery of Philo (*vit. Mos.* iii. 34, ὡς ἐπὶ ξηρᾶς ἀτραποῦ καὶ λιθώδους ἐδάφους—ἐκραυρώθη γὰρ ἡ ψάμμος καὶ ἡ σπορὰς αὐτῆς οὐσία συμφῦσα ἡνώθη).

Two more instances of faith are specially cited, both in connexion with the fall of Jericho (vv.[30. 31]). During the interval between the Exodus and the entrance into Canaan the writer, we are not surprised to find ($3^{16f.}$), notes not a single example of πίστις, but it is remarkable that neither here nor below (v.[32f.]) is there any allusion to Joshua.

[30] *It was by faith that the walls of Jericho collapsed, after being surrounded for only seven days.* [31] *It was by faith that Rahab the harlot did not perish along with those who were disobedient, as she had welcomed the scouts peaceably.*

The faith that had enabled Israel to cross the Red Sea in safety enabled them years later to bring the walls of a city crashing to the ground (v.[30]). There was no siege of Jericho; Israel simply marched round it for a week, and that act of faith in God's promise, against all probabilities, brought about the marvel. So the writer summarizes Jos 6^{1-20}. Judas Maccabaeus and his men also appealed, in besieging a town, to τὸν μέγαν τοῦ κόσμου δυνάστην, τὸν ἄτερ κριῶν καὶ μηχανῶν ὀργανικῶν κατακρημνίσαντα τὴν Ἰεριχὼ κατὰ τοὺς Ἰησοῦ χρόνους (2 Mac 12^{15}), and one Egyptian fanatic (for whom Paul was once mistaken, Acts 21^{38}) promised his adherents, in rebelling against the Romans, that the walls of Jerusalem would collapse at his word of command (Josephus, *Ant.* xx. 8. 6).

The faith of a community is now followed by the faith of an individual. The last name on the special list is that of a foreigner, an unmarried woman, and a woman of loose morals (v.[31]), in striking contrast to Sara and the mother of Moses The story is told in Jos 2[1-21] 6[25]. For ἡ πόρνη ("Ratio haec cur R. solita sit peregrinos excipere," Bengel) see below on 13[2]. A tendency to whitewash her character appears in the addition of ἐπιλεγομένη (א syr[hkl] Ephr.), which is also inserted by some codices in the text of Clem. Rom. 12[1]. Her practical faith (Ja 2[25]; Clem. Rom. 1[12] διὰ πίστιν καὶ φιλοξενίαν ἐσώθη), shown by her friendly (μετ' εἰρήνης) welcome to the spies, which sprang from her conviction that the God of Israel was to be feared, saved (συναπώλετο, cp. Sir 8[15]) her from the fate of her fellow-citizens (τοῖς ἀπειθήσασιν) who declined to submit to the claims of Israel's God. They are described by the same word as are the recalcitrant Israelites themselves (3[18]). Even Jewish priests were proud to trace their descent from Rahab; her reputation stood high in later tradition, owing to the life which followed this initial act of faith (cp. Mt 1[5]).

For lack of space and time the writer now passes to a mere summary of subsequent examples of faith (vv.[32f.]). Roughly speaking, we may say that vv.[33. 34] describe what the folk of old did by faith, vv.[35f.] what they did for faith.

[32] *And what more shall I say? Time would fail me to tell of Gideon, of Barak and Samson and Jephthah, of David and Samuel and the prophets—* [33] *men who by faith* (διὰ πίστεως) *conquered kingdoms, administered justice, obtained promises, shut the mouth of lions,* [34] *quenched the power of fire, escaped the edge of the sword, from weakness won to strength, proved valiant in warfare, and routed hosts of foreigners.*

Καὶ τί ἔτι (om. D*) λέγω (deliberative conjunctive) does not necessarily imply that Πρὸς Ἑβραίους was originally a sermon or address; it was a literary as well as an oratorical phrase. Thus Josephus uses a similar phrase in *Ant.* xx. 11. 1 (καὶ τί δεῖ πλείω λέγειν;). Faith did not die out, at the entry into Palestine. On the contrary, the proofs of faith are so rich in the later story of the People that the writer has no time for anything except a glowing abstract. Ἐπιλείψει γάρ με διηγούμενον ὁ χρόνος is one form of a common rhetorical phrase, though ἡ ἡμέρα is generally used instead of ὁ χρόνος. Three instances may be cited: Dion. Hal. *De Compositione Verb.* 4 (after running over the names of a number of authors) καὶ ἄλλους μυρίους, ὧν ἁπάντων τὰ ὀνόματα εἰ βουλοίμην λέγειν, ἐπιλείψει με ὁ τῆς ἡμέρας χρόνος: Demosth. *de Corona*, 324, ἐπιλείψει με λέγονθ' ἡ ἡμέρα τὰ τῶν προδότων ὀνόματα, and (out of several instances) Philo, *de Sacrif. Abelis et Caini*, 5, ἐπιλείψει μὲ ἡ ἡμέρα λέγοντα τὰ τῶν κατ' εἶδος ἀρετῶν ὀνόματα.

Διηγούμενον . . . περί, as, *e.g.*, in Plato's *Euth.* 6 C, πολλὰ περὶ τῶν θείων διηγήσομαι, and Philo's *de Abrah.* 44, ὧν ὀλίγῳ πρότερον ἔνια διεξῆλθον (= "gone over"). For με γάρ (א A D* 33. 547), γάρ με is rightly read by p13 Dc K L P W Clem. Chrys. etc. (cp. Blass, § 475. 2), though γάρ is omitted altogether by Ψ 216*. Six names are specially mentioned, to begin with. Gideon's crushing victory over the Ammonites echoes down later history (*e.g.* Is 9³ 10²⁶, Ps 83¹¹). The singling out of Barak is in line with the later Jewish tradition, which declined to think of him as a mere ally of Deborah; he was the real hero of the exploit. For example, some rabbis (cp. Targ. on Jg 5²³, Yalkut on Jg 42) gave him the high name of Michael, and praised this brave leader for his modesty in allowing Deborah to occupy so prominent a place. Later tradition also magnified Samson's piety and divine characteristics (*e.g.* Sotah 9*b*, 10*a*). Of all the four "judges" selected, Jephthah has the poorest reputation in Jewish tradition; he is censured for rashness, and his rank is comparatively insignificant. Augustine, however (*Quaest.* VII. xlix.), points out that the "spirit" came both on Jephthah (Jg 11²⁹· ³⁰) and on Gideon (8²⁷). Why these four names are put in this unchronological order (instead of Barak, Gideon, Jephthah, and Samson), it is impossible to guess; in 1 S 12¹¹ it is Gideon, Barak, Jephthah, and Samson, followed by Samuel. David here (**Δαυείδ τε**) belongs to the foregoing group, the only one of Israel's kings mentioned in the list. In Jewish tradition (*e.g.* Josephus, *Ant.* vi. 2, 2–3) Samuel's career was interpreted with quite martial fervour; he was credited with several victories over the Philistines. Hence he forms a transition between the previous heroes and the prophets, of which he was commonly regarded as the great leader (cp. Ac 3²⁴). **Ἄλλων** (+ τῶν?) is superfluously inserted before **προφητῶν** by syr^hkl pesh arm eth sah boh 69. 1288 Theod. Dam. In **οἳ διὰ πίστεως** (v.³³) the οἳ covers vv.³³· ³⁴, but διὰ πίστεως includes vv.³⁵⁻³⁸ as well, and is reiterated in v.³⁹. The following nine terse clauses, devoid of a single καί, begin by noting military and civil achievements. In **κατηγωνίσαντο βασιλείας**, καταγωνίζομαι (not a LXX term) is the verb applied by Josephus to David's conquests (in *Ant.* vii. 2. 2, αὐτῷ σῶσαι καταγωνισαμένῳ Παλαιστινοὺς δέδωκεν ὁ θεός); its later metaphorical use may be illustrated from *Mart. Pol.* 19² (διὰ τῆς ὑπομονῆς καταγωνισάμενος τὸν ἄδικον ἄρχοντα). **Ἠργάσαντο δικαιοσύνην** in the sense of 2 S 8¹⁵ (καὶ ἐβασίλευσεν Δαυεὶδ ἐπὶ Ἰσραήλ· καὶ ἦν ποιῶν κρίμα καὶ δικαιοσύνην ἐπὶ πάντα τὸν λαὸν αὐτοῦ) etc., the writer applying to this specific activity, for which πίστις was essential, a phrase elsewhere (cp. Ac 10³⁵) used for a general moral life. Such was their faith, too, that they had promises of God's help realized in their experience; this (cp. 6¹⁵) is the force of ἐπέτυχον ἐπαγγελιῶν. Furthermore, ἔφραξαν στόματα λεόντων, as in the case of Daniel (Dn $6^{18.23}$ ὁ θεός μου ἐνέφραξεν τὰ στόματα τῶν λεόντων, Theod.), ἔσβεσαν δύναμιν πυρός, as in the case of Daniel's three friends (Dn 3^{19-28}, 1 Mac 2^{59}, 3 Mac 6^{6}). In ἔφυγον στόματα μαχαίρης, the unusual plural of στόμα (cp. Lk 21^{24} πεσοῦνται στόματι μαχαίρης) may be due to the preceding στόματα rhetorically; it means repeated cases of escape from imminent peril of murder rather than double-edged swords (4^{12}), escapes, *e.g.*, like those of Elijah (1 K $19^{1f.}$) and Elisha (2 K $6^{14f.\ 31f.}$). In ἐδυναμώθησαν (p^{13} ℵ* A D* 1831; the *v.l.* ἐνεδυναμώθησαν was probably due to the influence of Ro 4^{20}) ἀπὸ ἀσθενείας, the reference is quite general; Hezekiah's recovery from illness is too narrow an instance.[1] The last three clauses are best illustrated by the story of the Maccabean struggle, where ἀλλότριοι is the term used for the persecutors (1 Mac 2^{7} etc.), and παρεμβολή for their hosts (1 Mac 3^{15} etc.). In παρεμβολὰς ἔκλιναν ἀλλοτρίων, παρεμβολή, a word which Phrynichus calls δεινῶς Μακεδονικόν, means a host in array (so often in 1 Mac and Polybius); κλίνω (cp. Jos. *Ant.* xiv. 15. 4, κλίνεται τὸ . . . κέρας τῆς φάλαγγος) is never used in this sense in the LXX.

What the heroes and heroines of πίστις had to endure is now summarized (vv.$^{35-38}$): the passive rather than the active aspect of faith is emphasized.

35 *Some were given back to their womankind, raised from the very dead; others were broken on the wheel, refusing to accept release, that they might obtain a better resurrection;* 36 *others, again, had to experience scoffs and scourging, aye, chains and imprisonment—* 37 *they were stoned . . . sawn in two, and cut to pieces; they had to roam about in sheepskins and goatskins, forlorn, oppressed, ill-treated* 38 *(men of whom the world was not worthy), wanderers in the desert and among hills, in caves and gullies.*

Ἔλαβον γυναῖκες[2] κτλ. (35) recalls such stories as 1 K $17^{17f.}$ and 2 K 4^{8-37} (καὶ ἡ γυνὴ . . . ἔλαβεν τὸν υἱὸν αὐτῆς καὶ ἐξῆλθεν); it was a real ἀνάστασις, though not the real one, for some other male beings became literally and finally νεκροί, relying by faith on a κρείσσων ἀνάστασις. Ἄλλοι δέ (like Sokrates in Athens: cp. Epict. iv. 1. 164–165, Σωκράτης δ' αἰσχρῶς οὐ σῴζεται . . . τοῦτον οὐκ ἔστι σῶσαι αἰσχρῶς, ἀλλ' ἀποθνήσκων σῴζεται) could only have saved their lives by dishonourably giving up their

[1] A more apt example is the nerving of Judith for her act of religious patriotism (cp. Rendel Harris, *Sidelights on NT Research*, 170 f.), though there is a verbal parallel in the case of Samson (Jg 16^{18} ἀπόστησει ἀπ' ἐμοῦ ἡ ἰσχύς μου καὶ ἀσθενήσω).

[2] The odd *v.l.* γυναικᾶς (p^{13} ℵ* A D* 33. 1912) may be another case (cp. Thackeray, 149, for LXX parallels) of -ας for -ες as a nominative form; as an accusative, it could only have the senseless meaning of "marrying" (λαμβάνειν γυναῖκας). Strong, early groups of textual authorities now and then preserve errors.

convictions, and therefore chose to suffer. This is a plain reference to the Maccabean martyrs. **Ἐτυμπανίσθησαν** (Blass prefers the more classical form in D* *ἀπετυμπανίσθησαν*), a punishment probably corresponding to the mediaeval penalty of being broken on the wheel. "This dreadful punishment consists," says Scott in a note to the thirtieth chapter of *The Betrothed*, "in the executioner, with a bar of iron, breaking the shoulder-bones, arms, thigh-bones and legs of the criminal, taking his alternate sides. The punishment is concluded by a blow across the breast, called the *coup de grâce*, because it removes the sufferer from his agony." The victim was first stretched on a frame or block, the *τύμπανον*[1] (so schol. on Aristoph. *Plut.* 476, *τύμπανα ξύλα ἐφ' οἷς ἐτυμπάνιζον· ἐχρῶντο γὰρ ταύτῃ τῇ τιμωρίᾳ*), and beaten to death, for which the verb was *ἀποτυμπανίζεσθαι* (*e.g.* Josephus, *c. Apionem*, i. 148, quoting Berossus, Λαβοροσοάρχοδος . . . *ὑπὸ τῶν φίλων ἀπετυμπανίσθη*: Arist. *Rhet.* ii. 5. 14, *ὥσπερ οἱ ἀποτυμπανιζόμενοι*, etc.). So Eleazar was put to death, because he refused to save his life by eating swine's flesh (2 Mac 6^{19} *ὁ δὲ τὸν μετ' εὐκλείας θάνατον μᾶλλον ἢ τὸν μετὰ μύσους βίον ἀναδεξάμενος αὐθαιρέτως ἐπὶ τὸ τύμπανον προσῆγεν*). It is this punishment of the Maccabean martyrs which the writer has in mind, as Theodoret already saw. The sufferers were "distracti quemadmodum corium in tympano distenditur" (Calvin); but the essence of the punishment was beating to death, as both Hesychius (*πλήσσεται, ἐκδέρεται, ἰσχυρῶς τύπτεται*) and Suidas (*ξύλῳ πλήσσεται, ἐκδέρεται, καὶ κρέμαται*) recognize in their definition of *τυμπανίζεται*. The hope of the resurrection, which sustained such martyrs **οὐ προσδεξάμενοι** (cp. 10^{34}) **τὴν ἀπολύτρωσιν**, is illustrated by the tales of Maccabean martyrs, *e.g.* of Eleazar the scribe (2 Mac $6^{21f.}$), urged to eat some pork *ἵνα τοῦτο πράξας ἀπολυθῇ τοῦ θανάτου*, and declining in a fine stubbornness; but specially of the heroic mother and her seven sons (*ibid.* $7^{1f.}$), who perished confessing *αἱρετὸν μεταλλάσσοντας ἀπὸ ἀνθρώπων τὰς ὑπὸ τοῦ θεοῦ προσδοκᾶν ἐλπίδας πάλιν ἀναστήσεσθαι ὑπ' αὐτοῦ . . . οἱ μὲν γὰρ νῦν ἡμέτεροι ἀδελφοὶ βραχὺν ἐπενέγκαντες πόνον ἀενάου ζωῆς ὑπὸ διαθήκην θεοῦ πεπτώκασιν*.

In v.[36] **ἕτεροι δὲ** (after *οἱ μέν . . . ἄλλοι δέ* in Matt 16^{14}) **πεῖραν ἔλαβον** (see on v.[29]) **ἐμπαιγμῶν** (cp. Sir 27^{28} *ἐμπαιγμὸς καὶ ὀνειδισμός*) **καὶ μαστίγων**—a hendiadys; the writer has in mind shameful tortures like those inflicted on the seven Maccabean brothers, as described in 2 Mac 7^1 (*μάστιξιν καὶ νευραῖς αἰκιζο-*

[1] Another word for the frame was *τροχός*, as in 4 Mac 9^{20}, where the eldest of the seven famous Jewish brothers is beaten to death. Hence the verb used by Philo (*in Flaccum*, 10) to describe the punishment inflicted on the Alexandrian Jews (Ἰουδαῖοι μαστιγούμενοι, κρεμάμενοι, τροχιζόμενοι, καταικιζόμενοι).

μένους . . . [7] ἦγον ἐπὶ τὸν ἐμπαιγμόν), although in this case the beating is not at once fatal, as the next words prove (ἔτι δὲ δεσμῶν καὶ φυλακῆς). The passage would be more clear and consecutive, however, if **ἕτεροι δέ** preceded **περιῆλθον** (in v.[37]), introducing the case of those who had not to suffer the martyrs' death. This would leave **ἐμπαιγμῶν** κτλ. as a reiteration or expansion of ἐτυμπανίσθησαν. Before **δεσμῶν καὶ φυλακῆς, ἔτι δέ** probably (cp. Lk 14^{26}) heightens the tone—not merely passing blows, but long durance vile: though the sense might be simply, "and further." In v.[37] **ἐλιθάσθησαν** (as in the case of Zechariah, 2 Ch 24^{20-22}, Mt 23^{35}) was the traditional punishment which ended Jeremiah's life in Egypt (Tertull. *Scorp.* 8); possibly the writer also had in mind the fate of Stephen (Acts 7^{58}). **Ἐπρίσθησαν** (Am 1^3 ἔπριζον πρίοσιν σιδηροῖς κτλ.) alludes to the tradition of Isaiah having being sawn in two with a wooden saw during the reign of Manasseh, a tradition echoed in the contemporary *Ascensio Isaiae* 5^{1-14} (Justin's *Dial.* cxx.; Tertull. *de Patientia*, xiv. etc.); cp. R. H. Charles, *The Ascension of Isaiah* (1900), pp. xlv–xlix.

After ἐλιθάσθησαν there is a primitive corruption in the text. Four readings are to be noted.
ἐπειράσθησαν, ἐπρίσθησαν : ℵ L P 33. 326 syr^{hkl}.
ἐπρίσθησαν, ἐπειράσθησαν : p^{13} A D Ψ 6. 104. 1611. 1739 lat boh arm.
ἐπειράσθησαν : fuld, Clem. Thdt.
ἐπρίσθησαν : 2. 327 syr^{vg} Eus. etc.

Origen apparently did not read ἐπειράσθησαν, if we were to judge from *Hom. Jerem.* xv. 2 (ἄλλον ἐλιθοβόλησαν, ἄλλον ἔπρισαν, ἄλλον ἀπέκτειναν μεταξὺ τοῦ ναοῦ καὶ τοῦ θυσιαστηρίου), but shortly before (xiv. 12) he quotes the passage verbally as follows: ἐλιθάσθησαν, ἐπρίσθησαν, ἐπειράσθησαν, ἐν φόνῳ μαχαίρας ἀπέθανον, though ἐπειράσθησαν is omitted here by H. In *c. Cels.* vii. 7 it is doubtful whether ἐπειράθησαν or ἐπειράσθησαν was the original reading. Eusebius omits the word in *Præp. Evang.* xii. 10 (583*d*), reading ἐλιθασθησαν, ἐπρίσθησαν, ἐν φόνῳ κτλ., and sah reads "they were sawn, they were stoned, they died under the sword." It is evident that ἐπειράσθησαν (written in some MSS as ἐπιρ.) as "were tempted" is impossible here; the word either was due to dittography with ἐπρίσθησαν or represents a corruption of some term for torture. Various suggestions have been made, *e.g.* ἐπηρώθησαν (mutilated) by Tanaquil Faber, ἐπράθησαν (sold for slaves) by D. Heinsius, ἐσπειράσθησαν (strangled) by J. Alberti, or ἐπέρθησαν (impaled) by Knatchbull. But some word like ἐπυρώ(άσ)θησαν (Beza, F. Junius, etc.) or ἐπρήσθησαν (Gataker)[1] is more likely, since one of the seven Maccabean brothers was fried to death (2 Mac 7^4), and burning was a punishment otherwise for the Maccabeans (2 Mac 6^{11}). It is at any rate probable that the writer put three aorists ending in -σθησαν together.

Death **ἐν φόνῳ μαχαίρης** (a LXX phrase) was not an uncommon fate for unpopular prophets (1 K 19^{10}, Jer 26^{23}); but the writer now passes, in **περιῆλθον** κτλ. ([37b. 38]), to the sufferings

[1] Or ἐνεπρήσθησαν, which is used by Philo in describing the woes of the Alexandrian Jews (*in Flaccum*, 20, ζῶντες οἱ μὲν ἐνεπρήσθησαν).

of the living, harried and hunted over the country. Not all the loyal were killed, yet the survivors had a miserable life of it, like Mattathias and his sons (1 Mac 2[28] ἔφυγον . . . εἰς τὰ ὄρη), or Judas Maccabaeus and his men, who had to take to the hills (2 Mac 5[27] ἐν τοῖς ὄρεσιν θηρίων τρόπον διέζη σὺν τοῖς μετ' αὐτοῦ, καὶ τὴν χορτώδη τροφὴν σιτούμενοι διετέλουν), or others during the persecution (2 Mac 6[11] ἕτεροι δὲ πλησίον συνδραμόντες εἰς τὰ σπήλαια). When the storm blew over, the Maccabeans recollected ὡς τὴν τῶν σκηνῶν ἑορτὴν ἐν τοῖς ὄρεσιν καὶ ἐν τοῖς σπηλαίοις θηρίων τρόπον ἦσαν νεμόμενοι (2 Mac 10[6]). They roamed, the writer adds, dressed **ἐν μηλωταῖς** (the rough garb of prophets, like Elijah, 1 K 19[13. 19]), **ἐν αἰγείοις δέρμασιν** (still rougher pelts). According to the *Ascensio Isaiae* (2[7f.]) the pious Jews who adhered to Isaiah when he withdrew from Manasseh's idolatry in Jerusalem and sought the hills, were "all clothed in garments of hair, and were all prophets." Clement (17[1]) extends the reference too widely: οἵτινες ἐν δέρμασιν αἰγείοις καὶ μηλωταῖς περιεπάτησαν κηρύσσοντες τὴν ἔλευσιν τοῦ Χριστοῦ· λέγομεν δὲ Ἠλείαν καὶ Ἐλισαιέ, ἔτι δὲ καὶ Ἰεζεκιήλ, τοὺς προφήτας· πρὸς τούτοις καὶ τοὺς μεμαρτυρημένους.

A vivid modern description of people clad in goatskins occurs in Balzac's *Les Chouans* (ch. i.): "Ayant pour tout vêtement une grande peau de chèvre qui les couvrait depuis le col jusqu'aux genoux. . . . Les mèches plates de leurs longs cheveux s'unissaient si habituellement aux poils de la peau de chèvre et cachaient si complétement leurs visages baissés vers la terre, qu'on pouvait facilement prendre cette peau pour la leur, et confondre, à la première vue, les malheureux avec ces animaux dont les dépouilles leur servaient de vêtement. Mais à travers les cheveux l'on voyait bientôt briller les yeux comme des gouttes de rosée dans une épaisse verdure ; et leurs regards, tout en annonçant l'intelligence humaine, causaient certainement plus de terreur que de plaisir."

Their general plight is described in three participles, **ὑστερούμενοι, θλιβόμενοι** (2 Co 4[8]), **κακουχούμενοι** (cp. 13[3], and Plut. *Consol. ad Apoll.* 26, ὥστε πρὶν ἀπώσασθαι τὰ πένθη κακουχουμένους τελευτῆσαι τὸν βίον). Κακοῦχειν only occurs twice in the LXX (1 K 2[26] 11[39] A), but is common in the papyri (e.g. *Tebt. Pap.* 104[22], B.C. 92). This ill-treatment at the hands of men, as if they were not considered fit to live (cp. Ac 22[22]), elicits a splendid aside—**ὧν οὐκ ἦν ἄξιος ὁ κόσμος.** Compare Mechilta, 5*a* (on Ex 12[6]): "Israel possessed four commandments, of which the whole world was not worthy," and the story of the bath qol in Sanhedr. 11. 1, which said, "One is here present who is worthy to have the Shekinah dwelling in him, but the world is not worthy of such." Κόσμος as in v.[7]; Philo's list of the various meanings of κόσμος (in *de aetern. mundi*, 2) does not include this semi-religious sense. Of the righteous, Wis 3[5] remarks: ὁ θεὸς ἐπείρασεν αὐτοὺς καὶ εὗρεν αὐτοὺς ἀξίους ἑαυτοῦ.

"There is a class of whom the world is always worthy and more than worthy: it is worthy of those who watch for, reproduce, exaggerate its foibles, who make themselves the very embodiment of its ruling passions, who shriek its catchwords, encourage its illusions, and flatter its fanaticisms. But it is a poor *rôle* to play, and it never has been played by the men whose names stand for epochs in the march of history" (H. L. Stewart, *Questions of the Day in Philosophy and Psychology*, 1912, p. 133).

In [38b] it was the not infrequent (cf. Mk 1[45]) confusion of ЄΝ and ЄΠΙ in ancient texts which probably accounted for ἐν being replaced by ἐπί (ἐφ') in p[13] ℵ A P 33. 88, etc.; ἐπί does not suit σπηλαίοις . . . ὀπαῖς, and the writer would have avoided the hiatus in ἐπὶ ἐρημίαις. Still, πλανώμενοι suits only ἐρημίαις καὶ ὄρεσιν, and ἐπί may have been the original word, used loosely like πλανώμενοι with σπηλαίοις κτλ. In Ps.-Sol 17[19] the pious ἐπλανῶντο ἐν ἐρήμοις, σωθῆναι ψυχὰς αὐτῶν ἀπὸ κακοῦ. For ὀπαῖς, cp. Ob [3] ἐν ταῖς ὀπαῖς τῶν πετρῶν. Σπήλαιον, like the Latin *spelunca* or *specus*, eventually became equivalent to a "temple," perhaps on account of the prominence of caves or grottoes in the worship of some cults.

Now for an estimate of this πίστις and its heroic representatives (vv.[39. 40])! The epilogue seems to justify God by arguing that the apparent denial of any adequate reward to them is part of a larger divine purpose, which could only satisfy them after death.

[39] *They all won their record* (μαρτυρηθέντες = ἐμαρτυρήθησαν in v.[2]) *for faith, but the Promise they did not obtain.* [40] *God had something better in store for us* (ἡμῶν emphatic); *he would not have them perfected apart from us.*

Some of these heroes and heroines of faith had had God's special promises fulfilled even in this life (*e.g.* vv.[11. 33]), but *the* Promise, in the sense of the messianic bliss with its eternal life (10[36. 37], cf. 6[17f.]), they could not win. Why? Not owing to any defect in their faith, nor to any fault in God, but on account of his far-reaching purpose in history; οὗτοι πάντες (again as in v.[13], but this time summing up the whole list, vv.[4-38]) οὐκ ἐκομίσαντο (in the sense of v.[13] μὴ κομισάμενοι; not a voluntary renunciation, as Wetstein proposes to interpret it—"non acceperunt felicitatem promissam huius vitae, imo deliberato consilio huic beneficio renunciaverunt et maluerunt affligi morique propter deum") τὴν ἐπαγγελίαν (in v.[13] *the* Promise was loosely called αἱ ἐπαγγελίαι, and the plural τὰς ἐπαγγελίας is therefore read here by A W 436. 1611). The reason for this is now given (v.[40]) in a genitive absolute clause, τοῦ θεοῦ περὶ ἡμῶν κρεῖττόν τι προβλεψαμένου (the middle for the active). Προβλέπειν only occurs once in the LXX (Ps 37[13] ὁ δὲ κύριος . . . προβλέπει ὅτι ἥξει ἡ ἡμέρα αὐτοῦ), and only here in the NT, where the religious idea makes it practically a Greek equivalent for *providere.*

Κρεῖττόν τι is explained by ἵνα μὴ χωρὶς ἡμῶν τελειωθῶσιν, which does not mean that "our experience was necessary to complete their reward," but that God in his good providence reserved the messianic τελείωσις of Jesus Christ until we could share it. This τελείωσις is now theirs (9^{15} 12^{23}), as it is ours—if only we will show a like strenuous faith during the brief interval before the end. This is the thought of $12^{1f.}$, catching up that of $10^{36f.}$. God deferred the coming of Christ, in order to let us share it (cp. 1 P $1^{10.\,20}$), his plan being to make room for us as well. The τελείωσις has been realized in Jesus; till he reappears (9^{28} $10^{12.\,37}$) to complete the purpose of God for us, we must hold on in faith, heartened by the example of these earlier saints. Their faith was only granted a far-off vision of the hoped-for end. We have seen that end realized in Jesus; therefore, with so many more resources and with so short a time of strain, we ought to be nerved for our endurance by the sense of our noble predecessors. It is not that we experience κρεῖττόν τι by our immediate experience of Christ (10^{14}), who fulfils to us what these former folk could not receive before his coming. This is true, but it is not exactly the point here. The κρεῖττόν τι is our inclusion in this People of God for whom the τελείωσις of Christ was destined, the privilege of the κρείττων διαθήκη. The writer does not go the length of saying that Christ suffered in the persons of these saints and heroes (as, *e.g.*, Paulinus of Nola, *Epist.* xxxviii. 3: "ab initio saeculorum Christus in omnibus suis patitur . . . in Abel occisus a fratre, in Noe irrisus a filio, in Abraham peregrinatus, in Isaac oblatus, in Jacob famulatus, in Joseph venditus, in Moyse expositus et fugatus, in prophetis lapidatus et sectus, in apostolis terra marique iactatus, et multis ac uariis beatorum martyrum crucibus frequenter occisus"), and this consideration tells against the theory of a "mystical" sense in v.^{26}. The conclusion of the whole matter rather is (vv.$^{39.\,40}$) that the reward of their faith had to be deferred till Christ arrived in our day. The τελείωσις is entirely wrought out through Christ, and wrought out for all. It covers all God's People (cp. 12^{23}), for now the Promise has been fulfilled to these earlier saints. But the writer significantly ignores any idea of their co-operation in our faith; we neither pray to them, nor they for us. Josephus interpreted the sacrifice of Isaac, as if Abraham reconciled himself to it by reflecting that his son would be a heavenly support to him (*Ant.* i. 13. 3, ἐκείνου, *i.e.* τοῦ θεοῦ, τὴν ψυχὴν τὴν σὴν προσδεχομένου καὶ παρ' αὐτῷ καθέξοντος· ἔσει τε μοι εἰς κηδεμόνα καὶ γηροκόμον . . . τὸν θεὸν ἀντὶ σαυτοῦ παρεσχημένος). Such ideas lie outside the range of our epistle, and there is significance in the fact that the writer never touches them.

In Clement of Alexandria's comment (*Strom.* iv. 16) on this passage, he quotes 10[32-39] (reading δεσμοῖς μου: ἑαυτούς: χρονιεῖ: δικαιός μου), then hurries on to 11[36]–12[2] (reading ἐλιθάσθησαν, ἐπειράσθησαν, ἐν φόνῳ μ. ἀπέθανον: ἐν ἐρημίαις: τὴν ἐπαγγελίαν τοῦ θεοῦ), and adds: ἀπολείπεται νοεῖν τὸ κατὰ παρασιώπησιν εἰρημένον μόνοι. ἐπιφέρει γοῦν· περὶ ἡμῶν κρεῖττόν τι προειδομένου τοῦ θεοῦ (ἀγαθὸς γὰρ ἦν), ἵνα μη χωρὶς ἡμῶν τελειωθῶσι. The collocation of τὴν ἐπαγγελίαν with τοῦ θεοῦ is a mistake.

From the ἡμῶν . . . ἡμῶν of the epilogue the writer now passes into a moving appeal to his readers (12[1f.]).

[1] *Therefore* (Τοιγαροῦν, as in 1 Th 4[8]), *with all this host of witnesses encircling us, we* (καὶ ἡμεῖς, emphatic) *must strip off sin with its clinging folds, to run our appointed course steadily* (δι' ὑπομονῆς), [2] *our eyes fixed upon Jesus as the pioneer and the perfection of faith—upon Jesus who, in order to reach his own appointed joy, steadily endured* (ὑπέμεινεν) *the cross, thinking nothing of its shame, and is now "seated at the right hand" of the throne of God.*

The writer now returns to the duty of ὑπομονή as the immediate exercise of πίστις (10[36f.]), the supreme inspiration being the example of Jesus (12[1-3]) as the great Believer, who shows us what true πίστις means, from beginning to end, in its heroic course (τὸν προκείμενον ἡμῖν ἀγῶνα).

The general phraseology and idea of life as a strenuous ἀγών, in the Hellenic sense (see on 5[14]), may be seen in many passages, *e.g.* Eurip. *Orest.* 846 f.:

πρὸς δ' Ἀργεῖον οἴχεται λεών,
ψυχῆς ἀγῶνα τὸν προκείμενον πέρι
δώσων, ἐν ᾧ ζῆν ἢ θανεῖν ὑμᾶς χρεών,

Herod. viii. 102 (πολλοὺς πολλάκις ἀγῶνας δραμέονται οἱ Ἕλληνες) and ix. 60 (ἀγῶνος μεγίστου προκειμένου ἐλευθέρην εἶναι ἢ δεδουλωμένην τὴν Ἑλλάδα), and especially in 4 Mac 14[5] πάντες (the seven martyrs), ὥσπερ ἐπ' ἀθανασίας ὁδὸν τρέχοντες, ἐπὶ τὸν διὰ τῶν βασάνων θάνατον ἔσπευδον, and Philo's *de migrat. Abrah.* 24, καὶ γὰρ Ἀβραὰμ πιστεύσας "ἐγγίζειν θεῷ" (Gn 18[23], cp. He 11[6]) λέγεται. ἐὰν μέντοι πορευόμενος μήτε κάμῃ (cp. He 12[3]) μήτε ῥαθυμήσῃ, ὡς παρ' ἑκάτερα ἐκτραπόμενος (cp. He 12[13]) πλανᾶσθαι τῆς μέσης καὶ εὐθυτενοῦς διαμαρτὼν ὁδοῦ, μιμησάμενος δὲ τοὺς ἀγαθοὺς δρομεῖς τὸ στάδιον ἀπταίστως ἀνύσῃ τοῦ βίου, στεφάνων καὶ ἄθλων ἐπαξίων τεύξεται πρὸς τὸ τέλος ἐλθών. The figure is elaborately worked out in 4 Mac 17[11-14] (ἀληθῶς γὰρ ἦν ἀγὼν θεῖος ὁ δι' αὐτῶν γεγενημένος. ἠθλοθέτει γὰρ τότε ἀρετὴ δι' ὑπομονῆς δοκιμάζουσα· τὸ νῖκος ἐν ἀφθαρσίᾳ ἐν ζωῇ πολυχρονίῳ. Ἐλεαζὰρ δὲ προηγωνίζετο· ἡ δὲ μήτηρ τῶν ἑπτὰ παίδων ἐνήθλει· οἱ δὲ ἀδελφοὶ ἠγωνίζοντο· ὁ τύραννος ἀντηγωνίζετο· ὁ δὲ κόσμος καὶ ὁ τῶν ἀνθρώπων βίος ἐθεώρει), where the Maccabean martyrs are athletes of the true Law; but the imagery is more rhetorical and detailed than in Πρὸς Ἑβραίους, where the author, with a passing touch of metaphor, suggests more simply and suggestively the same idea.

Ἔχοντες . . . ἀποθέμενοι . . . ἀφορῶντες, three participles with the verb after the second, as in Jude [20. 21]; but here the first, not the second, denotes the motive. **Τοσοῦτον**[1] (thrown forward, for emphasis) **ἔχοντες περικείμενον ἡμῖν νέφος μαρτύρων.** **Μαρτύρες** here, in the light of 11[2. 4. 5. 39], denotes those who have borne

[1] Τηλικοῦτον, ℵ* W.

personal testimony to the faith. Heaven is now crowded with these (12^{23}), and the record of their evidence and its reward enters into our experience. Such *πνεύματα δικαίων τετελειωμένων* speak to us (11^{4}) still; we are, or ought to be, conscious of their record, which is an encouragement to us (*καὶ ἡμεῖς*) *ἐπ' ἐσχάτου τῶν ἡμερῶν τούτων* (1^{2}). It is what we see in them, not what they see in us, that is the writer's main point; *περικείμενον* suggests that the idea of them as witnesses of our struggle (see the quot. from 4 Mac, above) is not to be excluded, but this is merely suggested, not developed. *Μάρτυς* is already, as in Rev 2^{13} etc., beginning to shade off into the red sense of "martyr" (cp. Kattenbusch in *Zeitsch. für neutest. Wissenschaft*, 1903, pp. 111 f.; G. Krüger, *ibid.*, 1916, pp. 264 f.; Reitzenstein in *Hermes*, 1917, pp. 442 f., and H. Delehaye in *Analecta Bollandiana*, 1921, pp. 20 f.), though the writer uses the word with a special application here, not as usually of the Christian apostles nor of the prophets, but of the heroes and heroines of the People in pre-Christian ages. He does not even call Jesus Christ *μάρτυς* (as does the author of the Johannine apocalypse).

The meaning of "witnesses of our ordeal" (*i.e.* spectators) is supported by passages like Epict. iv. 4. 31, *οὐδεὶς ἀγὼν*[1] *δίχα θορύβου γίνεται· πολλοὺς δεῖ προγυμναστὰς εἶναι, πολλοὺς [τοὺς] ἐπικραυγάζοντας, πολλοὺς ἐπιστάτας, πολλοὺς θεατάς*, and particularly Longinus, *de sublim.* xiv. 2, who, in arguing that many people catch their inspiration from others, notes: *τῷ γὰρ ὄντι μέγα τὸ ἀγώνισμα, τοιοῦτον ὑποτίθεσθαι τῶν ἰδίων λόγων δικαστήριον καὶ θέατρον, καὶ ἐν τηλικούτοις ἥρωσι κριταῖς τε καὶ μάρτυσιν ὑπέχειν τῶν γραφομένων εὐθύνας πεπαῖχθαι.* In *Educational Aims and Methods* (p. 28), Sir Joshua Fitch writes: "There is a remarkable chapter in the Epistle to the Hebrews, in which the writer unfolds to his countrymen what is in fact a National Portrait Gallery, as he enumerates, one by one, the heroes and saints of the Jewish history, and adds to his catalogue these inspiring words . . . [He 11$^{32-34}$]. And, finally, he draws this conclusion from his long retrospect . . . [He 12^{1}]. How much of the philosophy of history is condensed into that single sentence! It is suggestive to us of the ethical purpose which should dominate all our historical teaching. To what end do we live in a country whose annals are enriched by the story of great talents, high endeavours and noble sacrifices, if we do not become more conscious of the possibilities of our own life, and more anxious to live worthily of the inheritance which has come down to us?"

Νέφος (never in this sense in LXX) has its usual Greek meaning of "host" (Latin nimbus or nubes), as, *e.g.*, in Herod. viii. 109, *νέφος τοσοῦτο ἀνθρώπων.* In **ὄγκον ἀποθέμενοι πάντα καὶ τὴν εὐπερίστατον ἁμαρτίαν**, *ὄγκον* is thrown first for the sake of emphasis: "any encumbrance that handicaps us." The conjec-

[1] The broader conception of the moral life as an athletic contest recurs in Epict. iii. 25. 1–3, *σκέψαι, ὧν προέθου ἀρχόμενος, τίνων μὲν ἐκράτησας, τίνων δ' οὔ . . . οὐ γὰρ ἀποκνητέον τὸν ἀγῶνα τὸν μέγιστον ἀγωνιζομένοις, ἀλλὰ καὶ πληγὰς ληπτέον· οὐ γὰρ ὑπὲρ πάλης καὶ παγκρατίου ὁ ἀγὼν πρόκειται . . . ἀλλ' ὑπὲρ αὐτῆς εὐτυχίας καὶ εὐδαιμονίας.*

ture ὄκνον (P. Junius) is relevant, but superfluous; sloth is a hindrance, but the general sense of ὄγκος in this connexion is quite suitable. Compare Apul. *Apologia*, 19 ("etenim in omnibus ad vitae munia utendis quicquid aptam moderationem supergreditur, oneri potius quam usui exuberat"), and the evening prayer of the Therapeutae (Philo, *vit. Contempl* 3) to have their souls lightened from τοῦ τῶν αἰσθήσεων καὶ αἰσθητῶν ὄγκου. **Ὄγκος** had acquired in Greek literature the sense of pride, both bad and good, and it has been taken here (so sah = "having forsaken all pride") as an equivalent for pride in the sense of conceit (fastus), as, *e.g.*, by Bengel and Seeberg. But what the readers seem to have been in danger of was not arrogance so much as a tendency to grow disheartened. The metaphor is not "reducing our weight," though ὄγκος had sometimes this association with fleshiness; it refers to the weight of superfluous things, like clothes, which would hinder and handicap the runner. Let us strip for the race, says the writer. Put unmetaphorically, the thought is that no high end like **πίστις** is possible apart from a steady, unflinching resolve to do without certain things. What these encumbrances are the writer does not say (cp. 11[15. 25. 26]); he implies that if people will set themselves to the course of faith in this difficult world, they will soon discover what hampers them. In **καὶ τὴν εὐπερίστατον ἁμαρτίαν**, the article does not imply any specific sin like that of apostasy (v.[25]); it is ἁμαρτία in general, any sin that might lead to apostasy (*e.g.* v.[16]). The sense of εὐπερίστατος can only be inferred from the context and from the analogy of similar compounds, for it appears to have been a verbal adjective coined by the writer; at any rate no instance of its use in earlier writers or in the papyri has been as yet discovered. As the phrase goes with **ἀποθέμενοι**, the introductory καί linking **τὴν . . . ἁμαρτίαν** with ὄγκον, εὐπερίστατος probably denotes something like "circumstans nos" (vg), from περιϊστάναι (= cingere). The **εὐ** is in any case intensive. Theophylact suggested "endangering" (δι' ἣν εὐκόλως τις εἰς περιστάσεις ἐμπίπτει· οὐδὲν γὰρ οὕτω κινδυνῶδες ὡς ἁμαρτία), as though it were formed from περίστασις (distress or misery). Taken passively, it might mean (*a*) "popular," or (*b*) "easily avoided," or (*c*) "easily contracted." (*a*) περίστατος may mean what people gather round (περιστατέω) to admire, as, *e.g.*, in Isokrates, *de Permut.* 135 E, θαυματοποιΐαις ταῖς . . . ὑπὸ τῶν ἀνοήτων περιστάτοις γενομέναις, and εὐπερίστατον would then = "right popular." This is at any rate more relevant and pointed than (*b*), from περιΐσταμαι, which Chrysostom once suggested (τὴν εὐκόλως περιισταμένην ἡμᾶς ἢ τὴν εὐκόλως περίστασιν δυναμένην παθεῖν: μᾶλλον δὲ τοῦτο, ῥᾴδιον γὰρ ἐὰν θέλωμεν περιγενέσθαι τῆς ἁμαρτίας), though περίστατος does mean "admired," and ἀπερίστατος is sometimes, by way of contrast, "unsupported." On the other hand, ἀπερίστατος may mean "unencumbered," as in the contrast drawn by Maximus of Tyre (*Diss.* xx.) between the simple life (ἁπλοῦν βίον καὶ ἀπερίστατον καὶ ἐλευθερίας ἐπήβολον) and a life τῷ οὐχ ἁπλῷ ἀλλ' ἀναγκαίῳ καὶ περιστάσεων γέμοντι. The former life he declares was that of the golden age, before men worried themselves with the encumbrances of civilization. In the light of this, εὐπερίστατος might mean "which sorely hinders" (*i.e.* active), a sense not very different from (vg) "circumstans nos," or "which at all times is prepared for us" (syr). (*c*) is suggested by Theodoret, who rightly takes ἡ ἁμαρτία as generic, and defines εὐπερίστατον as εὐκόλως συνισταμένην τε καὶ γινομένην. καὶ γὰρ ὀφθαλμὸς δελεάζεται, ἀκοὴ καταθέλγεται, ἁφὴ γαργαρίζεται, καὶ γλῶσσα ῥᾷστα διολισθαίνει, καὶ ὁ λογισμὸς περὶ τὸ χεῖρον ὀξύῤῥοπος. But "easily caught" is hardly tense enough for the context. Wetstein, harking back to περίστατος and περίστασις, connects the adjective with the idea of the heroic onlookers. "Peccatum uestrum seu defectio a doctrina Christi non in occulto potest committi et latere; non magis quam lapsus cursoris, sed conspicietur ab omnibus. Cogitate iterum, spectatores adesse omnes illos heroas, quorum constantiam laudaui, quo animo uidebunt lapsum uestrum? qua fronte ante oculos ipsorum audebitis tale facinus committere?" But "open" or "conspicuous" is, again, too slight and light a sense. If any conjecture had to be accepted, εὐπερίσταλτον would be the best. Cp. the schol. on *Iliad*, ii. 183 (ἀπὸ δὲ χλαῖναν βάλε), χλαῖνα τετράγωνος χλαμὺς ἢ εἰς ὀξὺ λήγουσα· ἀπέβαλε δὲ αὐτὴν διὰ τὸ εὐπερίσταλτον. Hence Bentley's note: "Lego τὴν ὑπὲρ ἱκανὸν ἀπαρτίαν . . . immo potius εὐπερίσταλτον ἀπαρτίαν." In Soph. *Ajax*, 821, the hero says of the sword on which he is about to fall, "I have fixed it in the ground, εὖ περιστείλας, right carefully." The verbal adjective would therefore mean, in this connexion, "close-clinging," while ἀπαρτίαν (= burden) would be practically a synonym for ὄγκον.

Τρέχωμεν . . . ἀφορῶντες, for the motive-power in life comes from inward convictions. What inspires Christians to hold out and to endure is their vision of the unseen (cp. Herodian, v. 6. 7, ὁ δ' Ἀντωνῖνος ἔθεε . . . ἔς τε τὸν θεὸν ἀποβλέπων καὶ τοὺς χαλινοὺς ἀντέχων τῶν ἵππων· πᾶσάν τε τὴν ὁδὸν ἤνυε τρέχων ἔμπαλιν ἑαυτοῦ ἀφορῶν τε εἰς τὸ πρόσθεν τοῦ θεοῦ), as the writer has already shown (11[1f.]). **Τὸν προκείμενον ἡμῖν ἀγῶνα** is built on the regular (p. 193) phrase for a course being set or assigned; *e.g.* Lucian in *de Mercede Conduct.* 11, σοὶ δὲ ὁ ὑπὲρ τῆς ψυχῆς ἀγὼν καὶ ὑπὲρ ἅπαντος τοῦ βίου τότε προκεῖσθαι δοκεῖ: Plato's *Laches*, 182*a*, οὗ γὰρ ἀγῶνος ἀθληταί ἐσμεν καὶ ἐν οἷς ἡμῖν ὁ ἀγὼν πρόκειται κτλ., and Josephus, *Ant.* viii. 12. 3, οἷ προκειμένων αὐτοῖς ἄθλων, ἐπὰν περί τι σπουδάσωσιν, οὐ διαλείπουσι περὶ τοῦτ' ἐνεργοῦντες. For **ἀφορῶντες εἰς** (v.[2]), see Epictetus, ii. 19, where the philosopher says he wishes to make his disciples free and happy, εἰς τὸν θεὸν ἀφορῶντας ἐν παντὶ καὶ μικρῷ καὶ μεγάλῳ. An almost exact parallel occurs in the epitaph proposed by the author of 4 Mac (17^{10}) for the Maccabean martyrs, οἳ καὶ ἐξεδίκησαν τὸ ἔθνος εἰς θεὸν ἀφορῶντες καὶ μέχρι θανάτου τὰς βασάνους ὑπομείναντες. Ἀφορᾶν implies the same concentrated[1] attention as ἀποβλέπειν (see on 11^{26}): "with no eyes for any one or anything except Jesus." **Ἰησοῦν** comes at the end of the phrase, as in 2^{9}, and especially 3^{1}; the terms **τὸν τῆς πίστεως ἀρχηγὸν καὶ τελειωτήν** describe him as the perfect exemplar of **πίστις** in his earthly life (cp. 2^{13}), as the supreme pioneer (**ἀρχηγός** as in 2^{10}, though here as the pioneer of personal faith, not as the author of our faith) and the perfect embodiment of faith (**τελειωτής**, a term apparently coined by the writer). He has realized faith to the full, from start to finish. **Τελειωτής** does not refer to τελειωθῶσιν in 11^{40}; it does not imply that Jesus "perfects" our faith by fulfilling the divine promises.

In **ὃς ἀντὶ τῆς προκειμένης αὐτῷ χαρᾶς**, the χαρά is the unselfish joy implied in $2^{8.\ 9}$, "that fruit of his self-sacrifice which must be presupposed in order that the self-sacrifice should be a reasonable transaction. Self-sacrificing love does not sacrifice itself but for an end of gain to its object; otherwise it would be folly. Does its esteeming as a reward that gain to those for whom it suffers, destroy its claim to being self-sacrifice? Nay, that which seals its character as self-sacrificing love is, that this to it is a satisfying reward" (M'Leod Campbell, *The Nature of the Atonement*, p. 23). As Epictetus bluntly put it, ἐὰν μὴ ἐν τῷ αὐτῷ ᾖ τὸ εὐσεβὲς καὶ συμφέρον, οὐ δύναται σωθῆναι τὸ εὐσεβὲς ἔν τινι (i. 27. 14). So, in the Odes of Solomon 31^{8-12}, Christ says:

"They condemned me when I stood up . . .
But I endured and held my peace,
that I might not be moved by them.
But I stood unshaken like a firm rock,
that is beaten by the waves and endures.
And I bore their bitterness for humility's sake;
that I might redeem my people and inherit it."

Hence **ἀντί** (as in v.[16] ἀντὶ βρώσεως: cp. Plato's *Menex.* 237 A, ἄνδρας ἀγαθοὺς ἐπαινοῦντες, οἳ . . . τὴν τελευτὴν ἀντὶ τῆς τῶν ζώντων σωτηρίας ἠλλάξαντο) means, "to secure." The sense of

[1] Epictetus, in his praise of Herakles (iii. 24), declares that his hero lived and worked with a firm faith in Zeus the Father. "He considered that Zeus was his own father; he called Zeus father, and did everything with his eyes fixed on Zeus (πρὸς ἐκεῖνον ἀφορῶν ἔπραττεν ἃ ἔπραττεν)."

προκειμένης (cp. v.[1]) tells against the rendering of **ἀντὶ . . . χαρᾶς** as "instead of the joy which had been set before him," as though the idea were that of 11[25-26], either the renunciation of his pre-incarnate bliss (so Wetstein, von Soden, Windisch, Goodspeed, etc., recently), or the renunciation of joy in the incarnate life (so Chrysostom, Calvin), *i.e.* the natural pleasure of avoiding the way of the cross. This is a Pauline idea (2 Co 8[9], Phil 2[6. 7]), which the writer might have entertained; but (p. l) he never hints at it elsewhere, and the other interpretation tallies with the idea of 2[8. 9]. Inspired by this, Jesus **ὑπέμεινε** (+*τόν*, p[13] D*) *σταυρόν*—as we might say in English "a cross." Aristotle (*Nik. Eth.* ix. 1, 2) declares that courage is praiseworthy just because it involves pain, *χαλεπώτερον γὰρ τὰ λυπηρὰ ὑπομένειν ἢ τὰ ἡδέων ἀπέχεσθαι*: no doubt the end in view is pleasant (*τὸ κατὰ τὴν ἀνδρείαν τέλος ἡδύ*, cp. He 12[11]), but the end is not always visible. In **αἰσχύνης καταφρονήσας** it is not the horrible torture of the crucifixion, but its stinging indignity (cp. Gal 3[13] for an even darker view), which is noted as a hard thing; it was a punishment for slaves and criminals, for men of whom the world felt it was well rid (cp. 11[38a]). But Jesus did not allow either the dread or the experience of this to daunt him. He rose above "indignity and contumely, that is to say, all that would most touch that life which man has in the favour of man, and which strikes more deeply than physical infliction, because it goes deeper than the body—wounding the spirit" (M'Leod Campbell, *The Nature of the Atonement*, pp. 229, 230). Musonius (ed. Hense, x.) defined *ὕβρις* or *αἰσχύνη* as *οἷον λοιδορηθῆναι ἢ πληγῆναι ἢ ἐμπτυσθῆναι, ὧν τὸ χαλεπώτατον πληγαί*. But the special **αἰσχύνη** here is that of crucifixion. This, says the writer, Jesus did not allow to stand between him and loyalty to the will of God. It is one thing to be sensitive to disgrace and disparagement, another thing to let these hinder us from doing our duty. Jesus was sensitive to such emotions; he felt disgrace keenly. But instead of allowing these feelings to cling to his mind, he rose above them. This is the force of **καταφρονήσας** here, as in the last clause of St. Philip of Neri's well-known maxim, "Spernere mundum, spernere te ipsum, spernere te sperni." It is the only place in the NT where *καταφρονεῖν* is used in a good sense (true and false shame are noted in Sir 4[20. 21] *περὶ τῆς ψυχῆς σου μὴ αἰσχυνθῇς· ἔστιν γὰρ αἰσχύνη ἐπάγουσα ἁμαρτίαν, καὶ ἔστιν αἰσχύνη δόξα καὶ χάρις*). The climax is put in one of the writer's favourite quotations from the psalter; only this time he uses **κεκάθικεν** (perfect here alone for the more usual aorist, 1[3] 8[1] 10[12]) = and so has entered on his *χαρά*.

Jesus thus had to suffer worse than anything you have had to bear; this is the thought of vv.[3. 4], which round off the first movement of the appeal in 12[1f.] :—

[3] *Compare him who steadily endured* (ὑπομεμενηκότα) *all that hostility from sinful men, so as to keep your own hearts from fainting and failing.* [4] *You have not had to shed blood yet in the struggle against sin.*

The writer assumes, as in $5^{7f.}$, a close knowledge of the Passion story. Before proceeding to argue that suffering is a fruitful discipline, with which God honours them (v.[5f.]), he reminds them that as yet they have not had to face the worst (v.[4]). The metaphor of the race-course dies away into the general military metaphor of v.[4], where ἁμαρτία is half-personified as in 3^{13}. Ἀναλογίσασθε [1] (the γάρ is corroborative: "yes, ἀναλογίσασθε" κτλ.) is more than κατανοήσατε (3^{1}): "consider him and compare his treatment at the hands of these sinners (ἁμαρτωλῶν as in Mk 14^{41}) with what you are called to suffer." Τοιαύτην echoes σταυρόν and αἰσχύνης, and is explained by μέχρις αἵματος in the next verse, while ὑπομεμενηκότα is another aoristic perfect like κεκάθικεν.

Ἀντιλογίαν is used here of active opposition, as in Ps 17^{44} (ῥῦσαί με ἐξ ἀντιλογιῶν λαοῦ), where ℵ[ca] R read ἀντιλογίας, and in the papyri (e.g. *Tebt. P.* 138 [ii B.C.] ἀντιλογιάς μάχην). Like the verb (cp. Jn 19^{12}, Ro 10^{21}), the noun covers more than verbal opposition, as in Nu 20^{13} and Jude [11] τῇ ἀντιλογίᾳ τοῦ Κορέ. The words εἰς αὐτόν (or ἑαυτόν, A P syr[hkl] etc.: in semetipsum, vg.) have no special emphasis; all the writer means to say is that Jesus himself, Jesus in his own person, had to encounter malevolent opposition.

This is one of the places at which textual corruption began early. The curious *v.l.* ἑαυτούς finds early support in ℵ* D* (αὐτούς, p[13] ℵ[c] 33. 256. 1288. 1319*. 1739. 2127 Lat syr[vg] boh Orig.); p[13] ℵ* and D* go wrong here as in 11^{35}, D* and Lat as at 11^{23} (insertion). It is extremely unlikely that the reading arose from a recollection of passages like Nu 16^{37} (Korah, Dathan, and Abiram) ἡγίασαν τὰ πυρεῖα τῶν ἁμαρτωλῶν τούτων ἐν (*i.e.* at the cost of) ταῖς ψυχαῖς αὐτῶν, or Pr 8^{36} οἱ δὲ εἰς ἐμὲ ἁμαρτάνοντες ἀσεβοῦσιν εἰς τὰς ἑαυτῶν ψυχάς. The notion that an evil-doer really injured himself was a commonplace (*e.g.* M. Aurel. 9^{4} ὁ ἁμαρτάνων ἑαυτῷ ἁμαρτάνει· ὁ ἀδικῶν ἑαυτὸν ἀδικεῖ, the remark of Chrysippus quoted by Plutarch in *de Stoic. repugn.* xvi., ἀδικεῖσθαι ὑφ' ἑαυτοῦ τὸν ἀδικοῦντα καὶ αὐτὸν ἀδικεῖν, ὅταν ἄλλον ἀδικῇ, Aristotle in *Magn. Moral.* 1196*a*, ὁ ἄρα ταῦτα μὴ πράττων ἀδικεῖ αὐτόν, and Xen. *Hellen.* i. 7. 19, ἡμαρτηκότας τὰ μέγιστα εἰς θεούς τε καὶ ὑμᾶς αὐτούς); Philo works it out in *quod deter.* 15, 16. But there is no point in suggesting here, as this reading does, that the ἁμαρτωλοί were acting against their better selves, unconsciously injuring their own souls, as they maltreated Jesus. The writer deals with sin in a more straightforward and direct way, and, in spite of all arguments to the contrary (*e.g.* by Westcott, von Soden, Seeberg, Peake, Wickham), this seems a far-fetched idea here. It is like the similar interpretation of ἑαυτούς in 10^{34}, a piece of irrelevant embroidery; it "looks like the conceit which some reader wrote upon his margin" (A. B. Davidson). Theodoret took εἰς ἑαυτούς with ἀναλογίσασθε = "think to yourselves." Which is not natural, though the Ethiopic version follows this interpretation. In some early versions (*e.g.* sah arm) neither εἰς ἑαυτόν nor εἰς ἑαυτούς seems to be implied.

---

[1] Ἀναλογίζομαι, though not a LXX term, begins to be used in Hellenistic Judaism (*e.g.* Ps.-Sol 8^{7} ἀνελογισάμην τὰ κρίματα τοῦ θεοῦ) in a religious sense.

In ἵνα . . . ἐκλυόμενοι, ἐκλυόμενοι (ἐκλελυμένοι p[13] D*) might go with ταῖς ψυχαῖς ὑμῶν (cp. Polybius, xx. 4. 7, οὐ μόνον τοῖς σώμασιν ἐξελύθησαν, ἀλλὰ καὶ ταῖς ψυχαῖς), as readily as κάμητε (cp. Job 10[1] κάμνω δὲ τῇ ψυχῇ μου). Both verbs connect with it, to express the general sense of inward exhaustion and faint-heartedness; indeed, Aristotle uses both to describe runners relaxing and collapsing, once the goal has been passed: ἐπὶ τοῖς καμπτῆρσιν (at the goal of the race, not till then) ἐκπνέουσι καὶ ἐκλύονται· προορῶντες γὰρ τὸ πέρας οὐ κάμνουσι πρότερον (*Rhet.* iii. 9. 2). In v.[4] οὔπω (γάρ is superfluously added by D L 440. 491. 823 arm sah boh) κτλ. does not necessarily imply that they would be called upon to shed their blood in loyalty to their faith, as if martyrdom was the inevitable result of tenacity. Nor is the writer blaming them; he does not mean to suggest that if they had been truly decided for God against the world, they would by this time have suffered **μέχρις αἵματος**. He is shaming them, not blaming them. "Your sufferings have been serious and sharp (10[32f.]), but nothing to what others before you, and especially Jesus, have had to bear. Will you give way under a lesser strain than theirs?" The coming of the messiah was to be heralded by birth-pangs of trouble for his adherents on earth, and it might be supposed that the writer implies here: "The Coming One (10[37]) is near (12[26]), as is evident from your woes; do not fail, but be ready for him." But this line of thought is not worked out elsewhere by the writer, and is not necessary to his argument at this point. To fight μέχρις αἵματος is to resist to the death; cp. the cry of Judas Maccabaeus to his troops (2 Mac 13[14]), ἀγωνίσασθαι μέχρι θανάτου. Μέχρις αἵματος has the same meaning of a mortal combat, *e.g.* in Heliod. vii. 8, τῆς μέχρις αἵματος στάσεως.

Note another case of rhetorical alliteration in αἵμ. ἀντικ. . . . ἁμαρτ. ἀνταγωνιζόμενοι (cp. *Clem. Hom.* iv. 5, πρὸς τοσαύτην δύναμιν ἀνταγωνίσασθαι), and the use of ἀνταγωνίζεσθαι above (v.[1]) in the quot. from 4 Mac.

The connexion of thought in vv.[5f.] is: God has not yet asked from you the supreme sacrifice (v.[4]), and, besides (vv.[5f.]), any demand he makes upon your courage is in your highest interests.

[5] *And have you forgotten the word of appeal that reasons with you as sons?—*

> "*My son, never make light of the Lord's discipline,*
> *never faint* (ἐκλύου) *under his reproofs;*
> [6] *for the Lord disciplines the man he loves,*
> *and scourges every son he receives.*"

[7] *It is for discipline that you have to endure. God is treating you as sons; for where is the son who is not disciplined by his father?* [8] *Discipline is the portion* (μέτοχοι γεγόνασι, as 3[14]) *of all; if you get no discipline, then you are not sons, but bastards.* [9] *Why, we had fathers of our flesh to discipline us,*

and we yielded to them! Shall we not far more submit to the Father of our spirits, and so live? [10] *For while their discipline was only for a time, and inflicted at their pleasure, he disciplines us for our good, that we may share in his own holiness.* [11] *Discipline always seems for the time to be a thing of pain, not of joy; but those who are trained by it reap the fruit of it afterwards in the peace of an upright life.*

With the interrogative καὶ ἐκλέλησθε κτλ. (v.[5]) the writer opens his next argument and appeal. All such ὑπομονή means a divine παιδεία or moral training, which we have the honour of receiving from God. Instead of adducing the example of Jesus, however (see on $5^{7.8}$), he quotes from the book of Proverbs (vv.[5.6]), and then applies the general idea (vv.[7-11]). Ἐκλανθάνεσθαι (not a LXX term) in v.[5] is slightly stronger than the more common ἐπιλανθάνεσθαι, though it may be rhetorically chosen for the sake of assonance after ἐκλυόμενοι. The παράκλησις is personified rhetorically; Ἥτις (2^3) ὑμῖν (for the scripture applies to all believers) ὡς υἱοῖς διαλέγεται. It is the παράκλησις of God, who speaks as a father to his son (υἱέ μου), though in the original "son" is merely the pupil of the sage (personifying the divine wisdom). Παράκλησις in Alexandrian Judaism "is the regular term for 'an appeal' to an individual to rise to the higher life of philosophy" (Conybeare's ed. of Philo's *de vit. Contempl.*, p. 201). The quotation is from Pr $3^{11.12}$ (A):

υἱέ, μὴ ὀλιγώρει παιδείας Κυρίου,
μηδὲ ἐκλύου ὑπ' αὐτοῦ ἐλεγχόμενος·
ὃν γὰρ ἀγαπᾷ Κύριος παιδεύει (ἐλέγχει, B)
μαστιγοῖ δὲ πάντα υἱὸν ὃν παραδέχεται.

After υἱέ, μου is added (except by D* 31 Old Latin, Clem.), but otherwise the citation is word for word. Philo (*De Congressu. Erud.* 31) quotes the same passage to prove that discipline and hardship are profitable for the soul (οὕτως ἄρα ἡ ἐπίπληξις καὶ νουθεσία καλὸν νενόμισται, ὥστε δι' αὐτῆς ἡ πρὸς θεὸν ὁμολογία συγγένεια γίνεται. τί γὰρ οἰκειότερον υἱῷ πατρὸς ἢ υἱοῦ πατρί;). The LXX contains a double mistranslation. (*a*) It is at least doubtful if the Hebrew text of the second line means "be not weary of"; the alternative is a parallel to the first line, "scorn not." (*b*) It is certain that the second line of v.[6] originally ran, "he afflicts the man in whom he delights," or "and delights in him as a father in his son." Our writer, following the free LXX version, notes the twofold attitude of men under hardship. They may determine to get through it and get over it, as if it had no relation to God, seeing nothing of him in it. Stronger natures take this line; they summon up a stoical courage, which dares the world to do its worst to them. This is ὀλιγωρεῖν παιδείας Κυρίου. It ignores any divine meaning in the rough experience. Other natures collapse weakly (ἐκλύειν); they see God in the trial, but he seems too hard upon them, and they break down in self-pity, as if they were victims of an unkind providence. **Ἐλεγχόμενος . . . παιδεύει** is used, as in Rev 3[19] (*ὅσους ἐὰν φιλῶ ἐλέγχω καὶ παιδεύω*), of pointing out and correcting faults; **μαστιγοῖ**, as in Judith 8[27] (*εἰς νουθέτησιν μαστιγοῖ Κύριος τοὺς ἐγγίζοντας αὐτῷ*) and often elsewhere; **παραδέχεται**, in the sense of Lk 15[2]. In fact, the temper inculcated in this passage resembles that of Ps.-Sol 16[11f.], where the writer prays:

> *γογγυσμὸν καὶ ὀλιγοψυχίαν ἐν θλίψει μάκρυνον ἀπ᾽ ἐμοῦ,*
> *ἐὰν ἁμαρτήσω ἐν τῷ σε παιδεύειν εἰς ἐπιστροφήν . . .*
> *ἐν τῷ ἐλέγχεσθαι ψυχὴν ἐν χειρὶ σαπρίας αὐτῆς . . .*
> *ἐν τῷ ὑπομεῖναι δίκαιον ἐν τούτοις ἐλεηθήσεται ὑπὸ κυρίου.*

In **εἰς παιδείαν ὑπομένετε** (v.[7]), with which the writer begins his application of the text, the vigour is lost by the change of *εἰς* into **εἰ** (in a group of late cursives, including 5. 35. 203. 226[c]. 241. 242. 257. 337. 378. 383. 487. 506. 547. 623. 794. 917. 1319. 1831. 1891. 1898. 2127. 2143 + Theophyl.), and *ὑπομένετε* is indicative, not imperative.[1] To endure rightly, one must endure intelligently; there is a reason for it in God's relations with us (**ὡς υἱοῖς ὑμῖν προσφέρεται**). **Προσφέρεται** (cp. *Syll.* 371[13], i A.D.) is a non-biblical Greek term for "treating" or "handling" ("tractare, agere cum"); cp. *Syll.* 371[13], i A.D., and Latyschev's *Inscript. Antiq. Orae Septentrionalis*, i. 22[28] *τοῖς μὲν ἡλικιώταις προσφερόμενος ὡς ἀδελφός . . . τοῖς δὲ παισὶν ὡς πατήρ*); *τίς* goes with *υἱός*, as in Mt 7[9] (*τίς ἐστιν ἐξ ὑμῶν ἄνθρωπος*) etc., and *ἐστιν* after *υἱός* is rightly omitted by ℵ* A P W 104. 256 vg sah Origen.

A mood of bitter scepticism about the discipline of providence recurs in some contemporary Roman writers; both Lucan (*Pharsalia*, iv. 807 f., "Felix Roma quidem, civesque habitura beatos, | si libertatis superis tam cura placeret | quam uindicta placet") and Tacitus (*Hist.* i. 3, "nec enim umquam atrocioribus populi Romani cladibus magisve iustis indiciis adprobatum est non esse curae deis securitatem nostram, esse ultionem") speak as if the gods showed an unpaternal vindictiveness. But the idea of a fatherly providence was far-spread, both within and without Judaism. When our author argues: "You think that if God were fatherly, he would spare you these hardships? On the contrary, they are the proof of his wise affection"—he is not far from Seneca's position (in the *de Providentia*, iv. 7): "hos itaque deus quos probat, quos amat, indurat recognoscit, exercet." And in 2 Mac 6[12] the author bids his readers re-

[1] D takes *εἰς παιδείαν* with the foregoing *παραδέχεται*, as Hofmann does with *μαστιγοῖ*. This leaves *ὑπομένετε* (*ὑπομείνατε* D) in quite an effective opening position for the next sentence; but it is not the writer's habit to end a quotation with some outside phrase.

member τὰς τιμωρίας μὴ πρὸς ὄλεθρον, ἀλλὰ πρὸς παιδίαν τοῦ γένους ἡμῶν εἶναι. According to Sanhedr. 101*a* (cp. Sifre, Deut. 32), Rabbi Akiba comforted R. Eliezer on his sick-bed by explaining to him that "chastisements are precious," whereas the other three rabbis who accompanied him had only praised the sick man for his piety. There is a fine passage in Philo's *quod deter. potiori insid. soleat*, 39–40, where he argues that discipline at God's hands is better than being left to oneself in sin and folly; εὐτυχέστεροι δὲ καὶ κρείττους τῶν ἀνεπιτροπεύτων νέων οἱ μάλιστα μὲν ἐπιστασίας καὶ ἀρχῆς ἀξιωθέντες φυσικῆς, ἣν οἱ γεννήσαντες ἐπὶ τέκνοις κεκλήρωνται . . . ἱκετεύωμεν οὖν τὸν θεὸν οἱ συνειδήσει τῶν οἰκείων ἀδικημάτων ἐλεγχόμενοι, κολάσαι ἡμᾶς μᾶλλον ἢ παρεῖναι. Similarly, in *de sacrificantibus*, 11, he writes of parental care, human and divine, apropos of Deut 14[1] (υἱοί ἐστε κυρίῳ τῷ θεῷ ὑμῶν) δηλονότι προνοίας καὶ κηδεμονίας ἀξιωθησόμενοι τῆς ὡς ἐκ πατρός· ἡ δὲ ἐπιμέλεια τοσοῦτον διοίσει τῆς ἀπ' ἀνθρώπων ὅσονπερ, οἶμαι, καὶ ὁ ἐπιμελούμενος διαφέρει. Compare M. Aur. i. 17, τὸ ἄρχοντι καὶ πατρὶ ὑποταχθῆναι, ὃς ἔμελλε πάντα τὸν τῦφον ἀφαιρήσειν μου (cp. v. 31). When the king asks, in the *Epist. Arist.* 248, what is the supreme instance of neglect (ἀμέλεια), the Jew answers, εἰ τέκνων ἄφροντίς τις εἴη, καὶ μὴ κατὰ πάντα τρόπον ἀγαγεῖν σπεύδοι . . . τὸ δὲ ἐπιδεῖσθαι παιδείαν σωφροσύνης μετασχεῖν, θεοῦ δυνάμει τοῦτο γίνεται.

Jerome writes in his letter (*Epist.* xxii. 39) to Eustochium: "haec est sola retributio, cum sanguis sanguine conpensatur et redempti cruore Christi pro redemptore libenter occumbimus. quis sanctorum sine certamine coronatus est? Abel justus occiditur; Abraham uxorem periclitatur amittere, et, ne in inmensum uolumen extendam, quaere et invenies singulos diuersa perpessos. solus in deliciis Salomon fuit et forsitan ideo corruit. quem enim diligit dominus, corripit; castigat autem omnem filium, quem recipit." He often quotes this verse (6) in his letters of counsel and warning. Thus in lxviii. 1 he prefixes it with the remark, "magna ira est, quando peccantibus non irascitur deus." The modern parallel would be Browning's hero in *Christmas-Eve and Easter-Day* (pt. 2, xxxiii.), who is

> "happy that I can
> Be crossed and thwarted as a man,
> Not left in God's contempt apart,
> With ghastly smooth life."

In v.[8] **πάντες** (*sc.* υἱοὶ γνήσιοι) recalls **πάντα υἱόν** (v.[6]). **Νόθοι** are children born out of wedlock, who are left to themselves; the father is not sufficiently interested in them to inflict on them the discipline that fits his legitimate children for their place in the home. Νόθος (not a LXX term) seems to mean born of mixed marriages, in Wis 4[3] (cp. Aristoph. *Birds*, 1650–1652, νόθος γὰρ εἶ κοὐ γνήσιος . . . ὤν γε ξένης γυναικός). So Philo compares polytheists and lovers of material pleasure to τῶν ἐκ πόρνης ἀποκυηθέντων (*de Confus. ling.* 28), as distinguished from the sons of God. The double ἔστε (not ἦτε) makes the sentence more vivid; the writer supposes an actual case. In vv.[9. 10] the writer simply develops this idea of παιδεία, comparing the human and the divine methods. Hence εἶτα cannot mean here "further" (deinde); it is "besides," in the sense that it brings out another element in the conception.

Εἶτα might be taken interrogatively (=itane or siccine), to introduce an animated question (as often in Plato, *e.g. Leges*, 964*b*, *Theat.* 207*d*, *Sophist.* 222*b*), though we should expect a δέ in the second clause here or a καί before οὐ πολὺ μᾶλλον. Kypke suggests that εἶτα=εἰ δέ (quodsi) as, *e.g.*, in Jos. *B.J.* iii. 8. 5, εἶτ' ἂν μὲν ἀφανίσῃ τις ἀνθρώπου παρακαταθήκην, ἢ διάθηται κακῶς.

Παιδευτής only occurs once in the LXX, and there as a description of God (Hos 5[2] ἐγὼ δὲ παιδευτὴς ὑμῶν); in 4 Mac 9[6] (ὁ παιδευτὴς γέρων) it is applied to a man, as in Ro 2[20]. Καὶ ἐνετρεπόμεθα ("reverebamur," vg), we submitted respectfully to them (the object of the verb being πατέρας), as in Mt 21[37], not, we amended our ways (as in LXX, *e.g.* 2 Ch 7[14] and Philo's *quaest. in Gen.* 4[9] τὸ μὴ ἁμαρτάνειν μηδὲν τὸ παραμέγιστον ἀγαθόν· τὸ ἁμαρτάνοντα ἐντραπῆναι συγγένες ἐκείνου). In οὐ πολὺ μᾶλλον, the more common πολλῷ is read by D[c] K L, and after πολύ a few authorities (p[13] ℵ[c] D* 1739 Origen) supply the δέ which is strictly required after the preceding μέν. The description of God as τῷ πατρὶ τῶν πνευμάτων is unexpected. In the vocabulary of Hellenistic Judaism God is called ὁ τῶν πνευμάτων καὶ πάσης ἐξουσίας δυνάστης (2 Mac 3[24]), and "Lord of spirits" is a favourite Enochic title; but "spirits" here cannot mean angels (cp. Nu 16[22]). The contrast between τοὺς τῆς σαρκὸς πατέρας and τῷ πατρὶ τῶν πνευμάτων denotes God as the author of man's spiritual being; the expression is quite intelligible as a statement of practical religion, and is only rendered ambiguous when we read into it later ideas about traducianism and creationism, which were not in the writer's mind. Shall we not submit to Him, the writer asks, καὶ ζήσομεν (cp. 10[38] ζήσεται)? "Monemur hoc verbo nihil esse nobis magis exitiale quam si nos in Dei obsequium tradere recusemus" (Calvin). In v.[10] the assumption that the readers were mature men (εἴχομεν, v.[9]) is made explicit by πρὸς ὀλίγας ἡμέρας (till we became men). Πρός here, as in Wis 16[6] (εἰς νουθεσίαν δὲ πρὸς ὀλίγον ἐταράχθησαν) etc., means duration; it is not final, as if the parental discipline were with a view to the short, earthly life alone. Κατὰ τὸ δοκοῦν αὐτοῖς (as they chose) refers to the arbitrariness of the *patria potestas*. "Parents may err, but he is wise," as the Scottish metrical paraphrase puts it.

The writer has in mind the familiar *patria potestas* of the Romans, as in Terence's *Heauton Timoroumenos* (100: "vi et via pervolgata patrum";

204–207: "parentum iniuriae unius modi sunt ferme . . . atque haec sunt tamen ad virtutem omnia"), where one father is confessing to another how he had mishandled his boy (99 f.: "ubi rem rescivi, coepi non humanitus neque ut animum decuit aegrotum adulescentuli tractare"). Compare the remark of the Persian officer in Xenophon's *Cyropaedia* (ii. 2. 14), who argued that a man who set himself to make people laugh did less for them than a man who made them weep, and instanced fathers—κλαύμασι μέν γε καὶ πατέρες υἱοῖς σωφροσύνην μηχανῶνται. This is wholesome correction. But it was not always so. "Qur postremo filio suscenseam, patres ut faciunt ceteri?" old Demaenetus asks, in the *Asinaria* (49) of Plautus. Ovid's "durus pater" (*Amores*, i. 15. 17) was more than a tradition of literature. Pliny tells us, for example, that he had once to remonstrate with a man who was thrashing his son for wasting money on horses and dogs (*Epp.* ix. 12): "haec tibi admonitus immodicae seueritatis exemplo pro amore mutuo scripsi, ne quando tu quoque filium tuum acerbius duriusque tractares." There is also the story told by Aelian (*Var. Hist.* ix. 33) about the youth who, when asked by his father what he had learned from Zeno, was thrashed for failing to show anything definite, and then calmly replied that he had learned stoically to put up with a father's bad temper (ἔφη μεμαθηκέναι φέρειν ὀργὴν πατέρων καὶ μὴ ἀγανακτεῖν). Sons, says Dio Chrysostom (xv. 240 M), τρέφονται πάντες ὑπὸ τῶν πατέρων καὶ παίονται πόλλακις ὑπ' αὐτῶν. The general point of view is put by Epictetus (*Enchiridion*, 30, πατήρ ἐστιν· ὑπαγορεύεται ἐπιμελεῖσθαι, παραχωρεῖν ἀπάντων, ἀνέχεσθαι λοιδοροῦντος, παίοντος), and the connexion of "life" with παιδεία in Pr 4^{13} ἐπιλαβοῦ ἐμῆς παιδείας, μὴ ἀφῇς, ἀλλὰ φύλαξον αὐτὴν σεαυτῷ εἰς ζωήν σου: Pr 6^{23} λύχνος ἐντολὴ νόμου καὶ φῶς, καὶ ὁδὸς ζωῆς καὶ ἔλεγχος καὶ παιδεία, and Sir $4^{17f.}$.

Now for the contrast. **Ὁ δὲ** (God; *sc.* παιδεύει ἡμᾶς) **ἐπὶ τὸ συμφέρον** (cp. 1 Co 12^7; *Ep. Arist.* 125, συμβουλευόντων πρὸς τὸ συμφέρον τῶν φίλων), which is explained in **εἰς τὸ μεταλαβεῖν** (cp. 6^7) **τῆς ἁγιότητος αὐτοῦ.** **Ἁγιότης** is a rare term, which begins to appear late in Hellenistic Judaism (*e.g.* 2 Mac 15^2 τοῦ πάντα ἐφορῶντος μεθ' ἁγιότητος: *Test. Levi* 3^4 ὑπεράνω πάσης ἁγιότητος), and, except as a *v.l.* in 2 Co 1^{12}, occurs nowhere else in the NT. Here it denotes the divine life, to share in which is the outcome of **ὁ ἁγιασμὸς οὗ χωρὶς οὐδεὶς ὄψεται** (*i.e.* have a direct experience of) **τὸν κύριον** (v.[14]). The writer, in this contrast, is simply arguing that the divine education, which involves some suffering, as all παιδεία does, is more worthy of obedience from mature people than even the parental discipline to which, for all its faults of temper, they submitted during childhood. The sayings of Isokrates, that while the roots of παιδεία were bitter, its fruits were sweet, was a commonplace of ancient morals; the writer is going to develop it in a moment. Meantime he alludes to the equally well-known truth that παιδεία might involve severe physical treatment.

Two examples may be added of this doctrine that education involves a discipline which sometimes requires the infliction of pain. Maximus of Tyre (*Diss.* iv. 7), in arguing that the desire to give pleasure is by no means an invariable proof of true affection, asks: φιλοῦσιν δὲ που καὶ παῖδας πατέρες καὶ διδάσκαλοι μαθητάς· καὶ τί ἂν εἴη ἀνιαρότερον ἢ παιδὶ πατὴρ καὶ μαθητῇ διδάσκαλος; so Philo argues in *de Migrat. Abrah.* 20, σωφρονιστῶν ὡς ἔοικε τοῦτ᾽

ἐστι τὸ ἔθος, παιδαγωγῶν, διδασκάλων, γονέων, πρεσβυτέρων, ἀρχόντων, νόμων· ὀνειδίζοντες γάρ, ἔστι δ' ὅπου καὶ κολάζοντες ἕκαστοι τούτων ἀμείνους τὰς ψυχὰς ἀπεργάζονται τῶν παιδευομένων. καὶ ἐχθρὸς μὲν οὐδεὶς οὐδενί, φίλοι δὲ πᾶσι πάντες. In *de parent. col.* 4, he explains, διὰ τοῦτ' ἔξεστι τοῖς πατράσι καὶ κατηγορεῖν πρὸς τοὺς παῖδας καὶ ἐμβριθέστερον νουθετεῖν καί, εἰ μὴ ταῖς δι' ἀκοῶν ἀπειλαῖς ὑπείκουσι, τύπτειν καὶ προπηλακίζειν καὶ καταδεῖν.

In v.[11] the writer sums up what he has been saying since v.[5]. Discipline or **παιδεία πρὸς τὸ παρόν** (a classical Greek phrase = for the moment, *e.g.* Thuc. ii. 22, ὁρῶν αὐτοὺς πρὸς τὸ παρὸν χαλεπαίνοντας) **οὐ** (πᾶς . . . οὐ = absolute negative, not any) **δοκεῖ** (to human feelings and judgment) **χαρᾶς εἶναι ἀλλὰ λύπης** (to be a matter of, εἶναι with gen. as in 10[39]).

Πᾶσα μέν (ℵ* P 33. 93) and **πᾶσα δέ** (p[13] ℵ[c] A D[c] H K L Ψ 6. 326. 929. 1288. 1836 vg syr boh Chrys. etc.) practically mean the same thing, for the μέν is concessive ("of course") and δέ is metabatic. But probably it was the awkwardness of the double μέν that led to the alteration of this one. The other readings, **πᾶσα γάρ** (Cosm. (221 C) Jer. Aug.) and πᾶσα (D* 104. 460. 917 arm eth Orig. Cosm. (376 D)) are obviously inferior attempts to clear up the passage.

Ὕστερον δέ (cp. Pr 5[3. 4] (of the harlot) ἣ πρὸς καιρὸν λιπαίνει σου φάρυγγα· ὕστερον μέντοι πικρότερον χολῆς εὑρήσεις), but later on discipline yields fruit; it is not a stone flung down arbitrarily on human life, but a seed. By **καρπὸν εἰρηνικὸν δικαιοσύνης** the writer means fruit (καρπός as often = result or outcome), which consists in (genit. of apposition) δικαιοσύνη (as in 11[7] a generic term for the good life as a religious relationship to God). But why **εἰρηνικόν**? Possibly in contrast to the restiveness and pain (**λύπης**) of the period of discipline, when people are being trained (**γεγυμνασμένοις**); when the discipline does its perfect work, there is no friction between the soul and God. But there is also the suggestion of "saving" or "blissful." Philo quotes Pr 3[11. 12] (see above on v.[5]) as a saying of Solomon *the peaceful* (εἰρηνικός); the significance of this he finds in the thought that subjection and obedience are really a wholesome state for people who are inclined to be self-assertive, uncontrolled, and quarrelsome. He thinks that Noah is rightly called by a name denoting rest, since μετίασιν ἠρεμαῖον δὲ καὶ ἡσυχάζοντα καὶ σταθερὸν ἔτι δὲ καὶ εἰρηνικὸν βίον οἱ καλοκἀγαθίαν τετιμηκότες (*Abrah.* 5). To take εἰρηνικόν in some such sense (salutaris) would yield a good interpretation; and this is confirmed by the similar use of εἰρήνη in v.[14] and of the adjective in 3 Mac 6[32], where the Jews, in the ecstasy of their relief, χοροὺς συνίσταντο εὐφροσύνης εἰρηνικῆς σημεῖον. Those who stand their training reap a safe, sound life at last. In its social aspect, εἰρηνικόν could only refer to the brotherly love of the community; the writer might be throwing out a hint to his readers, that suffering was apt to render people irritable, impatient with one another's faults. The later record even of the martyrs, for example, shows that the very prospect of death did not always prevent Christians from quarrelling in prison. This may be the meaning of εἰρηνικόν in Ja 3[18], but it is out of keeping with the present context.

A close parallel to v.[11] is the saying of Aristotle (see above, for the similar remark of Isokrates), quoted by Diog. Laertius (v. 1. 18): τῆς παιδείας ἔφη τὰς μὲν ῥίζας εἶναι πικράς, γλυκεῖς δὲ τοὺς καρπούς. In *Epist. Arist.* 232, τοὺς γὰρ ἀπ' αὐτῆς (*i.e.* δικαιοσύνης) ἀλυπίαν κατασκευάζειν, though the ἀλυπία here is freedom from misfortune. Clem. Alex. (*Strom.* vii. 10. 56), after speaking of the time when we are delivered from the chastisements and punishments ἃς ἐκ τῶν ἁμαρτημάτων εἰς παιδείαν ὑπομένομεν σωτήριον [He 12[7]], adds: μεθ' ἣν ἀπολύτρωσιν τὸ γέρας καὶ αἱ τιμαὶ τελειωθεῖσιν ἀποδίδονται . . . καὶ θεοὶ τὴν προσηγορίαν κέκληνται οἱ σύνθρονοι τῶν ἄλλων θεῶν, τῶν ὑπὸ τῷ σωτῆρι πρώτων τεταγμένων, γενησόμενοι.

The writer now resumes the imperative tone (vv.[12f.]), with a blend of counsel and warning. The discipline of trouble is viewed under an active aspect; men must co-operate with God, exerting themselves to avoid sin (v.[1]) by the exercise of personal zeal and church-discipline. Otherwise, the results may be fatal. The exhortation broadens out here, resuming the tone and range of 10[25f.].

[12] *So* (διό as in 6[1]) "*up with your listless hands! Strengthen your weak knees!*" [13] *And* "*make straight paths for your feet*" *to walk in. You must not let the lame get dislocated, but rather make them whole.* [14] *Aim at peace with all—at that consecration without which no one will ever see the Lord;* [15] *see to it that no one misses the grace of God,* "*that no root of bitterness grows up to be a trouble*" *by contaminating all the rest of you;* [16] *that no one turns to sexual vice or to a profane life as Esau did—Esau who for a single meal* "*parted with his birthright.*" [17] *You know how later on, when he wanted to obtain his inheritance of blessing, he was set aside; he got no chance to repent, though he tried for it with tears.*

For the first time, since the hints in 3[12] 4[1] and 6[11], the writer alludes to differences of attainment in the little community. Hitherto he has treated them as a solid whole. But the possibility of individual members giving way has been voiced in 10[29], and now the writer ([13b]) widens his appeal; his readers are to maintain their faith not only for their own sakes but for the sake of those who at their side are in special danger of collapsing. The courage of their ὑπομονή is more than a personal duty; they are responsible for their fellow-members, and this involves the duty of inspiriting others by their own unswerving, unflagging faith. The admonition, as in 13[1f.], is addressed to the whole community, not to their leaders. The general aim of vv.[12. 13] is to produce the character praised by Matthew Arnold in his lines on Rugby Chapel:

"Ye move through the ranks, recall
The stragglers, refresh the out-worn . . .
Ye fill up the gaps in our files,
Strengthen the wavering line,

Stablish, continue our march,
On, to the bound of the waste,
On, to the City of God."

He begins in v.[12] by using scriptural language borrowed freely from Is 35[3] (ἰσχύσατε, χεῖρες ἀνειμέναι καὶ γόνατα παραλελυμένα), but in a form already current in Sir 25[32] (χεῖρες παρειμέναι καὶ γόνατα παραλελυμένα), and also from Pr 4[26] (ὄρθας τροχιὰς ποίει τοῖς ποσίν). This metaphorical language for collapsing in listless despair is common, *e.g.*, in Sir 2[12] where χεῖρες παρειμέναι is bracketed with "cowardly hearts," in Philo's description of the Israelites who longed to return to Egypt, οἱ μὲν γὰρ προκαμόντες ἀνέπεσον, βαρὺν ἀντίπαλον ἡγησάμενοι τὸν πόνον, καὶ τὰς χεῖρας ὑπ' ἀσθενείας ὥσπερ ἀπειρηκότες ἀθληταὶ καθῆκαν (*de Congressu Erud.* 29, cp. He 11[15]), and especially in the description of moral encouragement in Job 4[3. 4] εἰ γὰρ σὺ ἐνουθέτησας πολλοὺς, καὶ χεῖρας ἀσθενοῦς παρεκάλεσας, ἀσθενοῦντάς τε ἐξανέστησας ῥήμασιν, γόνασίν τε ἀδυνατοῦσιν θάρσος περιέθηκας. In Dt 32[36] παραλελυμένους is parallel to παρειμένους, and in Zeph 3[16] the appeal is θάρσει . . . μὴ παρείσθωσαν αἱ χεῖρές σου.[1] **Ἀνορθώσατε** (literally = straighten, renew) goes with **γόνατα** better than with **χεῖρας**, but the sense is plain. In v.[13], if **ποιήσατε** is read in the first clause, **καὶ τροχιὰς ὀρθὰς ποιήσατε τοῖς ποσὶν ὑμῶν** is a hexameter (p. lvii). By **τὸ χωλόν** the writer means "those who are lame," these crippled souls in your company.

Probably the ποιεῖτε of ℵ* P 33. 917. 1831 (Orig.) has been conformed, in ποιήσατε (ℵ[c] A D H K L, etc., Chrys.), to the preceding ἀνορθώσατε (so, *e.g.*, B. Weiss, in *Texte u. Untersuch.* xiv. 3. 4, 9, who declares that the older codices never yield any case of an original aor. being changed into a present), though some edd. (*e.g.* von Soden) regard ποιήσατε as the original text and ποιεῖτε as having been conformed to LXX (cp. Mt 3[3]).

As **ἰαθῇ δὲ μᾶλλον** shows, **ἐκτραπῇ** here has its medical sense (*e.g.* Hippol. *de offic. med.* 14, ὡς μήτε ἀνακλᾶται μήτε ἐκτρέπηται), not the common sense of being "turned aside" (as, *e.g.*, in Philo, *Quaest. in Exod.* 23[20] οἱ ἀφυλάκτως ὁδοιποροῦντες διαμαρτάνουσιν τῆς ὀρθῆς καὶ λεωφόρου ὡς πολλάκις εἰς ἀνοδίας καὶ δυσβάτους καὶ τραχείας ἀτραποὺς ἐκτρέπεσθαι· τὸ παραπλήσιόν ἐστιν ὅτε καὶ αἱ ψυχαὶ τῶν νεῶν παιδείας ἀμοιροῦσιν, and in M. Aurel. i. 7, καὶ τὸ μὴ ἐκτραπῆναι εἰς ζῆλον σοφιστικόν). In Od. Sol 6[14f.] the ministers of the divine grace are praised in similar terms for their service to weaker Christians:

"They have assuaged the dry lips,
And the will that had fainted they have raised up: . . .
And limbs that had fallen
They have straightened and set up."

[1] *Clem. Hom.* xii. 18, αἱ χεῖρες ὑπὸ δηγμάτων παρείθησαν.

But here it is the members as a whole who are addressed, and **τροχ. ὀρθας π. τ. ποσὶν ὑμῶν** means "keep straight" (*ποσίν*, dative = "for your feet")—it is the only way to help your fellow-members who have weakened themselves. Keep up the tone of your community, move in the right direction, to prevent any of your number from wavering and wandering. The straight path is the smooth path, it is implied; if any limping soul is allowed to stray from the straight course, under the influence of a bad example, he will be made worse instead of better. The admonition in *Test. Sim.* $5^{2.3}$ is interesting, as it suggests the train of thought here between vv.[12f.] and [16f.]:

ἀγαθύνατε τὰς καρδίας ὑμῶν ἐνώπιον Κυρίου
καὶ εὐθύνατε τὰς ὁδοὺς ὑμῶν ἐνώπιον τῶν ἀνθρώπων
καὶ ἔσεσθε εὑρίσκοντες χάριν ἐνώπιον Κυρίου καὶ ἀνθρώπων.
φυλάξασθε οὖν ἀπὸ τῆς πορνείας,
ὅτι ἡ πορνεία μήτηρ ἐστὶ τῶν κακῶν,
χωρίζουσα ἀπὸ τοῦ θεοῦ καὶ προσεγγίζοῦσα τῷ Βελίαρ.

The author of **Πρὸς Ἑβραίους** knows that the difficulties in the way of faith are more than mere despair. In 12^{1-11} he has been dealing with the need of cheerful courage under the strain of life; this leads to the appeal of v.[12]. But while there is nothing so infectious as cowardice or despair, he rapidly passes on, in vv.[13f.] (*καί κτλ.*), to warn his readers against some specific temptations in the moral life. He continues, in a third imperative (v.[14]), **εἰρήνην διώκετε** (an OT phrase, 1 P 3^{11}) **μετὰ πάντων.** Here *μετά* goes with *διώκετε* in the sense of "along with" (as in 11^{9} 13^{23}, for our author avoids *σύν*), and *πάντων* means "all the (other) *ἅγιοι*" (as in 13^{24}). The call is to make common cause with all the rest of the Christians in the quest for God's *εἰρήνη*, *i.e.* (see above on v.[11]) the bliss and security of a life under God's control. It is *εἰρήνη* in a sense corresponding to the older sense of felicity and prosperity on the ground of some (messianic) victory of God, practically as in Lk 1^{79} 19^{38} the Christian salvation; only this comprehensive sense does justice to the term here and in 13^{20}. Hence the following *καί* is almost = "even."

Εἰρήνη in a similar sense occurs repeatedly in the context of the passage already quoted from Proverbs: *e.g.* $3^{1.2}$ *υἱέ, ἐμῶν νομίμων μὴ ἐπιλανθάνου, τὰ δὲ ῥήματα μου τηρείτω σὴ καρδία· μῆκος γὰρ βίου καὶ ἔτη ζωῆς καὶ εἰρήνην προσθήσουσίν σοι . . .* 3^{9} *ἀπάρχου αὐτῷ ἀπὸ σῶν καρπῶν δικαιοσύνης . . .* $3^{16.17}$ *ἐκ τοῦ στόματος αὐτῆς ἐκπορεύεται δικαιοσύνη καὶ πάντες οἱ τρίβοι αὐτῆς ἐν εἰράνῃ . . .* 3^{23} *ἵνα πορεύῃ πεποιθὼς ἐν εἰρήνῃ πάσας τὰς ὁδούς σου.* After Pr 4^{26} (as quoted above) there follows the promise, *αὐτὸς δὲ τὰς ὀρθὰς ποιήσει τὰς τροχίας σου, τὰς δὲ πορείας σου ἐν εἰρηνῃ προάξει.*

The conventional interpretation takes **εἰρήνην** with **μετὰ πάντων** (*i.e.* all your members). This yields a fair sense, for a quarrelsome church is a real hindrance to effective faith; the quarrelsomeness here would be due to the presence of faulty persons, whose lapses were apt to be irritating, and what would break *εἰρήνη* (*i.e.* mutual harmony) in such cases is the spirit of harshness in dealing with faults, censoriousness, or aloofness, just as what makes for *εἰρήνη* is a concern for purity and goodness inspired by forbearance and patience. But all this is read into the text. There is no hint of such dangers elsewhere in Πρὸς Ἑβραίους as there is in 1 P 3[8f.] and Ro 12[16f.]. Our author is characteristically putting a new edge on an old phrase like *διώκετε εἰρήνην*.

What *εἰρήνη* specially involved is shown in **καὶ τὸν ἁγιασμόν** *κτλ.* Here **ἁγιασμός** is not to be identified with **σωφροσύνη** in the special sense of 13[4]; it is the larger "consecration" to God which all **ἅγιοι** must maintain. In fact, **διώκετε τὸν ἁγιασμόν** *κτλ.* is simply another description of the experience called "sharing in God's **ἁγιότης**" (v.[10]). **Χωρίς** generally precedes, here it follows, the word it governs (**οὗ**), either for the sake of the rhythm or to avoid a hiatus (**οὗ οὐδείς**). "To see the Lord," is an expression common in Philo for that vision of the Divine being which is the rare reward of those who can purify themselves from the sensuous (cp. H. A. A. Kennedy's *Philo's Contribution to Religion*, pp. 192 f.). **Κύριος** is God in vv.[5] and [6]; here, in view of 9[28], it might be Jesus (as 2[3]), though "to see God" (vg "deum") as a term for intimate personal fellowship is more adequate to the context. People must be on the alert against tendencies to infringe this **ἁγιασμός** (v.[15]); **ἐπισκοποῦντες**, one form and function of **παρακαλοῦντες** (10[25]), introduces three clauses, beginning each with **μή τις**, though it is not clear whether the third (v.[16]) is intended as an example of **μιανθῶσιν** or as a further definition of the second **μή τις** (**ῥίζα** *κτλ.*). The first clause, **μή τις ὑστερῶν** (*sc.* **ᾖ**) **ἀπὸ τῆς χάριτος τοῦ θεοῦ**, shows **ὑστερεῖν** (4[1]) with **ἀπό** as in Eccles 6[2] *ὑστερῶν . . . ἀπὸ πάντος οὗ ἐπιθυμήσει* (Sir 7[34] *μὴ ὑστέρει ἀπὸ κλαιόντων* has a different sense). In writing *ἀπὸ τῆς χάριτος τοῦ θεοῦ* the writer may have had already in mind the words of Dt 29[18] (*μὴ τίς ἐστιν ἐν ὑμῖν . . . τίνος ἡ διάνοια ἐξέκλινεν ἀπὸ κυρίου τοῦ θεοῦ ἡμῶν*), which he is about to quote in the next clause.

The rhetorical tone comes out in the two iambic trimeters *οὗ χωρὶς οὐδεὶς ὄψεται τὸν κύριον* and *ἐπισκοποῦντες μή τις ὑστερῶν ἀπό.*

The next clause, **μή τις ῥίζα πικρίας ἄνω φύουσα ἐνοχλῇ**, is a reminiscence of the warning against idolatry and apostasy in Dt 29[18], which A (as well as F*) preserves in this form, *μή τίς ἐστιν ἐν ὑμῖν ῥίζα πικρίας ἄνω φύουσα ἐνοχλῇ* (so B*: *ἐν χολῇ* B) *καὶ πικρίᾳ* (B*: *καὶ πικρία* B). The form is ungrammatical, for **ἐστιν** is superfluous, as is **καὶ πικρίᾳ**. On the other hand, the text of B yields no good sense, for a root can hardly be said to grow up **ἐν χολῇ**, and *καὶ πικρία* is left stranded; the alteration of **πικρίᾳ** in B* does not help matters, for it is not preceded by **ἐν χολῇ**.

Plainly the writer found something like the words of A in his text of the LXX; he may have omitted ἐστιν and καὶ πικρίᾳ. The confusion between -οχλη and χολη is intelligible, as ὄχλος and χόλος are confused elsewhere (Blass reads ἐν χολῇ here, which requires ᾖ or ἐστιν to be supplied). Ἐνοχλῇ is the present subjunctive of ἐνοχλεῖν, which is used in 1 Es 2^{19} (ἐνοχλοῦσα) and 2^{24} (ἐνοχλῆσαι) of rebellion disturbing and troubling the realm. As a general term for "troubling" or "vexing," it is common both in classical Greek and in the papyri, either absolutely or with an accusative, as, *e.g.*, Polystr. *Epicur.* (ed. C. Wilke) 8*b*. 4, οὐδ' ὑφ' ἑνὸς τούτων ἐνοχλησαμένους ἡμᾶς, the edict of M. Sempronius Liberalis (Aug. 29, 154 A.D.): ἐν τῇ οἰκείᾳ τῇ γεω[ργ]ίᾳ προσκαρτεροῦσι μὴ ἐνοχλεῖν (*BGU.* ii. 372), and Aristoph. *Frogs*, 709 f., οὐ πολὺν οὐδ' ὁ πίθηκος οὗτος ὁ νῦν ἐνοχλῶν. As for ῥίζα (of a person, as, *e.g.*, in 1 Mac 1^{10} καὶ ἐξῆλθεν ἐξ αὐτῶν ῥίζα ἁμαρτωλὸς Ἀντίοχος Ἐπιφανής) πικρίας (genitive of quality), the meaning is a poisonous character and influence (cp. Ac 8^{23}). The warning in Deuteronomy is against any pernicious creature in the community, who by cool insolence and infidelity draws down the divine sentence of extermination upon himself and his fellows. Here the writer thinks of people who consider that immediate gratification of their wishes is worth more than any higher end in life; they value their spiritual position as sons (vv.$^{5f.}$) so little, that they let it go in order to relapse on some material relief at the moment. Such a nature is essentially βέβηλος, devoid of any appreciation of God's privileges, and regarding these as of no more importance than sensuous pleasures of the hour. Under the bad influence of this (διὰ ταύτης, ℵ D K L Ψ 326, etc., as in 13^2: διὰ αὐτῆς, A H P 33. 424* syr^{hkl} boh Clem. etc., as in 11^4 12^{11}), all the rest (οἱ πολλοί, after one has been mentioned, as in Ro 5^{15} etc.) may be tainted (μιανθῶσι), and so (cp. on 10^{22}) rendered incapable of ὄψεσθαι τὸν Κύριον.

The third clause (v.^{16}) is μή τις (*sc.* ᾖ) πόρνος ἢ βέβηλος (for the collocation see Philo, *de Sacerdot.* 8, πόρνῃ καὶ βεβήλῳ σῶμα καὶ ψυχήν, and for this transferred sense of β. (= Lat. profanus) see Jebb-Pearson's *Fragments of Soph.* ii. 208); βέβηλος is only once applied to a person in the LXX, viz. in Ezk 21^{25} σὺ βέβηλε ἄνομε (= חָלָל), then to people like Antiochus (3 Mac $2^{2. 14}$) or (3 Mac 7^{15} τοὺς βεβήλους χειρωσάμενοι) recreant Jews. In adding ὡς Ἡσαῦ κτλ. the writer chooses the story of Esau, in Gn 25^{28-34} 27^{1-39}, to illustrate the disastrous results of yielding to the ἁμαρτία of which he had spoken in v.^{1}. There can be no ὑπομονή, he implies, without a resolute determination to resist the immediate pleasures and passions of the hour. As Cicero puts it in the *De Finibus*, i. 14, "plerique, quod tenere atque servare id quod ipsi statuerunt non possunt, victi et debilitati objecta specie voluptatis tradunt se libidinibus constringendos nec quid eventurum sit provident, ob eamque causam propter voluptatem et parvam et non necessariam et quae vel aliter pararetur et qua etiam carere possent sine dolore, tum in morbos graves, tum in damna, tum in dedecora incurrunt." But why choose Esau? Probably owing to rabbinic tradition, in which Esau is the typical instance of the godless who grow up among good people (Isaac and Rebekah) and yet do not follow their deeds, as Obadiah is of the good who grow up among the wicked (Ahab and Jezebel) and do not follow *their* deeds (Sifre 133 on Nu 27[1]). The rabbinic tradition[1] that Esau was sensual, is voiced as early as Philo, in the *de Nobilitate*, 4 (ὁ δὲ μείζων ἀπειθὴς ἐκ τῶν γαστρὸς καὶ τῶν μετὰ γαστέρα ἡδονῶν ἀκρατῶς ἔχων, ὑφ' ὧν ἀνεπείσθη καὶ πρεσβείων ἐξίστασθαι τῷ μετ' αὐτοῦ καὶ μετανοεῖν εὐθὺς ἐφ' οἷς ἐξέστη καὶ φονᾶν κατὰ τοῦ ἀδελφοῦ καὶ μηδὲν ἕτερον ἢ δι' ὧν λυπήσει τοὺς γονεῖς πραγματεύεσθαι), where Philo interprets the **μετάνοια** of Esau as simply regret for a bad bargain. Our author may have considered Esau a **πόρνος** literally—and in any case the word is to be taken literally (as in 13[4]), not in its OT metaphorical sense[2] of "unfaithful"—but the weight of the warning falls on βέβηλος, as is clear from the phrase **ἀντὶ βρώσεως μιᾶς** (cp. Gn 25[28] ἡ θήρα αὐτοῦ βρῶσις αὐτῷ). T. H. Green (*Prolegomena to Ethics*, § 96) points out that hunger was not the motive. "If the action were determined directly by the hunger, it would have no moral character, any more than have actions done in sleep, or strictly under compulsion, or from accident, or (so far as we know) the action of animals. Since, however, it is not the hunger as a natural force, but his own conception of himself, as finding for the time his greatest good in the satisfaction of hunger, that determines the act, Esau recognizes himself as the author of the act. . . . If evil follows from it, whether in the shape of punishment inflicted by a superior, or of calamity ensuing in the course of nature to himself or those in whom he is interested, he is aware that he himself has brought it on himself." The μιᾶς is emphatic: "id culpam auget, non misericordiam meretur" (Bengel).

In the quotation from Gn 25[33] (ἀπέδοτο δὲ Ἠσαὺ τὰ πρωτοτοκεῖα τῷ Ἰακώβ), **ἀπέδετο** (A C 623), as if from a form **ἀποδίδω** (cp. Helbing, 105), is preferred by Lachmann, B. Weiss, WH.

The warning is now (v.[17]) driven home. **Ἴστε**, indicative here (a literary Atticism, though Blass insists that it is chosen for the

[1] Jub 25[1. 8] (Esau tempting Jacob to take one of his own two sensual wives).

[2] Πορνεία has this sense, and so has the verb (*e.g.* Ps 73[27] ἐξωλέθρευσας πάντα τὸν πορνεύοντα ἀπὸ σοῦ).

sake of the rhythm, to assimilate **ἴστε γὰρ ὅτι καὶ με(τέπειτα)** to the closing words of the preceding sentence), recalls to the readers the scripture story with which they were so familiar. **Ἴστε ὅτι καὶ** (another item in his story) **μετέπειτα θέλων κληρονομῆσαι** (1 P 3^9) **τὴν εὐλογίαν** (=*πρωτοτόκια* as in 1 Ch $5^{1.2}$) **ἀπεδοκιμάσθη** (Jer 6^{30} *ἀπεδοκίμασεν αὐτοὺς Κύριος*: Ign. *Rom.* 8^3 *ἐὰν ἀποδοκιμασθῶ*). **Ἀποδοκιμάζεσθαι** is common in the Greek orators for officials being disqualified, but the rejection here is an act of God; Esau is a tragic instance of those who cannot get a second chance of *μετάνοια* (6^6). The writer has again the sombre, serious outlook which characterizes a passage like 6^{4-8}. The very metaphor of plant-growth occurs here as there, and *ἀπεδοκιμάσθη* recalls *ἀδόκιμος*. *Μετάνοια* is impossible for certain wilful sins; certain acts of deliberate choice are irrevocable and fatal. Why this was so, in Esau's case, is now explained; **μετανοίας γὰρ τόπον οὐχ εὗρε** (*εὑρίσκω*=obtain, with *ἐκζητεῖν* as often in LXX, *e.g.* Dt 4^{29}), **καίπερ μετὰ δακρύων** (emphatic by position) **ἐκζητήσας αὐτήν** (*i.e. μετανοίαν*. "*Μετανοίας τόπος* is, in fact, *μετάνοια*. . . . When *μετ. τόπον* is taken up again, the mere secondary *τόπος* disappears, and it is *αὐτήν*, not *αὐτόν*, agreeing with the great thing really sought," Alford). If the writer used his usual A text of the LXX, he would not have found any allusion to the tears of Esau in Gn 27^{38}, but the tears were retained, from the Hebrew, in Jub 26^{33}, in other texts of the LXX, and in Josephus (*Ant.* i. 18. 7, *πένθος ἦγεν ἐπὶ τῇ διαμαρτίᾳ. Καὶ αὐτοῦ τοῖς δάκρυσιν ἀχθόμενος ὁ πατήρ κτλ.*).[1] "Those tears of Esau, the sensuous, wild, impulsive man, almost like the cry of some 'trapped creature,' are among the most pathetic in the Bible" (A. B. Davidson). **Αὐτήν** refers to **μετανοίας**, not to **εὐλογίας** (which would require **μετανοίας . . . εὗρεν** to be taken as a parenthesis, a construction which is wrecked on the antithesis between **εὗρεν** and **ἐκζητήσας**). The **μετάνοια** is not a change in the mind of Isaac, which would require some additional words like **τοῦ πατρός**. Besides, Esau does not beseech Isaac to alter his mind. Nor can it refer to a change in God's mind. It is "a change of mind" on Esau's part, "undoing the effects of a former state of mind" (A. B. Davidson). Bitterly as Esau regretted his hasty action, he was denied any chance of having its consequences reversed by a subsequent *μετάνοια*; this is the writer's meaning. *Ἀδύνατον πάλιν ἀνακαινίζειν εἰς μετάνοιαν* is the law of God for such wilful offenders, and to try for a second *μετάνοια* is vain. Such is the warning that our author deduces from the tale of Esau.

[1] There is a striking parallel in *De Mercede Conductis*, 42, where Lucian describes an old man being met by *ἡ μετάνοια δακρύουσα ἐς οὐδὲν ὄφελος*.

This inexorable view agrees with Philo's idea (*Leg. Alleg.* iii. 75, πολλαῖς γὰρ ψυχαῖς μετανοίᾳ χρῆσθαι βουληθείσαις οὐκ ἐπέτρεψεν ὁ θεός) that some, like Cain[1] (*quod deter. pot.* 26, τῷ δὲ μὴ δεχομένῳ μετάνοιαν Καὶν δι' ὑπερβολὴν ἄγους), are too bad to repent, though Philo illustrates it here not from Esau, but from Lot's wife. In *de Spec. Leg.* ii. 5 he declares that luxurious spendthrifts are δυσκάθαρτοι καὶ δυσίατοι, ὡς μηδὲ θεῷ τῷ τὴν φύσιν ἵλεῳ συγγνώμης ἀξιοῦσθαι. In Jub 35^{14} Isaac tells Rebekah that "neither Esau nor his seed is to be saved." But the idea of Πρὸς Ἑβραίους is made still more clear by the use of **μετανοίας τόπον** as an expression for opportunity or chance to repent. This is a contemporary Jewish phrase; cp. Apoc. Bar 85^{12} ("For when the Most High will bring to pass all these things, there will not then be an opportunity for returning . . . nor place of repentance"), 4 Es 9^{12} ("while a place of repentance was still open to them, they paid no heed"), which goes back to Wis 12^{10} κρίνων δὲ κατὰ βραχὺ ἐδίδους τόπον μετανοίας (of God punishing the Canaanites). It is linguistically a Latinism,[2] which recurs in Clem. Rom. 7^{5} (ἐν γενεᾷ καὶ γενεᾷ μετανοίας τόπον ἔδωκεν ὁ δεσπότης τοῖς βουλομένοις ἐπιστραφῆναι ἐπ' αὐτόν) and Tatian (*Orat. ad Graecos*, 15, διὰ τοῦτο γοῦν ἡ τῶν δαιμόνων ὑπόστασις οὐκ ἔχει μετανοίας τόπον). But a special significance attaches to it in 4 Esdras, for example, where the writer (*e.g.* in $7^{102f.}$) rules out any intercession of the saints for the ungodly after death, in his desire to show that "the eternal destiny of the soul is fixed by the course of the earthly life" (G. H. Box, *The Ezra-Apocalypse*, pp. 154, 155). Here, as in the Slavonic Enoch (53^{1}), which also repudiates such intercession, "we may detect the influence of Alexandrine theology, which tended to lay all stress upon the present life as determining the eternal fate of every man." The author of Πρὸς Ἑβραίους shared this belief (cp. 9^{27}); for him the present life of man contains possibilities which are tragic and decisive. He ignores deliberately any intercession of saints or angels for the living or for the dead. But he goes still further, with Philo and others, in holding that, for some, certain actions fix their fate beyond any remedy. He regards their case as hopeless; characters like Esau, by an act of profane contempt for God, are rejected for ever, a second μετάνοια being beyond their reach.

The connexion (γάρ) between the finale (vv.$^{18-29}$) and what precedes lies in the thought that the higher the privilege, the higher the responsibility. In *Leg. Alleg.* iii. 1, Philo quotes Gn 25^{27} to prove that virtue's divine city is not meant for human passions; οὐ γὰρ πέφυκεν ἡ τῶν παθῶν θηρευτικὴ κακία τὴν ἀρετῆς πόλιν, wickedness banishing men from the presence and sight of God. But this line of thought is not in the writer's mind. It is more relevant to recall that Esau typifies exclusion from God in Jub 15^{30} ("Ishmael and his sons and his brothers and Esau, the Lord did not cause to approach Him"); yet even this is not needful to explain the turn of thought. The writer is continuing his grave warning. As vv.$^{14-17}$ recall the first warning of 6^{4-8}, so he now proceeds to reiterate the second warning of 10^{26-31}, reminding his readers that they stand in a critical position,

[1] Philo read μείζων ἡ αἰτία μου τοῦ ἀφεθῆναι in Gn 4^{13}.

[2] Livy, xliv. 10, "poenitentiae relinquens locum" (cp. xxiv. 26, "locus poenitendis"); cp. Pliny's *Epp.* x. 97, "ex quo facile est opinari, quae turba hominum emendari possit, si sit poenitentiae locus," where the phrase is used in quite a different sense, of a chance to give up Christianity.

in which any indifferences or disobedience to God will prove fatal. This is the note of vv.[25-29] in particular. But he leads up to the appeal by describing in a vivid passage the actual position of his readers before God (vv.[18-24]); their new status and environment appeals even more powerfully and searchingly for an unworldly obedience to God than the old status of the People.

[18] *You have not come* (**προσεληλύθατε**) *to what you can touch, to "flames of fire," to "mist" and "gloom" and "stormy blasts,* [19] *to the blare of a trumpet and to a Voice" whose words made those who heard it refuse to hear another syllable* [20] *(for they could not bear the command, "If even a beast touches the mountain, it must be stoned")*—[21] *indeed, so awful was the sight that Moses said, "I am terrified and aghast."* [22] *You have come* (**προσεληλύθατε**) *to mount Sion, the city of the living God, the heavenly Jerusalem, to myriads of angels in festal gathering,* [23] *to the assembly of the first-born registered in heaven, to the God of all as judge, to the spirits of just men made perfect,* [24] *to Jesus who mediates* (8[6] 9[15]) *the new covenant, and to the sprinkled blood whose message is nobler than Abel's.*

The passage moves through two phases (vv.[18-21] and [22-24]), contrasting the revelation at mount Sinai (2[2] 10[28]) with the new διαθήκη, the one sensuous, the other spiritual; the one striking terror with its outward circumstances of physical horror, the other charged with grace and welcome as well as with awe. The meditation and appeal are woven on material drawn from the LXX descriptions of the plague of darkness on Egypt (Ex 10[21f.] ψηλαφητὸν σκότος . . . ἐγένετο σκότος γνόφος θύελλα) and the theophany at Sinai (Dt 4[11] προσήλθετε καὶ ἔστητε ὑπὸ τὸ ὄρος· καὶ τὸ ὄρος ἐκαίετο πυρὶ ἕως τοῦ οὐρανοῦ, σκότος, γνόφος, θύελλα, φωνὴ μεγάλη, and Ex 19[12f.] προσέχετε ἑαυτοῖς τοῦ ἀναβῆναι εἰς τὸ ὄρος καὶ θιγεῖν τι αὐτοῦ· πᾶς ὁ ἁψάμενος τοῦ ὄρους θανάτῳ τελευτήσει . . . ἐν λίθοις λιθοβοληθήσεται ἢ βολίδι κατατοξευθήσεται· ἐάν τε κτῆνος ἐάν τε ἄνθρωπος, οὐ ζήσεται . . . καὶ ἐγίνοντο φωναὶ καὶ ἀστραπαὶ καὶ νεφέλη γνοφώδης ἐπ' ὄρους Σεινά, φωνὴ τῆς σάλπιγγος ἤχει μέγα· καὶ ἐπτοήθη πᾶς ὁ λαὸς ὁ ἐν τῇ παρεμβολῇ). In v.[18] the text is difficult and perhaps corrupt. **Ψηλαφωμένῳ ὄρει** would be equivalent to ψηλαφητῷ ὄρει, a tangible, material mountain; but as ὄρει is a gloss (added, from v.[22], by D K L 255 syr[hkl] arm Athan. Cosm. etc., either before or after ψηλ.), though a correct gloss, ψ. may be taken (*a*) either with **πυρί**, (*b*) or independently. In the former case, (*a*) two constructions are possible. (i) One, as in vg ("ad tractabilem et accensibilem ignem"), renders "to a fire that was material (or palpable) and ablaze"; (ii) "to what was palpable and ablaze with fire" (*πυρί* in an ablative sense). (i) is a daring expression, and the implied contrast (with v.[29]) is too remote. The objection to (ii) is that *πυρί* here, as in the OT, goes with the following datives. It is on the whole preferable (*b*) to take ψηλαφωμένῳ by itself (*sc.* τινι). The mountain could not be touched indeed (v.[20]), but it was a tangible object which appealed to the senses. This is the point of contrast between it and the **Σιὼν ὄρος**, the present participle being equivalent to the verbal adjective ψηλαφητός. Kypke connects ψ. with πυρί in the sense of "touched by lightning" ("igne tactum et adustum"), comparing the Latin phrase "fulmine tactum." But the Greek term is θίγγανειν, and in any case this interpretation really requires ὄρει, the mountain "sundering" under the lightning touch of God (Ps 144[5] etc.).

Two conjectures have been proposed, ὑψει νενεφωμένῳ by G. N. Bennett (*Classical Review*, vi. 263), who argues that this "would fit in exactly with the OT accounts, which represent the summit of the mountain as burnt with fire, while lower down it was enveloped in a dense cloud"; and πεφεψαλωμένῳ (ὄρει) by E. C. Selwyn (*Journal of Theological Studies*, ix. 133, 134) = "calcined" (a calcined volcano). Others (*e.g.* P. Junius) less aptly insert οὐ or μή before ψηλαφωμένῳ, to harmonize the phrase with v.[20].

In the rest of the description, **ζόφῳ** is a poetical word (cp. *de Mundo*, 400*a*, heaven πᾶντος ζόφου καὶ ἀτάκτου κινήματος κεχωρισμένον), which the writer prefers to σκότος. **Καὶ θυέλλῃ**—θύελλη, a hurricane, is defined by Hesychius as ἀνέμου συστροφὴ καὶ ὁρμὴ, ἢ καταιγίς (cp. Hom. *Od.* 5. 317), and in *de Mundo*, 395*a*, as πνεῦμα βίαιον καὶ ἄφνω προσαλλόμενον. In v.[19] **ἤχῳ** (ἤχη Ἀττικοί· ἦχος Ἕλληνες, Moeris) is a synonym for the LXX **φωνῇ**, which the writer intends to use immediately. Philo had already used ἦχος in *de Decalogo*, 11: πάντα δ' ὡς εἰκὸς τὰ περὶ τὸν τόπον ἐθαυματουργεῖτο, κτύποις βροντῶν μειζόνων ἢ ὥστε χωρεῖν ἀκοάς, ἀστραπῶν λάμψεσιν αὐγοειδεστάταις, ἀοράτου σάλπιγγος ἠχῇ πρὸς μήκιστον ἀποτεινούσῃ . . . πυρὸς οὐρανίου φορᾷ καπνῷ βαθεῖ τὰ ἐν κύκλῳ συσκιάζοντος. In *de Spec. Leg.* ii. 22 he explains that the φωνὴ σάλπιγγος announced to all the world the significance of the event. Finally, **καὶ φωνῇ ῥημάτων** (the decalogue in Dt 4[12]), **ἧς** (*i.e.* the φωνή) **οἱ ἀκούσαντες παρῃτήσαντο μὴ** (pleonastic negative as in Gal 5[7]; hence omitted by ℵ* P 467) **προστεθῆναι** (the active προσθεῖναι, in A, is less apt) **αὐτοῖς** (*i.e.* the hearers) **λόγον** (accus. and infinitive construction after μή, cp. Blass, § 429). The reference in v.[20] is to the scene described in Dt 5[23f.], where it is the leaders of the nation who appeal in terror to Moses to take God's messages and orders for them: καὶ νῦν μὴ ἀποθάνωμεν, ὅτι ἐξαναλώσει ἡμᾶς τὸ πῦρ τὸ μέγα τοῦτο, ἐὰν προσθώμεθα ἡμεῖς ἀκοῦσαι τὴν φωνὴν Κυρίου τοῦ θεοῦ ἡμῶν ἔτι, καὶ ἀποθανούμεθα. But in Ex 20[19] it is the people, as here, who appeal to Moses, μὴ λαλείτω πρὸς ἡμᾶς ὁ θεός, μὴ ἀποθάνωμεν. **Τὸ διαστελλόμενον** (in Ex 19[13], see above) is passive. **Διαστέλλομαι** is said by Anz (*Subsidia*, 326 f.) not to occur earlier than Plato; here, as in Jth 11[12] (ὅσα διεστείλατο αὐτοῖς ὁ θεός), of a divine injunction. In v.[21] **φανταζόμενον** is not a LXX term (for the sense, cp. Zec 10[1] κύριος ἐποίησεν φαντασίας, of natural phenomena like rain); it is used here for the sake of alliteration (φοβ. φαντ.). To prove that even Moses was affected by the terrors of Sinai, the writer quotes from Dt 9[19] ἔκφοβός εἰμι, adding rhetorically καὶ ἔντρομος. He forgets that Moses uttered this cry of horror, not over the fearful spectacle of Sinai but at a later stage, over the worship of the golden calf. For ἔντρομος, cp. 1 Mac 13[2] ἔντρομος καὶ ἔκφοβος (*v.l.* ἔμφοβος). The phrase ἔντρομος γενόμενος is applied by Luke to the terror of Moses at the φωνὴ Κυρίου out of the burning bush (Ac 7[32]).

Assonance led to ἔκτρομος (א D*) or ἔμφοβος (M 241. 255. 489. 547. 1739 Thdt.). Ἔντρομος was read by Clem. Alex. (*Protrept.* ix. 2).

The true position of Christians is now sketched (vv.[22-24]). Ἀλλὰ προσεληλύθατε Σιὼν ὄρει καὶ πόλει (11[10. 16]) θεοῦ ζῶντος, the author adding Ἰερουσαλὴμ ἐπουρανίῳ (11[16]) in apposition to πόλει, and using thus the archaic metaphors of Is 18[7], Am 1[2], Mic 4[1f.] etc., in his picture of the true fellowship. Paul had contrasted mount Sinai (=the present Jerusalem) with ἡ ἄνω Ἱερουσαλήμ. Our author's contrast is between mount Sion (=Ἱερουσαλὴμ ἐπουράνιος) and mount Sinai, though he does not name the latter. From the πόλις he now passes to the πολῖται.

In Chagiga, 12*b*, i. 33, Resh Lakish deduces from 1 K 8[13] and Is 63[15] that zebul, the fourth of the seven heavens, contains "the heavenly Jerusalem and the temple," *i.e.* as the residence of deity; while Ma'on, the fifth heaven, holds the "companies of ministering angels."

The second object of προσεληλύθατε is καὶ μυριάσιν (so En 40[1]: "I saw thousands of thousands and ten thousand times ten thousand before the Lord of spirits") ἀγγέλων, with which πανηγύρει must be taken, leaving the following καί to introduce the third object (v.[23]). The conception of the angels as μυριάδες goes back to traditions like those voiced in Ps 68[17] (τὸ ἅρμα τοῦ θεοῦ μυριοπλάσιον, χιλιάδες εὐθηνούντων· ὁ κύριος ἐν αὐτοῖς ἐν Σινά) and Dan 7[10] (μύριαι μυριάδες). Πανήγυρις was a term charged with Greek religious associations (cp. R. van der Loeff, *De Ludis Eleusiniis*, pp. 85 f.), but it had already been adopted by Greek Jews like the translators of the LXX and Josephus for religious festivals. Πανηγύρει describes the angelic hosts thronging with glad worship round the living God. Their relation to God is noted here, as in 1[14] their relation to human beings. Ἔνθα πανήγυρις ἐκεῖ χαρά, as Theophylact observes (ἱλαρᾶς εὐθυμίας, ἣν πανήγυρις ἐπιζητεῖ, Philo, *in Flacc.* 14); but the joy of Lk 15[10] is not specially mentioned. Chrysostom's suggestion is that the writer ἐνταῦθα τὴν χαρὰν δείκνυσι καὶ τὴν εὐφροσύνην ἀντὶ τοῦ γνόφου καὶ τοῦ σκότους καὶ τῆς θυέλλης. Augustine (*Quaest.* i. 168: "accessistis ad montem Sion et ad ciuitatem dei Hierusalem et ad milia angelorum exultantium") seems to imply not only that **πανηγύρει** goes with **ἀγγέλων**, but that he knew a text with some word like *πανηγυριζόντων* (Blass), as is further proved by boh ("keeping festival"), Orig^{lat} (laetantium, collaudantium), and Ambrose. There is a hint of this in Clem. Alex. *Protrept.* ix. 6, 7, *αὕτη γὰρ ἡ πρωτότοκος ἐκκλησία ἡ ἐκ πολλῶν ἀγαθῶν συγκειμένη παιδίων· ταῦτ' ἔστι τὰ πρωτότοκα τὰ ἐναπογεγραμμένα ἐν οὐρανοῖς καὶ τοσαύταις μυριάσιν ἀγγέλων συμπανηγυρίζοντα.*

The human *πολῖται* are next (v.[23]) described as **ἐκκλησίᾳ πρωτοτόκων ἀπογεγραμμένων ἐν οὐρανοῖς.** (For the collocation of angels and men, see En 39[5] "Mine eyes saw their [*i.e.* the saints'] dwellings with His righteous angels, and their resting-places with the holy"; the Enoch apocalypse proceeding to the intercession of the angels ("and they petitioned, and interceded, and prayed for the children of men") which the Christian writer deliberately omits.) The phrase describes what the author elsewhere calls ὁ λαός (*τοῦ θεοῦ*), but in two archaic expressions, chosen to emphasize what Paul would have called their election. They are *πρωτότοκοι* (as Israel had been *πρωτότοκος*, Ex 4[22] etc.), with a title to God's blessing (v.[16] *πρωτοτόκια*). The choice of the plural instead of the collective singular was due to the previous plural in *μυριάσιν ἀγγέλων*. In **ἀπογεγραμμένων ἐν οὐρανοῖς** there is a passing allusion to the idea of the celestial archives or register—a favourite poetical figure in which the Oriental expressed his assurance of salvation.[1] As in Lk 10[20] so here, the phrase refers to men on earth, to the church militant, not to the church triumphant; otherwise **ἐν οὐρανοῖς** would be meaningless.

This interpretation, which groups *πανηγύρει* with what precedes, is current in nearly all the early versions and Greek fathers, who generally assume it without question. The real alternative is to take *μυριάσιν* as further defined by *ἀγγέλων πανηγύρει καὶ ἐκκλησίᾳ πρωτοτόκων ἀπογεγραμμένων ἐν οὐρανοῖς.* This introduces and leaves *μυριάσιν* rather abruptly, and implies that angels alone are referred to (so recently Dods, von Soden, Peake, Seeberg), called *πρωτότοκοι* as created before men. But, while a later writer like Hermas (*Vis.* iii. 4) could speak of angels as *οἱ πρῶτοι κτισθέντες*, **ἀπογεγραμμένων** cannot naturally be applied to them. Hermas himself (*Vis.* i. 3) applies that term to men (*ἐγγραφήσονται εἰς τὰς βίβλους τῆς ζωῆς μετὰ τῶν ἁγίων*).

A fresh sweep of thought now begins ($^{23b-24}$). The writer is composing a lyrical sketch, not a law-paper; he reiterates the idea of the fellowship by speaking of God, men, and him by whom this tie between God and men has been welded, the allusion to Jesus being thrown to the end, as it is to form the starting-point for his next appeal (vv.$^{25f.}$). In **καὶ κριτῇ θεῷ πάντων** it is not possible, in view of 9[27] (*μετὰ δὲ τοῦτο κρίσις*) and of the punitive sense of **κρίνω** in 10[30], to understand **κριτής** as defender

[1] *Clem. Hom.* ix. 22, *τὰ ὀνόματα ἐν οὐρανῷ ὡς ἀεὶ ζώντων ἀναγραφῆναι.*

or vindicator (so, *e.g.*, Hofmann, Delitzsch, Riggenbach). The words mean "to the God of all (angels and men, the living and the dead, Ac 10^{42}), and to him as κριτής, to whom you must account for your life." It is implied that he is no easy-going God. The contrast is not between the mere terrors of Sinai and the gracious relationship of Sion, but between the outward, sensuous terror of the former and the inward intimacy of the latter—an intimacy which still involves awe. In the next phrase, **πνεύματα δικαίων** means the departed who have in this life been δίκαιοι in the sense of $10^{38f.}$; **τετελειωμένων** is added, not in the mere sense of "departed" (τελευτᾶν = τελειοῦσθαι, τελειοῦν), but to suggest the work of Christ which includes the δίκαιοι, who had to await the sacrifice of Christ before they were "perfected" (11^{40}). If this involves the idea of a descent of Christ to the under-world, as Loofs (*e.g.* in *ERE.* iv. 662) argues, it implies the group of ideas mentioned in 2^{14}, which may have lain in the background of the writer's thought. At any rate the "perfecting" of these δίκαιοι, their **τελείωσις**, was due to Jesus; hence (v.[24]) the writer adds, **καὶ διαθήκης νέας μεσίτῃ Ἰησοῦ** (again at the end, for emphasis), where νέας is simply a synonym for καινῆς (8^{8} etc.). The classical distinction between the two terms was being dropped in the κοινή. Τῆς νέας Ἱερουσαλήμ occurs in *Test. Dan* 5^{12}, and the two words are synonymous, *e.g.*, in *Test. Levi* 8^{14} (ἐπικληθήσεται αὐτῷ ὄνομα καίνον, ὅτι βασιλεὺς . . . ποιήσει ἱερατείαν νέαν). Indeed Blass thinks that the unexampled διαθήκης νεάς was due to a sense of rhythm; the author felt a desire to reproduce the — ⏑⏑ — — ⏑ — of the preceding ων τετελειωμένων.

In Cambodia (cp. *ERE.* iii. 164) those who are present at a death-bed all "repeat in a loud voice, the patient joining in as long as he has the strength, '*Arahan! Arahan!*' 'the saint! the just one!' (Pāli *arahaṃ*='the saint,' 'one who has attained final sanctification')." Bleek is so perplexed by καὶ πνευμ. δικ. τελ. coming between θεῷ and Ἰησοῦ that he wonders whether the author did not originally write the phrase on the margin, intending it to go with πανηγύρει or ἐκκλησίᾳ. The curious misreading of D d, τεθεμελιωμένων, underlies Hilary's quotation (*tract. in Ps.* 124: "ecclesia angelorum multitudinis frequentium—ecclesia primitivorum, ecclesia spirituum in domino fundatorum"). Another odd error, πνεύματι for πνεύμασι, appears in D (boh?) d and some Latin fathers (*e.g.* Primasius)—a trinitarian emendation (= 10^{29}).

In **διαθήκης νέας**, as in 13^{20}, the writer recalls the conception with which he had been working in the middle part of his argument (chs. 7–10); now he proceeds to expand and explain the allusion in **καὶ αἵματι ῥαντισμοῦ** ($9^{19f.}$) **κρεῖττον** (adverbial as in 1 Co 7^{38}) **λαλοῦντι παρὰ** (as in 1^{4} etc.) **τὸν Ἄβελ** (= τὸ[1] τοῦ Ἄβελ, cp. Jn 5^{36}). Reconciliation, not exclusion, is the note of the νέα διαθήκη. The blood of the murdered Abel (11^{4}) called out to

[1] τὸ Ἄβελ (genitive) was actually read by L and is still preferred by Blass.

God in En $22^{6f.}$ (where the seer has a vision of Abel's spirit appealing to God) for the extinction of Cain and his descendants. The κρεῖττον in Jesus here is that, instead of being vindictive and seeking to exclude the guilty, he draws men into fellowship with God (see p. xlii). The contrast is therefore not between the Voice of the blood of Jesus (λαλοῦντι) and the Voice of the decalogue (v.[19]), but between Jesus and Abel; the former opens up the way to the presence of God, the latter sought to shut it against evil men. The blood of martyrs was assigned an atoning efficacy in 4 Mac $6^{28f.}$ $17^{21f.}$; but Abel's blood is never viewed in this light, and the attempt to explain this passage as though the blood of Jesus were superior in redeeming value to that of Abel as the first martyr (so, *e.g.*, Seeberg), breaks down upon the fact that the writer never takes Abel's blood as in any sense typical of Christ's.

The application of vv.[18-24] now follows. Though we have a far better relationship to God, the faults of the older generation may still be committed by us, and committed to our undoing (vv.[25-29]).

[25] *See* (βλέπετε as 3^{12}) *that you do not refuse to listen to his voice. For if they failed to escape, who refused to listen to their instructor upon earth, much less shall we, if we discard him who speaks from heaven.* [26] *Then his voice shook the earth, but now the assurance is, "once again I will make heaven as well as earth to quake."* [27] *That phrase* (τὸ δέ as Eph 4^{9}), *"once again," denotes* (δηλοῖ, as in 9^{8}) *the removal of what is shaken (as no more than created), to leave only what stands unshaken.* [28] *Therefore let us render thanks that we get an unshaken realm; and in this way let us worship God acceptably*—[29] *but with godly fear and awe, for our God is indeed "a consuming fire."*

The divine revelation in the sacrifice of Jesus (λαλοῦντι) suggests the start of the next appeal and warning. From the celestial order, just sketched, the divine revelation (τὸν λαλοῦντα . . . τὸν ἀπ' οὐρανῶν) is made to us; instead of rejecting it, which would be tragic, let us hold to it. The argument is: God's revelation (v.[25]) implies a lasting relationship to himself (v.[28]); and although the present order of things in the universe is doomed to a speedy fall (v.[26]), this catastrophe will only bring out the unchanging realm in which God and we stand together (v.[27]). The abruptness of the asyndeton in (v.[25]) βλέπετε μή κτλ. adds to its force. Παραιτήσησθε . . . παραιτησάμενοι are only a verbal echo of παρῃτήσαντο κτλ. in v.[19]; for the refusal of the people to hear God except through Moses is not blamed but praised by God (Dt 5^{28}). The writer, of course, may have ignored this, and read an ominous significance into the instinctive terror of the people, as if their refusal meant a radical rejection of God. But this is unlikely. By παραιτησάμενοι τὸν χρηματίζοντα he means any obstinate rejection of what Moses laid down for them as the will of God. **Εἰ . . . οὐκ** (as was the fact) **ἐξέφυγον** (referring to the doom mentioned in 2^{2} 3$^{7f.}$ 10^{29}). As in 2^{3} (*πῶς ἡμεῖς ἐκφευξόμεθα*), **ἐκφεύγω** is used absolutely; the weaker *ἔφυγον* is read only by ℵ^{c} D K L M Ψ 104, etc. In the following words there are three possible readings. The original text ran: (*a*) **ἐπὶ γῆς παραιτησάμενοι τὸν χρηματίζοντα** (ℵ* A C D M d boh Cyr.), *ἐπὶ γῆς* being as often thrown to the front for the sake of emphasis. But the hyperbaton seemed awkward. Hence (*b*) *τὸν ἐπὶ γῆς παραιτησάμενοι χ.* (ℵ^{c} K L P Chrys. Thdt. etc.) and (*c*) *παραιτησάμενοι τὸν ἐπὶ γῆς χ.* (69. 256. 263. 436. 462. 467. 1837. 2005 vg) are attempts to make it clear that **ἐπὶ γῆς** goes with **τὸν χρηματίζοντα**, not with **παραιτησάμενοι**. The latter interpretation misses the point of the contrast, which is not between a rejection on earth and a rejection in heaven (!), but between a human oracle of God and the divine Voice *ἀπ' οὐρανῶν* to us. The allusion in *τὸν χρηματίζοντα* [1] is to Moses, as Chrysostom was the first to see. To refuse to listen to him is what has been already called *ἀθετεῖν νόμον Μωϋσέως* (10^{28}). As the Sinai-revelation is carefully described in 2^{2} as *ὁ δι' ἀγγέλων λαληθεὶς λόγος*, so here Moses is **ὁ χρηματίζων**, or, as Luke puts it, *ὃς ἐδέξατο λόγια ζῶντα δοῦναι* (Ac 7^{38}); he was the divine instructor of the *λαός* on earth. It is repeatedly said (Ex 20^{22}, Dt 4^{36}) that God spoke to the people at Sinai *ἐκ τοῦ οὐρανοῦ*, so that to take **τὸν χρηματίζοντα** here as God, would be out of keeping with **ἐπὶ τῆς γῆς**. The writer uses the verb in a wider sense than in that of 8^{5} and 11^{7}; it means "the man who had divine authority to issue orders," just as in Jer 26^{2} (*τοὺς λόγους οὓς συνέταξά σοι αὐτοῖς χρηματίσαι*), etc. He deliberately writes *τὸν χρηματίζοντα* of Moses, keeping *τὸν λαλοῦντα* as usual for God. Then, he concludes, **πολὺ** (altered, as in v.^{9}, to *πολλῷ* by D^{c} K L M P Ψ 226, or to *πόσῳ*, as in 9^{14}, by 255) **μᾶλλον** (*sc. οὐκ ἐκφευξόμεθα*) **ἡμεῖς οἱ τὸν** (*sc. χρηματίζοντα*) **ἀπ' οὐρανῶν ἀποστρεφόμενοι** (with accus. as 3 Mac 3^{23} *ἀπεστρέψαντο τὴν ἀτίμητον πολιτείαν*, and 2 Ti 1^{15} *ἀπεστράφησάν με πάντες*).

It is surprising that *οὐρανοῦ* (ℵ M 216. 424**. 489. 547. 623. 642. 920. 1518. 1872 Chrys.) has not wider support, though, as 9$^{23.\ 24}$ shows, there is no difference in sense.

In v.^{26} **οὗ ἡ φωνὴ τὴν γῆν ἐσάλευσε τότε** is another (cp. vv.$^{13.\ 14}$) unintentional rhythm, this time a pentameter. **Τότε**, *i.e.* at Sinai. But in the LXX of Ex 19^{18}, which the writer used, the shaking of the hill is altered into the quaking of the people, and Jg 5$^{4f.}$ does not refer to the Sinai episode. Probably the writer inferred an earthquake from the poetical allusions in Ps 114^{7}

[1] Cp. Jos. *Ant.* iii. 8. 8, Μωϋσῆς . . . ἐχρηματίζετο περὶ ὧν ἐδεῖτο παρὰ τοῦ θεοῦ.

(ἐσαλεύθη ἡ γῆ), Ps $68^{8f.}$ 77^{18}, when these were associated with the special theophany at Sinai. **Νῦν δὲ ἐπήγγελται** (passive in middle sense, as Ro 4^{21}) **λέγων**, introducing a loose reminiscence and adaptation of Hag 2^{6} (*ἔτι ἅπαξ ἐγὼ σείσω τὸν οὐρανὸν καὶ τὴν γῆν κτλ.*), where the prediction of a speedy convulsion of nature and the nations has been altered[1] in the LXX, by the introduction of **ἔτι**, into a mere prediction of some ultimate crisis, with reference to some preceding **σεῖσις**, *i.e.* for our writer the Sinai-revelation. The second and final *σεῖσις* is to be at the return of Jesus (9^{28}).

The anticipation of such a cosmic collapse entered apocalyptic. Thus the author of Apoc. Baruch tells his readers, "if you prepare your hearts, so as to sow in them the fruits of the law, it shall protect you when the Mighty One is to shake the whole creation" (32^{1}).

In $v.^{27}$ the Haggai prediction is made to mean the removal (**μετάθεσιν**, stronger sense than even in 7^{12}) **τῶν σαλευομένων** (by the *σεῖσις*). There is a divine purpose in the cosmic catastrophe, however; it is **ἵνα μείνῃ τὰ μὴ σαλευόμενα**, *i.e.* the **βασιλεία ἀσάλευτος** of the Christian order. For **ἀσάλευτος**, compare Philo, *de vit. Mosis*, ii. 3, *τὰ δὲ τούτου μόνου βέβαια, ἀσάλευτα, ἀκράδαντα . . . μένει παγίως ἀφ᾽ ἧς ἡμέρας ἐγράφη μέχρι νῦν καὶ πρὸς τὸν ἔπειτα πάντα διαμενεῖν ἐλπὶς αὐτὰ αἰῶνα ὥσπερ ἀθάνατα.* **Σείω** and **σαλεύω** are cognate terms (cp. *e.g.* Sir $16^{18.\,19}$ *ὁ οὐρανος . . . καὶ γὴ σαλευθήσονται . . . ἅμα τὰ ὄρη καὶ τὰ θεμέλια τῆς γῆς συσσείονται*). Here **σείσω** is changed into **σείω** by D K L P d arm and some cursives, probably to conform with the form of the promise in Hag 2^{21} (*ἐγὼ σείω τὸν οὐρ. καὶ τὴν γῆν*). The hint is more reticent, and therefore more impressive than the elaborate prediction of the Jewish apocalyptist in Apoc. Bar $59^{3f.}$: "but also the heavens were shaken at that time from their place, and those who were under the throne of the Mighty One were perturbed, when He was taking Moses unto Himself. For He showed him . . . the pattern of Zion and its measures, in the pattern of which was to be made the sanctuary of the present time" (cp. He 8^{5}). There is a premonition of the last judgment in En 60^{1}, as a convulsion which shook not only heaven, but the nerves of the myriads of angels.

"There have been two notable transitions of life," says Gregory of Nazianzus (*Orat.* v. 25), in the history of the world, *i.e.* the two covenants, "which are also called earthquakes on account of their arresting character" (*διὰ τὸ τοῦ πράγματος περιβόητον*); the first from idols to the Law, the second from the Law to the gospel. We bring the good news of yet a third earthquake, the transition from the present order to the future (*τὴν ἐντεῦθεν ἐπὶ τὰ ἐκεῖσε μετάστασιν, τὰ μηκέτι κινούμενα, μηδὲ σαλευόμενα*).[2]

---

[1] *i.e.* while Haggai predicts "it will be very soon," the LXX says "once again."

[2] Probably a reference to He 12^{26}.

Changes and crises may only serve to render a state or an individual more stable. Thus Plutarch says of Rome, in the disturbed days of Numa, *καθάπερ τὰ καταπηγνύμενα τῷ σείεσθαι μᾶλλον ἑδράζεται, ῥώννυσθαι δοκοῦσα διὰ τῶν κινδύνων* (*Vit. Num.* 8). But the writer's point in v.[27] is that there is an **ἀσάλευτος βασιλεία**[1] already present, in the fellowship of the new *διαθήκη*, and that the result of the cosmic catastrophe will simply be to leave this unimpaired, to let it stand out in its supreme reality and permanence. The passage is a counterpart to 1[10-12], where skies and earth vanish, though they are God's own *ἔργα*. So here, the writer puts in, by way of parenthesis, **ὡς πεποιημένων**. Kypke took **πεποιημένων**, "pro *πεποιημένην*, *sc.* *μετάθεσιν*," comparing Mt 5[19] where he regarded **ἐλαχίστων** as similarly equivalent to *ἐλαχίστην*. The word would then be a genitive absolute, connecting with what follows: "all this being done so that," etc. Even when *πεποιημένων* is taken in its ordinary sense, it is sometimes connected with **ἵνα** *κτλ.* (so, *e.g.*, Bengel and Delitzsch); the aim of creation was to replace the provisional by the permanent, the temporal by the eternal. A far-fetched interpretation. Even the conjecture (Valckenaer) *πεπονήμενων* (labouring with decay) is needless, though ingenious. In vv.[28. 29] the final word upon this prospect and its responsibilities is said. **Διό** (as in v.[12]), in view of this outlook (in v.[27]), **βασιλείαν ἀσάλευτον** (metaphorical, as, *e.g.*, Diod. Sic. xii. 29, *σπονδαὶ ἀσάλευται*) **παραλαμβάνοντες** (cp. 2 Mac 10[11] and *Epist. Arist.* 36, *καὶ ἡμεῖς δὲ παραλαβόντες τὴν βασιλείαν κτλ.*, for this common phrase) **ἔχωμεν χάριν** (*διό* with pres. subjunctive as in 6[1]). The unique and sudden reference to the primitive idea of **βασιλεία** (see Introd., p. xxxiii) may be a reminiscence of the scripture from which he has just quoted; the prediction about the shaking of heaven and earth is followed, in Hag 2[22], by the further assertion, *καὶ καταστρέψω θρόνους βασιλέων, καὶ ἐξολεθρεύσω δύναμιν βασιλέων τῶν ἐθνῶν.* Possibly our author regarded the prediction in Dn 7[18] (*καὶ παραλήψονται τὴν βασιλείαν ἅγιοι ὑψίστου καὶ καθέξουσιν αὐτὴν ἕως αἰῶνος τῶν αἰώνων*) as fulfilled already in the Christian church, though he does not mean by *βασιλείαν παραλαμβάνοντες* that Christians enter on their reign.

Why thankfulness (for this common phrase, see Epict. i. 2. 23, *ἔχω χάριν, ὅτι μου φείδῃ*, and *OP.* 1381[78] (2nd century) *διὰ θυσιῶν τῷ σώσαντι ἀπεδίδομεν χάριτας*) should be the standing order for them, the writer explains in **δι' ἧς** *κτλ.*; it is the one acceptable **λατρεύειν** (9[14]), or, as he puts it afterwards (13[15]), the real sacrifice of Christians. **Δι' ἧς λατρεύωμεν** (subj. cohortative in relative clause, like *στῆτε* in 1 P 5[12]) **εὐαρέστως** (not in LXX;

[1] Cp. Wis 5[15. 16] *δίκαιοι δὲ εἰς τὸν αἰῶνα ζῶσιν . . . λήμψονται τὸ βασίλειον τῆς εὐπρεπείας . . . ἐκ χειρὸς Κυρίου, ὅτι τῇ δεξιᾷ σκεπάσει αὐτούς.*

an adverb from the verb in the sense of $11^{5.6}$) τῷ θεῷ. The *v.l.* ἔχομεν (ℵ K P Lat syr^hkl eth etc.) is the usual (see Ro 5^1) phonetic blunder, though λατρεύομεν (ℵ M P syr^hkl arm) would yield as fair a sense as λατρεύωμεν (A C D L 33. 104 Lat sah etc.). In **μετὰ . . . δέους** he puts in a characteristic warning against presumption. There are three readings. (*a*) εὐλαβείας καὶ δέους, ℵ* A C D 256. 263. 436. 1912 sah boh syr^vg arm. (*b*) εὐλαβείας καὶ αἰδοῦς, ℵ^c M P Ψ 6. 104. 326. 1739 lat Orig. (*c*) αἰδοῦς καὶ εὐλαβείας, K L 462 syr^hkl Chrys. Thdt. The accidental doubling of αι (from καί) led to (*b*), especially as αἰδοῦς and εὐλαβεία were often bracketed together, and as δεός was a rare word (first popularized in Hellenistic Judaism by 2 Maccabees). **Εὐλαβεία** here as in 5^7 (cp. 11^7) of reverent awe. **Καὶ γὰρ ὁ θεὸς ἡμῶν πῦρ καταναλίσκον** (v.[29]). Not "for our God too is a πῦρ ἀν.," for the writer believed that the same God was God of the old διαθήκη and of the new; besides, this rendering would require **καὶ γὰρ ἡμῶν ὁ θεός**. The phrase is from Dt 4^{24} (Moses at Sinai to the Israelites) ὅτι Κύριος ὁ θεός σου πῦρ καταναλίσκον ἐστίν, θεὸς ζηλωτής (cp. 9^3), referring to his intense resentment of anything like idolatry, which meant a neglect of the διαθήκη. There is no allusion to fire as purifying; the author of Wisdom (16^{16}) describes the Egyptians as πυρὶ καταναλισκόμενοι, and it is this punitive aspect of God which is emphasized here, the divine ζῆλος (see p. xxxvi).

This is one of Tertullian's points (*adv. Marc.* i. 26–27) against the Marcionite conception of a God who is good-natured and nothing more: "tacite permissum est, quod sine ultione prohibetur . . . nihil Deo tam indignum quam non exsequi quod noluit et prohibuit admitti . . . malo parcere Deum indignius sit quam animadvertere. . . . Plane nec pater tuus est, in quem competat et amor propter pietatem, et timor propter potestatem? nec legitimus dominus, ut diligas propter humanitatem et timeas propter disciplinam." In Πρὸς Ἑβραίους there is no softening of the conception, as in Philo's argument (*de Sacrificantibus*, 8) that God's requirement is simply ἀγαπᾶν αὐτὸν ὡς εὐεργέτην, εἰ δὲ μή, φοβεῖσθαι γοῦν ὡς ἄρχοντα καὶ κύριον, καὶ διὰ πασῶν ἰέναι τῶν εἰς ἀρέσκειαν ὁδῶν καὶ λατρεύειν αὐτῷ μὴ παρέργως ἀλλὰ ὅλῃ τῇ ψυχῇ πεπληρωμένῃ γνώμης φιλοθέου καὶ τῶν ἐντολῶν αὐτοῦ περιέχεσθαι καὶ τὰ δίκαια τιμᾶν. In *de Decalogo*, 11, he spiritualizes the fire at Sinai thus: τοῦ πυρὸς τὸ μὲν φωτίζειν τὸ δὲ καίειν πέφυκεν (those who obey the divine laws being inwardly enlightened, those who disobey being inflamed and consumed by their vices), and closes the treatise (33) by enunciating his favourite doctrine that God never punishes directly but only indirectly (here by Δίκη, whose appropriate task is to punish those who disobey her liege Lord). Indeed he allegorizes the OT comparison of God to a flame (*Quaest. in Exod.* 24^{17} ὥσπερ δὲ ἡ φλὸξ πᾶσαν τὴν παραβληθεῖσαν ὕλην ἀναλίσκει, οὕτως, ὅταν ἐπιφοιτήσῃ εἰλικρινὴς τοῦ θεοῦ ἔννοια τῇ ψυχῇ πάντας τοὺς ἑτεροδόξους ἀσεβείας λογισμοὺς διαφθείρει, καθοσιοῦσα τὴν ὅλην διάνοιαν). The closest parallel to our passage lies in Ps.-Sol $15^{5f.}$ where the author declares that praise to God is the one security for man. Ψαλμὸν καὶ αἶνον μετ' ᾠδῆς ἐν εὐφροσύνῃ καρδιάς, καρπὸν χειλέων . . . ἀπαρχὴν χειλέων ἀπὸ καρδίας ὁσίας καὶ δικαίας, ὁ ποιῶν ταῦτα οὐ σαλευθήσεται εἰς τὸν αἰῶνα ἀπὸ (*i.e.* ὑπὸ) κακοῦ, φλὸξ πυρὸς καὶ *ὀργὴ ἀδίκων οὐχ ἅψεται αὐτοῦ, ὅταν ἐξέλθῃ ἐπὶ ἁμαρτωλοὺς ἀπὸ προσώπου κυρίου.*

With this impressive sentence **Πρὸς Ἑβραίους** really closes. But the writer appends (see Introd., pp. xxviii f.) a more or less informal postscript, with some personal messages to the community. A handful of moral counsels (vv.[1-7]) is followed by a longer paragraph (vv.[8-16]), and the closing personal messages are interrupted by a farewell benediction (v.[20]).

[1] *Let your brotherly love continue.* [2] *Never forget to be hospitable, for by hospitality* (διὰ ταύτης, as 12[15]) *some have entertained angels unawares.* [3] *Remember prisoners as if you were in prison yourselves; remember those who are being ill-treated* (11[37]), *since you too are in the body.*

Neither **φιλαδελφία** nor **φιλοξενία** is a LXX term, though the broader sense of the former begins in 4 Mac 13[23. 26] 14[1]. **Μενέτω** (cp. 6[10] 10[24. 32f.]), though its demands might be severe at times (cp. Ro 12[10], 1 P 1[22]; Clem. Ro 1[2]; Herm. *Mand.* 8[10]); the duty is laid as usual on members of the church, not specially on officials. In v.[2] a particular expression of this **φιλαδελφία** is called for. **Φιλοξενία** was practically an article of religion in the ancient world. The primary reference here in **τινες** is to Abraham and Sara (Gn 18[1f.]), possibly to Manoah (Jg 13[3f.]), and even to Tobit (Tob 12[15]); but the point of the counsel would be caught readily by readers familiar with the Greek and Roman legends of divine visitants being entertained unawares by hospitable people, *e.g.* Hom. *Odyss.* xvii. 485 f. (*καί τε θεοὶ ξείνοισιν ἐοικότες ἀλλοδαποῖσι | παντοῖοι τελέθοντες, ἐπιστρωφῶσι πόληας*, cp. Plat. *Soph.* 216 B); *Sil. Ital.* vii. 173 f. ("laetus nec senserat hospes | advenisse deum"), and the story of Philemon and Baucis (Ovid, *Met.* viii. 626 f.) alluded to in Ac 14[11]. In the Hellenic world the worship of Zeus Xenios (*e.g.* Musonius Rufus, xv. *a*, ὁ περὶ ξένους ἄδικος εἰς τὸν ξένιον ἁμαρτάνει Δία) fortified this kindly custom. According to Resh Lakish (Sota, 10*a*), Abraham planted the tree at Beersheba (Gn 21[33]) for the refreshment of wayfarers, and **φιλοξενία** was always honoured in Jewish tradition (*e.g.* Sabbath, 127. 1, "there are six things, the fruit of which a man eats in this world and by which his horn is raised in the world to come: they are, hospitality to strangers, the visiting of the sick," etc.). But there were pressing local reasons for this kindly virtue in the primitive church. Christians travelling abroad on business might be too poor to afford a local inn. Extortionate charges were frequent; indeed the bad repute which innkeepers enjoyed in the Greek world (cp. Plato's *Laws*, 918 D) was due partly to this and partly also to a "general feeling against taking money for hospitality" (cp. Jebb's *Theophrastus*, p. 94). But, in addition, the moral repute of inns stood low (Theophrastus, *Char.* 6[5] δεινὸς δὲ πανδοκεῦσαι καὶ πορνοβοσκῆσαι κτλ.); there is significance in the Jewish tradition preserved by Josephus (*Ant.* v. I. I) that Rahab ἡ πόρνη (11[31]) kept an inn. For a Christian to frequent such inns might be to endanger his character, and this consideration favoured the practice of hospitality on the part of the local church, apart altogether from the discomforts of an inn. ("In the better parts of the empire and in the larger places of resort there were houses corresponding in some measure to the old coaching inns of the eighteenth century; in the East there were the well-known caravanserais; but for the most part the ancient hostelries must have afforded but undesirable quarters. They were neither select nor clean," T. G. Tucker, *Life in the Roman World*, p. 20.) Some of these travellers would be itinerant evangelists (cp. 3 Jn [5-8]).

According to Philo the three wayfarers seen by Abraham did not at first appear divine (οἱ δὲ θειοτέρας ὄντες φύσεως ἐλελήθεσαν), though later on he suspected they were either prophets or angels when they had promised him the birth of a son in return for his splendid hospitality (*Abrah.* 22–23). "In a wise man's house," Philo observes, "no one is slow to practise hospitality: women and men, slaves and freedmen alike, are most eager to do service to strangers"; at the same time such hospitality was only an incident (πάρεργον) and instance (δεῖγμα σαφέστατον) of Abraham's larger virtue, *i.e.* of his piety. Josephus also (*Ant.* i. 11. 2) makes Abraham suppose the three visitors were human strangers, until at last they revealed themselves as divine angels (θεασάμενος τρεῖς ἀγγέλους καὶ νομίσας εἶναι ξένους ἠσπασατό τ' ἀναστὰς καὶ παρ' αὐτῷ καταχθέντας παρεκάλει ξενίων μεταλαβεῖν). It was ignorance of the classical idiom (cp. Herod. i. 44, ὑποδεξάμενος τὸν ξεῖνον φονέα τοῦ παιδὸς ἐλάνθανε βόσκων) in ἔλαθον ξενίσαντες, which led to the corruptions of ἔλαθον in some Latin versions into "latuerunt," "didicerunt," and "placuerunt." Note the paronomasia ἐπιλανθάνεσθε . . . ἔλαθον, and the emphatic position of ἀγγέλους. "You never know whom you may be entertaining," the writer means. "Some humble visitor may turn out to be for you a very ἄγγελος θεοῦ" (cp. Gal 4[14]).

Μιμνήσκεσθε (bear in mind, and act on your thought of) τῶν δεσμίων. Strangers come within sight; prisoners (v.[3]) have to be sought out or—if at a distance—borne in mind. Christian kindness to the latter, *i.e.* to fellow-Christians arrested for some reason or other, took the form either of personally visiting them to alleviate their sufferings by sympathy and gifts (cp. Mt 25[36], 2 Ti 1[16]), or of subscribing money (to pay their debts or, in the case of prisoners of war, to purchase their release), or of praying for them (Col 4[18] and 4[3]). All this formed a prominent feature of early Christian social ethics. The literature is full of tales about the general practice: *e.g.* Aristid. *Apol.* 15; Tertull. *ad Mart.* 1 f. and *Apol.* 39, with the vivid account of Lucian in the *de Morte Peregr.* 12, 13. This subject is discussed by Harnack in the *Expansion of Early Christianity* (bk. ii. ch. 3, section 5). Our author urges, "remember the imprisoned" **ὡς συνδεδεμένοι.** If ὡς is taken in the same sense as the following ὡς, the meaning is: (*a*) "as prisoners yourselves," *i.e.* in the literal sense, "since you know what it means to be in prison"; or (*b*) "as imprisoned," in the metaphorical sense of Diognet. 6, Χριστιανοὶ κατέχονται ὡς ἐν φρουρᾷ τῷ κόσμῳ. A third alternative sense is suggested by LXX of 1 S 18[1] (ἡ ψυχὴ Ἰωνάθαν συνεδέθη τῇ ψυχῇ Δαυίδ), but the absence of a dative after συνδεδεμένοι and the parallel phrase **ὡς ἐν σώματι** rule it out. Probably ὡς is no more than an equivalent for ὡσεί. Christians are to regard themselves as one with their imprisoned fellows, in the sense of 1 Co 12[26] εἴτε πάσχει ἓν μέλος, συμπάσχει πάντα τὰ μέλη. This interpretation tallies with 10[34] above (cp. Neh 1[3. 4]). It does not, however, imply that **ἐν σώματι,** in the next clause, means "in the Body (of which you and your suffering fellows are alike members"); for **ἐν σώματι** refers to the physical condition of liability to similar ill-usage. See Orig. *c. Cels.* ii. 23, τῶν τοῖς ἐν σώμασι (Bouhéreau conj. σώματι) συμβαινόντων, and especially Philo's words describing some spectators of the cruelties inflicted by a revenue officer on his victims, as suffering acute pain, ὡς ἐν τοῖς ἑτέρων σώμασιν αὐτοὶ κακούμενοι (*de Spec. Leg.* iii. 30). So in *de Confus. Ling.* 35, καὶ τῷ συμφορῶν ἀνηνύτων τῶν κακουχομένων (*i.e.* by exile, famine, and plague; cp. He 11[37]) οὐκ ἐνδεθεῖσαι χωρίῳ, σώματι.

Seneca (*Ep.* ix. 8) illustrates the disinterestedness of friendship by observing that the wise man does not make friends for the reason suggested by Epicurus, viz., to "have someone who will sit beside him when he is ill, someone to assist him when he is thrown into chains or in poverty," but "that he may have someone beside whom, in sickness, he may himself sit, someone whom he may set free from captivity in the hands of the enemy." The former kind of friendship he dismisses as inadequate: "a man has made a friend who is to assist him in the event of bondage ('adversum vincula'), but such a friend will forsake him as soon as the chains rattle ('cum primum crepuerit catena')." In *Ep. Arist.* 241, 242, when the king asks what is the use of kinship, the Jew replies, ἐὰν τοῖς συμβαίνουσι νομίζωμεν ἀτυχοῦσι μὲν ἐλαττοῦσθαι καὶ κακοπαθῶμεν ὡς αὐτοί, φαίνεται τὸ συγγενὲς ὅσον ἰσχῦόν ἐστι. Cicero specially praises generosity to prisoners, and charity in general, as being serviceable not only to individuals but to the State (*de Offic.* ii. 18, "haec benignitas etiam rei publicae est utilis, redimi e servitute captos, locupletari tenuiores").

4 *Let marriage be held in honour by all, and keep the marriage-bed unstained. God will punish the vicious and adulterous.*

5 *Keep your life free from the love of money; be content with what you have, for He* (αὐτός) *has said,*

"*Never will I fail you, never will I forsake you.*"

[6] *So that we can say confidently,*

"*The Lord is my helper* (βοηθός, cp. 2^{18} 4^{16}), *I will not be afraid. What can men do to me?*"

As vv.[1. 2] echo $10^{24.\ 32.\ 33}$, v.[4] drives home the πόρνος of 12^{16}, and vv.[5. 6] echo the reminder of 10^{34}. Evidently (v.[4]), as among the Macedonian Christians (1 Th 4^{3-9}), φιλαδελφία could be taken for granted more readily than sexual purity. **Τίμιος** (*sc.* ἔστω as in v.[5], Ro 12^9, the asyndeton being forcible) **ὁ γάμος ἐν πᾶσιν,** *i.e.* primarily by all who are married, as the following clause explains. There may be an inclusive reference to others who are warned against lax views of sexual morality, but there is no clear evidence that the writer means to protest against an ascetic disparagement of marriage. **Κοίτη** is, like the classical λέχος, a euphemistic term for sexual intercourse, here between the married; **ἀμίαντος** is used of incest, specially in *Test. Reub.* i. 6, ἐμίανα κοίτην τοῦ πατρός μου: Plutarch, *de Fluviis*, 18, μὴ θέλων μιαίνειν τὴν κοίτην τοῦ γεννήσαντος, etc.; but here in a general sense, as, *e.g.*, in Wisdom:

> μακαρία ἡ στεῖρα ἡ ἀμίαντος,
> ἥτις οὐκ ἔγνω κοίτην ἐν παραπτώματι,
> ἕξει καρπὸν ἐν ἐπισκοπῇ ψυχῶν (3^{13}),

and οὔτε βίους οὔτε γάμους καθαροὺς ἔτι φυλάσσουσιν,

> ἕτερος δ' ἕτερον ἢ λοχῶν ἀναιρεῖ ἢ νοθεύων ὀδυνᾷ (14^{24}).

In **πόρνους γὰρ καὶ μοιχούς** κτλ., the writer distinguishes between μοιχοί, *i.e.* married persons who have illicit relations with other married persons, and πόρνοι of the sexually vicious in general, *i.e.* married persons guilty of incest or sodomy as well as of fornication. In the former case the main reference is to the breach of another person's marriage; in the latter, the predominating idea is treachery to one's own marriage vows. The possibility of πορνεία in marriage is admitted in Tob 8^7 (οὐ διὰ πορνείαν ἐγὼ λαμβάνω τὴν ἀδελφήν μου ταύτην), *i.e.* of mere sexual gratification[1] as distinct from the desire and duty of having children, which Jewish and strict Greek ethics held to be the paramount aim of marriage (along with mutual fellowship); but this is only one form of πορνεία. In the threat **κρινεῖ** (as in 10^{30}) **ὁ θεός**, the emphasis is on ὁ θεός. "Longe plurima pars scortatorum et adulterorum est sine dubio, quae effugit notitiam iudicum mortalium . . . magna pars, etiamsi innotescat, tamen poenam civilem et disciplinam ecclesiasticam vel effugit vel leuissime persentiscit" (Bengel).

This is another social duty (cp. Philo, *de Decalogo*, 24). In view of the Epicurean rejection of marriage (*e.g.* Epict. iii. 7. 19), which is finely

[1] μὴ ἐν πάθει ἐπιθυμίας, as Paul would say (1 Th 4^5).

answered by Antipater of Tarsus (Stob. *Florileg.* lxvii. 25: ὁ εὐγενὴς καὶ εὔψυχος νέος . . . θεωρῶν διότι τέλειος οἶκος καὶ βίος οὐκ ἄλλως δύναται γενέσθαι, ἢ μετὰ. γυναικὸς καὶ τέκνων κτλ.), as well as of current ascetic tendencies (*e.g.*, 1 Ti 4³), there may have been a need of vindicating marriage, but the words here simply maintain the duty of keeping marriage vows unbroken. The writer is urging chastity, not the right and duty of any Christian to marry. Prejudices born of the later passion for celibacy led to the suppression of the inconvenient ἐν πᾶσι (om. 38. 460. 623. 1836. 1912* Didymus, Cyril Jerus., Eus., Athan., Epiphanius, Thdt.). The sense is hardly affected, whether γάρ (ℵ A D* M P lat sah boh) or δέ (C D^c Ψ 6 syr arm eth Clem., Eus., Didymus, Chrys.) is read, although the latter would give better support to the interpretation of the previous clause as an anti-ascetic maxim.

A warning against greed of gain (vv.$^{5, 6}$) follows the warning against sexual impurity. There may be a link of thought between them. For the collocation of sensuality and the love of money, see *Epict.* iii. 7. 21, σοὶ καλὴν γυναῖκα φαίνεσθαι μηδεμίαν ἢ τὴν σήν, καλὸν παῖδα μηδένα, καλὸν ἀργύρωμα μηθέν, χρύσωμα μηθέν: *Test. Jud.* 18, φυλάξασθε ἀπὸ τῆς πορνείας καὶ τῆς φιλαργυρίας . . . ὅτι ταῦτα . . . οὐκ ἀφίει ἄνδρα ἐλεῆσαι τὸν πλησίον αὐτοῦ, and Philo's (*de Post. Caini*, 34) remark, that all the worst quarrels, public and private, are due to greedy craving for ἢ εὐμορφίας γυναικὸς ἢ χρημάτων κτλ. In *de Abrah.* 26, he attributes the sensuality of Sodom to its material prosperity. Lucian notes the same connexion in *Nigrin.* 16 (συνεισέρχεται γὰρ μοιχεία καὶ φιλαργυρία κτλ., the love of money having been already set as the source of such vices). In 1 Co 5$^{10f.}$ Paul brackets οἱ πόρνοι with οἱ πλεονέκται, and πλεονεξία (cp. 1 Th 4⁶) as selfishness covers adultery as well as grasping covetousness. But the deeper tie between the two sins is that the love of luxury and the desire for wealth open up opportunities of sensual indulgence. In injuries to other people, Cicero observes (*de Offic.* i. 7. 24), "latissime patet avaritia." When Longinus describes the deteriorating effects of this passion or vice in character (*de Sublim.* 44), he begins by distinguishing it from mere love of pleasure; φιλαργυρία μὲν νόσημα μικροποιόν, φιληδονία δ' ἀγεννέστατον. Then he proceeds to analyse the working of φιλαργυρία in life, its issue in ὕβρις, παρανομία, and ἀναισχυντία.

'Αφιλάργυρος (the rebel Appianus tells Marcus Aurelius, in *OP.* xxxiii. 10, 11, that his father τὸ μὲν πρῶτον ἦν φιλόσοφος, τὸ δεύτερον ἀφιλάργυρος, τὸ τρίτον φιλάγαθος) **ὁ τρόπος** (in sense of "mores," as often, *e.g.*, M. Aurelius, i. 16, καὶ πᾶς ὁ τοιοῦτος τρόπος). **'Αρκούμενοι** is the plur. ptc. after a noun (as in 2 Co 1⁷, Ro 12⁹), and with **τοῖς παροῦσιν** reproduces a common Greek phrase for contentment, e.g. *Teles*, vii. 7, ἀλλ' ἡμεῖς οὐ δυνάμεθα ἀρκεῖσθαι τοῖς παροῦσιν, ὅταν καὶ τρυφῇ πολὺ διδῶμεν, and xxviii. 31, καὶ μὴ ἔχων οὐκ ἐπιποθήσεις ἀλλὰ βιώσῃ ἀρκούμενος τοῖς παροῦσιν. The feature here is the religious motive adduced in **αὐτὸς γὰρ**

εἴρηκεν (of God as usual, *e.g.*, 1[13]), a phrase which (cp. Ac 20[35] αὐτὸς εἶπεν) recalls the Pythagorean αὐτὸς ἔφα ("thus said the Master"). The quotation **οὐ μή σε ἀνῶ οὐδ' οὐ μή σε ἐγκαταλίπω** is a popular paraphrase of Jos 1[5] or Gn 28[15] (cp. Dt 31[8], 1 Ch 28[20]) which the writer owes to Philo (*de Confus. Ling.* 32), who quotes it exactly in this form as a λόγιον τοῦ ἵλεω θεοῦ μεστὸν ἡμερότητος, but simply as a promise that God will never leave the human soul to its own unrestrained passions. The combination of the aor. subj. with the first οὐ μή and the reduplication of the negative (for οὐδ' οὐ μή, cp. Mt 24[21]) amount to a strong asseveration. Note that the writer does not appeal, as Josephus does, to the merits of the fathers (*Antiq.* xi. 5. 7, τὸν μὲν θεὸν ἴστε μνήμῃ τῶν πατέρων Ἀβράμου καὶ Ἰσάκου καὶ Ἰακώβου παραμένοντα καὶ διὰ τῆς ἐκείνων δικαιοσύνης οὐκ ἐγκαταλείποντα τὴν ὑπὲρ ἡμῶν πρόνοιαν) in assuring his readers that they will not be left forlorn by God.

Ἐγκαταλείπω (so all the uncials except D) may be simply an orthographical variant of the true reading ἐγκαταλίπω (aorist subj.). In Dt 31[6] the A text runs οὐ μή σε ἀνῇ οὐδ' οὐ σε ἐγκαταλείπῃ, in Jos 1[5] οὐκ ἐγκαταλείπω σε οὐδὲ ὑπερόψομαί σε, and in Gn 28[15] οὐ μή σε ἐγκαταλείπω. The promise originally was of a martial character. But, as Keble puts it (*Christian Year*, "The Accession"):

> "Not upon kings or priests alone
> the power of that dear word is spent;
> it chants to all in softest tone
> the lowly lesson of content."

Ὥστε (v.[6]) **θαρροῦντας** (on the evidence for this form, which Plutarch prefers to the Ionic variant θαρσεῖν, cp. Crönert's *Memoria Graeca Herculanensis*, 133[2]) **ἡμᾶς** (om. M, accidentally) **λέγειν.** What God says to us moves us to say something to ourselves. This quotation from Ps 118[6] is exact, except that the writer, for the sake of terseness, omits the **καί** (=so) before **οὐ φοβηθήσομαι,** which is reinserted by ℵ[c] A D K L M syr[hkl] etc. For the phrase θαρροῦντας λέγειν, see Pr 1[21] (Wisdom) ἐπὶ δὲ πύλαις πόλεως θαρροῦσα λέγει: and for **βοηθός** and θαρρεῖν in conjunction, see Xen. *Cyr.* v. i. 25, 26, ἐπειδὴ δ' ἐκ Περσῶν βοηθὸς ἡμῖν ὡρμήθης . . . νῦν δ' αὖ οὕτως ἔχομεν ὡς σὺν μὲν σοὶ ὅμως καὶ ἐν τῇ πολεμίᾳ ὄντες θαρροῦμεν. Epictetus tells a man who is tempted (ii. 18. 29), τοῦ θεοῦ μέμνησο, ἐκεῖνον ἐπικαλοῦ βοηθὸν καὶ παραστάτην. This is the idea of the psalm-quotation here. Courage is described in Galen (*de H. et Plat. decr.* vii. 2) as the knowledge ὧν χρὴ θαῤῥεῖν ἢ μὴ θαῤῥεῖν, a genuinely Stoic definition; and Alkibiades tells, in the *Symposium* (221 A), how he came upon Sokrates and Laches retreating during the Athenian defeat at Delium καὶ ἰδὼν εὐθὺς παρακελεύομαί τε αὐτοῖν θαρρεῖν, καὶ ἔλεγον ὅτι οὐκ ἀπολείψω αὐτώ. In the touching prayer preserved in the *Acta Pauli* (xlii.), Thekla cries, ὁ θεός μου καὶ τοῦ οἴκου τούτου, Χριστὲ Ἰησοῦ ὁ υἱὸς τοῦ θεοῦ, ὁ ἐμοὶ βοηθὸς ἐν φυλακῇ, βοηθὸς ἐπὶ ἡγεμόνων, βοηθὸς ἐν πυρί, βοηθὸς ἐν θηρίοις.

According to Pliny (*Epp.* ix. 30: "primum est autem suo esse contentum, deinde, quos praecipue scias indigere sustentantem fouentemque orbe quodam societatis ambire") a man's first duty is to be content with what he has; his second, to go round and help all in his circle who are most in need. Epictetus quotes a saying of Musonius Rufus: *οὐ θέλεις μελετᾶν ἀρκεῖσθαι τῷ δεδομένῳ;* (i. 1. 27); but this refers to life in general, not to money or property in particular. The argument of our author is that instead of clinging to their possessions and setting their hearts on goods (10^{34}), which might still be taken from them by rapacious pagans, they must realize that having God they have enough. He will never allow them to be utterly stripped of the necessaries of life. Instead of trying to refund themselves for what they had lost, let them be content with what is left to them and rely on God to preserve their modest all; he will neither drop nor desert them.

Hitherto the community has been mainly (see on $12^{14f.}$) addressed as a whole. Now the writer reminds them of the example of their founders, dead and gone, adding this to the previous list of memories ($12^{1f.}$).

7 *Remember your leaders, the men who spoke the word of God to you; look back upon the close of their career, and copy their faith.*

Μνημονεύετε τῶν ἡγουμένων ὑμῶν οἵτινες (since they were the men who) **ἐλάλησαν ὑμῖν τὸν λόγον τοῦ θεοῦ.** The special function of these primitive apostles and prophets was to preach the gospel (cp. 1 Co 1^{17}) with the supernatural powers of the Spirit. Then the writer adds a further title to remembrance, their consistent and heroic life; they had sealed their testimony with their (ὧν κτλ.) blood. Ἡγούμενος, like ἄρχων, was a substantival formation which had a wide range of meaning; here it is equivalent to "president" or "leader" (cp. *Epp. Apollon.* ii. 69, ἄνδρας τοὺς ἡγουμένους ὑμῶν = your leading citizens, or prominent men, and Ac 15^{22}).[1] It was they who had founded the church by their authoritative preaching; ἐλάλησαν ὑμῖν τὸν λόγον τοῦ θεοῦ recalls the allusion to the σωτηρία which ὑπὸ τῶν ἀκουσάντων (*i.e.* Jesus) εἰς ἡμᾶς ἐβεβαιώθη (2^3). The phrase denotes, in primitive Christianity (*e.g.* Did. 4^1 where the church-member is bidden remember with honour τοῦ λαλοῦντος σοι τὸν λόγον τοῦ θεοῦ), the central function of the apostolic ministry as the declaration and interpretation of the divine λόγος. These men had died for their faith; **ἔκβασις** here, as in Wis 2^{17} (τὰ ἐν ἐκβάσει αὐτοῦ), is, like ἔξοδος, a metaphor for death as the close of life, evidently a death remarkable for its witness to faith. They had laid down their lives as martyrs. This proves that the allusion in 12^4 does not exclude some martyrdoms in the past history of the community, unless the reference here is supposed to mean

[1] In *Ep. Arist.* 310, of the headmen of the Jewish community at Alexandria.

no more than that they died as they had lived κατὰ πίστιν (11^{13}), without giving up their faith.

In Egypt, during the Roman period, "a liturgical college of πρεσβύτεροι or ἡγούμενοι was at the head of each temple" (*GCP*. i. 127), the latter term being probably taken from its military sense of "officers" (*e.g.* ἡγεμόνες τῶν ἔξω τάξεων).

Ἀναθεωροῦντες is "scanning closely, looking back (ἀνα-) on"; and **ἀναστροφή** is used in this sense even prior to Polybius; *e.g.* Magn. $46^{35. 44}$ (iii B.C.) and Magn. 165^{5} (i A.D.) διὰ τὴν τοῦ ἤθους κόσμιον ἀναστροφήν. As for **μιμεῖσθε**, the verb never occurs in the LXX except as a *v.l.* (B*) for ἐμίσησας in Ps 31^{6}, and there in a bad sense. The good sense begins in Wis 4^{2} (παροῦσάν τε μιμοῦνται αὐτήν), so far as Hellenistic Judaism goes, and in 4 Mac 9^{23} (μιμήσασθέ με) 13^{9} (μιμησώμεθα τοὺς τρεῖς τοὺς ἐπὶ τῆς Συρίας νεανίσκους) it is used of imitating a personal example, as here. In the *de Congressu Erudit.* 13, Philo argues that the learner listens to what his teacher says, whereas a man who acquires true wisdom by practice and meditation (ὁ δὲ ἀσκήσει τὸ καλὸν ἀλλὰ μὴ διδασκαλίᾳ κτώμενος) attends οὐ τοῖς λεγομένοις ἀλλὰ τοῖς λέγουσι, μιμούμενος τὸν ἐκείνων βίον ἐν ταῖς κατὰ μέρος ἀνεπιλήπτοις πράξεσι. He is referring to living examples of goodness, but, as in *de Vita Mos.* i. 28, he points out that Moses made his personal character a παράδειγμα τοῖς ἐθέλουσι μιμεῖσθαι. This stimulus of heroic memories belonging to one's own group is noted by Quintilian (*Instit. Orat.* xii. 2. 31) as essential to the true orator: "quae sunt antiquitus dicta ac facta praeclare et nosse et animo semper agitare conveniet. Quae profecto nusquam plura maioraque quam in nostrae civitatis monumentis reperientur. . . . Quantum enim Graeci praeceptis valent, tantum Romani, quod est maius, exemplis." Marcus Aurelius recollects the same counsel: ἐν τοῖς τῶν Ἐπικουρείων γράμμασι παράγγελμα ἔκειτο συνεχῶς ὑπομιμνήσκεσθαι τῶν παλαιῶν τινος τῶν ἀρετῇ χρησαμένων (xi. 26).

Human leaders may pass away, but Jesus Christ, the supreme object and subject of their faithful preaching, remains, and remains the same; no novel additions to his truth are required, least of all innovations which mix up his spiritual religion with what is sensuous and material.

8 *Jesus Christ is always the same, yesterday, to-day, and for ever.* 9 *Never let yourselves be carried away with a variety of novel doctrines; for the right thing is to have one's heart strengthened by grace, not by the eating of food—that has never been any use to those who have had recourse to it.* 10 *Our* (ἔχομεν as 4^{15}) *altar is one of which the worshippers have no right to eat.* 11 *For the bodies of the animals whose "blood is taken into the holy Place" by the highpriest as a "sin-offering, are burned outside the camp";* 12 *and so Jesus also suffered outside the gate, in order to sanctify the people* (cp. $10^{2f.}$) *by his own blood* (9^{12}). 13 *Let us go to him "outside the camp," then, bearing*

his obloquy [14] (*for we have no lasting city here below, we seek the City to come*). [15] *And by him "let us" constantly "offer praise to God" as our "sacrifice," that is, "the fruit of lips" that celebrate his Name.* [16] *Do not forget* (μὴ ἐπιλανθάνεσθε, as in v.[2]) *beneficence and charity either; these are the kind of sacrifices that are acceptable to God.*

V.[8] connects with what precedes and introduces what follows. Ἔχθες [1] refers to his life on earth (2[3] 5[7]) and includes the service of the original ἡγούμενοι; it does not necessarily imply a long retrospect. **Σήμερον** as in 3[15], and **ὁ αὐτός** as in 1[12]. The finality of the revelation in Jesus, sounded at the opening of the homily (1[1f.]), resounds again here. He is never to be superseded; he never needs to be supplemented. Hence (v.[9]) the warning against some new theology about the media of forgiveness and fellowship, which, it is implied, infringes the all-sufficient efficacy of Jesus Christ. **Διδαχαῖς** (6[2]) **ποικίλαις** (2[4] in good sense) **καὶ ξέναις μὴ παραφέρεσθε.** Παραφέρεσθαι (cp. Jude [12]) is never used in this metaphorical sense (swayed, swerved) in the LXX, where it is always literal, and the best illustration of ξέναις in the sense of "foreign to" (the apostolic faith) is furnished by the author of the epistle to Diognetus (11[1]), who protests, οὐ ξένα ὁμιλῶ . . . ἀλλὰ ἀποστόλων γενόμενος μαθητὴς γίνομαι διδάσκαλος ἐθνῶν. Such notions he curtly pronounces useless, **ἐν οἷς οὐκ ὠφελήθησαν οἱ περιπατοῦντες,** where ἐν οἷς goes with περιπατοῦντες; they have never been of any use in mediating fellowship with God for those who have had recourse to them. It is exactly the tone of Jesus in Mk 7[18].

Παραφέρεσθε was altered (under the influence of Eph 4[14]) into περιφέρεσθε (K L Ψ 2. 5. 88. 330. 378. 440. 491. 547. 642. 919. 920. 1867. 1872. 1908. arm sah). Περιπατήσαντες (ℵ[c] C D[c] K L M P syr[hkl] arm Orig. Chrys. etc.) and περιπατοῦντες (ℵ* A D* 1912 lat) are variants which are substantially the same in meaning, περιπατεῖν ἐν being used in its common sense = living in the sphere of (Eph 2[10] etc.), having recourse to.

The positive position is affirmed in **καλὸν κτλ.** (καλόν, as in 1 Co 7[1], Ro 14[21] etc.). "Καλός . . . denotes that kind of goodness which is at once seen to be good" (Hort on 1 P 2[12]), *i.e.* by those who have a right instinct. The really right and good course is **χάριτι βεβαιοῦσθαι τὴν καρδίαν,** *i.e.* either to have one's heart strengthened, or to be strengthened in heart (καρδίαν, accus. of reference). Bread sustains our physical life (ἄρτος καρδίαν ἀνθρώπου στηρίζει, Ps 104[15]), but καρδία here means more than vitality; it is the inner life of the human soul, which God's χάρις alone can sustain, and God's χάρις in Jesus Christ is everything (2[9] etc.). But what does this contrast mean? The explanation is suggested in the next passage (vv.[10-16]), which flows out of

[1] The forms vary; but this, the Attic spelling, has the best repute upon the whole (see W. G. Rutherford's *New Phrynichus*, pp. 370 f.), and strong support here in ℵ A C* D* M.

what has just been said. The various novel doctrines were connected in some way with βρώματα. So much is clear. The difficulty is to infer what the βρώματα were. There is a touch of scorn for such a motley, unheard of, set of διδαχαί. The writer does not trouble to characterize them, but his words imply that they were many-sided, and that their main characteristic was a preoccupation with βρώματα. There is no reference to the ancient regulations of the Hebrew ritual mentioned in 9^{10}; this would only be tenable on the hypothesis, for which there is no evidence, that the readers were Jewish Christians apt to be fascinated by the ritual of their ancestral faith, and, in any case, such notions could not naturally be described as ποικίλαι καὶ ξέναι. We must look in other directions for the meaning of this enigmatic reference. (*a*) The new διδαχαί may have included ascetic regulations about diet as aids to the higher life, like the ἐντάλματα καὶ διδασκαλίαι τῶν ἀνθρώπων which disturbed the Christians at Colossê. Partly owing to Gnostic syncretism, prohibitions of certain foods (ἀπέχεσθαι βρωμάτων, 1 Ti 4^3) were becoming common in some circles, in the supposed interests of spiritual religion. "We may assume," says Pfleiderer, one of the representatives of this view (pp. 278 f.), "a similar Gnostic spiritualism, which placed the historical Saviour in an inferior position as compared with angels or spiritual powers who do not take upon them flesh and blood, and whose service consists in mystical purifications and ascetic abstinences." (*b*) They may also have included such religious sacraments as were popularized in some of the mystery-cults, where worshippers ate the flesh of a sacrificial victim or consecrated elements which represented the deity. Participation in these festivals was not unknown among some ultra-liberal Christians of the age. It is denounced by Paul in 1 Co 10, and may underlie what the writer has already said in 10^{25}. Why our author did not speak outright of εἰδωλόθυτα, we cannot tell; but some such reference is more suitable to the context than (*a*), since it is sacrificial meals which are in question. He is primarily drawing a contrast between the various cult-feasts of paganism, which the readers feel they might indulge in, not only with immunity, but even with spiritual profit, and the Christian religion, which dispensed with any such participation. (*c*) Is there also a reference to the Lord's supper, or to the realistic sense in which it was being interpreted, as though participation in it implied an actual eating of the sacrificial body of the Lord? This reference is urged by some critics, especially by F. Spitta (*Zur Geschichte u. Litteratur des Urchristentums*, i. pp. 325 f.) and O. Holtzmann (in *Zeitschrift für die neutest. Wissenschaft*, x. pp. 251–260). Spitta goes wrong by misinterpreting v.[10] as though the σῶμα of Christ implied a sacrificial meal from which Jewish priests were excluded. Holtzmann rightly sees that the contrast between χάρις and βρώματα implies, for the latter, the only βρῶμα possible for Christians, viz. the Lord's body as a food. What the writer protests against is the rising conception of the Lord's supper as a φαγεῖν τὸ σῶμα τοῦ Χριστοῦ. On the day of Atonement in the OT ritual, to which he refers, there was no participation in the flesh of the sacrificial victim; there could not be, in the nature of the case (v.[11]). So, he argues, the σῶμα Χριστοῦ of our sacrifice cannot be literally eaten, as these neo-sacramentarians allege; any such notion is, to him, a relapse upon the sensuous, which as a spiritual idealist he despises as "a vain thing, fondly invented." A true insight into the significance of Jesus, such as he has been trying to bring out in what he has written, such as their earlier leaders themselves had conveyed in their own way, would reveal the superfluousness and irrelevance of these διδαχαί. As the writer is alluding to what is familiar, he does not enter into details, so that we have to guess at his references. But the trend of thought in vv.[10f.] is plain. In real Christian worship there is no sacrificial meal; the Christian sacrifice is not one of which the worshippers partake by eating. This is the point of v.[10]. The writer characteristically illustrates it from the OT ritual of atonement-day, by showing how the very death of Jesus outside the city of Jerusalem fulfilled the proviso in that ritual (vv.[11. 12]) that the sacrifice must not be eaten. Then he finds in this fact about the death of Jesus a further illustration of the need for unworldliness (vv.[13. 14]). Finally, in reply to the question, "Then have Christians no sacrifices to offer at all?" he mentions the two standing sacrifices of thanksgiving and charity (vv.[15. 16]), both owing their efficacy to Christ. Inwardness is the dominating thought of the entire paragraph. God's grace in Jesus Christ works upon the soul; no external medium like food is required to bring us into fellowship with him; it is vain to imagine that by eating anything one can enjoy communion with God. Our Lord stands wholly outside the material world of sense, outside things touched and tasted; in relationship to him and him alone, we can worship God. The writer has a mystical or idealistic bent, to which the sacramental idea is foreign. He never alludes to the eucharist; the one sacrament he notices is baptism. A ritual meal as the means of strengthening communion with God through Christ does not appeal to him in the slightest degree. It is not thus that God's χάρις is experienced.

The clue to v.[10] lies in the obvious fact that the θυσιαστήριον and the σκηνή belong to the same figurative order. In our spiritual or heavenly σκηνή, the real σκηνή of the soul, there is indeed a θυσιαστήριον ἐξ οὗ (partitive; cp. τὰ εἰς τοῦ ἱεροῦ ἐσθίου-

σιν, 1 Co 9^{13}) **φαγεῖν** (emphatic by position) **οὐκ ἔχουσιν ἐξουσίαν**[1] (1 Co 9^4) **οἱ τῇ σκηνῇ λατρεύοντες** (*λατρεύειν* with dative as in 8^5). It makes no difference to the sense whether *οἱ . . . λατρεύοντες* means worshippers (9^9 10^2) or priests (8^5), and the writer does not allegorize *θυσιαστήριον* as Philo does (*e.g.* in *de Leg. Alleg.* i. 15, *τῆς καθαρᾶς καὶ ἀμιάντου φύσεως τῆς ἀναφερούσης τὰ ἄμωμα τῷ θεῷ, αὕτη δέ ἐστι τὸ θυσιαστήριον*). His point is simply this, that the Christian sacrifice, on which all our relationship to God depends, is not one that involves or allows any connexion with a meal. To prove how impossible such a notion is, he (v.[11]) cites the ritual regulation in Lv 16^{27} for the disposal of the carcases of the two animals sacrificed **περὶ τῆς ἁμαρτίας** (*ὧν τὸ αἷμα εἰσηνέχθη ἐξιλάσασθαι ἐν τῷ ἁγίῳ ἐξοίσουσιν αὐτὰ ἔξω τῆς παρεμβολῆς καὶ κατακαύσουσιν αὐτὰ ἐν πυρί*). For a moment the writer recalls his main argument in chs. 7–10; in v.[10] Christ is regarded as the victim or sacrifice (cp. *προσενεχθείς* in 9^{28}), but here the necessities of the case involve the activity of the Victim. **Διὸ καὶ Ἰησοῦς κτλ.** (v.[12]). The parallel breaks down at one point, of course; his body was not burned up.[2] But the real comparison lies in **ἔξω τῆς πύλης** (*sc. τῆς παρεμβολῆς*, as Ex $32^{26.\,27}$). The Peshitto and 436 make the reference explicit by reading *πόλεως*, which seems to have been known to Tertullian (*adv. Jud.* 14, "extra civitatem"). The fact that Jesus was crucified outside Jerusalem influenced the synoptic transcripts of the parable in Mk 12^8 = Mt 21^{39} = Lk 20^{15}. Mark's version, *ἀπέκτειναν αὐτὸν καὶ ἐξέβαλον αὐτὸν ἔξω τοῦ ἀμπελῶνος*, was altered into (*ἐξέβαλον*) *ἐκβαλόντες αὐτὸν ἔξω τοῦ ἀμπελῶνος* (*καὶ*) *ἀπέκτειναν*. Crucifixion, like other capital punishments, in the ancient world was inflicted outside a city. To the writer this fact seems intensely significant, rich in symbolism. So much so that his mind hurries on to use it, no longer as a mere confirmation of the negative in v.[10], but as a positive, fresh call to unworldliness. All such sensuous ideas as those implied in sacrificial meals mix up our religion with the very world from which we ought, after Jesus, to be withdrawing. We meet Jesus outside all this, not inside it. In highly figurative language (v.[13]), he therefore makes a broad appeal for an unworldly religious fellowship, such as is alone in keeping with the *χάρις* of God in Jesus our Lord.

Τοίνυν (beginning a sentence as in Lk 20^{28} *τοίνυν ἀπόδοτε κτλ.*, instead of coming second in its classical position), let us join Jesus **ἔξω τῆς παρεμβολῆς**, for he is living. The thought of the

[1] The omission of *ἐξουσίαν* by D* M and the Old Latin does not affect the sense; *ἔχειν* then has the same meaning as in 6^{13}.

[2] The blood, not the body, of the victim mattered in the atonement ritual. Hence, in our writer's scheme of thought, as Peake observes, "while he fully recognises the fact of the Resurrection of Christ, he can assign it no place in his argument or attach to it any theological significance."

metaphor is that of Paul's admonition *μὴ συνσχηματίζεσθε τῷ αἰῶνι τούτῳ* (Ro 12²), and the words **τὸν ὀνειδισμὸν αὐτοῦ φέροντες** recall the warnings against false shame (11²⁶ 12²), just as the following (v.¹⁴) reason, **οὐ γὰρ ἔχομεν ὧδε** (in the present outward order of things) **μένουσαν**[1] **πόλιν ἀλλὰ τὴν μέλλουσαν ἐπιζητοῦμεν** recalls the ideas of 11¹⁰·¹⁴⁻¹⁶. The appeal echoes that of 4¹¹ *σπουδάσωμεν οὖν εἰσελθεῖν εἰς ἐκείνην τὴν κατάπαυσιν.* It is through the experiences of an unsettled and insulted life that Christians must pass, if they are to be loyal to their Lord. That is, the writer interprets *ἔξω τῆς παρεμβολῆς* figuratively ("Egrediamur et nos a commercio mundi huius," Erasmus). Philo had already done so (cp. specially *quod. det. pot.* 44), in a mystical sense: *μακρὰν διοικίζει τοῦ σωματικοῦ στρατοπέδου, μόνως ἂν οὕτως ἐλπίσας ἱκέτης καὶ θεραπευτὴς ἔσεσθαι τέλειος θεοῦ.* Similarly in *de Ebrietate*, 25, commenting on Ex 33⁷, he explains that by *ἐν τῷ στρατοπέδῳ* (= *ἐν τῇ παρεμβολῇ*) Moses meant allegorically *ἐν τῷ μετὰ σώματος βίῳ*, the material interests of the worldly life which must be forsaken if the soul is to enjoy the inward vision of God. Such is the renunciation which the writer here has in view. It is the thought in 2 Clem. 5¹ (*ὅθεν, ἀδελφοί, καταλείψαντες τὴν παροικίαν τοῦ κόσμου τούτου ποιήσωμεν τὸ θέλημα τοῦ καλέσαντος ἡμᾶς, καὶ μὴ φοβηθῶμεν ἐξελθεῖν ἐκ τοῦ κόσμου τούτου*) and 6⁵ (*οὐ δυνάμεθα τῶν δύο φίλοι εἶναι· δεῖ δὲ ἡμᾶς τούτῳ ἀποταξαμένους ἐκείνῳ χρᾶσθαι*). Only, our author weaves in the characteristic idea of the shame which has to be endured in such an unworldly renunciation.

The next exhortation in **v.¹⁵** (**ἀναφέρωμεν**) catches up **ἐξερχώμεθα**, as **δι' αὐτοῦ** carries on *πρὸς αὐτόν.* For once applying sacrificial language to the Christian life, he reminds his readers again of the sacrifice of thanksgiving. The phrase **καρπὸν χειλέων** explains (**τοῦτ' ἔστιν**) the sense in which **θυσία αἰνέσεως** is to be taken; it is from the LXX mistranslation (*καρπὸν χειλέων*) of Hos 14³ where the true text has פָּרִים (bullocks) instead of פְּרִי (fruit). In **ὁμολογούντων τῷ ὀνόματι αὐτοῦ**, *ὁμολογεῖν* is used in the sense of *ἐξομολογεῖσθαι* by an unusual[2] turn of expression. The *ὄνομα* means, as usual, the revealed personality. Probably there is an unconscious recollection of Ps 54⁸ (*ἐξομολογήσομαι τῷ ὀνόματί σου*); *θυσία αἰνέσεως*[3] is also from the psalter (*e.g.* 50¹⁴·²³). Ἀναφέρειν elsewhere in the NT is only used of spiritual sacrifices in the parallel passage 1 P 2⁵ *ἀνενέγκαι πνευματικὰς θυσίας εὐπροσδέκτους θεῷ διὰ Ἰησοῦ Χριστοῦ.* We have no sacri-

[1] In the sense of Aeneas (Verg. *Aen.* iii. 85, 86, "da moenia fessis | et genus et mansuram urbem"). Note the assonance *μένουσαν . . . μέλλουσαν.*

[2] But *ὁμολογεῖν τινι* occurs in 3 Es 4⁶⁰ 5⁵⁸ (A).

[3] In the LXX *ἐξομολόγησις* is generally preferred to *αἴνεσις* as an equivalent for תודה.

ficial meals, the writer implies; we do not need them. Nor have we any sacrifices—except spiritual ones. (The οὖν after δι' αὐτοῦ, which ℵ^c A C D^c M vg syr^hkl boh arm eth Orig. Chrys. etc. retain, is omitted by ℵ* D* P Ψ vt syr^vg; but ℵ* D* om. οὖν also 1 Co 6[7], as D in Ro 7[25]). The thought of 12[28] is thus expanded, with the additional touch that thankfulness to God is inspired by our experience of Jesus (δι' αὐτοῦ, as Col 3[17] εὐχαριστοῦντες τῷ θεῷ πατρὶ δι' αὐτοῦ); the phrase is a counterpart of **διὰ τοῦ ἀρχιερέως** in v.[11]. This thank-offering is to be made *διὰ παντὸς* (*sc.* *χρόνου*), instead of at stated times, for, whatever befalls us, we owe God thanks and praise (cp. 1 Th 5[16]). The Mishna (cp. Berachoth 5[4]) declares that he must be silenced who only calls upon God's name with thankfulness in the enjoyment of good (Berachoth 5[3] הָאוֹמֵר . . . עַל טוֹב יִזָּכֵר שְׁמֶךָ מוֹדִים מוֹדִים מְשַׁתְּקִין אוֹתוֹ).

The religious idea of thanksgiving was prominent in several quarters. According to Fronto (Loeb ed. i. p. 22) thank-offerings were more acceptable to the gods than sin-offerings, as being more disinterested: *μάντεων δὲ παῖδές φασιν καὶ τοῖς θεοῖς ἡδίους εἶναι θυσιῶν τὰς χαριστηρίους ἢ τὰς μειλιχίους.* Philo had taught (*de Plant.* 30) that *εὐχαριστία* is exceptionally sacred, and that towards God it must be an inward sacrifice: *θεῷ δὲ οὐκ ἔνεστι γνησίως εὐχαριστῆσαι δι' ὧν νομίζουσιν οἱ πολλοὶ κατασκευῶν ἀναθημάτων θυσιῶν—οὐδὲ γὰρ σύμπας ὁ κόσμος ἱερὸν ἀξιόχρεων ἂν γένοιτο πρὸς τὴν τούτου τιμήν—ἀλλὰ δι' ἐπαίνων καὶ ὕμνων, οὐχ οὓς ἡ γεγωνὸς ᾄσεται φωνή, ἀλλὰ οὓς ὁ ἀειδὴς καὶ καθαρώτατος νοῦς ἐπηχήσει καὶ ἀναμέλψει.* He proceeds (*ibid.* 33) to dwell on the meaning of the name Judah, *ὃς ἑρμηνεύεται κυρίῳ ἐξομολόγησις.* Judah was the last (Gn 29[35]) son of Leah, for nothing could be added to praise of God, nothing excels *ὁ εὐλογῶν τὸν θεὸν νοῦς.* This tallies with the well-known rabbinic saying, quoted in Tanchuma, 55. 2: "in the time of messiah all sacrifices will cease, but the sacrifice of thanksgiving will not cease; all prayers will cease, but praises will not cease" (on basis of Jer 33[1] and Ps 56[13]). The praise of God as the real sacrifice of the pious is frequently noted in the later Judaism (*e.g.* 2 Mac 10[7]).

In v.[16] the writer notes the second Christian sacrifice of charity. **Εὐποιία**, though not a LXX term, is common in Hellenistic Greek, especially in Epictetus, *e.g.* Fragm. 15 (ed. Schenk), *ἐπὶ χρηστότητι καὶ εὐποιίᾳ*; Fragm. 45, *οὐδὲν κρεῖσσον . . . εὐποιίας* (where the context suggests "beneficence"). **Κοινωνία** in the sense of charity or contributions had been already used by Paul (2 Co 9[13] etc.). To share with others, to impart to them what we possess, is one way of worshipping God. The three great definitions of worship or religious service in the NT (here, Ro 12[1. 2] and Ja 1[27]) are all inward and ethical; what lies behind this one is the fact that part of the food used in ancient OT sacrifices went to the support of the priests, and part was used to provide meals for the poor. Charitable relief was bound up with the sacrificial system, for such parts of the animals as were not burnt were devoted to these beneficent purposes. An equivalent must be provided in our spiritual religion, the writer suggests; if we have no longer any animal sacrifices, we must carry on at any rate the charitable element in that ritual. This is the force of μὴ ἐπιλανθάνεσθε. Contributions, *e.g.*, for the support of ἡγούμενοι, who were not priests, were unknown in the ancient world, and had to be explicitly urged as a duty (cp. 1 Co 9^{6-14}). Similarly the needs of the poor had to be met by voluntary sacrifices, by which alone, in a spiritual religion, God could be satisfied—τοιαύταις (perhaps including the sacrifice of praise as well as εὐποιία and κοινωνία) θυσίαις εὐαρεστεῖται (cp. $11^{5.\,6}$ 12^{28}) ὁ θεός. This counsel agrees with some rabbinic opinions (*e.g.* T. B. Sukkah, 59*b*: "he who offers alms is greater than all sacrifices"). The special duty of supporting the priesthood is urged in Sir $7^{30f.}$, but our author shows no trace of the theory that almsgiving in general was not only superior to sacrifices but possessed atoning merit before God (Sir 3^{14} ἐλεημοσύνη γὰρ πατρὸς οὐκ ἐπιλησθήσεται, καὶ ἀντὶ ἁμαρτιῶν προσανοικοδομηθήσεταί σοι). In the later rabbinic theology, prayer, penitence, the study of the Torah, hospitality, charity, and the like were regarded as sacrifices equivalent to those which had been offered when the temple was standing. Thus Rabbi Jochanan b. Zakkai (cp. Schlatter's *Jochanan ben Zakkai*, pp. 39 f.) consoled himself and his friends with the thought, derived from Hos 6^{6}, that in the practice of charity they still possessed a valid sacrifice for sins; he voiced the conviction also (*e.g.* b. baba bathra 10^{b}) that charity (צדקה) won forgiveness for pagans as the sin-offering did for Israel. In the Ep. Barnabas ($2^{7f.}$) the writer quotes Jer $7^{22.\,23}$ (Zec 8^{17}) as a warning to Christians against Jewish sacrifices (αἰσθάνεσθαι οὖν ὀφείλομεν τὴν γνώμην τῆς ἀγαθωσύνης τοῦ πατρὸς ἡμῶν ὅτ' ἡμῖν λέγει, θέλων ἡμᾶς μὴ ὁμοίως πλανωμένους ἐκείνοις ζητεῖν, πῶς προσάγωμεν αὐτῷ), but he quotes Ps 51^{19} as the description of the ideal sacrifice.

The tendency in some circles of the later Judaism to spiritualize sacrifice in general and to insist on its motive and spirit is voiced in a passage like Jth $16^{15f.}$:

> ὄρη γὰρ ἐκ θεμελίων σὺν ὕδασιν σαλευθήσεται,
> πέτραι δ' ἀπὸ προσώπου σου ὡς κηρὸς τακήσονται·
> ἔτι δὲ τοῖς φοβουμένοις σε σὺ εὐιλατεύεις αὐτοῖς·
> ὅτι μικρὸν πᾶσα θυσία εἰς ὀσμὴν εὐωδίας,
> καὶ ἐλάχιστον πᾶν στέαρ εἰς ὁλοκαύτωμά σοι·
> ὁ δὲ φοβούμενος τὸν κύριον μέγας διὰ παντός.

Also in a number of statements from various sources, of which that in *Ep. Arist.* 234 (τί μέγιστόν ἐστι δόξης; ὁ δὲ εἶπε· τὸ τιμᾶν τὸν θεόν· τοῦτο δ' ἐστὶν οὐ δώροις οὐδὲ θυσίαις, ἀλλὰ ψυχῆς καθαρότητι καὶ διαλήψεως ὁσίας) may be cited as a fair specimen. The congruous idea of bloodless sacrifices was common in subsequent Christianity. Thus the martyr Apollonius (*Acta Apollonii*, 44; Conybeare's *Monuments of Early Christianity*, pp. 47–48) tells the magistrate, "I expected . . . that thy heart would bear fruit, and that thou wouldst worship God, the Creator of all, and unto Him continually offer thy prayers by means of compassion; for compassion shown to men by men is a bloodless sacrifice and holy unto God." So Jerome's comment runs on Ps 15[4] οὐ μὴ συναγάγω τὰς συναγωγὰς αὐτῶν ἐξ αἱμάτων. Συνάγων, φησίν, συναγωγὰς ἐκ τῶν ἐθνῶν, οὐ δι' αἱμάτων ταύτας συνάξω· τοῦτ' ἔστιν, οὐ παρασκευάσω διὰ τῆς νομικῆς μοι προσέρχεσθαι λατρείας, δι' αἰνέσεως δὲ μᾶλλον καὶ τῆς ἀναμάκτου θυσίας (*Anecdota Maredsolana*, iii. 3. 123). Both in the Didache (14[1] κλάσατε ἄρτον καὶ εὐχαριστήσατε προσεξομολογησάμενοι τὰ παραπτώματα ὑμῶν, ὅπως καθαρὰ ἡ θυσία ὑμῶν ᾖ) and in Justin Martyr (*Dial.* 117, πάντας οὖν οἱ διὰ τοῦ ὀνόματος τούτου θυσίας, ἃς παρέδωκεν Ἰησοῦς ὁ Χριστὸς γίνεσθαι, τουτέστιν ἐπὶ τῇ εὐχαριστίᾳ τοῦ ἄρτου καὶ τοῦ ποτηρίου, τὰς ἐν παντὶ τόπῳ τῆς γῆς γινομένας ὑπὸ τῶν Χριστιανῶν, προλαβὼν ὁ θεὸς μαρτυρεῖ εὐαρέστους ὑπάρχειν αὐτῷ), the very prayers at the eucharist are called θυσίαι, but this belongs to a later stage, when the eucharist or love-feast became the rite round which collections for the poor, the sick, prisoners, and travelling visitors (vv.[1f.]) gathered, and into which sacrificial language began to be poured (cp. Justin's *Apol.* i. 66, 67). In Πρὸς Ἑβραίους we find a simpler and different line of practical Christianity.

Now for a word on the living **ἡγούμενοι** of the community (v.[17]), including himself (vv.[18. 19]).

[17] *Obey your leaders, submit to them; for they* (αὐτοί) *are alive to the interests of your souls, as men who will have to account for their trust. Let their work be a joy to them and not a grief—which would be a loss to yourselves.* [18] *Pray for me, for I am sure I have a clean conscience; my desire is in every way to lead an honest life.* [19] *I urge you to this* (*i.e.* to prayer) *all the more, that I may get back to you the sooner.*

The connexion of vv.[17f.] is not only with v.[7], but with vv.[8-16]. It would be indeed a grief to your true leaders if you gave way to these ποικίλαι καὶ ξέναι doctrines, instead of following men who are really (this is the force of αὐτοί) concerned for your highest interests. **Πείθεσθε** (cp. Epict. Fragm. 27, τὸν προσομιλοῦντα . . . διασκοποῦ . . . εἰ μὲν ἀμείνονα, ἀκούειν χρὴ καὶ πείθεσθαι αὐτῷ) **καὶ ὑπείκετε** (ὑπείκω is not a LXX term); strong words but justified, for the λόγος τοῦ θεοῦ which Christian leaders preached meant authoritative standards of life for the community (cp. 1 Co 4[17. 21] 14[37] etc.), inspired by the Spirit. Insubordination was the temptation at one pole, an overbearing temper (1 P 5[3]) the temptation at the other. Our author knows that, in the case of his friends, the former alone is to be feared. He does not threaten penalties for disobedience, however, as Josephus does (*c. Apionem*, ii. 194) for insubordination on the part of the Jewish laity towards a priest: ὁ δέ γε τούτῳ μὴ πειθόμενος ὑφέξει δίκην ὡς εἰς τὸν θεὸν αὐτὸν ἀσεβῶν. Rather, he singles out the highminded devotion of these leaders as an inducement to the rank and file to be submissive. **Αὐτοὶ γὰρ ἀγρυπνοῦσιν ὑπὲρ τῶν ψυχῶν ὑμῶν**, almost as Epictetus says of the true Cynic who zealously concerns himself with the moral welfare of men, ὑπερηγρύπνηκεν ὑπὲρ ἀνθρώπων (iii. 22. 95; he uses the verb once in its literal sense of a soldier having to keep watch through the night, iii. 24. 32).

The force of the phrase is flattened by the transference of ὑπὲρ τῶν ψυχῶν ὑμῶν to a position after ὡς λόγον ἀποδώσοντες (as A vg). The latter expression, ὡς (conscious that) λόγον ἀποδώσοντες (ὡς with fut. ptc. here only in NT), is used by Chrysostom, *de Sacerdotio*, iii. 18 (cp. vi. 1), to enforce a sense of ministerial responsibility (εἰ γὰρ τῶν οἰκείων πλημμελημάτων εὐθύνας ὑπέχοντες φρίττομεν, ὡς οὐ δυνησόμενοι τὸ πῦρ ἐκφυγεῖν ἐκεῖνο, τί χρὴ πείσεσθαι προσδοκᾶν τὸν ὑπὲρ τοσούτων ἀπολογεῖσθαι μέλλοντα;), but in Πρὸς Ἑβραίους the writer assumes that the ἡγούμενοι are doing and will do their duty. Any sadness which they may feel is due, not to a sense of their own shortcomings, but to their experience of wilfulness and error among their charges. Λόγον ἀποδιδόναι is more common in the NT than the equivalent λόγον διδόναι, which recurs often in Greek literature, *e.g.* in Plato's *Sympos.* 189*b*, πρόσεχε τὸν νοῦν καὶ οὕτως λέγε ὡς δώσων λόγον, or in the complaint of the Fayyum peasants (A.D. 207), who petition the local centurion that the disturbers of their work may be called to account: ἀξιοῦντες, ἐάν σοι δόξῃ, κελεῦσαι αὐτοὺς ἀχθῆναι ἐπὶ σε λόγον ἀποδώσοντας περὶ τούτου (*GCP.* i. $354^{25, 26}$). In Clem. Alex. *Quis div. salv.* 42, John says to the captain of the robbers, ἐγὼ Χριστῷ λόγον δώσω ὑπὲρ σοῦ.

The ἵνα clause (ἵνα μετὰ χαρᾶς τοῦτο ποιῶσιν καὶ μὴ στενάζοντες) goes back to πείθεσθε . . . ὑπείκετε. The members have it in their power to thwart and disappoint their ἡγούμενοι. Τοῦτο π. refers to ἀγρυπνοῦσιν, and the best comment on καὶ μὴ στενάζοντες is in Denny's hymn:

"O give us hearts to love like Thee,
Like Thee, O Lord, to grieve
Far more for others' sins than all
The wrongs that we receive."

The last four words, ἀλυσιτελὲς γὰρ ὑμῖν τοῦτο, form a rhetorical litotes, as when Pindar (*Olymp.* i. 53) remarks, ἀκέρδεια λέλογχεν θαμινὰ κακαγόρος. It would be a "sore loss" to them if their lives failed to answer the hopes and efforts of their ἡγούμενοι, hopes like those implied in 6^{9} and 10^{39}. Ἀλυσιτελές ("no profit") is probably used after λόγον ἀποδώσοντες with its sense of "reckoning." Compare the use of the adverb in Theophrastus, viii. 11 (οὐ γὰρ μόνον ψεύδονται ἀλλὰ καὶ ἀλυσιτελῶς ἀπαλλάττονσι), and the dry remark of Philo (*in Flaccum*, 6), speaking about the attempt of the Alexandrian anti-Semites to erect images in Jewish places of worship, when he says that Flaccus might have known ὡς οὐ λυσιτελὲς ἔθη πάτρια κινεῖν! The term lent itself to such effective under-statements, as in Philo's aphorism (*Fragments of Philo*, ed. J. Rendel Harris, p. 70) τὸ ἐπιορκεῖν ἀνόσιον καὶ ἀλυσιτελέστατον.

The next word (v.[18]) is about himself. **Προσεύχεσθε** (continue praying) **περὶ** (cp. 2 Mac 1[6] *καὶ νῦν ὧδέ ἐσμεν προσευχόμενοι περὶ ὑμῶν*) **ἡμῶν** (plural of authorship), **πειθόμεθα** (a modest confidence: "whatever some of you may think, I believe") **γὰρ ὅτι καλὴν συνείδησιν ἔχομεν.** He is conscious of a keen desire (*θέλοντες* as in 12[17]) to act in a straightforward, honest way; hence he can ask their prayers. Hence also they may feel confident and eager about praying for him. The writer chooses *καλήν* (cp. on v.[9]) instead of *ἀγαθήν* as his adjective for *συνείδησιν*, probably for the sake of assonance with the following *καλῶς*, perhaps also to avoid the hiatus after *ὅτι.* When he adds, **ἐν πᾶσιν** (here neuter) **καλῶς θέλοντες ἀναστρέφεσθαι** (a phrase which occurs in the Pergamos inscript. 459[5] *καλῶς καὶ ἐνδόξως ἀναστραφῆναι*, in the 1st century B.C. inscription (Priene, 115[5]) *ἀναστρεφόμενος ἐν πᾶσιν φιλ[ανθρώπως]*, and in Epict. iv. 4. 46, *ἑορτὴν ἄγειν δύνασαι καθ' ἡμέραν, ὅτι καλῶς ἀνεστράφης ἐν τῷδε τῷ ἔργῳ*, etc.), the language recalls that of 2 Co 1[11. 12] where Paul appeals for the help of his readers' prayers and pleads his honesty of conscience (*τὸ μαρτύριον τῆς συνειδήσεως ἡμῶν, ὅτι . . . ἀνεστράφημεν κτλ.*). Perhaps the writer is conscious that his readers have been blaming him, attributing (say) his absence from them to unworthy motives, as in the case of Paul (*e.g.* 1 Th 2[18], 2 Co 1[17f.]). This may be the feeling which prompts the protest here and the assurances in vv.[19. 23]. "I am still deeply interested in you; my absence is involuntary; believe that."

Καί is inserted before *περί* by D vt Chrys. (possibly as a reminiscence of 1 Th 5[25]), *i.e.* pray as well as obey ("et orate pro nobis," d); this would emphasize the fact that the writer belonged to the *ἡγούμενοι.* But the plural in v.[18] is not used to show that the writer is one of the *ἡγούμενοι* mentioned in v.[17], for whom the prayers of the community are asked. He was one of them; *ἡμῶν* here is the literary plural already used in 5[11] 6[9. 11]. There are apt parallels in Cicero's *de Officiis*, ii. 24 ("Quem nos . . . e Graeco in Latinum convertimus. Sed toto hoc de genere, de quaerenda, de collocanda pecunia vellens etiam de utenda"), and *OP.* x. 1296 (the letter of a boy to his father), *ποιῶ . . . φιλοπονοῦμεν καὶ ἀναψυχόμεν.* *Πειθόμεθα* (*πείθομαι* 256. 1319. 2127) has been changed into **πεποίθαμεν** by ℵ[c] C[c] D Ψ W 6. 104. 263. 326 (Blass), probably because the latter ("we are confident") is stronger than *πείθομεθα*, which (cp. Ac 26[26]) only amounts to "we believe" (though implying "we are sure"). Retaining *πειθόμεθα*, A. Bischoff (*Zeits. für die neut. Wiss.* ix. 171 f.) evades the difficulty by altering the order of the words: *προσεύχ. περὶ ἡμῶν· καλὴν γὰρ συν. ἔχομεν, ὅτι πείθομεθα ἐν πᾶσιν κ. θ. ἀναστρέφεσθαι, i.e.* taking *ὅτι* as "because."

As in Philem [22], the writer's return is dependent on his friends' prayers (v.[19]); specially (see p. 17) let them intercede with God for his speedy restoration to them, **ἵνα τάχιον ἀποκατασταθῶ ὑμῖν** (cp. *OP.* 1[81] (A.D. 49–50) *ἀποκατεστάθη μοι ὁ υἱός*). *Τάχιον* may mean "the sooner" (*i.e.* than if you did not pray) or simply "soon" (as in v.[23], where, as in Hellenistic Greek, it has lost its comparative meaning). What detained the writer, we cannot tell. Apparently (v.[23]) it was not imprisonment.

A closing prayer and doxology, such as was not uncommon in epistles of the primitive church (*e.g.* 1 Th 5[23], 1 P 5[11]), now follows. Having asked his readers to pray for him, he now prays for them.

[20] *May the God of peace "who brought up" from the dead our Lord* (7[14]) *Jesus* (see p. lxiii), "*the*" *great* "*Shepherd of the sheep, with the blood of the eternal covenant,*" [21] *furnish you with everything that is good for the doing of his will, creating in your lives by Jesus Christ what is acceptable in his own sight! To him* (i.e. God) *be* (sc. εἴη) *glory for ever and ever. Amen.*

Ὁ θεὸς τῆς εἰρήνης means the God of saving bliss (see on 12[11]), εἰρήνη being taken in a sense like the full OT sense of the secure prosperity won by the messianic triumph over the hostile powers of evil (cp. 2[14] 7[2]). There is no special allusion here, as in Paul's use of the phrase (Ro 15[33], 2 Co 13[11] etc.), to friction in the community; the conflict is one in which God secures εἰρήνη for his People, a conflict with evil, not strife between members of the church. The method of this triumph is described in some OT phrases, which the writer uses quite apart from their original setting. The first quotation is from Is 63[11] ποῦ ὁ ἀναβιβάσας ἐκ τῆς γῆς τὸν ποιμένα τῶν προβάτων, which the writer applies to Jesus—his only reference to the resurrection (cp. on vv.[11. 12]). But there is no need (with Blass) to follow Chrysostom in reading τῆς γῆς here for νεκρῶν. With **ἀναγεῖν** in this sense, **ἐκ νεκρῶν** (so Ro 10[7]) or some equivalent (ἐξ ᾅδου, Ps 30[4], Wis 16[13], Joseph. *Ant.* vi. 14. 2) is much more natural. In **τὸν ποιμένα τῶν προβάτων τὸν μέγαν**, ὁ μέγας is applied to him as in 4[14] 10[21]. The figure of the ποιμήν, which never occurs in Paul, plays no rôle in our author's argument as it does in 1 Peter (2[25] 5[4]); he prefers ἱερεύς or ἀρχηγός, and even here he at once passes to the more congenial idea of the διαθήκη. Jesus is the great Shepherd, as he has made himself responsible for the People, identifying himself with them at all costs, and sacrificing his life in order to save them for God. But as death never occurs in the OT description of the divine shepherd, not even in the 23rd Psalm, the writer blends with his quotation from Isaiah another—**ἐν αἵματι διαθήκης αἰωνίου**, a LXX phrase from Zech 9[11] (ἐν αἵματι διαθήκης σου ἐξαπέστειλας δεσμίους σου), Is 55[3] (διαθήσομαι ὑμῖν διαθήκην αἰώνιον), etc. Ἐν αἵματι διαθήκης αἰωνίου goes with ἀναγαγών, not with τὸν ποιμένα, in which case τόν would need to be prefixed to the phrase. Jesus was raised to present his blood as the atoning sacrifice which mediated the διαθήκη (9[11. 24f.]). To the resurrection (cp. on v.[12]) is thus ascribed what elsewhere in the epistle is ascribed to the εἰσελθεῖν εἰς τὰ ἅγια. But as the stress falls on αἰωνίου, then more is implied than that apart from the *αἷμα* no *διαθήκη* could have been instituted. In reality the thought resembles that of 9^{14} (*ὃς διὰ πνεύματος αἰωνίου ἑαυτὸν προσήνεγκεν . . . καθαριεῖ τὴν συνείδησιν ἡμῶν . . . εἰς τὸ λατρεύειν θεῷ ζῶντι*), where **εἰς τὸ** *λατρεύειν θεῷ* corresponds to **εἰς τὸ ποιῆσαι τὸ θέλημα αὐτοῦ** below; *ἐν κτλ.* is "equipped with," not "in virtue of." This interpretation is in line with the author's argument in chs. 7–10. "Videtur mihi apostolus hoc belle, Christum ita resurrexisse a mortuis, ut mors tamen eius non sit abolita, sed aeternum vigorem retineat, ac si dixisset: Deus filium suum excitavit, sed ita ut sanguis, quem semel in morte fudit, ad sanctionem foederis aeterni post resurrectionem vigeat fructumque suum proferat perinde ac si semper flueret" (Calvin). In **καταρτίσαι** (the aor. optative)[1] *κτλ.*, there is a parallel to the thought of Ph 2^{13}. *Εἰς τὸ ποιῆσαι τὸ θέλημα αὐτοῦ* recalls the language of 10^{36}, and **διὰ Ἰησοῦ Χριστοῦ** goes with **ποιῶν**: the power of God in our lives as for our lives (v.[20]) works through the person of Jesus Christ. To take *διὰ* 'Ι. Χ. with **τὸ εὐάρεστον ἐνώπιον αὐτοῦ** yields an unobjectionable sense, corresponding to the thought of v.[15]. But *τὸ . . . αὐτοῦ* stands quite well by itself (cf. 1 Jn 3^{22}).

The writer makes no such use of the shepherd and flock metaphor as, *e.g.*, Philo had done. The Jewish thinker (*Vit. Mos.* i. 11) argues that the calling of a shepherd is the best preparation for anyone who is to rule over men; hence "kings are called *shepherds of their people*" as a title of honour. He also interprets the sheep as the symbol of a nature which is capable of improvement (*de sacrif. Abel.* 34, *προκοπῆς δὲ πρόβατον, ὡς καὶ αὐτὸ δηλοῖ τοὔνομα, σύμβολον*). The classical habit of describing kings as shepherds of their people would help to make the metaphor quite intelligible to readers of non-Jewish origin. Compare, *e.g.*, the saying of Cyrus (Xenophon, *Cyropaedia*, viii. 2. 14), that a good shepherd resembled a good king, *τόν τε γὰρ νομέα χρῆναι ἔφη εὐδαίμονα τὰ κτήνη ποιοῦντα χρῆσθαι αὐτοῖς, ᾗ δὴ προβάτων εὐδαιμονία, τόν τε βασιλέα ὡσαύτως εὐδαίμονας πόλεις καὶ ἀνθρώπους ποιοῦντα χρῆσθαι αὐτοῖς.*

Παντί was soon furnished with the homiletic addition of **ἔργῳ** (C K M P syr sah arm eth Chrys. Thdt. etc.), or even *ἔργῳ καὶ λόγῳ* (A, from 2 Th 2^{17}). *Ποιῶν* has either *αὐτῷ* (ℵ* A C* 33* 1288 boh) or *ἑαυτῷ* (Greg. Nyss.) or *αὐτός* (d 1912) prefixed. Hort, admitting that "it is impossible to make sense of *αὐτῷ*" (B. Weiss, Blass = *ἑαυτῷ*), maintains that *αὐτός* is original. It is a homiletic insertion, out of which *αὐτῷ* arose by corruption. *Ἡμῖν* (ℵ D M Ψ 33. 104. 181. 326. 917. 927. 1288. 1739. 1912, etc. syr^{vg} sah boh arm) is merely an error for **ὑμῖν**, due to the preceding *ἡμῶν*.

A personal postscript (vv.[22-24]) is now added, as 1 P 5^{12-14} after $5^{10.\ 11}$.

22 *I appeal to you, brothers* ($3^{1.\ 12}$ 10^{19}), *to bear with this appeal of mine. It is but a short letter.*

---

[1] This lonely occurrence of the optative points to its tendency after the LXX to disappear; thus, apart from *μὴ γένοιτο*, it only occurs once in a writer like Epictetus (iii. 5. 11).

[23] *You must understand that our brother Timotheus is now free. If he comes soon, he and I will see you together.*
[24] *Salute all your leaders and all the saints. The Italians salute you.*
[25] *Grace be with you all. Amen.*

The Timotheus referred to (in v.[23]) is probably the Timotheus who had been a colleague of Paul. The other allusions have nothing to correspond with them in the data of the NT. But there is no ground for supposing that vv.[22-25] were added, either by the writer himself (Wrede) or by those who drew up the canon, in order to give a Pauline appearance to the document (see Introd., pp. xxviii f.). Seeberg's reasons for regarding vv.[22-25] as a fragment of some other note by the same writer are that [23b] implies not a church but a small group of Christians, and that vv.[18. 23] presuppose different situations; neither reason is valid. The style and contents are equally unfavourable to Perdelwitz's theory, that vv.[22-25] were added *brevi manu* by some one who wrote out a copy of the original λόγος παρακλήσεως and forwarded it to an Italian church.

In v.[22] **ἀνέχεσθε**, for which ἀντέχεσθε (J. Pricaeus apud Tit 1[9]) is a needless conjecture, takes a genitive (as in 2 Ti 4[3] τῆς ὑγιαινούσης διδασκαλίας οὐκ ἀνέξονται, and in Philo, *quod omnis probus*, 6, καὶ πῶς πατρὸς μὲν ἢ μητρὸς ἐπιταγμάτων παῖδες ἀνέχονται, γνώριμοι δὲ ὧν ἂν ὑφηγηταὶ διακελεύωνται). It has been flattened into ἀνέχεσθαι (infinitive as in 1 P 2[11]) by D* Ψ vg arm 181. 436. 1288. 1311. 1873, etc. (Blass). A written homily may be like a speech (Ac 13[15]), a **λόγος τῆς παρακλήσεως** (cp. on 12[5]); παράκλησις echoes **παρακαλέω** He is not the only early Christian writer who mildly suggested that he had not written at undue length (cp. *e.g.* 1 P 5[12] δι' ὀλίγων ἔγραψα, παρακαλῶν κτλ.; Barn 1[5. 8]) **Καὶ γὰρ** ("etenim" as 4[2]) **διὰ βραχέων** (*sc.* λόγων) **ἐπέστειλα**[1] (epistolary aorist) **ὑμῖν.** Διὰ βραχέων was a common phrase in this connexion; *e.g.* Lucian's *Toxaris*, 56 (πειστέον καὶ ταῦτά σοι νομοθετοῦντι καὶ διὰ βραχέων λεκτέον, μὴ καὶ κάμῃς ἡμῖν τῇ ἀκοῇ συμπερινοστῶν). Πρὸς Ἑβραίους may be read aloud easily in one hour. The writer has had a good deal to say (πολύς, 5[11]), and he has now said it. Not I hope, he adds pleasantly, at too great length! As for the δυσερμήνευτος λέγειν, that is another question which he does not raise here. He is not pleading for a patient reading, because he has had to compress his argument into a short space, which makes it hard to follow, owing to its highly condensed character. What he does appear to anticipate is the possibility of his readers resenting the length at which he has

[1] For ἐπέστειλα (here as in Ac 15[20] 21[25]; Theophr. 24[13] ἐπιστέλλων μὴ γράφειν κτλ. = "write," "send a letter"), see Laqueur's *Quaest. Epigraph. et Papyr. Selectae*, 16 f. (ἐπιστέλλειν = "communicare aliquid cum aliquo sive per hominem sive per epistolam").

written. When the younger Pliny returned a book to Tacitus, with some criticisms upon its style and matter, he said he was not afraid to do so, since it was those most deserving praise whc accepted criticism patiently ("neque enim ulli patientius reprehunduntur quam qui maxime laudari merentur," *Epp.* vii. 20). The author of Πρὸς Ἑβραίους might have taken this line, for he has done justice to the good qualities of his friends (*e.g.* $6^{9f.}$ 10^{39} $13^{1f.}$), even in reproving them for backwardness and slowness. But he prefers to plead that his words have not been long; his readers surely cannot complain of being wearied by the length of his remarks. Not long before, Seneca had made the same kind of observation to Lucilius (*Ep.* xxxviii. 1) about short letters being more effective than lengthy discussions. "Merito exigis ut hoc inter nos epistularum commercium frequentemus, plurimum proficit sermo, quia minutatim inrepit animo . . . aliquando utendum est et illis, ut ita dicam, concionibus, ubi qui dubitat inpellendus est: ubi vero non hoc agendum est ut velit discere sed ut discat, ad haec submissiora uerba ueniendum est. facilius intrant et haerent: nec enim multis opus est, sed efficacibus." But Seneca's practice was not always up to his theory in this respect. His Stoic contemporary Musonius Rufus gave examples as well as precepts of brevity, which were more telling (*e.g.* ὅστις δὲ πανταχοῦ δεῖται ἀποδείξεως καὶ ὅπου σαφῆ τὰ πράγματά ἐστιν, ἢ διὰ πολλῶν ἀποδείκνυσθαι βούλεται αὐτῷ τὰ δι' ὀλίγων δυνάμενα, παντάπασιν ἄτοπος καὶ δυσμαθής, ed. Hense, pp. 1, 2). The literary critic Demetrius considered that the length of a letter should be carefully regulated (τὸ δὲ μέγεθος συνεστάλθω τῆς ἐπιστολῆς, *De Elocut.* 228); letters that were too long and stilted in expression became mere treatises, συγγράμματα, as in the case of many of Plato's, whereas the true ἐπιστολή, according to Demetrius (*ibid.* 231), should be φιλοφρόνησις in a brief compass (σύντομος). Which would apply to Πρὸς Ἑβραίους. Erasmus comments: "Scripsi paucis, ut ipse vos brevi visurus." He may have, but he does not say so.

In v.[23] γινώσκετε is imperative; he is conveying a piece of information. See, *e.g.*, *Tebt. P.* 37^2 (73 B.C.) γίνωσκε Κεφαλᾶν . . . προσεληλυθέναι Δημητρίῳ: *ibid.* 12^2 (118 B.C.) 36^2 56^5. The construction with the participle is common (*e.g.* Lk 8^{46}); you must understand τὸν ἀδελφὸν ἡμῶν (omitted by א^c D$^{b. c}$ K P Ψ 6 Chrys. etc.) Τιμόθεον ἀπολελυμένον, *i.e.* "is (set) free," not necessarily from prison. The general sense, ranging from "is free" to "has started," may be illustrated, *e.g.*, from the application of a woman to leave Alexandria via Pharos (*OP.* $1271^{4.5}$, iii A.D.: ἀξιῶ γράψαι σε τῷ ἐπιτρόπῳ τῆς Φάρου ἀπολῦσαι με κατὰ τὸ ἔθος), or from *BGU.* i. 27^{12-15} (καθ' ἡμέραν προσδεχόμ[ε]θα διμισσωρίαν ὥστε ἕως σήμερον μηδέναν ἀπολελύσθαι τῶν μετὰ σίτου), where ἀ. = "has set out," as in Ac 28[25] (ἀπελύοντο). The interpretation of the next words μεθ' οὗ ἐὰν τάχιον ἔρχηται ὄψομαι ὑμᾶς depends upon whether Timotheus is supposed to join the writer or to journey straight to the community addressed. In the latter case, the writer, who hopes to be coming soon (v.[19]) himself, looks forward to meeting him there. In the former case, they will travel together. It is natural to assume that when the writer sent this message, Timotheus was somewhere else, and that he was expected ere long to reach the writer. For ὄψομαι = visit, see 3 Jn [14] ἐλπίζω δὲ εὐθέως ἰδεῖν σε, etc. Ἐὰν τάχιον ἔρχηται may mean either, "as soon as he comes," or "if he comes soon." The latter suits the situation implied in v.[19] better. The writer (in v.[19]) asks the prayers of his readers, that some obstacle to his speedy return may be removed. If this obstacle were the hindrance that kept Timotheus from joining him on a journey which they had already planned to the church (Riggenbach), he would have said, "Pray for Timotheus, I cannot leave for you till he rejoins me." But the idea is: as the writer is rejoining his friends soon (he hopes), he will be accompanied by Timotheus, should the latter arrive before he has to start. Written advice is all very well, but he hopes soon to follow up this λόγος παρακλήσεως with personal intercourse, like Seneca in *Ep.* vi. 5 ("plus tamen tibi et uiua vox et convictus quam oratio proderit. in rem praesentem uenias oportet, primum quia homines amplius oculis quam auribus credunt, deinde quia longum iter est per praecepta, breue et efficax per exempla").

The greeting comes as usual last (v.[24]). Ἀσπάσασθε κτλ. is an unusual turn, however; the homily was evidently sent to the community, who are told to greet all their ἡγούμενοι. This finds its nearest parallel in Paul's similar injunction (Ro 16[3f.]) to the Ephesian Christians to salute this and that eminent member of their circle. Still, no other NT church is bidden to salute its leaders; and though the writer plainly wishes to reinforce his counsel in v.[17], the πάντας suggests that the persons addressed were "part of the whole church of a large city . . . a congregation attached to some household" (Zahn); they are to convey the writer's greetings to all the leaders of the larger local church—and to all their fellow-members (καὶ πάντας τοὺς ἁγίους being more intelligible, in the light of a passage like Ph 4[21] ἀσπάσασθε πάντα ἅγιον). To his personal greetings he now adds greetings from some Italians. In οἱ ἀπὸ τῆς Ἰταλίας, ἀπό may have its usual sense of "domiciled at" (practically = ἐν), as, *e.g.*, in *OP.* i. 81 (A.D. 49–50), where τῶν ἀπ' Ὀξυρύγχων means "the inhabitants of Oxyrhynchus," or in Πλῆνι . . . ἀπὸ Φμαῦ, *i.e.* at Phmau (ostracon of A.D. 192, quoted in Deissmann's *Light from the East*, p. 186). If it thus means residents in Italy, the writer is in Italy himself. But οἱ ἀπὸ τῆς Ἰταλίας, on the analogy of Ac 21^{27} (οἱ ἀπὸ τῆς Ἀσίας Ἰουδαῖοι), might equally well mean Italians resident for the time being outside Italy; in this case the writer, who is also abroad, is addressing some Italian community, to which their countrymen forward greetings. Grammatically, either rendering is possible, and there is no tradition to decide the question. Perhaps οἱ ἀπὸ τῆς Ἰταλίας is more natural, however, as a description of some Italian Christians abroad who chanced to be in the same locality as the writer and who take this opportunity of sending their greetings by him to an Italian community. If the writer was in Italy, we should have expected πάντες οἱ ἀπὸ τῆς Ἰταλίας, considering the size of Italy and the scattered Christian communities there at this period.

The final benediction, ἡ χάρις (*sc.* ἔστω or εἴη) μετὰ πάντων ὑμῶν (Tit 3^{15}, 2 Ti 4^{22}) has a liturgical ἀμήν, which is omitted by ℵ* W fuld sah 33; the homily was, of course, intended to be read aloud at worship.

INDEXES.

I. INDEX GRAECITATIS.

Words marked * are peculiar in NT to Hebrews.
,, ,, † occur only in quotations from LXX.
,, ,, ‡ are peculiar in NT to Luke (gospel, Acts) and Hebrews.
,, ,, [Paul] [T] [P] are only used elsewhere in NT by Paul, or in the Pastoral Epistles, or in 1 Peter.

II. SUBJECTS AND AUTHORS.

III. QUOTATIONS OR REMINISCENCES OF THE OLD TESTAMENT.

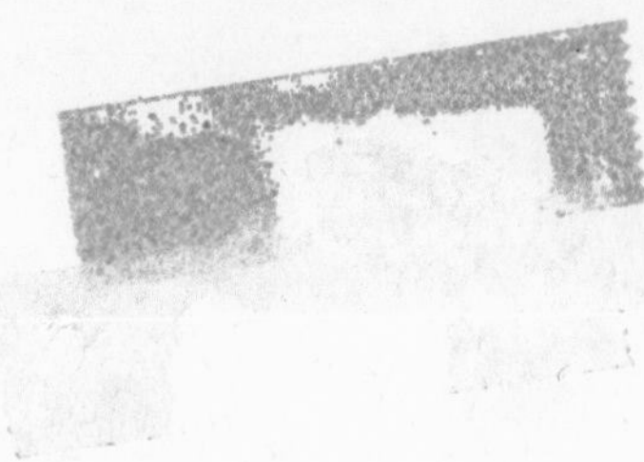